Handbook of Research on Revisioning and Reconstructing Higher Education After Global Crises

Shalin Hai-Jew
Kansas State University, USA

A volume in the Advances in Higher Education and Professional Development (AHEPD) Book Series

Published in the United States of America by
    IGI Global
    Information Science Reference (an imprint of IGI Global)
    701 E. Chocolate Avenue
    Hershey PA, USA 17033
    Tel: 717-533-8845
    Fax: 717-533-8661
    E-mail: cust@igi-global.com
    Web site: http://www.igi-global.com

Copyright © 2023 by IGI Global. All rights reserved. No part of this publication may be reproduced, stored or distributed in any form or by any means, electronic or mechanical, including photocopying, without written permission from the publisher. Product or company names used in this set are for identification purposes only. Inclusion of the names of the products or companies does not indicate a claim of ownership by IGI Global of the trademark or registered trademark.

Library of Congress Cataloging-in-Publication Data

Names: Hai-Jew, Shalin, editor.
Title: Handbook of research on revisioning and reconstructing higher education
  after global crises / Shalin Hai-Jew, editor.
Description: Hershey PA : Information Science Reference, [2023] | Includes
  bibliographical references and index. | Summary: "This edited book
  focuses on the work of reconceptualizing and rebuilding institutions of
  higher education after crises, such as the severe challenges of the
  SARS-CoV-2 / COVID-19 pandemic, with harsh effects on the faculty,
  staff, students, and the institutions themselves in various ways and
  discusses how the schools adapt and reposition during a challenging
  time"-- Provided by publisher.
Identifiers: LCCN 2022039937 (print) | LCCN 2022039938 (ebook) | ISBN
  9781668459348 (hardback)| ISBN   9781668459355 (ebook)
Subjects: LCSH: Education, Higher--Aims and objectives. | Internet in
  higher education. | COVID-19 Pandemic, 2020---Social aspects.
Classification: LCC LB2322.2 .P39 2023 (print) | LCC LB2322.2 (ebook) |
  DDC 378--dc23/eng/20220916
LC record available at https://lccn.loc.gov/2022039937
LC ebook record available at https://lccn.loc.gov/2022039938

This book is published in the IGI Global book series Advances in Higher Education and Professional Development (AHEPD) (ISSN: 2327-6983; eISSN: 2327-6991)

British Cataloguing in Publication Data
A Cataloguing in Publication record for this book is available from the British Library.

All work contributed to this book is new, previously-unpublished material. The views expressed in this book are those of the authors, but not necessarily of the publisher.

For electronic access to this publication, please contact: eresources@igi-global.com.

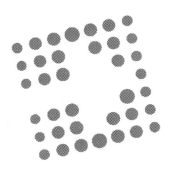

Advances in Higher Education and Professional Development (AHEPD) Book Series

Jared Keengwe
University of North Dakota, USA

ISSN:2327-6983
EISSN:2327-6991

Mission

As world economies continue to shift and change in response to global financial situations, job markets have begun to demand a more highly-skilled workforce. In many industries a college degree is the minimum requirement and further educational development is expected to advance. With these current trends in mind, the **Advances in Higher Education & Professional Development (AHEPD) Book Series** provides an outlet for researchers and academics to publish their research in these areas and to distribute these works to practitioners and other researchers.

AHEPD encompasses all research dealing with higher education pedagogy, development, and curriculum design, as well as all areas of professional development, regardless of focus.

Coverage

- Adult Education
- Assessment in Higher Education
- Career Training
- Coaching and Mentoring
- Continuing Professional Development
- Governance in Higher Education
- Higher Education Policy
- Pedagogy of Teaching Higher Education
- Vocational Education

IGI Global is currently accepting manuscripts for publication within this series. To submit a proposal for a volume in this series, please contact our Acquisition Editors at Acquisitions@igi-global.com or visit: http://www.igi-global.com/publish/.

The Advances in Higher Education and Professional Development (AHEPD) Book Series (ISSN 2327-6983) is published by IGI Global, 701 E. Chocolate Avenue, Hershey, PA 17033-1240, USA, www.igi-global.com. This series is composed of titles available for purchase individually; each title is edited to be contextually exclusive from any other title within the series. For pricing and ordering information please visit http://www.igi-global.com/book-series/advances-higher-education-professional-development/73681. Postmaster: Send all address changes to above address. Copyright © 2023 IGI Global. All rights, including translation in other languages reserved by the publisher. No part of this series may be reproduced or used in any form or by any means – graphics, electronic, or mechanical, including photocopying, recording, taping, or information and retrieval systems – without written permission from the publisher, except for non commercial, educational use, including classroom teaching purposes. The views expressed in this series are those of the authors, but not necessarily of IGI Global.

Titles in this Series

For a list of additional titles in this series, please visit: www.igi-global.com/book-series

Collaborative Models and Frameworks for Inclusive Educator Preparation Programs
Beverly Sande (Prairie View A&M University, USA) and Charles William Kemp (Shawnee State University USA)
Information Science Reference • © 2022 • 244pp • H/C (ISBN: 9781668434437) • US $215.00

Instilling Diversity and Social Inclusion Practices in Teacher Education and Curriculum Development
Olga María Alegre de la Rosa (University of La Laguna, Spain) and Luis Miguel Villar Angulo (University of Seville, pain)
Information Science Reference • © 2022 • 252pp • H/C (ISBN: 9781668448120) • US $215.00

Rethinking Perception and Centering the Voices of Unique Individuals Reframing Autism Inclusion in Praxis
Jessica Block Nerren (California State University, San Bernardino, USA)
Information Science Reference • © 2022 • 287pp • H/C (ISBN: 9781668451038) • US $215.00

Handbook of Research on Practices for Advancing Diversity and Inclusion in Higher Education
Eleni Meletiadou (London Metropolitan University, UK)
Information Science Reference • © 2022 • 451pp • H/C (ISBN: 9781799896289) • US $270.00

Self-Care and Stress Management for Academic Well-Being
Karis L. Clarke (Clark Atlanta University, USA)
Information Science Reference • © 2022 • 302pp • H/C (ISBN: 9781668423349) • US $215.00

Preparing Agriculture and Agriscience Educators for the Classroom
Andrew C. Thoron (Abraham Baldwin Agricultural College, USA) and R. Kirby Barrick (University of Florida, USA (retired))
Information Science Reference • © 2022 • 381pp • H/C (ISBN: 9781668434208) • US $215.00

New Models of Higher Education: Unbundled, Rebundled, Customized, and DIY
Aaron M. Brower (University of Wisconsin Extended Campus, USA & University of Wisconsin-Madison, USA) and Ryan J. Specht-Boardman (University of Wisconsin Extended Campus, USA)
Information Science Reference • © 2022 • 425pp • H/C (ISBN: 9781668438091) • US $240.00

Contributions of Historically Black Colleges and Universities in the 21st Century
Anisah Bagasra (Kennesaw State University, USA) Alison Mc Letchie (South Carolina State University, USA) and Jonathan Wesley (Independent Researcher, USA)
Information Science Reference • © 2022 • 359pp • H/C (ISBN: 9781668438145) • US $215.00

701 East Chocolate Avenue, Hershey, PA 17033, USA
Tel: 717-533-8845 x100 • Fax: 717-533-8661
E-Mail: cust@igi-global.com • www.igi-global.com

List of Contributors

Abdin, Md. Minhazul / *University of Rajshahi, Bangladesh* 122
Arán Sánchez, Ana / *Escuela Normal Rural Ricardo Flores Magón, Mexico* 288
Arcand, Carolyn / *University of New Hampshire, USA* 1
Banerjee, Shayantani / *Amity University, Ranchi, India* 161
Cannon, Jessica A. / *University of Central Missouri, USA* 22
Chilala, Sheilas K. / *Mulungushi University, Zambia* 144
Dotterweich Bryan, Lisa / *Western Iowa Tech Community College, USA* 102
Ebben, Maureen / *University of Southern Maine, USA* 1
Hai-Jew, Shalin / *Kansas State University, USA* 34, 205, 305, 320, 369
Hapsari, Eky Kusuma / *Universitas Negeri Jakarta (UNJ), Indonesia* 85
Hastowohadi, Hastowohadi / *Akademi Penerbang Indonesia (API), Banyuwangi, Indonesia* 85
Ibrahim, Yaacob / *Singapore Institute of Technology, Singapore* 186
Kumar, Navinandan / *Amity University, Ranchi, India* 161
Kumar, Nilesh / *Amity University, Ranchi, India* 161
Manzoor, Amir / *Karachi School of Business and Leadership, Karachi, Pakistan* 171
McNeal, Ramona Sue / *University of Northern Iowa, USA* 102
Meishar-Tal, Hagit / *Holon Institute of Technology (HIT), Israel* 276
Mokhtar, Intan Azura / *Singapore Institute of Technology, Singapore* 186
Moonga, Fred / *University of Eswatini, Eswatini* 144
Moonga, Ireen / *Mulungushi University, Zambia* 144
Muyuni, Audrey / *Mulungushi University, Zambia* 144
Perez Vila, Angel / *University of North Florida, USA* 400
Roy, Goutam / *University of Rajshahi, Bangladesh* 122
Schmeida, Mary / *Kent State University, USA* 102
Schott, Glorianne / *University of Southern Maine, USA* 1
Soleimani, Rana / *University of North Florida, USA* 400
Syropoulos, Apostolos / *Greek Molecular Computing Group, Greece* 385
Tupper, Judith / *University of Southern Maine, USA* 1
Tuzcu, Muteber / *Yeditepe University, Turkey* 261
Zhang, Justin Zuopeng / *University of North Florida, USA* 400
Zina, Ayushi / *Amity University, Ranchi, India* 161

Table of Contents

Preface xviii

Acknowledgment xxvii

Section 1
Student-Centeredness in Teaching and Learning

Chapter 1
Humanizing the Online Classroom: Lessons From the Pandemic Crisis 1
Maureen Ebben, University of Southern Maine, USA
Carolyn Arcand, University of New Hampshire, USA
Judith Tupper, University of Southern Maine, USA
Glorianne Schott, University of Southern Maine, USA

Chapter 2
Revisioning Accessibility in Higher Education Post COVID-19 22
Jessica A. Cannon, University of Central Missouri, USA

Chapter 3
"Future Is Yours": Motivating Online Learners in Higher Education Through a Package of Goods
(in the COVID-19 Pandemic) 34
Shalin Hai-Jew, Kansas State University, USA

Chapter 4
Exploring Students' Perceptions in Hybrid Vocational English Task-Based Language Teaching in
Indonesia Higher Education: A Transitivity Analysis 85
Hastowohadi Hastowohadi, Akademi Penerbang Indonesia (API), Banyuwangi, Indonesia
Eky Kusuma Hapsari, Universitas Negeri Jakarta (UNJ), Indonesia

Section 2
Global Economic Struggles in the Pandemic

Chapter 5
Affordability and State Support for Higher Education 102
Ramona Sue McNeal, University of Northern Iowa, USA
Lisa Dotterweich Bryan, Western Iowa Tech Community College, USA
Mary Schmeida, Kent State University, USA

Section 3
Post-Pandemic Education in Resource Constrained-Environments

Chapter 6
Transition to Blended Learning in a Limited Resource Setting: Administrators' and Teachers'
Perceptions 122
    Goutam Roy, University of Rajshahi, Bangladesh
    Md. Minhazul Abdin, University of Rajshahi, Bangladesh

Chapter 7
Higher Education in the Aftermath of the Pandemic: Lessons From Zambia and Eswatini 144
    Fred Moonga, University of Eswatini, Eswatini
    Sheilas K. Chilala, Mulungushi University, Zambia
    Ireen Moonga, Mulungushi University, Zambia
    Audrey Muyuni, Mulungushi University, Zambia

Chapter 8
Impact of Technology on Educational Patterns: Virtual vs. Traditional Pedagogy 161
    Shayantani Banerjee, Amity University, Ranchi, India
    Ayushi Zina, Amity University, Ranchi, India
    Navinandan Kumar, Amity University, Ranchi, India
    Nilesh Kumar, Amity University, Ranchi, India

Chapter 9
Student Intention to Use Online Library Services of a Locked-Down University: A Quantitative
Study 171
    Amir Manzoor, Karachi School of Business and Leadership, Karachi, Pakistan

Section 4
Social Organizing in the Teeth of an Unfolding Global Pandemic

Chapter 10
Community Awareness and Leadership Among Singapore Youths Amidst a COVID-19
Landscape 186
    Intan Azura Mokhtar, Singapore Institute of Technology, Singapore
    Yaacob Ibrahim, Singapore Institute of Technology, Singapore

Section 5
Working on Inclusion

Chapter 11
Navigating Inequitable (Mis)Treatment and Racist Harassment in Higher Education During the
COVID-19 Pandemic: A Self-Decentered Autoethnographic Case 205
    Shalin Hai-Jew, Kansas State University, USA

Section 6
Building Back Better...and Better

Chapter 12
Online Education and Student Satisfaction: Insight From Student Perceptions Towards Online Education Quality 261
Muteber Tuzcu, Yeditepe University, Turkey

Chapter 13
From Routine Mode to Emergency Mode and Back: Reflections on Israeli Online Teaching and Learning in Higher Education After the COVID-19 Period 276
Hagit Meishar-Tal, Holon Institute of Technology (HIT), Israel

Chapter 14
Experiences and Challenges of Indigenous Students in Higher Education During the Pandemic 288
Ana Arán Sánchez, Escuela Normal Rural Ricardo Flores Magón, Mexico

Chapter 15
What to Keep, What to Discard: Remaking an Instructional Design Service Post Pandemic 305
Shalin Hai-Jew, Kansas State University, USA

Section 7
Harnessing Motion for More Effective Applied Learning

Chapter 16
Infographics for Information Conveyance: A Light History From Early Days (Stasis) to Today (Motion, Interactive, Immersive) 320
Shalin Hai-Jew, Kansas State University, USA

Chapter 17
Going Through the Motions: A Partial Survey of Public Online Multimodal Motion Infographics for Higher Ed 369
Shalin Hai-Jew, Kansas State University, USA

Chapter 18
Using Motion Infographics to Teach Computer Programming Concepts 385
Apostolos Syropoulos, Greek Molecular Computing Group, Greece

Chapter 19
Motion Infographics for Stakeholder Engagement: A Content-Marketing Perspective 400
Angel Perez Vila, University of North Florida, USA
Rana Soleimani, University of North Florida, USA
Justin Zuopeng Zhang, University of North Florida, USA

Conclusion 415

Compilation of References 416

About the Contributors 484

Index 490

Detailed Table of Contents

Preface xviii

Acknowledgment xxvii

Section 1
Student-Centeredness in Teaching and Learning

Chapter 1
Humanizing the Online Classroom: Lessons From the Pandemic Crisis 1
    Maureen Ebben, University of Southern Maine, USA
    Carolyn Arcand, University of New Hampshire, USA
    Judith Tupper, University of Southern Maine, USA
    Glorianne Schott, University of Southern Maine, USA

The global calamity of the COVID-19 pandemic accelerated the shift from face-to-face learning to online learning ushering in pedagogical experimentation and innovation. This chapter advocates for the importance of a humanizing approach to the online classroom. Humanizing is conceptualized as a pedagogical orientation and practice in which person-to-person connections and the relational qualities of teaching and learning are intentionally prioritized. Four areas are discussed: 1) the adoption of new practices for the creation of authentic learning experiences, 2) the development of humanizing approaches for the assessment of student learning, 3) the recognition of student mental wellness as a humanizing practice, and 4) the leverage of educational frameworks to build connection. The aim is to expand the conversation regarding the opportunities and challenges for humanizing online learning.

Chapter 2
Revisioning Accessibility in Higher Education Post COVID-19 22
    Jessica A. Cannon, University of Central Missouri, USA

One impact of the COVID-19 pandemic and complications from the virus is a significant increase in the number of people with cognitive and physical disabilities. Higher education has been slow to fully engage with accessibility measures, pursuing an on-demand individual accommodation model rather than broader accessibility from the outset. Recent legal decrees reinforce the expectation that broad accessibility is the new standard. Educational institutions can choose to act with deliberate attention to becoming leaders in implementing new accessibility practices and resources. A proactive approach increases the formal and informal educational opportunities for a broader audience of learners, as well as setting an example for how society at large can become more supportive of disabilities. This chapter outlines several ways higher education can adapt and lead this effort.

Chapter 3

"Future Is Yours": Motivating Online Learners in Higher Education Through a Package of Goods (in the COVID-19 Pandemic) 34

    Shalin Hai-Jew, Kansas State University, USA

Globally, learners around the world have had to move from face-to-face (F2F) learning to full "emergency online learning" in many cases, such as in higher education. In "emergency online teaching," instructors have been learning about how to support learners; however, with the slowing of the acute phases of the pandemic, many learners have dropped out, many for good. One of the most important strategies to retain online learners on their learning tracks involves a package of learning goods that position learners for the future in the near-, mid-, and far-terms. The core idea here is that "future pull" is alluring, and it supports learner persistence in online (and offline) learning. This work describes the mix of elements for creating just such a package in the contemporaneous moment based on the abductive logic study of instructional design work of the past several years for online learning during the COVID-19 pandemic at a Midwestern university.

Chapter 4

Exploring Students' Perceptions in Hybrid Vocational English Task-Based Language Teaching in Indonesia Higher Education: A Transitivity Analysis 85

    Hastowohadi Hastowohadi, Akademi Penerbang Indonesia (API), Banyuwangi, Indonesia
    Eky Kusuma Hapsari, Universitas Negeri Jakarta (UNJ), Indonesia

The transition from online to hybrid instruction has been implemented in recent years in response to vocational institution policy in the higher education context of Indonesia in order to implement student engagement in the wake of the COVID-19 outbreak. To address this issue, the authors sought to develop vocational English materials that incorporated hybrid instruction into a task-based approach that encourages independent student learning. The authors investigated and analyzed the responses of students learning vocational English to support our teaching and learning quality as a result of the implementation of the hybrid system. With an emphasis on vocational English tasks, it is hoped that this study will make a practical contribution to the teaching practice in Indonesian higher education during the transition from online to hybrid instructions.

Section 2
Global Economic Struggles in the Pandemic

Chapter 5

Affordability and State Support for Higher Education 102

    Ramona Sue McNeal, University of Northern Iowa, USA
    Lisa Dotterweich Bryan, Western Iowa Tech Community College, USA
    Mary Schmeida, Kent State University, USA

The COVID-19 pandemic has helped to accelerate an already declining rate in college enrollment in the U.S. tuition, and college fees have continued to outpace inflation, pricing some students out of higher education. State appropriations can help offset the cost of college, but state support varies significantly. While some states have been creative in promoting college affordability by adoption programs including bans on scholarship displacement and promise programs, others have reduced funding. Why has the state-level response differed so significantly? In exploring this question, this chapter examines the influence of state-level factors on state appropriations for higher education for the years 2010 through 2020. Pooled cross-sectional time series data that controls for variation between states and over time is used.

Section 3
Post-Pandemic Education in Resource Constrained-Environments

Chapter 6
Transition to Blended Learning in a Limited Resource Setting: Administrators' and Teachers' Perceptions 122
>   *Goutam Roy, University of Rajshahi, Bangladesh*
>   *Md. Minhazul Abdin, University of Rajshahi, Bangladesh*

From the online learning experiences during the COVID-19 pandemic, the higher educational institutions of Bangladesh are considering integrating online education into traditional face-to-face learning. Research showed several challenges in implementing blended learning strategies, including having limited resources. This chapter explores how the administrators and teachers at the higher education institutes of Bangladesh could start blended learning with limited resources. The administrators and teachers of two universities in Bangladesh, who were directly involved in the decision-making process, were interviewed. The findings showed that while the administrators and teachers were willing to start blended learning, there were several challenges due to the limited resources aligned with the problems of online education. Administrators and teachers considered blended education as a way to respond to an education disruption caused by emergencies such as natural disasters, political unrest, and pandemics. This chapter provides some recommendations.

Chapter 7
Higher Education in the Aftermath of the Pandemic: Lessons From Zambia and Eswatini 144
>   *Fred Moonga, University of Eswatini, Eswatini*
>   *Sheilas K. Chilala, Mulungushi University, Zambia*
>   *Ireen Moonga, Mulungushi University, Zambia*
>   *Audrey Muyuni, Mulungushi University, Zambia*

The COVID-19 pandemic negatively affected people's health and wellbeing and stretched their coping capacities with potential for multiple long-term psychosocial effects. Social interactions were inexorably affected if not altered. Education was probably the second most affected despite the young age-group due to the large number of people involved – teachers and supporting staff. Most low-income countries of Africa have young populations, which may explain the relatively low COVID-19 mortality rates on the continent. The focus in this chapter is higher education in the aftermath of the pandemic. The authors discuss how higher education institutions (HEIs) in the countries under discussion navigated the pandemic and remodelled to attain their objectives during and after the pandemic. They argue that the pandemic had enduring negative and positive effects. They conclude that although digitisation in learning and teaching in HEIs was underway, the pandemic accelerated its uptake.

Chapter 8

Impact of Technology on Educational Patterns: Virtual vs. Traditional Pedagogy............................ 161

Shayantani Banerjee, Amity University, Ranchi, India
Ayushi Zina, Amity University, Ranchi, India
Navinandan Kumar, Amity University, Ranchi, India
Nilesh Kumar, Amity University, Ranchi, India

With innovations in technology, educational practices and expectations are changing at a rapid pace. The virtual reality on electronic devices is at a stark contrast with traditional classroom teaching and ethics. This chapter aspires to trace the changes that the use of ICT tools has brought to conventional pedagogy, teacher's adaptability, and teacher's anxiety in coping with the inclination of education toward technology. For the study, various sets of data were collected from different institutions, and then the data were observed. Apart from ICT tools, the popularity of social media elicits teachers to explore its educational use. However, the tempting distraction of this technology could make teachers anxious about its pedagogical use. Thus, the aim of this chapter will be to analyze the impact of technology on factors like school culture versus online teaching, attitude towards social media, professional development of teachers, learning goals, and content-building in the curriculum.

Chapter 9

Student Intention to Use Online Library Services of a Locked-Down University: A Quantitative
Study 171

Amir Manzoor, Karachi School of Business and Leadership, Karachi, Pakistan

The COVID-19 pandemic had a drastic impact on the teaching and learning practices of universities around the globe. To comply with the new normal, universities shifted their teaching and learning activities online. Academic libraries also shifted their services online. However, in many cases, the students enrolled in universities during COVID-19 era had no prior experience of online library services. This study investigated the factors that drive or inhibit these students' use of online library services. Various recommendations and implications for library management are reported.

Section 4
Social Organizing in the Teeth of an Unfolding Global Pandemic

Chapter 10

Community Awareness and Leadership Among Singapore Youths Amidst a COVID-19
Landscape 186

Intan Azura Mokhtar, Singapore Institute of Technology, Singapore
Yaacob Ibrahim, Singapore Institute of Technology, Singapore

The COVID-19 pandemic has changed how businesses operate, how people work, and the way people socialize and interact. The changes that needed to be made were significant and did not happen easily. However, the COVID-19 pandemic also presented opportunities for creativity to flourish, innovations to happen, and kindness and magnanimity to be extended to one another. In Singapore, an island-nation city-state, significant changes had to be implemented to ring-fence the spread of infections and ensure the local economy and healthcare system could cope with the impact of the pandemic. At the forefront of some of these changes were the youths. Young people with creative ideas, boundless energy, and a strong sense of social cause and fairness led initiatives that had significant and positive impact on those most vulnerable. In this chapter, the backdrop of the evolution of a values-based education system in Singapore and its impact on the younger generation of Singaporeans is discussed followed by examples of youth-led initiatives in Singapore amidst a COVID-19 landscape.

Section 5
Working on Inclusion

Chapter 11
Navigating Inequitable (Mis)Treatment and Racist Harassment in Higher Education During the COVID-19 Pandemic: A Self-Decentered Autoethnographic Case 205
Shalin Hai-Jew, Kansas State University, USA

The SARS-CoV-2/COVID-19 pandemic (late 2019 to the present) brought to the fore latent and externalized forms of racism and bias and xenophobia. The author experienced a range of inequitable mistreatment and racist harassment in her workplace in higher education during this time, including from her direct supervisor who engaged in a racist microassault along with excess work assignments (the work of several individuals or multiple FTEs) during multiple years of the pandemic. This work uses a self-decentered auto-ethnography to explore practical ways to address racism and discrimination in the workplace, through clear documentation, honest in-lane reportage, and other efforts up an escalatory ladder. This work highlights the challenges of working towards a solution in a bureaucracy with a mix of apparently conflicting objectives and foremost to protect the institution against lawsuits and negative publicity.

Section 6
Building Back Better...and Better

Chapter 12
Online Education and Student Satisfaction: Insight From Student Perceptions Towards Online Education Quality 261
Muteber Tuzcu, Yeditepe University, Turkey

The phenomenon of online education cannot be accepted as new, but the immediate change from an in-class environment to an online environment is new because of COVID-19 restrictions. The aim of the study is whether students are satisfied with online education during the COVID-19 period to determine the factors that affect students' satisfaction with online education during the period and to find service quality gaps and students' satisfaction based on the gap model. As higher education institutions try to cope with a competitive advantage and maintain service quality, feedback from students is valuable to increase the effectiveness of educational plans and implement future intentions. Students are aware that unusual circumstances bring both advantages and disadvantages. Not being present in the class environment is counted as both a positive and negative thing by students. Overall, students feel satisfied with online education during the lockdown period.

Chapter 13
From Routine Mode to Emergency Mode and Back: Reflections on Israeli Online Teaching and Learning in Higher Education After the COVID-19 Period 276
Hagit Meishar-Tal, Holon Institute of Technology (HIT), Israel

This chapter analyses Israeli higher education institutions' transitions from campus learning to online learning due to the COVID-19 pandemic and critically discusses the transition back to routine campus-based learning. The chapter reviews the state of online teaching in pre-COVID-19 academia, the changes required during lockdowns and social distancing restrictions, and the essential difference between routine and emergency online teaching. It also discusses the consequences of returning to campus-based learning and ways to leverage the changes that took place during the COVID-19 period and adapt them to routine mode again.

Chapter 14
Experiences and Challenges of Indigenous Students in Higher Education During the Pandemic 288
Ana Arán Sánchez, Escuela Normal Rural Ricardo Flores Magón, Mexico

This chapter describes and analyzes the experiences of indigenous students of higher education during the COVID-19 pandemic. They are undergraduates of the bachelor's degree of elementary education who attend a public university located in the north of Mexico, as part of an affirmative action policy that began in 2017. Through the phenomenological method, with an interpretative framework and qualitative approach, this research examines the testimonies of 15 key informants using in-depth interviews, in order to convey the academic challenges they went through during the school lockdown and isolation period of the health emergency caused by the SARS-COV-2 virus, including the development of their dissertation to obtain their degree. The chapter reveals the extreme difficulties they experienced due to the lack of suitable computer equipment, internet connection, and absence of an adequate digital competence. For the ones that had to do their thesis report in order to graduate, having to write their theses in a second language meant an additional obstacle as well.

Chapter 15
What to Keep, What to Discard: Remaking an Instructional Design Service Post Pandemic............ 305
Shalin Hai-Jew, Kansas State University, USA

As humanity seems to be moving ahead from the novel SARS-CoV-2/COVID-19 pandemic, people are reckoning with the changes adopted during the high-stress period, of unprecedented threats to lives and health, lockdowns and reopenings, social tensions, and political strife. Instructional design (ID) work at a university also underwent some seminal changes. This work explores what changes to keep and what to discard, based on a SWOT (strengths, weaknesses, opportunities, and threats) analysis and a grounding of some 17 years of ID work and decades of prior college and university teaching work.

Section 7
Harnessing Motion for More Effective Applied Learning

Chapter 16
Infographics for Information Conveyance: A Light History From Early Days (Stasis) to Today
(Motion, Interactive, Immersive) 320
Shalin Hai-Jew, Kansas State University, USA

To help the world emerge from the COVID-19 pandemic, an older tool has come back to the fore: analog and digital informational graphics. Infographics (information + graphics) have been used for many decades to convey data, knowledge, information, and learning. In the latest phase, there are now motion (animated) and interactive and immersive infographics that offer richer ways. This work explores the basic mechanisms of information conveyance in infographics from early days through the contemporaneous moment with the richer. Finally, a summary graphic captures the general sequence in the design, development, and deployment of modern motion, interactive, and/or immersive infographics.

Chapter 17
Going Through the Motions: A Partial Survey of Public Online Multimodal Motion Infographics
for Higher Ed 369
    Shalin Hai-Jew, Kansas State University, USA

With the learning slippage that occurred in the aftermath of the SARS-CoV-2/COVID-19 pandemic, learning advantages that may be achieved are a topic of special interest. The popularization of online learning has riveted focus to digital learning methods and contents. In formal higher education, various contemporary digital infographics are in use: static, motion, interactive, and immersive. This work explores some of the publicly available and open infographics used in formal learning in higher education to better understand these digital contents. The search for "infographics" is based on a popular referatory for web-hosted digital learning resources, but with a new search feature that goes beyond the curated and peer-reviewed contents that captures the newest relevant contents from the web. The works are analyzed for modalities, topics, pedagogical value, and design for transience to protect against cognitive overload. This is an exploratory research work.

Chapter 18
Using Motion Infographics to Teach Computer Programming Concepts 385
    Apostolos Syropoulos, Greek Molecular Computing Group, Greece

Although programming languages are expressive tools, their expressive power is quite limited. A direct consequence of this is that novice users have difficulty grasping the basic programming constructs mainly because there is a discrepancy between natural languages and programming languages (e.g., How do we express common human tasks in Python?). A relatively easy way to tackle this discrepancy is to use motion infographics. However, when pupils and students are familiar with abstraction, a basic idea of computational thinking, then one can use motion infographics that show familiar objects and/or ideas that should be used to teach the corresponding programming constructs. The author has used this approach to create motion infographics that explain conditional and repetitive constructs. However, this does not really work with recursion as one has to resort to the use of trees to explain this programming concept. All the motion infographics presented here have been produced with XeLaTeX, an open source tool that can be used to produce excellent printed/electronic documents.

Chapter 19
Motion Infographics for Stakeholder Engagement: A Content-Marketing Perspective 400
    Angel Perez Vila, University of North Florida, USA
    Rana Soleimani, University of North Florida, USA
    Justin Zuopeng Zhang, University of North Florida, USA

This chapter aims to summarize the design considerations of motion infographics to engage stakeholders from the perspective of content marketing. Specifically, the authors synthesize and illustrate the role of motion infographics in facilitating content marketing and promoting stakeholder engagement. This research fills the gap by proposing a multidisciplinary area by exploring the relationships between motion infographics, content marketing, and stakeholder engagement. It provides valuable guidelines for practitioners to design and implement motion infographics in these relevant contexts.

Conclusion 415

Compilation of References 416

About the Contributors 484

Index 490

Preface

The idea for *Handbook of Research on Revisioning and Reconstructing Higher Education After Global Crises* started early in the pandemic when it was clear that the SARS-CoV-2 / COVID-19 pandemic would be highly disruptive and have long-term implications on humanity. This was based on the behaviors of the pathogenic agent and known human responses to mass-scale health threats (often befuddlement and even apathy). Indeed, as the world slowly emerges from the lockdowns and mass-fear and broken social relationships (and various games of "us vs. them," "insider vs. outsider"), we are learning about the fragility of social agreements and political compacts (with wars breaking out in the pandemic). State-side, democracy itself has been challenged from within and without and has shown some weaknesses, some fragility. We are learning about backwards steps in terms of learning. We are seeing setbacks in personal finances. The psychological defensiveness from a sense of actual threat to life will likely last for a long time even after the pathogenic agent has receded in terms of being a potent threat. The world has shifted on its axis.

I have spent decades of my career in higher education, from right after my graduation with my first graduate degree back in the mid-1980s when I was 20…and through decades of teaching in higher education…to the present, when I work as an instructional designer and researcher.

The call went out in February 2022. I offered a brainstorm of possible topics:

##

CRISES AFFECTING HIGHER EDUCATION
>   Higher education and particular crises and vulnerabilities
>   Historical crises affecting higher education globally or regionally
>   Crises affecting business sector serving higher education

ASSESSING DAMAGES AND LOSSES FROM THE COVID-19 PANDEMIC
>   Affected dimensions in higher education
>   Social connections in higher education
>   Opportunity costs of the COVID-19 pandemic
>   Global damage from the COVID-19 pandemic
>   Permanent vs. temporary losses to higher education from the COVID-19 pandemic

RECONCEPTUALIZATIONS OF HIGHER EDUCATION AFTER CRISIS / CRISES
>   Revisioning the roles of higher education into the near-, mid- and long-term futures
>   Strategic planning for higher education
>   Investments in higher education

Preface

HUMAN RESOURCES IN HIGHER EDUCATION
    Changing staffing in higher education
    Dynamics in human resources during the pandemic
    Addressing mental health, stress, and demoralization in crises
    Integrating remote workers in higher education post-pandemic
    Keeping the peace and compromise in roiling politics

DESIGNED CURRICULUM AND PROGRAMMING
    Redesigning programming for effectiveness in higher education
    Evolving curricular designs post-pandemic
    Interdisciplinarity in a time of crisis

EMERGENCY ONLINE LEARNING (EOL)
    Lessons from emergency online learning (EOL)
    Virtual labs

ADDRESSING LEARNING GAPS
    Identifying learning gaps in sequence of learning
    Accelerating learning
    Reconfiguring curriculums
    Promoting creative thinking
    Supporting interconnectivity in online learning
    Returning to face-to-face (F2F) learning in a context of biosafety concerns
    Blended learning in a time of COVID-19 pandemic
    Flipped classrooms in a time of COVID-19 pandemic
    Encouraging formal, nonformal, and informal learning (as complementarities)

ONLINE LEARNING
    Role of online education in higher education post-pandemic
    Creating remote communities online

DISCIPLINE-SPECIFIC ADVANCEMENTS
    Discipline history and advancements
    Methods and practices

RESEARCH AND DEVELOPMENT (R&D) AND INNOVATIONS
    Promoting research and development (R&D) and other innovations in universities post-pandemic
    Expressive arts and innovations
    Protecting intellectual property (IP) in universities post-pandemic

TECHNOLOGIES AND THEIR DEPLOYMENT
    Information technology services (ITS) in higher education
    Virtuality and higher education

LIBRARY SCIENCES
Provisioning of library resources and services
Acquisitions of resources for libraries
Archival of resources and contents

ATHLETICS
Collegiate sports
Sports clubs

PERFORMATIVE AND DRAMATIC ARTS
Arts performances
Dance
Concerts
Arts shows

REBUILDING CAMPUS LIFE
Events
Gatherings
Social connections

STRATEGIC AND TACTICAL PARTNERSHIPS
Working with (un)enlightened government and state resources for higher education
Partnering with organizations
Partnering with government
Partnering with businesses

NEW BRANDING for HIGHER EDUCATION
Brand burnishment / refurbishment
Brand differentiation (and competitive advantage) between institutions of higher education

TUITIONS AND AFFORDABILITY
Affordable higher education for the masses

PROMOTION OF HIGHER EDUCATION CULTURES
Pomp and circumstances
Sub-cultures and evolutions

ATHLETICS AND SPORTS TRADITIONS
Sporting events
Kinesiology and related studies

ENROLLMENT STRATEGIES
Enrollment strategies for higher education post-pandemic

Preface

INTERNATIONAL STUDENTS
  Providing supports for international students in universities and colleges post-pandemic
  Attracting international students in higher education post-pandemic

BROAD AND TARGETED SUPPORT FOR STUDENTS
  Student support services post-pandemic
  Bridging digital divides with supports
  Promoting student clubs in a time of COVID-19

ACADEMIC HONESTY
  Supporting academic honesty in higher education post-pandemic

RESIDENTIAL LIVING
  Residential living on campus for students post-pandemic
  Off-campus living supports for students post-pandemic

SOCIAL SUPPORTS
  Developing peer support for students post-pandemic
  Supporting faculty and staff in higher education post-pandemic
  Re-socialization of peoples in higher education post-pandemic

FACING DOWN THE INDIVIDUAL AND COLLECTIVE TRAUMA
  Recovery from mass trauma in higher education

CAREER DEVELOPMENT FOR LEARNERS
  Supporting career development in higher education post-pandemic

PHENOMENA DISINTERMEDIATING HIGHER EDUCATION
  Challenges to higher education

FUND-RAISING AND PATRONAGE, ENDOWMENTS
  Alumni support
  Corporate support
  Event-based fund-raising
  Endowment management

PREPARING FOR THE NEXT CRISES
  Tactical making up for lost time
  Planning and resourcing for organizational resilience
  Strengthening human resources
  Competitive advantages in time spent under lockdown and reopening cycles

##

Preface

In response to the call, several dozen people proposed ideas, and less than half came through with a draft chapter some eight months later. Some wrote from experiences. Others built on theory. Others conducted various research studies. Some drew on multiple sources.

There are themes about the importance of caring for students as whole individuals. There is focus on ensuring accessibility for learners, including those suffering from the debilitating effects of "long COVID." There is emphasis on harnessing learner motivations for learning. Indeed, the return to higher education has been challenging, with many deciding not to return ever. The move to online learning, with various technologies, was another focus. The affordability of higher education garnered some much-needed attention. A number of works focused on administrators and teachers and learners making do with limited resources in a time of global emergency. One work touched on anti-Asian hatred that manifested in a workplace. A number of works explored what changes to continue adopting even post-disaster. Then, there is a final section on a pedagogical approach to enhance learning, in this case, using motion resources. The last part is from a project that was being edited at the same time but did not have sufficient accepted works to fully make. This section reads as a bit of an add-on because it is. However, the works align with the theme of revisioning higher education post-disaster, with improved ways to enhance learning.

The global calamity of the COVID-19 pandemic accelerated the shift from face-to-face learning to online learning ushering in pedagogical experimentation and innovation. Chapter 1 advocates for the importance of a humanizing approach to the online classroom. Humanizing is conceptualized as a pedagogical orientation and practice in which person-to-person connections and the relational qualities of teaching and learning are intentionally prioritized. Four areas are discussed: 1) the adoption of new practices for the creation of authentic learning experiences, 2) the development of humanizing approaches for the assessment of student learning, 3) the recognition of student mental wellness as a humanizing practice, and 4) the leverage of educational frameworks to build connection. The aim is to expand the conversation regarding the opportunities and challenges for humanizing online learning.

Chapter 2

One impact of the COVID-19 pandemic and complications from the virus is a significant increase in the number of people with cognitive and physical disabilities. Higher education has been slow to fully engage with accessibility measures, pursuing an on-demand individual accommodation model rather than broader accessibility from the outset. Recent legal decrees reinforce the expectation that broad accessibility is the expectation. Educational institutions can choose to act with deliberate attention to becoming leaders in implementing new accessibility practices and resources. A proactive approach increases the formal and informal educational opportunities for a broader audience of learners, as well as setting an example for how society at large can become more supportive of disabilities. Chapter 2 outlines several ways higher education can adapt and lead this effort.

Globally, learners around the world have had to move from face-to-face (F2F) learning to full "emergency online learning" in many cases, such as in higher education. In "emergency online teaching," instructors have been learning about how to support learners; however, with the slowing of the acute phases of the pandemic, many learners have dropped out, many for good. One of the most important strategies to retain online learners on their learning tracks involves a package of learning goods that position learners for the future in the near-, mid-, and far-terms. The core idea here is that "future pull" is alluring, and it supports learner persistence in online (and offline) learning. Chapter 3 describes the mix of elements for creating just such a package in the contemporaneous moment based on the abductive logic study of instructional design work of the past several years for online learning during the COVID-19 pandemic at a Midwestern university.

xxii

Preface

The transition from online to hybrid instruction has been implemented in recent years in response to vocational institution policy in the higher education context of Indonesia in order to implement student engagement in the wake of the COVID-19 outbreak. To address this issue, the authors of Chapter 4 sought to develop Vocational English materials that incorporated hybrid instruction into a task-based approach that encourages independent student learning. The authors investigated and analyzed the responses of students learning vocational English to support our teaching and learning quality as a result of the implementation of the hybrid system. With an emphasis on vocational English tasks, it is hoped that this study will make a practical contribution to the teaching practice in Indonesian higher education during the transition from online to hybrid instructions.

The COVID-19 pandemic has helped to accelerate an already declining rate in college enrollment in the U.S. Tuition and college fees have continued to outpace inflation, pricing some students out of higher education. State appropriations can help offset the cost of college, but state support varies significantly. While some states have been creative in promoting college affordability by adoption programs including bans on scholarship displacement and promise programs, others have reduced funding. Why has the state-level response differed so significantly? In exploring this question, this chapter examines the influence of state-level factors on state appropriations for higher education for the years, 2010 through 2020. Pooled cross-sectional time series data that controls for variation between states and over time is used in Chapter 5.

From the online learning experiences during the COVID-19 pandemic, the higher educational institutions of Bangladesh are considering integrating online education into traditional face-to-face learning. Research showed several challenges in implementing blended learning strategies, including having limited resources. This chapter explores how the administrators and teachers at the higher education institutes of Bangladesh could start blended learning with limited resources. The administrators and teachers of two universities in Bangladesh, who are directly involved in the decision-making process, were interviewed. The findings showed that while the administrators and teachers were willing to start blended learning, there were several challenges due to the limited resources aligned with the problems of online education. Administrators and teachers considered blended education as a way to respond to an education disruption caused by emergencies such as natural disasters, political unrest, and pandemics. Chapter 6 provides some recommendations.

The COVID-19 pandemic negatively affected people's health and wellbeing and stretched their coping capacities with potential for multiple long-term psychosocial effects. Social interactions were inexorably affected if not altered. Education was probably the second most affected despite the young age-group due to the large number of people involved - teachers and supporting staff. Most low-income countries of Africa, have young populations which may explain the relatively low COVID-19 mortality rates on the continent. The focus in Chapter 7 is higher education in the aftermath of the pandemic. It is discussed how Higher Education Institutions (HEIs) in the countries under discussion navigated the pandemic and remodeled to attain their objectives during and after the pandemic. It is argued that the pandemic had enduring negative and positive effects. The chapter concludes that although digitization in learning and teaching in HEIs was underway, the pandemic accelerated its uptake.

With innovations in technology, educational practices and expectations are changing at a rapid pace. The virtual reality on electronic devices is at a stark contrast with traditional classroom teaching and ethics. Chapter 8 aspires to trace the changes that the use of ICT tools has brought to conventional pedagogy, teacher's adaptability, and teacher's anxiety in coping with the inclination of education toward

xxiii

technology. For the study, various set of data was collected from different institutions, and then the data was observed. Apart from ICT tools, the popularity of social media elicits teachers to explore its educational use. However, the tempting distraction of this technology could make teachers anxious about its pedagogical use. Thus, the aim of this paper will be to analyze the impact of technology on factors like school culture versus online teaching, attitude towards social media, professional development of teachers, learning goals, and content-building in the curriculum.

COVID-19 pandemic had drastic impact on teaching and learning practices of universities around the globe. To comply with the new normal, universities shifted their teaching and learning activities online. Academic libraries also shifted their services online. However, in many cases the students enrolled in universities during COVID-19 era, had no prior experience of online library services. Chapter 9 investigates the factors that drives or inhibit these students' use of online library services. Various recommendations and implications for library management are reported.

The COVID-19 pandemic has changed how businesses operate, how people work, and the way people socialize and interact. The changes that needed to be made were significant and did not happen easily. However, the COVID-19 pandemic also presented opportunities for creativity to flourish, innovations to happen, and kindness and magnanimity to be extended to one another. In Singapore, an island-nation city-state, significant changes had to be implemented to ring-fence the spread of infections, and ensure the local economy and healthcare system could cope with the impact of the pandemic. At the forefront of some of these changes were the youths. Young people with creative ideas, boundless energy, and a strong sense of social cause and fairness, led initiatives that had significant and positive impact on those most vulnerable. In Chapter 10, the backdrop of the evolution of a values-based education system in Singapore and its impact on the younger generation of Singaporeans, is discussed, followed by examples of youth-led initiatives in Singapore, amidst a Covid-19 landscape.

The SARS-CoV-2 / COVID-19 pandemic (late 2019 to the present) brought to the fore latent and externalized forms of racism and bias and xenophobia. The author experienced a range of inequitable mistreatment and racist harassment in her workplace in higher education during this time, including from her direct supervisor who engaged in a racist microassault along with excess work assignments (the work of several individuals or multiple FTEs) during multiple years of the pandemic. This work uses a self-decentered auto-ethnography to explore practical ways to address racism and discrimination in the workplace, through clear documentation, honest in-lane reportage, and other efforts up an escalatory ladder. Chapter 11 highlights the challenges of working towards a solution in a bureaucracy with a mix of apparently conflicting objectives and foremost to protect the institution against lawsuits and negative publicity.

Chapter 12 covers how the phenomenon of online education cannot be accepted as new but the immediate change from an in-class environment to an online environment is new because of COVID-19 restrictions. The aim of the study is whether students are satisfied with online education during the COVID-19 period, to determine the factors that affect students' satisfaction with online education during the period, and to find out service quality gaps and students' satisfaction based on the gap model. As higher education institutions try to cope with a competitive advantage and maintain service quality, feedback from students is valuable to increase the effectiveness of educational plans and implement future intentions. Students are aware that unusual circumstances bring both advantages and disadvantages. Not being present in-class environment is counted as both a positive and negative thing by students. Overall, students feel satisfied with online education during the lockdown period.

Preface

Chapter 13 analyses Israeli higher education institutions' transition from campus learning to online learning due to the COVID-19 pandemic and critically discusses the transition back to routine campus-based learning. The paper reviews the state of online teaching in pre-COVID-19 academia, the changes required during lockdowns and social distancing restrictions, and the essential difference between routine and emergency online teaching. It also discusses the consequences of returning to campus-based learning and ways to leverage the changes that took place during the COVID-19 period and adapt them to routine mode again.

Chapter 14 describes and analyzes the experiences of indigenous students of higher education during the COVID-19 pandemic. They are undergraduates of the bachelor's degree of elementary education, who attend a public university located in the north of Mexico, as part of an affirmative action policy that began in 2017. Though the phenomenological method, with an interpretative framework and qualitative approach, this research examines the testimonies of 15 key informants using in-depth interviews, in order to convey the academic challenges they went through during the school lockdown and isolation period of the health emergency caused by the SARS-CoV-2 virus, including the development of their dissertation to obtain their degree. The chapter reveals the extreme difficulties they experienced due to the lack of suitable computer equipment, internet connection and absence of an adequate digital competence. For the ones that had to do their dissertation in order to graduate, having to write their thesis in a second language meant an additional obstacle as well.

As humanity seems to be moving ahead from the novel SARS-CoV-2 / COVID-19 pandemic, people are reckoning with the changes adopted during the high-stress period, of unprecedented threats to lives and health, lockdowns and reopenings, social tensions, and political strifes. Instructional design (ID) work at a university also underwent some seminal changes. Chapter 15 explores what changes to keep and what to discard, based on a SWOT (strengths, weaknesses, opportunities, and threats) analysis and a grounding of some 17 years of ID work and decades of prior college and university teaching work.

To help the world emerge from the COVID-19 pandemic, an older tool has come back to the fore: analog and digital informational graphics. Infographics (information + graphics) have been used for many decades to convey data, knowledge, information, and learning. In the latest phase, there are now motion (animated) and interactive and immersive infographics that offer richer ways to. Chapter 16 explores the basic mechanisms of information conveyance in infographics from early days through the contemporaneous moment with the richer. Finally, a summary graphic captures the general sequence in the design, development, and deployment of modern motion, interactive, and / or immersive infographics.

With the learning slippage that occurred in the aftermath of the SARS-CoV-2 / COVID-19 pandemic, learning advantages that may be achieved are a topic of special interest. The popularization of online learning has riveted focus to digital learning methods and contents. In formal higher education, various contemporary digital infographics are in use: static, motion, interactive, and immersive. This work explores some of the publicly available and open infographics used in formal learning in higher education to better understand these digital contents. The search for "infographics" is based on a popular referatory for web-hosted digital learning resources, but with a new search feature that goes beyond the curated and peer-reviewed contents that captures the newest relevant contents from the Web. The works are analyzed for modalities, topics, pedagogical value, and design for transience to protect against cognitive overload. Chapter 17 is an exploratory research work.

xxv

Although programming languages are expressive tools, still their expressive power is quite limited. A direct consequence of this is that novice users have big difficulties to grasp the basic programming constructs mainly because there is a discrepancy between natural languages and programming languages (e.g., how do we express common human tasks in Python?). A relatively easy way to tackle this discrepancy is to use motion infographics. However, when pupils and students are familiar with abstraction, a basic idea of computational thinking, then one can use motion infographics that show familiar objects and/or ideas that should be used to teach the corresponding programming constructs. Chapter 18 uses this approach to create motion infographics that explain conditional and repetitive constructs. However, this does not really work with recursion as one has to resort to the use of trees to explain this programming concept. All the motion infographics presented here have been produced with XeLaTeX, an open source tool that can be used to produce excellent printed/electronic documents.

Chapter 19 aims to summarize the design considerations of motion infographics to engage stakeholders from the perspective of content marketing. Specifically, we synthesize and illustrate the role of motion infographics in facilitating content marketing and promoting stakeholder engagement. This research fills the gap by proposing a multidisciplinary area by exploring the relationships between motion infographics, content marketing, and stakeholder engagement. It provides valuable guidelines for practitioners to design and implement motion infographics in these relevant contexts.

Something as earthshaking as a global disaster, all at once, experienced in a rolling simultaneity, helps people reconsider their lives and the speed of time. It helps one consider what is relevant. Reprieves are short. At any one time in the world, various parts are in crisis, and populations are under duress. How the world's peoples respond in various sectors have huge implications for how humanity recovers or does not.

Handbook of Research on Revisioning and Reconstructing Higher Education After Global Crises is really about asking these questions and working towards consensus and creative dissensus answers.

Thanks to all those who have contributed to this text. I am grateful for their generosity in sharing their expertise. I am grateful for their patience as they went through the double-blind peer editing process and the revisions. I also appreciate that they reviewed the works of their peers.

Thanks to IGI Global for the many opportunities to publish, edit, and collaborate. I could not have asked for a more supportive publisher.

Shalin Hai-Jew
Kansas State University, USA
October 2022

Acknowledgment

Thank you to the respective researchers and research teams who contributed to this work.

Humanity is served well by those who think and act smart and fast in and after crises.

This book is dedicated to those who bring the fight every day to keep order and protect people. It is not often that we realize just how disordered and socially unjust the world can become without human smarts, agency, ethics, and good will.

Section 1
Student–Centeredness in Teaching and Learning

Chapter 1
Humanizing the Online Classroom:
Lessons From the Pandemic Crisis

Maureen Ebben
https://orcid.org/0000-0001-8620-372X
University of Southern Maine, USA

Carolyn Arcand
University of New Hampshire, USA

Judith Tupper
https://orcid.org/0000-0001-7332-7336
University of Southern Maine, USA

Glorianne Schott
University of Southern Maine, USA

ABSTRACT

The global calamity of the COVID-19 pandemic accelerated the shift from face-to-face learning to online learning ushering in pedagogical experimentation and innovation. This chapter advocates for the importance of a humanizing approach to the online classroom. Humanizing is conceptualized as a pedagogical orientation and practice in which person-to-person connections and the relational qualities of teaching and learning are intentionally prioritized. Four areas are discussed: 1) the adoption of new practices for the creation of authentic learning experiences, 2) the development of humanizing approaches for the assessment of student learning, 3) the recognition of student mental wellness as a humanizing practice, and 4) the leverage of educational frameworks to build connection. The aim is to expand the conversation regarding the opportunities and challenges for humanizing online learning.

DOI: 10.4018/978-1-6684-5934-8.ch001

Copyright © 2023, IGI Global. Copying or distributing in print or electronic forms without written permission of IGI Global is prohibited.

INTRODUCTION

Whether by choice or by necessity, most college faculty have now had experience with online education. For many, their initial pandemic instructional experiences could be characterized as emergency remote teaching, a pedagogical approach that is antithetical to high-quality online learning. As Dean and Director of Online Programs at the University of Kentucky, Jay Miller (2022), puts it, "There is a difference between educating online and online education" (n.p.). Although the experiences of remote learning during the pandemic were variable, the shift to online education brought with it new insights, supporting continued innovation and expansion of the online classroom (Villasenor, 2022). Even learning activities that were typically conducted in person have become hybrid (Lempres, 2022). Changing and growing in new ways, what is the role of online education in higher education in the wake of the COVID-19 crisis?

An important direction for online education pertains to the relational aspects of teaching and learning. That is the human-to-human connections that occur between teachers and students, and students and students, that solidify learning and help form lasting memories of the classroom experience. We call these interactional processes "humanizing the classroom," and consider them essential aspects of high-quality online pedagogy.

Felton and Lambert (2020) underscore the power of human relationships in higher education pedagogy. Interactions between students and instructors "positively influence learning, retention, and graduation rates, [and contribute to] critical thinking, identity development, communication skills, and leadership abilities" (p. 5). Indeed, human relationships are not only "the beating heart of higher education," but "learning and well-being are intimately, inseparably connected" (Felton & Lambert, 2020, p. 163). In the shift to remote learning necessitated by the pandemic, "being a human" has been a rallying cry for faculty who sought to interact meaningfully with students. These faculty sought to realize Felton and Lambert's (2020) pandemic-inspired exhortation that "no matter the future, let's challenge ourselves to make relationship-rich education a reality for all of our students" (p. 165).

There may be unique challenges to achieving relationship-rich education in the online context. Online teaching occurs in a digital space that circumscribes the kinds of interactions that may be available. It is important to recognize that our efforts toward humanizing the online classroom are always situated within the particular material conditions and social circumstances of both instructors and students. Internet connections, bandwidth, equipment capabilities, software, platforms, and so on constitute material resources that may be unevenly available to students and faculty. Along with its materiality, the online classroom is a space for the person-to-person intersubjective experiences of teachers and learners. It is shaped by intellectual, emotional, and psychological human capacities that express, build, and sustain relationships and connections. Given the material and social features of online modalities, how can faculty humanize the online classroom?

CHAPTER PREVIEW

A worthwhile facet of the post-pandemic is the perspective that allows faculty to appraise their experiences with online learning to inform teaching and learning practices going forward. In this chapter, four college professors respond to Felton and Lambert's (2020) challenge by exploring the questions: How can faculty humanize the online classroom? What does that look like in practice? We are full-time and part-time faculty in all career stages (early-, mid-, late-career), teaching undergraduate and graduate students across a range of disciplines in the humanities and social sciences including communication and media studies, public policy and administration, and public health at the 4-year university and 2-year community college levels in the Midwest and the northeast regions of the U.S. We share our experiences and pedagogies around humanizing the online classroom.

In each of the four vignettes, we explicate our pedagogical orientations, practical strategies, and outcomes of efforts toward humanizing the online classroom. Our discussions draw on research coupled with our pandemic teaching experiences to offer fruitful ways in which the online classroom may be humanized for the post-pandemic future. The focus is on four (4) areas: 1) adopting new practices for the creation of authentic learning experiences, 2) developing humanizing approaches for the assessment of student learning, 3) recognizing and fostering student mental wellness as a humanizing practice, and 4) leveraging learning frameworks to build connection.

1. *Creating authentic learning experiences* demonstrates how the pandemic prompted the adoption of new online teaching methods aimed at providing busy students with authentic opportunities for engagement.
2. *Developing humanizing approaches for the assessment of student learning* explores novel ways in which instructors can assess student learning in online classrooms during times of significant stress for both faculty and students.
3. *Recognizing and fostering student mental wellness as a humanizing practice* considers how the pandemic crisis brought increased awareness of the role of mental health in student success and advocates for pedagogical orientations that center student mental wellness, particularly in the online context.
4. *Leveraging learning frameworks for connection* offers strategies for using technology to promote relationship-rich online learning.

We acknowledge that there are more than four aspects to humanizing the online classroom. Our aim here is to open a conversation. We invite others to add to, critique, refute, and engage in lively discourse to develop this dialogue further. A wider range of voices and experiences will broaden and enrich our understandings of the complex relational and pedagogical dynamics involved in cultivating relationship-rich online education experiences. This chapter is a contribution toward the goal of articulating some of the opportunities and challenges for authentic and connected classroom experiences in ways that are meaningful and responsive to the ever-changing circumstances of teaching and learning in higher education.

HUMANIZING THE ONLINE CLASSROOM

Expanding on Best Practices in Teaching and Learning to Meet the Moment (Carolyn Arcand)

As the COVID-19 pandemic led to widespread stay-at-home orders in spring 2020, most college students and professors transitioned to online courses (Lederman, 2020). The large-scale shift to virtual education heightened typical challenges to fostering student engagement online. As an instructor in Public Policy and Public Administration graduate programs, I taught most of my courses in person (and a few online) prior to the pandemic. Since spring 2020, I have moved most of my courses online. The pandemic prompted me to reexamine best practices in online teaching while considering the challenges that the pandemic presented to my students when adapting from an in-person to an online format.

Online Education and Best Practices Prior to the Pandemic

Online courses have traditionally provided benefits, and presented challenges, for higher education. Benefits include technology which enables instructors to utilize multiple teaching methods (e.g., recorded lecture videos, online discussions, face-to-face video conferences) to address students' varied learning styles and provide them with enhanced flexibility (Davis et al., 2022). Despite these benefits, evidence from bachelor's degree programs suggests that students tend to perform worse in online courses relative to courses held in a physical classroom (Alpert et al. 2016; Cellini & Grueso, 2021). Generally, older students with strong overall GPAs are more likely to succeed in online courses (Clark, 2013). Students with less academic preparation tend to perform worse in online settings (Cellini, 2021). Graduate students typically have better online course completion rates relative to undergraduates (Gering et al., 2018).

Best practices for online teaching had been developed by experts for decades leading up to the pandemic. For example, globally recognized nonprofit *Quality Matters* utilizes extensive research to create and update rubrics that institutions and instructors can use to improve the quality of online courses. Practices described in these rubrics include presenting an easy-to-use course website with instructions for course navigation and expectations of students, using a variety of assessment methods, and clearly specifying criteria for evaluation of students' work (Quality Matters, n.d.). Award-winning online faculty describe best practices including designing each course with the target student audience in mind (e.g., traditional first-year undergraduates or adult graduate students who are employed full-time), fostering student interaction and community using different types of media, using a range of assessment formats, and communicating regularly with students (Martin et al., 2019). Students note the importance of opportunities for social connection and assignments that involve engaging in their local communities as valuable components in online courses (Boling et al., 2012). Best practices that emphasize communication and community-building between instructors and students work to directly foster a humanized online learning experience. Practices that encourage the use of accessible materials, clear criteria, and adoption of different types of assessment methods indirectly humanize the online classroom by respecting the time, diverse learning styles, and varied assessment strengths and preferences held by students.

Instructor and Student Responses to the Pandemic

The shift to online learning in Spring 2020 led most instructors to adopt new teaching methods and change the types of assignments that they asked students to complete (Lederman, 2020). Most instructors reported that the move to online learning made it difficult to engage with students (June, 2020). As I revised my courses early in the pandemic, I listened closely to my students' anecdotal accounts of managing uncertainty and paid attention to emergent research on the impact of the pandemic on student circumstances more broadly.

Students described the shift to online learning as creating challenges to their motivation and learning (Davis et al., 2022). For example, when campus closures led many residential undergraduates to move back home with their parents they had to take on responsibilities such as housework and caring for or homeschooling their younger siblings, in addition to coursework (Morris et al., 2021; von Keyserlingk

Humanizing the Online Classroom

et al., 2021). Students also experienced issues with reliable internet and adjustment to new (perhaps shared) workspaces (Gillis & Krull, 2020).

Many students who were employed faced decreased wages and lost jobs (Aucejo et al., 2020). Non-traditional students–those who are older, financially independent, do not hold a traditional high school diploma, have children, attend school part-time and/or work full-time (National Center for Education Statistics, n.d.) --reported having financial challenges and reducing the number of courses taken (Babb et al., 2021). Graduate students experienced concerns around employment, financial stability, and the health and well-being of their families (Kee, 2021).

Amplifying Best Practices to Directly and Indirectly Humanize the Online Classroom

My approach to engaging with students in online courses as we all navigated the pandemic was influenced by hearing about these challenges as they were occurring. I wanted to be responsive to the upheavals students were experiencing in their family, work, and academic lives. I did not want my online courses to create additional navigational challenges for them; rather, I sought to create a seamless and intuitive course presence online. Beyond this, I hoped to provide opportunities for authentic connection during a time of isolation. Each of these goals involved planning to either indirectly or directly humanize my online teaching. To this end, I worked to normalize caregiving as a valid reason for students to request accommodations, optimized my course content for ease of access and flexibility, and regularly provided optional opportunities for live student-teacher connection.

Normalizing Accommodations for Caregiving

I have always been supportive of students taking additional time on assignments to attend to extenuating circumstances around illness, family, or employment. However, the pandemic created the first instance in which *I* had to ask my students for additional flexibility around my own family obligations. In 2020, I was a parent to an infant and a toddler and juggling my work with family responsibilities amidst daycare closings and childhood illnesses created a scenario where I regularly had to rearrange my office hours or scheduled class meetings (both held via video conference) to attend to emergent family circumstances. I announced that I am a caregiver and that I would need to reschedule meetings or may take extra time to grade assignments if my children's school or daycare was closed or they were home sick. At the same time, I encouraged students to reach out and ask for flexibility if they needed time to take care of a relative, friend, or themselves. More than ever before, students did reach out to request extra time when they or a family member were ill or in need of care. Instances of needing extra time to accommodate care provision were much more commonly reported by my students, relative to employment-related circumstances. In the future, I plan to maintain the practice of announcing that I may need flexibility due to my caregiving responsibilities and encouraging students to request flexibility around their own.

Optimizing Course Content for Ease of Access and Flexibility

To enhance ease of access and flexibility (i.e., to make sure my course structures were not creating navigational headaches for students), I streamlined weekly course content modules. I put everything that students needed for a given week (links to reading assignments, lecture videos, handouts, homework assignments, etc.) on one page of the course website. I used a common format for all weekly content modules and for presenting assignment instructions. This cut down on the amount of time students would need to spend searching for items or working to understand instructions. I also gave students more flexibility around completing assignments. As an example, for one class students were given 10 homework assignments, but only the top 9 homework assignment grades were counted. This format gave students the flexibility to skip a homework assignment when needed, without worrying about a negative impact on their final grade.

Providing Optional Opportunities for Live Student-Teacher Connection

Finally, I thought it was important to provide students with regular, optional opportunities for live connection to help mitigate the isolation that accompanied stay-at-home orders. To create these opportunities, I restructured my courses to build in weekly or biweekly class discussions over video conference. Students were instructed to either attend a live video conference meeting and participate in an online discussion, or complete an alternative assignment (e.g., write an essay addressing the discussion questions from class) for participation credit. I announced that I would open all class meetings ten minutes early and invited students to drop in early to chat with me and others before class. Additionally, I held live video conferences during office hours each week and posted an announcement reminding students that they could drop in to meet with me on days that office hours were held. These announcements included a link for easy access to the office hours video conference. Class meetings, early drop-in chats, and office hours have all been remarkably well-attended. My students have reported that they enjoy having the opportunity to connect with each other and discuss course material live, rather than in a typed asynchronous discussion thread.

The changes that I made sought to amplify existing best practices to humanize my online classroom in response to the intensified student circumstances and day-to-day uncertainty created by COVID-19. These changes have been well-received and will ideally continue to evolve beyond the pandemic.

Making Space for Student Connectedness and Measurement of Active Learning (Judith Tupper)

During the early lockdown period of the pandemic, we came to understand the precarious position of many students. Some quickly fell into food and housing insecurities. Adult learners, responsible for their household income, were unable to support their families and encountered difficult choices concerning employment, childcare, and remote learning for their children. In many cases, personal illness, illness in family members, and mental health concerns required the complete focus of students' time, finances, and emotional capacities. Life priorities shifted for both students and faculty. The attention to course readings, assignments, tests, and grades simply did not rise to the top of these many concerns (Slade et al., 2021). In the face of these changing priorities, instructors reconsidered assessment with adaptations that usually involved reductions in student workload, and the jettisoning of group work and presentations (Johnson et al., 2020).

But even the "best practice" online instructional design may not alleviate the special cause variance that arises through student, faculty, and family member illness, financial pressures, housing shortages, food insecurities, internet instability, escalating inflation, mental health concerns, and societal domestic and foreign unrest. Inequities in student basic needs that existed prior to the pandemic were amplified by this upheaval (Jankowski, 2020). Many of my students described their general state of *dis-ease* and

Humanizing the Online Classroom

disconnection during the height of the COVID-19 disruption as well as a continuing sense of malaise as the pandemic continued.

What can we learn from assessment strategies during an unprecedented time of higher education disruption? Some innovations have the potential to vastly improve student assessment while connecting the student to their peers, faculty, institution, wider community, and personal career goals.

Student Connectedness is Tied to Student Performance

As discussed in this chapter, student connectedness is associated with less anxiety and better academic performance. Being lonely increases the chances of poor academic performance in students with worse mental health. Online students will be more successful academically and have improved mental health through a sense of connectedness to their university and emotional intimacy with at least one significant person at the university (Di Malta et al., 2022; Giusti et al., 2021). Some students will thrive on social connectedness (group discussions, group tutorials, and student communities), and other students, with lower academic performance, may rely on a one-to-one relationship with their instructor to feel connected. How can asynchronous online courses increase student connectedness through assessment strategies? I share some specific strategies that I used during the first years of the pandemic that support student engagement, connectedness, and the measurement of learning objectives that I plan to continue to use in the future. The online course can be a meaningful place of learning as one of my students shared on a course evaluation.

There is some magic that happens in this class that I can't fully explain. As a class, we have never met, have never heard each other's voices, or even seen each other's faces on screen. But this is an intimate class, where people feel comfortable sharing thoughts, stories, and wishes. It embodies the words "learning community".

Assessment Strategies to Increase Academic Engagement and Student Connectedness

Student connectedness is central to the fiber of the online course community. Building the learning community early in courses through pre-course communications and "coffee shoppe" discussion boards of mutual introduction set the stage for relationships between students and instructors and student peer relationships. Thoughtful prompts for introductions may include personal information to humanize the instructor and build relationships between participants. I have found it well worth the time to respond individually to each student and weave shared experiences and future course topics, setting the stage for an active learning community and relevance to career goals.

Instructors are at the helm of the culture and tempo of online courses. Students should come to know the value and meaning of working together and experience the benefits of the learning community. Establishing the "we" through weekly modules with multiple grading activities and personalized feedback will enhance active learning and diminish the self-study feeling that some students report in online courses. Reminding students that "we" travel as a team through content and experience lessons and conversations together reinforces the learning community.

Creating Opportunities for Success

As an online student, and later, an online instructor, I've learned that effective and engaging course design includes clear learning objectives, ideally mapped to professional competencies. Establishing clear expectations at the start of courses through detailed syllabi, course announcements, and grading rubrics are general tools of the trade. Humanizing the online classroom does not imply any short-change of academic integrity. Students appreciate reasonable boundaries as long as expectations–and consequences–are addressed and explained thoroughly. With a creative variety of brief weekly assessment opportunities, there should be little reason or opportunity for cheating or plagiarism. Every short assessment is an opening for individualized student connections and monitoring of progress towards learning goals and objectives.

While exacting standards of student accountability and performance may be overwhelming initially for already depleted students, tools for success can be embedded in every lesson, activity, and assessment. For example, "starter" templates can set students up for successful submission. The fatigued student may demonstrate learning in the template and capture the essence of the assignment while avoiding excess time formatting. It should also be transparent that student success is the instructor's goal.

Authentic and Personalized Communication with Students

Another key strategy to humanize assessment in an online course is generous and frequent personalized feedback during grading. Grading rubrics are likely a necessity, but it is authentic feedback that keeps students engaged. Regular positive feedback for student work is a tonic for stressed students and will keep students returning to the course to check on their assessments. It is especially effective to acknowledge individual performance improvement, comment on evidence of scaffold learning, and how content knowledge and skill acquisition applies to student career interests and goals. Supportive and personalized feedback also includes acknowledging student task persistence (i.e., assignment completion and timeliness) even when the learning objectives have not been fully met. Students value personalized feedback and have remarked on its importance:

She makes each student feel that they are her only student and makes an effort to connect with all of us, during each assignment/discussion board. I had more interaction, and connectivity with [instructor] than I have had in in-person classes!

Instructors should seek creative and varied assessments to engage students with different learning styles. Supplying a plethora of brief grading opportunities rewards active participation and can smooth out a miss or two. I give students opportunities to self-test to assess understanding. Open book quizzes are helpful to self-check learning acquisition, reinforce concepts and content vocabulary, and add points towards final grades.

How to help academically struggling students? I work to stay present and act quickly when students start to check out. Gently coaxing them back at an early point may avoid common grading challenges later in the semester. Adult learners appreciate flexibility as they manage the unpredictability of their own lives and those of their families. Establishing late submission policies with modest point reductions afford students a way to "catch-up." I have also added a simple request to assignment submissions at key points in the semester. I ask students to "check- in'' when submitting the assignment. (e.g., Tell me how you are doing in the text box. How is the class going for you?) In my experience, this quick check-in is well received and often reveals ways to support students and deepen their connection to the content and learning community.

Building Engaging Discussion Forums

Graded discussion forums, for better or worse, are a ubiquitous element of online pedagogy. It can be debated that during disruptive times such as the pandemic, discussion boards may be considered a particular burden and waste of precious time and emotional energy. Yet these forums, when purposeful, afford a sense of currency and engagement with real-time events, along with frequent and low-risk grading opportunities. Key elements of successful group discussion assessments include establishing a rhythm and flow of initial posts and responses to weekly prompts. I suggest modeling engagement through regular instructor postings. For example, I ask questions and remind students that responses to the instructor are also part of the grading rubric. Carefully watch for signs of disengagement. If students struggle to take part due to time constraints or other pressures, it can be overwhelming to see other students moving ahead without them. I remind students that they do not have to read all posts each week but can choose to make different connections each week.

Adding Student-directed Assessments

Grading opportunities can also be student-directed. Depending on the level of individual student fatigue, student-directed assessments can be motivating and meaningful, or conversely, a stress-added burden. Instructors may consider frameworks that support student-directed assessment such as portfolio products, competency checklists, career-specific assignments, with just-in-time design. One simple student-directed assessment strategy is to assign a brief one-page paper in which the student reflects on a specific course learning objective and discusses the application of the content to their chosen career plans. Reflective assignments can be rewarding to students who have worked hard to engage with course content and can articulate the applied purpose of the learning experience.

Partners in the Learning Community During Uncertain Times and Beyond

Instructors can effectively respond to challenges of assessing online student learning during times of crisis by returning to core tenets of student assessment. Coupled with opportunities for student connectedness with peers and instructors, authentic assessment is directly tied to student learning objectives, active learning activities, and professional competencies. Students can be engaged in assessment through a variety of strategies that acknowledge and respect changing priorities, need for flexibility, differing learning styles, and shared experiences of learning and adapting. Instructors can be genuine, honest, and supportive with students and connect creative online course assessments aligned with carefully designed learning objectives. I plan to bring forward these assessment strategies that promote connectedness, flexibility, and individualized feedback in my post-pandemic online teaching.

Recognizing and Fostering Student Mental Wellness as a Humanizing Practice (Maureen Ebben)

In this section, I propose a revisioning orientation to student mental health that humanizes and reframes mental wellness as a matter of equity. I ask: what would taking student mental health seriously mean for how we perform our teaching and learning roles? The health effects of the COVID-19 pandemic on the mental wellbeing of college students have been profound. A systematic review of empirical research on college student mental health found that college students "reported feeling more anxious, depressed, fatigued, and distressed than prior to the pandemic" (Elharake et al., 2022). For many, the trauma of the pandemic years brought heightened levels of stress and grief with lingering impacts (Everett, 2021). Although college student mental health was increasingly recognized as important on many university campuses, the pandemic spotlighted its centrality in student persistence and success.

Humanizing Mental Wellness as a Matter of Equity

Mental wellness is a key component of student success. Socioeconomic aspects of students' identities such as race, class, gender, ethnicity, and so on are readily understood to be important elements that can help or hinder student persistence. Mental health also needs to be included in this constellation of factors. Further, it is important to recognize that such intersectional dimensions of students' backgrounds and identities shape their experiences of mental health. For example, students of color, low-income students, and LGBTQI+ students experience depression and other mental health challenges at higher rates (Anderson, 2020).

In recent years, many colleges and universities have expanded their efforts around diversity, equity, and inclusion (DEI) through initiatives that seek to put equity at the center of student services and pedagogical approaches with recognition of the wide range of student backgrounds and experiences (Ivery, 2022). However, missing from many of these efforts is an explicit recognition of mental wellness as another component of equity. For example, some students arrive at college possessing skills with emotional regulation, self-knowledge, and an array of tried-and-true coping strategies. Other students are in the early stages of becoming aware of or developing skills for managing stress and anxiety. Like other elements that comprise persons' intersectional identities, mental health needs to be acknowledged and included in equity initiatives to promote student (and faculty) mental wellness.

Equality vs. Equity

What might the inclusion of mental wellness in humanizing pedagogical efforts toward equity look like? Equity scholars and advocates note that equity is not the same as equality (Phuong et al., 2017). *Equality* in pedagogy means that all students are treated the same, with the same materials, time, methods, assessments, and so forth. Those students who are the brightest, most motivated, and least burdened tend to be the ones to rise to the top and succeed. *Equity* approaches, however, focus not so much on the equality of treatment, but on the achievement of equality of outcomes. There is recognition that students come from a wide range of backgrounds and experiences and that they have a variety of needs (Ebben & Blewett, 2021). Working to address mental wellness from an equity perspective is a more complicated and challenging endeavor than addressing mental wellness from an equality approach. But it is worth the time

Humanizing the Online Classroom

and effort to think seriously about developing practices that take into account students' socioemotional needs in teaching and learning.

Building on Pandemic Teaching Experiences for More Humanizing Practices

Teaching during the pandemic years meant reconfiguring classes, practices, and policies. Some changes were welcomed by students while other changes resulted in unintended confusion, anxiety, and stress. Consider, for example, a course staple such as an attendance policy. Often strict before the pandemic, attendance policies became more generous as faculty and students experienced the roller-coaster ride of pandemic twists and turns. After the first year of the pandemic, however, many colleges sought to return to "normal" with some online classes becoming more hybrid through a mix of in-person and online components. To enforce this return to a kind of normalcy, attendance was insisted upon by many instructors giving rise to "the attendance conundrum" in which students face a range of complex and idiosyncratic course attendance policies (Supiano, 2022). An additional layer of uncertainty occurred as students were told by university officials (and public health experts) that if they were exposed to or tested positive for COVID-19 they should self-isolate for several days. It was often difficult for students to identify the proper course of action. Should they attend class? Should they stay home? Experiencing a loss of choice and personal agency, many students felt increased anxiety that exacerbated mental health challenges during an already fraught time. A routine and seemingly minor course component, such as an attendance policy, may compound student stress depending on how it is formulated and implemented.

Equitable Design

Hopefully, the worst days of the pandemic are behind us, but students still face an array of differing course policies and practices, whether regarding attendance or other aspects of course logistics and expectations. The answer is not uniformity, but thoughtful design. Options and flexibility can assuage student stress. Instructors teaching asynchronous, hybrid, or high-flex classes, that are online or partially online, offer latitude for how students can access course information and participate (Berube 2022). Student choice of modalities for engagement and participation without fear of negative consequences may promote mental wellness, as expressed by this undergraduate: "Sometimes, students wake up feeling depressed and need to lie in bed all day. We shouldn't feel like the reason is invalid" (in Supiano, 2022).

Rather than dismiss such a statement, what would it mean if we took it seriously? How do the structures and practices that we establish around our course policies intersect with student mental wellness? Some students regard course policies that make, for example, class attendance mandatory as a form of able-ism. That is, the policies privilege the minds and bodies of persons who are unencumbered by maladies of any sort. If faculty establish mandatory course requirements regarding attendance, and other course activities, how can instructors ensure that the policies are equitable for all students?

As the pandemic eases and higher education institutions seek to reinvigorate their on-campus student learning and living experiences, it is clear that some students want to stay remote for mental health reasons. Online and hybrid modalities are the preferred choice for students of color and students with disabilities as "68 percent of Black students and 60 percent of Hispanic students feel positive about online learning, and the transition to virtual learning has offered some students with disabilities new educational modalities" (Pressley, 2022). Students of color and students with disabilities report being subjected to fewer microaggressions (i.e., discriminatory interpersonal interactions) as online students compared to what they typically endure in face-to-face classes and in-person activities. Chief diversity officer, Raechele Pope, from the University at Buffalo states, "There is significant data, both anecdotal and from empirical studies, suggesting that being away from those [biased] experiences may have positive mental health effects" (in Pressley, 2022). How can we revision education to play a positive role in maintaining–ideally, enhancing–the mental health of students?

Humanizing Policies for Mental Wellness

Remembering what we did during the pandemic and building on the best changes may humanize our practices to promote student mental wellness. How, for example, do we retain the increased flexibility that was a hallmark of learning during the pandemic? I have found that if I loosen up attendance policies (whether for synchronous video conference class meetings or in-person class meetings), students still attend. I discovered that if I grant extensions (when justifiably warranted) students do not abuse this generosity. In fact, students often welcomed the recognition of their humanity, sending me thank you notes and emails of appreciation. More importantly, I found that students were mentally restored and able to academically engage in the class more effectively.

Teaching as Relational

The relational aspect of teaching and learning cannot be overstated. Teaching is a relational act. During the pandemic, feelings of loneliness and experiences of existential uncertainty about the course of the pandemic in the midst of a social milieu of civil and political unrest posed challenges for mental wellness and learning. As college instructor, Cantu-Wilson, observes, "We don't know the depth to which students felt isolated. I don't think we understand how severe the impact was to their psyches, to their hearts" (in Tamez-Robledo et al., 2022). Intentional community-building efforts that seek to recognize students as whole persons can help to heal these deleterious effects. Guided by trauma-informed principles (Salis & Rhodes, 2021), pedagogical practices can work to create safe environments with student-to-student and student-instructor relationships of support allowing for student voice, choice, and empowerment.

Prioritizing Mental Wellness

One way that I build toward student voice, choice, and empowerment is to include the option of "mental health days" in my course syllabus. Students are allowed mental health time off with no penalties. While I had included mental health days in my syllabi before the pandemic, now I make a point to use this policy in all of my classes and to amplify the policy in discussions with students to model and normalize the fact that restoration of mental health is essential and should be built into the academic rhythms of the semester.

It is also important to remember that faculty are not solely responsible for student mental wellness. We can partner with colleagues. For example, embedding mental health resources into online classes is an approach that could be expanded. Just as librarians are often tied to specific courses to provide literacy and research skills, so, too, campus personnel and services around mental wellness could have a presence in online classes, increasing students' awareness of and access to vital resources. Mental wellness is complex, but there are steps we can take to champion it. A good place to start is by asking, how can humanizing practices contribute to student mental wellness?

Using Learning Frameworks to Promote Connection (Glorianne Schott)

Since the start of the COVID-19 pandemic, I have intentionally leveraged the affordances of online learning frameworks to help students to feel more connected to each other and the course. Here, I discuss two (2) such frameworks: 1) Community of Inquiry (CoI), and 2) Universal Design for Learning (UDL). I summarize the pedagogical assumptions of each and share my experiences about how they can be used to foster connection and promote humanizing effects for the online classroom.

Community of Inquiry (CoI) Framework

The Community of Inquiry (CoI) framework promotes human connection through design elements that enhance three types of presence in online learning: 1) social presence (i.e., the ability of learners to project their personal characteristics), 2) teaching presence (i.e., the ability of the instructor to communicate through course design, direct instruction, and facilitation of discourse), and 3) cognitive presence (i.e., the ability of students to construct meaning through sustained communication) (Garrison, 2006). The tools enabled through the CoI framework create an "optimal online learning experience for students" because they promote forms of presence that "facilitate critical thinking, critical inquiry among students, and meaningful discourse among students and faculty" (Singh et al., 2022, p. 15). I discuss some humanizing practices that I use that draw on the principles of the CoI framework below.

Introductions and Discussions

Instead of using a written self-introduction, or one in which I just look at a camera and speak, I introduce myself to my students using video clips from *Google Earth* along with drone footage from the region where I live. In my accompanying narrative, I share information about my background and include upbeat music to set the tone for the open connection I am trying to establish. I teach 1,600 miles away from some of my students, so use of the map and drone footage situates my location in relation to them. To initiate peer-to-peer connections, students are asked to share a short video introducing themselves. I provide students with a choice of prompts, and we use tools like *Padlet, Flipgrid,* and *Voicethread.* These applications work well for the introductions because they are user-friendly and embedded into the class learning management system. Students' efforts to get acquitted with these apps are a worthwhile investment of their time since students use the same audio and video tools throughout the semester to submit their assignments.

To foster meaningful discussions, I divide students into small groups. This is easily accomplished by most learning management systems. I have found that assigning discussion prompts to small groups of 6 to 8 students is less intimidating than requiring students to post in a large thread of over 40 students. The small groups can continue for the remainder of the semester, or new groups can be formed every few weeks. Within the small discussion groups, I assign task roles to students such as moderator, questioner, skeptic, and reporter (Nilson & Goodson, 2018). These roles allow for robust discussions on the given topics while promoting interpersonal connections and group cohesion.

Assignments and Grading

Student engagement–or lack thereof–was a significant factor in student satisfaction and perceptions of learning during the pandemic (Baber, 2020). For this reason, it is important to get "buy in" from students that the course topic is relevant to them, and the course modality, such as online, is an effective way to learn the subject matter. Strong teaching presence when communicating instructions and expectations for the course is often instrumental to student success (Nilson & Goodson, 2018). When we think about teaching presence in an online class, two main functions often come to mind: assigning things and grading things. However, our teaching style and relational tone may become robotic as we share PDFs of instructions and check boxes in grading rubrics. Learning management systems, and other technologies, provide the opportunity to personalize feedback to students–and in ways that can conveniently be linked to the gradebook. For example, recording audio and video feedback allows a student to hear our voice, especially our tone, which is likely to be more friendly than if the student were reading typed words on a page. I have found that providing enhanced personalized feedback leads to more conversation with students about specific aspects of their learning. These conversations, in turn, strengthen relational connections and contribute to students' persistence, motivation, and success in the course.

Universal Design for Learning (UDL) Framework

Another framework that informs course design and really hits at the heart of humanizing online learning is Universal Design for Learning (UDL). The goal of UDL is to address barriers that arise from systemic or other causes, and that result in inequitable learning opportunities and outcomes (Novak, 2022). As the pandemic continued into the third and fourth semesters, it required instructors to listen more closely to what was happening in the lives of students. Students faced myriad challenges that affected their ability to complete coursework including illness, lack of finances, social isolation, and death of a loved one to name a few. These obstacles became potential barriers to student learning. Many students, who previously had progressed smoothly through an educational program, now faced problems that prevented them from completing assignments and meeting deadlines. When I encountered situations in which I needed to make adjustments for a student, I considered how I could make adjustments while maintaining consistency and fairness for other students in the course. I needed to rethink many of my policies and make appropriate modifications that could be offered to, and benefit, all students, not just one. Universal Design for Learning guided me in making changes to my course design and delivery in ways that were equitable, promoting connection and community.

Course design based on UDL is guided by three principles in which an instructor: 1) provides multiple means of representation that gives learners choice in how they acquire information and knowledge; 2) provides multiple means of expression to allow learners various means of demonstrating what they know, and 3) provides multiple means of engagement by offering alternative ways for learners to be involved with course content, peers, and the instructor (Boothe et al.. 2018). Another important element of the UDL framework is its focus on the identification of barriers. Novak (2022) presents three guiding questions for instructors to ask in course design: 1) what do all learners need to know or be able to do? 2) what barriers may prevent students from learning? and 3) how can instructors design flexible ways for all students to learn and share what they know? Overcoming barriers means giving students more than one way to meet course objectives (Thibodeau, 2021).

Variety of Modalities

Given the proliferation of educational tools and applications, I was able offer course content in a variety of modalities. For example, in each module of my course, I presented content and materials in written, audio, and video formats. Students also had the option to engage in discussions through a choice of modalities including text, audio, and/or video. Interestingly, for discussions, students frequently selected audio over video. I provided students with apps such as *Vocaroo, Talk & Comment*, and *Mote* to record and share their audio clips in the class discussion forums. This approach provided a means of expression for learners who prefer to communicate with audio, and our relational connections were strengthened by the experience of hearing each student's distinctive voice.

Adding variability to how students can demonstrate their knowledge is another humanizing way to expand choice. For example, I redesigned an assignment so that students could decide how to present their work. Given this option, some students submitted a standard essay, while others used a question-and-answer format; several created presentations. While the criteria in the grading rubric remained the same, students had the flexibility to present their learning in novel and engaging ways that contributed to building community. For example, leading up to the due date for the assignment, I scaffolded a series of interactions in which students shared about their work process. Students not only discussed their topic, but also how they were using particular modalities for the assignment. They also exchanged information about the primary and secondary resources they found helpful, their favorite websites, and assisted each other with learning and using MLA and APA citation styles. Even though these were individual assignments, as students moved through the ups and downs of the learning process together, relational connections were enhanced.

The pandemic made me more aware of student needs. Utilizing the CoI and UDL learning frameworks were essential for helping me to address students' needs in humanizing ways. Each semester, I receive one or two letters from a college representative outlining the accommodations necessary for certain students to have the greatest opportunity for success. During the pandemic, I examined these requests more closely to reflect on whether the accommodation was something that would benefit all students. For example, I considered whether my due dates and time limits on assessments were arbitrary, or were the set deadlines necessary? What would happen if all students had the ability to take an assessment without the distraction and pressure of a clock ticking down in the corner? Following Burgstahler (2022), "infusing UDL into all aspects of higher education is an important step toward ensuring equity" (p. 1). As colleges and universities move through the pandemic crisis, learning frameworks like CoI and UDL offer humanizing ways to reinvigorate higher education.

FUTURE RESEARCH DIRECTIONS

This chapter discussed some ways in which humanizing orientations and practices can contribute to high-quality online education with a focus on four (4) themes: 1) a reexamination of pedagogical choices, particularly around course practices and student-instructor modes of communication, (2) a humanizing approach to the assessment of student learning, (3) the importance of increased awareness of student mental health to center student mental wellness with supportive pedagogical strategies, and 4) the intentional use of learning frameworks to foster instructor-student connection and create community. This is but a start. Future research can build on these perspectives and explore other ways in which online education can be humanizing.

For example, one important aspect of this work that needs further investigation entails soliciting a broad, representative sample of student reactions and responses to changes in online teaching that occurred as a result of the pandemic. What worked best for students? Where might students identify areas for improvement in humanizing their learning experiences? There may be salient differences in preferences across varied student groups.

Another facet of future research may involve compiling an extensive catalog of instructors' work towards humanizing their online classrooms during the pandemic. In what ways were existing frameworks and best practices revised? How did assessment practices change? What new methods were adopted for supporting students' mental health? How did these approaches vary when teaching different groups of students (e.g., undergraduates, graduate students, and nontraditional students)? These methods could be distilled into a new set of best practices for humanizing the online classroom.

A final area for further research may target how online education could be humanized for the instructors themselves. What lessons might be learned from the pandemic in terms of supporting instructors, whose own lives changed dramatically in the midst of a global crisis? Can pandemic-inspired innovation help colleges more effectively support instructors in balancing their own mental health and caregiving responsibilities with teaching obligations? Revisioning support of instructors' wellbeing through a humanizing lens will foster better teaching practices and, in turn, a higher-quality learning environment for students.

CONCLUSION

The global calamity of the COVID-19 pandemic accelerated the shift from face-to-face learning to online learning ushering in pedagogical experimentation and innovation. We now occupy a distinctive space from which to reflect on the crisis and consider what we have discovered about online learning and how those ideas might inform our teaching and learning practices going forward. In this chapter, we have argued for the importance of a humanizing approach to online learning. We conceptualize humanizing as a pedagogical orientation and practice in which human connections and the relational qualities of teaching and learning are intentionally prioritized. Our discussion has addressed four (4) areas: 1) adopting new practices for the creation of authentic learning experiences, 2) developing humanizing approaches for the assessment of student learning, 3) recognizing and fostering student mental wellness as a humanizing practice, and 4) leveraging learning frameworks for connection.

We acknowledge that there are additional topics and strategies that are important to consider in the quest to achieve a more humanized online classroom. This chapter is intended to expand the conversation. As technology continues to evolve, we must work to continually build humanity into new methods of online teaching. A proactive approach is needed, with attention to student and instructor experiences and larger institutional support structures. This work will strengthen the online teaching and learning environment and enhance equity in the classroom. We invite others to build on the ideas and perspectives articulated here as we engage in efforts to revison and reconstruct higher education after the pandemic crisis.

REFERENCES

Alpert, W., Couch, K., & Harmon, O. (2016). A randomized assessment of online learning. *The American Economic Review*, *106*(5), 378–382. doi:10.1257/aer.p20161057

Anderson, G. (2020, September 16). *More pandemic consequences for underrepresented students.* Inside Higher Ed. https://www.insidehighered.com/news/2020/09/16/low-income-and-students-color-greatest-need-pandemic-relief

Aucejo, E., French, J., Araya, M., & Zafar, B. (2020). The impact of COVID-19 on student experiences and expectations: Evidence from a survey. *Journal of Public Economics*, *191*, 104271. Advance online publication. doi:10.1016/j.jpubeco.2020.104271 PMID:32873994

Babb, S., Rufino, K., & Johnson, R. (2022). Assessing the effects of the COVID-19 pandemic on nontraditional students' mental health and well-being. *Adult Education Quarterly*, *72*(2), 140–157. doi:10.1177/07417136211027508 PMID:35520881

Baber, H. (2020). Determinants of students' perceived learning outcome and satisfaction in online learning during the pandemic of COVID19. *Journal of Education and e-learning Research, 7*(3), 285-292. doi:10.20448/journal.509.2020.73.285.292

Berube, M. (2022). Cut students some slack already. *The Chronicle of Higher Education.* https://www-chronicle-com.wv-o-ursus-proxy01.ursus.maine.edu/article/cut-students-some-slack-already

Boling, E. C., Hough, M., Krinsky, H., Saleem, H., & Stevens, M. (2012). Cutting the distance in distance education: Perspectives on what promotes positive, online learning experiences. *Internet and Higher Education*, *15*(2), 118–126. doi:10.1016/j.iheduc.2011.11.006

Boothe, K. A., Lohmann, M. J., Donnell, K. A., & Hall, D. D. (2018). Applying the principles of universal design for learning (UDL) in the college classroom. *The Journal of Special Education Apprenticeship*, *7*(3). Retrieved June 29, 2022, from https://scholarworks.lib.csusb.edu/josea/vol7/iss3/2/

Burgstahler, S. (2022). *Universal design as a framework for diversity, equity, and inclusion initiatives in higher education.* Disabilities, Opportunities, Internetworking, and Technology. https://www.washington.edu/doit/universal-design-framework-diversity-equity-and-inclusion-initiatives-higher-education

Cellini, S. (2021, August 13). *How does virtual learning impact students in higher education?* Brookings. https://www.brookings.edu/blog/brown-center-chalkboard/2021/08/13/how-does-virtual-learning-impact-students-in-higher-education/

Cellini, S., & Grueso, H. (2021). Student learning in online college programs. *American Educational Research Association Open*, *1*(7), 1–18. 10.1177%2F23328584211008105

Clark, M. (2013). *Student success and retention: Critical factors for success in the online environment* (Publication No. 444) [Doctoral dissertation, University of North Florida]. University of North Florida Digital Commons.

Davis, L., Sun, Q., Lone, T., Levi, A., & Xu, P. (2022). In the storm of COVID-19: College students' perceived challenges with virtual learning. *Journal of Higher Education Theory and Practice*, 22(1), 66–82. doi:10.33423/jhetp.v22i1.4964

Di Malta, G., Bond, J., Conroy, D., Smith, K., & Moller, N. (2022). Distance education students' mental health, connectedness and academic performance during COVID-19: A mixed-methods study. *Distance Education*, 43(1), 97–118. doi:10.1080/01587919.2022.2029352

Ebben, M., & Blewett, L. (2021). Post-pandemic anxiety: Teaching and learning for student mental wellness in communication. In J. Valenzano (Ed.), *Post-pandemic pedagogy: Predicting the change to come* (pp. 129–147). Rowman and Littlefield.

Elharake, J. A., Akbar, F., Malik, A. A., Gilliam, W., & Omer, S. B. (2022). Mental health impact of COVID-19 among children and college students: A systematic review. *Child Psychiatry and Human Development*. Advance online publication. doi:10.100710578-021-01297-1 PMID:35013847

Everett, S. (Ed.). (2021). Editor's introduction. In S. Everett (Ed.), *Trauma-informed teaching: Cultivating healing-centered ELA classrooms* (pp. 9-12). National Council of Teachers of English. https://ncte.org/wp-content/uploads/2022/06/Trauma-Informed-Teaching-.pdf

Felton, P., & Lambert, L. (2020). *Relationship-Rich Education: How Human Connections Drive Success in College*. Johns Hopkins University Press.

Garrison, D. R. (2006). Online collaboration principles. *Journal of Asynchronous Learning Networks*, 10(1), 25–34. doi:10.24059/olj.v10i1.1768

Gering, C. S., Sheppard, D. K., Adams, B. L., Renes, S. L., & Morotti, A. A. (2018). Strengths-based analysis of student success in online courses. *Online Learning*, 22(3), 55–85. doi:10.24059/olj.v22i3.1464

Gillis, A., & Krull, L. (2020). COVID-19 Remote Learning Transition in Spring 2020: Class Structures, Student Perceptions, and Inequality in College Courses. *Teaching Sociology*, 48(4), 283–299. doi:10.1177/0092055X20954263

Giusti, L., Mammarella, S., Salza, A., Del Vecchio, S., Ussorio, D., Casacchia, M., & Roncone, R. (2021). Predictors of academic performance during the covid-19 outbreak: Impact of distance education on mental health, social cognition and memory abilities in an Italian university student sample. *BMC Psychology*, 9(1), 1–17. doi:10.118640359-021-00649-9 PMID:34526153

Ivery, C. (2022, March 18). *Pandemic and racial reckoning reframe equity imperative for community colleges*. Diverse Issues in Higher Education. https://www.diverseeducation.com/opinion/article/15289683/pandemic-and-racial-reckoning-reframe-equity-imperative-for-community-colleges

Jankowski, N. A. (2020). *Assessment during a crisis: Responding to a global pandemic*. National Institute for Learning Outcomes Assessment. https://www.learningoutcomesassessment.org/wp-content/uploads/2020/08/2020-COVID-Survey.pdf

Johnson, N., Veletsianos, G., & Seaman, J. (2020). US Faculty and Administrators' Experiences and Approaches in the Early Weeks of the COVID-19 Pandemic. *Online Learning*, 24(2), 6–21. doi:10.24059/olj.v24i2.2285

Humanizing the Online Classroom

June, A. (2020, June 8). *Did the scramble to remote learning work? Here's what higher ed thinks.* The Chronicle of Higher Education. https://www.chronicle.com/article/did-the-scramble-to-remote-learning-work-heres-what-higher-ed-thinks

Kee, C. (2021). The impact of COVID-19: Graduate students' emotional and psychological experiences. *Journal of Human Behavior in the Social Environment*, *31*(1-4), 476–488. doi:10.1080/10911359.2020.1855285

Lederman, D. (2020, April 22). *How teaching changed in the (forced) shift to remote learning.* Inside Higher Education. https://www.insidehighered.com/digital-learning/article/2020/04/22/how-professors-changed-their-teaching-springs-shift-remote

Lempres, D. (2022, May 12). *Is hybrid learning here to stay in higher ed?* EdSurge. https://www.edsurge.com/news/2022-05-12-is-hybrid-learning-here-to-stay-in-higher-ed

Martin, F., Ritzhaupt, A., Jumar, S., & Budhrani, K. (2019). Award-winning faculty online teaching practices: Course design, assessment and evaluation, and facilitation. *The Internet and Higher Education*, *42*, 34–43. doi:10.1016/j.iheduc.2019.04.001

Matters, Q. (n.d.). *Specific review standards from the QM Higher Education Rubric* (6th ed.). https://www.qualitymatters.org/sites/default/files/PDFs/StandardsfromtheQMHigherEducationRubric.pdf

Miller, J. (2022, May 19). BLOG: UK online principles, priorities, wild possibilities. *University of Kentucky News*. https://uknow.uky.edu/campus-news/blog-uk-online-principles-priorities-wild-possibilities

Morris, M., Kuehn, K., Brown, J., Nurius, P., Zhang, H., Sefidgar, Y., Xu, X., Riskin, E., Dey, A., Consolvo, S., & Mankoff, J. (2021). College from home during COVID-19: A mixed-methods study of heterogeneous experiences. *PLoS One*, *16*(6), e0251580. Advance online publication. doi:10.1371/journal.pone.0251580 PMID:34181650

National Center for Education Statistics. (n.d.). *Nontraditional undergraduates/Highlights.* https://nces.ed.gov/pubs/web/97578a.asp#:~:text=A%20nontraditional%20student%20was%20identified,or%20did%20not%20obtain%20a

Nilson, L. B., & Goodson, L. A. (2018). *Online teaching at its best: Merging instructional design with teaching and learning research.* Jossey-Bass.

Novak, K. (2022). *UDL Now! A teacher's guide to applying universal design for learning in today's classrooms* (3rd ed.). CAST, Inc.

Phuong, A. E., Nguyen, J., & Marie, D. (2017). Evaluating an adaptive equity-oriented pedagogy: A study of its impacts in higher education. *The Journal of Effective Teaching*, *17*(2), 5–44. Retrieved June 29, 2022, from https://uncw.edu/jet/articles/vol17_2/phuong.html

Pressley, J. (2022, May 25). *Online learning can help minimize racism and ableism in and out of the classroom.* EdTech. https://edtechmagazine.com/higher/article/2022/05/online-learning-can-help-minimize-racism-and-ableism-and-out-classroom

Salis, F., & Rodhes, B. (2021). Trauma informed care during a global pandemic: Synergies and multidisciplinary boundaries for working with childhood, adolescence, senility and disability. *Education Sciences & Society-Open Access*, *12*(1), 149–163. Advance online publication. doi:10.3280/ess1-2021oa11822

Singh, J., Singh, L., & Matthees, B. (2022). Establishing Social, Cognitive, and Teaching Presence in Online Learning—A Panacea in COVID-19 Pandemic, Post Vaccine and Post Pandemic Times. *Journal of Educational Technology Systems*, *51*(1), 28–45. Advance online publication. doi:10.1177/00472395221095169

Slade, C., Lawrie, G., Taptamat, N., Browne, E., Sheppard, K., & Matthews, K. E. (2021). Insights into how academics reframed their assessment during a pandemic: Disciplinary variation and assessment as afterthought. *Assessment & Evaluation in Higher Education*, *47*(4), 588–605. doi:10.1080/02602938.2021.1933379

Supiano, B. (2022, January 20). The attendance conundrum: Students find policies inconsistent and confusing. They have a point. *The Chronicle of Higher Education*. https://www.chronicle.com/article/the-attendance-conundrum

Tamez-Robledo, N., Koenig, R., & Young, J. (2022, May 17). *The pandemic's lasting lessons for colleges, from academic innovation leaders*. EdSurge. https://www.edsurge.com/news/2022-05-17-the-pandemic-s-lasting-lessons-for-colleges-from-academic-innovation-leaders

Thibodeau, T. (2021, June 6). *The science and research behind the UDL framework*. Novak Education. https://www.novakeducation.com/blog/the-science-and-research-behind-the-udl-framework#:~:text=The%20Introduction%20of%20Universal%20Design,Center%20for%20Applied%20Specialized%20Technology

Villasenor, J. (2022, February 10). *Online college classes can be better than in-person ones. The implications for higher ed are profound.* Brookings. https://www.brookings.edu/blog/techtank/2022/02/10/online-college-classes-can-be-better-than-in-person-ones-the-implications-for-higher-ed-are-profound/

von Keyserlingk, L., Yamaguchi-Pedroza, K., Arum, R., & Eccles, J. (2022). Stress of university students before and after campus closure in response to COVID-19. *Journal of Community Psychology*, *50*(1), 285–301. doi:10.1002/jcop.22561 PMID:33786864

KEY TERMS AND DEFINITIONS

Ableism: Practices that privilege the minds and bodies of persons unencumbered by maladies of any sort.

Assessment: Strategies to measure achievement of learning objectives.

Authentic Learning: Active application of knowledge and skills gained in the classroom to real-world issues and problems.

Caregiving: The work of looking after oneself and/or others through activities such as cooking, cleaning, and emotional support.

Community of Inquiry (CoI): A pedagogical framework for fostering learning experiences through three forms of presence: 1) cognitive presence, 2) social presence, and 3) teaching presence.

Equity: Approach that focuses on the achievement of equal outcomes with recognition that different people may need different supports to reach the same outcome.

Humanizing the Online Classroom

Humanizing: Building empathy, respect, and equity into a process.

Mental Health: State of psychological and emotional wellbeing.

Relationship-Rich Education: Pedagogical orientation and practice in which the human connections and relational qualities of teaching and learning are intentionally prioritized in ways that promote learning.

Social Presence: The ability to identify with a group, communicate purposefully in a trusting environment, and develop relationships through individual personalities.

Universal Design for Learning (UDL): A pedagogical approach that seeks to accommodate the needs and abilities of all learners, especially through the elimination of unnecessary hurdles in the learning process.

Chapter 2
Revisioning Accessibility in Higher Education Post COVID-19

Jessica A. Cannon
https://orcid.org/0000-0002-3618-4409
University of Central Missouri, USA

ABSTRACT

One impact of the COVID-19 pandemic and complications from the virus is a significant increase in the number of people with cognitive and physical disabilities. Higher education has been slow to fully engage with accessibility measures, pursuing an on-demand individual accommodation model rather than broader accessibility from the outset. Recent legal decrees reinforce the expectation that broad accessibility is the new standard. Educational institutions can choose to act with deliberate attention to becoming leaders in implementing new accessibility practices and resources. A proactive approach increases the formal and informal educational opportunities for a broader audience of learners, as well as setting an example for how society at large can become more supportive of disabilities. This chapter outlines several ways higher education can adapt and lead this effort.

INTRODUCTION

It is frightening to be faced with a medical condition or life situation that is unpredictable, uncontrollable, life altering, and life threatening. But that does not make it unnatural. What is natural is to feel the good and the bad that is life. What is not natural is to suppress realities that we all in one form or another will face. (Barragann and Nusbaum, 2017, p. 53)

Eduardo Barragann (2017) speaks here about living with disability, yet his words also reflect the experiences of millions who were infected with the SARS-CoV-2 COVID-19 virus. Two years into the pandemic, early medical research demonstrates that the effects of COVID-19 can be both temporary (weeks) and long-term (months, years, to perhaps permanent) in nature. Infection impacts human physi-

DOI: 10.4018/978-1-6684-5934-8.ch002

Copyright © 2023, IGI Global. Copying or distributing in print or electronic forms without written permission of IGI Global is prohibited.

Revisioning Accessibility in Higher Education Post COVID-19

ology as well as cognitive function, and complications increase in frequency and severity with multiple infections by COVID-19 variants. As governments, businesses, and education systems push to 'return to normal,' infections continue as the virus mutates. Even if COVID-19 becomes endemic in the future, daily news reports show that many individuals—of all age groups—have temporary or long-term disabilities resulting from COVID-19. Acute and post-acute or "long-Covid" symptoms meet the definition of disability as set forth in the Americans with Disabilities Act (1990): "a physical or mental impairment that substantially limits one or more major life activities" (U.S. Department of Justice, n.d.). COVID-19 may become the agent of change that compels society to recognize and deliver equal access as a civil right for all people because the virus disables so many. This chapter focuses first on synthesizing the medical literature on COVID-19 symptoms as it impacts education, then explores the problems with the existing accommodations-approach to disability in higher education. In many ways, higher education is already behind in providing broader accessibility instead of one-off individual accommodations (Dolmage, 2017; Bolt, 2017; Kerschbaum, Eisenman, and Jones, 2017), and this chapter closes by proposing several actionable steps to change common structural, cultural, and instructional barriers.

BACKGROUND

Medical Research on Acute and Post-Acute COVID-19 Symptoms

Medical research on COVID-19 continues to identify and define the consequences of infection, although the symptoms and immune responses are generally grouped into two categories: acute (immediate symptoms and reactions with the initial infection) and post-acute sequelae (commonly called long-COVID). Both short- and long-term symptoms are relevant concerns in the education setting because even "mild" initial infection can still cause effects that range from asymptomatic to debilitating illness that requires weeks of isolation and rest. Long-COVID, while still being defined and studied, likewise can impact students of all ages for months or years with cognitive and physical disabilities (National Institutes of Health, 2022). Therefore, it is critical to follow the medical research to understand the symptoms of COVID-19 and their potential impact on the design and delivery of learning experiences. This is particularly important in higher education where an Individualized Education Plan (IEP) model used in K-12 education in the United States is *not* present to ameliorate gaps between student needs and institutional, program, or technology structures.

Most people are familiar with the worst acute COVID-19 symptoms requiring hospitalization from watching news reports. These symptoms occur in roughly 5 percent (critical intensive care) to 15 percent of cases (the overall hospitalization rate among those infected with early strains of the virus) (Basu-Ray, Adeboye, and Soos, 2022). For other cases not requiring hospitalization, acute symptoms often included viral upper respiratory illnesses, gastrointestinal issues, headaches and confusion, or alteration of taste and smell (Basu-Ray, Adeboye, and Soos, 2022). The primary immune response by the body can also lead to Cytokine Release Syndrome where severe inflammation and organ damage results from an individual's own immune response to fight the virus. Even in mild or totally asymptomatic infections, COVID-19 has been shown to leave damage to the heart, lungs, kidneys, and other organs. Complications from this damage can appear immediately or months and years later (Basu-Ray, Adeboye, and Soos, 2022; Fraser et al., 2022). In short, "mild" acute infections are not mild for everyone; the acute infection period can impact faculty, staff, and students' abilities to engage in education for weeks or even months.

Understanding long-COVID is the focus of the RECOVER Initiative, a research collaborative created by the National Institutes of Health. The RECOVER Initiative, or Researching COVID to Enhance Recovery, includes over 30 research teams at hospitals across the United States that are all working with the public to identify and treat symptoms of long-COVID (National Institutes of Health, 2022). Boston Medical Center (2022), a participant in the RECOVER Initiative, describes long-Covid saying: "despite recovery from initial infection, many patients continue to experience a number of symptoms—including fatigue, shortness of breath, brain fog, sleep disorders, fevers, gastrointestinal symptoms, abnormal blood clotting, loss of taste and/or small, anxiety, and depression. These symptoms collectively are now referred to as a condition called post-acute sequelae of SARS-CoV-2 (PASC) or 'long Covid.' Even if someone did not experience symptoms during their initial infection, PASC is still relevant because a patient could still experience long-term effects from infection."

Two years into the pandemic, there are several longitudinal studies that elaborate on the effects of long-COVID. One meta-analysis and review of this medical research shows over fifty long-term effects of COVID (Lopez-Leon et al., 2021). The review found that 80 percent of individuals infected with COVID-19 experienced at least one long-term symptom. Several of the most-often reported symptoms involve fatigue, headaches, attention disorder and memory loss, all of which significantly impact the ability to focus and learn. Symptoms reported in 10 percent or more of cases are summarized in Table 1 (Lopez-Leon et al., 2021).

The review notes that this information is based on 15 studies from around the world with patient cohorts that ranged from 102 to almost 45,000 participants. The studies examined adults ranging in age from 17 to 87 years and the follow-up time ranged from 14 to 110 days. Additionally, these studies predominantly focused on initial variants of COVID-19, not Omicron (Lopez-Leon et al., 2021). A second preliminary meta-analysis recently published showed increased risks for psychotic disorder, cognitive deficit, dementia, and epilepsy in the delta and omicron waves of the virus as well (Taquet et al., 2022). There are important take-aways in these studies for higher education. *At least one in ten persons* infected, and often more than that, experienced long-term symptoms that would impact their ability to work or study in significant ways.

Beyond physiological pain and symptoms that could limit movement and daily activities, symptoms like fatigue, headaches, attention disorder, memory loss, hearing loss, anxiety, depression, and sleep disorder are all issues that would seriously impact an individual in a learning environment—and in many cases, patients had more than one of these symptoms. Additional studies are ongoing and look specifically at the neurological long-term complications of COVID-19 using MRI and functional MRI scanners. These studies are trying to pinpoint differences in the brains of patients who develop long-term symptoms including fatigue, "fuzzy brain," or confusion (Brigham and Women's Hospital, 2022). One early neurological study shows damage in the brains of deceased COVID-19 patients akin to damage caused by Alzheimer's disease, damage which they hypothesize may be a potential cause of some 'brain fog' and confusion reported among COVID-19 survivors (Reiken et al., 2022). All of these symptoms potentially increase with repeated infections of COVID-19 variants.

While research is still revealing the ways that COVID-19 impacts human physiology and cognitive function, higher education needs to plan to provide these individuals with support. Beyond accommodating physical spaces like dorms and classrooms to address mobility and stamina issues students may face after COVID-19 infection, faculty and staff will need to provide a greater quantity and quality of digital access to campus resources as well as redesigning course content and assessments. Existing research on assisting individuals with traumatic brain injuries (TBI) or cognitive impairments has largely not been incorporated into the discussion of accessibility in higher education. Neurodivergence is increasingly important, and will be even more so with COVID-19, making existing K-12 research on cognitive disabilities and military research on TBI a beneficial starting point for planning how to adapt adult learning environments moving forward.

Table 1. Long-term effects of COVID-19 reported in 10 percent or more of patients.

Symptom	Percent of Patients Reporting
Fatigue	58%
Headache	44%
Attention Disorder	27%
Hair Loss	25%
Dyspnea	24%
Aguesia	23%
Anosmia	21%
Polypnea	21%
Cough	19%
Joint Pain	19%
Sweat	17%
Memory Loss	16%
Chest Pain or Discomfort	16%
Nausea	16%
Hearing Loss and Tinnitus	15%
Anxiety	13%
Depression	12%
Weight Loss	12%
Digestive Disorders	12%
Fever	11%
Sleep Disorder	11%
Pain	11%
Resting Heart Rate Increase	11%
Palpitations	11%
Reduced Pulmonary Capacity	10%

Current Issues and the Expectations for Accessibility

The Rehabilitation Act of 1973, the Americans with Disabilities Act (1990), and Section 508 of the Rehabilitation Act (signed into law in 1998) establish the legal requirements for accessibility. Higher education, whether a private institution offering educational services to the public (Title III) or a public institution that receives federal funding (Title II), falls under the requirements for equal access to all programs and services under the ADA. With the development of the Internet, Section 508 was added to the Rehabilitation Act to specify that digital resources must also be created with the accessibility of end-users in mind. This means that materials must be accessible through a variety of senses and navigation tools to permit users with disabilities to access the content that other non-disabled users are able to access. The United States Access Board (n.d.) maintains guides for compliance with federal legislation focusing both on physical spaces and on access in digital settings. The Access Board has proposed aligning Section 508 requirements with levels A and AA on the Web Content Accessibility Guidelines (WCAG) 2.0 standards, making WCAG 2.0 a solid starting point for guidance on digital accessibility (W3C, n.d.).

Many colleges and universities follow on-demand individual accommodation models for addressing accessibility in learning environments. The problems inherent with individualized accommodations after a student has enrolled in a course have been critically reviewed (Dolmage, 2017; Kerschbaum, Eisenman, and Jones, 2017). A common refrain from students and researchers is that this approach forces the individual to disclose their disability repeatedly as they navigate campus and various courses. Individuals with disabilities are then at the whim of each person they must interact with to receive the specified accommodation based on how others perceived disability and accommodation. This is because despite the law (de jure), the institutional systems (de facto) at universities frequently do not or cannot provide adequate accommodation or simply fail to require employees to provide the accommodations. This model is designed to adjust after-the-fact on an individual on-demand basis, rather than designed to be accessible and inclusive from the outset—be it a physical space, an extracurricular activity, or a course. Beginning in 2013, legal actions against several universities show the Department of Justice and the Office of Civil Rights altering expectations for higher education to provide equal access under the ADA precisely because of this issue. And, with increasing demand for accessible learning environments (because of COVID-19 or simply greater awareness of the law), understanding these revised expectations and practices is a necessity for all administrators, staff, and faculty.

Two important cases involve Atlantic Cape Community College and Wichita State University. The Consent Decree from the Office of Civil Rights to Atlantic Cape Community College in 2015 requires accessible materials to be available to students from the outset of a course rather than on-demand after a course has begun. The decree from the United States District Court for the District of New Jersey (2015) specifically defines accessible as "fully and equally accessible to, and independently useable by, blind individuals, so that the blind students and faculty members are able to acquire the same information, engage in the same interactions, and enjoy the same services as sighted students and faculty with substantially equivalent ease of use." It applies the requirements to "all individuals who provide any course-related instruction to ACCC students, including, but not limited to, professors, instructors, other faculty, and teaching assistants." And, the decree applied the expectations to all electronic or technology systems on campus, including not just learning management systems and course materials but also search engines, databases, office equipment, and information kiosks.

The National Federation for the Blind arrived at a second agreement in 2016 with Wichita State University. This agreement pushes accessibility expectations further by stating "equally effective" and "timely" access should be available to *all* materials across the campus—from course delivery in all formats to websites and even extracurricular opportunities. The agreement requires "providing the same information to students with disabilities to meet the same result, gain the same benefit, and reach the same level of achievement as any other student" (Resolution Agreement, 2016). Equally effective is defined here as "the alternative format or medium communicates the same information in as timely as fashion as does the original format or medium" (Resolution Agreement, 2016). A similar case involved Southern

Oregon University, and cases involving individuals who are deaf were also settled against the University of California Berkeley, Harvard, and MIT with similar expectations placed on the universities involved (Resolution Agreement, 2015; DRA v. University of California Berkeley, 2013; National Association of the Deaf v. Harvard and Massachusetts Institute of Technology, 2015). These agreements collectively show high expectations for access that existing on-demand individual accommodations practices cannot easily meet. Higher education must shift to implementing accessibility as a core value so that all digital and physical spaces on campus include accessible design from the outset.

Improving Accessibility through Structural, Cultural, and Instructional Change

Accessibility is a multi-layered issue with a long history of structural resistance in higher education. As David Bolt (2017) argues,

in the academy we are becoming increasingly appreciative of access requirements, which are essential, but recognizing the foundational achievements, ideas, knowledge, influence, experience, and/or authority of those of us who identify or are labelled as disabled proves profoundly difficult for some non-disabled colleagues, as though a fundamental order would be disrupted. This threat to ableism is the basis for all resistance to disability studies (p. 2).

Resistance often focuses not just on the study of disability but also on acknowledging and incorporating individuals with disabilities into the institutional culture and activities.

One example of a current issue is simply the pathway students must follow to incorporation or engagement in the campus community. Institutional practices assume that students can afford to seek lengthy medical testing and documentation for the disability. It also assumes self-disclosure is somehow an innocuous single event protected by anonymity in an office of accessibility. Instead, disclosure of disability in higher education is often multiple disclosures to multiple offices and individuals (including faculty, staff, and peers). In each instance of disclosure, the person receiving the information places their own definitions of disability onto the individual seeking accommodation. Often, for example with faculty, this involves an untrained person with limited knowledge of disability deciding if the accommodation is "fair" or even "necessary at all" and acting according to those personal prejudices and beliefs. In a concrete example, this could be a faculty member denying someone with mobility issues more time to take a test, making it impossible for the individual show what they know because they simply can't write as quickly as another student (and creating a violation of the student's civil rights and approved accommodation). The student might not be able to report that, as some might immediately suggest, if it is a major course and they need to continue to work with that faculty member for fear of retribution. This can become a traumatic and convoluted process for the student with the disability, creating a structural barrier requiring individuals to prove or defend their disability needs rather than accessing something that is a basic civil right (Sanchez, 2017). Furthermore, not all students or adults have documentation or a diagnosis, and in the case of long-COVID, there are currently no clear definitions of the condition or treatments. Ultimately, then, compliance with the law and to better support the growing number of individuals with disabilities requires higher education to approach accessibility through practices that create equal access from the start and do not demand disclosures to various offices, faculty, and staff across campuses.

SOLUTIONS AND RECOMMENDATIONS

Improving conditions for those with disabilities in higher education will continue to be a complex and evolving process requiring the input of professionals from a variety of disciplines. This chapter provides some modest suggestions for reimagining how higher education might better accommodate individuals through structural, cultural, and instructional revisions.

First, policy and structural changes are needed. Faculty, staff, and student guides, and other related campus policies, must make it clear that providing accessible content for students (even content created by other students within a course) is a requirement. This fits with many campuses' diversity, equity, and inclusion initiatives that are ongoing, although accessibility is sometimes forgotten as part of the DEI movement. Beyond reforming policies, to help create structural change and support faculty and students in designing with accessibility in mind, is to create a campus-wide collaborative team that examines and participates in decision-making that can impact accessibility issues. For example, one option is to model the collaborative teams that already assist individuals in the consultative medicine and Individualized Education Program (IEP) models. Consultative medicine involves a multi-disciplinary team of specialists that treat "patients with puzzling ailments who fall through the cracks of established health care systems" (Geng, Verghese, and Tilburt, 2021). This model was used by several medical institutions across the United States—for example, the Mayo Clinic, the Undiagnosed Diseases Network, the Cleveland Clinic National Consultation Service, and Stanford Consultative Medicine—even before COVID-19, but it has become the standard for centers participating in the RECOVER Initiative to research and treat long-COVID symptoms.

Similarly, students under the age of 18 seeking IEP plans in public education or adults seeking assistance for education, workplace training, life skills, or assistive technologies after age 18 are paired with a social work team to facilitate finding and obtaining resources in their community. Specialists involved in these teams can include speech pathologists, assistive technologists, grants writers, and medical professionals, among others. This kind of collaborative team seen in both examples is an ideal for model for higher education. Accessibility is usually a separate office (sometimes only under HR for faculty and staff) that does not have integration with the day-to-day operations of the university, whereas a collaborative team focused on accessibility could better allocate resources and connect students, staff, and faculty with support.

A collaborative team approach to accessibility in higher education could take many forms, although expanding the function and staffing of existing accessibility offices or instructional design centers is a logical first step. Ideally, the team would be involved or represented in the procurement process for all technology and physical public spaces (including classroom design and set-up). In addition, the team would also support faculty in learning about accessibility requirements and facilitate remediation of course materials with the faculty and library. Finally, the team would work with students to ensure all campus courses and activities are accessible.

This team model moves beyond accommodating individual requests in that the goal is to educate the campus community and create accessible environments before they are even needed. Removing the structural barriers before students arrive on campus provides greater access and less stress for both documented and undocumented disabilities. It also gives faculty a direct connection to help in building accessible learning environments, a resource that is sometimes not available when faculty receive an accommodation letter and do not know what to do. And it creates a group on campus responsible for oversight and implementation of new policies or resources, tasks that the frequently understaffed accessibility office or instructional design teams may not be able to complete in the current configurations common for these offices in universities. An ideal team focused on accessibility for a campus could include experts in assistive technology, education technologies, instructional design, accessibility and advocacy, grant writing, web design, faculty and staff representatives, student representatives, and a legal representative. The collaborative team would be charged with turning policies into action, which is where many institutions fall short.

Other structural changes are needed as well, even beyond what we typically envision when accessibility comes to mind. Policies for sick leave and course extensions or incomplete grades need clarification and expansion. Fatigue, limited mobility, and frequent highs and lows in recovery from COVID-19 requires greater flexibility in workloads and hours. How can a student missing a month of work continue in the course or in a program without a way to withdraw or put the course on hold? Rethinking the traditional time frames allotted to semesters and incomplete grades is necessary, and it provides clearer paths forward (to degree completion or continuing to work for the university) for students and faculty or staff. In fact, these conditions already impact individuals with chronic illness and other disabilities, and these individuals often have no recourse but to push through pain, sleep disorders, anxiety, and depression with limited or no support from campus officials to maintain their education or work positions. Like the student with difficulty writing used as an example earlier, there needs to be clear institution-wide guidance on providing access to prevent the issues with multiple disclosures and staff or peers being able to deny implementing accessible practices based on assumptions that these conditions are somehow a failure of individual work ethic or determination rather than recognizing them as medical issues and providing accessibility adjustments as a civil right for the individual. In fact, individuals with disabilities are often very resilient and hardworking because they have had to hide or overcome disabilities in life to get by in society. Nevertheless, they should not have to negotiate daily or weekly with a multitude of individuals in varying power-relationships (think student-faculty, for example) to receive an accommodation.

CHANGING CULTURES

Moving beyond structural changes and related to this discrimination, another critical step is to increase awareness of access issues among faculty, staff, and students. Creating a culture where disability is part of diversity and not seen as a separate office or group of people is important to building a truly inclusive community. For example, Wichita State University in response to their agreement with the National Federation of the Blind, implemented a training process for all faculty, staff, and students. These were also offered as continuing education courses to the community at a nominal fee. Courses taught basic accessibility practices, and specifically how to create accessible content files and captioning multimedia materials. This approach helps to increase awareness of the struggles faced by individuals with disabilities and to highlight best practices in courses, campus activities, and peer-to-peer file and material sharing that can involve everyone on campus in making the community stronger and more accessible. Additional workshops discussing the stigma and issues surrounding disclosure and addressing ableism in daily life would also support changing cultures on college campuses. Often, leaders from organizations like the National Federation of the Blind can connect universities with local professionals who can serve as consultants or speak to the campus community about their experience. It is important for the cultural change to impact not just faculty and staff but to also include students. Students also need to create and share accessible resources with peers in coursework and apply these values of inclusivity in activities across campus. Meaningful change in campus cultures could be measured by something like accessibility compliance in campus digital resources, greater engagement and participation by individuals with disabilities in the broader campus extracurricular events, and qualitative studies of student experiences.

Instructional Change

Ultimately, a campus revolves around the instructional mission and increasing instructional design and instructional support are mission critical to increasing accessibility in higher education. Structurally, institutions in higher education need to provide software and campus spaces that are accessible. The proposed collaborative team discussed earlier could help integrate accessibility specialists into various campus processes like procurement, which is important to ensure that faculty and students are using learning management software, education technologies, and campus reporting software that is ADA compliant and flexible to the needs of students and faculty. Procurement does not always weight accessibility high or require certain provisions be met, so including personnel focused on making sure all purchases are inclusive and adaptive to accessibility needs is necessary for campuses to improve in this area. In addition to stable and usable platforms, however, institutions also need to provide the instructional design infrastructure to support the creation of effective and accessible learning environments.

Qualified instructional design staff, or the collaborative accessibility team outlined in this chapter, must be available for training and direct support of faculty. Faculty are often willing to redesign courses with accessibility in mind, and to provide variety in course content and assessments. But they were not necessarily taught how to do these things in their own graduate training or teaching experience. It is, in fact, a failure of the higher education system itself that faculty are taught how to research and innovate in their fields but not necessarily how to be effective teachers in that field in graduate studies, even though the goal of many graduate programs is for their students to land tenure-track positions in universities where they will teach in some form or another. Faculty need support in learning and applying accessibility and pedagogical practices, and this is where a partnership between faculty and instructional designers is key. Instructional designers can bring expertise on education technologies, WCAG standards for accessible materials, instructional theories like Universal Design for Learning, and accessible practices to the discussion of course design. This impacts not just online or hybrid courses but all modalities because all courses use learning management systems and deliver content to students (and increasingly in digital and multimedia formats). Instructional designers also can teach faculty about cognitive load and modern pedagogical practices like spaced retrieval and interleaving. Instructional designers, or a campus-wide team focused on accessibility, are best situated to keep up with the evolving research literature on accessibility and share it with faculty or with policy makers.

It is worth noting here that courses cannot simply be built by instructional designers as shells for the subsequent input of content material. Faculty, as subject matter experts, bring content but they also bring deeper understanding of trends in the field, how it applies to students' lives, and ways to innovate with the subject and its applications in society. These are elements of the motivation that keep students engaged in the classroom. Faculty also understand what types of assessments will best facilitate learning in their field. Thus, the ever-critical recruitment and retention expectations of higher education require both the internal course design support that instructional designers can provide as well as the spark and expertise that faculty bring.

Revisioning Accessibility in Higher Education Post COVID-19

Finally, the culture and design of the course needs to be flexible. There are already students in courses with chronic illnesses, sleep disorders, attention disorder, memory issues, traumatic brain injuries, and anxiety and depression. COVID-19 is simply increasing the number of students with these conditions. Faculty, working with instructional designers, must account for cognitive impairments and develop alternative paths to demonstrating learning or accessing content. This includes spaced retrieval and repetition, consideration of cognitive loads in the work and tasks assigned, and flexibility with deadlines. Anyone who has felt "brain fog" from COVID-19, or simply felt overwhelmed by the multitude of things to address simultaneously while teaching during the pandemic, can understand how these limitations affect work. Learning does not occur on a set timetable; by providing alternative paths to learning outcomes through multiple ways to demonstrate content mastery or skills, course design becomes more accessible. And by providing these from the outset of a course, students are not required to self-disclose disabilities—for example, 'outing' themselves to classmates and professors to obtain a notetaker—to be included in the higher education community.

FUTURE RESEARCH DIRECTIONS

Additional research on the impact of COVID-19 on cognition is necessary in the medical community before educators can begin to assimilate that literature with existing work on the impact of cognitive impairments on learning, memory, and other physiological aspects of human thought. In addition, understanding how COVID-19 and long-COVID impact the organs, including the heart and the common fatigue symptoms, are crucial as well. Beyond COVID-specific research, exciting advances in cognitive neuroscience and cognitive psychology over the last decade are increasingly applied in educational research and theories, particularly with the use of functional MRI technologies to see "real time" imaging of brain function (Means, Bakia, and Murphy, 2014; Mayer, 2002). This information has even been distilled into resources to help teach students how to learn more effectively (McGuire, 2018; Zakrajsek, 2022). Future researchers will, hopefully, continue to add to this growing body of applied learning best practices.

CONCLUSION

Medical research on COVID-19 is ongoing, however early studies demonstrate complications from the virus that will expand the number of individuals with disabilities. The existing model in higher education based on individual accommodations made after a class begins is no longer tenable. Recent legal decrees and agreements requiring timely and equal access to all facets of campus life and instruction result in a need for higher education institutions to adopt an accessibility model where access is built into courses, activities, and the campus spaces before students even arrive for the semester. Higher education has an opportunity to lead the implementation of a new model for accessibility, one that focuses on collaborative teams and support networks for faculty, staff, and students. By implementing structural changes to policies, access to instructional design training, direct support in course design, and efforts to change the culture of campuses to be more inclusive of disability, institutions of higher education ultimately will increase student engagement and success for everyone.

REFERENCES

Barragan, E., & Nusbaum, E. (2017). Perceptions of disability on a postsecondary campus: Implications for oppression and human love. *Negotiating disability: Disclosure and higher education*, 39-56.

Basu-Ray, I., Adeboye, A., & Soos, M. P. (2022). Cardiac manifestations of coronavirus (COVID-19). StatPearls Publishing.

Bolt, D. (2017). Introduction: Avoidance, the academy, and activism. In Disability, Avoidance and the Academy (pp. 1-8). Routledge.

Boston Medical Center. (2022). *RECOVER long COVID study*. Retrieved from https://www.bmc.org/infectious-diseases/recover-long-covid-study

Brigham and Women's Hospital. (2022). *Long-term neurological complications of COVID-19*. https://www.brighamandwomens.org/campaigns/physicians/understanding-long-term-effects-of-covid-19

Dolmage, J. T. (2017). *Academic ableism: Disability and higher education*. University of Michigan Press.

DRA versus University of California Berkeley. (2013). https://www.sdbor.edu/administrative-offices/academics/aac/Documents/5.BSettlementbetweentheUniversityofCalifornia-BerkeleyandDisability-RightsAdvocatesAAC0613.pdf

Fraser, M., Agdamag, A. C. C., Maharaj, V. R., Mutschler, M., Charpentier, V., Chowdhury, M., & Alexy, T. (2022). COVID-19-Associated Myocarditis: An Evolving Concern in Cardiology and Beyond. *Biology (Basel)*, *11*(4), 520. doi:10.3390/biology11040520 PMID:35453718

Geng, L. N., Verghese, A., & Tilburt, J. C. (2021). Consultative medicine-an emerging specialty for patients with perplexing conditions. *The New England Journal of Medicine*, *385*(26), 2478–2484. doi:10.1056/NEJMms2111017 PMID:34936744

Kerschbaum, S. L., Eisenman, L. T., & Jones, J. M. (Eds.). (2017). *Negotiating disability: Disclosure and higher education*. University of Michigan Press. doi:10.3998/mpub.9426902

Lopez-Leon, S., Wegman-Ostrosky, T., Perelman, C., Sepulveda, R., Rebolledo, P. A., Cuapio, A., & Villapol, S. (2021). More than 50 long-term effects of COVID-19: A systematic review and meta-analysis. *Scientific Reports*, *11*(1), 1–12. doi:10.103841598-021-95565-8 PMID:34373540

Mayer, R. E. (2002). Multimedia learning. *Psychology of Learning and Motivation*, *41*, 85–139. doi:10.1016/S0079-7421(02)80005-6

McGuire, S. Y. (2018). *Teach yourself how to learn: Strategies you can use to ace any course at any level*. Stylus Publishing, LLC.

Means, B., Bakia, M., & Murphy, R. (2014). *Learning online: What research tells us about whether, when and how*. Routledge. doi:10.4324/9780203095959

National Association of the Deaf v. Harvard and MIT. (2015). Retrieved from https://www.nad.org/2015/02/17/nad-sues-harvard-and-mit-for-discrimination-in-public-online-content/

National Institutes of Health. (2022). *Recover: Researching COVID to enhance recovery*. Retrieved from https://recovercovid.org/

Reiken, S., Sittenfeld, L., Dridi, H., Liu, Y., Liu, X., & Marks, A. R. (2022). Alzheimer's-like signaling in brains of COVID-19 patients. *Alzheimer's & Dementia*, *18*(5), 955–965. doi:10.1002/alz.12558 PMID:35112786

Resolution Agreement. (2015). *National Federation of the Blind*. Retrieved from https://nfb.org/images/nfb/documents/pdf/higher-ed-toolkit/sou-agreement.pdf

Resolution Agreement. (2016). *National Federation of the Blind*. Retrieved from https://www.wichita.edu/services/mrc/access/_documents/wichita-state-agreement-redacted.pdf

Sanchez, R. (2017). Doing disability with others. *Negotiating disability: Disclosure and higher education*, 211-225.

Taquet, M., Sillett, R., Zhu, L., Mendel, J., Camplisson, I., Dercon, Q., & Harrison, P. J. (2022). Neurological and psychiatric risk trajectories after SARS-CoV-2 infection: An analysis of 2-year retrospective cohort studies including 1 284 437 patients. *The Lancet. Psychiatry*, *9*(10), 815–827. doi:10.1016/S2215-0366(22)00260-7 PMID:35987197

United States District Court for the District of New Jersey. (2015). *Consent Decree*. http://www.atlantic.edu/documents/nfb_lanzailotti_atlantic_cape_consent_decree.pdf

U.S. Access Board. (n.d.). *Guidance Documents*. https://www.access-board.gov/guidance.html

U.S. Department of Justice. (n.d.). *A Guide to Disability Rights Law*. https://www.ada.gov/cguide.htm

W3C. (n.d.). *Web Content Accessibility Guidelines 2.0*. https://www.w3.org/TR/WCAG20/

Zakrajsek, T. D. (2022). *The New Science of Learning: How to Learn in Harmony With Your Brain*. Stylus Publishing, LLC.

Chapter 3
"Future Is Yours":
Motivating Online Learners in Higher Education Through a Package of Goods (in the COVID–19 Pandemic)

Shalin Hai-Jew
https://orcid.org/0000-0002-8863-0175
Kansas State University, USA

ABSTRACT

Globally, learners around the world have had to move from face-to-face (F2F) learning to full "emergency online learning" in many cases, such as in higher education. In "emergency online teaching," instructors have been learning about how to support learners; however, with the slowing of the acute phases of the pandemic, many learners have dropped out, many for good. One of the most important strategies to retain online learners on their learning tracks involves a package of learning goods that position learners for the future in the near-, mid-, and far-terms. The core idea here is that "future pull" is alluring, and it supports learner persistence in online (and offline) learning. This work describes the mix of elements for creating just such a package in the contemporaneous moment based on the abductive logic study of instructional design work of the past several years for online learning during the COVID-19 pandemic at a Midwestern university.

INTRODUCTION

The advent of the SARS-CoV-2 / COVID-19 pandemic resulted in global-scale movements of learners from K-12 through higher education to online learning, in order to protect people against the ravages of a novel airborne pathogen passed from person-to-person. In wealthier and more developed countries, the technological infrastructure for such learning—learning management systems, social media apps, built-in tutoring systems, social robots, wireless connectivity, unhindered Internet and Web access, secure grade systems, virtual labs for learning, and others—were somewhat more built out than for lesser developed countries. For many, COVID-19 is seen as leading to "a formidable academic disaster

DOI: 10.4018/978-1-6684-5934-8.ch003

Copyright © 2023, IGI Global. Copying or distributing in print or electronic forms without written permission of IGI Global is prohibited.

"Future Is Yours"

around the world, particularly in low and middle-income countries" (Chandrasiri & Weerakoon, 2021, p. 3), with many students disconnected socially from others, isolated, stressed, and not learning at prior rates of achievement. Students have disappeared from the school rolls at every level. Learning retention is dependent on many factors in more normal circumstances: individual attitudes and dispositions, practical matters (such as the availability of time and money) (Merriam & Caffarella, 1999, p. 55), social supports, psychosocial factors (Merriam & Caffarella, 1999, pp. 56 - 57), institutional barriers, and learner motivations. For example, one seminal study grouped learners as "*goal-oriented* learners, who use education as a means of achieving some other goal; *activity-oriented* learners, who participate for the sake of the activity itself and the social interaction; and *learning-oriented* participants, who seek knowledge for its own sake" (Houle, 1961, as cited in Merriam & Caffarella, 1999, p. 54). In many countries, those who have higher education degrees are often a minority. A mass-level crisis, such as a pandemic, magnifies the challenges.

Various headwinds emerge during a pandemic. There are the practical survival ones—literally staying alive, maintaining housing, retaining work, and acquiring food and drink. There is the issue of both social and personal focus. Governments struggled to provide public education, and learners struggled to learn. In a time of mass crisis, to use a colloquialism, citizens are "not okay." Mental health is a common challenge (Rasmussen, et al., 2022). Many governments have been seen as ineffectual to their citizenry. The unfortunate circumstances enable the holding of natural social experiments, such as to better understand the efficacy of learning online under emergency circumstances. Fully online learning, hybrid (or blended) learning, and face-to-face learning are thought to offer different levels of support to learners. Online learning and hybrid learning are both thought to require students to have more self-regulated learning skills (van Alten, Phielix, Janssen, & Kester, 2021, p. 1) because there are fewer structural and social supports for the learning. Learning motivation is defined as "an established pattern of pursuing goals, beliefs, and emotions" (Ford, 1992, as cited in Law, Geng, & Li, 2019, p. 2). Both remote learning methods require technological savvy (Yilmaz, 2017, p. 260) and the infrastructure to enable the work. Learners need to know how to express their own social presence online (in learning management systems or LMSes, in virtual worlds, on video, and so on), and they need to have a cognitive presence through which they express their learning and interact with others. In different localities, both faculty and learners have varying experiences with online learning; in some cases, the pandemic forced makeshift efforts.

This chapter suggests that "future pull," defined here as "the draw and attraction of a future that may motivate actions in the present," may serve as an overarching strategy to enhance both online student motivation and their retention. In this approach, there is the near-, mid-, and far-future. The near-term future involves the one to six years (covering the higher education learning span); the mid-term future involves post-graduation and the first five years of professional life; the far-term future involves the first six to ten years and onwards of a profession. The suggestion of a hopeful future may seem like a radical suggestion in a context when the next day is not guaranteed, and large numbers of people are dying of the infection. Still, in reality, a majority of learners will survive the pandemic and advance their lives along a constructive path. This "future pull" approach has been used as an instructional design impetus in one shop in a Midwestern university during the pandemic.

REVIEW OF THE LITERATURE

For years, the seminal "no significant difference" study and follow-on database (located at https://deta-research.org/research-support/no-significant-difference/) served as a core understanding that distance or online learning was as effective as face-to-face learning. Over the years, additional empirical studies have been conducted about online learning. Student engagement is a critical element for their success in online learning. One study has formalized and shored up an operational definition of student engagement, and this includes four dimensions: "behavioral, cognitive, social, and emotional" (Ayouni et al., 2021, p. 1). Several general understandings have emerged in this space. One is that there is often high attrition in online learning, particularly in massive open online courses (MOOCs) and in automated learning ones. For online learners to retain in MOOCs, they need an "online academic hardiness" (Kuo, Tsai, & Wang, 2021, p. 1) as a psychological resource; they require "the courage that is needed to turn stressful changes from burdens into advantageous growth in online environments" (Kuo, Tsai, & Wang, 2021, p. 1).

Even in free courses for continuing education, there are challenges with retention. One study examined whether the cost is mitigated through either a tuition waiver or a refund to see which provided better incentives for the learning and found that "refunds outperformed waivers in promoting long-term learning, due to the monetary cost incurred in the former instance (even if it was refundable)" (Lee & Yeung, 2021, p. 1). Those offered "a free refund (vs. waiver) were less likely to drop out, spent more time reading the learning materials, and were more likely to return to the learning activity during the post-experimental phase" (Lee & Yeung, 2021, p. 1). External incentive structures matter. The researchers write: "…the waiver drew more attention to the incentive and reduced attention to the learning benefits, but the refund preserved the latter consideration" (Lee & Yeung, 2021, p. 1), perhaps by showing the cost of the "free" course and triggering cost-benefit considerations (p. 12).

Student perseverance and attrition patterns have also been studied in the usage of self-paced learning using open educational resources (OERs).

The results revealed that at the student level, student engagement with video lectures, self-assessment, social tools, and additional videos relevant to solved test items significantly predicted student usage duration. At the teacher level, teachers' use of teacher resources was positively associated with student usage duration. An additional analysis of student and teacher total usage time indicated that, compared with heavy users, light and medium users were more likely to discontinue their engagement in the long term if their teachers did not use the platform. (Kim et al., 2020, p. 1)

This research suggests the importance of encouraging heavy usage of OERs and of teacher use of OERs to encourage extended enduring usage of these resources. There are interrelationships between teacher and student usage of OERs in this case.

One study found "the significant mediating effect of commitment on behavioral, emotional and cognitive engagement in learning MOOCs" (Kuo, Tsai, & Wang, 2021, p. 1). Another study identified factors that motivated and demotivated continuance in MOOC learning.

An examination of student statements related to motivations revealed that knowledge, work, convenience, and personal interest were the most frequently coded nodes…On the other hand, lack of time was the most prevalently coded barrier for students. Other barriers and challenges cited by the interviewed

"Future Is Yours"

learners included previous bad classroom experiences with the subject matter, inadequate background, and lack of resources such as money, infrastructure, and internet access. (Shapiro et al., 2017, p. 35)

Learners who already earned a bachelor's degree "were more positive than learners who had not completed a college degree or those who had an advanced degree, and this was a highly statistically significant result" (Shapiro et al., 2017, p. 47). Prior successful persistence may have helped learners even as they may have experienced frustration in the online learning (Shapiro et al., 2017, p. 47). A different study also found that graduate students have "higher levels of critical thinking and lower levels of procrastination" than the undergraduate students studying online (Artino & Stephens, 2009, p. 146).

In a study involving business students, soft skills including "self-regulated learning strategies, motivation, and social skills" were measured (Tseng, Yi, & Yeh, 2019, p. 179). The researchers found that graduate students had higher levels of soft skills than undergraduate ones, "especially in self-regulation and motivation. Likewise, students with managerial experiences demonstrated a higher level of soft skills" (Tseng, Yi, & Yeh, 2019, p. 179). Soft skills factors predicted some 34% of the variance in student learning outcomes in a statistically significant way in this study. As such, enabling learners to acquire and practice soft skills will benefit the learning.

Another core tenet has long been that learner intrinsic motivations are important for goal setting, self-efficacy, and learning. For autonomous online learning environments, learners who are "highly motivated, self-regulated" tend to fare better in their learning (Artino & Stephens, 2009, p. 146). Online and blended (hybrid) learning environments are thought to provide less structure and fewer supports for learners, so online learners need to be more self-directed and autonomous to be successful in their learning. One recent study suggests that learner academic performance in blended / hybrid learning is mostly based on internal factors with the learner and external conditions. The researchers found that "a low proportion of variance is explained by the behavior-based indicators, while a significant proportion of variability stems from the learners' internal conditions" (Jovanović et al., 2021, p. 1). Event logs in online learning systems may be less revelatory of learner performance since behavior is less revelatory. They write: "…when variability in external conditions is largely controlled for (the same institution, discipline, and nominal pedagogical model), students' internal state is the key predictor of their course performance" (Jovanović et al., 2021, p. 1). Students' internal conditions "explain a large proportion of the variability in their learning outcomes" (Jovanović et al., 2021, p. 11). Learning motivation "plays a vital role in enhancing the enrolment but does not directly influence learning performance in a blended learning setting" (Law, Geng, & Li, 2019, p. 1).

It is important to have instruction and peer rationales for the importance of the learning to support online learners' motivations and achievement. There are social elements to how online learners regard online course materials in the short-term, and these ideas affect their performance.

Both peer and instructor rationales positively influenced students' interest in and perceived utility value of upcoming course content in the short term, but only peer rationales increased students' applied knowledge and final grades at the end of the semester. Unexpectedly, peer rationales also decreased students' relatedness to instructors. Qualitative results suggest that peer rationales may influence achievement by way of identification processes, while instructor rationales focus students' attention on content. (Shin, Ranellucci, & Roseth, 2017, p. 184)

Learners invest more into their studies when they understand the potential utility of the learning to their futures; however, the research did not find evidence of "long-term change in students' perceptions of value and interest, as neither time nor the experimental conditions changed students' perceptions of utility value, intrinsic value, interest in course topics, or interest in future courses" (Shin, Ranellucci, & Roseth, 2017, p. 195). An earlier study, based on structural equation modeling, found "evidence for the mediating effect of need satisfaction between contextual support and motivation/self-determination" (Chen & Jang, 2010, p. 741). Learners needed to perceive that their needs were being satisfied in online learning in order to experience a sense of self-determination and drive. However, "motivation/self-determination failed to predict learning outcomes" (Chen & Jang, 2010, p. 741). In fact, the structural equation modeling found that "the path from self-determination…to learning outcome was insignificant across all fitted models" (Chen & Jang, 2010, p. 750). Finally, there was support for the observation that "intrinsic motivation, extrinsic motivation, and amotivation are distinctive constructs" (Chen & Jang, 2010, p. 741).

Learners fare better when there is a fit between their identity and the learning contents. Researchers observe:

…when students perceived higher meaning of the learning contents in a particular learning situation, they experienced less frustration…and boredom…, which is in line with the assumption that a misfit between learning contents and the individual's identity correspond with negative emotional experiences… In turn, when students perceived a higher usefulness for their future job, they experienced more enjoyment… and hope…" (in alignment with utility value-interventions). (Berweger, Born, & Dietrich, 2022, p. 6)

This study also found that "expectancy-value appraisals are positively associated with positive emotions and negatively with negative emotions" (Berweger, Born, & Dietrich, 2022, p. 1). Students experienced positive emotions in learning situations "with high intrinsic and utility value, but not in situations of high attainment value" (Berweger, Born, & Dietrich, 2022, p. 1). Students' perceived costs of engaging moderated the relationship between "expectancy and frustration and boredom" at the situation level (Berweger, Born, & Dietrich, 2022, p. 1). Situations with high success expectancy "related positively to the momentary experience of enjoyment and hope, and negatively to frustration" (Berweger, Born, & Dietrich, 2022, p. 4). Students need to feel that a learning situation is controllable in order to be able to anticipate success and experience "higher enjoyment…and hope…, and lower frustration…" (Berweger, Born, & Dietrich, 2022, p. 6). Finally, they observe: "…students with high intrinsic value tended to experience fewer frustrating…and boring situations. Furthermore, as predicted, students who repeatedly experienced negatively valanced situations (i.e., high costs) also tended to experience more frustration…and boredom…" (Berweger, Born, & Dietrich, 2022, p. 7)

Sociality and Online Learning

Social relationships matter in online learning. One space for social engagement are discussions. Learners engaging in group-oriented learning tasks "had more diverse learning sentiments and interaction patterns, and deeper interactions with regard to learning sentiments" (Huang, Han, Li, Jong, & Tsai, 2019, p. 1). The dynamic learning sentiments included (1) generation, (2) collision and integration, (3) refinement, and (4) stability (Huang et al., 2019, p. 1). The social interactions benefit by enabling more complex online learning as shown by lag sequential analysis of evolving sentiments over time. Eight

"Future Is Yours"

"significant sentiment sequences" were identified: "positive" -> "insightful", "negative" -> "insightful," "confused" -> "insightful", "negative" -> "joking," "neutral" -> "positive," "negative" -> "negative," "neutral" -> ["neutral" and "joking" -> "joking"] (Huang et al., 2019, pp. 8 - 9). Online interaction patterns are suggestive of students maintaining "a level of consistency when others shared or compared opinions" (Huang, Han, Li, Jong, & Tsai, 2019, p. 9). Learners were seen to address differences of opinions through "negotiation and co-construction of knowledge" (Huang et al., 2019, p. 9). Their socially supportive responses to shared jokes "strengthened the cohesion" and "enhanced learners' interactions" (Huang et al., 2019, p. 9).

Meeting Learner Needs

Another study explored the effects of "need satisfaction and need dissatisfaction in online learning contexts" in order to test a motivation and learning model (Wang et al., 2019, p. 114). This study aligned with prior findings from face-to-face (F2F) learning contexts in that "need satisfaction and need dissatisfaction demonstrated distinctive effects on students' motivation and learning outcomes in online learning contexts" (Wang et al., 2019, p. 114). Here, online learning was seen as providing relatively low-quality teaching. Further, "need satisfaction was related primarily to the perception of gains in perceived knowledge transfer, need dissatisfaction was related more closely to students' course grades. In accordance with our findings, previous researchers have demonstrated that need satisfaction mediated the association between autonomy support and autonomous motivation, whereas need frustration mediated the relations between controlling teaching and controlled motivation (Haerens et al., 2015, as cited in Wang et al., 2019, p. 123). Need satisfaction was associated with "self-determined motivation), and need dissatisfaction was more associated with "non-self-determined motivation," with each having different effects on student learning outcomes and different types of motivation: "The higher-order thinking skill aligns with the brighter side of motivation, while the course grade is vulnerable to the darker side aspects" (Wang et al., 2019, p. 123). Learning to tests may lead to behaviors that are not conducive to long-term learning and innovation.

Assessing Signs of Online Learner Motivations

Learner motivation has long been a critical aspect of learner achievement. Motivation levels of leaners "differentially predict engagement" across different types of technology enhanced learning (TEL) (Dunn & Kennedy, 2019, p. 104). Intrinsic motivations "predict engagement, whilst extrinsic motivations predict usage" (Dunn & Kennedy, 2019, p. 104); while engagement predicted grades, usage did not. There were even more nuanced findings in terms of learning performance. When the technologies in TEL were broken out, "the use of social media groups was a significant predictor of grade, whereas reviewing lecture slides/recordings, reading additional content and using course blogs/discussion boards were not" (Dunn & Kennedy, 2019, p. 104). Focusing only on the usage of TEL may not be helpful to understanding learner performance online. There is a need to identify what technologies are most effect for harnessing for learning and what pedagogical usages they may be put to.

Another study posits that learners' patterns of accessing online learning materials may speak to particular learning patterns and learning performance, based on available trace data and event logs on learning management systems. In general, the most commonly accessed learning materials include "lecture slides, video lectures, shared assignments, and forum messages" (Li & Tsai, 2017, p. 286). Some patterns of online content access emerged:

First, the students viewed the learning materials related to their classroom lectures (i.e., lecture slides and video lectures) for longer and more often than other learning materials (i.e., shared assignments and posted messages). Second, although the students spent a great deal of time viewing the online learning materials, most did not use annotation tools. Third, students' viewing behaviors showed great variety and were clustered into three behavior patterns: 'consistent use students' who intensively used all of the learning materials, 'slide intensive use students' who intensively used the lecture slides, and 'less use students' who infrequently used any learning material. (Li & Tsai, 2017, p. 286)

The different behavior patterns were associated with variant motivations and learning performances. Consistent use students were seen to have higher motivations and were willing to invest "more time and effort in learning and completing their tasks" (Li & Tsai, 2017, p. 295); these students gained higher homework scores than "slide intensive use students," but the two groups achieved similar exam scores (Li & Tsai, 2017, p. 295). The researchers also found that "32% of the students in this study were labeled as 'less use students' as they infrequently accessed the online learning materials" which aligns with prior studies (Li & Tsai, 2017, p. 294). This study found that "intrinsic goal orientations, self-efficacy, and task value" showed significant differences in outcomes (Li & Tsai, 2017, p. 295).

Embedded Pedagogies in Online Learning

Certainly, online learning involves various types of embedded pedagogies. Another study explored learner actions in self-directed online environments, without the presence of high-touch (live instructors), and particularly how they engaged in guided inquiry. A core requirement for successful learning in such a context involves engaging with the content behaviorally and processing the content cognitively "for more effective learning to occur" (Al Mamun, Lawrie, & Wright, 2022, p. 15). The researchers write:

Students interacted with scaffolded guided-inquiry online modules designed through application of a predict-observe-explain-evaluate framework. Quantitative data (engagement measures) were collected through digital artifacts and qualitative data (student reflections and activity) through interviews and student written responses. A diversity in learning approaches was observed as a result of individual learners' differences in their prior online experiences and existing chemistry knowledge. Learners' individual differences also influenced student engagement in terms of persistence, systematic investigation and understanding of the science concepts. (Al Mamun, Lawrie, & Wright, 2022, p. 1)

Less experienced learners were found to possibly experience cognitive overload when engaging simulations. The study found that "students with prior simulation experience demonstrated more efficient, skilled interactions in exploring and understanding the simulations" (Al Mamun, Lawrie, & Wright, 2022, p. 16).

Online learning contexts are seen to benefit learners by providing various supports for learners. One study identified three groups of learners from among heterogeneous adult learners: those with high, moderate, and low self-regulated learning styles, and high variances of self-regulated subscales among the three groups. They write: "…only achievement motivation—more specifically, attainment

"Future Is Yours"

and utility value—predicts profile membership" (Vanslambrouck et al., 2019, p. 126). To bolster learner self-regulated learning, instructors are asked to use authentic tasks in the learning and to model "online interaction and information sharing" (Vanslambrouck et al., 2019, p. 126).

The importance of active, authentic, and applied learning for aerospace engineering students is shown to affect learner motivations, both intrinsic and extrinsic. The subject matter is challenging already, and the project-based learning often harnesses "hard problems" to spark the imagination and inspire hard work by the learners. The most salient motivators for aerospace engineering students were the following: "intrinsic motivators such as sense of accomplishment, a feeling of progress, personal and intellectual growth, enjoyment of studies, self-confidence and responsibility" and "the practical utility of the acquired knowledge and the opportunities provided by the teachers to surpass difficult tasks, to perform well-defined activities in whose definition students can participate and to establish relationships with other classmates" and "academic conditions related with the available resources, the tradeoff between efforts and rewards, the evaluation methods and the teacher's ability to perform the tutorial labor and to motivate students" (López-Fernández et al., 2019, p. 349). The assignments need to be in the zone of proximal development of the respective learners to provide flow learning instead of triggering either boredom or frustration.

One study explored the latent self-regulated learning profiles of 8th grade students based on their activities in an online course. They identified…

…five distinct SRL profiles from low completion and no activity to full completion and very high activity. In addition, students in the profile who showed low SRL activity achieved significantly worse learning outcomes than students in the three profiles with higher SRL activity. Finally, we explored whether SRL activity profile membership can be explained by student characteristics (i.e., self-reported SRL, motivation, and price knowledge). None of the student-level variables predicted profile membership… (van Alten et al., 2021, p. 1)

This work aligns with many others about the importance of self-regulated learning skills to learner achievement.

Teacher Motivations in Online Teaching and Learning

Other studies have explored teacher motivations for online learning. One study examined the relationships "among teachers' motivational beliefs, motivational regulation, and their learning engagement in online professional learning communities" (Zhang & Liu, 2019, p. 145). The researchers found that "teachers' perceived task value positively predicted their online learning engagement" (Zhang & Liu, 2019, p. 145). Further, the teachers' motivational regulation "played a partial mediating role in the predicting power of perceived task value to learning engagement" (Zhang & Liu, 2019, p. 145).

Teachers engage more constructively in the online teaching when they see the work as part of their professional development and general teaching. Another study engaged online and blended learning (OBL). These researchers suggest that awareness of students in their diversities can enable more effective and customized online and offline teaching. To that end, researchers have examined "the reasons and values that students in a teacher training program in higher education attribute to their participation in OBL" (Vanslambrouck et al., 2018, p. 33). This work identified three motivational profiles of learners, informed by variances in terms of intrinsic motivation, identified regulation, introjected regulation, external regulation, and amotivation (Vanslambrouck et al., 2018, p. 36). General values linked to participation in hybrid education include the following: intrinsic values ("learning pleasure, content interest, job performing pleasure"), attainment value ("self-esteem, social affirmation, satisfying old needs"), utility value ("teaching job, financially, time, feel good," and costs ("workload, relationship risks, mental issues") (Vanslambrouck et al., 2018, p. 36). Inductively identified categories for the value of OBL include the following: intrinsic values ("self-study, working with technology, social contact"), attainment value ("independent learning, social motivation"), utility value ("flexible learning, face-to-face moments, new skills"), and costs ("personal sacrifices, high effort in distance moments, high effort for social help, technology") (Vanslambrouck et al., 2018, p. 36).

The harnessing of online peer assessment has been studied as an innovative evaluation method for instructors and learners. One study was conducted to assess "student self-efficacy and motivation in online peer assessment learning environments" (Tseng & Tsai, 2010, p. 164). The study that found that "...the students' responses also showed that they were highly confident and strongly intrinsically motivated when participating in an online peer assessment learning environment" (Tseng & Tsai, 2010, p. 164). The research identified a "reciprocal relationship between students' self-efficacy and motivation in an online peer assessment learning environment" (Tseng & Tsai, 2010, p. 164). In a dance course, peer feedback was found to have constructive effects on the learning. There were three online peer-feedback modes: "videos with peer comments, videos with peer ratings, and videos with mixed mode (i.e., peer ratings plus peer comments)" (Hsia, Huang, & Hwang, 2016, p. 55). The researchers found that "in terms of dance skills, peer ratings could improve the students' group performance, while the mixed mode improved individuals' learning performance" (Hsia, Huang, & Hwang, 2016, p. 55). The researchers explain additional findings:

In terms of learning motivation and self-efficacy, the correlation analysis shows that the students' intrinsic motivation, self-efficacy and dance skill performance were positively correlated. Via analyzing the peer feedback content, it was found that the feedback provided by the mixed mode group was of better quality than that provided by the 'peer comments' group; that is, the former provided more detailed feedback to individuals than the latter. Furthermore, it was found that the scores provided by the mixed mode group were highly related to those provided by the teachers, while those provided by the 'peer ratings' group were not. The online user behavior analysis further shows that the integration of peer commenting, and peer rating is able to promote students' willingness to participate in online learning activities. (Hsia, Huang, & Hwang, 2016, p. 55)

Another team used a newer "online interactive peer-review approach" in a flipped learning course to give voice to both the assessor and "assessees" in an online learning context. They write:

The results indicated that integrating the online interactive peer-review learning approach could not only strengthen the NP (nurse practitioners) students' knowledge and clinical skills but could also significantly improve their critical thinking tendency and reflective thinking. (Lin et al., 2021, p. 1)

This learning approach led to improvements in higher order thinking and improved problem-solving. Learners who engage in effective reflection tend to have better learning performance outcomes. In online learning, understanding feedback is important. One study found six conceptual metaphors related to feedback:

"Future Is Yours"

feedback is a treatment, feedback is a costly commodity, feedback is coaching, feedback is a command, feedback is a dialogue, and feedback is a learner tool. (Jensen, Bearman, & Boud, 2021, p. 1)

Each of the metaphors "offers a coherent frame of entailments related to the roles and responsibilities of online instructors and online learners as well as some bigger assumptions about what role feedback should play in online teaching and learning" (Jensen, Bearman, & Boud, 2021, p. 1). Feedback can be constructive, or non-constructive. The researchers write:

Of these dominant metaphors, four align with feedback practices that are considered inappropriate among feedback researchers, because they entail that the instructor is the main agent in the feedback process, and that the feedback provided to learners automatically leads to learning. The exceptions are FEEDBACK IS DIALOGUE and FEEDBACK IS A LEARNER TOOL, which both align well with what is increasingly accepted as good practice. (Jensen, Bearman, & Boud, 2021, pp. 10 - 11)

Certainly, there are diverse practices and sources around feedback for learners.

A study of English as a Foreign Language (EFL) learners at the tertiary level examined student personality (based on the Big Five personality traits) and the association of such traits with online learning motivation and online learning satisfaction. The results showed that personality traits "were correlated with online satisfaction, and that extraversion and conscientiousness were the two important traits among the Big Five in predicting motivation and satisfaction. Also, motivation was a strong predictor of satisfaction. Five constructs of motivation, including escape, social contact, desire to learn, self-development and academic progress, were significantly related to satisfaction" (Shih et al., 2013, p. 1152). Individual dispositions are associated with certain behavioral patterns in online learning.

Being able to engage socially via online mechanisms may be another competitive advantage for online learning. "Social ability" in online learning is found to be comprised of five elements: perceived peer social presence, written communication skills, instructor social presence, "comfort with sharing personal information," and social navigation (Yang et al., 2006, p. 277). These researchers found that "different motivational constructs vary in their relationships with the multiple social ability factors" (Yang et al., 2006, p. 277). More complex associations were identified:

Intrinsic goal orientation is related to perceived peers (sic) social presence. Self-efficacy explains the variance of perceived instructor social presence and comfort with sharing personal information. Task value is associated with social navigation and both perceived peers and instructor social presence. (Yang et al., 2006, p. 277)

Various pedagogies and technologies have also been associated with effectiveness in online learning. One approach involves instructor-created podcasting as a method for engaging learners. This study explored "attention, relevance, confidence, and satisfaction" of learners (Bolliger, Supranakorn, & Boggs, 2010, p. 714) and found "strong positive relationships between all subscales" (p. 714). Students were "moderately motivated by the use of podcasts in their online courses" (Bolliger, Supranakorn, & Boggs, 2010, p. 714). The researchers also found "statistically significant differences in student motivation based on gender, class standing, and prior online learning experience" (Bolliger, Supranakorn, & Boggs, 2010, p. 714). The experiencing of the podcasts helped learners feel more connected to their instructors (p. 718), and the design of the podcasts to enhance their relevance was found to be important. The researchers identified seven themes in terms of improvements to the podcasts, based on the following: "content selection, length of files, inclusion of additional podcasts, use of videos, access and development of files, or requests not to integrate them" (Bolliger, Supranakorn, & Boggs, 2010, p. 719).

Another technical approach involves the usage of gamification elements, such as badging, to improve learner motivations. One study examined various badging conditions--"no badges, badges visible to peers, badges only visible to students themselves" as the three research conditions. They write: "The results show that badges have less impact on motivation and performance than is commonly assumed. Independent of condition, students' intrinsic motivation decreased over time. Contrary to expectation, the badges that could only be viewed by the students themselves were evaluated more positively than those that could also be viewed by others" (Kyewski & Krämer, 2018, p. 25). The finding of intrinsic motivations as being more powerfully motivating than extrinsic ones align with prior research.

Over the years, then, online learning, blended/hybrid learning, and face-to-face learning have existed with efficacious learning.

ONLINE LEARNING IN A PANDEMIC

The sudden onset of the SARS-CoV-2 / COVID-19 pandemic forced a mass exodus from shared physical spaces (and shared "airspace") to virtual learning. This meant that faculty had to shift to "emergency online teaching" (EOT), and learners had to go to "emergency online learning" (EOL). Many ended up engaging "crisis-driven digitalization."

Different faculty were prepared differently for the sudden shift to online learning from the pandemic. Researchers found that the "learning approach goals of faculty were positively associated with perceiving the shift to online learning as a positive challenge and as useful for their own competence development. Conversely, performance (appearance) avoidance and work avoidance goals were negatively related to student ratings of teaching quality" (Daumiller et al., 2021, p. 1). How instructors adapted to the remote teaching and learning impacted "burnout/engagement and student evaluations of teaching quality" (Daumiller et al., 2021, p. 7). Many teachers taught without the benefit of much training, leaving learners without "well-planned online learning" in many cases (Lorenza & Carter, 2021, p. 1). The research literature only mentioned one planned approach to help students adapt to online learning, in a blended chemistry course. This planned process is dubbed Discover, Learn, Practice, Collaborate and Assess (DLPCA) (Lapitan et al., 2021, p. 116).

Lessons Learned from the Global Health Crisis

In the time of the pandemic, various studies have been conducted on online learning and blended / hybrid learning. The shift to remote learning, given the need for people to socially distance, took many by surprise and resulted in challenges: "technological, mental health, time management, and balance between life and education" (Maqableh & Alia, 2021, p. 1). A third of learners in one study were dissatisfied with the online learning experience, in alignment with a number of other studies. A third were also not satisfied with the "digital platforms' online learning experience functionality" (Maqableh & Alia, 2021, p. 10). The most important factors identified as barriers to effective learning were "a distraction and reduced focus, psychological issues, and management issues" (Maqableh & Alia, 2021, p. 1). This study found

"Future Is Yours"

"many unsatisfied students with the online learning experience, learning materials, interactions with colleagues and teachers, and exams and quizzes" (Maqableh & Alia, 2021, p. 10).

How well-prepared learners are to engage live online learning in an emergency context has been studied. Asia was "one of the earliest regions to implement live online learning" with the onset of the SARS-CoV-2 / COVID-19 pandemic Tang et al., 2021, p. 1) and so is a region of interest in this context. One research team explored "learning motivation, learning readiness and student's self-efficacy in participating in live online learning" during the outbreak (Tang et al., 2021, p. 1). Their data showed that postgraduate student preparedness scores were higher than for undergraduate and sub-degree students (Tang et al., 2021, p. 1). They found readiness for live online learning were based on five factors: "technology readiness, learner control, online communication self-efficacy, self-directed learning, and motivation for learning" (five measured items) (Tang et al., 2021, p. 9). For effective instructor-led online education, the learning should be designed to promote learner motivation and agency (Tang et al., 2021, p. 13).

Demographic factors have been implicated in terms of (non)preparedness for the abrupt shift to online learning. There are those with particular motivational and behavioral processes, who are "more likely to select into online (OL) than face-to-face (F2F) courses" (McPartian et al., 2021, p. 1). Student enrolment "indicates the initial motivation and commitment of students" (Law, Geng, & Li, 2019, p. 7). There are also those "less likely to perform well in OL courses" (McPartian et al., 2021, p. 1). They write:

University students…reported their reasons for OL course selection: university constraints, specific need for flexibility, general preference for flexibility, and learning preferences. (McPartian et al., 2021, p. 1)

Their self-selection was informed by "motivation, behavior, and performance" (McPartian et al., 2021, p. 1). Other patterns emerged. Online students "who said they had a specific need for flexibility created by the costs of competing responsibilities spent more time on non-academic activities (e.g., working, commuting), less time on academic activities (e.g., study groups), and ultimately performed worse when compared to F2F peers" (McPartian et al., 2021, p. 1). Demographically, these poorer performers in the study were "especially likely to be women, older, and part-time" (McPartian et al., 2021, p. 1).

Some researchers suggest that prior uses of the Internet and high technology devices prepared the learning population for online learning in the pandemic crisis (Rusli, Rahman, & Abdullah, 2020, p. 1). Prior self-managed online learning—heutagogy—may have also increased population preparedness. The "digital divide" between the wealthy and the poor, the urban and the rural, also affected learner preparedness in the shift to remote learning. Researchers have found that "differences exist between rural and urban students in habitus (i.e., intrinsic motivation) and forms of capital, including cultural (i.e., e-learning self-efficacy) and social capital (i.e., parental support and teacher support), which are the main causes of the digital outcome divide" (Zhao et al., 2021, p. 1). They also found that "e-learning self-efficacy, intrinsic motivation, and parental support" were dominant factors in the rural-urban digital income divide in terms of electronic learning (Zhao et al., 2021, p. 1). In some cases, gaps may be mediated; in others, they become unbridgeable.

For learners to be successful in their online courses, an important factor involves their level of satisfaction. One study examined the ties between learner satisfaction and other variables, during the COVID-19 pandemic.

The results showed that the mean (standard deviation) score of satisfaction with e-learning in the students was 20.75 (2.13) and 59% of them had undesirable satisfaction. There was a significant relationship between satisfaction with e-learning and variables of gender and history of attending online classes before Covid-19. Regarding the four aspects of e-learning, there was a statistically significant difference between the two groups of students with desirable satisfaction and undesirable satisfaction. The results revealed that the mean scores of dimensions of teaching and learning, feedback and evaluation, flexibility and appropriateness, and workload among students with desirable satisfaction were higher than students with undesirable satisfaction. (Yekefallah et al., 2021, p. 1)

The researchers note the importance of creating quality online learning experiences for learners, given the lack of clarity about how long the pandemic might drag on. The researchers found that 59% of the surveyed learners experienced "undesirable satisfaction" with the online learning. There were also demographic elements at play: females were more satisfied than males; those with a history of attending online classes were more satisfied than those that didn't; and a majority preferred the familiar, or the face-to-face learning (Yekefallah et al., 2021, p. 3). Others have noted the importance of student-perceived teaching quality critical in blended learning, and in both online and offline learning (Law, Geng, & Li, 2019, p. 8).

In the first few weeks of emergency online learning, based on semi-guided essays written by learners and analyzed for contents, researchers found that learners appreciated "cost- and time-effectiveness, safety, convenience and improved participation" as positives" (Hussein et al., 2020, p. 1). Negatives included "distraction and reduced focus, heavy workload, problems with technology and the internet, and insufficient support from instructors and colleagues" (Hussein et al., 2020, p. 1).

College students' use and acceptance of "emergency online learning" due to COVID-19 were found to be based on a mix of factors, including "attitude, affect, and motivation; perceived behavioral control (ease of use of technology, self-efficacy, and accessibility), and cognitive engagement" (Aguilera-Hermida, 2020, p. 1). The researcher found that "attitude, motivation, self-efficacy, and use of technology play a significant role in the cognitive engagement and academic performance of students" (Aguilera-Hermida, 2020, p. 1). Many learners experienced the challenges of "a lack of motivation and negative emotions" (Aguilera-Hermida, 2020, p. 5) in the transition to online learning. The author suggests the importance of having a positive attitude and of seeing the pandemic as temporary. The researcher writes:

Content is important, but without the proper conditions, students may have a negative experience again and their cognitive engagement can drop. Educators must be mindful of these circumstances and promote a positive attitude, encourage motivation, and invite students to rely on their previous knowledge. (Aguilera-Hermida, 2020, p. 7)

Instructors need to empathize with learners and support their endeavors. Given the sense of a lack of support structure for the virtual and blended / hybrid types of learning, researchers have suggested that self-regulated learning is "crucial for academic success" (Vanslambrouck et al., 2019, p. 126).

In blended adult education, with a broad diversity of learners, varying levels of self-regulated learning skills are also expected. One study found three main profiles in such as group: low, moderate, and high SRL. An effective learning experience should include tailored SRL support to each level. The researchers write:

"Future Is Yours"

The three profiles differ significantly in terms of the scores of all SRL subscales. Furthermore, only achievement motivation—more specifically, attainment and utility value—predicts profile membership. These results inform educational practice about opportunities for supporting and enhancing SRL skills. Anticipating attainment and utility value, time management, and collaboration with peers are all recommended. (Vanslambrouck et al., 2019, p. 126)

Another study explored ways that training programs enhance university students' academic performance, self-regulated learning strategies, and motivations. A broad meta-analysis explored the effects of "extended self-regulated learning training programs on academic performance, self-regulated learning strategies, and motivation of university students" (Theobald, 2021, p. 1). The researcher found the following training effects:

The largest effect sizes were obtained for metacognitive strategies (g – 0.40) and resource management strategies (g – 0.39) followed by academic performance (g – 0.37), motivational outcomes (g – 0.35), and cognitive strategies (g – 0.32). Training effects varied for specific self-regulated learning strategies and ranged between 0.23 (rehearsal) and 0.61 (attention and concentration). Moderator analyses revealed differential training effects depending on course design characteristics. Feedback predicted larger training effects for metacognitive and resource management strategies as well as motivation. Cooperative learning arrangements predicted larger training effects for cognitive and metacognitive strategies. The provision of learning protocols predicted larger training effects for resource management strategies. Moreover, training programs based on a metacognitive theoretical background reported higher effects sizes for academic achievement compared to training programs based on cognitive theories. Further, training programs that targeted older students and students with lower prior academic achievement showed larger effect sizes for resource management strategies. To conclude, self-regulated learning training programs enhanced academic performance, self-regulated learning strategies, and motivation of university students. (Theobald, 2021, p. 1).

Learners were able to enhance their self-regulated learning strategy usage (Theobald, 2021, p. 12) and their "metacognitive and resource management strategies" but with different average effects from different strategies (Theobald, 2021, p. 13). Learners also had increased intrinsic motivation from SRL training programs.

There are dedicated tools to help learners engage online self-regulation of their learning, including important tasks such as goal setting and planning. One study found that "task duration in which learners' goals can be attained (e.g., within one short session or over multiple weeks) might influence the effectiveness of MCII" ("mental contrasting and implementation intentions") otherwise (Wong et al., 2021, p. 1). There were mixed findings otherwise.

Flipped classrooms have also been hypothesized to be less motivating to learners and to provide less learner satisfaction. One study found that "students' e-learning readiness" was "related to their satisfaction and motivation while undertaking academic tasks" in the flipped classroom (Yilmaz, 2017, p. 251). The identified sub-factors for e-learning readiness include "computer self-efficacy, internet self-efficacy, online communication self-efficacy, self-directed learning, learner control and motivation towards e-learning" (Yilmaz, 2017, p. 256). Flipped classrooms come in different variations to support "learning performance, motivation, teacher-student interaction and creativity" (Tsai et al., 2020, p. 1). One study compared a gamified vs. non-gamified flipped classroom. The researchers observed differences in the learner experiences and learning outcomes:

…the students were positive regarding perceived competence, autonomy, and relatedness, better performance, and were able to achieve good achievement during the tests. The survey results reveal that the gamified flip-class setting fostered better motivation and engagement. Particularly, students motivated to compete and beat other students during the gamification activities by collecting points and badges as many as possible. Four main themes emerged from the qualitative interviews, namely, (1) pre-class learning motivation, (2) pre-class competition, (3) students' learning autonomy, and (4) students' social engagement. (Zainuddin, 2018, p. 75)

A gamified flipped classroom was designed to meet the basic psychological needs of learners as defined by self-determination theory such as "competency, autonomy and relatedness" (Zainuddin, 2018, p. 75). Learners are training for independent study (Zainuddin, 2018, p. 86).

Another work used the Big 5 personality traits to understand which learners were better adapted to shifting to online learning during the COVID-19 pandemic. The quality of adaptation was seen to include "their quality of motivation, subjective well-being, self-efficacy, online engagement, and online satisfaction" (Audet et al., 2021, p. 1). They summarize: "Results showed that conscientiousness and openness to experience were associated with higher self-efficacy and with different forms of autonomous motivation for online learning. Conscientiousness was related to identified motivation, whereas openness to experience was related to intrinsic motivation. In contrast, neuroticism was related to increases in controlled motivation. Only openness to experience was strongly related to engagement with online learning and higher levels of subjective well-being" (Audet et al., 2021, p. 1).

One study found that first-year students in the EOL context experienced a lonely struggle with autonomy and unmet psychological needs. This study found challenges in the transition:

The results show negative effects of lacking internet connectivity and concurrence of learning and home spaces but positive effects of ceased commute between home and campus. Teachers' implementation of digital learning opportunities was perceived as adequate but did not sufficiently address the overwhelming increase in students' autonomy and decrease in social relatedness. Students' self-regulation skills as well as skills to initiate and maintain social contacts for interactive learning activities and for motivational support emerged as crucial aspects. Many students were not able to cope appropriately, and students' need satisfaction during emergency online teaching appeared to be related to students' prior need satisfaction resulting in five groups of students, with two being relatively resilient and three being vulnerable to the disruptions of regular onsite teaching. (Eberle & Hobrecht, 2021, p. 1)

The online course builds provided insufficient attention to student autonomy and social relating. The "loss of university libraries as learning spaces" led to various challenges in meeting learner needs for "competence and social relatedness" (Eberle & Hobrecht, 2021, pp. 8 - 9). In these times, teachers themselves were facing challenges of workloads, new learning, and other issues. A study of medical college students found that student "attitudes and perceived preparedness for online learning were moderate, while perceived barriers were high" in the shift to online learning during the pandemic (Muflih et al., 2021, p. 1). This study found some obstacles to successful online learning: "an unstable Internet connection, a lack of motivation, and a lack of instructions (Muflih et al., 2021, p. 1).

"Future Is Yours"

Researchers have also estimated students' online learning satisfaction during the pandemic, and they ranked the levels at low, moderate, and high. They found correlations between various dimensions and online learning satisfaction:

The correlational analysis implied online learning self-efficacy to be significantly and positively associated with online learning satisfaction while general anxiety and fear of COVID-19 were significantly and negatively related to online learning satisfaction. The discriminant analysis revealed the emergence of three online learning satisfaction levels from online self-efficacy, general anxiety, and fear of COVID-19. (Al-Nasa'h, Awwad, & Ahmad, 2021, p. 1)

The research team identified the essential nature of "online learning self-efficacy towards online learning satisfaction" (Al-Nasa'h, Awwad, & Ahmad, 2021, p. 1), a core finding which aligns with other works. Finally, they found high online learning satisfaction levels occurred "with high online self-efficacy, moderate general anxiety, and low fear of COVID-19" (Al-Nasa'h, Awwad, & Ahmad, 2021, p. 1). This is one of the few works that brings in COVID-19 directly as a defined factor (causing duress) in the study while others place it apart of the environment leading to the need for online learning. Another insight is that some moderate anxiety is necessary for developing satisfaction with distance learning (Al-Nasa'h, Awwad, & Ahmad, 2021, p. 5). Learners, to be effective, need to alleviate some of the psychological distress from the difficult circumstances of the pandemic (Al-Nasa'h, Awwad, & Ahmad, 2021, p. 5).

Some Technologies in the Emergency Online Learning Space

Various technology platforms were harnessed during the pandemic: learning management systems, massive open online courses (MOOCs), social media, gamified systems, homework study systems, performance dashboards, and others. Many extracted online learning data to understand learner test cases in order to enable adaptive "control options to an individual level of knowledge" (Petrovskaya et al., 2020, p. 656). With the computerization of so many data points of learners, one study found that learner mood and time of day had an impact on student performance (positive moods had salutary performance benefits); further, they found that "sleep hours and perceived energy level" were not found to have a significant effect on student performance (Kaur, Kumar, & Kaushal, 2021, p. 12). Artificial intelligence (AI) is used to customize online learning based on informative data points and constellations of select data.

In one endeavor, researchers examined the effects of exposing learners to their own learning data through Learning Analytics Dashboards (LADs) to enhance self-regulated learning. This study measured different motivation factors: "mastery, performance-approach, and performance-avoid"; the self-regulated learning measures included the following: "academic self-concept, instrument goals, control expectation, effort and persistence, and memorizing study strategies" (Aguilar et al., 2021, p. 6). They write:

The finding that advisor use of Early Warning System (EWS) indicators in meetings between academic advisors and students "was negatively associated with the rate of decrease of students' reporting of using memorizing strategies but positively related when students' performance was compared to that of their peers. (Aguilar et al., 2021, p. 1)

Rote memorization is often considered a superficial approach that does not lead to deep learning unless it is combined with actual understanding. Learning Analytics Dashboards (LADs) were found to have complex and differing effects on different learners. How advisors harnessed the information had varying effects on learners, too:

What is clear, however, is that this inverse relationship speaks to the power of comparison for academically vulnerable students at an elite institution. Indeed, the only significant predictor of students' negative change in mastery orientation was the students' self-report that their advisor compared them to other students. As with students' change in performance-avoid orientation, our analysis indicates that advisors logging into the EWS and viewing students' pages was predictive of students' a kind of 'buffering' relationship, i.e., advisors logging into the EWS was associated with their students slowing the decrease of the reported use of memorization strategies to learn. (Aguilar et al., 2021, p. 7)

One public medical school even built their own LMS to meet their learner needs, in a low- to middle-income country. Researchers conducted a study of learner receptivity to the tailored LMS, with the finding that learning on this customized LMS "appeared to be accepted, useful, user-friendly, and effective" among the research participants / medical students (Thepwongsa et al., 2021, p. 1).

Online Social Presences to Meet Learner Needs

University students directly experienced the absence of their teachers in the emergency online teaching modality and expressed their loss of learning from that absence (Lorenza & Carter, 2021, p. 5). Many learners missed the direct student-teacher interactions in the online classes (Selvaraj et al., 2021, p. 5). Student-instructor rapport is critical for effective learning, both offline and online. Rapport building by instructors is seen as "a two-pronged process of initiating and subsequently maintaining rapport with students" (Flanigan, Akcaoglu, & Ray, 2022, p. 1). There are various strategies employed: "During the first weeks of the semester, these instructors rely upon connecting, information sharing, and common grounding behaviors to initiate a sense of rapport from their students. Going forward throughout the semester, these instructors rely upon attentive and courteous behaviors while providing learners with personalized instruction to maintain rapport" (Flanigan, Akcaoglu, & Ray, 2022, p. 1). A study on blended learning found the following: "Teaching presence was found to have direct positive impacts on the cognitive presence and social presence, and indirect positive impacts on teaching performance" (Law, Geng, & Li, 2019, p. 1)

Teachers are central to the learning endeavor. One study found the following:

Perceived teacher support was found to have a broad range of direct and mediated effects on students' motivations for e-learning. Effort beliefs were consistent predictors of task value and ability beliefs after accounting for auto-lagged effects. E-learning completion was chiefly predicted by ability beliefs. (Fryer & Bovee, 2016, p. 21)

Tutors also influence learners' motivation "to learn a foreign language": "If the tutor is friendly and seems interested in guiding the student, in an empathetic environment, the student may have a better disposition to complete the activities of the virtual course…a high motivation must be characterized by autonomous behaviors, that is, an intrinsic motivation" (Fandiño & Velandia, 2020, p. 1 and p. 7). Certainly, in a time of mass aloneness, the human connections and interpersonal warmth created in online learning can be especially important.

"Future Is Yours"

In Developing Countries

Many have expressed a broad preference for "regular" classes instead of online ones (Selvaraj et al., 2021, p. 5). A fifth of participants in one study expressed an interest in having their institutes re-open during the pandemic "possibly out of concern of the time they are wasting instead of completing their courses" (Selvaraj et al., 2021, p. 7). They experienced online learning as so inadequate that they felt that they were wasting time. The online learning was spotty in various developing countries. One mixed methods research study found the following:

The quantitative finding showed that the students did not experience a constant online teaching and learning during the COVID-19 pandemic. It also revealed that the COVID-19 pandemic devastatingly affected students' learning in higher education in Afghanistan. In addition, the qualitative finding revealed that the students had problems with Internet and technological facilities in their learning and they suggested that the Ministry of Higher Education should design and introduce a practical online platform which will be free and accessible with a poor Internet connection because some of the students live in areas where the Internet speed is very slow. (Noori, 2021, p. 1)

One study focused on how university students in a developing country engaged with their learning during the pandemic. The researcher identified three key themes:

The three themes and sub-themes described were: (a) personal, with sub-themes of challenge, curiosity, self-determination, satisfaction and religious commitment; (b) social, with sub-themes of relationships, imspiration, and well-being of self and others; and (c) environmental, with sub-themes of facilities and conditioning. (Rahiem, 2021, p. 1)

Learners were driven by their intrinsic "consequential aspirations, not by a controlled motivation, nor were they motivated by a reward, a penalty, or a rule that propelled them" (Rahiem, 2021, p. 1).

The setbacks from the pandemic may well be counted in a variety of ways and for years to come. Online learners have reported a psychological toll and excessive stresses in the "social laboratory" of online learning during a pandemic (Lemay, Bazelais, & Doleck, 2021, p. 1). A number of studies has identified various lacks in the online learner experience in 2020–2022 (and counting through the present).

The social design of online learning may enable basic learner needs satisfactions in online learning environments. These include teaching presence and social presence, to communicate social-contextual communications in online learning.

Findings indicated that perceived teaching presence was a significant positive predictor of the basic psychological needs for autonomy, competence, and relatedness, with greater contribution than social presence to the perceived satisfaction of the need for competence. Social presence was also a significant positive predictor of the three basic psychological needs, with greater contributions than teaching presence on the perceived satisfaction of the needs for autonomy and relatedness. These results point to the significance of both teaching presence and social presence as two key online presences that can positively influence students' basic psychological needs satisfaction, which is known to be crucial to higher-quality self-determined motivation and engagement. (Turk, Heddy, & Danielson, 2022, p. 1)

Here, autonomy is defined as "sense of control, self-endorsement, self-direction, volition" and competence as "sense of mastery, sense of progress, sense of achievement" (Turk, Heddy, & Danielson, 2022, p. 2). The researchers also identified a potential link between social presence and learners' needs for social relatedness ("need to belong, need to connect, need to be cared about by others") (Turk, Heddy, & Danielson, 2022, p. 3). Teacher presence online was found to significantly influence learner autonomy (Turk, Heddy, & Danielson, 2022, p. 11) and learners' "perceived competence" (p. 11), in alignment with studies in face-to-face learning. Learners' social presence "significantly predicted perceived relatedness" (Turk, Heddy, & Danielson, 2022, p. 11).

Another work explored factors that inform how students evaluate online learning during the pandemic. A positive involved lessened time needed for commuting. Nationality was found to determine "their assessment of online studying and the frequency of participation in online courses" (Szopiński & Bachnik, 2022, p. 1) in business. The researchers also observe that "...the student engagement variable determines the current evaluation of online studying, the change in frequency of participation since the introduction of online classes, and the preferred mode of study (online or offline)" (Szopiński & Bachnik, 2022, p. 1).

Another study identified the importance of "learning activity use," which "explained students' performance at the end of the semester beyond their learning prerequisites and prior achievement" and prior knowledge (Bosch, Seifried, & Spinath, 2021, p. 1). Learner motivation is seen as fueling student willingness to engage in learning activities. Students who valued the topic (educational psychology) used more learning activities as well (Bosch, Seifried, & Spinath, 2021, p. 1). The researchers note that many students had high intentions to use many learning activities early in the semester but ended up using much less. Finally, the researchers note the importance of student learning behaviors on their "potential to determine their own success" (Bosch, Seifried, & Spinath, 2021, p. 1). Learner expectancies for possible gains from the learning were "not associated with the use of learning activities" even as those who valued the subject engaged the learning activities more (Bosch, Seifried, & Spinath, 2021, p. 9).

A survival analysis approach was used in a study of learners who shifted from in-person learning to online learning due to school closures in the pandemic. They found increases in student enrollments in online learning in the face of the pandemic but also the finding that the "proportion of students engaged also decreased more rapidly over time" based on a survival analysis of student data (Spitzer et al., 2021, p. 1). The researchers studied "how many students remain active learners for how long" in the online learning (Spitzer et al., 2021, p. 8), as an indicator of student perseverance.

Among learners in a large developing country, learner reactions to the shift to online learning were captured. The researchers found that "students prefer recorded classes with quiz at the end of each class to improve the effectiveness of learning. The students opined that flexibility and convenience of online classes makes it attractive option, whereas broadband connectivity issues in rural areas makes it a challenge for students to make use of online learning initiatives" (Muthuprasad et al., 2021, p. 1). The learning needed to be practical for those studying agricultural topics. The learners found the online courses more difficult than traditional ones because of "the technological constraints, delayed feedback and inability of the instructor to handle effectively the Information and Communication Technologies" (Muthuprasad et al., 2021, p. 11).

Ruggedizing Learners to Enable Persistence

An "adversity quotient" is defined as "a person's ability to manage difficulties and transform obstacles into opportunities" (Safi'i et al., 2021, p. 1). One study points to this quotient as a necessary tool for

"Future Is Yours"

effective online learning online during the pandemic. This factor is found to affect student learning autonomy, achievement motivation, and ultimately their learning performance (Safi'i et al., 2021, p. 1). They elaborate:

Adversity quotient affects students' achievement motivation through three indicators, namely, receiving advice that achievement is possible..., the recognition of students that the learning materials taught support student achievement...and the students' thinking that learning materials in school are closely related to their achievement... (Safi'i et al., 2021, p. 5)

Learners' adversity quotients are seen as affecting offline and online learning. The level of adversity quotient affecting "students' learning autonomy are enacted through three indicators: "students' ability to determine their own learning goals," the selection of learning skills to fit the learner, and "student learning standards" (Safi'i et al., 2021, p. 6).

One study suggests that it is detrimental to "sanitize" project management education by removing difficulties. The researchers suggest that harnessing "desirable difficulties" may enhance the learning by bringing a sense of the real world into the "practice-relevant online learning" (van der Hoorn & Killen, 2021, p. 1). There is value to "embracing unpredictability, and authenticity" can have a constructive effect on learning. The researchers write:

In response to COVID-19 restrictions, we moved an interactive role-play online and explored the resultant learning through analysis of student performance and students' individual reflections. Findings suggest that the online role-play boosted learning by exposing students to a challenging environment, which included tasks that stretched their capabilities and thus enhanced the level of "Desirable Difficulties". Drawing on the concepts of Desirable Difficulties and 'role-play-as-rehearsal', we discuss the benefits of formative 'testing' and propose a new concept: 'role-play-as testing'. (van der Hoorn & Killen, 2021, p. 1)

The virtualization of practice through online learning was seen to be effective (van der Hoorn & Killen, 2021).

Resilience is seen as a byproduct of academic self-efficacy (ASE), in another study. More specifically, there were positive correlations between academic self-efficacy and "resilience and social support" (Warshawski, 2022, p. 1). Some differences were found in the research variables based on "students' gender, cultural group and their perceived difficulty in studies" (Warshawski, 2022, p. 1), among the nurse educators. The finding showed "positive moderate correlations...between ASE and resilience, ASE and social support, and between resilience and social support" (Warshawski, 2022, p. 6).

Researchers have hypothesized that "intellectual humility enhanced academic performance via stronger intrinsic motivation and greater receptivity to feedback" (Wong & Wong, 2021, p. 1). In their research, they found "...a small, positive indirect effect of intellectual humility on academic performance through receptivity to feedback, where more intellectually humble students were more receptive to coursework feedback in that they perceived it as constructive and engaged with it more and had subsequently higher GPAs" (Wong & Wong, 2021, p. 1). They also found that intellectual humility positively predicted intrinsic motivation, but it "was not significantly predictive of academic performance" ...but a path analysis suggested that "intellectual humility may facilitate academic performance via active engagement and learning behavior underpinning effective self-regulation" (Wong & Wong, 2021, p. 1). This study used an instrument to measure intellectual humility including "independence of intellect and ego, openness to revising one's viewpoints, respect for others' viewpoints, and lack of intellectual overconfidence" (Wong & Wong, 2021, p. 3).

As to studies of burnout from online distance learning during the pandemic, researchers found that "psychological capital" is beneficial in an academic context (Barratt & Duran, 2021, p. 1). Social support was found to moderate the relationship between psychological capital and "learner engagement and burnout" among postgraduate distance learning students (Barratt & Duran, 2021, p. 1). Those with psychological capital have "self-efficacy, optimism, hope, and resilience" and is a composite construct (Barratt & Duran, 2021, p. 2). Those with more psychological capital engage in the online learning more and experience burnout less.

Harnessing Powerful Technologies and Socio-technical Capabilities

Online learning is enabled through various core technologies like learning management systems (LMSes) and social media, among others.

Gamification in Online Student Learning Performance

A playful relaxed psychological state may enhance learning and mediate anxieties. Roleplaying has been harnessed for in-class motivation through "physical attendance and practical guided work" (Topîrceanu, 2017, p. 41). The insights from face-to-face learning have been moved to an online learning platform built around gamification concepts. This system does not involve grading or "negative feedback." It uses the narratives of "heroes, accumulated experience, levels, level-ups, achievements, quests, guilds, and other representative elements taken from role-playing games" with particular positive foci (Topîrceanu, 2017, p. 41). Students collaborate in "guilds" (Topîrceanu, 2017, p. 45). Such gamified approaches enable "friendly academic experience" (Topîrceanu, 2017, p. 46).

Leaderboards are a feature of gamified learning. Their design may affect how students see their own positionality in relation to other students in terms of course performance. One study was conducted among postgraduate students to see if there were differential effects based on whether absolute (showing a student's position in comparison to everyone else in the course) or relative (showing a student's position in relation to a few "neighbors" closest to them) leaderboards were used. The researchers write: "Results suggest that the absolute leaderboard helps intensify students' sense of comparison and competitiveness more than the relative leaderboard" (Bai et al., 2021, p. 1).

Conversely, in the relative leaderboard class, students ranked in the top third tended to display better learning performance than their peers in the lower two thirds did. Students who ranked in different positions showed similar levels of course engagement and intrinsic motivation for learning. (Bai et al., 2021, p. 1)

Those who ranked at the top often engaged in upward comparison of learners, bolstering the idea that there may be more competition at the top. The researchers conducted qualitative analyses and found that "the students ranked in the bottom third preferred anonymous (vs. public) comparison on an absolute leaderboard but favored public (vs. anonymous) comparison on a relative leaderboard" (Bai et al., 2021,

"Future Is Yours"

p. 1). The top-ranked participants showed "a significantly higher level of interest/enjoyment than the bottom-ranked students at the end of the semester" (Bai et al., 2021, p. 10). They conclude:

The absolute leaderboard highlights both winners (proximity to a standard, i.e., near the number one ranking) and losers (away from a standard), enabling all users to view other participant's (sic) progression, which can dampen the level of interest/enjoyment among the bottom-ranked participants. (Bai et al., 2021, p. 10)

Friendly competition can be harnessed with constructive motivations for learners, such as in a gamified context. Gamification can spark both intrinsic and extrinsic motivations through leaderboards which show individual and group progress in leaderboards (Zainuddin, 2018, p. 86). Gamification elements may include "badges, social interactions, points, and leaderboards" (Xu et al., 2021, p. 444), among others.

Another study found that "game-based learning in distance learning cannot act as a mediator in enhancing the students' achievement" (Wardoyo et al., 2021, p. 1). There are mixed effects of gamified learning. This latter study did find that "technological knowledge, educational competence, (and) computer skills" are critical for technology-based learning" (Wardoyo et al., 2021, p. 1).

Social Media Technologies

In an emergency online learning context, instructors sometimes went to existing technologies. Some instructors harness various social media applications to enhance the online learning courses. One study explored the openness of learners to using the WhatsApp app to support learning. Drivers that contribute to learner acceptance of the technology and connectedness to online learning include "students' perceived usefulness, availability of learning support, motivation, and connectedness with their friends" (Mulyono, Suryoputro, & Jamil, 2021, p. 1).

Another group used the Kahoot! platform in their online classes during the pandemic to increase learner attention and participation. They used Kahoot! Games "carried out for the different topics of a university subject" (Martín-Sómer, Moreira, & Casado, 2021, p. 154). They found that "the transfer from face-to-face to remote teaching had produced a general decrease in interest that can be mitigated by performing Kahoot! games" (Martín-Sómer, Moreira, & Casado, 2021, p. 154).

A research study finding that the addition of a "social robot" and "gamification" elements separately did not result in any significant increase in engagement or motivation, and further, when the two elements were combined as additions, there was "lower engagement" (Donnermann et al., 2021, p. 1)

Social Robots

One study explored the effects from the addition of a "social robot" and "gamification" elements in an online learning context. Separately, these did not result in any significant increase in engagement or motivation, and further, when the two elements were combined as additions, there was "lower engagement" (Donnermann et al., 2021, p. 1). The infusion of technology into online learning may not necessarily have a positive learning effect.

Augmented Reality (AR)

Augmented reality (AR) has been harnessed to enhance student motivation in engineering education. In this discipline, learners often learn by doing as a central pedagogical approach. To understand concepts, learner benefit from visualizing and interacting with the concepts and phenomena. AR is thought to be able to stand in the gap by providing hands-on interactive learning with "images, videos and texts" (Kaur, Mantri, & Horan, 2020, p. 883). This study found that AR contributed to learner motivation in terms of "attention, relevance, confidence, satisfaction" (Kaur, Mantri, & Horan, 2020, p. 884). Various technologies have been harnessed to meet the pandemic moment.

Machine Language Translation Systems

Some students for whom English was not a first language used machine translation systems to read books written originally in the English for their studies at one medical university. One study explored the "perceived ease of use, learning motivations for English, and foreign language reading anxiety" in this context. The researchers found that "overall, using machine translation systems produced benefits, including increasing the students' motivation to learn English and further decreasing their anxiety when it comes to reading textbooks written in English" (Tsai & Liao, 2021, p. 1). The machine translation systems offered cognitive scaffolding for the learners. Learners were seen to move away from the usage of such tools once they gained more English fluency.

By Discipline Area

Some of the pandemic-era studies of online learning may be appreciated within their particular disciplines.

In Language-based Learning

One study focused on the goal-oriented active learning (GOAL) system used to promote reading engagement, self-directed learning behavior, and motivation in extensive reading. This study found that high self-directed learning ability students demonstrated significantly more reading engagement, SDL (self-directed learning) behaviors, motivation, and autonomy for extensive reading than those with low SDL ability" (Li et al., 2021, p. 1). The researchers write that a self-directed learning support environment can be highly useful to support "foreign language learning in the schools; however, the affective and behavioral outcomes created by the environment were affected to varying degrees by the levels of students' SDL ability" (Li et al., 2021, p. 1). Those with high self-directed learning ability "engaged in more planning and monitoring interactions in the GOAL system" and engaged more in extensive reading (Li et al., 2021, p. 9) as compared to those with lower SDL abilities.

One study focused on the power of a "positive future image of their language learning" and an interest in English culture having a "better self-regulatory capacity in online learning environments" (Zheng et al., 2018, p. 144). Those who learn English so as to "avoid negative academic results" were found to be less motivated to engage online self-regulated learning (Zheng et al., 2018, p. 144). Finally, the researchers also found that learners with positive online learning experiences tended to be more flexible and independent in their self-regulatory learning process" (Zheng et al., 2018, p. 144).

"Future Is Yours"

Social presence in a Community of Inquiry Framework includes the ability of learners to engage as real people with each other, including teachers and learners. In a study of online writing instruction, student reflections during the online course (during the pandemic) showed various themes: "social presence, social comfort, attitudes about online learning, and social learning" (Stewart, 2021, p. 1). This work suggests that "simply inviting students to 'feel real' or positioning yourself as a 'real' instructor is not sufficient for establishing the types of social interactions that composition studies values" (Stewart, 2021, p. 1). Authentic learning requires additional structural and other elements for full building of community of inquiries for learning writing online. In the C of I model, the educational experience is created as an intersection of social presence, cognitive presence, and teaching presence.

Another study explored the effects of an online collaboration tool for college students to enhance their academic writing skills. The researchers found that "college students with underdeveloped language skills can benefit from a well-structured online intervention supporting a collaborative learning environment for academic writing" (Li & Mak, 2022, p. 1).

In an online foreign language learning context during COVID-19, students benefitted when they had access to printed materials vs. "studying purely online"; the learners appreciated the ability to take notes and highlight various parts (Klimova, 2021, p. 1787). Students who participated in this research expressed the sense of irreplaceability of face-to-face courses for foreign language learning. Further, the sense of social distance in online learning may be a demotivator for learning. The researchers found that "no or only a small compensatory foreign language instruction took place during the school lockdowns" (Klimova, 2021, p. 1789). Teachers teaching online were found to need to be more present to be effective in their online teaching.

Another study focused on learner motivations and self-regulated learning in online language learning courses. The motivation for language learning is based on a "complex combination of cognitive and social aspects" (Lin, Zhang, & Zheng, 2017, p. 76). While the researchers found that "increased use of online learning strategy may help to improve student satisfaction, perceived progress, and final grades" (Lin, Zhang, & Zheng, 2017, p. 83), the research suggests that motivations alone did not have an obvious impact on assessed performance.

One study examined the motivations of Vietnamese students to acquire English as a non-native language. The motivations were defined as the following: "obtaining a good job in the future, achieving success in academic studies, maintaining effective communications with foreigners, having personal enjoyment, and being influenced by other people" (Van Nguyen & Habók, 2021, p. 1). These learners tended to be "more internally (rather than externally) motivated" but also showed "strong motivational intensity to learn English and enhance their language competence" (Van Nguyen & Habók, 2021, p. 1). Further, the researchers found "a strong positive relationship between internal motivation and motivational intensity, whereas there was a weak positive correlation between external motivation and motivational intensity" (Van Nguyen & Habók, 2021, p. 1).

In a European country, during the early stages of the outbreak, social presence was seen as especially important in an English as a Foreign Language course. The researchers found that "explicit acknowledgement of others in the learning environment was the most prevalent and seemed to boost affective and cohesive effects. Furthermore, the findings illustrated the importance students placed on having in-class opportunities to express their frustrations" (Alger & Eyckmans, 2022, p. 1). The venting provided an outlet for learner frustrations. Off-task talk, and self-disclosures are important for cohesion among the learners (Alger & Eyckmans, 2022).

In Mathematics Learning

One study explored whether learner motivational and emotional orientations mattered in learner self-regulation in a university mathematics course moved from face-to-face lectures to online learning based on "crisis-driven digitalization" context. In a field where chalk boards (or white boards for the more cutting-edge) are *de rigueur,* the shift to online was "a radical shift" (Reinhold et al., 2021, p. 1). The researchers identified two clusters of students "differing in mathematics related interest, anxiety, self-concept, and work ethics" (Reinhold et al., 2021, p. 1), what they termed "more promising" and "less promising." The "more promising" were those with "higher expectation of success, higher need for face-to-face social interaction, and less preference for online learning formats after the pandemic situation than students from the less promising cluster" (Reinhold et al., 2021, p. 1). Students in the "less promising cluster" reported "below average interest in mathematics, above average mathematics anxiety, a below average self-concept regarding mathematics and below average work ethics" (Reinhold et al., 2021, p. 4). Learners in the different clusters "did not differ significantly in their subjective task value, their learning outside of course structures, and their appreciation of digital learning formats" (Reinhold et al., 2021, p. 1). A critical factor was that "a positive general attitude towards learning with ICT was the key element influencing students' coping with learning in the pandemic situation" (Reinhold et al., 2021, p. 1). Interestingly, students in the more promising group "were eager to return to face-to-face instruction" (Reinhold et al., 2021, p. 1).

In mathematics, there are certain learning behaviors that are particularly conducive to learning success. One such positive learning behavior involves reading supplemental materials related to wrong answers, so as to correct misconceptions. It helps to review the contents of a test afterwards. Also, making references to other students' learning strategies may be beneficial to the learning of math (Hwang, Wang, & Lai, 2021, p. 1). Ideally, learners would take a cyclic approach, with four recurring stages of self-regulation: self-evaluation, goal setting, strategy adoption, and monitoring (in a cyclic approach) (Hwang, Wang, & Lai, 2021, p. 4). This work takes a social regulation online learning framework as compared to a more conventional individual self-regulation framework to improve learner learning motivations and strategies (p. 15). This study explored whether the social approach enabled higher competencies but found that "the learning performance of the learners who used the social regulation-based online learning framework were not significantly better than those of the learners who used the conventional self-regulated learning framework in the fields of confidence in learning mathematics and mathematics anxiety" (Hwang, Wang, & Lai, 2021, p. 16). There were advances in self-regulation, however. Those who used the social regulation-based online learning framework "not only performed more learning behaviors than the control group students but had more actions of self-modification and notes organization" (Hwang, Wang, & Lai, 2021, p. 16).

One study explored the efficacy of an online mathematics homework system, particularly the "see similar example" (or "practice another version" or PAV) feature. They summarize:

Findings indicate students used similar examples to troubleshoot, to check if they were on the right track, and to see the form of the answer. Students also sought to unpack the reasoning in solution steps, used solutions as templates for solving their own problems, and sometimes copied answers. One student did a 'see similar example' problem for more practice. Students' goals included completing the homework, maximizing their score, and understanding the content. (Dorko, 2021, p. 1)

"Future Is Yours"

In mathematics, studying similar examples can be a positive approach to learning comprehension and performance. These do often require learner opt-in and investment in study. One study looked at the transition to online education for high school students. This study found the following:

...online education has positive but limited impacts on test scores on average, particularly those in the subject of math within the natural sciences track; top-tier students are most positively affected by online education; and the benefits of online education vary among students with different backgrounds. (Zhang, Zhao, & Zhou, 2021, p. 1)

There was also the finding that online learning time "has a significant negative effect for some students in certain subjects" (Zhang, Zhao, & Zhou, 2021, p. 1).

In Statistics Learning

How peers support each other in an online learning context is seen to enhance learner motivation and performance, such as in a statistic learning course (Razak & See, 2010). In an online statistics course, instructors used efficacy building strategies to support learner self-efficacy for cognitive, motivational, and affective outcomes. Four sources of self-efficacy were identified: "anxiety coping, modeling, mental practice, and effort feedback" (Huang, Mayer, & Usher, 2020, p. 1). The research team found that "the four strategies worked effectively in combination, significantly improving transfer test scores..., increasing self-efficacy ratings..., and reducing task anxiety ratings..., as compared with the control condition" (Huang, Mayer, & Usher, 2020, p. 1). They note that "no motivational strategy alone was effective" but powerful only in combination (Huang, Mayer, & Usher, 2020, p. 1).

In Physics Learning

In one university physics course, the instructors launched an AI-enabled gamified online learning application to address the "head, hands, and heart" of each learner, the full student, "to first encourage and motivate participation, stimulate practice, and strengthen the students' domain knowledge of physics" (Tan & Cheah, 2021, p. 1). The researchers emphasize the importance of instructional design to consider the full dimensionality of learners. The effectiveness of this innovative tool is being assessed with follow-on research.

In Nursing and Other Health Science Professions

In a nursing course, various factors affected student engagement in online learning: "Techno-pedagogical skills were considered very important for faculty and important for students. For both faculty and students, self-directed learning skills were important, and peer-assisted learning (PAL)" enabled "fair symmetry" for collaborative learning (Elshami et al., 2022, p. 1). In this context, the learners in this context expressed a preference for "pre-recorded educational material" which could be consumed at the learners' own pace (Elshami et al., 2022, p. 1). Another study also focused on nursing students, this time, on their learning flow during the COVID-19 pandemic. The researchers summarize:

The factors affecting the learning flow of nursing students during the COVID-19 pandemic were their self-regulated learning ability...; learning motivation...; self-efficacy in clinical practice; and lecture type, or a mixture of recorded and real-time video lectures...As a result of the qualitative study, eight categories and 22 subcategories were derived. The eight categories are: a lack of preparation in the starting of virtual classes due to the COVID-19 pandemic, adapting and growing in a new learning environment, enhancing nursing knowledge and skills through virtual clinical training, self-regulation difficulties when studying alone due to social distancing, difficulty concentrating when learning online, disadvantages of virtual learning, concerns about academic performance, and missing opportunities to enjoy college life. (Park & Seo, 2021, p. 1)

There were unique insights to the particular context. Students were "concerned that they would be unable to fully establish their competence to work as actual hospital nurses due to a lack of clinical practice" (Park & Seo, 2021, p. 1). Designers of the online learning could benefit the student experience by creating ways to bridge to effective clinical practice skills.

Another study in the COVID-19 era focused on student nurses in an online course. This work studied the relationship "among critical thinking, self-directed learning, and problem-solving in student nurses taking online classes" (Song, Lee, & Lee, 2022, p. 1). The researchers found "significant positive correlations among critical thinking, self-directed learning, and problem-solving" (Song, Lee, & Lee, 2022, p. 1). Also, self-directed learning "had a significant mediating effect on the relationship between critical thinking and problem-solving ability" (Song, Lee, & Lee, 2022, p. 1) in this context of so-called "genre pedagogy."

Does peer learning have effects on nursing students' learning outcomes in an electrocardiogram assignment? In one experimental study, students were divided into a peer learning group vs. a self-directed learning group to see if there would be a difference in learning flow, interpretation skills, and self-confidence, in their web-based education. Learners in both groups improved on learning flow, interpretation, and self-confidence; however, they did not show any "significant pretest-posttest differences in learning flow, interpretation skills, or self-confidence between the two groups" (Ko, Issenberg, & Koh, 2022, p. 1).

Several studies involving nursing students focused on their well-being. One study used a self-administered survey to understand the impact of COVID-19 on the psychosocial well-being and learning of nursing and midwifery undergraduate students (Rasmussen et al., 2022, p. 1). The major identified themes were the following: "psychosocial impact of the pandemic, adjustment to new modes of teaching and learning, and concerns about course progression and career underpinned by lack of motivation to study, feeling isolated, and experiencing stress and anxiety that impacted on students' well-being and their ability to learn and study" (Rasmussen et al., 2022, pp. 1-2). There were appreciations for the "different and flexible teaching modes that allowed them to balance their study, family, and employment responsibilities. Support from academic staff and clinical facilitators / mentors combined with clear and timely communication of risk management related to personal protective equipment (PPE) in a healthcare facility, were reported to reduce students' stress and anxiety. (Rasmussen et al., 2022, p. 2).

Still another study focused on training inexperienced nurses to address the "great risk of sexual harassment" through an e-book intervention for the experimental group and a video and brochure for the control group (Chang et al., 2021, p. 1). The training is to enable nurses to mitigate such harassment and not to go to self-blame or other counter-productive responses.

"Future Is Yours"

In nurse educator education, researchers explored whether online course duration had different effects on the graduate nurse educator students' engagement in their community of inquiry.

High mean scores on the questionnaire showed that a community of inquiry was established regardless of course duration. However, there were differences in terms of the social and teaching presence subscales but not in the cognitive presence subscale suggesting that students in the traditional course were better able to establish the type of rapport with each other that increased comfort and engagement with peer interactions. Independent t-tests revealed statistically significant differences in perceptions of time to complete course activities. Students in the 16-week course were more likely to report that they had adequate time to complete course teachings, think critically about course content, complete course assignments and thoughtfully engage in course discussion and that they performed their best on assignments. (Tiedt, Owens, & Boysen, 2021, p. 1)

This work supports the traditional longer course duration vs. "an intensive 8-week format because it allows for students to build a better rapport and greater student engagement with the course materials and peers" (Tiedt, Owens, & Boysen, 2021, p. 1). Respective social presence and social connectedness are important. Also, acceleration of the learning may force students to quickly complete the work, without sufficient reading and reflection (Tiedt, Owens, & Boysen, 2021).

One qualitative case study based on online interviews focused on undergraduate radiography students' experiences with learning during the pandemic. Two themes were identified: "(1) Maintaining balance in the new 'normal'; (2) Enablers for an inclusive learning environment" (Gumede & Badriparsad, 2022, p. 193). In the shift to online teaching and learning, many felt that they were "required to adjust without adequate consideration of the prerequisites of the process, such as device and data availability" (Gumede & Badriparsad, 2022, p. 193). The shift was seen as an opportunity for digital literacy, to better position the discipline beyond the crisis. Radiography learning occurs in a context of ever-present stress and "overwork" (Gumede & Badriparsad, 2022, p. 198).

In health science courses that were evaluated for student attitudes about teaching and learning outcomes in various learning modalities, one researcher has found that learners prefer team-based learning and a collaborative learning pedagogy "rather than face-to-face lectures" in hybrid courses. Students also appreciated the "flexibility, convenience, and control over the delivery of content" (Alabdulkarim, 2021, p. 5382). The study also found learner enjoyment of virtual classrooms and the enabled technologies in blended learning (Alabdulkarim, 2021, p. 5381).

Another study, this time involving health sciences undergraduate students, found a preference to use smartphones to access online learning during the COVID-19 outbreak. They also used Zoom as "the most utilized online communicating platform" (Chandrasiri & Weerakoon, 2021, p. 1) in this time period. These learners also experienced a positive perception towards online learning (Chandrasiri & Weerakoon, 2021, p. 1). Still, the researchers suggest that "remedial actions" may be in order to make up for lost learning experiences such as fewer interactive sessions and a lack of clinical training (Chandrasiri & Weerakoon, 2021, p. 5).

In Public Administration Education

One researcher conducted a SWOT (Strengths, Weaknesses, Opportunities, Threats) analysis of public administration education online during the pandemic. One major finding was of the critical socializing roles of university campuses and face-to-face education. Also: "…self-actualization is indispensable for revealing the real potential and the creativity of students" (Hergüner, 2021, p. 1). In online learning, students were frustrated by the sense that the interactions were "anti-social" (Hergüner, 2021, p. 4). Besides the lack of learner motivation, other "threats" to the online learning process were "technical difficulties" and "student immobility" (not clearly defined) (Hergüner, 2021, pp. 4 - 5). Online education was not seen as enabling "community formation" in the same way as in-class teaching (Hergüner, 2021, p. 5).

In Library and Information Sciences Learning

One study explored the readiness of students in library and information sciences for the shift to online learning during the pandemic. The learners "were sufficiently prepared for online learning during the COVID-19 lockdown in the country," and they were "motivated to learn online, were receptive to new ideas, learned from their mistakes, and were willing to interact and engage with their fellow students while learning online" (Rafique et al., 2021, p. 5). Important factors for successful learning online were computer self-efficacy, self-directed learning, learner control, learning motivation, and "online communication self-efficacy" (Rafique et al., 2021, p. 6). Not all the learners were equally prepared. Finally, the researchers found that postgraduate students "exhibited a higher readiness towards computer/ internet, online communications self-efficacy, and learning motivation than undergraduates and graduate students" (Rafique et al., 2021, p. 8).

In Billiards Studies

An intervention in billiards learning using mobile flipped learning was tested and found to be effective. The approach involved "scaffolding, questioning, interflow, reflection and comparison" (SQIRC) (Lin, Hsia, & Hwang, 2021, p. 1). This study found significant improvement in student performance on "billiards striking strategies, self-efficacy, and learning motivation" based on their learning from video-recorded activities "with reflection and comparison guidance" (Lin, Hsia, & Hwang, 2021, p. 1).

Maladaptive Attitudes and Behaviors for Online Learning

Online learners have been profiled by similarity clusters to better understand online learning dynamics. One study explored the effect of learner motivation on their achievement, emotions, and academic performance. This work found three latent profiles of learner approaches, based on control-value theory, with learners labeled on their orientations with different levels of adaptivity in terms of achievement in learning. They write: "High control-enjoyment students reported greater success and expected better grades than low control-boredom and low value-boredom students, and out-performed low-control-boredom students on all tests" (Parker et al., 2021, p. 1). The researchers suggest that ambiguity in motivation is a risk factor for learners, who benefit from focus and direction. What is maladaptive to online learning? Low control-boredom and low value-boredom profiles are risky: "The low control-boredom maladaptive profile (very low control appraisals, high boredom and anxiety) predicted adverse achievement perceptions and performance. The low value-boredom profile was ambiguous inasmuch that it exhibited a maladaptive emotion profile but predicted achievement perception and performance outcomes that do not necessarily suggest they are motivationally at-risk" (Parker et al., 2021, p. 10). Of the participants in the study, 44% were identified as maladaptive in terms of orientation (Parker et al.,

"Future Is Yours"

2021, p. 11). There may be learning interventions to shift maladaptive psychosocial profiles to more constructive approaches.

Another work profiled learners based on their "online assignment motivation" based on achievement goal theory (focused on mastery and performance-approach goals) and expectancy-value theory (focused on achievement goals and their value for the learner and the likelihood of the goal being achieved). This approach focuses on the value of the focal goal and the learners' self-confidence in their ability to reach that goal. This study identified four learner profiles: "*High Motivation, Moderate Motivation, Low Goal Orientation/Moderate Expectancy-Value,* and *Very High Goal Orientation/Very Low Expectancy-Value*" (Xu, 2022, p. 1). This study also resulted in the finding that "profile membership was associated with self-regulation of online assignment behavior, including handling distraction, arranging the environment, managing time, monitoring motivation, emotion management, and cognitive reappraisal" (Xu, 2022, p. 1). Learners need to promote "multiple motivational beliefs to better support self-regulation of online assignment behavior" (Xu, 2022, p. 1).

Another work involved the identification of regulation profiles during computer-supported collaborative learning. This study examined their profiles with students' performance, motivation, and self-efficacy for learning. Three regulation profiles were identified: "'all-round-oriented and affirming regulator' (AOAR), 'social-oriented and elaborating regulator' (SOER), and 'individual-oriented and passive regulator' (IOPR)" (De Backer et al., 2021, p. 1). The learners with the different regulation profiles "differed significantly in their conceptual understanding, motivation for learning, and self-efficacy beliefs" (De Backer et al., 2021, p. 1). In order to engage learners with different regulation profiles, various "customized metacognitive scaffolds" should be built into computer-supported collaborative learning" (CSCL) contexts (De Backer et al., 2021, p. 1). Interestingly, more than half of the CSCL participants were 'all-round-oriented and affirming regulator' (AOAR); less than a third were 'social-oriented and elaborating regulator' (SOER); and the 'individual-oriented and passive regulators' (IOPR) were the remainder (De Backer et al., 2021, p. 12).

Project group learning was the focus of another study, this one involving project management students. The learning mix that would be effective involved learner "ownership of self-chosen projects and regular feedback from the supervisor" which led to "hard work, intrinsic motivation and learning in all phases of the project" (Nordahl-Pedersen & Heggholmen, 2022, p. 791). Ideally, learners would work in a context of "considerable autonomy within a tight framework" for effective communities of learning (Nordahl-Pedersen & Heggholmen, 2022, p. 791).

Instructors that take a homogenous approach in online teaching and learning risk disregarding "the heterogeneity in students' cognitive and motivational characteristics" (Dietrich et al., 2021, p. 1). This study explored the effects of individualized learning design as an intervention to see what the effects might be on "students' motivation (self-concept, self-efficacy, intrinsic and utility task values), on their performance, and…on their professional development with regard to inclusive education" (Dietrich, Greiner, Weber-Liel, Berweger, & Kämpfe, 2021, p. 1). The researchers found "…the intervention positively affected the self-concepts of effort avoidant students" (Dietrich et al., 2021, p. 1). An individualized approach "also positively impacted students' attitudes and self-efficacy towards inclusive education, but had no effect on course performance, course-related self-efficacy and task values" (Dietrich et al., 2021, p. 1), in a blended learning course for student teachers.

Dealing with Learner Procrastination

Why do college students procrastinate in online learning? asks another research team. If students did not see the learning contents as relevant or the technologies as usable, these perceptions informed their senses of "task value and emotional cost," which informed whether or not they engaged in academic procrastination. Conscientiousness was also a predictor of academic procrastination, for those with lower levels of conscientiousness (Cheng & Xia, 2021, p. 1). They write: "Perceived instructor engagement and peer interaction did not predict academic procrastination" (Cheng & Xia, 2021, p. 1). Procrastination in online courses was seen as a "complex phenomenon" that "stemmed from the interrelationships between college students' perceptions of learning context, personal characteristics, and motivational beliefs" (Cheng & Xia, 2021, p. 1). The perceived usability of technology was significantly associated with "all motivational beliefs" and was "a significant predictor of academic self-efficacy and emotional cost" even after "controlling for the other facets of perceived course structures and conscientiousness" Cheng & Xia, 2021, p. 9). A surprise finding was that "academic self-efficacy was not significantly associated with academic procrastination" Cheng & Xia, 2021, p. 9). Under emotional duress, learners may procrastinate in a maladaptive way to relieve the related tension Cheng & Xia, 2021, p. 10), so helping learners deal with their stresses may be important.

A different study explored the learning experiences of procrastinators during the pandemic based on exploratory research. Procrastinators are thought to be thrown off by the lessened structure in online learning and the change in the learning environment from a physical space to a virtual one. The lower levels of social engagement may also be challenging. One finding: "The procrastinators are encountering a higher degree of challenges related to motivation as opposed to non-procrastinators" (Melgaard et al., 2022, p. 117). Other themes from the study of online learning include the observation that procrastinators "are more anxious about exams and grades as compared to non-procrastinators" and further that "extreme procrastinators" have "major challenges with structuring their everyday routines, while non-procrastinators thrive and positively use the time to study" (Melgaard et al., 2022, p. 120). The uses of "online lectures" have negatively affected the participation of both procrastinators and non-procrastinators (Melgaard et al., 2022, p. 120) and an even more negative impact on extreme procrastinators; on the other hand, synchronous delivery "has a positive impact on non-procrastinators" (Melgaard et al., 2022, p. 120). The researchers also found that "non-procrastinators report achieving relatively better results as compared to their prior performance while procrastinators on the other hand report no decline in their results" (Melgaard et al., 2022, p. 121).

Another work connects procrastination (as a disposition) with ineffective self-regulated learning and ineffective online learning during the coronavirus lockdown. One study found that "procrastination is negatively related to 6 sub-constructs of self-regulated online learning: task strategy, mood adjustment, self-evaluation, environmental structure, time management, and help-seeking" (Hong, Lee, & Ye, 2021, p. 1). Procrastination here is defined as "purposeful but needless delay in completing academic tasks" (Hong, Lee, & Ye, 2021, p. 5).

Another work explores how to help students learn optimally, such as through the use of interpolated pre-questions in video learning. The research team writes: "...after controlling for prior knowledge, students with high achievement motivation benefitted more from the pre-questions than students with low achievement motivation. Among students with high achievement motivation, there was longer fixation duration to the learning materials and better transfer in the pre-questions condition than in the no-questions condition, but these differences based on video type were not apparent among students with

"Future Is Yours"

low achievement" (Yang et al., 2021, p. 1). The benefit is seen in transfer of learning in one context to a different one rather than learning memory retention. They write:

Eye-tracking data showed that although all students searched more efficiently when viewing the instructional video with interpolated pre-questions than the video with no questions, students with high achievement motivation who watched the video with pre-questions paid attention to learning content for a longer period and had better transfer scores compared to students with low achievement motivation who watched the same video. (Yang et al., 2021, p. 7)

One study extracted university learner profiles from an online learning space based on the dimension of learning engagement and identified five clusters: "highly-engaged self-driven online contributors, moderately engaged self-driven online viewers, less engaged self-driven online learners, highly engaged course-driven online learners, and less engaged course-driven online learners" (Binali, Tsai, & Chang, 2021, p. 1).

One variable that may be indicative of effective higher order thinking and learning involves innovation practices and innovation artifacts in engineering. The compared learning modalities include "asynchronous online" vs. "an on-campus synchronous face-to-face (F2F) course" during the pandemic. They write:

Findings indicated that both F2F and online students self-reported similar levels of innovative behavioral tendencies. Yet, the F2F students received higher mean scores on innovation, compared with the online students, in both individual assignments and team projects. (Usher, Barak, & Haick, 2021, p. 1)

They did find that the online students "received lower mean scores on both team and individual creations" as compared to their F2F learning counterparts (Usher, Barak, & Haick, 2021, p. 7). This work suggests that it would be helpful to support learners in collaborating remotely and to support innovative learning online.

Another study focused on the creativity of postgraduate students. The core question involved whether autonomous motivation of the postgraduate learner had an effect on the learners' innovations. The measure of "autonomous motivation" had an effect on the creativity of postgraduate students (Wang, Wang, & Zhu, 2022, p. 1). The provision of supervisory innovation support by teachers was also important.

Harnessing Pedagogical Designs to Meet Online Learner Psychological Needs

Instructors can build a blended or hybrid synchronous learning context to support student motivation. Instructors may harness "pedagogical, social, and technical affordances" to recreate learning environments that are "motivating and engaging," ideally to enable deep cognitive engagement (Shi, Tong, & Long, 2021, p. 1). The researchers studied the effects of these affordances:

This study found that pedagogical affordance had positively predictive effects on both intrinsic and extrinsic motivation. The remote students who perceived high level of pedagogical affordance in the BSLE would result in high intrinsic and extrinsic learning motivation. Conversely, if they perceived low level of pedagogical affordance, they would present insufficient learning motivation. (Shi, Tong, & Long, 2021, p. 11)

One pandemic-era intervention for high school students in online learning involved gratitude, based on the academic benefits of gratitude (seen as "a catalyst of well-being and desirable psychological outcomes") (Valdez, Datu, & Chu, 2022, p. 1). The instructor harnessed a Facebook-based gratitude intervention, which was found to have an effect on "academic motivation and engagement." Specifically, the "…students who were assigned to the intervention condition had higher scores than those in the control condition, on autonomous motivation, controlled motivation, and cognitive engagement" (Valdez, Datu, & Chu, 2022, p. 1). A qualitative research phase involved findings "that Facebook-based gratitude intervention increased such learning outcomes because this intervention could promote social support, motivation, positive thinking, and desire to pay back parents and other significant people" (Valdez, Datu, & Chu, 2022, p. 1). There are benefits to "designing online gratitude interventions via social media" to "boost positive learning processes and outcomes" (Valdez, Datu, & Chu, 2022, p. 1).

Another work described the harnessing of social media to influence student knowledge sharing and learning performance, based on social cognitive theory and connectivism theory. The researchers hypothesize that social media may influence higher education learners' motivations, such as "reputation and altruism," which may affect knowledge sharing and learning performance (Hosen et al., 2021, p. 1). This model was validated empirically, with findings that "social media functions (documents exchange, virtual communication, and knowledge formation) and individual motivation (reputation) are core factors" that higher education institutions may use "to encourage knowledge sharing" for learning improvements (Hosen et al., 2021, p. 1).

Pedagogically, another study found that harnessing the predict-observe-explain (POE) approach of inquiry-based learning as applied to earth sciences heightened primary school learners' science learning, their critical thinking, and their self-confidence (Hong et al., 2021, p. 1).

Online learning data was used in another study that examined the power of task-value scaffolding to help learners experience intrinsic motivation for their studies. The study focused on a predictive learning analytics dashboard (LAD) and examined learner statistics related to "anxiety, motivation, and performance" in an online statistics course. The results…

showed that task-value scaffolding had a negative impact on learners' computation anxiety and attitudes towards statistics in comparison to the control group. On the other hand, the treatment had no significant influence on other aspects of statistics anxiety, motivation, and learning outcomes. (Valle et al., 2021, p. 1)

The findings are counter to some prior research, which suggested that emphasizing task-value might trigger learner intrinsic motivations and sense of autonomy. Here, "task-value scaffolding embedded in LADs can have detrimental effects on learners" (Valle et al. 2021, p. 1). Perhaps that emphasis might stress the learners.

Another work described an online scenario-based learning intervention, replete with feedback and reflection. The study explored whether this learning intervention led to student teachers' senses of self-efficacy and "emotional, motivational, and cognitive classroom readiness." The three conditions were: scenario-based learning only, scenario-based learning with feedback, and scenario-based learning with feedback and reflection, with the latter two as the experimental conditions. They write:

The findings indicated that, compared to the control group, both intervention conditions had a significant positive effect on cognitive classroom readiness. A significant positive effect on self-efficacy was found for intervention group 2. Overall, our research demonstrates the potential of an easy-to-implement online

"Future Is Yours"

intervention in enhancing self-efficacy and classroom readiness and points towards the importance of combining feedback and reflection within online scenario-based learning activities. (Bardach et al., 2021, p. 1)

How online learners perceive a course affects their level of effort and ultimate learning achievements. Students reported decreased effort when they either saw the course as too easy or when they thought "it was going to take a lot of time and the course was difficult" (Jones, Krost, & Jones, 2021, p. 1).

This study highlights the importance of designing courses that (a) interest students in the course activities, (b) foster perceptions of caring between the instructor and students, (c) are at an appropriate level of difficulty, and (d) provide a reasonable workload with considerations for students with time constraints. (Jones, Krost, & Jones, 2021, p. 1)

Proper design may affect perceptions and enable more effective engagement. The strongest predictors of learner effort in a course were their level of interest in the topic and their sense of caring from the instructor. Then: "The remaining predictors, empowerment, usefulness, success, and cost did not significantly predict student effort when all of the variables were included in the model at once" (Jones, Krost, & Jones, 2021, p. 4). Student grades predicted directly by student effort and indirectly predicted by their "interest" and the caring expressed by their instructors (Jones, Krost, & Jones, 2021, p. 4).

One study of a semester of university student learning focused on their motivational regulation and autonomous motivation, "exploring both between and within person components" (Garn & Morin, 2021, p. 1). The researchers write:

Participants...from one large class reported motivation in two-week intervals over the course of one semester. Bivariate latent curve models with structured residuals revealed rates of change in motivational regulation and autonomous motivation were not linear, declining across the first ten weeks of the semester then bouncing back in the final month. Between-person effects of individual change demonstrated mirroring relationships of latent intercepts and slopes across the semester. Within-person findings revealed that autonomous motivation was a negative predictor of future motivation regulation. Students' grade point average only predicted students' beginning level of motivational regulation. It appears that students with higher states of autonomous motivation view motivation regulation as unnecessary or even a potential threat to their learning pleasure and satisfaction. (Garn & Morin, 2021, p. 1)

Another study explored whether there were motivation -performance tradeoffs in online learning. The researchers describe their work:

First exam and final class grades were obtained. We compared online and on-campus students in reported use of strategies to enhance the importance of studying-related outcomes (goals-defined) and to enhance the studying experience (experience-defined). The latter included an Internet-based strategy (i.e., making studying more enjoyable by exploring class web page). Online and on-campus students did not differ in reported use of outcome-focused strategies but online students were more likely to report exploring the class web page. For online students, greater exploration was associated with higher interest but lower first exam grades, which predicted final interest and grades. (Sansone et al., 2012, p. 141)

To wit, the researchers found "trade-offs between maintaining interest and performance" in online learning (Sansone et al., 2012, p. 141). They also discovered additional interrelationships:

For all students, reminding oneself about the importance of good grades was highly rated, followed closely by working to see the usefulness of learning the topic for real life. In fact, all three goals-defined motivational strategies were rated above the midpoint, indicating that no matter the context, students attempted to enhance their motivation to study by focusing on potential positive outcomes. (Sansone et al., 2012, p. 147)

Enhancing motivation in the learning did show a negative association with performance. The Internet may generate interest in the topic, but it may also distract from the learning based on its usage.

In one study, the use of prompts to activate learner self-regulation in online courses during the pandemic only resulted in "small effects" in terms of "a declarative knowledge and transfer test, even as the "prompted groups showed different online learning behavior than the control group" (Schumacher & Ifenthaler, 2021, p. 1). The use of trace data from the online learning platform was "rather limited" (Schumacher & Ifenthaler, 2021, p. 11).

Another innovation to support student learning involved the use of the Dynamic Concept Maps (DCMs) approach to "stimulate in students the processes of mutual interaction and hybridization between digital artefacts…and analog artefacts (books)…so as to encourage the development of significant learning" (Marzano & Miranda, 2021, p. 1) in online learning. This intervention was found to reduce study time.

One study explored the management of student risk in online settings through multiple elements: "digital literacy, parental mediation," and self-control (Purnama et al., 2021, p. 1). Certainly, children who had to go online en masse for learning were sometimes exposed to some of the darker elements of the Web and Internet. A different study explored the effects of ego depletion on online learning. Ego depletion can occur when people have experienced "frequent or excessive acts of self-control" which minimizes their ability to enact "subsequent acts of self-control (Greene et al., 2022, p. 1). Interestingly, even after "a rigorous ego-depletion treatment…no detectable group differences" were found "in terms of either process or product data" (Greene et al., 2022, p. 1).

"Future is Yours": Motivating Online Learners in Higher Education through a Package of Goods (in the Pandemic)

This study, then, was set up in the following way, with a review of the literature, then the capture of instructional design information during the two prior years of the pandemic, and coding of the data. This general sequence is shown in Figure 1.

In the early phases of the pandemic (2020), as the U.S. government was struggling to understand the capabilities of the novel SARS-CoV-2 / COVID-19 and to set in place proper policies, in-person education continued apace until March 2020 at the target Midwestern university. At that time, students were asked not to return from spring break. They were asked to move out of the residence halls. All the courses shifted to online learning.

"Future Is Yours"

Figure 1. Diagram of "Future Pull" Research (cross-functional diagram)

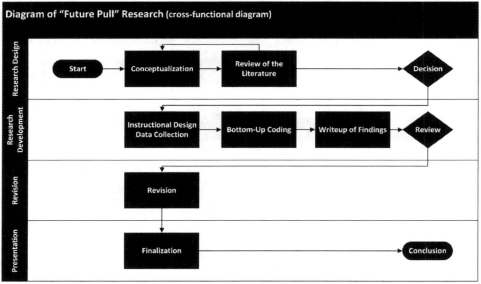

At that time, early support for faculty involved faculty trying to adjust to the learning management system (LMS) as the main site for learning, whereas before it was just an addendum to in-person courses in many cases. [It was used by many as a site for grade recording and the direct exporting of grades into grade recording systems.] The university strove to provide laptops, digital scanners, and other equipment to faculty who needed the technologies. [As with wireless fidelity or wi-fi providers, additional help was not provided for setup.] Those who may have wanted to access digital cameras, tripods, and such, on loan, no longer had access because in-person meetings were so fraught with biosafety hazards. The library's services went virtual, in a move that seemed smooth given that they had long been providing library services to distance learners already. Some faculty did not have access to wireless networks at home because they lived in the countryside, and many students also lacked access, often due to financial challenges. There were jokes / non-jokes about freeriding wireless at low-cost hotel parking lots. Hotspot devices were sent out to some. As more information about the high transmissibility and pathogenicity of the virus emerged, the public went on their own self-imposed lockdowns, often even before the government edicts came down. Spending time face-to-face with others, even family, felt like high risk, and people started to avoid each other assiduously where they could. Those providing essential services strove to acquire masks and to socially distance, so as to protect themselves and others around them. As the first year passed, remote employees started to be slowly hired again, and they had to be onboarded.

As to instructional design questions, faculty asked how they could create equivalency of learning for a live demo in a laboratory with expensive equipment. Others asked how to enable field trips and field work, especially in contexts where virtual "fields" were not available. [One faculty member dug a trench in her backyard in order to show students something of ground strata. She received her 20 seconds of fame when she microblogged herself standing in a large hole and lecturing about the soil sub-surface.]]

Based on the literature review and hands-on instructional design work during the two years and a quarter of work during the COVID-19 pandemic, and abductive logic, some observations have been made about what goes into the package of goods for conveying the "future is yours" message to learners. These are shown in Table 1. Each element may have effects on the following: learning content, assignments, activities, guest speakers, projects, communications (messaging, calendaring, work feedback, and others), and policies, among others.

Table 1. A package of goods for "Future is Yours" messaging and preparation for online learners during the COVID-19 pandemic

Term	Learner Goals	Pedagogical Interventions (as a Package of Goods)
Near-Term Future (1 – 6 Years)	• Self-efficacy • Self-regulation • Communications skills • Socio-technical skills • Social connections • Explorations of self-identity • Academic and professional belongingness	• Acclimatizing to the learning management system (LMS) and respective technologies • Technological enablements • Harnessing of third-party tools (as relevant to the learning) • Support to define and articulate learner goals (knowledge, skills, and abilities) • Clear directions • Clear and basic language • Opt-in help resources • Files in multiple modalities • Accessibility • Social supports • Students as audiences for each other's capabilities and work • A culture of civility and mutual respect • Elicitation of unique learner voices • Adaptive and customized engagement with learners • Defined study calendars • Incremental steps for larger-scale assignments (scaffolded work) • Sufficient and appropriate learning feedback • Sharing of prior works by prior learners (with legal releases) • Student clubs (online) • Virtual events • Campus life (albeit virtual) • Engaging timely issues (that are relevant in the present and mid-term future) • Engaging aesthetics and friendliness for the learning space as a "social hangout" • Open-source texts to enable free or low-cost access to learning materials • Effective socio-technical technologies • Mapped paths to a profession (and filling of knowledge gaps for learners) • Field research • Funding of research • Professional apprenticeships
Mid-Term Future (graduation and 5 years into a career)	• Social connections • Explorations of self-identity • Academic and professional belongingness • Entry to various professions of interest • Development of the full and well-rounded person • Innovations, contributions to a field	• Social learning activities • Practice of soft skills • Problem-based learning, authentic learning • Engagement of the local world in the learning (local to learners) • Student-informed assessments (agency), participatory design (vs. passive consumption of the pre-designed learning alone) • Accessible contents • Effective socio-technical technologies • Connections with professionals in the field; recommendations (in various forms, from letters to memos and others) • Funding of research, co-published research
Far-Term Future (6 – 10 years into a career, onwards)	• Explorations of self-identity • Entry to various professions of interest • Professional advancement • Innovations, contributions to a field	• Problem-based learning, authentic learning • Practice of soft skills • Work-based experiences, apprenticeships • Open "hard" / difficult questions in the discipline • Professional ties, networking • Guest speakers (from the professions) • Electronic portfolios • Resumes and *curriculum vitae* • Accessible contents • Effective socio-technical technologies • Funded research, co-published research

70

"Future Is Yours"

The contents in Table 1 are written generally to be inclusive of various types of higher educational learning. One insight here is that in a time of mass global disruption, students go online not only to learn but to find social company, find affirmations for the self, understand their own identities, engage with their instructor and peers in meaningful ways, expand their KSAs (knowledge, skills, and abilities), and achieve their various goals. They may be driven by their intrinsic motivations (self-development, self-identity, autonomy, and others) and extrinsic motivations (social recognition by others, extra credit, a paying job), and others. During the pandemic, some enrolled in higher education in order to acquire scholarship and grant funds on which to live.

DISCUSSION

To be clear, teachers and other staff faced many challenges during the pandemic. There was not an actual playbook for how to adapt to a world gone awry from a deadline airborne pathogen. To adapt, under threat, many went back to the familiar and the proverbial back foot. They often paid out-of-pocket for their home offices and equipment. They faced a heavy workload. Many were asked to take on excessive roles, worked inhumane hours including on nights and weekends, and experienced burnout and even left the profession. There were new technologies to be learned, new pedagogical approaches, and discipline-based demands. While many were able to maintain senses of normalcy and civility and professionalism and care in difficult budgetary and social environments, not all were able to do so. [The university leadership modeled an ethic of care in powerful ways by monitoring COVID-19 in the community and on campus, providing healthcare, and going with the best science while balancing staff and student needs for some autonomy.] Many experienced personal ego depletion and fatigue. For many teachers, they could not find the optimism about a glowing future for themselves, much less for others. In this time of testing, not all made it to the other side.

However, some teachers were able to call on colleagues to offer live virtual events. [Others simply cleared the slate of all such events because the logistics just felt too challenging, with intellectual property concerns and requisite rights releases, technology troubleshooting, and other factors.] Some were able to adapt by meeting learners where they were at and based on their unique needs, given the importance of understanding learners as individuals, with different mixes of characteristics and motivations (Xu, 2022). Instructors would do well to emphasize the importance of the topic for the student learning, given that "…perceived content relevance is a strong predictor of students' learning in online learning environments" (Cheng & Xia, 2021, p. 9). Instructors also need to simultaneously raise learner confidence in their ability to achieve the related learning goals. It is important for learners to not be afraid of difficulty in order to learn more optimally (Yang et al., 2021, p. 7). Another important message is that it is a "happening world" out there even though students may have temporally been sidelined due to the pandemic, unfair as that is. Instructors need to have hope for the future and the conviction of their imaginations to support student learning. In the pandemic, with so many disruptions to government, the economy, social ties, and higher education, and with so much social distancing and lockdowns, the virtual has to stand in the real for most. Finally, the most important point is that learning is about building for the future; this effort is actual. Instructors do well to thread the connections, so learners may be uplifted and encouraged and inspired, especially in difficult rough patches (even if these challenging times run for years). Learners should see what is possible, so they can imagine "multiple horizons" for their own self-determined futures.

FUTURE RESEARCH DIRECTIONS

"Future pull" likely has different motivation power in the near-term (first one to six years in higher education to cover the undergraduate and perhaps graduate span), mid-term (post-higher education and the first five years of a profession), and far-term futures (the first six to ten years in a profession and beyond). Future pull likely evolves over time, too, with the individual and groups defining what serves as inspiration and "pull." Learning is lifelong, and the design of motivations—intrinsic and extrinsic—is continuous.

For future research, there is a number of open questions:

- Are there continuing through-lines of motivations for all phases of higher education? Professional life? Both?
  - How can these be built and maintained for enabling lifelong learning, learner productivity, health, and innovation?
- What are strategies for individuals to maintain their intrinsic motivations through their various life phases?
  - Are there particular types of intrinsic motivations that lead to original innovations and effective world-changing contributions?
- What sorts of financial incentives promote retention in learning for learner-paid courses? [as compared to the structuring of free courses with financial incentives that promote "lasting learning motivation" (Lee & Yeung, 2021, p. 1)]
- Are there anti "future pulls," and what are these? [For example, teaching old materials can be highly demotivating for learners. Learners want cutting-edge, not outdated.] What are ways to design these constructively (to discourage negative attitudes and actions into the future)?
- What about "future pull" in future crisis conditions? How can societal continuity be better prepared for, including in the education space? Are there ways to design these to be more compelling and supportive of learners at every level?
- How can all education stakeholders be encouraged to view the future with hope and clarity and specificity, when so much of human energy is focused on survival in the present? How can present-distortions be harnessed to engage a fast-arriving future?
- How can instructors in higher education bring the draw and the charisma to attract learners and to keep their attention? To attract external moneys from businesses and government entities? How can the staff and administration at universities support these endeavors?

The challenges are many-fold in normal times, much less during a global pandemic.

CONCLUSION

During a pandemic, the world is fundamentally and critically disrupted. People's prior senses of order—from government, from laws, from social safety nets, from social connections—are challenged. In some cases, various aspects of the world do actually break down, sometimes irretrievably. [The outbreak of a hot war is an example. Political opportunists and opportunists of all stripes emerge into contexts of apparent weakness and chaos.] For university students, they are moved from the pathogen-dangerous physical real space into virtual learning management systems (LMSes) and other online spaces for everything educational and social. They may lose momentum in their ambitions and objectives.

This work suggests that "future pull" is a powerful way to align and structure online learning to retain learners who may be facing sharp headwinds against continuing learning and continuing progressions towards a career. "The "future is yours" framework can be interpreted fairly broadly based on the particular teaching and learning context. What motivates particular target groups of learners will differ. This work notes that "future pull" is about creating effective learning that pulls learners into the future and then messaging around that clearly, to encourage learner persistence.

DEDICATION

This work is dedicated to all the students who stuck it out through the difficult years of the SARS-CoV-2 / COVID-19 pandemic. I am in awe of your strength and grit. The world can be a very tough place, and your character and knowledge and skills should hold you in good stead.

REFERENCES

Aguilar, S. J., Karabenick, S. A., Teasley, S. D., & Baek, C. (2021). Associations between learning analytics dashboard exposure and motivation and self-regulated learning. *Computers & Education*, *162*(104085), 1–11. doi:10.1016/j.compedu.2020.104085

Aguilera-Hermida, A. P. (2020). College students' use and acceptance of emergency online learning due to COVID-19. *International Journal of Educational Research Open*, *1*(100011), 1–8. doi:10.1016/j.ijedro.2020.100011 PMID:35059662

Al Mamun, M. A., Lawrie, G., & Wright, T. (2022). Exploration of learner-content interactions and learning approaches: The role of guided inquiry in the self-directed online environments. *Computers & Education*, *178*(104398), 1–22. doi:10.1016/j.compedu.2021.104398

Al-Nasa'h, M., Awwad, F. M, & Ahmad, I. (2021). Estimating students' online learning satisfaction during COVID-19: A discriminant analysis. *Heliyon*, *7*(12), 1 - 7.

Alabdulkarim, L. (2021). University Health Sciences students rating for a blended learning course framework. *Saudi Journal of Biological Sciences*, *28*(9), 5379–5385. doi:10.1016/j.sjbs.2021.05.059 PMID:34466118

Alger, M., & Eyckmans, J. (2022). "I took physical lessons for granted": A case study exploring students' interpersonal interactions in online synchronous lessons during the outbreak of COVID-19. *System*, *102716*, 1–18. doi:10.1016/j.system.2021.102716

Artino, A. R. Jr, & Stephens, J. M. (2009). Academic motivation and self-regulation: A comparative analysis of undergraduate and graduate students learning online. *The Internet and Higher Education*, *12*(3-4), 146–151. doi:10.1016/j.iheduc.2009.02.001

Audet, É. C., Levine, S. L., Metin, E., Koestner, S., & Barcan, S. (2021). Zooming their way through university: Which Big 5 traits facilitated students' adjustment to online courses during the COVID-19 pandemic. *Personality and Individual Differences*, *180*(110969), 1–5. doi:10.1016/j.paid.2021.110969

Ayouni, S., Hajjej, F., Maddeh, M., & Alotaibi, S. (2021). Innovations of materials for student engagement in online environment: An ontology. *Materials Today: Proceedings*, 1–7. doi:10.1016/j.matpr.2021.03.636

Bai, S., Hew, K. F., Sailer, M., & Jia, C. (2021). From top to bottom: How positions on different types of leaderboard may affect fully online student learning performance, intrinsic motivation, and course engagement. *Computers & Education*, *173*, 104297. doi:10.1016/j.compedu.2021.104297

Bardach, L., Klassen, R. M., Durksen, T. L., Rushby, J. V., Bostwick, K. C., & Sheridan, L. (2021). The power of feedback and reflection: Testing an online scenario-based learning intervention for student teachers. *Computers & Education*, *169*(104194), 1–17. doi:10.1016/j.compedu.2021.104194

Barratt, J. M., & Duran, F. (2021). Does psychological capital and social support impact engagement and burnout in online distance learning students? *The Internet and Higher Education*, *100821*, 1–9. doi:10.1016/j.iheduc.2021.100821

Berweger, B., Born, S., & Dietrich, J. (2022). Expectancy-value appraisals and achievement emotions in an online learning environment: Within-and between-person relationships. *Learning and Instruction*, *77*(101546), 1–9. doi:10.1016/j.learninstruc.2021.101546

Binali, T., Tsai, C. C., & Chang, H. Y. (2021). University students' profiles of online learning and their relation to online metacognitive regulation and internet-specific epistemic justification. *Computers & Education*, *175*(104315), 1–16. doi:10.1016/j.compedu.2021.104315

Bolliger, D. U., Supanakorn, S., & Boggs, C. (2010). Impact of podcasting on student motivation in the online learning environment. *Computers & Education*, *55*(2), 714–722. doi:10.1016/j.compedu.2010.03.004

Bosch, E., Seifried, E., & Spinath, B. (2021). What successful students do: Evidence-based learning activities matter for students' performance in higher education beyond prior knowledge, motivation, and prior achievement. *Learning and Individual Differences*, *91*(102056), 1–12. doi:10.1016/j.lindif.2021.102056

Chandrasiri, N. R., & Weerakoon, B. S. (2021). Online learning during the COVID-19 pandemic: Perceptions of Allied Health Sciences undergraduates. *Radiography*, 1–5. PMID:34893435

Chang, T. S., Teng, Y. K., Chien, S. Y., & Tzeng, Y. L. (2021). Use of an interactive multimedia e-book to improve nursing students' sexual harassment prevention knowledge, prevention strategies, coping behavior, and learning motivation: A randomized controlled study. *Nurse Education Today*, *104883*, 1–7. doi:10.1016/j.nedt.2021.104883 PMID:34218069

Chen, K. C., & Jang, S. J. (2010). Motivation in online learning: Testing a model of self-determination theory. *Computers in Human Behavior*, *26*(4), 741–752. doi:10.1016/j.chb.2010.01.011

Cheng, S. L., & Xie, K. (2021). Why college students procrastinate in online courses: A self-regulated learning perspective. *The Internet and Higher Education*, *50*, 100807. doi:10.1016/j.iheduc.2021.100807

Daumiller, M., Rinas, R., Hein, J., Janke, S., Dickhäuser, O., & Dresel, M. (2021). Shifting from face-to-face to online teaching during COVID-19: The role of university faculty achievement goals for attitudes towards this sudden change, and their relevance for burnout/engagement and student evaluations of teaching quality. *Computers in Human Behavior*, *118*(106677), 1–10. doi:10.1016/j.chb.2020.106677

De Backer, L., Van Keer, H., De Smedt, F., Merchie, E., & Valcke, M. (2021). Identifying regulation profiles during computer-supported collaborative learning and examining their relation with students' performance, motivation, and self-efficacy for learning. *Computers & Education*, 104421.

Dietrich, J., Greiner, F., Weber-Liel, D., Berweger, B., Kämpfe, N., & Kracke, B. (2021). Does an individualized learning design improve university student online learning? A randomized field experiment. *Computers in Human Behavior*, *122*, 106819. doi:10.1016/j.chb.2021.106819

Donnermann, M., Lein, M., Messingschlager, T., Riedmann, A., Schaper, P., Steinhaeusser, S., & Lugrin, B. (2021). Social robots and gamification for technology supported learning: An empirical study on engagement and motivation. *Computers in Human Behavior*, *121*(106792), 1–9. doi:10.1016/j.chb.2021.106792

Dorko, A. (2021). How students use the 'see similar example' feature in online mathematics homework. *The Journal of Mathematical Behavior*, *63*(100894), 1–25. doi:10.1016/j.jmathb.2021.100894

Dunn, T. J., & Kennedy, M. (2019). Technology Enhanced Learning in higher education; motivations, engagement and academic achievement. *Computers & Education*, *137*, 104–113. doi:10.1016/j.compedu.2019.04.004

Eberle, J., & Hobrecht, J. (2021). The lonely struggle with autonomy: A case study of first-year university students' experiences during emergency online teaching. *Computers in Human Behavior*, *121*(106804), 1–11. doi:10.1016/j.chb.2021.106804

Elshami, W., Taha, M. H., Abdalla, M. E., Abuzaid, M., Saravanan, C., & Al Kawas, S. (2022). Factors that affect student engagement in online learning in health professions education. *Nurse Education Today*, *110*, 105261. doi:10.1016/j.nedt.2021.105261 PMID:35152148

Fandiño, F. G. E., & Velandia, A. J. S. (2020). How an online tutor motivates E-learning English. *Heliyon*, *6*(8), 1 - 7.

Flanigan, A. E., Akcaoglu, M., & Ray, E. (2022). Initiating and maintaining student-instructor rapport in online classes. *The Internet and Higher Education*, *53*(100844), 1–11.

Fryer, L. K., & Bovee, H. N. (2016). Supporting students' motivation for e-learning: Teachers matter on and offline. *The Internet and Higher Education*, *30*, 21–29. doi:10.1016/j.iheduc.2016.03.003

Garn, A. C., & Morin, A. J. (2021). University students' use of motivational regulation during one semester. *Learning and Instruction*, *74*(101436), 1–10. doi:10.1016/j.learninstruc.2020.101436

Greene, J. A., Duke, R. F., Freed, R., Dragnić-Cindrić, D., & Cartiff, B. M. (2022). Effects of an ego-depletion intervention upon online learning. *Computers & Education*, *177*(104362), 1–14. doi:10.1016/j.compedu.2021.104362

Gumede, L., & Badriparsad, N. (2022). Online teaching and learning through the students' eyes–Uncertainty through the COVID-19 lockdown: A qualitative case study in Gauteng province, South Africa. *Radiography*, *28*(1), 193–198. doi:10.1016/j.radi.2021.10.018 PMID:34785145

Hergüner, B. (2021). Rethinking public administration education in the period of pandemic: Reflections of public administration students on online education through a SWOT analysis: Rethinking public administration education. *Thinking Skills and Creativity*, *100863*, 1–8. doi:10.1016/j.tsc.2021.100863

Hong, J. C., Hsiao, H. S., Chen, P. H., Lu, C. C., Tai, K. H., & Tsai, C. R. (2021). Critical attitude and ability associated with students' self-confidence and attitude toward "predict-observe-explain" online science inquiry learning. *Computers & Education*, *166*(104172), 1–14. doi:10.1016/j.compedu.2021.104172

Hong, J. C., Lee, Y. F., & Ye, J. H. (2021). Procrastination predicts online self-regulated learning and online learning ineffectiveness during the coronavirus lockdown. *Personality and Individual Differences*, *174*(110673), 1–8. doi:10.1016/j.paid.2021.110673 PMID:33551531

Hosen, M., Ogbeibu, S., Giridharan, B., Cham, T. H., Lim, W. M., & Paul, J. (2021). Individual motivation and social media influence on student knowledge sharing and learning performance: Evidence from an emerging economy. *Computers & Education*, *104262*, 1–18. doi:10.1016/j.compedu.2021.104262

Hsia, L. H., Huang, I., & Hwang, G. J. (2016). Effects of different online peer-feedback approaches on students' performance skills, motivation and self-efficacy in a dance course. *Computers & Education*, *96*, 55–71. doi:10.1016/j.compedu.2016.02.004

Huang, C. Q., Han, Z. M., Li, M. X., Jong, M. S. Y., & Tsai, C. C. (2019). Investigating students' interaction patterns and dynamic learning sentiments in online discussions. *Computers & Education*, *140*(103589), 1–18. doi:10.1016/j.compedu.2019.05.015

Huang, X., Mayer, R. E., & Usher, E. L. (2020). Better together: Effects of four self-efficacy-building strategies on online statistical learning. *Contemporary Educational Psychology*, *63*(101924), 1–14. doi:10.1016/j.cedpsych.2020.101924 PMID:33041461

Hussein, E., Daoud, S., Alrabaiah, H., & Badawi, R. (2020). Exploring undergraduate students' attitudes towards emergency online learning during COVID-19: A case from the UAE. *Children and Youth Services Review*, *119*(105699), 1–7. doi:10.1016/j.childyouth.2020.105699

Hwang, G. J., Wang, S. Y., & Lai, C. L. (2021). Effects of a social regulation-based online learning framework on students' learning achievements and behaviors in mathematics. *Computers & Education*, *160*(104031), 1–19. doi:10.1016/j.compedu.2020.104031

Jensen, L. X., Bearman, M., & Boud, D. (2021). Understanding feedback in online learning–A critical review and metaphor analysis. *Computers & Education*, *173*(104271), 1–12. doi:10.1016/j.compedu.2021.104271

Jones, B. D., Krost, K., & Jones, M. W. (2021). Relationships between students' course perceptions, effort, and achievement in an online course. *Computers and Education Open*, *2*(100051), 1–10. doi:10.1016/j.caeo.2021.100051

Jovanović, J., Saqr, M., Joksimović, S., & Gašević, D. (2021). Students matter the most in learning analytics: The effects of internal and instructional conditions in predicting academic success. *Computers & Education*, *104251*, 1–13. doi:10.1016/j.compedu.2021.104251

Kaur, D. P., Mantri, A., & Horan, B. (2020). Enhancing student motivation with use of augmented reality for interactive learning in engineering education. *Procedia Computer Science*, *172*, 881–885. doi:10.1016/j.procs.2020.05.127

Kaur, P., Kumar, H., & Kaushal, S. (2021). Affective state and learning environment based analysis of students' performance in online assessment. *International Journal of Cognitive Computing in Engineering*, *2*, 12–20. doi:10.1016/j.ijcce.2020.12.003

Kim, D., Lee, Y., Leite, W. L., & Huggins-Manley, A. C. (2020). Exploring student and teacher usage patterns associated with student attrition in an open educational resource-supported online learning platform. *Computers & Education*, *156*, 103961. doi:10.1016/j.compedu.2020.103961

Klimova, B. (2021). An insight into online foreign language learning and teaching in the era of COVID-19 pandemic. *Procedia Computer Science*, *192*, 1787–1794. doi:10.1016/j.procs.2021.08.183 PMID:34630743

Ko, Y., Issenberg, S. B., & Roh, Y. S. (2022). Effects of peer learning on nursing students' learning outcomes in electrocardiogram education. *Nurse Education Today*, *108*(105182), 1–6. doi:10.1016/j.nedt.2021.105182 PMID:34741917

Kuo, T. M. L., Tsai, C. C., & Wang, J. C. (2021). Linking web-based learning self-efficacy and learning engagement in MOOCs: The role of online academic hardiness. *The Internet and Higher Education*, *100819*, 1–15. doi:10.1016/j.iheduc.2021.100819

Kyewski, E., & Krämer, N. C. (2018). To gamify or not to gamify? An experimental field study of the influence of badges on motivation, activity, and performance in an online learning course. *Computers & Education*, *118*, 25–37. doi:10.1016/j.compedu.2017.11.006

Lapitan, L. D. Jr, Tiangco, C. E., Sumalinog, D. A. G., Sabarillo, N. S., & Diaz, J. M. (2021). An effective blended online teaching and learning strategy during the COVID-19 pandemic. *Education for Chemical Engineers*, *35*, 116–131. doi:10.1016/j.ece.2021.01.012

Law, K. M., Geng, S., & Li, T. (2019). Student enrollment, motivation and learning performance in a blended learning environment: The mediating effects of social, teaching, and cognitive presence. *Computers & Education*, *136*, 1–12. doi:10.1016/j.compedu.2019.02.021

Lee, Y. H., & Yeung, C. (2021). Incentives for learning: How free offers help or hinder motivation. *International Journal of Research in Marketing*. 1 - 16.

Li, H., Majumdar, R., Chen, M. R. A., & Ogata, H. (2021). Goal-oriented active learning (GOAL) system to promote reading engagement, self-directed learning behavior, and motivation in extensive reading. *Computers & Education*, *104239*, 1–11. doi:10.1016/j.compedu.2021.104239

Li, J., & Mak, L. (2022). The effects of using an online collaboration tool on college students' learning of academic writing skills. *System*, *102712*, 1–14. doi:10.1016/j.system.2021.102712

Li, L. Y., & Tsai, C. C. (2017). Accessing online learning material: Quantitative behavior patterns and their effects on motivation and learning performance. *Computers & Education*, *114*, 286–297. doi:10.1016/j.compedu.2017.07.007

Lin, C. H., Zhang, Y., & Zheng, B. (2017). The roles of learning strategies and motivation in online language learning: A structural equation modeling analysis. *Computers & Education*, *113*, 75–85. doi:10.1016/j.compedu.2017.05.014

Lin, H. C., Hwang, G. J., Chang, S. C., & Hsu, Y. D. (2021). Facilitating critical thinking in decision making-based professional training: An online interactive peer-review approach in a flipped learning context. *Computers & Education*, *173*(104266), 1–25. doi:10.1016/j.compedu.2021.104266

Lin, Y. N., Hsia, L. H., & Hwang, G. J. (2021). Promoting pre-class guidance and in-class reflection: A SQIRC-based mobile flipped learning approach to promoting students' billiards skills, strategies, motivation and self-efficacy. *Computers & Education*, *160*(104035), 1–18. doi:10.1016/j.compedu.2020.104035

López-Fernández, D., Ezquerro, J. M., Rodríguez, J., Porter, J., & Lapuerta, V. (2019). Motivational impact of active learning methods in aerospace engineering students. *Acta Astronautica*, *165*, 344–354. doi:10.1016/j.actaastro.2019.09.026

Lorenza, L., & Carter, D. (2021). Emergency online teaching during COVID-19: A case study of Australian tertiary students in teacher education and creative arts. *International Journal of Educational Research Open*, *2*(100057), 1–8. doi:10.1016/j.ijedro.2021.100057 PMID:35059667

Maqableh, M., & Alia, M. (2021). Evaluation online learning of undergraduate students under lockdown amidst COVID-19 pandemic: The online learning experience and students' satisfaction. *Children and Youth Services Review*, *128*(106160), 1–11. doi:10.1016/j.childyouth.2021.106160

Martín-Sómer, M., Moreira, J., & Casado, C. (2021). Use of Kahoot! to keep students' motivation during online classes in the lockdown period caused by Covid 19. *Education for Chemical Engineers*, *36*, 154–159. doi:10.1016/j.ece.2021.05.005

Marzano, A., & Miranda, S. (2021). Online learning environments to stimulate in students the processes of mutual interaction between digital and analog artefacts to enhance student learning. *MethodsX*, *8*(101440), 1–9. doi:10.1016/j.mex.2021.101440 PMID:34430329

McPartlan, P., Rutherford, T., Rodriguez, F., Shaffer, J. F., & Holton, A. (2021). Modality motivation: Selection effects and motivational differences in students who choose to take courses online. *The Internet and Higher Education*, *49*(100793), 1–14. doi:10.1016/j.iheduc.2021.100793

Melgaard, J., Monir, R., Lasrado, L. A., & Fagerstrøm, A. (2022). Academic procrastination and online learning during the COVID-19 pandemic. *Procedia Computer Science*, *196*, 117–124. doi:10.1016/j.procs.2021.11.080 PMID:35035617

Merriam, S. B., & Caffarella, R. S. (1999). *Learning in Adulthood: A Comprehensive Guide* (2nd ed.). Jossey-Bass Publishers.

Muflih, S., Abuhammad, S., Al-Azzam, S., Alzoubi, K. H., Muflih, M., & Karasneh, R. (2021). Online learning for undergraduate health professional education during COVID-19: Jordanian medical students' attitudes and perceptions. *Heliyon*, *7*(9), e08031. doi:10.1016/j.heliyon.2021.e08031 PMID:34568607

Mulyono, H., Suryoputro, G., & Jamil, S. R. (2021). The application of WhatsApp to support online learning during the COVID-19 pandemic in Indonesia. *Heliyon*, *7*(8), 1 - 8.

Muthuprasad, T., Aiswarya, S., Aditya, K. S., & Jha, G. K. (2021). Students' perception and preference for online education in India during COVID-19 pandemic. *Social Sciences & Humanities Open, 3*(1), 1 - 11.

Noori, A. Q. (2021). The impact of COVID-19 pandemic on students' learning in higher education in Afghanistan. *Heliyon*, *7*(10), 1 - 9.

Nordahl-Pedersen, H., & Heggholmen, K. (2022). What promotes motivation and learning in project management students? *Procedia Computer Science*, *196*, 791–799. doi:10.1016/j.procs.2021.12.077

Park, J., & Seo, M. (2021). Influencing factors on nursing students' learning flow during the COVID-19 pandemic: A mixed method research. *Asian Nursing Research,* 1 - 10.

Parker, P. C., Perry, R. P., Hamm, J. M., Chipperfield, J. G., Pekrun, R., Dryden, R. P., Daniels, L. M., & Tze, V. M. (2021). A motivation perspective on achievement appraisals, emotions, and performance in an online learning environment. *International Journal of Educational Research*, *108*(101772), 1–16. doi:10.1016/j.ijer.2021.101772

Petrovskaya, A., Pavlenko, D., Feofanov, K., & Klimov, V. (2020). Computerization of learning management process as a means of improving the quality of the educational process and student motivation. *Procedia Computer Science*, *169*, 656–661. doi:10.1016/j.procs.2020.02.194

Purnama, S., Ulfah, M., Machali, I., Wibowo, A., & Narmaditya, B. S. (2021). Does digital literacy influence students' online risk? Evidence from Covid-19. *Heliyon*, *7*(6), 1 - 6.

Rafique, G. M., Mahmood, K., Warraich, N. F., & Rehman, S. U. (2021). Readiness for Online Learning during COVID-19 pandemic: A survey of Pakistani LIS students. *The Journal of Academic Librarianship*, *47*(3), 1 - 10.

Rahiem, M. D. (2021). Remaining motivated despite the limitations: University students' learning propensity during the COVID-19 pandemic. *Children and Youth Services Review*, *120*(105802), 1–14. doi:10.1016/j.childyouth.2020.105802 PMID:33318719

Rasmussen, B., Hutchinson, A., Lowe, G., Wynter, K., Redley, B., Holton, S., Manias, E., Phillips, N., McDonall, J., McTier, L., & Kerr, D. (2022). The impact of COVID-19 on psychosocial well-being and learning for Australian nursing and midwifery undergraduate students: A cross-sectional survey. *Nurse Education in Practice*, *58*(103275), 1–9. doi:10.1016/j.nepr.2021.103275 PMID:34922092

Razak, R. A., & See, Y. C. (2010). Improving academic achievement and motivation through online peer learning. *Proceedings of WCLTA 2010,* 358 – 352.

Reinhold, F., Schons, C., Scheuerer, S., Gritzmann, P., Richter-Gebert, J., & Reiss, K. (2021). Students' coping with the self-regulatory demand of crisis-driven digitalization in university mathematics instruction: Do motivational and emotional orientations make a difference? *Computers in Human Behavior*, *120*(106732), 1–10. doi:10.1016/j.chb.2021.106732

Rusli, R., Rahman, A., & Abdullah, H. (2020). Student perception data on online learning using heutagogy approach in the Faculty of Mathematics and Natural Sciences of Universitas Negeri Makassar, Indonesia. *Data in Brief*, *29*(105152), 1–6. doi:10.1016/j.dib.2020.105152 PMID:32025542

Safi'i, A., Muttaqin, I., Hamzah, N., Chotimah, C., Junaris, I., & Rifa'i, M. K. (2021). The effect of the adversity quotient on student performance, student learning autonomy and student achievement in the COVID-19 pandemic era: evidence from Indonesia. *Heliyon, 7*(12), 1 – 8.

Sansone, C., Smith, J. L., Thoman, D. B., & MacNamara, A. (2012). Regulating interest when learning online: Potential motivation and performance trade-offs. *The Internet and Higher Education*, *15*(3), 141–149. doi:10.1016/j.iheduc.2011.10.004

Schumacher, C., & Ifenthaler, D. (2021). Investigating prompts for supporting students' self-regulation–A remaining challenge for learning analytics approaches? *The Internet and Higher Education*, *49*(100791), 1–12. doi:10.1016/j.iheduc.2020.100791

Selvaraj, A., Radhin, V., Nithin, K. A., Benson, N., & Mathew, A. J. (2021). Effect of pandemic based online education on teaching and learning system. *International Journal of Educational Development*, *85*(102444), 1–11. doi:10.1016/j.ijedudev.2021.102444 PMID:34518732

Shapiro, H. B., Lee, C. H., Roth, N. E. W., Li, K., Çetinkaya-Rundel, M., & Canelas, D. A. (2017). Understanding the massive open online course (MOOC) student experience: An examination of attitudes, motivations, and barriers. *Computers & Education*, *110*, 35–50. doi:10.1016/j.compedu.2017.03.003

Shi, Y., Tong, M., & Long, T. (2021). Investigating relationships among blended synchronous learning environments, students' motivation, and cognitive engagement: A mixed methods study. *Computers & Education*, *168*(104193), 1–15. doi:10.1016/j.compedu.2021.104193

Shih, H. F., Chen, S. H. E., Chen, S. C., & Wey, S. C. (2013). The relationship among tertiary level EFL students' personality, online learning motivation and online learning satisfaction. *Procedia: Social and Behavioral Sciences*, *103*, 1152–1160. doi:10.1016/j.sbspro.2013.10.442

Shin, T. S., Ranellucci, J., & Roseth, C. J. (2017). Effects of peer and instructor rationales on online students' motivation and achievement. *International Journal of Educational Research*, *82*, 184–199. doi:10.1016/j.ijer.2017.02.001

Song, Y., Lee, Y., & Lee, J. (2022). Mediating effects of self-directed learning on the relationship between critical thinking and problem-solving in student nurses attending online classes: A cross-sectional descriptive study. *Nurse Education Today*, *109*(105227), 1–5. doi:10.1016/j.nedt.2021.105227 PMID:34972030

Spitzer, M. W. H., Gutsfeld, R., Wirzberger, M., & Moeller, K. (2021). Evaluating students' engagement with an online learning environment during and after COVID-19 related school closures: A survival analysis approach. *Trends in Neuroscience and Education*, *25*(100168), 1–8. doi:10.1016/j.tine.2021.100168 PMID:34844697

"Future Is Yours"

Stewart, M. K. (2021). Social presence in online writing instruction: Distinguishing between presence, comfort, attitudes, and learning. *Computers and Composition, 62*, 102669. doi:10.1016/j.compcom.2021.102669

Szopiński, T., & Bachnik, K. (2022). Student evaluation of online learning during the COVID-19 pandemic. *Technological Forecasting and Social Change, 174*, 121203. doi:10.1016/j.techfore.2021.121203 PMID:34531617

Tan, D. Y., & Cheah, C. W. (2021). Developing a gamified AI-enabled online learning application to improve students' perception of university physics. *Computers and Education: Artificial Intelligence, 2*(100032), 1–10. doi:10.1016/j.caeai.2021.100032

Tang, Y. M., Chen, P. C., Law, K. M., Wu, C. H., Lau, Y. Y., Guan, J., He, D., & Ho, G. T. (2021). Comparative analysis of Student's live online learning readiness during the coronavirus (COVID-19) pandemic in the higher education sector. *Computers & Education, 168*(104211), 1–17. doi:10.1016/j.compedu.2021.104211 PMID:33879955

Theobald, M. (2021). Self-regulated learning training programs enhance university students' academic performance, self-regulated learning strategies, and motivation: A meta-analysis. *Contemporary Educational Psychology, 66*(101976), 1–19. doi:10.1016/j.cedpsych.2021.101976

Thepwongsa, I., Sripa, P., Muthukumar, R., Jenwitheesuk, K., Virasiri, S., & Nonjui, P. (2021). The effects of a newly established online learning management system: The perspectives of Thai medical students in a public medical school. *Heliyon, 7*(10), 1 - 7.

Tiedt, J. A., Owens, J. M., & Boysen, S. (2021). The effects of online course duration on graduate nurse educator student engagement in the community of inquiry. *Nurse Education in Practice, 55*(103164), 1–8. doi:10.1016/j.nepr.2021.103164 PMID:34371480

Topîrceanu, A. (2017). Gamified learning: A role-playing approach to increase student in-class motivation. *Procedia Computer Science, 112*, 41–50. doi:10.1016/j.procs.2017.08.017

Tsai, M. N., Liao, Y. F., Chang, Y. L., & Chen, H. C. (2020). A brainstorming flipped classroom approach for improving students' learning performance, motivation, teacher-student interaction and creativity in a civics education class. *Thinking Skills and Creativity, 38*(100747), 1–11. doi:10.1016/j.tsc.2020.100747

Tsai, P. S., & Liao, H. C. (2021). Students' progressive behavioral learning patterns in using machine translation systems–A structural equation modeling analysis. *System, 101*(102594), 1–13. doi:10.1016/j.system.2021.102594

Tseng, H., Yi, X., & Yeh, H. T. (2019). Learning-related soft skills among online business students in higher education: Grade level and managerial role differences in self-regulation, motivation, and social skill. *Computers in Human Behavior, 95*, 179–186. doi:10.1016/j.chb.2018.11.035

Tseng, S. C., & Tsai, C. C. (2010). Taiwan college students' self-efficacy and motivation of learning in online peer assessment environments. *The Internet and Higher Education, 13*(3), 164–169. doi:10.1016/j.iheduc.2010.01.001

Turk, M., Heddy, B. C., & Danielson, R. W. (2022). Teaching and social presences supporting basic needs satisfaction in online learning environments: How can presences and basic needs happily meet online? *Computers & Education*, *104432*, 1–15. doi:10.1016/j.compedu.2022.104432

Usher, M., Barak, M., & Haick, H. (2021). Online vs. on-campus higher education: Exploring innovation in students' self-reports and students' learning products. *Thinking Skills and Creativity*, *42*(100965), 1–10. doi:10.1016/j.tsc.2021.100965

Valdez, J. P. M., Datu, J. A. D., & Chu, S. K. W. (2022). Gratitude intervention optimizes effective learning outcomes in Filipino high school students: A mixed-methods study. *Computers & Education*, *176*(104268), 1–16. doi:10.1016/j.compedu.2021.104268

Valle, N., Antonenko, P., Valle, D., Dawson, K., Huggins-Manley, A. C., & Baiser, B. (2021). The influence of task-value scaffolding in a predictive learning analytics dashboard on learners' statistics anxiety, motivation, and performance. *Computers & Education*, *173*, 104288. doi:10.1016/j.compedu.2021.104288

van Alten, D. C., Phielix, C., Janssen, J., & Kester, L. (2021). Secondary students' online self-regulated learning during flipped learning: A latent profile analysis. *Computers in Human Behavior*, *118*(106676), 1–13. doi:10.1016/j.chb.2020.106676

van der Hoorn, B., & Killen, C. P. (2021). Stop sanitizing project management education: Embracing Desirable Difficulties to enhance practice-relevant online learning. *Project Leadership and Society*, *2*(100027), 1–9. doi:10.1016/j.plas.2021.100027

Van Nguyen, S., & Habók, A. (2021). Vietnamese non-English-major students' motivation to learn English: from activity theory perspective. *Heliyon*, *7*(4), 1 - 11.

Vanslambrouck, S., Zhu, C., Lombaerts, K., Philipsen, B., & Tondeur, J. (2018). Students' motivation and subjective task value of participating in online and blended learning environments. *The Internet and Higher Education*, *36*, 33–40. doi:10.1016/j.iheduc.2017.09.002

Vanslambrouck, S., Zhu, C., Pynoo, B., Lombaerts, K., Tondeur, J., & Scherer, R. (2019). A latent profile analysis of adult students' online self-regulation in blended learning environments. *Computers in Human Behavior*, *99*, 126–136. doi:10.1016/j.chb.2019.05.021

Wang, C., Hsu, H. C. K., Bonem, E. M., Moss, J. D., Yu, S., Nelson, D. B., & Levesque-Bristol, C. (2019). Need satisfaction and need dissatisfaction: A comparative study of online and face-to-face learning contexts. *Computers in Human Behavior*, *95*, 114–125. doi:10.1016/j.chb.2019.01.034

Wang, H., Wang, L., & Zhu, J. (2022). Moderated mediation model of the impact of autonomous motivation on postgraduate students' creativity. *Thinking Skills and Creativity*, *100997*, 1–11. doi:10.1016/j.tsc.2021.100997

Wardoyo, C., Satrio, Y. D., Narmaditya, B. S., & Wibowo, A. (2021). Do technological knowledge and game-based learning promote students achievement: Lesson from Indonesia. *Heliyon*, *7*(11), 1 - 8.

Warshawsk, S. (2022). Academic self-efficacy, resilience and social support among first-year Israeli nursing students learning in online environments during COVID-19 pandemic. *Nurse Education Today*, *105267*, 1–6. doi:10.1016/j.nedt.2022.105267

Wong, I. H., & Wong, T. T. (2021). Exploring the relationship between intellectual humility and academic performance among post-secondary students: The mediating roles of learning motivation and receptivity to feedback. *Learning and Individual Differences*, *88*(102012), 1–8. doi:10.1016/j.lindif.2021.102012

Wong, J., Baars, M., He, M., de Koning, B. B., & Paas, F. (2021). Facilitating goal setting and planning to enhance online self-regulation of learning. *Computers in Human Behavior*, *106913*, 1–15. doi:10.1016/j.chb.2021.106913

Xu, J. (2022). A profile analysis of online assignment motivation: Combining achievement goal and expectancy-value perspectives. *Computers & Education*, *177*(104367), 1–17. doi:10.1016/j.compedu.2021.104367

Xu, J., Lio, A., Dhaliwal, H., Andrei, S., Balakrishnan, S., Nagani, U., & Samadder, S. (2021). Psychological interventions of virtual gamification within academic intrinsic motivation: A systematic review. *Journal of Affective Disorders*, *293*, 444–465. doi:10.1016/j.jad.2021.06.070 PMID:34252688

Yang, C. C., Tsai, I. C., Kim, B., Cho, M. H., & Laffey, J. M. (2006). Exploring the relationships between students' academic motivation and social ability in online learning environments. *The Internet and Higher Education*, *9*(4), 277–286. doi:10.1016/j.iheduc.2006.08.002

Yang, J., Zhang, Y., Pi, Z., & Xie, Y. (2021). Students' achievement motivation moderates the effects of interpolated pre-questions on attention and learning from video lectures. *Learning and Individual Differences*, *91*(102055), 1–9. doi:10.1016/j.lindif.2021.102055

Yekefallah, L., Namdar, P., Panahi, R., & Dehghankar, L. (2021). Factors related to students' satisfaction with holding e-learning during the Covid-19 pandemic based on the dimensions of e-learning. *Heliyon*, *7*(7), 1 - 6.

Yilmaz, R. (2017). Exploring the role of e-learning readiness on student satisfaction and motivation in flipped classroom. *Computers in Human Behavior*, *70*, 251–260. doi:10.1016/j.chb.2016.12.085

Zainuddin, Z. (2018). Students' learning performance and perceived motivation in gamified flipped-class instruction. *Computers & Education*, *126*, 75–88. doi:10.1016/j.compedu.2018.07.003

Zhang, S., & Liu, Q. (2019). Investigating the relationships among teachers' motivational beliefs, motivational regulation, and their learning engagement in online professional learning communities. *Computers & Education*, *134*, 145–155. doi:10.1016/j.compedu.2019.02.013

Zhang, Y., Zhao, G., & Zhou, B. (2021). Does learning longer improve student achievement? Evidence from online education of graduating students in a high school during COVID-19 period. *China Economic Review*, *70*, 101691. doi:10.1016/j.chieco.2021.101691

Zhao, L., Cao, C., Li, Y., & Li, Y. (2021). Determinants of the digital outcome divide in E-learning between rural and urban students: Empirical evidence from the COVID-19 pandemic based on capital theory. *Computers in Human Behavior*, *107177*, 1–15.

Zheng, C., Liang, J. C., Li, M., & Tsai, C. C. (2018). The relationship between English language learners' motivation and online self-regulation: A structural equation modelling approach. *System*, *76*, 144–157. doi:10.1016/j.system.2018.05.003

KEY TERMS AND DEFINITIONS

Future Pull: The draw and attraction of a future that may motivate actions in the present, with the future defined in phases from the present moment (near-, mid-, and far-term futures).

Motivation: Intrinsic or extrinsic inspirations by a person or a group to take particular purposive actions.

Chapter 4

Exploring Students' Perceptions in Hybrid Vocational English Task–Based Language Teaching in Indonesia Higher Education:
A Transitivity Analysis

Hastowohadi Hastowohadi
Akademi Penerbang Indonesia (API), Banyuwangi, Indonesia

Eky Kusuma Hapsari
Universitas Negeri Jakarta (UNJ), Indonesia

ABSTRACT

The transition from online to hybrid instruction has been implemented in recent years in response to vocational institution policy in the higher education context of Indonesia in order to implement student engagement in the wake of the COVID-19 outbreak. To address this issue, the authors sought to develop vocational English materials that incorporated hybrid instruction into a task-based approach that encourages independent student learning. The authors investigated and analyzed the responses of students learning vocational English to support our teaching and learning quality as a result of the implementation of the hybrid system. With an emphasis on vocational English tasks, it is hoped that this study will make a practical contribution to the teaching practice in Indonesian higher education during the transition from online to hybrid instructions.

INTRODUCTION

This chapter presents a blended strategic implementation of task-based language instruction within vocational English content in a hybrid setting. It was centered on providing a conceptual and analytic framework that would be utilized in this study to unearth a wealth of information on how vocational

DOI: 10.4018/978-1-6684-5934-8.ch004

Copyright © 2023, IGI Global. Copying or distributing in print or electronic forms without written permission of IGI Global is prohibited.

English was implemented in the hybrid classroom setting and how the students perceived the task-based as an interconnector among the lecturer (etic and emic perspective), the students, and the teaching and learning materials that encapsulate and support English class. We obtained the respondents' opinions and provided a robust account of their interpretation. The stories of the participants will contribute to the future application in Indonesian higher education of vocations that accommodate various perspectives of language learning context and goals.

BACKGROUND

In the last two years, higher education institutions have focused on online or distance learning due to the COVID-19 pandemic. Policy changes that loosen learning in higher education can be implemented remotely and face-to-face, and have demanded lecturers adapt to the new learning system. The Ministry of Education and Culture (Kemendikbud) confirms that the permit for face-to-face learning activities at universities and polytechnics/community academics in the even semester of the 2020/2021 Academic Year can be carried out in a mixed manner (hybrid learning) (Kemdikbud, 2020, December 2). The higher education context is in progress from the third convergence; the strengths are social, technical, and intellectual. It encourages higher education to the tipping point of a significant transformation (Garrison & Vaughan, 2008). Therefore, hybrid teaching needs to be carried out to facilitate the learning needs of students in the transition mode. The merging of online and face-to-face (FTF) instruction has been increasingly used to overcome the challenges associated with the need for a new pedagogy. Therefore, there is a need for a fundamental redesign based on a hybrid system (Lin, 2014). It is expected that hybrid teaching will maintain the continuity of student independent learning in the transition period from full-online to hybrid mode.

A learning atmosphere that demands student independence needs to be carried out during this pandemic. Therefore, lecturers need to seek an approach that maximizes the potential for autonomous learning. To mediate this, the researchers have implemented vocational task-based language teaching (TBLT) in the aviation English course. In this vocational English task-based language teaching, the lecturer makes efforts to maximize vocational learning activities with tasks, combining synchronous and asynchronous learning and the use of technology 2.0 in class. TBLT is a way of teaching languages and a robust area of inquiry that adheres to the concept of tasks related to curriculum design such as materials, teaching, and testing (Jackson O.D., 2022). Most importantly, TBLT epitomizes the notion of a classroom that should be responsive to students' need for using language in the real world. In this perspective, the authors try to connect learning activities with the real world so that interactions for learning with the target language for communicative purposes can be conveyed.

Hence, the authors synchronize hybrid teaching with vocational TBLT to enrich interaction in a higher vocational setting. It indicates the nuance of vocational purpose to sharpen students' educational background to master aviation English. It showcases the link between the need to learn specific skills in terms of vocational English and mediated-task-based language teaching. Hence, this would change the landscape of English activities and it would foster the students' more active coping with teaching material. Constructivist learning approaches can serve as a bridge between practical vocational knowledge and theoretical knowledge in the context of vocational English classes (Storevik, 2015). In line with this, the real-life learning activities in vocational English have to be linked with constructivism as an approach to portraying a miniature classroom of nature.

LITERATURE REVIEW

Online Education

Online education has become primarily concerned with teaching and learning approaches in rapid and transformational education changes. Communication and information technologies have become more feasible in terms of online education in higher education settings. This dynamic education landscape has attracted immense interest from researcher-educators on online education. In similar vein, Dziuban, Picciano, Graham, and Moskal (2016) portray the massive evolution of online education in four phases using primarily USA context: 1990s (Internet propelled distance education), 2000–2007 (increasing use of Learning Management Systems –LMS), 2008–2012 (growth of Massive Open Online Courses – MOOCs), and beyond with growth of online higher education enrollments outpacing traditional higher education enrollments. Nowadays, universities offer online programs to advance technology making it easy to implement and apply. Online education entails a robust support for implementing hybrid mode for higher education students.

Hybrid Mode

Hybrid courses derive from online and face-to-face classes that synergize the advantage of both. It incorporates available technologies in providing asynchronous and synchronous delivery options to online discussion boards such as Facebook, Whatsapp, etc. Furthermore, the hybrid mode deals with interaction, engagement, strongest satisfaction, perceived usefulness, and continuance intention. In the hybrid mode, the teacher-educator is in charge of using pre-recorded learning materials and self-made materials which are presented by life conferencing like ZOOM or a combination of both (Wang, Liu, & Tian, 2021). The flexibility of these technologies provides more instant interactions and supervision (Klass, 2003). By providing asynchronous learning resources such as pre-recorded, students could be able to initiate making decisions of replay time and place to learn in learning (Keller, 2007). Therefore, the hybrid mode offers tons of learning activities in either synchronous or asynchronous settings. First and foremost, the hybrid mode enables learners a better understanding of knowledge and complex concepts that point to synchronous and asynchronous learning scenarios.

English As a Second Language (ESL)

In a broader sense, English as a second language (ESL) is a set of instructional experiences and related materials organized around a framework that has to deal with an articulated purpose, goals/standards, and outcomes. Furthermore, an ESL would include content as well as second language competencies referring to its goals and standards. Inserting a language program into curriculum content should be in line with the goal. Snow and Brinton (1988) emphasized that when language programs are attached to the specific content course, students are apparently to engage in reading, writing, and study skills. Therefore, students who enroll in aviation English should survive in their second language setting. In comparison, ESL students and non-ESL students meet difficulty in the course because of the high level of communication skills that are needed (Jalili-Grenier & Chase, 1997). Memmer and Worth (1991) suggest that students more actively participate in a conversation ecology where they can practice the language.

METHOD

The research design employs qualitative narrative inquiry that exposes the stories of human participants. It aims to guide us in looking for social phenomena situated in the classroom. It showcases how they get immersed and build up the perception of what they had from the entire starting point of the story to the end. The reality of students and teachers as members of the community of classroom practice in the educational landscape is the definition of the classroom as micro-socio-cultural. In this respect, students were engaged by hybrid vocational English task-based material in which they got in touch with synchronous and asynchronous activities. The researchers wanted to examine the students' perceptions in an aviation English class that used hybrid vocational English task-based instruction in an Indonesian higher education setting. The research question is:

- How do the students perceive hybrid vocational English task-based in higher education settings in Indonesia?

From this, the researchers were eager to analyze the result of this study by using a systemic functional linguistic approach to transitivity analysis. Transitivity is used for studying representative concepts and how it portrays a text. The study hoped to expose the students' experience as long as the hybrid vocational English task-based approach has been implemented to respond to the higher institution policy.

RESEARCH DESIGN

The researchers use a narrative inquiry research design to set up participants' stories as a co-collaborator in defining social phenomena that occur in this story. Analytical practice rooted in social and humanities disciplines in some inquiry investigations takes various forms (Daiute& Lightfoot 2004). "Narrative" in qualitative research may be a fitting term given to any text or discourse, or, it may be the text used in the context of a mode of inquiry (Chase, 2005). The researcher's role is to get immersed with the participants as living data to dig out specific information in a narrative manner. Handoyo Puji Widodo (Personal Communication, July 27, 2020) pointed out that the narrative inquiry design emphasizes life experiences influenced by social and cultural contexts and the time dimension. The researchers positioned an insider perspective to gain vivid data from participants in order to arrange a holistic story.

DATA ANALYSIS

To examine students' perceptions of the implementation of hybrid vocational English task-based language teaching, the data was collected through questionnaires and semi-structured interviews. All of these encounters were digitally recorded via the WhatsApp and Zoom applications. The data was transcribed, sorted out, and labeled as narrative-finding themes. To interpret the data, the researchers used thematic data analysis and transitivity analysis as part of a systemic functional linguistic approach. Referring to Braun & Clarke (2006), the researchers conducted the thematic data analysis by following the steps: (1) classifying and coding the data; (2) sorting out the data collection to get relevant findings; (3) analyzing the findings; and (4) making sense of the findings.

FINDINGS AND DISCUSSION

The voices of six participants were arranged on purpose in a narrative inquiry with four-appealing themes as a result of analyzing thematically. These students recounted their original narratives in response to questions designed by the researchers to elicit a variety of participant voices. In the following paragraphs, each theme is elaborated with an emphasis on the transitivity coding:

Starting the Hybrid Teaching and Learning Process

Starting in the even semester of 2021, the Indonesian higher institution has been implementing hybrid teaching and learning to respond to the current transition from pandemic to endemic. Therefore, the authors planned to rearrange the teaching and learning program for the academic year preparation by infusing task-based language learning into the vocational lesson plan. At the beginning of the lesson, one of us explained to the students the implementation of a hybrid teaching and learning program. The responses of the students as the participants of this study are as follows:

L recounted the first time she met the incidental learning using the hybrid system:

I (Participant) started *(Material) my learning journey this semester with a different mode* of *(Relational) learning called a hybrid system.* My lecturer *(Participant)* instructed *(Verbal/Material) us to follow* both *(Relational) synchronous and asynchronous learning activities as well as face-to-face learning settings in the classroom.*

From this excerpt, the transitivity perspective describes that she ought to relate hybrid systems with her learning trip. She also needed to be concerned with both online and face-to-face classroom activities 'instructed' as verbal material to strengthen this point.

S concluded what he understood from the lecturer's explanation about hybrid learning:

My lecturer *(Participant)* instructed *(Material/Verbal) us to undergo hybrid learning in this even semester* because *(Relational) it was the transition era* from *(Relational) pandemic to endemic; we should do both* online and face-to-face learning mode *(Cir-Place).* I *(Participant)* understood *(Material) it was the reality* that *(Relational) I need to adapt as soon as possible.*

The material verbal indicates that he absorbed the lecturer's instruction which is shown by 'instructed' due to the transition from pandemic to endemic and he needs to scrutinize the hybrid's nature; how to deal with the instructions. It is explained by the relational aspect 'from' and circumstance place 'online and face to face learning mode'.

T remembered a different focus when listening to the lecturer:

I (Participant) knew (Material) from *(Relational) my lecturer, when* I *(Participant) personally* asked *(Material) him why did* we *(Participant)* move *(Mental/verbal) to hybrid learning,* my lecturer *(Participant)* said *(Material) that it was the higher education policy* of *(Material) Indonesia to respond to the current situation of COVID-19 outbreak around the globe.*

This excerpt captured the relational aspect 'from' which links to vocational English material that he considered was a must because of the higher education policy it is shown by the material process 'said' which was caused by the current COVID-19 outbreak.

In addition, P agreed to participate in the hybrid learning. He stated:

I *(Participant)* would be thinking *(Mental/Material)* of *(Relational) my study could be done by obeying hybrid learning mode.* I *(Participant)* perceived *(Mental/Material)* that *(Relational) was the best mode in this present time by conducting both online and offline classroom settings.*

P agreed to follow a hybrid learning mode to continue his study because he was aware of the unpredictable situation of COVID-19. It can be shown from 'would be thinking' as the mental-material process which means that should proceed with his learning in a hybrid mode; he should study both online and offline.

However, J did not straightly accept what was told by the lecturer. He narrated:

I (Participant) felt *(Material) curious about why hybrid learning would occur, and my lecturer answered that it was caused by the consideration of moving from a pandemic to an endemic situation. To respond to that,* hybrid learning *(Actor)* is considered *(Mental/Material) to be the appropriate solution for the current time. It was a must that* I *(Participant)* should spend *(Material) my study both online and offline.*

On the contrary, J never expected to meet with hybrid learning because he wanted to have face-to-face classroom interaction instead of blending between online and offline settings. It can be interpreted by the material word 'felt' that J needs to consider the solution because of the current condition; it is explained by the material process 'should spend' which means he needed to adopt this new learning change.

Finally, K was aware of the current teaching and learning situation. He said:

I *(Participant)* thought *(Mental/material) that* I *(Participant)* would meet *(Material) fully* face-to-face learning encounter,*(Cir-place) but the learning becomes hybrid.* I (Participant) knew *(Material)* I *(Participant)* should obey *(Mental/Material) my higher institution policy to respond to uncertain COVID-19 impact.*

The mental-material process 'thought' shows that K ought to run hybrid learning which is connected by the other mental-material 'should obey' that indicates higher education policy in responding COVID-19 outbreak.

Adopting Vocational English Task-based Learning

The following narrative of participant voices is about the implementation of task-based learning in professional English. The primary objective of this campaign is to create a new pedagogical environment in which students can gain authentic experience with a meaning-making strategy, a case study, and solutions supported by the authentic text. It is in line with the nature of task-based, Ellis (2009) provides that students should certainly rely on their completion of the activity by using their resources. The enchanted expression occurred beneath the voice transcription of the participants.

'L' narrated her understanding of the new method in learning aviation English:

Exploring Students' Perceptions in Hybrid Vocational English Task-Based Language Teaching

I (Participant) <u>suppose</u> (Material) vocational English task-based is concerned <u>with</u> (Relational) building specific areas of English, especially in our department that focuses on aviation English. <u>I</u> (Participant) <u>should create</u> (Material/Verbal) our own learning activities <u>which</u> (Relational) are <u>meaningful</u> (Cir)to the purpose of our subject.

For her, vocational English task-based is indeed to build up constructive understanding which is shown by the circumstance aspect 'meaningful'. Hence, it should hone her subject aviation English mastery that is supported by the relational aspect 'with'.

S seems to agree with the idea of using authentic materials. He expressed his opinion:

Yeah, <u>the idea with vocational English</u> (Actor) <u>is</u> (Material) <u>good</u>. (Cir) <u>I</u> (Participant) <u>could absorb</u> (Material)in this aviation terminology and <u>I</u>(Participant) <u>need to experience</u>(Mental/Material) <u>authentic text</u>. (Cir) <u>I</u> (Participant) <u>should grapple</u> (Mental/Material) with <u>these kinds of learning activities</u>. (Cir)

The tasks of vocational English help him to sharpen aviation terminology by building up the use of authentic material that can be shown by the circumstance parameter 'good'. Then, he used the material process 'absorb' which indicates he was eager to master his subject and stressed out by circumstance phrase 'authentic material' to explain the use of learning sources.

T commented on the new learning method that seems to suit his ideas of learning vocational English:

<u>Vocational English for me</u> *(Actor)* <u>was quite enjoyable</u> *(Material)* <u>because</u> *(Relational)* <u>it</u> *(Participant)* <u>directed</u> *(Material)* *me to explore* <u>the major terms used in the flight operation officer department</u>. *(Cir)* <u>The subject (Actor)</u> <u>is</u> *(Material)* *aviation English, and* <u>my lecturer</u> *(Participant)* <u>invited</u> *(Mental/Material) us to dive* <u>into</u> *(Relational)* <u>meaning-making strategy, deal with authentic text, and focus on solving problems</u> *(Cir)* <u>by</u> *(Relational) doing certain learning activities.*

The task-based on vocational English assisted him to explore and sharpen his knowledge about flight operation, especially in aviation English; it can be seen from the material process 'was quite enjoyable' and related it to the circumstance parameter 'the major terms used in flight operation officer department'.

P had a similar opinion on the new method that could help him to become a better learner of aviation English:

I (Participant) <u>struggled out (Mental/Material)</u> *to study* <u>aviation English</u>.*(Cir) I (Participant)* <u>planned</u> *(Material)to get to know* <u>about</u> *(Relational)* <u>aviation English terms and their usage in a practical way</u>. *(Cir)*

He knew that through learning via the tasks which were given by his lecturer, he wanted to initially improve his aviation English knowledge. It can be seen from the mental-material process 'struggled out 'and it is explained by the circumstance parameter 'aviation English'.

J expressed his idea about the requirement of learning aviation English:

<u>The term vocational English</u> *(Actor)* <u>was</u> *(Material) something new. <u>I</u> (Participant) <u>met</u> (Material) this term when* <u>my lecturer</u> *(Participant)* <u>explained</u> *(Material) to me* <u>that</u> *(Relational)* <u>we</u> *(Participant)* <u>would like to immerse</u> *(Material)* <u>in aviation English learning activities</u>;*(Cir)* <u>we</u> *(Participant)* <u>need to pursue</u> *(Material)* <u>our identity as flight operation officer students</u> *(Cir)* <u>that</u> *(Relational)* <u>are connected</u> *(Mate-*

rial) with *(Relational)* authentic materials and meaning-making strategies *(Cir) upon overall learning interaction in even semester.*

J felt that the tasks helped him in mastering aviation English. The material process 'met' portrays how he felt motivated, however, the other material process 'would like to immerse' explains that he was engaged to learn aviation English which is best explained by the circumstance parameter 'in aviation English learning activities.

Meanwhile, K made assumptions about the difference between the previous and the recent semester lessons.

I *(Participant)* met *(Material)* a new subject in this even semester, *(Cir) in contradictory, previous se-mester I was dealing with general English.* It *(Participant)* was *(Material) totally different subject* that *(Relational)* I *(Participant)* need to develop *(Mental/Material) my knowledge* in constructing my identity as a flight operation officer student. *(Cir)* I *(Participant)* would meet *(Material)* with both *(Relational) theoretical and practical use of vocational terminology* in terms of aviation English. *(Cir)*

On another side, K assumed that his current learning was completely different; previously, he dealt with general English. The tasks made him aware of his identity and that he should pursue his goal to work in the field of the aviation industry so ought to improve aviation English mastery through theoretical and practical use of vocational English as it is best explained by the mental-material process 'need to develop'.

Activating Autonomous Learning

In this theme, we were concerned with digging out the stunning finish of the students in activating their autonomous learning in terms of hybrid learning encounters. The six participants vividly depicted the scaffolding processes, which are explicitly explained through some sequential stages; the lecturer described and elaborated the tasks into three main steps; they are the pre, main, and post activities that guide the students in completing the learning activities independently or in groups.

L recalled the lecturer's teaching steps as follows:

My lecturer *(Participant)* emphasized *(Mental/Material) on letting us know how to run our learning activities* through *(Relational)* some details instructions. *(Cir)* He (Participant) put *(Material) the learn-ing instructions* as *(Relational) magnetic center for us to catch the way to finish the study.* In one of his teaching, *(Cir)* my lecturer *(Participant)* let *us watch spontaneous speaking steps until the recording session and he would like to push us to complete the activity.*

She perceived learning tasks as lightened guidance to complete her independent learning through spontaneous activities. It can be seen from the mental-material process 'emphasized' which means struggling out and eager to do spontaneous speaking that can be done both ways, online and offline; she could perform in front of the class and or by recording. It is best described by the circumstance parameter 'some detailed instructions.'

S reflected on his experience with the new methods of learning English:

Exploring Students' Perceptions in Hybrid Vocational English Task-Based Language Teaching

Learning to scaffold *(Actor)* was *(Material)* something important (Cir) *for me* because *(Relational) this semester,* I *(Participant)* studied *(Material) English both* online and offline. *(Cir)For instance,* my lecturer *(Participant)* instructed *(Material) me to get immersed* with *(Relational)* photovoice;*(Cir) he showed us how to use the photo and sound it. Firstly,* he *(Participant)* told *(Material) us the photovoice terms and its requirements, then* he *(Participant)* instructed *(Material) us to take the picture by ourselves then posted* to *(Relational)* the Facebook *(Cir-place)* by *(Relational) doing recording or presenting* in front of the class, *(Cir-place) after that,* he *(Participant)* took *(Material)* some *(Relational)* steps to complete the spontaneous speaking. *(Cir) He just gave me prompting questions, such as "what is the picture talking about, how did you capture the picture, how did you work with the tool," etc.*

S considered that clear learning instructions made him aware of taking the route to sharpen his photovoice speaking ability through the vocational learning material. The circumstance aspect showcases his awareness of 'something important' and he relates to photovoice which is one learning activity to sharpen his understanding of aviation English.

T enjoyed one of the new learning strategies applied in the classroom:

I *(Participant)* found *(Material) the literature circle* was *(Material) a milestone to step up vocational English material and it was quite challenging to gain.* My lecturer *(Participant)* explained *(Material) to me* what *(Relational) were the learning skills and tools that need to be achieved. For instance,* I *(Participant)* acted *(Mental/Material)* as *(Relational) a story reader and summarizer;* my lecturer *(Participant)* described *(Mental/Material) me as quite literate with certain stories* related to *(Relational) my flight operation officer department.*

He regarded that learning vocational English via literature circle was his main consideration; he would not be able to literate with vocational English material if he did not understand the roadmap of literature circle activities such as being a summarizer and story reader. The scaffolding process should be clear to follow to enact autonomous learning. It is explained as mental-material 'described' and relates to the flight operation officer department.

'P' replied to our question regarding the implementation of vocational English in hybrid circumstances. He portrayed his experience with his new learning of paraphrasing:

In one of the vocational learning activities,*(Cir)* I *(Participant)* was interested in *(Mental/Material) understanding* how to *(Relational) paraphrase vocational English text.* I *(Participant)* was asked *(Material)* to *(Relational) copy the original text then move to Google translate and* change *(Material)* the structure in the Indonesian language, *(Cir) then moved to English as a target language.* These steps *(Actor)* were required *(Material) to complete paraphrasing. Lastly,* we *(Participants)* were instructed *(Mental/Material) to do the same thing* with *(Relational) different texts.*

He perceived learning tasks as lightened guidance to complete his independent learning through spontaneous activities. It can be seen from the mental-material process 'emphasized' which means struggling out and eager to do spontaneous speaking that can be done both ways, online and offline; he could perform in front of the class and or by recording. It is best described by the circumstance parameter 'some detailed instructions.

Another new way of learning was expressed by J who seemed to enjoy it:

I *(Participant)* noticed *(Material)* that *(Relational) learning something has to be easy, and my lecturer taught me how to deal with it.* He *(Participant)* gave *(Material) me a tricky lesson* with *(Relational) spidergram. Finally,* I *(Participant)* implemented *the (Mental/Material) method to scaffold my vocational English material.* I *(Participant)* learned *(Mental/Material) 'Higher Order Thinking Skills'* through *(Relational) spidergram.*

He was convinced that being able to scaffold made him understand the instructions on vocational English material. The material process 'noticed' describes his eagerness to learn independently via Higher Order Thinking Skills and relates to spidergram.

The concluding remark of this section was made by 'K,' who simply stated that knowing how to complete vocational English learning material in an asynchronous manner was the impetus for constructing the activity. He was aware that student-centered learning must play a crucial role in fostering independence in the classroom. He posted his idea regarding visual analysis that can be applied to oral communication. He recalled:

I *(Participant)* was *(Material) thankful that my lecturer gave me an insightful notice on* how *(Relational)* to describe *(Mental/Material)* weather forecast *(Cir)* by *(Relational) doing a speaking activity through visual analysis.* My lecturer *(Participant)* asked *(Material) me* to *(Relational) do gestures, gaze, and focus on the presenter in the image* that *(Relational) was describing the weather forecast.*

Reflecting the Vocational Task-based Learning

The final theme seals the lineup of previous stories that were told by the six participants. Reflective practice is an unavoidable part of a robust learning quality that encapsulates the overall part of learning experiences. The participants were eager in narrating their original stories that close up vocational learning experiences with some strong-symbolic arguments, as follows:

The female student, L, admitted the benefit of having a new way of learning:

This *(Actor)* was *(Material)* the best part of the learning quality *(Cir)* that *(Relational)* I *(Participant)* should chase *(Mental/Material)* in my aviation English. *(Cir)* I *(Participant)* pondered *(Mental/Material) both* face-to-face and online classes, *(Cir) yet,* I *(Participant)* need to follow up *(Mental/Material)* on *(Relational) what* I *(Participant)* need to improve. *(Material)* Since the beginning of my aviation English, *(Cir-loc-time)* I *(Participant)* found *(Material) the tasks* were *(Material)* quite complex; *(Cir)* I *(Participant)* need to *(Material) always ask my lecturer* about *(Relational)* reading annotation *(Cir)* because *(Relational)* the task *(Participant)* instructed *(Mental/Material) us* to *(Relational) read and reread the target text and I was in charge to check it seriously.*

The transitivity perspective analyzes the hybrid vocational English task-based scaffold should be easier to catch up. Besides, she should ask when she meets difficulty understanding the instruction. It can be seen from the material process phrase 'quite complex' that indicates her problem in understanding the task. However, she can always ask for help from her lecturer about it.

Exploring Students' Perceptions in Hybrid Vocational English Task-Based Language Teaching

S was surprised when he was required to write a reflective essay at the end of the lesson. He elaborated on that.

I *(Participant)* thought *(Mental/Material)* after *(Relational)* the end of the class,*(Cir-time) would not any other activity, surprisingly,* my lecturer *(Participant)* instructed *(Mental/Material) me to sharpen my learning goal* with *(Relational)* reflective practices.*(Cir)* It *(Actor)* was *(Material)* helpful *(Cir)* for *(Relational) me to improve my weaknesses on that learning goal.* One of my weaknesses *(Actor)* was concerning *(Mental/Material)* on *(Relational) aviation terminology,* my lecturer *(Participant)* suggested *(Mental/Material) to improve my vocabulary acquisition* by *(Relational)* blending reading intensively with paraphrasing.*(Cir)* I *(Participant)* noticed *(Mental/Material)* with *(Relational)* air navigation material *(Cir)that I need to enhance it.*

The last part of this vocational English course was concerned with improving his learning quality in aviation English class. 'T' was aware of this part because he needed to achieve his learning goal as well as the learner's identity as a flight operation cadet. Therefore, his lecturer pushed him to reflect after the end of the class via book-note.

I *(Participant)* dreamed *(Mental/Material) of working* as *(Relational)* a flight operation officer, *(Cir) and this was my real dream a long time ago.* Reflection *(Actor)* is *(Material)* a pedagogical aspect *(Cir)* that *(Relational)* I *(Participant)* need to shape *(Mental/Material)* as *(Relational) my cadet identity.* In the future,*(Cir-time)* reflecting on vocational English learning *(Actor)* will benefit *(Mental/Material) me to communicate easier* in *(Relational)* flight operation job encounters.*(Cir)* He *(Participant)* pointed out *(Verbal/Material)* that *(Relational) building reading literacy* was *(Material)* a key point *(Material) to improving his understanding* of *(Relational)* vocational English text. *(Cir) So,* this focus *(Actor) literally* was *(Material)* his *(Relational)* concern. *(Cir)*

'P' concluded that reflection was something vital for him to improve his learning quality:

I *(Participant)* must admit *(Mental/Material)* that *(Relational)* I *(Participant)* did not know *(Mental/ Material)* what reflection was.*(Cir) But,* my lecturer *(Participant)* gave *(Material) me an analogy* that *(Relational) when I went to a party, I should see myself in the mirror to see my physical appearance. It made sense to me, and finally, I found reflection was a good intention to enhance the quality of my vocational English in terms of task-based language learning.*

In another story that was set up by 'J' in his narration about the reflective practice on the task-based activity, he commented:

I *(Participant) immensely* love *(Mental/Material) my department and identity* as *(Relational)* a flight operation cadet. *(Cir) Indeed,* I *(Participant)* would like to hone *(Verbal/Material) my understanding of my aviation English* through *(Relational) certain activities such as the literature circle that was taught* by *(Relational) my lecturer in this class. This is what* I *(Participant)* reflected *(Mental/Material)* during *(Relational) that* semester. *(Cir)*

'K' truly loved to improve his English through task-based activity. He reflected that:

I *(Participant)* was *(Material)* admittedly sure that through *(Relational)* task-based *(Cir)* I *(Participant)* could improve *(Mental/Material)* my learning quality better, and rehearsal *(Actor)* was *(Material)* a peak point to leveling up my *(Relational)* English skills.*(Cir)* Speaking *(Actor)* was *(Material)* my *(Relational)* concern.*(Cir)*

SOLUTION AND RECOMMENDATIONS

As was pointed out in the introduction to this paper, the research recommends that the students encourage authentic material resources and link to learning-independency; they equip their learning with a reading scaffolding process to vocational English. However, reflection is a gatekeeper in opening critical thinking development. It is hoped to encourage the parallel session of task-based approach toward autonomous learning in using 2.0 learning devices as well as face-to-face learning directions. In line with the hybrid nature, it keeps the students dealing with tons of real and virtual activities that are attached to the blending between online and offline learning atmosphere. Therefore, the tasks should involve the hybrid learning paradigm. As it is stated by one of the participants, 'vocational English task-based is concerned with building specific areas of English, especially in our department that focuses on aviation English'. Hence, the tasks should accommodate vocational English material as well as learning modes for the students (face-to-face and online settings). Another participant said, 'It was a must that I should spend my time studying both online and offline.' It can be interpreted from the two participants' voices that the vocational English tasks should be linked with hybrid nature; It should emphasize the autonomous choice of students' learning to create meaningful activities and the systematic mastery of basic knowledge. As it was pointed out by the participants' voices 'I found the literature learning circle was a milestone to step up vocational English material'. From the transitivity analysis result, it can be said that the literature circle method should connect to hybrid vocational English material to maintain the nature of the learning paradigm in the post-pandemic era. Technically, the students should be equipped with a strong wifi-connection in order to support zoom-online learning as well as an asynchronous support system. If the wifi-connection is still poor, the institution should create an LMS system or other learning media in asynchronous mode to activate independent learning by showing clear guidance in completing vocational English tasks such as the use of photovoice that can be done by presenting in front of the class or by doing self-vlog and upload it to Facebook. A participant said that 'to take the picture by ourselves then post it to Facebook' by doing self-record or presenting in front of the class which means that he perceived that Facebook can mediate him to do asynchronous mode. To do so, the photovoice entails some prompting questions to elaborate and explain the photo(s) coherently. Clearly, an approach that prioritizes 'process over product' is a feature of TBLT that draws most of the experiential learning.

In Fact, tailoring task-based with vocational English is an important matter to fit with a hybrid setting. Additionally, the students will be best provided with authentic material in terms of constructive learning methods; the lecturer should engage the students with life experience in aviation English materials engaged by critical thinking teaching instructions. In addition, Hybrid is also in line with a cooperative and communicative approach that enables the students to interact between student-students and teacher-students relationship (Wu, Zheng, and Zhai, 2021) Certainly, vocational English has to deal with a fully furnished hybrid that emphasizes on meaning-making (Harper and Widodo, 2018) as well as interactional

Exploring Students' Perceptions in Hybrid Vocational English Task-Based Language Teaching

processes that occurred in language use (Ellis 2009, p. 227). These bundles of recommendations are purely the core of engaging vocational English classes in a hybrid setting; it will certainly be needed higher institution support as well as the lecturer's teaching creativity with the authentic material in a task-based language teaching approach.

These findings suggest that hybrid teaching in vocational English task-based should focus on, first of all, choosing materials. The materials should meet with the identity of students in flight operation officer jobs that relate to the professional certifications as their ultimate profession. Then, the learning activities should engage the students' active participation in both physical and emotional aspects. It means that the lecturer should enclose the replication of online learning into the real world as it is called virtual activity. It is supported by one of participants 'J' that he considered getting into face-to-face learning and it could be represented as virtual reality. Secondly, infusing certain learning strategies such as a literature circle activity encourages the students to practice and develop the skills and strategies of good readers. It aims to help the students get immersed in reading literacy throughout the study in a hybrid setting. In addition, it would assist them in understanding the text and context in aviation English in terms of the meaning-making approach which is of task-based nature. In short, the emotional facet of the students in hybrid mode has to have occurred in learning materials as well as the approach of meaning-making as it is considered to be a task-based language teaching context. These will contribute to the global context in determining and infusing hybrid vocational English task-based language teaching mode.

FUTURE RESEARCH DIRECTION

Finally, areas for further research could concern building up support between vocational English lecturers with the institution in managing an application that accommodates the task-based language teaching approach; LMS or learning media are plausible options. It should be done in order to overcome problems in online learning such as poor internet connectivity. Moreover, the zoom application is possible to be done in a certain time; it should be employed to run synchronous mode. In a further sense, the teaching methods should be variative, a clear and vivid-teaching scaffold, as well as robust vocational English material that brings the students to get immersed with bundles of communicative, cooperative, and constructive learning activities. The area of exploring and developing other teaching approaches; including the teaching instructions and activities in the Post COVID-19 era will be the focus of future research direction. The task-based data-driven will be a reference in exploring future students' voices to be interpreted to fit with hybrid learning settings and vocational English tasks.

CONCLUSION

The study presented narrative inquiry to the participants who were involved in arranging robust data on how hybrid vocational English task-based has been implemented. In this chapter, the findings show that hybrid vocational English task-based language teaching has been contributing to the teaching transition from online to offline in an unprecedented moment of the COVID-19 outbreak. Indeed, as a vocational English lecturer that had arranged the teaching activities, it would significantly have directed the students to explore vocational learning goals. During the course, the participants have been adjusted to follow vocational task-based learning instruction from the lecturer which focuses on both online and offline classroom atmospheres. These blending teaching and learning settings were linked to the need of the current possible situation to integrate with the pedagogical aspect of vocational English task-based language teaching. However, the teaching activities should be variative and the instructions should intercede with the student's needs in their ongoing study to build up a comprehensive, communicative, and constructive manner (Stevick, 1996; Wu, Zheng, and Zhai, 2021).

The study suggested being aware of vocational English content which includes the task-based approach. Importantly, the choices regarding lesson content become more meaningful. Combining real and virtual, paying attention to learners' active construction and communication are the focus in preparing vocational English material connecting to English as a second language paradigm. To meet these expectations, the constructivist approach is needed to implement hybrid teaching, for instance, teaching English with authentic material. Moreover, the communicative approach needs to be inserted in teaching vocational English. For example, the students may use the literature circle by creating infographic flyers and presenting them to their classmates during Q and A sessions. This would attract them in the communicative and constructive aspect. As stated by 'J' and 'S' in their narration, they wanted to blend real learning activities and communicative and constructive ways of completing their lesson in aviation English.

The contribution to this study is to empower collaboration with aviation instructors and English lecturers to set up and create vocational English material as well as conceptualize the teaching tasks for online and offline activities that provide clear learning evaluation to students as co-collaborator for improving vocational English task-based language teaching in the future plan. It is recommended that the lecturer and higher education institutions should promote collaborative teaching material and tasks that use technology 2.0 for hybrid teaching. Secondly, enriching meaning-making learning strategy by using authentic material in vocational English terms is a strategy to make students feel motivated, and aware of their identity as the student of flight operation officers. It is potentially hoped to enhance their motivation as well as their English application in their future job. Teaching vocational English via a task-based should maintain teaching technique variations in order to make the students actively participate in the study, such as implementing a literature circle activity that promotes individual and team performance and it can be applied on synchronous and asynchronous as well as face-to-face classroom interaction effectively. These practical contributions are hopefully implemented and applied in the future studies of hybrid vocational English task-based language teaching in Indonesia.

REFERENCES

Braun, V., & Clarke, V. (2006). Using thematic analysis in psychology. *Qualitative Research in Psychology*, *3*(2), 77–101. doi:10.1191/1478088706qp063oa

Chase, S. E. (2005). Narrative inquiry: Multiple lenses, approaches, voices. In N. K. Denzin & Y. S. Lincoln (Eds.), *The SAGE Handbook of Qualitative Research* (pp. 651–679). SAGE.

Daiute, C., & Lightfoot, C. (Eds.). (2004). *Narrative analysis: Studying the development of individuals in society*. SAGE. doi:10.4135/9781412985246

Dziuban, C., Picciano, A. G., Graham, C. R., & Moskal, P. D. (2016). *Conducting research in online and blended learning environments: New pedagogical frontiers.* Routledge, Taylor & Francis Group.

Ellis, R. (2009). Task-based Language Teaching: Sorting out the Misunderstandings. *International Journal of Applied Linguistics, 19*(3), 221–246. doi:10.1111/j.1473-4192.2009.00231.x

Garrison, D. R., & Vaughan, N. D. (2008). *Blended learning in higher education: Framework, principles, and guidelines.* Jossey-Bass/Wiley.

Harper, J., & Widodo, H. P. (2018). Perceptual mismatches in the interpretation of task-based ELT materials: A micro-evaluation of a task-based English lesson. *Innovation in Language Learning and Teaching.* Advance online publication. doi:10.1080/17501229.2018.1502773

Jackson, D. O. (2022). *Task-Based Language Teaching.* Cambridge University Press. doi:10.1017/9781009067973

Jalili-Grenier, F., & Chase, M. (1997). Retention of nursing students with English as a second language. *Journal of Advanced Nursing, 25*(1), 199–203. doi:10.1046/j.1365-2648.1997.1997025199.x PMID:9004030

Keller, C. (2007). *Virtual learning environments in higher education: A study of user acceptance.* Institutionen för ekonomisk och industriell utveckling.

Klass, B. (2003, May 30). *Streaming media in higher education: Possibilities and pitfalls.* Campus Technology. https://campustechnology.com/articles/2003/05/streaming-media-in-higher-education-possibilities-and-pitfalls.aspx

Lin, O. (2014). Student views of hybrid learning. *Journal of Computing in Teacher Education, 25*(2), 57-66. .10784610 doi:10.1080/10402454.2008

Memmer, M. K., & Worth, C. C. (1991). Retention of English-as-a-second-language (ESL) students: Approaches used by 21 generic baccalaureate nursing programs. *The Journal of Nursing Education, 30*(9), 389–396. doi:10.3928/0148-4834-19911101-04 PMID:1663540

Republik Indonesia. (2020, December 3). Kementerian Pendidikan dan Kebudayaan » Republik Indonesia. Retrieved September 30, 2022, from https://www.kemdikbud.go.id/main/blog/2020/12/perkuliahan-dapat-dilakukan-secara-tatap-muka-dan-dalam-jaringan-tahun-2021

Snow, M. A., & Brinton, D. M. (1988). Content-based language instruction: Investigating the effectiveness of the adjunct model. *TESOL Quarterly, 22*(4), 553–574. doi:10.2307/3587256

Stevick, E. (1996). *Memory, meaning and method.* Newbury House.

Storevik, M. (2015). *A study of vocationalisation of English in Norwegian upper secondary schools. "Why do I need Norwegian and English? I'm training to become a carpenter"* [Master thesis]. Retrieved from https://bora.uib.no/bora-xmlui/handle/1956/10611

Wang, X., Liu, T., Wang, J., & Tian, J. (2021). Understanding Learner Continuance Intention: A Comparison of Live Video Learning, Pre-Recorded Video Learning and Hybrid Video Learning in COVID-19 Pandemic. *International Journal of Human-Computer Interaction*. Advance online publication. doi:10.1080/10447318.2021.1938389

Wu, G., Zheng, J., & Zhai, J. (2021). Individualized learning evaluation model based on hybrid teaching. *International Journal of Electrical Engineering Education*, 1–15. doi:10.1177/0020720920983999

Section 2
Global Economic Struggles in the Pandemic

Chapter 5

Affordability and State Support for Higher Education

Ramona Sue McNeal
University of Northern Iowa, USA

Lisa Dotterweich Bryan
Western Iowa Tech Community College, USA

Mary Schmeida
Kent State University, USA

ABSTRACT

The COVID-19 pandemic has helped to accelerate an already declining rate in college enrollment in the U.S. tuition, and college fees have continued to outpace inflation, pricing some students out of higher education. State appropriations can help offset the cost of college, but state support varies significantly. While some states have been creative in promoting college affordability by adoption programs including bans on scholarship displacement and promise programs, others have reduced funding. Why has the state-level response differed so significantly? In exploring this question, this chapter examines the influence of state-level factors on state appropriations for higher education for the years 2010 through 2020. Pooled cross-sectional time series data that controls for variation between states and over time is used.

INTRODUCTION

The COVID-19 pandemic challenged government agencies at all levels to find creative ways to deliver public service. Following a declaration of a pandemic by the World Health Organization (WHO) in March 2020, schools moved online. During the 2020-2021 academic year, higher education in the U.S. used a combination of in-person, online, and hybrid methods to provide instruction. In the following academic year, schools returned to in-person delivery (College Board, 2021). Returning to in-person classes has not meant that colleges resumed where they left off in March 2020. Higher education re-

DOI: 10.4018/978-1-6684-5934-8.ch005

Copyright © 2023, IGI Global. Copying or distributing in print or electronic forms without written permission of IGI Global is prohibited.

Affordability and State Support for Higher Education

turned to a series of challenges; among the issues they face in 2022-2023 school year are affordability, campus safety, and free speech.

State legislatures submitted numerous bills during the 2022 legislative session that impact how colleges and universities will be able to operate in the 2022-2023 school year. Campus safety has become a priority in many state legislatures. Ten states legislatures reviewed bills on sexual assault on campus while six considered making hazing a criminal offense. In addition, in at least eight states, legislatures debated proposals that would expand concealed carry provisions on college campuses. Free speech was also a hot button issue. While over fourteen states had proposed bills on the general topic of free speech, several considered legislations on the teaching of topics considered contentious such as critical race theory (Smalley, 2022).

Affordability has been and remains a top education issue even with state budgets bouncing back from the pandemic. Although there had been a positive trend in state funding for higher education prior to the COVID-19 outbreak, it has not been sufficient to counter other developments. States and local governments had increased funding for higher education for eight consecutive years through the 2019-2020 academic year after four years of decreasing monies (College Board, 2021, p.3). As important as state and local appropriations are, tuition and fees remain the largest source of funding for four-year institutions. Student enrollments are critical to the financial well-being of higher education. Unfortunately, public four-year institutions saw a drop of 66,640 students (1%) and public 2-year institutions saw a drop of 323,420 students (8%) between fall 2019 and fall 2020 (College Board, 2021, p.3). After years of continued growth in the number of international students, there was a 10% drop in the number of international students between fall 2019 and fall 2020 (College Board, 2021, p.7). Additionally, inflation continues to be a concern. Although U.S. Secretary of Treasury Janet Yellen made optimistic prediction regarding the risk of inflation in 2021, it is currently running at a near four-decade high. Secretary Yellen attributed the unexpected spike in inflation to the length of the pandemic and the war in Europe (Liptak, 2022). During the 2020-2021 academic year, colleges worked to contain the cost of tuition and fees. Many either froze both or had minimal increases. With the combination of falling student enrollments and continued inflation there is a pressure on institutions to increase tuition and fees (Smalley, 2022).

Fees and tuition are only part of the story; income inequality has also affected college affordability. Between the years 1990 and 2020, American families in the upper quartile income brackets saw an average income increase of 57% while the lower quartile only experienced a 12% increase in average income (College Board, 2021, p.3). At the same time, the cost of higher education has been rising at a rate faster than inflation. The published tuition and fees at a public four-year school is 2.58 times higher for the 2021-2022 academic year relative to the 1991-1992 academic year after adjusting for the Consumer Price Index or CPI (College Board, 2021, p.12). In 1984, the cost of attending a four-year public college was roughly equal to 16.4% of the medium family income; by 2011, the cost had risen to 33.5 percent (Delaney, 2014, p.57). It is becoming more difficult for students from lower income brackets to afford higher education. In addition, costs beyond tuition and fees (including housing, transportation, childcare, and food) are making it less likely that these students will finish their degrees (Castleman & Meyer, 2019). Whether or not a student graduates, they will most likely be faced with substantial student loans to repay after leaving school. A 2020 *Forbs* report found that the country's student loan debt was at $1.56 trillion; the only national consumer debt larger than student loans was mortgage debt (Friedman, 2020).

Income inequalities among college students has manifested itself in different ways; for example, food insecurity is now an issue that colleges are trying to address. Food insecurity among college students has grown to the point that it has caught the attention of state legislatures. For example, during the 2022

103

legislative session, two states (New Jersey and California) considered proposals to expand Supplemental Nutrition Assistance Program (SNAP) to include benefits for college students. In addition, in six other states bills were introduced to help reduce hunger on campuses through other strategies (Smalley, 2022). For example, the state of Louisiana enacted House bill 888 on June 18, 2022, requiring the Board of Regency to institute a process for colleges to be designated as a Hunger Free Campus and to establish a Hunger Free Grant Program (National Conference of State Legislatures [NCSL], 2022). As with the issue of food insecurity, homelessness and the lack of affordability housing is now a serious problem confronting college students. Research finds that approximately 45% of college students experience some form of housing insecurity with 10% that are either homeless or at the risk of becoming homeless (Broton, 2020, p.25). Finally, there have been demographic changes to the student population that are complicating the issue of college affordability. Today, more college students are from low-income families; are older or have at least one child. These demographic factors increase the demand for financial assistance and add additional costs such as childcare to the price of attending college (Castleman & Meyer, 2019).

Although the federal government provides some financial assistance to higher education, state-level subsidies to public universities remains a dominate factor in off-setting the cost of fees and tuition to students. There are economic arguments for states to provide support to higher education. According to Human Capital Theory, government investment in education can contribute to economic growth as well as help reduce inequalities based on income and race (Denison, 1962; Becker, 1964). While there is economic justification for contributing to higher education, state legislators must weigh the value of subsidizing higher education against funding other state programs. The response at the state-level on how much government contributes to higher education varied significantly. While differences in wealth among the various states should play an important role in policy adoption in this issue area, they cannot alone account for differences in state-level funding. The goal of this research is to determine why the states have judged the value of funding higher education so differently. Following the agenda setting and policy adoption literature, this chapter will examine the impact of political influences, state resources, and the demands or needs within the states on funding (Mooney & Lee, 1995; 2000; Hwang & Grey, 1991). In exploring this topic, state-level educational appropriations for higher education will be examined from 2010 through 2020. Pooled cross-sectional time series data that controls for variation between states and over time will be used.

BACKGROUND

The COVID-19 pandemic worsened the already existing inequalities in education based on income and race through the "digital divide" or gaps in Internet usage, skills, and access. Although the U.S. has made significant strides in closing these gaps, communities still exist without access to the Internet that is inexpensive, dependable or with high-speed connections (Goldberg, 2022). According to the Pew Research Center, some K-12 students faced a digital "homework gap" once classes moved online. Among their findings was that approximately 12% of students had to use public Wi-Fi to do their homework because they lacked Internet access at home. The "homework gap" was more pronounced among Black and low-income teens. Approximately one-in-five Black teens reported having to use public Wi-Fi to do their homework while one-in-four teens living in households with an annual income under $30,000 did not have Internet access at home (Auxier & Anderson, 2020). The inequalities continued when schools reopened in the fall of 2020. Parents in higher income families were better able to protect their children

Affordability and State Support for Higher Education

from COVID-19 by sending them to small private schools or forming "learning pods" (also known as "pandemic pods" or microschools"). These terms describe an informal group of parents; often they were formed to hire a full-time tutor to teach their children (Samuels & Prothero, 2020). The pandemic also increased the impact of income inequalities among college students. For example, colleges in Montana could not simply address COVID-19 by moving their classes online. Montana is a rural state where only 63.3% of the citizens have broadband access, 12.7% of the residents do not have home computers and 21% do not have Internet access at home (Frank et al, 2021, p.186). Many college students in Montana faced a digital "homework gap" like their K-12 counterparts. College libraries such at the Montana State University library worked creatively to overcome the digital "homework gap" through strategies including lending laptops, iPads, and wireless hotspots (Frank et al, 2021).

The digital "homework gap" is only one example of the negative effects COVID-19 had on higher education. In addition, the decline in community college enrollment that began in 2010 (American Association of Community Colleges, 2019) continued and was exacerbated by the pandemic. While four-year colleges were experiencing increases in enrollment among traditional aged students since 2010 (National Center for Education Statistics, 2022), they also saw a drop in student enrollment during the pandemic. According to the Bureau of Labor Statistics, before 2020, higher education officials could rely on 65% of each year's graduating high school seniors to enroll in a postsecondary institution. In 2020, that percentage dropped to 62.7% of graduating seniors, and, in 2021, to 61.8% of graduating seniors (Bauman, 2022). National Student Clearinghouse Research Center (NSCRC) data confirms this drop in enrollment. Recent data from the NSCRC shows that there has been a fifth consecutive semester of enrollment declines across higher educational institutions in the United States. Since spring 2020, undergraduate enrollment has decreased by nearly 1.4 million students. Data shows that community colleges faced the steepest decline, a 7.8% drop since spring 2021. Public four-year colleges experienced a 3.4% drop since the previous spring. Private nonprofit four-year colleges experienced 1.7% decline in enrollment since spring 2021. Especially alarming is the finding that Black first-time freshman enrollment dropped 6.5% since the previous spring. This group was the only demographic to experience a decline in first-time freshman enrollment (Moody, 2022).

The pandemic did not cause the decline in college enrollment, but it did help to accelerate it. Income inequality and tuition and fees that continue to outpace inflation are causing high school students to question whether they should attend college. Jaschik (2022) references at survey conducted by Youth-Truth, a nonprofit, where 22,000 members of the class of 2022 were asked about their post-graduation plans and compared the survey results to a similar survey given to the class of 2019, the last high school class to graduate before the pandemic. The percentage of Latino students who wanted to go to college decreased from 79% in 2019 to 71% in 2022. The percentage of Black students who expressed interest in attending college fell from 79% in 2019 to 72% in 2022. Also, the percentage of male students who wanted to attend college decreased from 74% in 2019 to 67% in 2022 (Jaschik, 2022). These findings call into question the perceived value of postsecondary education by college age students. In fact, Doug Shapiro, the Vice-President, Research and Executive Director of the NSCRC said the five semesters of consecutive enrollment decline "…suggests that there is a broader questioning of the value of college and particularly concerns about student debt and paying for college and the potential labor market returns" (Moody, 2022).

How widespread is the belief that college education is overvalued? According to the Pew Research Center, roughly 62% of Americans adults over 25 do not have a four-year college degree (Parker, 2021). A 2021 survey conducted by the Pew Research Center of adults over 25 years of age found a complex set of reasons why more Americans do not have a college degree. As suggested by other research, the economy is an important factor. Of the 4,475 adults without a bachelor's degree and not enrolled in college, 42% said not being able afford a four-year college degree and 36% said they needing to work to support their family were major reasons why they did not have a four-year degree. An additional 23% said they didn't need a four-year degree for their career while 29% said they did not want to go to college. Finally, 20% listed never considered it and 13% listed did not think they could get into college as reasons for not having a degree (Parker, 2021). Although these survey results suggest that economic factors are the driving force behind dropping enrollments, there are also other issues related to beliefs about the value of higher education.

HIGHER EDUCATION IN A FEDERAL SYSTEM

States are not the only level of government that provides financial assistance to higher education. The federal government also provides funding to higher education but has typically restricted its role to various forms of student financial aid with limited assistance to institutions through mechanisms such as funding for research. Federal student aid has not kept up with inflation; for the 2020-2021 academic year, total student aid decreased 32% relative to the 2010-2011 academic year in inflation related dollars. Among the federal aid programs that continue to shrink are Pell Grants which fell by 39% and veteran's benefits which fell by 3% (College Board, 2021, p.4). The trend in shrinking federal student aid has temporally shift course. Recognizing the economic impact of the pandemic, Congress passed the Coronavirus, Aid, Relief, and Economic Security (CARES) Act (Public Law 116-136) on March 27, 2020. As part of the $2.2 trillion in economic assistance, $14 billion was given to the Office of Postsecondary Education as the Higher Education Emergency Relief Fund (HEERF). (U.S. Department of Education, 2021). These funds were intended to provide relief to colleges and students enduring unanticipated costs associated with the pandemic. Fifty percent of HEERF I funds were required to be utilized as emergency financial aid to students (June, 2020). HEERF funds were allocated to students for expenses related to the changes in campus operations resulting from the pandemic rather than financial need stemming from COVID-19 (NASFAA, 2022a). The remaining funds could be used for institutional costs. In addition to providing monies to support higher education during the pandemic, the CARES Act aided students by waiving interested on student loan payments through September 30, 2020, which was extended through the ended of January 2022 (College Board, 2021, p.8).

In January 2021, an additional $21.2 billion was allocated to higher education by legislation passed by Congress and signed into law by former President Trump in December 2020. These funds were made available to institutions under the Coronavirus Response and Relief Supplemental Appropriations (CRRSA) Act and are known as HEERF II funds. This legislation requires institutions to spend at least as much of the money on student grants that was required in the CARES Act funding allocated the previous year (Murakami, 2021). According to HEERF II guidelines, funds can be used to cover emergency student costs such as tuition, food, housing, health care, and childcare (NASFAA, 2022b). HEERF II provisions allowed colleges and universities to spend greater amounts of the funds received in 2021 on institutional costs than in 2020 (Murakami, 2021). Institutions were allowed to use funds to pay for expenses related to the coronavirus such as lost revenue, reimbursement for previous expenses, technological costs related to distance learning, faculty and staff training, payroll, student support activities related to the pandemic, and for further financial aid grants to students (NASFAA, 2022b).

Affordability and State Support for Higher Education

HEERF III funds were made available to colleges and universities as part of the American Rescue Plan signed into law by President Biden on March 11, 2021. HEERF III provided $39.6 billion in aid to institutions (Office of Postsecondary Education, 2022). Public and non-profit institutions of higher learning were required to spend fifty percent of HEERF III funds on student grants whereas for-profit institutions are required to devote 100% of funds to student grants. Furthermore, institutions must use part of their HEERF III funding for putting evidence-based practices into place to observe and suppress the virus in accordance with public health recommendations. Colleges and universities must also use funds to contact financial aid applicants regarding the chance to receive a financial aid adjustment due to circumstances such as recent unemployment of a family member. HEERF II rules for allowable spending generally apply to HEERF III. In March 2021, the Biden Administration announced that unspent HEERF I monies, originally allocated under the CARES Act, would be subject to HEERF III rules (NASFAA, 2022c).

Although the CARES Act helped both higher education institutions and students through the pandemic, it is a stimulus package enacted to help during a crisis and is not meant to be ongoing aid for education. With dropping enrollments and increased student debt, public opinion polls indicate that the public wants the federal government to go further in solving the college affordability problem. The *52nd Annual PDK Poll of the Public Attitudes Toward the Public Schools* taken before the 2020 presidential election found that 60% of adults and 70% of parents said that public education was highly important to their decision on who to vote for president. In addition, 77% of those surveyed wanted Washington to focus more on college affordability (Starr, 2020, p. K2). Concerns over college affordability also drew the attention of the two major parties. The Democratic Party platform included several strategies for addressing college affordability including increasing federal funding for childcare on college campuses; creating programs to address food insecurity on campuses and making community colleges and trade schools tuition free (Democratic Party, 2020). The Republican Party did not adopt a new platform in 2020 but elected to ratify the 2016 platform. In the 2016 (and readopted 2020) platform, the Republican Party recognized that student debt had become unsustainable. Unlike the Democratic Party, they attributed the problem of student debt to the federal student loan program and called on the federal government to turn student loans over to the private sector (Ballotpedia, 2020).

What are some of the major federal policies used to promote college affordability? An early example of federal involvement in higher education is the Servicemen's Readjustment Act (1944) (Public Law 78-346). The act signed into law by on June 22, 1944, by President Franklin Roosevelt provided federal funds to WWII veterans for education, housing, and unemployment insurance. It was not conceived as a higher education policy but was adopted because the National Resource Planning Board feared that many of returning soldiers would become unemployed leading to a possible economic depression. Although the act was meant to prevent a postwar depression, it had a significant impact on higher education. After its first seven years, over eight million veterans received funds for education including support for four-year degrees, community college and trade school. Although the act expired in 1956, it has been extended several times (National Archives, 2022).

The federal government increased its role in higher education following the launch of Sputnik *I* (first artificial earth satellite) on October 4, 1957, by the former Soviet Union. This event raised fears that the United States was falling behind the Soviet Union in military strength and technology. In response the federal government increasing research grants to higher education through federal agencies including the National Science Foundation, and National Institute of health (Jencks & Riesman, 1968). In addition, the federal government adopted the 1958 National Defense Education Act (Public Law 85-864) with

107

the underlying goals of improving the American Education system and encourage more students to seek college educations. Among the provisions of the act was the National Defense Student Loan Program later renamed the Federal Perkins Loan Program. Further increasing the role of the federal government, the Higher Education Act of 1965 (Public Law 89-329) was passed as part of President Lyndon Johnson's Great Society Program. The goal of the act was to expand opportunities for all to obtain a higher education. To achieve this goal, Title IV of this act and its subsequent revisions spearheaded several student aid programs including Pell Grants, and federal direct loans. Initially federal loans were meant to act as an investment to help students out of poverty. During the 2019-2020 school year, 55 percent of college graduates receiving a bachelor's degree from a public four-year institution left with an average debt of $26,700 with figures higher for those graduating from a four-year private nonprofit institution (College Board, 2021, p.43). This level of student loan debt is causing some to question the value of higher education (Moody, 2022).

PROMOTING AFFORDABILITY AT THE STATE-LEVEL

States vary in their commitment to higher education; for some state legislatures promoting higher education is lower on their list of priorities while others have gone beyond increasing appropriations to improve the affordability of postsecondary education. Among the strategies implemented at the state-level to increase college affordability are bans on scholarship displacement, promise programs varying in design, and free college applications for high schoolers as part of their graduation requirement. Although legislation on scholarship displacement bans was introduced at the federal level, states have begun enacting or introduced their own versions of these laws. Scholarship displacement bans are based on the situation where private scholarship, grants, loans, or other financial assistance may impact the student's eligibility for institutional financial aid awards and the amount of the award (H.R. 5380, p. 2). In response, the United States House of Representatives, September 27, 2021, introduced H.R. 5380, the Helping Students Plan for College Act of 2021. This bill would require higher education institutions to "notify students of the impact of private scholarships and grants on eligibility for institutional financial aid." The Helping Students Plan for College Act of 2021 would support student use of financial aid that they are not receiving under the Title IV, Student Assistance, of the Higher Education Act of 1965. Title IV is to assist high school graduates of financial need through opportunity grants, who otherwise would not be able to benefit by postsecondary or higher education (H.R. 5380, p. 3-4; Public Law 89-329, 1965, p. 1232). At the state level, Maryland (2017) became an early adopter of banning scholarship displacement by public colleges by limiting the conditions that institutions can reduce financial aid. Recently, the state of Illinois introduced House Bill 5311, the Scholarship Displacement Act to be applied following the 2022-2023 school year, which sets parameters on permitting a higher education public institution to reduce a student's financial aid because of awarded private scholarships to the student. Among the parameters is permission to reduce the student's financial aid if all sources of aid exceed the student's need (State of Illinois, January 28, 2022). In California, the California Ban on Scholarship Displacement Act of 2021 defines private scholarships as supplemental assistance that "do not supplant, gift aid, grants, scholarships, tuition waivers, and fellowship stipends provided by institutions of higher education to California students who have financial need" (California Legislature, 2022, 70046(b); NCSL, 2022).

Promise programs are a popular state programs that offer higher education scholarships to students who otherwise could not attend postsecondary institutions. They are merit-based scholarships that require students to meet certain grade requirements. This strategy has become widespread; sometimes referred to as promise communities in states with expanded number of programs. The Kalamazoo Promise in Michigan (2005) is an example of a promise program designed to meet the needs of a local community and is offered to students living and graduating from a Kalamazoo Public School district. For students that meet its academic requirements, this program can cover tuition and mandatory fees for eligible Michigan institutions (The Kalamazoo Promise, n.d.). Recently, the Mississippi House Bill 147, was introduced and if passed would establish the Mississippi Promise Scholarship Act. This scholarship and mentoring program seek to increase the number of postsecondary education students in the state by offering students with a last-dollar scholarship that covers tuition cost and fees not covered by Pell or other state funds. It is applicable to any Mississippi institution public or private offering an Associates Program (Mississippi Legislature, 2022, para 1; NCSL, 2022). In North Carolina, the Senate Bill 706 amendment, establishes the state's Community College Promise Scholarship Program. The purpose of this specific program includes using the state educational resources to the fullest, creating options for students on educational and careers, cost-savings for the state, and to develop a competitive workforce (North Carolina General Assembly, 2021, Section 1, Part 5(a); NCSL, 2022).

While some states are placing a ban or parameters on student scholarship displacement, or establishing a promise program, others are passing laws mandating high school students fill out a free application for federal student aid as a high school graduation requirement. Nebraska for example will begin free application completion and submission to the U.S. Department of Education with the 2022-2023 school year (Nebraska Legislature, January 8, 2021; NCSL, 2022). Among other states, New York offers free federal student aid applications as part of high school graduation requirements (State of New York, January 6, 2021; NCSL,2022). Similar in South Carolina, as part of high school graduation requirements, students must complete a free application for federal aid before graduating (South Carolina General Assembly, January 12, 2021; NCSL, 2022).

BALANCE WHEEL MODEL

Rising student debt has drawn the attention of both the public and political actors; nevertheless, this does not guarantee that government actors will address the problem. Rochefort, and Cobb (1994) argue that certain characteristics of an issue determine whether the public perceives it to be a substantial enough problem that the government needs to address it. These traits: causality, severity, incidence, proximity, and crisis are key elements that influence whether an issue is recognized as a public problem. Issues are more likely to be perceived as warranting government action when the public reaches consensus that institutional failures are the cause, that the consequences of a lack of government action are severe, that the problem occurs with frequency, and/or that it closely affects many people (1994, p.16). Times of crisis such as a pandemic can focus attention by combining dimensions of proximity and severity in the public mind.

The literature on policy adoptions suggests specific categories of variables are central to explaining the variation in state-level policy (Mooney & Lee, 1995; 2000; Hwang & Grey, 1991). Early research found that measures of state wealth was important to policy adoption (Walker, 1969; Gray, 1973) while later studies (Meier, 1994; Mooney & Lee, 1995) suggest that both politics and public demand/need are also important in explain policy action. The type of policy often dictates which of these factors play a more dominate role in explaining legislative action. Policy action associated with funding higher education has been described as cyclical and tied to the economy. According to the Balance Wheel Model, when the economy is good, state legislatures will increase monies for higher education at a faster rate than other government services. The reverse is also true, when states face an economic downturn, they are more likely to decrease funding to higher education at a higher rate than other budget categories. This pattern has been attributed to tuition being an alternative source of financing for higher education; for other items in the state budget, there might not be another source of funding (Delaney, 2014). This suggests that measures of state wealth will be more significant than measures of politics and public demand/need.

In the following section, this chapter examines factors identified by the policy adoption and agenda setting literature as impacting policy change including political influences, state resources, and the demands or needs of citizens (Mooney & Lee, 1995; 2000; Hwang & Grey, 1991). This paper explores state funding of higher education from 2010 through 2020; this timeframe was chosen to examine changes in state funding that include two economic crises (the Great Recession and the COVID-19 pandemic).

EMPIRICAL MODELS: DATA AND METHODS

The focus of this chapter is to explore the factors that influence differences among states in the amount of money allocated to higher education. The dependent variable is public higher education appropriations per Full Time Equivalent (FTE) student by state created by dividing state educations appropriations by net FTE enrollment (State Higher Education Executive Officers Association [SHEEO], 2021). Because public need/demand (Meier, 1994; Mooney & Lee, 1995; 2000) has been found to be an important factor in predicting policy adoption, student share measured as the proportion of total education revenues at public institutions that come from students and their families lagged by one year was included (SHEEO, 2021). The early literature on policy diffusion and adoption (Walker, 1969; Savage, 1978) found that state wealth and urbanization were important predictors of policy action. To control for measures of state wealth, gross state product, per capita personal income and urbanization were included. Gross state product and per capita personal income are measured over time in millions of dollars (Bureau of Economic Analysis, 2021) while urbanization is measured by the percent of the population living in urban areas (Iowa Community Indicators Program, 2022). Based on the early policy adoption literature and the Balance Wheel Model, it is expected that states with greater wealth are more likely to increase funding for higher education. Legislative professionalism was also included as a measure of state resources. It is expected that more professional legislatures will be leaders in policy adoptions because they are more likely to possess expertise in the various policy areas. This variable is measured using an index created by the NCSL (2021) and consists of a three-point scale ranging from part-time to full-time and is based on salary, staff, and time-in-session of the 50 state legislatures.

Because the literature (Meier, 1994; Mooney & Lee, 1995) suggest that the political environment is important in explaining policy decisions, controls were included for political actors. Among the controls is political culture which can influence perception of the proper role of government. Elazar (1984) argues that the ethnic and religious backgrounds of those who originally settled in the U.S. help to determine the political culture of the various regions. States in the northern region of the United States were settled by groups including the Puritans who believed that the role of government was to assure that the public interest was carried out (moralistic political culture). The middle section of the country was settled by individuals who viewed the role of government as a service provider (individualistic political culture) while those in the southern portion of the United States and rural areas saw the job of government as one

Affordability and State Support for Higher Education

of maintaining the status quo (traditionalistic political culture). Two variables were added for moralistic and individualistic political cultures with each coded 1 for the specific form of political culture and 0 otherwise. Traditionalistic political culture serves as the reference group.

Research (Kousser, 2005) argues that the relationship among policymaking institution also influences policy outcomes. Among these institutional actors is the governor whose ability to influence policy is associated with his/her level of institutional power. To control for variation among states, a five-point scale for the institutional power of state governors was included ranging from 1 which indicates the governor has weak power to 5 which signifies that the governor has strong power based on the state's constitution and statutes (Donovan, Mooney, & Smith, 2013). Because policies to address college affordability are popular with constituents, it is expected that governors will promote them in an election year. To control for the impact of gubernatorial elections, a dummy variable was included coded 1 if it is a gubernatorial election year and 0 otherwise. Party competition has also been found to influence policy adoption. Research (e.g., Garand, 1985; Barrilleux, 2000) suggests that in states where neither party dominates, policies are more reflective of public demand. The Ranney Index, a measure of party control which ranges from 0 (total Republican Party control) to 1(total Democratic Party control) was included (Thomas, & La Raja, 2012; 2017). Because women in state legislatures have been found to be associated with more progressive policies (Orey et al., 2006), states with a greater percentage of female legislators may be more likely to support increasing funding for higher education. The presence of women legislators is measured using the percent women in a state legislature for each year (Center for American Women and Politics, 2021). Finally, controls were included for region. The College Board (2016, p. 12) found regional variations in the extent that increases in tuition and fees outpace inflation. For example, while state in the middle region of the U.S. saw a 27% increase in tuition and fees over a ten-year period, the West saw a 66% increase during the same timeframe. To control for these regional differences, dummy variables were added for Northeast, Midwest, and South, while West serves as the reference group.

FINDINGS AND DISCUSSION

In Table 1, the dependent variable is coded so that higher scores are associated with a greater state funding for higher education. Since the dependent variable is measured over time pooling the fifty states and is continuous, cross-sectional time series analysis is used. The findings in Table 1 are only partially consistent with the Balance Wheel Model that argues that state-funding for higher education is primarily tied to economic conditions (Delaney, 2014). As expected, legislative professionalism and per capita personal income were significant and positively related to state appropriations for higher education. However, gross state product was unrelated appropriations and percent urban was significant and negatively related to funding. Both results are inconsistent with early research that found state wealth was an important determinate of policy adoption (Walker, 1969; Gray, 1973) and the Balance Wheel Model. While gross state product was used as a measure of wealth in this model, it might be possible that per capita personal income is a better measure and may be overshadowing the impact of gross state product. Although urbanization is typically used as an indicator of wealth, in this circumstance it might be acting as a measure of need. Rural states with dispersed populations may need to pay more for the same services as urban states because they cannot take advantage of economy of scale.

As expected, gubernatorial institutional power and election years were positively associated with increased appropriations for higher education. Inconsistent with the literature, were the results that the percent women in the state legislature, and party competition were unrelated to funding for higher education. One explanation is that fiscal policy is an area where the governor has greater institutional power compared to the state legislature. In most states, the governor is charged with estimating revenues and proposing the budget for the following year. This allows the governor to set funding priorities (Krause & Melusky, 2012).

Table 1. State-level higher education's appropriations, 2010-2020

Variables	Higher Education Appropriations	
	β (se)	**p>|z|**
Political constraints		
Moralistic political culture [i,t]	**-1614.05(758.18)**	**.033**
Individualistic political culture [i,t]	981.45(725.38)	.176
Gubernatorial election year [i,t]	**144.05(66.28)**	**.030**
Gubernatorial institutional power [i,t]	**333.03(186.90)**	**.076**
% women in the state legislature [i,t]	-5.49(11.19)	.624
Party competition [i,t]	199.22(556.06)	.720
State resources		
Per capita personal income [i,t]	**.18(.009)**	**.000**
Gross state product [i,t]	-.0003(.0003)	.276
Urban population (%) [i,t]	**-64.26(14.03)**	**.000**
Legislative professionalism [i,t]	**558.16(261.81)**	**.033**
Demands/needs		
Student share (lagged) [i,t]	**-9220.72(705.63)**	**.000**
Regions		
Northeast	**-2594.02(611.38)**	**.000**
Midwest	**-1802.37(526.41)**	**.001**
South	**-2109.07(710.71)**	**.003**
Constant	**7516.14(1309.54)**	**.000**
Wald Chi^2 (14) Number of Panels N	999.97 50 550	.0000

Note: Panel corrected cross-sectional time series data for the 50 states. Unstandardized coefficients are presented with standard errors in parenthesis. Subscript i contains the unit to which the observations belong, in this case the state, and controls for variation in state legislative activity between the states. Subscript t represents the time or year the variable was measured.

The finding that states with a moralistic political culture provided less funding for higher education was not anticipated. Because states with a moralistic political culture were settled by individuals who believe that the role of government was to assure that the public interest was carried out, it was expected

Affordability and State Support for Higher Education

that these states would be more likely to provide more funding for higher education. There are several possible explanations for this result. States with an individualist political culture were settled by members of the middle class who wanted to increase their social standing. During the colonial period, many felt that education was one avenue for improving social status (Cremin, 1970). The finding that these states provide greater levels of funding for higher education is not unrealistic. More difficult to explain is the finding that states with a traditionalist political culture provide greater funding than states with a moralistic political culture. Settlers in these states were described as aristocratic. During the colonial period, there was limited education available to poor families in these states and wealthy families sent their children to private schools or boarding schools in England (Cremin, 1970). This outcome seems to be indicative of current educational goals and not based on political culture. The measure for lagged student share is negatively related to funding. This indicates that following time periods where students and their families are dealing with higher college costs, states respond by providing less funding. It also suggests that following a period where students and their families are paying relatively lower college costs, the state increases funding for higher education. This implies that funding for higher education is not responding to student needs but is instead tied to the economy. This is consistent with the Balance Wheel Model. Finally, there is support for the argument that there are regional differences in funding for higher education with states in the West providing greater funding for higher education. Since many states in the West are rural, this could be because they cannot take advantage of economy of scale.

FUTURE RESEARCH DIRECTIONS

This chapter explores state-level funding for higher education. The results of this study suggest that state resources, and the economy plays an important role in funding while demand/need is unrelated, and the impact of political factors is mixed. The literature on state appropriations for higher education argues that funding is primarily explained by economic conditions. This chapter, however found that political actors including the governor can play an important role along with other factors including geography and political culture. While this chapter adds new insight into the topic of state-level funding for higher education, there are ways that future studies can improve upon it. Because the literature on funding suggests that the economy dominates other factors, additional controls for the economic should be added. This study primarily used indicators of state wealth but controls including those related to inflation could enhance the model. There are other sources of education funding including the federal government; future studies should explore whether changes in funding from other sources impacts state government behavior. Better measures of need/demand may also help to improve understanding of state actions. It may be useful to include indicators for student enrollment and student debt. Finally, this chapter began with a discussion of how the COVID-19 pandemic has impacted higher education, but it examines the years 2010-2020. This timeframe can only provide a limited understanding of the impact of COVID-19 pandemic. As more data because available, future investigations will be better able to explore the influence of this event on higher education.

CONCLUSION

The COVID-19 pandemic challenged both K-12 and higher education to find new strategies for delivering classes. Schools moved forward during the pandemic with a combination of in-person, online, and hybrid methods to provide instruction. This was not a smooth process. The move to online and hybrid classes made it evident that the "digital divide" still exists in the United States and other countries. Although the U.S. has come along way in closing the digital divide, parts of the country (particularly rural communities) do not have access to the Internet that is inexpensive, dependable or with high-speed connections (Goldberg, 2022). Some students faced a digital "homework gap" once classes moved online. Because some students do not have Internet access or even computers at home, they had to rely on public Wi-Fi to do schoolwork. This helped to accelerate the ongoing decline in college enrollments brought on by college costs that continue to outpace inflation. The prospect of pay off long term student debts and the difficulties associated with taking classes during the pandemic left some questioning the value of a college degree. The federal government responded in several ways. The first was the passage of the CARES Act on March 27, 2020. It provided $2.2 trillion in economic stimulus, with $14 billion allocated to helping support higher education (U.S. Department of Education, 2021). Recently, the federal government has passes legislation to further address the digital divide and its impact on higher education. As part of President Biden's $65 billion "Internet for All" initiative to expand Internet access, more than $10 million in grants will be allocated to expand high-speed Internet access to minority-serving colleges and universities (National Telecommunications and Information Administration [NTIA], July 22, 2022).

Although these actions represent initiatives by the federal government to address the impact of the pandemic on higher education; state-level subsidies to public universities remains the dominate factor in containing college costs. How do states decides how much funding to appropriate for higher education? The Balance Wheel Model argues that state financing is driving by economics; when the economy is good, and the state has surplus resources they spend more on higher education and less when state budgets are tight. The findings from this study support this model in part. Two measures of state wealth (per capita income and legislative professionalism) were significant and positive while gross state product was not significant and percent urban was negatively related to funding. The finding that percent urban was negatively related to funding suggests that in this variable is acting as measure of need in this model. Rural states with dispersed populations may have to pay more for the same services as urban states because they cannot take advantage of economy of scale. These results suggest that economic conditions as well as geography matter. Also supporting the Balance Wheel Model is the finding that lagged student share is negatively related to appropriations implying that funding for higher education is not responding to student needs but is based on state revenues. Contradictory to the Balance Wheel Model was the finding that several political and geographical factors (political culture, regional differences, institutional power of the governor and gubernatorial elections) also influenced state appropriation for higher education. These results suggest that the economic conditions play a significant role in explain appropriations, but it is not the only factor. Because of the governor's budgetary role in the state, he/she can set funding priorities. In addition, other factors including belief about the proper role of the government among citizens and geography can constrain budget decisional.

REFERENCES

American Association of Community Colleges. (2019). *Community college enrollment crisis? Historical trends in community college enrollment.* Retrieved from https://www.aacc.nche.edu/wp-content/uploads/2019/08/Crisis-in-Enrollment-2019.pdf

Auxier, B., & Anderson, M. (2020). *As schools close due to the coronavirus, some U.S. students face a digital 'homework gap."* Retrieved from https://www.pewresearch.org/fact-tank/2020/03/16/as-schools-close-due-to-the-coronavirus-some-u-s-students-face-a-digital-homework-gap/

Ballotpedia. (2020). *The Republican Party Platform, 2020.* Retrieved from https://ballotpedia.org/The_Republican_Party_Platform,_2020

Barrilleux, C. (2000). Party strength, party change, and policy making in the American states. *Party Politics*, *6*(1), 61–73. doi:10.1177/1354068800006001004

Bauman, D. (April 28, 2022*). 3 things we learned from the latest federal employment and enrollment report.* Retrieved from https://www.chronicle.com/article/3-things-we-learned-from-the-latest-federal-employment-and-enrollment-report

Becker, G. (1964). *Human Capital.* Columbia University Press.

Broton, K. M. (2020). A review of estimates of housing insecurity and homelessness among students in U.S. higher education. *Journal of Social Distress and the Homeless*, *29*(1), 25–38. doi:10.1080/10530789.2020.1677009

Bureau of Economic Analysis. (2021). *GDP by state.* Retrieved from https://www.bea.gov/data/gdp/gdp-state

California Legislature. (2022). *California Assembly Bill 288.* 2021-2022 Regular Session.

Castleman, B., & Meyer, K. (2019). Financial constraints & collegiate student learning: A behavioral economics perspective. *Daedalus*, *148*(4), 195–216. doi:10.1162/daed_a_01767

Center for American Women and Politics. (2021). *State-by-state information.* Retrieved from https://cawp.rutgers.edu/facts/state-state-information

College Board. (2016). *Trends in college pricing, 2016.* Retrieved from https://research.collegeboard.org/media/pdf/trends-college-pricing-2016-full-report.pdf

College Board. (2021). *Trends in college pricing and student aid, 2021.* Retrieved from https://research.collegeboard.org/media/pdf/trends-college-pricing-student-aid-2021.pdf

Cremin, L. (1970). *American education: The colonial experience, 1607-1783.* Harper & Row.

Delaney, J. A. (2014). The Role of state policy in promoting college affordability. *The Annals of the American Academy of Political and Social Science*, *655*(1), 56–78. doi:10.1177/0002716214535898

Democratic Party. (2020). *Where we stand: Providing world-class education in every zip code.* Retrieved from https://democrats.org/where-we-stand/party-platform/providing-a-world-class-education-in-every-zip-code/

Denison, E. (1962). *Sources of economic growth in America*. Committee for Economic Development.

Doyle, W. R. (2007). Public opinion, partisan identification, and higher education policy. *The Journal of Higher Education*, *78*(4), 369–401. doi:10.1353/jhe.2007.0021

Elazar, D. J. (1984). *American federalism: A view from the states* (3rd ed.). Harper and Row.

Frank, J., Salsbury, M., McKelvey, H., & McLain, R. (2021). Digital equity & inclusion strategies for libraries: Promoting student success for all learners. *The International Journal of Information, Diversity, & Inclusion*, *5*(3), 185–205.

Friedman, Z. (February 3, 2020). *Student loan debt statistics in 2020: A record $1.6 trillion*. Retrieved from https://www.forbs.com/sites/zackfriedman/2020/02/03/student-loan-debt-statistics/#4bb54987281f

Garand, J. (1985). Partisan change and shifting expenditure priorities in the American states, 1945-1978. *American Politics Quarterly*, *13*(4), 355–391. doi:10.1177/1532673X8501300401

Goldberg, R. (2022). *New NTIA data show barriers to closing the digital divide, achieving digital equality*. Retrieved from https://www.ntia.doc.gov/blog/2022/new-ntia-data-show-enduring-barriers-closing-digital-divide-achieving-digital-equity

Gray, V. (1973). Innovations in the states: A diffusion study. *The American Political Science Review*, *67*(4), 1174–1185. doi:10.2307/1956539

House of Representatives 5380. (2021). *Helping Students Plan for College Act of 2021*. 117th Congress (2021-2022).

Hwang, S., & Grey, V. (1991). External limits and internal determinates of state public policy. *Political Research Policy*, *44*(2), 277–299.

Iowa Community Indicators Program. (2022). *Urban Percentage of Population for States, Historical*. Retrieved from https://www.icip.iastate.edu/tables/population/urban-pct-states#:~:text=Urban%20Percentage%20of%20the%20Population%20for%20States%2C%20Historical,%20%2087.5%20%2048%20more%20rows%20

Jaschik, J. (2022). *Decline in male, Black, and Latino students planning on college*. Retrieved from https://www.insidehighered.com/admissions/article/2022/05/23/male-black-and-latino-high-school-students-may-not-be-college-bound?v2

Jencks, C., & Riesman, D. (1968). *The academic revolution*. University of Chicago Press.

June, A. W. (2020). *Congress gave colleges billions. Who got what?* Retrieved from https://www.chronicle.com/article/congress-gave-colleges-billions-who-got-what

Kousser, T. (2005). *Term limits and the dismantling of state legislative professionalism*. Cambridge University Press.

Krause, G., & Melusky, B. (2012). Concentrated power: Unilateral executive authority and fiscal policy-making in the American states. *The Journal of Politics*, *74*(1), 98–112. doi:10.1017/S0022381611001149

Liptak, K. (2022). *Treasury Secretary concedes she was wrong on 'path inflation would take'*. Retrieved from https://www.msn.com/en-us/news/politics/treasury-secretary-concedes-she-was-wrong-on- path-that-inflation-would-take/ar-AAXWmGD?ocid=uxbndlbing

Lowi, T. (1964). American business, public policy, case studies, and political theory. *World Politics*, *16*(4), 677–715. doi:10.2307/2009452

Meier, K. (1994). *The politics of sin: drugs, alcohol, and public policy*. Sharpe.

Mississippi Legislature. (2022). *Mississippi House Bill 147*. 2022 Regular Session.

Moody, J. (2022). *A 5th straight semester of enrollment declines*. Retrieved from https://www.inside-highered.com/news/2022/05/26/nsc-report-shows-total-enrollment-down-41-percent?v2

Mooney, C., & Lee, M. (1995). Legislating morality in the American states: The case of pre-Roe abortion regulation reform. *American Journal of Political Science*, *39*(3), 599–627. doi:10.2307/2111646

Mooney, C., & Lee, M. (2000). The influence of values on consensus and contentious morality policy: U.S. death penalty reform, 1956-82. *The Journal of Politics*, *62*(1), 223–239. doi:10.1111/0022-3816.00011

Murakami, K. (2021). *Billions in Aid Head to Colleges*. Retrieved from https://www.insidehighered.com/news/2021/01/15/education-department-releases-billions-aid-colleges#:~:text=The%20U.S.%20Education%20Department%20on,through%20emergency%20student%20grants%20again

National Archives. (2022*). Servicemen's Readjustment Act*. Retrieved from https://www.archives.gov/milestone-documents/servicemens-readjustment-act

National Association of Student Financial Aid Administrators. (2022a). *NASFAA higher education emergency relief reference page*. Retrieved from https://www.nasfaa.org/covid19_heerf

National Association of Student Financial Aid Administrators. (2022b). *NASFAA higher education emergency relief fund ii (HEEF II) reference page*. Retrieved from https://www.nasfaa.org/heerf_ii

National Association of Student Financial Aid Administrators. (2022c). *NASFAA higher education emergency relief fund iii (HEEF III) reference page*. Retrieved from https://www.nasfaa.org/heerf_iii

National Center for Education Statistics. (2022). *College enrollment rates*. Retrieved from https://nces.ed.gov/programs/coe/indicator/cpb

National Conference of State Legislatures. (2021). *Full-and-part-time legislatures*. https://www.ncsl.org/research/about-state-legislatures/full-and-part-time-legislatures.aspx

National Conference of State Legislatures. (2022). *Postsecondary Bill Tracking Database*. Retrieved from https://www.ncsl.org/research/education/postsecondary-bill-tracking-database.aspx

National Telecommunications and Information Administration. (2022). *Biden Administration announces more than $10 million in grants to expand high-speed Internet to minority-serving colleges and universities*. Retrieved from https://www.internetforall.gov/sites/default/files/2022-07/DOC-NTIA-CMC-Award-Announcement-Press-Release-7.22.22.pdf

Nebraska Legislature. (2021) *Nebraska Legislative Bill 200*. 107th Legislature.

North Carolina General Assembly. (2021). *North Carolina Senate Bill 706*. Session 2021.

Office of Postsecondary Education. (2021). *Cares Act: Higher education emergency relief fund*. Retrieved from https://www2.ed.gov/about/offices/list/ope/caresact.html#:~:text=This%20bill%20allotted%20%242.2%20trillion,Emergency%20Relief%20Fund%2C%20or%20HEERF

Orey, B., Smooth, W., Adams, K., & Harris-Clark, K. (2006). Race and gender matter: Refining models of legislative policy making in state legislatures. *Journal of Women, Politics & Policy, 28*(3-4), 97–119. doi:10.1300/J501v28n03_05

Parker, K. (2021). *What's behind the growing gap between men and women in college completion?* Retrieved from https://www.pewresearch.org/fact-tank/2021/11/08/whats-behind-the-growing-gap-between-men-and-women-in-college-completion/

Public Law 116-136 (2020). *Coronavirus, Aid, Relief, and Economic Security Act*.

Public Law 78-346 (1944). *Servicemen's Readjustment Act*.

Public Law 85-864 (1958). *National Defense Education Act*.

Public Law 89-329 (1965). *Higher Education Act of 1965*.

Rochefort, D. A., & Cobb, R. W. (1994). *The politics of problem definition*. University Press.

Samuels, C., & Prothero, A. (July 29, 2020). *Could the 'Pandemic Pod' be a lifeline to parents or a threat to equality?* Retrieved from https://www.edweek.org/ew/articles/2020/07/29/could-the-pandemic-pod-be-a-lifeline.html

Savage, R. (1978). Policy innovativeness as a trait of American states. *The Journal of Politics, 40*(1), 212–219. doi:10.2307/2129985

Smalley, A. (2022). *Legislative preview: Affordability, free speech among trends in higher education*. Retrieved from https://www.ncsl.org/research/education/legislative-preview-affordability-free-speech-among-trends-in-higher-education-magazine2022.aspx

Starr, J. P. (2020). Public school priorities in a political year: The 52nd Annual PDK Poll of the Public's Attitudes Toward the Public Schools. *Phi Delta Kappan, 102*(1), K1–K16. doi:10.1177/0031721720956844

State Higher Education Executive Officers Association. (2021). State Higher Education Finance: FY 2020. Author.

State of Illinois. (2022). *Illinois House 5311*. 102nd General Assembly.

State of New York. (2021). *New York A 361*. 2021-2022 Regular Sessions.

The Kalamazoo Promise. (n.d.) *The Kalamazoo Promise*. Retrieved from https://www.kalamazoopromise.com

Thomas, C., & La Raja, J. (2012). Parties and elections. In V. Gray, R. Hanson, & T. Kousser (Eds.), *Politics in the American states: A comparative analysis* (10th ed., pp. 63–104). CQ Press.

Affordability and State Support for Higher Education

Thomas, C., & La Raja, J. (2017). Parties and elections. In V. Gray, R. Hanson, & T. Kousser (Eds.), *Politics in the American states: A comparative analysis* (11th ed., pp. 57–98). CQ Press.

U.S. Department of Education. (2021). *CARES Act: Higher education emergency relief fund.* Retrieved from https://www2.ed.gov/about/offices/list/ope/caresact.html

Walker, J. (1969). The diffusion of innovation among the American states. *The American Political Science Review, 63*(3), 880–899. doi:10.2307/1954434

ADDITIONAL READING

Andrews, R. J., & Stange, K. M. (2019). Price regulation, price discrimination, and equality of opportunity in higher education: Evidence from Texas. *American Economic Journal. Economic Policy, 11*(4), 31–65. doi:10.1257/pol.20170306

Conger, D., & Dickson, L. (2017). Gender imbalance in higher education: Insights for college administrators and researchers. *Research in Higher Education, 58*(2), 214–230. doi:10.100711162-016-9421-3

Greenstein, D. I. (2019). The future of undergraduate education: Will differences across sectors exacerbate inequality? *Daedalus, 148*(4), 108–137. doi:10.1162/daed_a_01763

Hillman, N. W., Fryar, A. H., & Crespín-Trujillo, V. (2018). Evaluating the impact of performance funding in Ohio and Tennessee. *American Educational Research Journal, 55*(1), 144–170. doi:10.3102/0002831217732951

Husted, T. A., & Kenney, L. W. (2018). The effect of reduced support from state government on research in state universities. *Journal of Education Finance, 44*(2), 164–174.

Melguizo, T., Witham, K., Fong, K., & Chi, E. (2017). Understanding the relationship between equity and efficiency: Towards a concept of funding adequacy for community colleges. *Journal of Education Finance, 43*(2), 195–216.

Newfield, C., & Douglass, J. A. (2020). Future of American higher education. *Issues in Science and Technology, 36*(4), 12–13.

Ortagus, J. C., & Yang, L. (2018). An examination of the influence of decreases in state appropriations on online enrollment at public universities. *Research in Higher Education, 59*(7), 847–865. doi:10.100711162-017-9490-y

Rof, A., Bikfalvi, A., & Marques, P. (2022). Pandemic-accelerated digital transformation of a born digital higher education institution: Towards a customized multimode learning strategy. *Journal of Educational Technology & Society, 25*(1), 124–141.

Soliz, A. (2018). The effects of the expansion of for-profit colleges on student enrollments and outcomes at community colleges. *Educational Evaluation and Policy Analysis, 40*(4), 631–652. doi:10.3102/0162373718795053

KEY TERMS AND DEFINITIONS

Balance Wheel Model: Theory that argues that when the economy is good, state legislatures will increase monies for higher education at a faster rate than other government services. The reverse is also true, when states face an economic downturn, they are more likely to decrease funding to higher education at a faster rate than other budget categories.

CARES Act (2020): A $2.2 trillion economic stimulus bill passed by Congress in response to the economic impact of the COVID-19 pandemic.

Digital Divide: Disparities in Internet usage, skills, and access based on factors including race, income, and the rural/urban divide.

Digital "Homework Gap": Disparities in Internet access based on factors including race, income, and the rural/urban divide that result in students having difficulty completing their homework and keeping up with classes.

Higher Education Act of 1965: Federal act passed during the Johnson Administration as part of the Great Society Program meant to help more Americans obtain a college degree.

Human Capital Theory: An economic theory that argues that government investment in education can contribute to economic growth as well as help reduce inequalities based on income and race.

Servicemen's Readjustment Act (1944): Federal act passed in 1944 providing returning soldiers with funds for education and training, housing, and unemployment insurance.

Section 3
Post–Pandemic Education in Resource Constrained–Environments

Chapter 6

Transition to Blended Learning in a Limited Resource Setting:
Administrators' and Teachers' Perceptions

Goutam Roy

ⓘ https://orcid.org/0000-0001-7355-044X
University of Rajshahi, Bangladesh

Md. Minhazul Abdin
University of Rajshahi, Bangladesh

ABSTRACT

From the online learning experiences during the COVID-19 pandemic, the higher educational institutions of Bangladesh are considering integrating online education into traditional face-to-face learning. Research showed several challenges in implementing blended learning strategies, including having limited resources. This chapter explores how the administrators and teachers at the higher education institutes of Bangladesh could start blended learning with limited resources. The administrators and teachers of two universities in Bangladesh, who were directly involved in the decision-making process, were interviewed. The findings showed that while the administrators and teachers were willing to start blended learning, there were several challenges due to the limited resources aligned with the problems of online education. Administrators and teachers considered blended education as a way to respond to an education disruption caused by emergencies such as natural disasters, political unrest, and pandemics. This chapter provides some recommendations.

INTRODUCTION

In recent years, technology has made blended education more manageable and accessible. The advancement of technology over the past few decades has been rapid (El-Ghalayini & El-Khalili, 2011); therefore, the technological explosion affects daily life activities in several ways. However, technology has also had a more significant impact on education. Across the world, educational institutions have more access to

DOI: 10.4018/978-1-6684-5934-8.ch006

Copyright © 2023, IGI Global. Copying or distributing in print or electronic forms without written permission of IGI Global is prohibited.

technology leading to a shift toward integrating it into education (Alijani et al., 2014; Roy et al., 2021). Due to more accessibility of technology, the transition from traditional learning to online and blended learning has accelerated.

In most cases, traditional learning refers to the teaching and learning process completed in real-time in both teacher and student presence in a specific infrastructure (Nortvig et al., 2018). Online learning refers to the teaching-learning process using various online or technological tools where the location of the teacher-students and time of the day will be flexible (Jnr et al., 2019; Nortvig et al., 2018; Senn, 2008). In addition, online learning provides flexibility to both the teacher and the student and creates a self-learning environment for the student.

Although students are very interested in various teaching methods of online learning, there are several challenges to online learning (Allen et al., 2007). Teaching-learning activities like field work, group collaboration and observations are better conducted directly in the classroom. Besides, students who are not skilled in technology may face problems in online learning (Senn, 2008). Such challenges are observed for the teachers too. Therefore, to take advantage of traditional face-to-face and online learning, many teachers have incorporated both simultaneously (Woodworth & Applin, 2007). Combining online and blended learning has significantly reduced traditional face-to-face learning time (Garrison & Vaughan, 2012).

Blended learning refers to the combination of traditional face-to-face and online learning (Alijani et al., 2014; El-Ghalayini & El-Khalili, 2011; Nortvig et al., 2018; Wong et al., 2014;). Blended learning is also expected to improve students' communication, information literacy, creativity, collaboration skills, and ability to use digital technologies (Zurita et al., 2015).

Blended learning has several advantages. It develops various skills among students, increases their interest and satisfaction in learning, and provides opportunities for peer learning (Cleveland-Innes & Wilton, 2018). Learning activities incorporating 21st Century skills with blended learning may also provide meaningful education since learners can integrate new information with their existing knowledge and ideas (Zurita et al., 2015). Several studies showed that students prefer blended learning for its easy access to teaching-learning resources, efficient and faster contact with instructors, and capacity to pay attention in class (Szadziewska & Kujawski, 2017). Blended learning also gives students flexibility in learning and accelerates learning outcomes. It also develops various skills for students to use resources effectively (Poon, 2013). Similar to this, blended learning can engage students in building and applying their knowledge in real-life situations (Smyth et al., 2012). It is also stated that blended learning strengthens the connection between student participation and experience in learning (Ghazal et al., 2018).

Education is considered as a process of acquiring and imparting knowledge through teaching and learning. Blended learning means imparting and gaining knowledge through traditional face-to-face and online methods. This learning system emphasises many aspects and ways of learning and teaching. Blended learning has become an umbrella term (Hrastinski, 2019). Additionally, it was stated that blended learning had evolved a variety of concepts and approaches, including various pedagogical theories, teaching strategies, technological advancements and real-time duties (Driscoll, 2002). However, these mixes do not accord with the most popular definitions of blended learning.

Although there are many advantages, it may be challenging for administrators and teachers to transition to blended education, particularly in a low-resource setting. The Bangladeshi universities faced various challenges in running online teaching-learning activities during COVID-19 due to the lack of preparedness and experience and shortage of resources (Roy et al., 2021). As one of the features of blended learning is online learning activities, therefore, to succeed in blended learning activities, there must be adequate technological, human, and logistical resources. There is also a challenge in implementing blended learning in higher education institutions which has limited resources, such as Bangladesh. Particularly, institutions are facing various challenges in developing resources to implement blended learning successfully (Akçayır & Akçayır, 2018). They are facing challenges such as online technology adoption and its maintenance costs and acquiring appropriate modern technology for educational programs. Brown (2016) mentioned that institutions are facing challenges in integrating new technologies that are compatible and flexible with existing technologies. Limitations of appropriate infrastructure and technology cause difficulties for successful blended learning implementation. Considering limited resource settings as potential challenges towards blended learning implementation, this article discussed the administrators' and teachers' perceptions of transition to blended learning considering the context of Bangladesh.

BLENDED LEARNING

The phrase 'blended learning' is used often; however, it has several definitions. There is confusion about what it truly means (Oliver & Trigwell, 2005). In most cases, blended learning combines online and face-to-face instruction (Boelens et al., 2015; Garrison & Vaughan, 2012; Graham, 2013). Though blended learning refers to the combination of traditional face-to-face and online learning, its meaning has gradually been transformed into a broader aspect of blended learning. Lalima and Dangwal (2017) define blended learning as combining online and traditional learning and promoting collaborative and informal learning. According to Haijian et al. (2011), blended learning combines the best parts of conventional and online learning, making teaching more effective by integrating different learning theories. Picciano (2006) stated that blended learning is a structured and pedagogically valuable method of instruction that combines face-to-face learning with online learning.

According to Oliver and Trigwell (2005), blended learning is not well-defined and inappropriately used in most situations. Previously, blended learning was used to describe classroom training and e-learning activities (Graham, 2013). Nowadays, this learning strategy is getting recognition as a flexible, hybrid or integrated approach (Garrison & Kanuka, 2004; Moskal et al., 2013). Some researchers and academics identified a specific percentage for face-to-face and online learning. For instance, Jnr et al. (2019) opined that there should be 30 per cent traditional learning and 70 per cent online interaction while adopting blended learning. However, Owston et al. (2018) argued that 80 per cent of online and 20 per cent of face-to-face learning are enough to make blended learning successful.

Although there is no set definition for blended learning, several definitions are commonly used in scientific publications (Hrastinski, 2019). One of those given by Graham (2006): "blended learning systems combine face-to-face instruction with computer-mediated instruction" (p. 5). Similarly, Garrison and Kanuka (2004) stated: "the thoughtful integration of classroom face-to-face learning experiences with online learning experiences" (p. 96).

Challenges of Blended Learning

The challenges of online learning and the same of blended learning are interconnected. Some common challenges of online learning are lack of necessary infrastructure, lack of preparation of institutions, lack of resources, and lack of technology, particularly at the rural level (Dubey & Pandey, 2020). These challenges also apply to blended learning as well. While adopting blended learning, several challenges have been identified, such as: "lack of policy; lack of faculty support, lack of technological and computer skills; large class sizes; and inadequate technological resources" (Tshabalala et al., 2014, p. 108). Besides, the lack of teachers and staff training on technology is a common challenge in online and blended education (Tshabalala et al., 2014).

There are several differences between the challenges of online learning and the challenges of blended learning. In a proper online learning environment, students spend much time on screens (Domingues-Montanari, 2017). As a result, the motivation and enthusiasm of the students toward online education decreases, which leads the students to drop out (Aragon & Johnson, 2004). On the contrary, blended learning combines traditional and online learning, reducing screen time (Garrison & Vaughan, 2012). As a result, students' interest and satisfaction in blended learning have increased, and it has given them opportunities for peer learning (Cleveland-Innes & Wilton, 2018). It has also been observed that the contact or interaction between students and teachers decreased due to online classes for a long time (Islam & Habib, 2022).

One of the challenges of online learning is that many poor students cannot afford online education tools (Adedoyin & Soykan, 2020); however, blended learning provides face-to-face opportunities. That is why the challenge is less faced in the blended learning environment. In addition, there is an opportunity to attend teaching-learning activities directly, such as field work, group collaboration and observations (Senn, 2008).

Students have to endure various financial, social and emotional pressures due to being outside the regular schooling schedule in online education (Suneeth et al., 2021). In contrast, blended learning allows educational activities to occur outside the conventional classroom setting and makes learning materials accessible for students from anywhere and at any time to accomplish their academic goals (Kibby, 2007). It is believed that students who attend online classes for a long time get tired and lose focus in class (Panday, 2020). Learners have the opportunity to learn independently in a blended learning environment. Blended learning also enables students to learn autonomously (Glazer, 2012; Linder, 2016). Therefore, considering the effectiveness of blended learning, various researchers have agreed that blended learning might be more effective than traditional learning or online learning (Smith & Hill, 2019).

The transition to blended learning is increasing around the world. As a result, developing countries face various challenges (Ahmed, 2013). Such common challenges in implementing blended and online learning are also observed in Bangladesh. Al-Amin et al. (2021) identified those such as lack of technical resources, poor internet connection, high cost and psychological factors.

The Recent Development of Blended Learning in Higher Education

Higher education has embraced blended learning over the past decade, creating a sense of transformation in the education sector (Alammary et al., 2014). Blended learning has revolutionised higher education and provided students with meaningful learning experiences (Garrison & Kanuka, 2004). For these reasons, higher education institutions (HEIs) are adopting blended learning.

Blended learning is widely recognised as a powerful pedagogical technique (Kenney & Newcombe, 2011). To researchers, blended learning is considered a new traditional model in education (Ross & Gage, 2006) or new normal in course delivery (Norberg et al., 2011). Graham (2013) acknowledged that "many institutions of higher education that are in the awareness/exploration stage would like to transition to adoption/early implementation" (p. 11). Graham (2013) also suggested exploring this transformation in future.

The digitalisation of society has changed employee expectations for skill development throughout their employment (OECD, 2019). So, there is increasing pressure on higher education institutions to conduct technology-based education to keep pace with the times and meet the diverse academic needs of students. That is why the HEIs are beginning to acknowledge that blended learning may improve the quality of teaching and learning. Because of this, several institutions have included blended learning initiatives to improve quality (Lim, 2019). HEIs are incorporating blended learning into the teaching-learning process to increase student engagement and make learning more effective (Kaleta et al., 2007; Garnham & Kaleta, 2002; Vaughan, 2007).

One of the reasons higher education institutions are interested in blended learning is that it increases access to the learning environment and minimises the educational expenditures of the institution. The most significant reason is that higher education institutions implement blended learning for their pedagogical improvement (Graham, 2006). An advantage of blended learning is that students have expressed a satisfactory attitude towards it, and there is control over learning (Garnham & Kaleta, 2002; Vaughan, 2007;). Another advantage is that many students can be accumulated simultaneously (Kizi & Ferdinantovna, 2022). Blended learning facilitates the accessibility of students at the higher education level and provides accessibility for institutions to students (Piper, 2010; Vaughan, 2007). In addition, blended learning reduces the teacher's lecturing time in the classroom and provides more time for the teacher to facilitate the students' various learning problems, skills, and creative thinking. (Kizi & Ferdinantovna, 2022).

According to Carbonell et al. (2013), blended learning is a practical approach for academic staff as it allows flexibility in their work. In this case, the face-to-face part creates opportunities to reflect pedagogically and develop various skills. However, teachers are adopting the blended learning method due to the increased flexibility and access to course resources (Graham, 2013). It also minimises the logistical cost of the institution while reducing the time spent in the classroom for both the teachers and students (Poon, 2012). It is also argued that conventional education cannot address the individual needs of every student due to an improper teacher-student ratio (Masadeh, 2021). Due to its reliance on the yearly assessment, the conventional education system cannot address the difficulties of irregular students (Lalima & Dangwal, 2017), which established the need for blended learning.

Kizi and Ferdinantovna (2022) added that blended learning was vital in continuing education programs during the Covid-19 pandemic. During the COVID era, educational institutions had to consider alternatives to traditional teaching-learning. As a result, many countries globally have chosen blended learning as an option (Masadeh, 2021). Many universities quickly adopted blended learning as it was challenging to conduct education in a face-to-face learning environment during Covid-19 (Bryson & Andres, 2020). Therefore, it can be said that blended learning has brought a significant change in the modern education system, particularly to the HEIs.

Blended Learning in Bangladesh

Online education is not widespread in Bangladesh; however, a growing interest in distance education since the 1990s has been observed. Since its establishment in 1992, Bangladesh Open University has provided various distance education programs through e-books, radio, television, and the Internet. Bangladesh Open University can be considered one of the pioneers of e-learning in Bangladesh (Chowdhury

Transition to Blended Learning in a Limited Resource Setting

& Behak, 2022). According to Trines (2019), the Open University is essential in providing education to previously underserved rural people. However, while many universities worldwide are offering Massively Open Online Courses (MOOCS) courses, Bangladesh is still behind in this regard (Roy, 2018; Sohail, 2018). This situation changed during the COVID-19 pandemic. The pandemic has brought significant changes to the higher education system in Bangladesh and introducing both MOOCs and blended learning can be an appropriate solution to continue teaching-learning activities, particularly in an emergency.

Like various educational institutions worldwide, all educational institutions in Bangladesh were closed due to the COVID-19 pandemic. The universities were closed from March 2020, and the students' academic life was at stake (Islam & Habib, 2022). In this situation, online education was considered the most appropriate approach for continuing education (Shahriar et al., 2021). Considering these aspects, the University Grants Commission of Bangladesh (UGC) has instructed all universities to conduct online teaching-learning activities (The Daily Star, 2020a; The Financial Express, 2020). Many universities, particularly private ones, have responded to the UGC's directives and started online education programs (Roy et al., 2021; The Daily Star, 2020b). After the response to online education, universities, especially private universities, shifted all their academic activities like classes, exams, results, and admissions online (Abdullah, 2020; The Daily Star, 2020a). The UGC also published some guidelines on May 07, 2020 (Abdullah, 2020). The public universities started their online learning activities at a later period.

In a survey conducted during the COVID-19 period, Islam et al. (2020) demonstrated that 40 per cent of students attended online classes, and nearly 50 per cent of students could not participate due to inadequate devices. Although many students have overcome the device crisis, they have struggled to afford high-priced internet packages. Due to the poor Internet system and disruption of electricity in most rural areas of Bangladesh, many measures have not been effective (Tithi, 2021). Based on the experiences during the COVID-19 pandemic, the UGC believes blended learning could be a good option for the future. Therefore, they provide specific guidelines for implementing blended learning to meet future challenges and improve the learning process at the higher education level. To make blended learning more accessible and practical, the UGC formulated the Blended Learning Policy, which was approved on February 27, 2022 (The Financial Express, 2022). It is expected that the universities of Bangladesh will consider this guideline and start blended learning activities.

Although Bangladesh is progressing well in terms of prosperity and development (World Bank, 2022), education in Bangladesh lags for various reasons (Aka, 2021; Banu et al., 2018; Nath et al., 2014). Several times, education has been disrupted due to political unrest and natural calamities. The higher education institutions in Bangladesh are sometimes closed due to student politics (Zaman, 2014). In addition, Bangladesh is a country prone to natural disasters. Every year, river bursts, floods, cyclones, and tidal waves are common occurrences, and people's lives are affected due to these (Sandulache, 2019). These disasters also impact education. For example, disasters disrupt educational programs, damage school infrastructure, and displace students and families (Quayyum & Chowdhury, 2016). Educational institutions were also closed due to calamities at various times. Mainly Students bear the suffering of this (The Daily Star, 2022b). Bangladesh had no standard guidelines to keep the education system functioning in various emergencies (Quayyum & Chowdhury, 2016).

Blended learning activities can be an appropriate solution to avert the session lag created in the post-COVID era and reduce financial losses in the education sector (Chowdhury & Behak, 2022). There is no substitute for blended learning to advance the country technologically and continue education during emergencies. In realising this, the Ministry of Education, Bangladesh, has taken several initiatives to incorporate blended learning strategies in both secondary and higher education levels. While a guideline for blended learning has already come out for the HEIs of Bangladesh, the ministry has been working on a specific framework for secondary education too. However, as already discussed, educational institutions lack adequate resources; therefore, it is a matter of investigation to understand how the administrators and teachers could run their teaching-learning activities in limited resource settings. This book chapter is going to explore this based on the perception of the administrators and teachers of two HEIs.

METHODOLOGY

This book chapter is written from a larger project dataset in which the main issues of the investigation were the opportunities and challenges of blended learning in the context of the Bangladeshi HEIs. While the main study considered both quantitative and qualitative approaches to data collection, the findings of this book chapter are taken from the qualitative part only. Two universities, a public and a private, situated in north Bangladesh were considered for data collection. From each university, two departments from the Social Science faculty were sampled purposively. From each department, two senior teachers who are also part of the administration process of their respective departments were interviewed. Therefore, a total of eight teachers were the sample of this study. On the other hand, four administrators from each university, such as Vice-Chancellor or Pro-Vice Chancellors, Deans of the Social Science Faculty, Institutional Quality Assurance Cell (IQAC) directors and Information and Communication Technology (ICT) directors, were interviewed. They were purposively selected as they took the policy-level decisions for their respective universities. All the interviewed teachers and administrators, except a teacher, had a PhD in their respective field and had at least ten years of teaching experience. Among them, all were male except one, and all teachers and administrators actively contributed to the decision-making process for their respective departments and universities. The entire study protocol was reviewed and approved by the Research Proposal Evaluation Committee of the Institute of Education and Research, University of Rajshahi, Rajshahi, Bangladesh.

Participant-specific semi-structured interview guidelines were used for the interview sessions. Both authors explained the objective of the study project to the participants. Upon written consent from the participants, the interviews were started and recorded using an audio recorder. The average duration of the interview sessions was 50 minutes, ranging from 45 to one hour. The recorded interviews were transcribed, and inductive thematic analysis was employed to get the themes from the participants' responses. The authors carefully read all the responses, and coding was employed for a similar group of responses. The raw data were checked several times to ensure the correctness, and both the authors made the codes independently and then, the codes were compared, discussed and then finalised. The codes were categorised and clustered based on the potential connection and possibility of integration (Cohen et al., 2019). The sub-themes and themes were created during the second round of analysis. During this analysis, data reduction, coding expression/term, and verification of conclusions were continued simultaneously until the conclusions were drawn.

Findings

From the responses, five themes have been identified: motivation, preparedness, resources, implementations and challenges.

Motivation

All the administrators and teachers of both public and private universities showed a positive attitude towards implementing blended learning in their universities. They thought blended learning activities must be implemented to keep pace with the digital transition. The participants, in their discussions, also highlighted the effective use of blended learning activities to support education programs, particularly in emergency situations. Administrators felt that implementing blended learning could allow teachers flexibility in education programs. This learning strategy would give teachers more time to spend on productive work. To keep up with the changing world, the university administrators showed their interest in implementing a blended learning program in their respective universities as soon as possible. They also thought that it had been possible to prevent cost and time wastage of various programs, such as academic meetings, syndicate meetings, etc. Administrations strongly believe that blended operations would bring these benefits if implemented. The vice-chancellor of the private university said,

To survive the fourth industrial revolution, we must get used to technology now, and blended learning will play a significant role in forming this habit. We must run both virtual and physical platforms simultaneously. We have realised the benefits of keeping them running simultaneously. For example, during the Covid period, we are doing our various meetings online. The time and the amount of financial cost for each session have been minimised, and at the same time, we can arrange multiple discussions on the same day, where the attendance level is also the same. Moreover, various activities are being arranged online frequently. If you compare the activities to the previous period, you will see that the ratio has increased significantly, and the students also enjoy it very much. That's why I am motivated to start blended learning activities.

Similarly, the pro-vice chancellor of the public university said,

First of all, we have to be motivated. If the normal situation does not prevail, we must take some process to keep the university's reading and learning process normal. We want the students, teachers, and staff of the university to know where their difficulties are and where their complications are. Let us not only think of the issues in the form of problems but also give them in the form of suggestions and think about how to solve them. In this way, they can help the administration and also help the faculty and department. Then I believe our university will be better for any emergency. The university will not lag. We are interested in starting blended learning.

Teachers also thought that online teaching-learning activities during the COVID-19 pandemic created a scope to integrate online modalities, and blended learning could be considered the best approach to continue online activities. The teachers thought that their activities during COVID-19 had already created a base which would be helpful to start blended learning activities. All the teachers opined that, except for some practical or lab-based activities, a part of the syllabus could be taught online, and they showed their interest in being a part of this. Teachers also mentioned that as they already provided online teaching with low resources, therefore, low resources might not be a big challenge for them. A teacher at the public university said,

Through blended learning, we teachers and students can keep pace with the digital transition. I am definitely interested in joining the blended learning program. What I understand is that some master's students want to enter the job. Many of them told me that if there were online classes, they could have attended the classes besides doing the job in Dhaka. I think in some cases, but not always, in higher education, we should have this opportunity, especially at the master's level. I would feel comfortable if such a program is kept in the master's field.

Preparedness

While the administrators were motivated to start blended learning in their universities, all the administrators confessed that they were not fully prepared for blended learning. They also mentioned three types of preparedness needed to be ensured: teachers' capacity development, physical facility and resources, policy and guidelines. The public university administrators expressed that, along with the teachers and students, administrators also needed to be prepared for implementing blended learning. A customised short training considering the context of low resources could be helpful for them. They expected such an initiative from the UGC. Public university administrators mentioned that implementing blended learning at the university level could be possible if there was a transformation of the existing policies and infrastructure of the university, adequate resource support, and a positive attitude from all regarding blended learning. They thought except for the resource support, the other things were in favour of them. On the other hand, the private university administrators thought that though they lacked readiness, however, this could not create any problem as they could cope with the situation rapidly. An administrator of the private university mentioned that during COVID-19, they provided training not only to the teachers and students but also to the officials; therefore, he believed that their university had already started working to prepare all personnel. He thought that limited resources would not be a major problem to begin with because they were in practice, and they continued the online activities even after starting face-to-face activities after the lockdown. An administrator of the private university said,

At the beginning of COVID, we purchased Microsoft Teams software to switch to online learning. They gave us training in software management. Initially, our teachers and students faced problems, but later they continued teaching-learning activities smoothly. Our IT department has appointed a new workforce to make online teaching-learning more effective and smoother during Covid. An experienced director has also been appointed.

Similarly, the public university teachers thought that as they had some experiences with online education during the COVID-19 pandemic using minimal resources, it would not be challenging to start blended learning using the same resources. Similar findings were found from the responses of the private university teachers. They also thought that they could begin blended learning activities as they were familiar with the technological issues; however, they expected some specific training concerning blended learning pedagogy to make the effort successful. Limited resources might not be a problem, according to them, as they knew how to overcome the problems. Therefore, while there was a lack in terms of preparedness, both the teachers and administrator thought that this problem could be fixed easily, and they were very enthusiastic about starting blended learning activities.

Resources

According to the public university administrators, they already had a specific software for the online class provided by the UGC; however, they needed to incorporate a customised learning management system. The ICT director of the public university mentioned that resources were not only related to technological issues but financial and policy-related issues needed to be addressed. According to him, technological problems could be solved quickly; however, it was necessary to increase other resources. An administrator of a public university said,

We have to change the complete structure of our university to implement blended learning. We have already informed the UGC. We have also planned to increase our allocation for this structural change. We have already provided a plan and budget to bring the university's 11 residential halls and academic buildings under a sustainable internet system. However, I do not think starting blended learning activities within the existing resources would be difficult. At least we can start.

The status of the private university was ahead, according to the responses of the private university administrators. They mentioned that the classrooms of each department were digitally equipped. They just needed to fix some problems such as continuous electricity and the speed of internet connections.

Teachers of both public and private universities mentioned that they expected some resources from the administrators; however, existing resources could be used to start a blended learning activity. Teachers of both types of universities mentioned that some of their ICT equipment had a low capacity to be upgraded. Without these, teaching-learning activities might be hampered. For instance, some computers had low configuration, and some software needed more resources. They demanded updated ICT equipment. A teacher at the private university said, "To start the blended learning, I do not think the university has a major problem in terms of equipment. Our administrators repeatedly said that if any more equipment is needed, the university will provide it." Similarly, a teacher at the public university mentioned,

I think that at some point in the future, we will have to go to blended learning. Many of our students in developed countries still work and study on their own. Many teachers are busy with academic or personal matters. Also, when his family is sick or if he stays at home when he is sick, I think there should be an opportunity for blended learning. At this stage, we can start using the existing resources. However, we have to keep a certain percentage for blended learning. For example, we can keep 30 per cent online and the remaining 70 per cent offline.

Implementation

The public university administrators informed that they had already started some processes related to online education that would also be helpful in starting the blended learning activities. According to them, they started spending more budget to improve the ICT-related infrastructure. For instance, they started working to ensure stable and high-speed internet in all residence halls so students could participate in online activities from their residences. Besides, the administrators informed that they had the plan to build at least one smart classroom for each department so that blended learning activities could be started; however, this could take some more time. The pro-vice-chancellor of the public university informed that they would review the blended learning guideline made by UGC and were thinking of introducing specific software for teaching and assessment purposes. For that, they also submitted their additional needs to the UGC. According to the public university administrators, this process would start soon; therefore, they were on the right way to implementing blended learning. An administrator of the public university commented,

As you know, we have already instructed all teachers to engage students online to some extent in addition to offline activities. We have seen the Blended Learning Policy formed by the UGC. We are reviewing it. We will design the master's level in a blinded manner so that students can work alongside their studies.

The administrators of the private university echoed the same. The vice-chancellor of the private university informed that, as a start, they were thinking of starting blended learning activities for the master's students. After gaining experience, they would extend it to both undergraduate and postgraduate students. "Not only the teaching-learning activities, but we are also working for online seminars, symposiums, and conferences which will help us to attain competence to ensure an effective blended learning environment", according to the vice-chancellor of the private university.

Public university teachers thought starting blended learning activities at this moment was possible despite some challenges. They believed that the COVID period familiarised them with online activities with low resources. Teachers recommended specifying a certain percentage of online-offline in blended learning activities, which would increase over time. The same findings were found in the responses of private university teachers. They also focused on changing the mindset of the teachers and students before starting the implementation process. According to them, the strengths of blended learning needed to be discussed with the students, which could make the implementation process more manageable. A teacher at the public university said,

I do not think there will be many obstacles from university teachers in implementing blended learning. I think blended learning can be entirely successful only if the existing obstacles are overcome. For example, high-speed internet is very important to run blended learning properly. I saw a few days ago that the mobile phone companies in Bangladesh could not provide real 4G though 70%-80% of internet users use mobile internet. Broadband internet is still costly. We can start blended learning now; however, the problems need to be addressed.

Challenges

The administrators and teachers also discussed the challenges, and they identified a number of challenges which could be fixed easily. According to them, some challenges could be fixed by themselves, while others would be overcome over the period. The public university administrators mentioned that they had to formulate a plan aligned with blended learning and then make a budget accordingly. This would not be a difficult task, according to them. According to the administrators, the main challenges had the compatible device for the students and the cost and speed of internet connection. Administrators informed that they were working to fix this problem. They already started to provide short loans to the students so they could buy necessary devices; however, they expected an initiative from the UGC and Ministry of Education for issues related to the internet. A dean of the public university said:

The academic council has prepared and passed a policy regarding the online examination. We consulted with our teachers before forming this policy. The government is already working on implementing blended learning. The government has arranged low-interest loans for students. Besides, they should consider providing affordable internet packages by contracting with telecom companies. So, I think the problems are going to be solved soon.

An administrator of the public university proposed that we could launch blended education on a small scale and then gradually extend it. According to him, this might be the best solution at this moment. He also proposed that universities could take the assignments online, and once the students got habituated, the entire assessment system could be online. One of the administrators from the private university proposed that extending the computer lab period might be a solution. Students with no device could use the computer lab for their studies. Besides, gradually increasing the number of computers with internet connection each year could be another solution, according to the administrators of both public and private universities. The vice-chancellor of the private university said, "Many students do not have devices. I have spoken to the board of trustees and requested them to provide laptops from the university. They have also agreed."

Teachers thought differently. According to them, the technological capability of the teachers and students was the major challenge. However, they also thought that students could easily overcome this challenge as they were young and could learn quickly. This problem could be seen among some senior teachers unfamiliar with the technological updates. They also thought this challenge could be overcome by engaging the senior teachers in offline activities while the junior teachers could work on the online modalities. Another challenge raised by the teachers was related to pedagogy. According to them, teaching online was different from face-to-face teaching. With the teachers' existing knowledge, blended learning activities could be started; however, eventually, all the teachers needed to be trained in line with the pedagogy related to ICT and education.

DISCUSSION

Higher education is currently transitioning towards a blended alternative to traditional learning (Alammary et al., 2014; Garrison & Kanuka, 2004). Universities in Bangladesh have addressed the disruptions caused by the COVID-19 pandemic through online learning. This chapter examined the perceptions and thoughts of administrators and teachers at Bangladeshi universities regarding the transition to blended education in a limited resources setting. Study results indicate that, despite limited resources, teachers perceived blended learning as positive.

During the COVID-19 pandemic, public university teachers initiated online teaching-learning programs on their own initiative. Many teachers were newly introduced to online teaching-learning without training or prior experience; however, they found online learning activities engage students, motivating them to blended learning (Roy et al., 2021). It was understood that teachers' previous experience using technology has a significant role in their perception of blended learning (Dečman, 2015; Saleem et al., 2016). On the other hand, since COVID, there have been instructions to start online classes at private universities. Although many private university teachers did not have prior technology expertise, they became proficient through training provided by their IT department. Their skills and experience in using technology helped to develop a positive attitude toward blended learning (Dečman, 2015; Kocaleva et al., 2014). The public university teachers highlighted the challenge of insufficient access to resources. In contrast, private university teachers felt that those were sufficient to conduct online teaching and learning activities during the COVID-19 period. Both are interested in starting with the existing resources and are willing to take on the challenges.

It has emerged that the teachers of both public and private universities have a positive attitude towards the transition to blended education. This is similar to several studies (Aji et al., 2020; Rasmitadila et al., 2020). They also acknowledged the necessity of blended learning to respond to education programs in emergencies. Teachers want blended learning to continue post-Covid since it provides flexibility to teachers. Private university teachers consider blended learning beneficial in increasing their understanding. They have acquired knowledge of various educational and online tools during COVID. It is believed that blended learning will lead to greater prosperity for them. Besides, the blended learning program will also allow students to engage in service along with their studies. Teachers at both universities emphasise acquiring the digital skills of the students through blended learning (Chowdhury & Behak, 2022).

Surprisingly, teachers from both public and private universities agree that implementing blended learning in universities is possible. According to teachers, government and university authority support play an essential role in successful blended learning implementation. According to the teachers, technological and pedagogical issues must be worked on to implement blended learning effectively. It is observed that public university teachers were able to take classes online but could not take any exams. Therefore, they emphasised the importance of flexibility in evaluation to implement blended education successfully. Besides, they suggested sharing all course materials with students, along with online course records, so that if a student encounters a problem, they can resolve it independently, which is vital in designing blended learning. On the other hand, teachers in private universities emphasise customisation in offline academic activities like in-courses, presentations, group work, theoretical discussions, etc. Besides, they showed interest in conducting various online meetings-seminars, symposiums, and conferences, which helped them connect with the students. Educators agree in both public and private universities that blended learning will occur by taking some academic activities offline and remaining online simultaneously. Besides, teachers in public and private universities highlighted extracurricular activities and online soft skill development for students.

Like other countries, public university teachers feel that teacher inefficiency in online teaching-learning is a big challenge in implementing blended education (Bower et al., 2015; Brown, 2016; Hung & Chou, 2015). In response to this challenge, teachers' training in acquiring ICT skills is necessary (Al-Ayed & Al-Tit, 2021). The teachers also reported that they should be provided training by a pedagogical expert on online teaching-learning. Besides, the teachers think that the government and the administration should come forward to eliminate the problems related to devices and the internet for rural students. It is important to note that even though private university administrators have no previous experience, they have received training in a short time. Furthermore, later training has been arranged for all levels of staff and employees of the university. It is easily understood that private universities can switch to online learning faster than public universities. Private university administrators consider their activities successful as they have enriched themselves with sufficient resources to run blended learning activities further. However, in the case of the public university, there is a kind of barrier or setback of financial resources. Public universities have to depend on government or UGC allocations for financial matters.

Interestingly, public and private university administrators have realised the importance of blended learning. They express interest in adopting blended learning to cope with the digital transition that is taking place in higher education in today's world (Al-Ayed & Al-Tit, 2021; Mahmood et al., 2022).

Transition to Blended Learning in a Limited Resource Setting

Besides, the administrators of both universities mentioned blended learning to deal with the education crisis in emergencies. Similarly, private university administrators expressed interest in blended learning implementation to avoid wasting working hours in crisis moments. According to private university administrators, transitioning to blended learning will minimise the cost of their various academic activities like meetings, seminars, etc. On the other hand, administrators from public universities emphasise that blended learning will increase flexibility in teachers' work (King & Arnold, 2012). Teachers can also take classes even if they have a meeting or other work. In addition, the transition to blended learning will encourage teachers to spend time on more productive activities.

There are various resource barriers to implementing blended learning in the public university, including infrastructural challenges, excessive student numbers, lack of workforce, and lack of technology similar to other countries (Tshabalala et al., 2014). Administrators believe that implementing blended learning in the university is possible if these barriers can be overcome. The university administration has announced plans and activities to eliminate these barriers and implement blended learning. The university administration will make infrastructural changes to implement blended learning in the university. They have already informed the UGC as well. They also planned to set up one digital classroom in each department of the university. On the other hand, the private university has digital classrooms and plans to digitise their new campus fully. Apart from this, the administration has instructed the teachers to carry out academic activities online and offline to implement blended learning. The university plans to design the master's courses on a blended basis in the future so that students can engage in work while studying. In addition, both public and private university administrators have called for reforming existing policies to implement blended learning. The administrators from both universities have expected the government's support in this regard. While private universities talked about providing devices to students, public universities have emphasised government loan assistance for students. In the transition to blended learning, administrators of both private and public universities are concerned about limited resources. Everyone agreed that a blended learning strategy in higher education should be strengthened with better help.

RECOMMENDATIONS

Based on the findings and discussions above, it can be concluded that university administrators and teachers in Bangladesh support the transition to blended learning. They all consider blended learning as a path to rebuild higher education in the post-Covid era and a way to survive in the digital technology transition. To ensure a proper blended learning environment in the Bangladeshi HEIs, four specific recommendations are provided:

1. Based on the blended learning guideline by the UGC, all universities should produce university-specific policies and guidelines to start blended learning activities considering their particular context, university philosophy and existing resources. This will help the universities to understand their own capacity and resources as well, and therefore, making a realistic plan would be possible.
2. As limited resource is evident, universities should make short-term and long-term realistic plans to overcome the problems. This plan should also contain the teachers' and students' preparedness that includes necessary training for both groups. Besides, the departmental curriculum should be revised

in line with the blended learning policies and guidelines. The departments and the Institutional Quality Assurance Cell could work jointly to prepare such a plan.

3. Instead of starting blended learning activities university-wide, universities could start an experimental project on a department or two. Based on the experience of this pilot project, universities should extend this learning approach to other departments.

4. A lack of research on blended learning considering the context of HEIs in Bangladesh is evident. Therefore, conducting necessary research projects on various components of blended learning is recommended, eventually supporting the universities in the implementation process.

CONCLUSION

Through blended learning, just as teachers get flexibility in their work, flexibility will also come in higher education administrative management. This could enable all of them to work more productively. Administrators and teachers recommend expanding blended education beyond just teaching-learning activities. All the administrators and teachers identified blended education as a practical approach, particularly in emergent situations. Learning through the blended approach could prevent waste of time, and it can be expected that teachers and students will be more efficient and skilled in technology. Besides, blended learning could make the teachers and students more productive and create opportunities to work alongside teaching and studying.

ACKNOWLEDGMENT

The authors would like to thank the Institute of Education and Research, University of Rajshahi, Rajshahi, Bangladesh, for allocating funds for the primary research project. This book chapter is an output of this project. The authors also like to thank Associate Professor Dr. Happy Kumar Das, Institute of Education and Research, University of Rajshahi, Rajshahi, Bangladesh, for reading the first draft and for his comments, feedback and suggestions.

REFERENCES

Abdullah, M. (2020, April 30). Dipu Moni: Private universities can conduct exams, admissions online. *Dhaka Tribune*. https://archive.dhakatribune.com/bangladesh/education/2020/04/30/dipu-moni-students-need-to-be-kept-engaged-to-prevent-depression

Adedoyin, O. B., & Soykan, E. (2020). Covid-19 pandemic and online learning: The challenges and opportunities. *Interactive Learning Environments*, 1–13. doi:10.1080/10494820.2020.1813180

Ahmed, S. M. Z. (2013). A survey of students' use of and satisfaction with university subscribed online resources in two specialised universities in a developing country. *Library Hi Tech News*, *30*(3), 6–8. doi:10.1108/LHTN-02-2013-0010

Aji, W. K., Ardin, H., & Arifin, M. A. (2020). Blended learning during pandemic CoronaVirus: Teachers' and students' perceptions. *IDEAS: Journal on English Language Teaching and Learning, Linguistics and Literature, 8*(2), 632–646. doi:10.24256/ideas.v8i2.1696

Aka, A. M. (2021, February 18). Time for a radical rethinking of our education system. *The Daily Star.* https://www.thedailystar.net/opinion/news/time-radical-rethinking-our-education-system-2046741

Akçayır, G., & Akçayır, M. (2018). The flipped classroom: A review of its advantages and challenges. *Computers & Education, 126*, 334–345. doi:10.1016/j.compedu.2018.07.021

Al-Amin, M., Zubayer, A. A., Deb, B., & Hasan, M. (2021). Status of tertiary level online class in Bangladesh: Students' response on preparedness, participation and classroom activities. *Heliyon, 7*(1), e05943. doi:10.1016/j.heliyon.2021.e05943 PMID:33506126

Al-Ayed, S. I., & Al-Tit, A. A. (2021). Factors affecting the adoption of blended learning strategy. *International Journal of Data and Network Science*, 267–274. doi:10.5267/j.ijdns.2021.6.007

Alammary, A., Sheard, J., & Carbone, A. (2014). Blended learning in higher education: Three different design approaches. *Australasian Journal of Educational Technology, 30*(4). Advance online publication. doi:10.14742/ajet.693

Alijani, G., Kwun, O., & Yu, Y. (2014). *Effectiveness of blended learning in KIPP New Orleans' Schools.* https://www.semanticscholar.org/paper/Effectiveness-of-Blended-Learning-in-KIPP-New-Alijani-Kwun/7b8b10d66fcb2184655106a16a8df23a46ac7cdf

Allen, I., Seaman, J., & Garrett, R. (2007). *Blending in: The extent and promise of blended education in the United States.* Sloan Consortium.

Aragon, S., & Johnson, E. (2004). *Factors influencing completion and non-completion of community college online courses.* https://www.learntechlib.org/primary/p/12019/

Banu, F. A. L., Roy, G., & Shafiq, S. (2018). Analysing bottlenecks to equal participation in primary education in Bangladesh: An equity perspective. In R. Chowdhury, M. Sarkar, F. Mojumdar, & R. M. Moninoor (Eds.), *Engaging in educational research: Revisiting policy and practice in Bangladesh* (pp. 39–64). Springer Singapore. doi:10.1007/978-981-13-0708-9_3

Boelens, R., Van Laer, S., De Wever, B., & Elen, J. (2015). *Blended learning in adult education: Towards a definition of blended learning.* https://biblio.ugent.be/publication/6905076/file/6905079.pdf

Bower, M., Dalgarno, B., Kennedy, G. E., Lee, M. J. W., & Kenney, J. (2015). Design and implementation factors in blended synchronous learning environments: Outcomes from a cross-case analysis. *Computers & Education, 86*, 1–17. doi:10.1016/j.compedu.2015.03.006

Brown, M. (2016). Blended instructional practice: A review of the empirical literature on instructors' adoption and use of online tools in face-to-face teaching. *The Internet and Higher Education, 31*, 1–10. Advance online publication. doi:10.1016/j.iheduc.2016.05.001

Bryson, J. R., & Andres, L. (2020). Covid-19 and rapid adoption and improvisation of online teaching: Curating resources for extensive versus intensive online learning experiences. *Journal of Geography in Higher Education, 44*(4), 608–623. doi:10.1080/03098265.2020.1807478

Carbonell, K. B., Dailey-Hebert, A., & Gijselaers, W. (2013). Unleashing the creative potential of faculty to create blended learning. *The Internet and Higher Education*, *18*, 29–37. doi:10.1016/j.iheduc.2012.10.004

Chowdhury, M. K., & Behak, F. B. (2022). Online higher education in Bangladesh during Covid-19: It is challenges and prospects. *Journal of Ultimate Research and Trends in Education*. https://www.semanticscholar.org/paper/Online-Higher-Education-in-Bangladesh-during-It-is-Chowdhury-Behak/ab48203efc4528ae39d3e4c97ca874cb27dd6fee

Cleveland-Innes, M., & Wilton, D. (2018). *Guide to blended learning*. Commonwealth of Learning (COL). https://oasis.col.org/handle/11599/3095

Cohen, L., Manion, L., & Morrison, K. (2011). *Research methods in education* (7th ed.). Routledge.

Dečman, M. (2015). Modeling the acceptance of e-learning in mandatory environments of higher education: The influence of previous education and gender. *Computers in Human Behavior*, *49*, 272–281. doi:10.1016/j.chb.2015.03.022

Domingues-Montanari, S. (2017). Clinical and psychological effects of excessive screen time on children. *Journal of Paediatrics and Child Health*, *53*(4), 333–338. doi:10.1111/jpc.13462 PMID:28168778

Driscoll, M. (2002). *Blended learning: Let's get beyond the hype*. IBM Global Services.http://www-07.ibm.com/services/pdf/blended_learning.pdf

Dubey, P., & Pandey, D. (2020). Distance learning in higher education during pandemic: Challenges and opportunities. *International Journal of Indian Psychology*, *8*(2), 43–46.

El-Ghalayini, H., & El-Khalili, N. (2011). An approach to designing and evaluating blended courses. *Education and Information Technologies*. Advance online publication. doi:10.100710639-011-9167-7

Garnham, C., & Kaleta, R. (2002). Introduction to hybrid courses. *Teaching with Technology Today*, *8*(6), 5. https://hccelearning.files.wordpress.com/2010/09/introduction-to-hybrid-course1.pdf

Garrison, D. R., & Kanuka, H. (2004). Blended learning: Uncovering its transformative potential in higher education. *The Internet and Higher Education*, *7*(2), 95–105. doi:10.1016/j.iheduc.2004.02.001

Garrison, D. R., & Vaughan, N. D. (2012). *Blended learning in higher education: Framework, principles, and guidelines*. John Wiley & Sons.

Ghazal, S., Al-Samarraie, H., & Aldowah, H. (2018). "I am Still Learning": Modeling LMS critical success factors for promoting students' experience and satisfaction in a blended learning environment. *IEEE Access: Practical Innovations, Open Solutions*, *6*, 77201. doi:10.1109/ACCESS.2018.2879677

Glazer, F. S. (2012). *Blended learning: Across the disciplines, across the academy*. Stylus Sterling. https://styluspub.presswarehouse.com/browse/book/9781579223243/Blended%20Learning

Graham, C. (2013). Emerging practice and research in blended learning. In Handbook of Distance Education (pp. 333–350). doi:10.4324/9780203803738.ch21

Graham, C. R. (2006). Blended learning systems: Definition, current trends, and future directions. In C. J. Bonk & C. R. Graham (Eds.), *Handbook of Blended Learning: Global Perspectives, Local Designs* (pp. 3–21). Pfeiffer Publishing.

Haijian, C., Hexiao, H., Wang, L., Chen, W., & Kunru, J. (2011). Research and application of blended learning in distance education and teaching reform. *I.J. Education and Management Engineering, 3*, 67-72. https://www.mecs-press.org/ijeme/ijeme-v1-n3/IJEME-V1-N3-10.pdf

Hrastinski, S. (2019). What do we mean by blended learning? *TechTrends, 63*(5), 564–569. doi:10.100711528-019-00375-5

Hung, M. L., & Chou, C. (2015). Students' perceptions of instructors' roles in blended and online learning environments: A comparative study. *Computers & Education, 81*, 315–325. doi:10.1016/j.compedu.2014.10.022

Islam, D. M. S., Tanvir, K., Salman, M., & Amin, D. M. (2020). *Online classes for university students in Bangladesh during the Covid-19 pandemic- is it feasible?* https://www.tbsnews.net/thoughts/online-classes-university-students-bangladesh-during-covid-19-pandemic-it-feasible-87454

Islam, M. T., & Habib, T. (2022). Barriers of adopting online learning among the university students in Bangladesh during Covid-19. *Indonesian Journal on Learning and Advanced Education, 04*(1), 71–91. doi:10.23917/ijolae.v4i1.15215

Jnr, B. A., Kamaludin, A., Romli, A. M., Raffei, A. F. M., Phon, D. N. E., Abdullah, A., Ming, G., Shukor, N. A., Nordin, M. S., & Baba, S. (2019). Exploring the role of blended learning for teaching and learning effectiveness in institutions of higher learning: An empirical investigation. *Education and Information Technologies*. Advance online publication. doi:10.100710639-019-09941-z

Kaleta, R., Skibba, K., & Joosten, T. (2007). Discovering, designing, and delivering hybrid courses. In A. G. Picciano, & C. Dzuiban (Eds.), *Blended Learning Research Perspectives*. The Sloan Consortium. Retrieved January 10, 2022, from https://www.scirp.org/%28S%28351jmbntvnsjt1aadkposzje%29%29/reference/referencespapers.aspx?referenceid=1427102

Kenney, J., & Newcombe, E. (2011). Adopting a blended learning approach: Challenges encountered and lessons learned in an action research study. *Online Learning, 15*(1). Advance online publication. doi:10.24059/olj.v15i1.182

Kibby, M. D. (2007). □*Hybrid teaching and learning: Pedagogy versus pragmatism.* https://scholar.google.com.au/citations?view_op=view_citation&hl=th&user=qKa3xU4AAAAJ&citation_for_view=qKa3xU4AAAAJ:u5HHmVD_uO8C□□□□□□□□□□□□□□□□□□□□

King, S. E., & Arnold, K. C. (2012). Blended learning environments in higher education: A case study of how professors make it happen. *Mid-Western Educational Researcher, 25*(1), 44–59. https://www.mwera.org/MWER/volumes/v25/issue1-2/v25n1-2-King-Arnold-GRADUATE-STUDENT-SECTION.pdf

Kizi, T. M. Y., & Ferdinantovna, M. H. (2022). What is blended learning? What are the benefits of blended learning? *Theory and Analytical Aspects of Recent Research, 1*(5), 735–738.

Kocaleva, M., Stojanovic, I., & Zdravev, Z. (2014). *Research on UTAUT application in higher education institutions*. Academic Press.

Lalima, & Dangwal, K. L. (2017). Blended learning: An innovative approach. *Universal Journal of Educational Research, 5*(1). https://eric.ed.gov/?id=EJ1124666

Lim, C. (2019). *Driving, sustaining and scaling up blended learning practices in higher education institutions: A proposed framework*. https://www.researchgate.net/publication/337068663_Driving_sustaining_and_scaling_up_blended_learning_practices_in_higher_education_institutions_a_proposed_framework

Linder, K. E. (2016). *The blended course design workbook: A practical guide*. Stylus Publishing, LLC.

Mahmood, S., Lodhi, H., & Fatima, Q. (2022). Transition to blended learning: Teachers' pedagogical beliefs, practices and challenges. *Harf-O-Sukhan, 6*(2), 253-270. Retrieved from https://harf-o-sukhan.com/index.php/Harf-o-sukhan/article/view/506

Masadeh, T. S. Y. (2021). Blended learning: Issues related to successful implementation. *International Journal of Scientific Research and Management, 9*(10), 1897–1907. doi:10.18535/ijsrm/v9i10.el02

Moskal, P., Dziuban, C., & Hartman, J. (2013). Blended learning: A dangerous idea? *The Internet and Higher Education, 18*, 15–23. doi:10.1016/j.iheduc.2012.12.001

Nath, S. R., Roy, G., Rahman, M. H., Ahmed, K. S., & Chowdhury, A. M. R. (2014). New Vision Old Challenges: The State of Pre-primary Education in Bangladesh. In M. Mohsin, M. G. Mostafa & A. Begum (Eds.), Campaign for Popular Education (CAMPE). Academic Press.

Norberg, A., Dziuban, C., & Moskal, P. (2011). A time based blended learning model. *On the Horizon, 19*(3), 207–216. doi:10.1108/10748121111163913

Nortvig, A. M., Petersen, A. K., & Balle, S. (2018). *A literature review of the factors influencing e-learning and blended learning in relation to learning outcome, student satisfaction and engagement.* https://www.semanticscholar.org/paper/A-literature-review-of-the-factors-influencing-and-Nortvig-Petersen/1462df81936e74422d9d365b851c769a72784222

OECD. (2019). *Education at a Glance 2019: OECD Indicators*. OECD. doi:10.1787/f8d7880d-

Oliver, M., & Trigwell, K. (2005). Can 'Blended Learning' be redeemed? *E-Learning and Digital Media, 2*(1), 17–26. doi:10.2304/elea.2005.2.1.17

Owston, R., York, D., & Malhotra, T. (2018). Blended learning in large enrolment courses: Student perceptions across four different instructional models. *Australasian Journal of Educational Technology*. Advance online publication. doi:10.14742/ajet.4310

Panday, P. K. (2020, September 2). Online classes and lack of interactiveness. *Daily Sun*. https://www.daily-sun.com/printversion/details/502935

Picciano, A. (2006). Blended learning: Implications for growth and access. *Journal of Asynchronous Learning Networks, 10*(3). Advance online publication. doi:10.24059/olj.v10i3.1758

Piper, T. H. (2010). *What policy changes do experts recommend K-12 instructional leaders enact to support the implementation of online instruction and learning?* (Doctoral Dissertation). https://www.proquest.com/openview/591508c78e9964e2168c757ae82abab8/1?pq-origsite=gscholar&cbl=18750&diss=y

Poon, J. (2012). Use of blended learning to enhance the student learning experience and engagement in property education. *Property Management, 30*(2), 129–156. Advance online publication. doi:10.1108/02637471211213398

Poon, J. (2013). Blended learning: An institutional approach for enhancing students' learning experiences. *Journal of Online Learning and Teaching, 9*(2), 271–288. https://dro.deakin.edu.au/view/DU:30057995

Quayyum, M. A., & Chowdhury, O. M. A. (2016, September 4). Natural disasters and uninterrupted education. *The Daily Star.* https://www.thedailystar.net/op-ed/natural-disasters-and-uninterrupted-education-1280044

Rasmitadila, R., Widyasari, W., Humaira, M., Tambunan, A., Rachmadtullah, R., & Samsudin, A. (2020). Using blended learning approach (BLA) in inclusive education course: A study investigating teacher students' perception. *International Journal of Emerging Technologies in Learning, 15*(2), 72–85. doi:10.3991/ijet.v15i02.9285

Ross, B., & Gage, K. (2006). Blended learning: Global perspectives from WebCT and our customers in higher education. In C. J. Bonk & C. R. Graham (Eds.), *Handbook of blended learning: Global perspectives, local designs* (pp. 155–168). Pfeiffer.

Roy, G. (2018). *Massive open online courses among Bengali-speaking people: Participation patterns, motivations and challenges about data analysis* [Master's thesis, University of Twente]. Student Theses. https://essay.utwente.nl/76043/

Roy, G., Babu, R., Kalam, M. A., Yasmin, N., Zafar, T., & Nath, S. R. (2021). *Response, readiness and challenges of online teaching amid COVID-19 pandemic: the case of higher education in Bangladesh.* Educational and Developmental Psychologist. doi:10.1080/20590776.2021.1997066

Saleem, N., Al-Suqri, M., & Ahmed, S. (2016). Acceptance of Moodle as a teaching/learning tool by the faculty of the department of Information Studies at Sultan Qaboos University, Oman based on UTAUT. *International Journal of Knowledge Content Development and Technology, 6*(2), 5–27. doi:10.5865/IJKCT.2016.6.2.005

Sandulache, S. (2019, October 13). *Natural disaster in Bangladesh.* Adrabangladesh. https://www.adrabangladesh.org/single-post/2019/10/13/natural-disaster-in-bangladesh

Senn, G. J. (2008). *Comparison of face-to-face and hybrid delivery of a course that requires technology skills development.* https://www.researchgate.net/publication/220590646_Comparison_of_Face-To-Face_and_Hybrid_Delivery_of_a_Course_that_Requires_Technology_Skills_Development

Shahriar, S. H. B., Arafat, S., Sultana, N., Akter, S., Khan, M. M. R., Nur, J. E. H., & Khan, S. I. (2021). The transformation of education during the corona pandemic: Exploring the perspective of the private university students in Bangladesh. *Asian Association of Open Universities Journal, 16*(2), 161-176. https://www.emerald.com/insight/content/doi/10.1108/AAOUJ-02-2021-0025/full/html

Smith, K., & Hill, J. (2019). Defining the nature of blended learning through its depiction in current research. *Higher Education Research & Development, 38*(2), 383–397. doi:10.1080/07294360.2018.1517732

Smyth, S., Houghton, C., Cooney, A., & Casey, D. (2012). Students' experiences of blended learning across a range of postgraduate programmes. *Nurse Education Today, 32*(4), 464–468. doi:10.1016/j.nedt.2011.05.014 PMID:21645947

Sohail, E. (2018, January 26). A digital education for a digital Bangladesh? *Dhaka Tribune*. https://archive.dhakatribune.com/opinion/2018/01/26/digital-education-digital-bangladesh

Suneeth, B. G., Kashyap, S., Reddy, G. M., & Kaushal, V. (2021). Resilience adaptations in tourism education for the post-COVID-19 era - a study of India. In *Tourism Destination Management in a Post-Pandemic Context* (pp. 291–302). Emerald Publishing Limited. doi:10.1108/978-1-80071-511-020211020

Szadziewska, A., & Kujawski, J. (2017). *Advantages and disadvantages of the blended-learning method used in the educational process at the faculty of management at the University of GDANSK, in the opinion of undergraduate students.* doi:10.21125/iceri.2017.1051

The Daily Star. (2020a). Conduct academic activities online during closure: UGC to universities. *The Daily Star.* https://www.thedailystar.net/country/news/conduct-academic-activities-online-during-closure-ugc-universities-1884748

The Daily Star. (2020b). UGC urges univs to continue classes online. *The Daily Star.* https://www.thedailystar.net/city/news/ugc-urges-univs-continue-classes-online-1885063

The Financial Express. (2020). *UGC suggests universities introducing online education.* The Financial Express. https://thefinancialexpress.com.bd/national/ugc-suggests-universities-introducing-online-education-1584975932

The Financial Express. (2022). *UGC directs implementation of blended learning.* The Financial Express. https://thefinancialexpress.com.bd/education/ugc-directs-implementation-of-blended-learning-1655035062

Tithi, N. (2021, September 26). Blended learning is what we will need in the coming days. *The Daily Star.* https://www.thedailystar.net/opinion/interviews/news/blended-learning-what-we-will-need-the-coming-days-2183941

Trines, S. (2019, January 8). *Education in Bangladesh.* https://wenr.wes.org/2019/08/education-in-bangladesh

Tshabalala, M., Ndeya-Ndereya, C., & Merwe, T. (2014). Implementing blended learning at a developing university: Obstacles in the way. *Electronic Journal of E-Learning, 12*, 101–110. https://eric.ed.gov/?id=EJ1020735

Vaughan, N. (2007). Perspectives on blended learning in higher education. *International Journal on E-Learning, 6*(1), 81–94. https://www.learntechlib.org/index.cfm?fuseaction=Reader.ViewAbstract&paper_id=6310

Wong, L., Tatnall, A., & Burgess, S. (2014). A framework for investigating blended learning effectiveness. *Education + Training, 56*(2/3), 233–251. Advance online publication. doi:10.1108/ET-04-2013-0049

Woodworth, P., & Applin, A. A. (2007). *A hybrid structure for the introductory computers and information technology course.* Semantic Scholar. https://www.semanticscholar.org/paper/A-hybrid-structure-for-the-introductory-computers-Woodworth-Applin/780faf868da6760f9f915602a3b37acad1703d2a

World Bank. (2022). *Overview.* World Bank. https://www.worldbank.org/en/country/bangladesh/overview

Zaman, F. (2014, November 27). "Student Politics" in Bangladesh. *The Daily Star*. https://www.thedailystar.net/student-politics-in-bangladesh-52187

Zurita, G., Hasbun, B., Baloian, N., & Jerez, O. (2015). A blended learning environment for enhancing meaningful learning using 21st century skills. In G. Chen, V. Kumar, Kinshuk, R. Huang, & S. C. Kong (Eds.), Emerging Issues in Smart Learning (pp. 1–8). Springer. doi:10.1007/978-3-662-44188-6_1

KEY TERMS AND DEFINITIONS

Administrator: Refers to a person appointed to take final decisions for the organisation. Administrators manage the institution's overall activities based on the goals and objectives. They have to conduct organisational activities more than teaching-learning activities and plan and implement the overall transformation of the educational institution.

Blended Learning: Blended learning refers to blending all traditional face-to-face educational activities with online or distance activities embedded with technology. It is not limited to teaching-learning only and also addresses all academic activities of higher education institutions, such as educational management, educational reformation, decision making and education policy-making.

Education Transition: This term is defined as a general process of changing existing modes of education. It includes the reconstruction and transformation of the whole educational process. Reconstruction and transformation occur within the context or environment of education, teacher, student, and administrator perceptions and insights, policy-making, and policy implementation. Modernisation of education is achieved through the education transition.

Higher Education Institutions: Indicate the formal institutions that provide both undergraduate and postgraduate degrees. The institution can be run by the government or by privately. It contributes to the country's development by creating a workforce. It is a complete set of staff, teachers, administrators, infrastructures, and policies.

Online Education: It indicates a form of distance education embedded with technology and the internet. Educational activities are carried out using digital technologies and the internet. Online education includes various things in the teaching-learning process, such as audio, visual, animation, and virtual environments. It gives a more flexible teaching-learning environment than traditional education.

Perception: Refers to the ability to see, hear, or become aware of something through the senses. It also indicates how something is regarded, understood, or interpreted. It also can be defined as a skill by which we consider or evaluate something. It influences our decision-making and leads us to problem-solving.

Resources: Refers to available sources or supplies of staff, expertise, and other assets to support or aid an action. It can be in the form of money, expertise, staff, technology, logistics, etc., that facilitates the execution of an idea or action.

Teachers: Refers to a person appointed by the institution to teach the students. Besides, teachers play the role of a facilitator to strengthen our learning. Apart from academic activities, they had to conduct many organisational activities, including research.

Chapter 7
Higher Education in the Aftermath of the Pandemic:
Lessons From Zambia and Eswatini

Fred Moonga

https://orcid.org/0000-0001-6401-7643
University of Eswatini, Eswatini

Sheilas K. Chilala
Mulungushi University, Zambia

Ireen Moonga
Mulungushi University, Zambia

Audrey Muyuni
Mulungushi University, Zambia

ABSTRACT

The COVID-19 pandemic negatively affected people's health and wellbeing and stretched their coping capacities with potential for multiple long-term psychosocial effects. Social interactions were inexorably affected if not altered. Education was probably the second most affected despite the young age-group due to the large number of people involved – teachers and supporting staff. Most low-income countries of Africa have young populations, which may explain the relatively low COVID-19 mortality rates on the continent. The focus in this chapter is higher education in the aftermath of the pandemic. The authors discuss how higher education institutions (HEIs) in the countries under discussion navigated the pandemic and remodelled to attain their objectives during and after the pandemic. They argue that the pandemic had enduring negative and positive effects. They conclude that although digitisation in learning and teaching in HEIs was underway, the pandemic accelerated its uptake.

DOI: 10.4018/978-1-6684-5934-8.ch007

Copyright © 2023, IGI Global. Copying or distributing in print or electronic forms without written permission of IGI Global is prohibited.

Higher Education in the Aftermath of the Pandemic

INTRODUCTION

The COVID-19 pandemic affected many aspects of humanity globally since its emergence in late 2019. It may be too early to write about its aftermath as it is still being reported in some parts of the world in August 2022 at the time of writing. Nonetheless, its impact is evident globally. The pandemic has had more than just health implications in that people's coping capacities were overstretched with potential for multiple enduring psychosocial and other effects. Social interactions were severely affected if not altered. Aside from health, education was probably the second most affected sector due to the large number of people associated with it, that is, the school-going age-group and teachers involved as well as supporting staff. The closure of schools for extended periods severely impacted on the welfare of the school-going age group as it restricted their interactions with their friends at school.

Azvedo et al. (2020) estimated that the pandemic left more than a billion students out of school. According to UNICEF (2021), this represents 94 percent of students worldwide while a third could not access remote learning. Thus, although the school-going age was less at risk from the pandemic whose fatality was said to increase with age, (United Nations, 2020; Remuzzi and Remuzzi, 2020), the education sector has a large number of young people globally. Most low-income countries of Africa, including the two under discussion have young populations which may explain low COVID-19 mortality on the continent. As discussed later in this chapter, majority of the victims who experienced the negative effects of the pandemic such as domestic and sexual abuse as well as orphanhood, were young people. These vices escalated when schools were closed at the height of the pandemic.

The higher education sector in developing countries, which is our focus, was facing some challenges prior to the pandemic. The challenges included but were not limited to increased enrolments, reduced public funding, and competition for resources. Therefore, the pandemic exacerbated these challenges and even added more. Some learners dropped out of school; some delayed their completion while others completed under difficult circumstances. Without doubt, there were also losses in the quality of education as most Higher Education Institutions (HEIs) were using online learning and teaching for the first time with limited capacities and resources. Conversely, employment opportunities and earning prospects are likely to be delayed and compromised which is likely to result in long term challenges over the life course. Azvedo et al (2020) estimated that, the closure of schools during the pandemic is likely to lead to about $872 losses in annual earnings for this cohort.

As the pandemic heightened, all HEIs closed; some immediately switched to online learning and teaching; while others had to wait, mobilise resources, and build capacities of learners and educators before adopting it. Over time, online teaching and learning has become the sole mode of continuing with education during the health crisis. The switch to online teaching and learning was not straight forward as discussed later in this chapter. There were inevitable challenges in access and affordability of ICT resources, utilisation of online and other ICT resources, poor connectivity, among others. These challenges were not exclusive to students, the teaching staff also struggled with these, not to mention issues of assessment quality and academic integrity.

In discussing higher education in the aftermath of the pandemic, this chapter will focus on the higher education trinity of teaching and learning; research and innovation; and community engagement or social contribution. That is, how HEIs in the countries under discussion remodelled the attainment of these objectives during and after the pandemic, the sustainability of those measures and further plans for the future with or without the pandemic. Other areas of focus will be on partnerships and support from government and the private sector. The former is critical in the attainment of the three objectives and even in enhancing digitalisation in teaching and learning and administration. Although HEIs includes both universities and colleges, in this chapter, we use it mainly to refer to universities. In the next section, we discuss the backgrounds of higher education in Zambia and Eswatini - the two countries this chapter is focused on, and how these two countries under discussion are suitable for and relevant to the current topic.

BACKGROUND

Although the countries under discussion are different in many ways, including geographic size, and economic activities, and to some extent culture, they have some commonalities that make them suitable for analysis in the context of reconstructing higher education in the aftermath of the global crisis. Foremost, both are land-locked (a new and positive narrative is that they are land-linked) countries which make them reliant on neighbouring countries for trade and travel. It also means that even if one of them could have been able to implement some unique preventive measures to avert the crisis, say regarding travel restrictions or tourism in which both are rich, they would not implement those measures without consultations with other countries in the region to which they are linked.

The two countries were also experiencing similar economic crises prior to the pandemic. For instance, Zambia defaulted on its huge debt for the first time while Eswatini sought financial support from the International Monetary Fund (IMF) to avert the COVID-19 crisis (IMF, 2020). Therefore, both were in economic crisis before, during and after the pandemic which means public HEIs dependent on government for support in these countries faced challenges leading to poor attainment of their core objectives. Additionally, Zambia held a crucial general election in August 2021 that saw a change of government. Crucial because the country was sliding backwards economically, politically, and socially due to poor governance. Prior to the general elections, there was unprecedented political violence by the then ruling party supporters against opposition party supporters, and reckless borrowing. Economic fundamentals were poorly managed. For instance, inflation was 22% at the end of 2021 (World Bank, 2022), while the country's currency was trading poorly against major currencies such as the United States Dollar (1$= 22.6 Zambian Kwacha) on June 30, 2021, (Bank of Zambia, 2022).

After the August 2021 general elections, the new government set priority on education and health, making the former freely available up to grade 12 while employing 30,496 teachers and 11, 276 health workers in the first year in office (Shalubala, 2022). However, there has been little emphasis on higher education except for increased government support to vulnerable students through the education loan system. An additional 2,232 bursaries were provided to university student applicants (Mkhala, 2022). Nonetheless, it would stress the budget to cater for the whole education spectrum in one year. It was not clear at the time of writing in September 2022, whether or not the Zambian government would allocate more resources to higher education in the second budget which would be presented in October 2022.

Eswatini on the other hand experienced pro-democracy political demonstrations in June 2021 (Mthembu, 2022) that led to the looting and burning of shops and other trading places as well as school infrastructure. Thus, the combination of political violence and the pandemic negatively impacted the financing and management of HEIs in the country. Political violence combined with the pandemic led to successive rescheduling of the academic calendar. Thus, the two countries are important in analysing the 'revisioning and reconstruction of higher education after the global crises.

Higher Education in the Aftermath of the Pandemic

Most public HEIs in the countries under discussion are reliant on tuition fees and grants from government for their operations. Given that students were away from campuses during the pandemic, they could not pay these fees as when on campus. Grants from governments also plummeted as governments experienced similar if not more economic challenges (Paul et al. 2021). As mentioned earlier, the two countries had economic challenges even before the pandemic (Geda, 2021). Importantly, most funds were channelled to COVID-19 response. For example, funding in the Global Partnership for Education (GPE) partner countries (to which the two countries under discussion are members) was prioritised in the four (4) areas namely, distance learning during school closures, teacher training of online teaching, provision of Water, Sanitation and Hygiene (WASH) materials, and support to vulnerable populations (ADEA, 2021).

Most infrastructure development and renovations were suspended (except ICT and distance learning infrastructure which were priorities) due to scarcity of resources as the sector was reliant on borrowing (Geda, 2021). Besides, online teaching and learning enhanced by the pandemic may reduce the need for physical infrastructure such as classrooms (Moonga, et al. 2022). Watermeyer (2021) further notes, apart from residences, there may be no need of constructing new buildings in the near future because online teaching and learning do not require large lecture rooms. Other modes of generating income such as research and innovation as well as partnership were also affected as most of the world remained closed. All these factors negatively affected the operations of HEIs thereby necessitating revisioning in the *modus operandi* of HEIs during and after the pandemic.

Despite the negative effects, the pandemic also affected the higher education sector in some positive and progressive ways. One of the most transformative positive effects of the pandemic was accelerated digitalisation in teaching and learning and others forms of human transactions. As Moonga (2022) notes, the pandemic enhanced digitalization of teaching and learning whose uptake had been low and slow in most HEIs in low-income countries. Characterised as 'disruptive innovation' by Christensen in 1995 (cited in Kaplan and Haenlein, 2016, p. 442), in its formative years, digitalisation was slow especially in resource constrained countries of the south. However, it rescued the education sector during the pandemic from possible collapse by providing Technological Enhanced Learning (TEL) and teaching through various virtual platforms.

Unlike other innovations, digitalisation and in particular online learning and teaching enhanced by the pandemic can be characterised as forced innovation because without the pandemic, its uptake would have remained low and slow. Thus, its speedy adoption during the pandemic enabled the education sector to move along other sectors of society such as business entities in utilising digital technology. Online learning and teaching also made it easier for physically challenged students to participate in lessons in the virtual environment, requiring limited movement (Basilaia and Kvavadze, 2020). Moreover, its flexible nature meant that both learners and teachers would catch-up with lessons at their convenient time in the comfort of their rooms or homes. Next, we discuss higher education in Zambia, thereafter, higher education in Eswatini.

MAIN FOCUS OF THE CHAPTER

Higher Education in Zambia

In Zambia, Higher Education is regulated by the Higher Education Authority (HEA), a grant aided institution established under the Higher Education Act No. 4 of 2013. The mandate of the Authority is to provide for the registration, accreditation, and regulation of both private and public HEIs and promoting quality assurance. The Act defines higher education as tertiary education leading to the award of a certificate, diploma, bachelor's degree, postgraduate diploma, master's degree, or doctorate degree, while as a HEI is defined as an institution that provides higher education on a full-time, part-time or distance learning basis (Higher Education Act No. 4 of 2013).

In the same Act, a Public HEI means a university or college which is owned by the Government or a local authority and is financed with public funds, while a private HEI is one which is not owned by the Government or local authority and is not financed with public funds. Based on 2021 HEA report, there are 54 private and 9 public registered HEIs, and 963 accredited programs (HEA, 2022). Among the HEIs, the University of Zambia is the oldest, established in 1965 after Zambia's political independence. It was followed by the Copperbelt University and Mulungushi University established in 1987 and 2008 respectively. Although most of the HEIs provided higher education on a full-time, part-time or e-learning basis, the most common mode of learning and teaching used prior to the pandemic is the traditional face-to face and distance learning.

Teaching and Learning During and After the Pandemic

On 18th March 2020, Zambia recorded the first two COVID-19 cases while the first death was on 2nd April 2020 (Reuters Staff, April 2, 2020). Following these developments, government implemented restrictions. This meant that the traditional face-to-face (F2F) or in-person learning, and teaching was suspended as all HEIs were abruptly closed in an effort to contain the pandemic. However, some HEIs only suspended physical classes but continued with virtual or online classes to avoid disruption of the academic calendar. On-line learning and teaching were rarely used prior to the pandemic.

Online learning and teaching were initially shunned by both lecturers and students due to challenges with resources associated with it as well as limited technological proficiency among learners and teachers (Ferreira-Meyers, et al. 2020). But with time, it became a mode of choice particularly because there were no other options. As the pandemic eased, blended learning became more prominent. Even distance and continuing education that were looked down upon in the past, have become important due to the unprecedented global pandemic. By and large, the experience of COVID-19 has heightened the need for research on its impact on HEIs globally as students' access and participation in learning during the pandemic were negatively affected (Mishra, Gupta, and Shree; 2020).

In Zambia, e-learning platforms such as Moodle which had been introduced in some HEIs prior to the pandemic (but used sparingly), were quickly adopted in some public and private universities such as Mulungushi University and ZICAS respectively. Therefore, such HEIs did not experience major disruptions at the onset of the pandemic. Both lecturers and students had been oriented on how to use this model (Mphahlele, 2020). Although the University of Zambia and the Copperbelt University (the oldest and biggest public universities) initially closed, they, like many other universities, instructed teaching staff to urgently prepare and deliver their lessons online, a challenge and opportunity that could not be

Higher Education in the Aftermath of the Pandemic

evaded during the pandemic (Lufungulo, Mwila, Mudenda, Kampamba, Chulu and Hikaambo, 2021; Ali, 2020; Dhawan, 2020).

Challenges and Opportunities with Online Learning and Teaching

As mentioned earlier, online learning had challenges. For instance, where lecturers managed to arrange interactive classes on-line, some students hardly participated due to power outages, unreliable access to Internet, lack of e-learning devices (such as smart phones and computers), and lack of internet data. This was exacerbated by stress, anxiety, isolation (Handel et al, 2020) and general unfavorable academic conditions at home, coupled with poor ICT skills (Chola et al., 2020; Kombe and Mtonga, 2021). Nonetheless, e-learning tools have played a crucial role during this pandemic, helping schools and universities facilitate student learning and teaching during the closure of universities (Subedi et al., 2020).

Changes in learning and teaching affected different learners and teachers in different ways. Some learners and educators found it difficult to adapt whereas others quickly adapted to the new methods and environment. As Doucet et al (2020) observed, different subjects and age-groups require different approaches to online learning and teaching. For instance, adult (mature) learners adapted much slower compared to young learners. Similarly, students taking practice-based courses also adapted slower than their counterparts taking theory-based subjects. However, this is often the case even for F2F learning and teaching. Therefore, benefits and challenges of online learning and teaching varied from person to person and from one subject to another.

Due to financial challenges exacerbated by the pandemic, some students could not afford to pay tuition fees as many households experienced challenges (Mwale & Chita, 2020; UNDP, 2020). Therefore, they could not be registered because they could only do so after paying. Non-registration, in turn, hindered their active participation or access to learning materials since this was dependent on one being a registered student and registration requires payment of a specified minimum amount. However, as mentioned earlier, even before the COVID-19 pandemic, some universities in Zambia were already facing significant challenges in meeting the required resources for universal access to quality education as a basic human right and in line with the fourth (4th) Sustainable Development Goal (SDG) - inclusive and equitable quality education (United Nations, 2015). Thus, COVID-19 exacerbated the already compromised situation in some HEIs. Students from poor and vulnerable families experienced challenges disproportionately. They had limited access to ICT resources such as smart phones, laptops and tablets, among others, required to access the necessary materials for online learning even when some may have been proficient in ICT.

A study at Mulungushi University in Zambia, (Kombe and Mtonga, 2021), revealed that, students who participated in e-learning reported different levels of participation. About 33 per cent indicated that they were 'very involved' compared to 62 per cent who were 'rarely' to 'very rarely' involved. For the 5 per cent of students who reported not participating in e-learning, the findings suggested that they were eager to participate but excluded due to various challenges. The same study indicated that many students (78%) reported borrowing ICT devices they were using during e-learning from their parents, friends, and other relatives, confirming the struggles vulnerable students encounter during on-line learning (Kombe and Mtonga, 2021).

Despite the earlier negative experiences with online learning and teaching, there is hope in this once neglected if not shunned pedagogy. It was reassuring during the pandemic how some HEIs demonstrated forward-thinking and resilience under difficult conditions. For instance, during the lockdown, some of the HEIs embarked on ambitious strategies to cultivate interest of their members of staff and students

149

who were technophobic to embrace digital teaching and learning by doing most transactions online (Moonga, et al. 2022). These efforts paid-off as no time was lost in the academic calendar in the case of Mulungushi University.

Students and Staff Training and Support

In an effort to ensure success of online programs, the management in different HEIs embarked on training and retraining academic staff and students in Technology Enhanced Learning (TEL) and teaching to enhance their capacities in the implementation of e-learning. A series of training programs for lecturers and students were rolled out to enhance interaction through various e-learning platforms with less difficulties. For instance, video lessons on how to use Moodle (the official e-Learning platform for most HEIs) were provided to both staff members and students, especially the new ones. Mulungushi university for example increased the number of Moodle licences to facilitate a conducive environment for e-learning. Other platforms that were mostly used for online learning and teaching include, Google meet and WhatsApp. The latter was the most frequently used platform at the university (41%), followed by Zoom (21%) with Moodle at (4%). Moodle was the least preferred platform because students reported not being familiar with it in addition to having some difficulties accessing it due to technical challenges such as poor internet connectivity (Kombe and Mtonga, 2021).

Apart from training of staff and students in ICT, some HEIs also invested in modern equipment such as Video Conferencing Facility (VCF), that was required to facilitate e-learning. Like many other universities in less developed countries, Mulungushi university did not have much equipment that could be used for e-learning prior to COVID-19 pandemic. Despite budgetary limitations, the university also had to provide lecturers with data bundles to allow for smooth running of classes whenever required.

Additionally, to relieve the burden of data bundles on the part of the students, the university in partnership with mobile phone service providers supported all students with free 100 megabytes (MB) bundles to enable them access Moodle, the university's official e-learning platform. This was later extended to unlimited access to Moodle by the students after the university partnered with a local mobile network provider. To supplement the unlimited access to Moodle, Mulungushi university and the University of Zambia also provided Educational Tablets (Edu Tabs) to students on credit. This again was a momentous effort by these HEIs to ensure undisrupted learning and teaching despite limited resources.

Despite these laudable arrangements put in place by HEIs to cushion e-learning and teaching costs during the pandemic, the study at Mulungushi University (Kombe and Mtonga, 2021) revealed that, all the students who participated in the study never mentioned this offer. This might mean that the students may not have been aware of some of the services offered by the university due to inadequate communication (Kombe and Mtonga, 2021) and might have affected the achievements of equal access to quality education. Field education discussed next was even more challenging.

Field Education

Although most HEIs managed to navigate teaching and learning during the pandemic, the programmes with fieldwork or field education components experienced more challenges. Field education is critical in the attainment of professional competencies and skills in professions such as Education, Nursing, Medicine, Social work and Law among others. Such professions refer to field education as the *signature pedagogy* (Olson-Morrisson et al., 2015) because a student in these fields cannot start practising without doing supervised field practice as stipulated in the accreditation standards. The Council of Social Work Education, (2008) defines signature pedagogy as a central form of instruction and learning to socialise students to perform the role of a practitioner ...it contains pedagogical norms with which to connect and integrate theory and practice (cited in Wayne et al., 2010, p.327).

In Zambia, the social work field practice is divided into rural and urban placements. The former is used at lower levels and is developmental oriented while the latter is used at higher levels and is clinical, administrative, and evaluative oriented. In both cases, close supervision of students is a necessity. Health-care professionals worked throughout the pandemic period and therefore it should have been rewarding to their students' field education. Their profession entails working in such risky environments with clear liability procedures. But in the case of medical social work or students placed in health care facilities, there were challenges of who takes liability in an event a student or supervisor contracted COVID-19 (Buchanan & Bailey-Belafonte, 2021). Rural placements had more challenges during the pandemic because students involved are often first timers who need more orientation and close supervision.

Communication challenges and the crucial aspect of interacting with community members were particularly challenging. Nonetheless, given that Zambia did not implement a complete lockdown, some activities went on with minor interruptions. Therefore, field education was not completely abandoned. It was conducted remotely or virtually dependent on the levels of supervision required and the working arrangements adopted by the hosting agency. Most organisations adopted the 'work from home' policy during the pandemic while conducting meetings virtually. When the pandemic eased, employees alternated in reporting for work physically. Thus, students doing fieldwork had to fit in such arrangements.

Examinations

Challenges with online examinations were much more than those in teaching and learning because chances of cheating when a student is writing from their room are much higher. Perhaps this is an aspect where HEIs need to be innovative through artificial intelligence to monitor examinations in real time before a next possible crisis. Nonetheless, there are some like Mulungushi university managed to navigate the academic calendar during the pandemic including conducting examinations on-line. However, as expected, there were numerous challenges such as failure to upload the examination answer sheet within the stipulated period of time and delayed access to the examination question paper by some students due to power cuts and poor internet connectivity among other factors.

Some HEIs only piloted online examinations for selected courses while others postponed examinations until the crisis eased. Despite the challenges experienced during the pandemic, most HEIs succeeded in navigating the pandemic because they devised innovative ways of learning and teaching and general communication. Even after COVID-19 eased, many HEIs continued with blended learning and teaching, that is, F2F and online as a way of benefiting from the advantages of each mode while reducing the disadvantages of each.

Higher Education in Eswatini

Higher education in Eswatini is governed by the Higher Education Act of 2013. Therein, higher education is defined as 'all learning programmes commenced after secondary education and leading to a higher qualification' (Higher Education Act, 2013). Conversely, HEI is defined in the same Act as any registered or conditionally registered, private, or public institution that provides higher education on full-time, part-time or long-distance basis. The Eswatini Higher Education Council (ESHEC) established in 2015 under the foregoing Act is the main regulatory body for HEIs. There are eight (8) HEIs in Eswatini. Three (3) of them are universities (1 public and 2 private). The biggest and oldest is the University of Eswatini (UNESWA) formerly the University of Swaziland (UNISWA). There are also five (5) colleges of education, three (3) of which are public while two (2) are private as per Education policy of 2018 (The Kingdom of Eswatini, 2018).

Teaching and Learning During and After the Pandemic

Historically, learning and teaching has been conducted through F2F or in-person basis globally serve for distance education whose development heralded online learning and teaching in many ways. It was later piloted in many HEIs around the world. The utilisation of online learning and teaching was enhanced during the pandemic due to limited options. Like any other country in the world, Eswatini was not spared by the COVID-19 crisis or pandemic as used interchangeably in this chapter. The government of Eswatini declared a state of public emergency on 17th March 2020 (Dlamini, 2020), three (3) days after the first COVID-19 case was diagnosed. Subsequently, the government amended the Disaster Management Act of 2006 to Disaster Management (Coronavirus-COVID-19) Regulations 2020, to accommodate and enhance public health measures around the pandemic (The Kingdom of Eswatini, 2020). The declaration of a public emergency meant closure of businesses and other human activities including learning and teaching. Only shops selling food and other necessities, essentials for children and pharmacies were left to operate under strict guidelines. Almost one month after the first confirmed case, the first COVID-19-related death was announced on 13th April, 2020 (Nkosi, 2020). It was hard to imagine how the situation would be even if the pandemic ended. The uncertainty was forbearing. By 10th August 2022, there were 73,316 confirmed cases, 1,419 deaths cumulatively, while 319,384 people had been vaccinated representing 33.7 percent of the whole population (Ministry of Health, 2022).

HEIs in low-income countries are vulnerable to economic shocks especially those reliant on public funding which in most cases is inadequate and often received late. Since the diagnosis of the first case, the impacts of the pandemic have been many and varied. Among the notable impacts of the pandemic in Eswatini was a surge in Gender-Based Violence (GBV) cases and teenage pregnancies. GBV cases rose from 1,420 in January 2020 to 9, 399 in September 2020 (Partner relations Team, 2020). Approximately 261 girls from 280 primary and high schools got pregnant during the partial lockdown (Dlamini, 2020). Although no statistics were available for HEIs learners, a similar pattern is highly likely. Such risky behaviour undoubtedly could have exposed some to Sexually Transmitted Diseases (STDs) in addition to dropping out of the school system. Additionally, the pandemic orphaned 5,200 children, thus doubling the number of orphans in ten (10) months the country from July 2021 to May 2022 (Mkhonta, 2022). This increased the number of those requiring social protection which was already under stress.

The primary objective of HEIs is learning and teaching. As alluded to earlier, learning and teaching has historically been conducted through the traditional F2F or in-person. However, open and flexible learning has also been used for more than three centuries (Casey 2008). It started as correspondence education using posted learning materials, moved to broadcasting and later to asynchronous computer conferencing (Anderson & Simpson, 2012) but has evolved over the years. It was enhanced and became the key method of teaching and learning during the pandemic. Moodle was adopted by the University of Eswatini as the official online mode of learning and teaching while Zoom, Microsoft Teams were designated for meetings. Emails, WhatsApp, and SMS were retained for communication. Thus, the most

Higher Education in the Aftermath of the Pandemic

transformative effect of the pandemic has been Technology Enhanced Learning (TEL). Both synchronous and asynchronous learning and teaching were used and would continue to be used post the COVID-19 crisis. For example, instead of closing schools and HEIs when students are rioting, learning and teaching would continue online while learners are at home.

Challenges and Opportunities of Online Learning and Teaching

TEL has not been advantageous to everyone. Challenges regarding access to the internet and afford-ability of electronic resources as well as ICT proficiency, were expected. Although teaching staff were equipped with online teaching methods which evidently improved their proficiency, challenges with assessments and quality assurance as well as plagiarism remained of great concern. These too were re-solved with time. When the pandemic eased in 2021, sitting arrangements were spaced for F2F learning and teaching. Overall, switching to online learning and teaching was easier and faster in private HEIs than in public ones due to lengthy and slow bureaucratic decision-making processes in the latter as well as resource constraints.

Students and Staff Training and Support

Although some staff were already conversant with online learning, the university of Eswatini through the Directorate of distance education and faculty of education embarked on training academic staff in online teaching methodologies. Other measures include partnership with mobile and internet providers to subsidise internet data for students. Support to academic staff was still in the pipeline when normal learning and teaching resumed.

Field Education

Experiential learning is a critical aspect of professional training in which concepts and theories are integrated with practice during field education. It is perhaps one of the most affected areas in HEIs be-cause of the requirement for physical presence that accords the learner supervision by both the field and academic supervisor. However, such practices were interrupted or could not be embarked upon. Thus, like full-time employees, student trainees had to work from home most of the time as prescribed by their host agencies. This subtracted a great deal from the physical presence requirement. In some instances, especially when the lockdown was relaxed, students would report for their practicum two or three days in a week. As such periods for field education had to be extended in order to offset the reduced weekly contact time. It also meant that field reports and theses deadlines had to be extended. For non-completing students, their field education was either postponed or they were given some similar assessments to undertake such as a long paper to write whichever was more feasible.

However, field practice challenges did not start with the pandemic, they existed even before. They included among others limited resources in universities and host agencies, increased enrolments, and fewer placement opportunities (Ayala et la., 2018). At the university of Eswatini, remote supervision was adopted for social work students. Despite these challenges, there are some social work services that were already being implemented through the use of ICT. For example, most countries are developing and piloting comprehensive electronic registers and service delivery for social protection and other social service benefits. For example, social cash transfer beneficiaries were receiving the monthly or

153

bi-monthly benefits through mobile money or vouchers. In case management, case conferencing, in which a caseworker holds a teleconference meeting with the client or service user, and sometimes other stakeholders or professionals, was being used virtually even before the pandemic. Even tele-counselling existed before the pandemic. All these were important areas where students would be placed for field education. Those in education were in an even more advantageous situation since most learning and teaching were done online. So, they could practice this pedagogy both as students and as student teachers. However, all these online methods and services are limited by internet connectivity, ICT literacy, and client's or user's attitude towards online services (Buchanan and Bailey-Belafonte, 2021). As such, most vulnerable clients or users, majority of whom are social work service beneficiaries could not be reached and therefore excluded from benefits and services meant for them.

Examinations

Although other assessments were done online, no online examination was conducted online at the university of Eswatini in 2020. Instead, physical or in-person examinations with spaced sitting arrangements were conducted to first and final year students while other levels like second and third years progressed using coursework assessments (continuous assessments) done online. As Richardson (2015) noted, assessment by course work may less likely cause possible risks to academic standards. Both students and staff were already used to coursework assessments which were adopted during the pandemic and could easily be checked against plagiarism. These measures were implemented after postponement of examinations could no longer help the situation. Below we discuss how HEIs in the two countries carried out the other two mandates of research and innovation, and community engagement or social contribution.

Research and Innovation

Access to research funds was a challenge before, during and after the pandemic in the countries under discussion due to limited funding locally. As mentioned earlier, the emergence of the pandemic had both challenges and opportunities for HEIs to prove their utility and relevance to society with regard to knowledge generation and innovation. However, their capabilities in these areas were constrained because governments and philanthropic organisations withheld funding for these purposes (DeMathews et al., 2020) serve for COVID-19-related solutions. The university of Eswatini through the Department of Chemistry, manufactured sanitisers while the Department of Consumer Science and Design, manufactured face masks from clothing material as surgical masks became scarce at the onset of the pandemic. The school of health sciences facilitated sensitisation of the public COVID-19 preventive measures and general public health. However, resources for research declined tremendously during the pandemic. Doing research itself also became a challenge as telephone interviews and online distribution of questionnaire became the norm. Challenges with these measures are well documented (Bryman, 2016).

Community Engagement or Social Contribution

HEIs and many other organisations around the world collaborate with communities around them to which they are part for mainly ethical and legal reasons (Bowen, 1953 cited in Ankit & El-Sakran, 2020). But there could be more. This is because of the many benefits that these organisations derive from surrounding communities as well as the negative effects such as environmental pollution they cause through their

Higher Education in the Aftermath of the Pandemic

activities to those communities. These engagements are commonly referred to as community or Corporate Social Responsibility (CRS). CRS is useful for a good reputation and competitive advantage of an HEI (Sengupta, Blessinger & Mahoney, 2020). HEIs in the countries under discussion contributed to their surrounding communities by sensitizing community members with COVID-19 preventive measures and distributing face masks and hand sanitisers because some community members could neither access nor afford these on the market. Some university facilities were either used as testing centres for COVID-19 or for quarantining those diagnosed with it since students were not on campus.

FUTURE RESEARCH DIRECTIONS

COVID-19 will go down in history as a global health crisis that revolutionised ICT not for health care purposes, but for other aspects of human transactions, chiefly, education and trade. Even, after the pandemic, HEIs will not have to close if there is a problem. They will have the option for online or blended learning. The option for online learning will also reduce the pressure for space and infrastructure in the face on increasing enrolments. It will also solve the problem of rescheduling the academic calendar each time a university closed due to student riots or other problems.

Although the countries under discussion were less affected by the pandemic in early 2020 due to the dominance of young populations as mentioned earlier, more HEIs in these countries and the African region in general were closed for prevention purposes (Marinoni, et al. 2020). This could have probably prevented the pandemic from spreading further. However, resource constraints could have made the impact of closures felt much more than in USA, Asia and Europe where the effects of the pandemic were more pronounced. The scarcity of research resources during the pandemic became worse among HEIs in resource constrained countries.

As argued earlier, the pandemic did not only have negative effects despite the loss of many human lives and an indelible mark if not reconfiguring society in some ways. It ignited many innovations in teaching and learning and other human transactions and interactions. Although many HEIs had been piloting and in some cases consolidating online teaching and learning, through their distance education institutes or directorates, they had to scale-up during the pandemic because of limited options. Premised on flexibility and convenience to both the learner and teacher, online learning was revolutionised during the pandemic. The pandemic also awakened HEIs to the need for alternative ways of carrying out various human transactions and to the transient nature, if not fallacy, of normalcy. The resounding revival of digital technology in teaching and learning as well as research has been a milestone that has long term implications on research and innovation. Online research can no longer be questioned because it gained prominence and demonstrated relevance and reliability during the pandemic.

CONCLUSION

The pandemic negatively affected many aspects of people's lives, chiefly social, health and education as well as economies. The time and opportunities lost during the pandemic may take time to recover if at all. The higher education system which is our focus had challenges such as decline in grants, rising enrolments, and demand for infrastructure even before the pandemic. These challenges were compounded by the crisis. Various innovative online measures were adopted in teaching and learning, field education and even examinations by some HEIs. Online teaching and learning have been a success story in many respects. However, a lot of innovations are required in field education and examinations in order to uphold quality standards. Although digitisation in learning and teaching in HEIs was well underway, it would not have happened at such pace without the pandemic. Most other initiatives including those adopted in field education would not have been adopted without the pandemic. Therefore, it unboxed people's thinking about traditional ways of doing things.

Quality assurance may have been compromised in one way or another, but that is the reality that the pandemic brought about. Therefore, new and digitally oriented methods of quality assurance such as using anti-plagiarism soft wares (which were already being used before the pandemic) need to be enhanced as well as artificial intelligence especially in monitoring the conduct of examinations. By and large, the innovative and progressive challenges occasioned by the pandemic need to be nurtured.

To achieve equitable access to inclusive and quality education for all as per Sustainable Development Goal (SDG) number four (4) (United Nations, 2015), there is a need to devise deliberate measures to ensure that vulnerable learners are accepted, supported, and have access to all lessons in order for them to succeed in their learning. This would also foster the achievement of Sustainable Development Goal (SDG) number ten (10), 'reduced inequalities' (United Nations, 2015).

ACKNOWLEDGMENT

This research received no funding from any funding agency in the public, commercial, or not-for-profit sectors. However, we convey our sincere appreciation to the sources we consulted.

REFERENCES

ADEA, AU/CIEFFA, & APHRC (2021). *Financing Education in Africa during the COVID-19 Pandemic.* ADEA, AU/CIEFFA, APHRC.

Ali, W. (2020). Online and Remote Learning in Higher Education Institutes. A Necessity in Light of COVID-19 Pandemic. *Higher Education Studies, 10*(3), 16–25. doi:10.5539/hes.v10n3p16

Anderson, B., & Simpson, M. (2012). History and heritage in distance education. *Journal of Open. Flexible and Distance Learning, 16*(2), 1–10.

Ankit, A., & El-Sakran, T. (2020). Corporate Social Responsibility: Reflections on Universities in the United Arab Emirates. In E. Sengupta, P. Blessinger, & C. Mahoney (Eds.), *Civil Society and Social Responsibility in Higher Education: International Perspectives on Leadership and Strategies* (pp. 15–32). Emerald Publishing Ltd. doi:10.1108/S2055-364120200000024004

Ayala, J., Drolet, J., Fulton, A., Hewson, J., Letkemann, L., Baynton, M., Elliott, G., Judge-Stasiak, A., Blaug, C., Gérard Tétreault, A., & Schweizer, E. (2018). Field education in crisis: Experiences of field education coordinators in Canada. *Social Work Education, 37*(3), 281–293. doi:10.1080/02615479.20 17.1397109

Higher Education in the Aftermath of the Pandemic

Azevedo, J. P., Hasan, A., Goldemberg, D., Geven, K., & Iqbal, S. A. (2021). Simulating the potential impacts of COVID-19 school closures on schooling and learning outcomes: A set of global estimates. *The World Bank Research Observer*, *36*(1), 1–40.

Bank of Zambia. (2022). *Daily ZMW/USD exchange rates.* https://www.boz.zm/historical-series-of-daily-zmw-usd-exchange-rates-zmw.htm

Basilaia, G., & Kvavadze, D. (2020). Transition to online education in schools during a SARS-CoV-2 coronavirus (COVID-19) pandemic in Georgia. *Pedagogical Research*, *5*(4), 10. doi:10.29333/pr/7937

Bryman, A. (2016). *Social research methods.* Oxford University Press.

Buchanan, C. S., & Bailey-Belafonte, S. J. (2021). Challenges in adapting Field placement during a Pandemic: A Jamaican Perspective. *International Social Work*, *64*(2), 285–288. doi:10.1177/0020872820976738

Casey, D. M. (2008). The historical development of distance education through technology. *TechTrends*, *52*(2), 45–51. doi:10.100711528-008-0135-z

Chola, R., Kasimba, P., George, R., & Rajan, R. (2020). Covid-19 and e-learning: Perception of freshmen level physics students at Lusaka apex medical university. *International Journal of Academic Research and Development*, *15*(19), 67–76.

Council of Social Work Education. (2008). *Educational Policy and Accreditation Standards.*

DeMatthews, D., Knight, D., Reyes, P., Benedict, A., & Callahan, R. (2020). From the field: Education research during a pandemic. *Educational Researcher*, *49*(6), 398–402. doi:10.3102/0013189X20938761

Dhawan, S. (2020). Online Learning a Panacea in the Time of COVID-19 Crisis. *Journal of Education Technology*, *49*(1), 5–22.

Dlamini, S. (2020). 261 Teenage Pregnancies during Lockdown. Mbabane: Eswatini Observer.

Doucet, A., Netolicky, D., Timmers, K., & Tuscano, F. J. (2020). *Thinking about pedagogy in an unfolding pandemic: An Independent Report on Approaches to Distance Learning during COVID-19 School Closure.* Academic Press.

Ferreira-Meyers, K., Biswalo, P., Maduna, S., Ngcobo, L., & Dlamini-Zwane, N. (2020). Selected case studies from Eswatini: dealing with the COVID-19 pandemic in the education sectors. In *Digital 2020 online* (pp. 255–276). https://www.researchgate.net/profile/Upasana-Singh/publication/348355099_digiTAL_2020_proceedings/

Government of the Republic of Zambia. (2013). *Higher Education Act No. 4 of 2013.* Government Printers.

Händel, M., Stephan, M., Gläser-Zikuda, M., Kopp, B., Bedenlier, S., & Ziegler, A. (2020). Digital readiness and its effects on higher education students' socio-emotional perceptions in the context of the COVID-19 pandemic. *Journal of Research on Technology in Education*, 1–13.

Higher Education Authority. (2022). *State of Higher Education in Zambia, 2021 Report.* Author.

International Monetary Fund. (2020). *IMF Executive Board Approves US $ 110.4 Million in Emergency Support to The Kingdom of Eswatini to Address the COVID-19 Pandemic.* Press Release NO. 20/274. IMF.

Kaplan, A. M., & Haenlein, M. (2016). Higher Education and the Digital Revolution: About MOOCs, SPOCs, Social Media, and the Cookie Monster. *Business Horizons, 59*(4), 441–450. doi:10.1016/j.bushor.2016.03.008

Kombe, C. L., & Mtonga, D. E. (2021). Challenges and Interventions of e-learning for Under- resourced Students amid Covid-19 Lockdown: A Case of a Zambian Public University. *Journal of Student Affairs in Africa, 9*(1), 23–39. doi:10.24085/jsaa.v9i1.1426

Lufungulo, E., Mwila, K., Mudenda, S., Kampamba, M., Chulu, M., & Hikaambo, C. (2021). Online Teaching during COVID-19 Pandemic in Zambian Universities: Unpacking Lecturers' Experiences and the Implications for Incorporating Online Teaching in the University Pedagogy. *Creative Education, 12*(12), 2886–2904. doi:10.4236/ce.2021.1212216

Marinoni, G., vant Land, H., & Jenssen, T. (2020). The Impact of COVID-19 on Higher Education around the World: IAU Global survey report. Paris: International Association of Universities (IAU).

Ministry of Health. (2022). *COVID-19: Daily Information updated, 21ˢᵗ July 2022*. Ministry of Health.

Mishra, L., Gupta, T., & Shree, A. (2020). Online teaching-learning in higher education during the lockdown period of the COVID-19 pandemic. *International Journal of Educational Research Open, 1*, 100012. doi:10.1016/j.ijedro.2020.100012 PMID:35059663

Mkhala, T., (2022). *Government allocates Faith's K65M to Students' bursaries*. Lusaka: News Diggers.

Mkhonta, N. (2022, Aug.). 5200 Children Orphaned by COVID-19 Pandemic. *Eswatini Times*.

Moonga, F. (2020). Civil Society Organisations, Higher Education Institutions, and Corporate Social Responsibility in Zambia. In Leadership Strategies for Promoting Social Responsibility in Higher Education (pp. 33-44). Emerald Publishing.

Moonga, F. (2022). Africa's University Landscape: Embracing Digital Transformation. In A. Kaplan (Ed.), *Digital Transformation and Disruption of Higher Education* (pp. 60–72). doi:10.1017/9781108979146.008

Moonga, F., Mabundza, L., & Hlatshwayo, P. (2022). Post COVID-19 Reforms in Higher Education in Eswatini. In Education reform in the Aftermath of the COVID-19 Pandemic (pp. 158-175). IGI Global.

Mphahlele, R. S. (2020). Online learning support in a ubiquitous learning environment. In Managing and designing online courses in ubiquitous learning environments (pp. 1-18). IGI Global. doi:10.4018/978-1-5225-9779-7.ch001

Mthembu, M. V. (2021). Pro-Democracy protests in the Kingdom of Eswatini 2018-2019. In E. R. Sanches (Ed.), *Popular Protest, Political Opportunities and Change in Africa* (pp. 200–217). Routledge.

Muleya, G., Simui, F., Mundende, K., Kakana, F., Mwewa, G., & Namangala, B. (2019). Exploring learning cultures of digital immigrants in technologically mediated postgraduate distance learning mode at the University of Zambia. *Zambia ICT Journal, 3*(3), 1–10. doi:10.33260/zictjournal.v3i2.83

Mwale, N., & Chita, J. (2020). Higher education and programme delivery in the context of COVID-19 and institutional closures: Student responses to the adoption of e-Learning at a public university in Zambia. In Technology-based teaching and learning in higher education during the time of COVID-19 (pp. 9-33). CSSALL Publishers (Pty) Ltd.

Nkosi, L. (2020). *Ministry of Health Press statement COVID-19 Update, 17th April, 2020*. Ministry of Health.

Olson-Morrison, D., Radohl, T., & Dickey, G. (2019). Strengthening Field Education: An Integrated Model for Signature Pedagogy in Social Work. *InSight: A Journal of Scholarly Teaching, 14*, 55-73.

Partner Relations Team. (2020). *Update on the Impact of COVID-19 to Eswatini*. Bulembu Ministries.

Paul, B. V., Finn, A., Chaudhary, S., Mayer Gukovas, R., & Sundaram, R. (2021). *COVID-19, Poverty, and Social Safety Net Response in Zambia*. Policy Research Working Paper, 9571. Washington, DC: The World Bank.

Remuzzi, A., & Remuzzi, G. (2020). COVID-19 and Italy: What next? *Lancet, 395*(10231), 1225–1228. doi:10.1016/S0140-6736(20)30627-9 PMID:32178769

Richardson, J. T. (2015). Coursework versus examinations in end-of-module assessment: A literature review. *Assessment & Evaluation in Higher Education, 40*(3), 439–455. doi:10.1080/02602938.2014.919628

Sengupta, E., Blessinger, P., & Mahoney, C. (2020). Introduction to Leadership Strategies for promoting Social Responsibility in Higher Education. In E. Sengupta, P. Blessinger, & C. Mahoney (Eds.), *Civil Society and Social Responsibility in Higher Education: International Perspectives on Leadership and Strategies* (pp. 3–13). Emarald Publishing Ltd. doi:10.1108/S2055-364120200000024003

Shalubala, C. (2022). Successful Teacher Recruitment Excites Government. Lusaka: News Diggers.

Staff, R. (2020). Zambia Records First Coronavirus Death. *Reuters*, (April), 2.

Subedi, S., Nayaju, S., Subedi, S., Shah, S. K., & Shah, J. M. (2020). Impact of e-learning during CO-VID-19 pandemic among nurshing students and teachers of Nepal. *International Journal of Science and Healthcare Research, 5*(3), 68–76.

The Kingdom of Eswatini. (2013). *Higher Education Act, 2013*. Author.

The Kingdom of Eswatini. (2018). *National Education and Training Sector Policy*. Author.

The Kingdom of Eswatini. (2020). The Disaster Management (Coronavirus-COVID-19) Regulations 2020. Author.

UNFPA. (2020). *Eswatini Population projections report, 2017-2038*. https://eswatini.unfpa.org/sites/default/files/pub-pdf/eswatini_population_projections_report_2017-2038.pdf

UNICEF. (2021). *Responding to COVID-19: UNICEF annual report 2020*. UNICEF.

United Nations. (2015). *Sustainable Development Goals (SDGs): The 2030 Agenda for Sustainable Development*. United Nations.

United Nations. (2020). *Shared Responsibility, Global Solidarity: Responding to the socioeconomic impacts of COVID-19*. United Nations.

United Nations Development Programme. (2020). *A Rapid Socioeconomic Assessment of COVID-19 in Eswatini*. UNDP.

Wayne, J., Bogo, M., & Raskin, M. (2010). Field education as the signature pedagogy of social work education. *Journal of Social Work Education*, *46*(3), 327–339. doi:10.5175/JSWE.2010.200900043

World Bank. (2022). *Inflation, consumer prices (annual %) - Zambia*. Author.

Chapter 8
Impact of Technology on Educational Patterns:
Virtual vs. Traditional Pedagogy

Shayantani Banerjee
Amity University, Ranchi, India

Ayushi Zina
Amity University, Ranchi, India

Navinandan Kumar
Amity University, Ranchi, India

Nilesh Kumar
Amity University, Ranchi, India

ABSTRACT

With innovations in technology, educational practices and expectations are changing at a rapid pace. The virtual reality on electronic devices is at a stark contrast with traditional classroom teaching and ethics. This chapter aspires to trace the changes that the use of ICT tools has brought to conventional pedagogy, teacher's adaptability, and teacher's anxiety in coping with the inclination of education toward technology. For the study, various sets of data were collected from different institutions, and then the data were observed. Apart from ICT tools, the popularity of social media elicits teachers to explore its educational use. However, the tempting distraction of this technology could make teachers anxious about its pedagogical use. Thus, the aim of this chapter will be to analyze the impact of technology on factors like school culture versus online teaching, attitude towards social media, professional development of teachers, learning goals, and content-building in the curriculum.

DOI: 10.4018/978-1-6684-5934-8.ch008

Copyright © 2023, IGI Global. Copying or distributing in print or electronic forms without written permission of IGI Global is prohibited.

INTRODUCTION

Information and Communications Technology has changed the face of education system. It is rightly said that technology has impacted every sphere of life. Education sector forms a major part of our lives and it is needless to say that technological advancements have made their way in it. Earlier it was unthinkable to conduct classes without a classroom set-up. But technology has enabled us to conduct classes from our homes which reach the homes of our students. Technology and pedagogy are closely connected through a continuous feedback loop, and it is in the integration of new technologies and related practices into existing ecologies that opportunities and challenges arise (Fawns, 2018).

The failure to meet such integration preserve traditional academic practices and values (Feenberg, 2017; Rose, 2017). Technology is neither a negative nor a positive force, rather a part of the landscape in which education is enacted. Technological "solutions", like virtual learning environments (VLEs), create pressures, implicit or explicit, to use them. Such environments make many educational practitioners unsure of their responses towards the values imparted by traditional pedagogy, which can be defined as a "pre-technology education context in which the teacher is the sender or the source, the educational material is the information or message, and students is the receiver of the information." (Mbodila, Munienge, and Muhandji, 2012)

The traditional pedagogy relies completely on the teacher. The teacher is the facilitator who instructs the students what to do, with the help of chalk-and-talk or marker-and-white board. The students depend entirely on their notebooks or books for the retention of information given in the classroom while the teacher prescribes the activities. Its limited effectiveness in teaching and learning has been explained by Mbodila, Munienge, and Muhandji (2012) in the following words:

In this method, the learner's skill, knowledge and practice is of little value, therefore teaching methods are educational and people learn what society expects from them. So the curriculum is homogeneous.

The importance of the transition towards technology-based pedagogy is intensified when the institutionalised status of physical classroom is considered. Instruction in such classrooms is an integral part of both the behavioural and the normative social structure (Hardy, 1983) of higher education. The teaching -learning environment, that is pedagogical ecology, of the traditional classroom includes a set of prescribed social roles and normative expectations that not only shape behaviour but also confer greater status and power to particular social actor. (Jaffee, 1997). The introduction of the new virtual learning environment leaves us with the question whether this will represent a pedagogical ecology that reinforces or alters these established pedagogical roles and behaviours. The mode of instructional technology is proliferating rapidly and this in turn has a transformative impact on teaching and learning (Reiser, 2001; Mc Donald and Postle, 1999)

This instructional technology, commonly termed as "the virtual classroom" (Hiltz, 1994) is defined as a video conferencing tool where instructors (teachers) and participants (students) engage with each other using the learning material. Being an online learning platform, it allows live interaction between the teacher and the student. Nevertheless, unforeseen situations like, low battery of the device or poor internet connectivity, do cause hindrance in the learning process. Even the setup of the house enabling the learning process plays a major role in facilitating the process as people engaged in online learning need a space of their own which might be a constraint in many of the houses.

Impact of Technology on Educational Patterns

However, online learning, also termed as 'digital education', 'e-learning', 'technology-enhanced learning' etc. is mostly portrayed as inherently positive. Information and Communications technology has made its way into learning process. The use of PowerPoint in explaining lessons is fairly common these days. Most schools have projectors to facilitate these. The blackboards were replaced by the whiteboards. Now the whiteboards are being replaced by the web boards. Instead of the regular whiteboards, we now have interactive whiteboards. The reason behind this is the emphasis on students' involvement in the learning process. The teachers also try to use different tools or games to make the learning process entertaining. Kahoot, Answer Garden, WordArt, Wordaizer are just a few apps which are used by the teachers to extract answers from students. The use of such tools involves children in the teaching and learning process. The focus is on making the students capable of deriving their own answers and interpretations rather than blindly taking down notes and copying what the teachers dictate.

There is promising evidence that digital tools can, where effectively used, build skills in interactivity and collaboration, critical thinking and leadership for secondary age learners. These are considered to be vital skills by employers. There is promising evidence too that for secondary age learners, digital resources coupled with digital tools can increase knowledge and understanding of career pathways, applying for work, and working environments. These resources can make it easier for employers to provide help and support to learners. (The Scottish Government, 2015)

There has been a tendency to consider traditional pedagogy to be superior and in Feenberg's (2017, p. 366) words, "… there is little doubt that well prepared teachers under good conditions can be effective in sustaining a true equivalent of classroom interaction." Feenberg went on to propose blended learning as a way to negotiate the divide between technology-driven instruction and human endeavour and in doing so, seems to have conceded to a persistent notion that face-to-face learning is something that can- in the right circumstances- be just as good, but not better. (Fawns, 2018). At the same time, it is also believed that instructional technology has great potential for facilitating more innovative educational methods. Through convenient information gathering and sharing, it can promote innovative teaching methods such as cooperative learning (Lan, Sung & Chang, 2007; Roschelle et al., 2010), exploratory learning outside the classroom (Liu et al., 2012), and game-based learning (Klopfer et al., 2012). Such educational patterns will not only help in subject-content learning but also facilitate the development of communication, problem-solving, creativity and other high-level skills among students (Warschauer, 2007)

In the 21ˢᵗ century, ICT (Information Communication Technology) has offered different techniques to expedite the online learning process while making traditional pedagogy seem less impactful. As Yelland (2005) argued, the traditional pedagogical ecology does not promote productivity in the workplaces of today's society. This argument was supported by Grimus (2000) who said, "by teaching ICT skills, students are prepared to face future development based on proper understanding." (p.362) Some of the most crucial roles played by the use of ICT learning process is the enhancement of student skills, motivation and knowledge, assistance in completing learning tasks and the provision to facilitate a more smoothed and compound view of abstract concept. (Mbodila, Munienge, and Muhandji, 2012). A problem-based learning, promoting critical and analytical thinking is the need of the times. The use of ICT is instrumental in this case as it helps in creating a learner-centred environment. Unlike traditional pedagogy which follows a direct flow of information from teacher to the students, ICT offers a variety of models in teaching and learning. This enables the teachers to play the role of a facilitator helping them to transform their teaching practices.

Impact of Technology on Educational Patterns

ICT promotes deep learning in numerous ways and many of the shortcomings of traditional pedagogy are overcome by the use of ICT. It develops in the students the ability to question, investigate and construct new information. Irrespective of their location, the teachers and students can collaborate and interact. ICT- Supported learning provides students with the opportunity to work with the people of different cultural backgrounds. Having an integrative approach to teaching and learning, the use of ICT promotes the manipulation of existing information, creating real-world products. It is more exploratory in nature and therefore, recognized different learning pathways and various ways of articulation of knowledge. While improving your imagination isn't one of the most common benefits, reading can greatly boost your imagination. Think of the worlds you are immersed in and the characters you encounter while reading a novel. These worlds and characters stimulate the part of your brain that houses your imagination, allowing you to imagine what the places and people look like by imagining the words.

When you start reading a book, you usually don't immediately have a picture in your head. However, by the time you finish the book, you can easily imagine the whole world and characters filling the book. Reading books is all due to the stimulation of the brain that reading produces. Heavy readers will know the feeling of losing themselves in the world of novels. It's a wonderful feeling.

The imagination is a powerful tool that can be useful in all aspects of life. While it may not be considered as often, it is the imagination that allows us to empathize with people. This empathy can help at work or even at home. Since reading is an excellent way to enhance your imagination, it's no wonder that books have been a favorite for so many years. However, after a period of adjustment, online teaching can become second nature and the offer can improve as a result. As professors become accustomed to the bells and whistles associated with this technology, they will come to appreciate certain freedoms or additional technical capabilities that are lacking in conventional classrooms.

For example, in a huge lecture hall, it's logistically difficult for students to split into smaller groups and then get everyone back together in time. Within Zoom, the ease of creating virtual breakout rooms removes those hurdles, making it easy to dispel the lengthy passivity of listening to a lecture with interactive sessions. This is arguably a more effective approach that offsets the depersonalizing tendencies of technology and also affirms students' active involvement in their own learning.

In other words, digital tools allow schools to integrate some horizontal learning into vertical learning environments. However, without a vibrant campus—a physical platform for unplanned interactions—the spontaneity of horizontal learning would largely disappear.

Because horizontal learning cannot be mandated, it still happens more easily in spaces designed for social interactions. Research suggests the disappearance of the campus would be a huge loss for students.

Overall Impact of Using ICT During Online Learning on the Students of Ranchi

Jharkhand is a tribal dominated belt. The tribal population in India as per the 2011 census is 10.43 crore, constituting about 8.6% of the total population and 89.97% of them live in rural areas. Scheduled Tribes constitute 26.2 percent of Jharkhand's total population according to census 2011. A sample study of the responses of 120 students from various schools and colleges of Ranchi reflects how being a tribal or non-tribal, age group, availability of Online learning platforms, use of ICT tools in online classes etc. affects the learning process of the students of Ranchi.

Impact of Technology on Educational Patterns

Methods of the Study

Data has been gathered through various techniques and methods for this research. Analytical approaches like interviews with teachers, discussions and questionnaires filled out by students were employed. Quantitative data sources included surveys and qualitative data included interviews with teachers, students, schools and higher education organizations. Secondary data sources like journals, books and information and communication technologies in education were also explored.

RESULTS

Findings and Analysis

The responses of females have exceeded those of males by 47.5% and the responses have mostly been received from the age group of 16-25 years. Covid brought with it a revolutionary change in the use of ICT enabled pedagogical tools. The responses on the utility of using ICT enabled pedagogical tools are presented in the following table.

Table 1.

Data Observed	Options	Numbers/ Response	% Percentage
Gender	Male	21	26.25
	Female	59	73.75
Age	16-20	35	43.75
	21-25	39	48.75
	26 and above	4	5
ICT tools such as (Moodle, Myquiz, Kahoot, Padlet) used	Yes	45	56.25
	No	35	43.75
Any e- exam system used	Yes	71	88.75
	No	9	11.25
Technology for information presentation (eg: Powerpoint, digital media)	Yes	77	96.25
	No	3	3.75
Technology help in personal productivity	Yes	78	97.5
	No	2	2.5
Level of Satisfaction using technology in classroom	Highly satisfactory	23	28.75
	Satisfactory	41	51.25
	Neutral	15	18.75
	Unsatisfactory	1	1.25

Impact of Technology on Educational Patterns

While the survey clearly states that 56.3% of the schools and colleges in Jharkhand use ICT tools, there are still quite a large number of schools/ colleges that need to adopt the change. In spite of this, the shift to e-examinations has been exponential. 96.3% of the schools and colleges in Jharkhand have adopted the mode of teaching through PowerPoint presentations and use of other digital media. 97.5% of the students surveyed accepted that the use of technology enhances personal productivity. In terms of administration and classroom management, 96.3% of the schools and institutions make use of technology. A mixed response was received when students shared their experience of using technology in classroom. While 51.2% students were highly satisfied using ICT tools in classroom, 28.7% found it satisfactory and 18.8% students were neutral about it. On being interviewed, they acknowledged the difficulty in adapting to technology without prior training. However, the majority, that is, 90% of the students, accepted the fact that the use of ICT tools in the classroom increases their overall performance. Each of the students surveyed endorsed using internet technology for exploring the topics of their academic interest. Although 82.5% of the students find no difficulty in handling technological tools, yet a traditional classroom is a preferred arrangement with 55% of the students endorsing traditional classrooms to be more informative.

Figure 1. Outcome of the use of ICT tools in Schools and Higher Education Institutions of Ranchi:

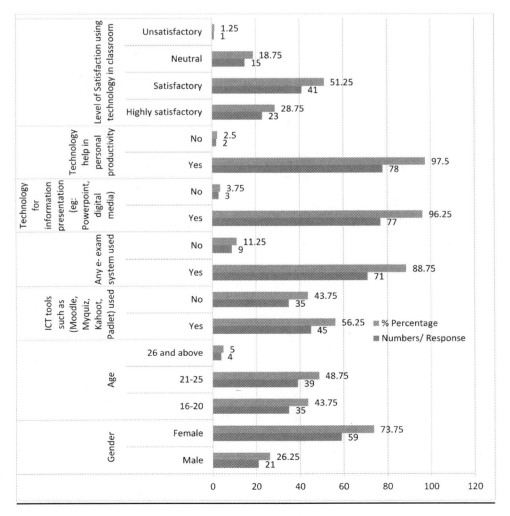

Impact of Technology on Educational Patterns

A specific survey was conducted in the higher education institutions of Ranchi to develop a comparative analysis on the impact of the use of technology in pedagogy among tribal and non-tribal students. The responses are recorded in table 2:

Data Observed	Options	Numbers/ Response	% Percentage
Gender	Male	77	64.16
	Female	43	35.83
Age	15-20	38	31.66
	20-25	46	38.33
	25-30	22	18.34
	30-35	14	11.67
Are you a tribal student	Tribal	96	80
	Non- Tribal	24	20
Level of Education	10th	0	0
	12th	16	13.33
	Graduation	60	50
	Post Graduation	43	35.83
	PhD	1	0.83
Tools used	Padlet	0	0
	kahoot	0	0
	Google classroom	9	7.5
	MS Teams	86	71.66
	Zoom	25	20.83
Measurement ICT (Learning Activities)	Outstanding	23	19.16
	Good	64	53.34
	Satisfactory	32	26.66
	Poor	1	0.83

96% of the students surveyed turned out to be tribals, 60% of which were pursuing graduation and 43& of them were pursuing post-graduation. 55% of them acknowledged that being a tribal or a non-tribal bear no consequence on the absorption of knowledge gained through the use of ICT tools. MS Teams has been found to be most widely used ICT learning tool in Ranchi, a very important aspect of fair-treatment by teachers in ICT enabled virtual classrooms was raised and 85% of the students agreed that virtual classrooms provide a greater scope for fair treatment of students by teachers, irrespective of their tribal identity.

Impact of Technology on Educational Patterns

Figure 2. Impact of the use of Technology among tribal and non-tribal students in Ranchi:

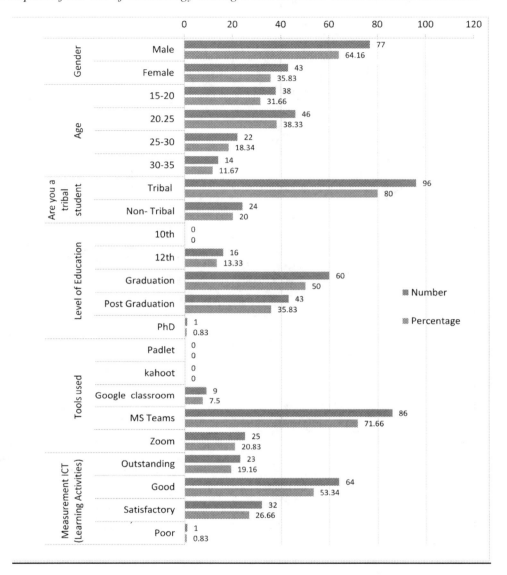

CONCLUSION

This research paper not only examines the shift in the pattern of pedagogy after the use of ICT tools in the schools and higher education institutions, with special reference to Ranchi but also determines the effectiveness of the use of ICT tools during teaching- learning process. The study shows how education is detecting a significant change regarding access, equity and quality in India, accelerating this transition by the exponential growth of ICT in the world's educational systems (Dubey & Sinha, 2021). The research indicated that, though most of the institutions have adopted ICTs in classrooms, the utilisation needs to expand so as to provide quality interactive education. In spite of its limitations, creativity in digital environment knows no bounds. The responses recorded through the surveys clearly indicate that

Impact of Technology on Educational Patterns

educational institutions that have adopted ICT have taken a step forward in improving the quality of higher education and in turn, the quality of research. Both the advantages and disadvantages of technology are addressed in the national education policy of 2020. Therefore, bridging the digital gap is necessary for the overall development of education sector.

REFERENCES

Dubey, M., & Sinha, K. (2021). Role Of Information Communication Technology In Higher Education In Ranchi. *Elementary Education Online*, *20*(6), 1074–1074.

Fawns, T., & O'Shea, C. (2018, May). Distributed learning and isolated testing: tensions in traditional assessment practices. In *Proceedings of the 2018 Networked Learning Conference* (pp. 132-139). Academic Press.

Feenberg, A. (2017). The online education controversy and the future of the university. *Foundations of Science*, *22*(2), 363–371. doi:10.100710699-015-9444-9

Grimus, M. (2000, August). ICT and multimedia in the primary school. In *16th conference on educational uses of information and communication technologies, Beijing, China* (pp. 21-25). Academic Press.

Hardy, C. (1983). *Organizations: Rational*. Natural and Open Systems.

Hiltz, S. R. (1994). *The virtual classroom: Learning without limits via computer networks*. Intellect Books.

Jaffee, D. (1997). Asynchronous learning: Technology and pedagogical strategy in a distance learning course. *Teaching Sociology*, *25*(4), 262–277. doi:10.2307/1319295

Klopfer, E., Sheldon, J., Perry, J., & Chen, V. H. (2012). Ubiquitous games for learning (UbiqGames): Weatherlings, a worked example. *Journal of Computer Assisted Learning*, *28*(5), 465–476. doi:10.1111/j.1365-2729.2011.00456.x

Lan, Y. J., Sung, Y. T., & Chang, K. E. (2007). A mobile-device-supported peer-assisted learning system for collaborative early EFL reading. *Language Learning & Technology*, *11*(3), 130–151.

Liu, T. C., Lin, Y. C., Tsai, M. J., & Paas, F. (2012). Split-attention and redundancy effects on mobile learning in physical environments. *Computers & Education*, *58*(1), 172–180. doi:10.1016/j.compedu.2011.08.007

Mbodila, M., & Muhandji, K. (2012, July). The use of ICT in Education: a comparison of traditional pedagogy and emerging pedagogy enabled by ICTs. *Proceedings of the 11th International Conference on Fontier in Education*.

McDonald, J., & Postle, G. (1999). Teaching online: Challenge to a reinterpretation of traditional instructional models. AusWeb99, Lismore, NSW.

Reiser, R. A. (2001). A history of instructional design and technology: Part I: A history of instructional media. *Educational Technology Research and Development*, *49*(1), 53–64. doi:10.1007/BF02504506

Roschelle, J., Rafanan, K., Bhanot, R., Estrella, G., Penuel, B., Nussbaum, M., & Claro, S. (2010). Scaffolding group explanation and feedback with handheld technology: Impact on students' mathematics learning. *Educational Technology Research and Development*, *58*(4), 399–419. doi:10.100711423-009-9142-9

Rose, E. (2017). Cause for optimism: Engaging in a vital conversation about online learning. *Foundations of Science*, *22*(2), 373–376. doi:10.100710699-015-9445-8

The Scottish Government. (2015). *Literature Review on the Impact of Digital Technology on Learning and Teaching*. ICF Consulting Services Ltd.

Warschauer, M. (2007). The Paradoxical Future of Digital Learning. *Learning Inquiry*, *1*, 41–49.

Yelland, N. (2005). The future is now: A review of the literature on the use of computers in early childhood education (1994-2004). *AACE Review*, *13*(3), 201–232.

Chapter 9
Student Intention to Use Online Library Services of a Locked–Down University:
A Quantitative Study

Amir Manzoor

https://orcid.org/0000-0002-3094-768X

Karachi School of Business and Leadership, Karachi, Pakistan

ABSTRACT

The COVID-19 pandemic had a drastic impact on the teaching and learning practices of universities around the globe. To comply with the new normal, universities shifted their teaching and learning activities online. Academic libraries also shifted their services online. However, in many cases, the students enrolled in universities during COVID-19 era had no prior experience of online library services. This study investigated the factors that drive or inhibit these students' use of online library services. Various recommendations and implications for library management are reported.

INTRODUCTION

Libraries are the place of knowledge collection and information storage catalogued for its potential users. The Internet has enabled libraries to reach more people and provide easier access to required information. However, this has not changed the basic function of libraries. Academic libraries are a cornerstone in learning institutions. In Spring 2020, COVID-19 pandemic forced a wide majority of colleges and universities to go online (Kelly & Columbus, 2020; Cox, 2020; Mashroofa, 2021; Alajmi, 2019). In this scenario, academic libraries faced significant challenges in providing continued access to library services by students. Many libraries implemented various measures to continue their operations in compliance with COVID-19 safety protocol (Breeding, 2020). While researchers have studied the provision of online library services (Perera & Suraweera 2021; Fernando & Senevirathne 2021; Almaiah & Alismaiel,

DOI: 10.4018/978-1-6684-5934-8.ch009

Copyright © 2023, IGI Global. Copying or distributing in print or electronic forms without written permission of IGI Global is prohibited.

2019) the examination of new university students' intention to use (ITU) these online services is still missing. This examination is important to determine whether online libraries were able to satisfy the needs of students in the time where students were forced to confine themselves (Kelly & Columbus, 2020). Therefore, this study examines the factors influencing students' intention to use the online library services during the lock-down.

LITERATURE REVIEW

An online library is a library without walls in which a significant proportion of the resources does not exist in tangible form but is accessible electronically. An online library is a collection of services that supports users in creating, dealing and sharing information and organization/presentation of information objects. The collection of information artifacts is available for access via digital format. There are various services provided by online libraries including remote reference services. Online library services offer multiple advantages including quick addition to the collection, quality control, Improved search, quicker access to information, and reduced bureaucracy (Ameen et al., 2019). Online libraries are highly dynamic and able to hold inter-linked, multimedia objects as well. Online libraries support documents and significant meta-data which can be extracted automatically. From access control point of view, online libraries can be distributed and ubiquitous and their physical/logical organizations can be separated (Chung et al., 2010). Online libraries can support multiple layers of access control. Online libraries can support two-way user-communication and quick interaction. Online libraries support symmetric search, complex interactions, navigation, and social filtering (Sharon & Frank, 2020; Asabere et al., 2021).

COVID-19 pandemic caused physical libraries to move their operations online to serve the requirements of their users i.e., students, faculty, and researchers. In the era of Internet, academic libraries face significant complex challenges to meet the needs of their stakeholders (Cox, 2020; Lee & Lehto, 2013; Lwoga & Sife, 2018; Mohamad Rosman et al., 2021; Nguyen et al., 2021). This was because of rapid increase in the sources of information and changes in the behavior of library users (Hinchliffe & Wolff-Eisenberg, 2020; Ghazal et al., 2018). To meet this challenge, libraries made significant changes to adopt to this new norm of VOVID-19. Some libraries utilized their existing online platforms while others developed their online capabilities (Breeding, 2020; Kelly & Columbus, 2020; Breeding, 2020; Rahman & Mohezar, 2020; Rivo & Žumer, 2022). Libraries also started integrating their online systems with online learning management systems (LMS) of the universities (Nicholas & Tomeo, 2005; Johnson, Trabelsi, & Fabbro, 2008; Moncrieff, Macauley, & Epps, 2007; Hwee & Yew, 2018; Rosman et al., 2019; Shivdas et al., 2020; Soltani-Nejad et al., 2020; Teo et al., 2019; Tyagi et al., 2022; Wibowo, 2019). Providing library services online was not easy task. The libraries were not sure that whether they would be able to provide all their services effectively and efficiently to satisfy the users. In the online learning mode, fewer students visited the libraries physically. Rather, students demanded round the clock access to information (Dilevko & Gottlieb, 2002; Moyo, 2004; Gardner & Eng, 2005; Allen & Seaman, 2008; Allen & Seaman, 2008; Isibika & Kavishe, 2018).

The rapidly changing technology landscape has brought significant changes the way students seek information and now majority of students prefer online library resources (Tipton, 2002; Kelley & Orr, 2003; Moyo, 2004; Walters, 2004; Liu & Yang, 2004; Kennedy, 2005; Stephan et al., 2006; Williamson et al., 2007; Nicholas, 2008; Brandt, 2008; Ilahi et al., 2019). It was reported that convenience was the most significant that drove students' use of online library resources (Brandt, 2008). Researchers argue that an increasing number of students accessing information online coupled with rise in the number of online learning platforms mean that academic libraries need creative and collaborative efforts to satisfy the needs of students (Johnson, Trabelis & Fabbro, 2008; Silipigni, 2008; Khan et al., 2022; Omotayo & Haliru, 2020; Pinho et al., 2020; Rafique et al., 2018, 2020, 2021).

Technology Acceptance Model (TAM) and Online Library Services

To study the students' acceptance and use of smartphones in distance education, this study employs TAM (Davis, 1989) which is one of the most cited and widely used behavioral intention model that focuses on factors that affect users' use of technology and predict acceptance or resistance to end-user system. There exist various variations of TAM. However, all focusses on factors that impacts users' acceptance of technology-based systems (Padilla-Meléndez, 2008). According to TAM, two factors determine technology acceptance by its users: perceived usefulness and perceived ease of use (Davis, 1993). Behavioral intention (BI) leads users to use the technology. The online library services can be considered a web-based information system that its end-users (i.e., students) will either accept or reject.

Perceived Ease of Use (PEOU)

PEOU of technology is an important predictor of technology use. The concept of PEOU stems from self-efficacy theory (Bandura,1982). It is defined as the extent to which prospective user perceive how easy it is to use the system (Davis et al., 1989; Venkatesh, 1999). When PEOU is high, the user acceptance of the system increases. When users think that a system provides them information relevant to the tasks in their hands, it is more likely that users perceive the system's more effective and easier to use (Park et al., 2009; Stockham & Turtle, 2004). User's PEOU of a system influences user's PU of system. The user's PU of system in turn influences user's attitude towards and ITU.

Perceived Usefulness (PU)

PU is defined as the extent to which an individual believes that use of a system would enhance his/her performance on a given task. The PU is influenced by the extent to which a system can improve users' productivity. A study found that Internet skills positively correlated with PU (Cheung & Huang, 2005). Users' ITU is likely affected by user's PU of the system (Davis et al., 1989). Literature suggest that PU has significant impact on BI (Jackson et al., 1997; Agarwal & Prasad, 1999; Hu et al., 1999; Yi & Hwang, 2003; De Rosa et al., 2006).

Relevance

In this study, relevance is defined as the perceived match between online library content and student's information needs or the extent to which online library services (the system) provides users (the students) the required information (Schamber et al., 1990; Venkatesh & Davis, 2000; Hong et al., 2002; Thong et al., 2002; Shih, 2004; Vaidyanathan, Sabbaghi, & Bargellini, 2005; Park et al., 2009). Higher the relevance of system, higher the PU of the system would be (Gluck, 1996). Also, higher relevance means the users are more likely to perceive the system effective and easy to use (Janes, 1994; Shih, 2004). The relevance of system is also important for user's BI to use the system. When users find the system more relevant, they are encouraged to use the system to find more information needed to complete their tasks (Spink, Greisdorf, & Bateman, 1998).

Visibility

In this study, visibility is operationalized as the degree to which online library services (the system) is observable by students (the users). Visibility is very important when the system is being used first time by the users because users may not be aware of the availability of the new system. Increased visibility means, it is more likely that users will perceive the system more useful (Thong et al., 2022; Hong et al., 2002). Further, a highly visible system is more likely to enhance user's ITU (Moore & Benbasat, 1991). Therefore, we predict that high visibility of online library services will increase students' perception on its usefulness and consequently enhance their ITU.

Self-Efficacy (SE)

In general, SE is defined a person's judgment of his/her capabilities to perform a given task. In this study, SE is operationalized as an individual's perception of efficacy in using a system. SE plays important roles in determining a person's behavior. Literature suggests that user's computer self-efficacy has significant impact on user's PEOU and subsequent use and acceptance of the system (Venkatesh & Davis, 1996; Venkatesh & Davis, 2000).

CONCEPTUAL FRAMEWORK AND RESEARCH HYPOTHESES

Figure 1 shows the conceptual framework used in this study.

Figure 1. Conceptual Framework

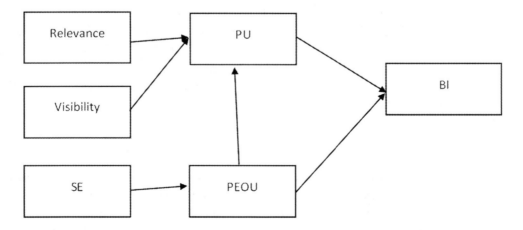

Following are the research hypotheses of this study.

- H1: PU has a significant impact on students' BI to use online library services.
- H2: PEOU has a significant impact on students' BI to use online library services.
- H3: PEOU of use has a significant impact on PU of online library services.
- H4: Relevance of online library services has a significant impact on the PU of online library services.
- H5: Visibility of online library services has a significant impact on the PU of online library services.
- H6: SE of students has a significant impact on PEOU of online library services.

METHODOLOGY

Research Instrument

The data for this study was collected using a questionnaire. The measures used in the questionnaire were adapted from available literature. Specifically, the scale used to measure PU, PEOU, and BI towards usage were adopted from Davis et al., (1989), Adams, Nelson, and Todd (1992), Chin and Todd (1995), Szajna (1996), Corwin (1998), Wallace (1998), and Venkatesh and Davis (2000). The scale used to measure relevance, visibility, and self-efficacy were adopted from Park et al., 2009. A five-point Likert scale (where 1 = strongly disagree to 5= strongly agree) was used to measure all items. There were two parts of the questionnaire. The first part contained questions to collect demographic data. The second part contained items used to measure the variables included in the research framework.

Sampling Design

This questionnaire was administered on a sample of university students in Karachi. These students were selected using snowball sampling technique. The participants of this study were first year undergraduates' who were enrolled various universities of Karachi for the year 2020/2021. The participants of the study had basic internet and computer skills. However, they had received no formal library orientation program prior to their joining university. The final sample consisted of 148 participants. The sample was balanced where 48.7% of participants were female and 51.3% were male.

DATA ANALYSIS AND RESULTS

We used confirmatory factor analysis (CFA) to establish construct reliability and validity. SmartPSLS statistical software was used for all statistical analyses. Multiple regression analysis and path analysis were used to examine the hypothesized relationships.

Instrument Validation

The model was tested to ascertain reliability of the research instrument. The procured specified by Cronbach (1951) was used to measure the internal consistency of the research instrument. As shown in Table 1, the values of Cronbach's alpha for all measures used in the research instrument were above .70 (Nunnally & Bernstein, 1994). Therefore, the research instrument was considered reliable.

Table 1. Reliability statistics

Measure	Cronbach's Alpha
BI	0.794
PEOU	0.922
PU	0.899
Relevance	0.744
SE	0.869
Visibility	0.812

Hypothesis Testing

H1 proposed PU has a significant impact on students' BI to use online library services. Looking at Table 3, we see that path coefficient of PU -> Behavioral Intention was 0.078 with p-value = 0.000. Therefore, H1 was supported. H2 and H3 proposed that PEOU has a significant impact on BI to use and PU, respectively. Looking at 3, we see that path coefficient of PEOU -> Behavioral Intention is 0.681 with p-value=0.000 and path coefficient of PEOU -> PU was .079 with p-value =0.000. Hence, H2 and H3 are supported. H4 proposed that relevance of online library services has a significant impact on the PU of online library services. Looking at Table 3, we see that path coefficient of Relevance -> PU was .407 with p-value =0.000. Hence, H4 is supported. H5 proposed that visibility of online library services has a significant impact on the PU of online library services. Looking at Table 3, we see that path coefficient of Relevance -> PU was .220 with p-value =0.005. Hence, H5 is supported. H6 proposed that SE of students has a significant impact on PEOU of online library services. Looking at Table 3, we see that path coefficient of Relevance -> PU was .383 with p-value =0.000. Hence, H6 is supported.

Table 2. R square values

	Original Sample	Sample Mean	Standard Deviation	T Statistics	P Values
BI	0.510	0.521	0.071	7.190	0.000
PEOU	0.147	0.159	0.050	2.944	0.003
PU	0.343	0.367	0.063	5.441	0.000

Student Intention to Use Online Library Services of a Locked-Down University

Table 3. Path coefficients

	Original Sample	Sample Mean	Standard Deviation	T Statistics	P Values
PEOU -> BI	0.681	0.685	0.058	11.711	0.000
PEOU -> PU	0.079	0.074	0.081	0.985	0.000
PEOU -> BI	0.078	0.079	0.078	0.994	0.000
Relevance -> PU	0.407	0.419	0.068	5.960	0.000
SE -> PEOU	0.383	0.394	0.063	6.054	0.000
Visibility -> PU	0.220	0.223	0.078	2.825	0.005

The two predictors i.e., PU and PEOU together explained more than 50% variation in the students' BI to use online library services ($R^2 = 0.510$, p< 0.001). PEOU was a direct and most significant predictor of BI. Relevance was the direct and most significant predictor of students' PU of online library services. Findings indicate that recognition of benefits and PEOU of online library services drive students' ITU.

CONCLUSION

The present study aims to examine the factors that drive students' intention of using online library services. The PU emerged as the most significant indicator of students' ITU. PEOU was also a significant indicator. Relevance and visibility were significant indicators of students' PU of online library services. self-efficacy was the significant indicator of students' PEOU. Self-efficacy was a significant predictor of student's PEOU. The findings suggest that library management should work on enhancing students' belief that online library services are useful for them. This belief will drive students continued use of these services. Library management should also work to make online library services more accessible and easier to use. That would increase the students use the online library services. The orientation of new students on online library services is very important. Library management should ascertain whether students have the required computer skills to use online library services. This would help increase student's self-efficacy and subsequently enhance students' PEOU of online library services.

Practical and Managerial Implications

There are two major implications of this study. First, the academicians and practitioners can use the conceptual model of this study to predict the factors that could enhance the use of online library services in their respective context. The results of this study can serve as guidelines for designing online library services and systems. The researchers can also use the conceptual model as a tool to gauge students' acceptance of online library services. Doing so, they could minimize the risks that students would reject the online library services. Early detection of risks would enable system designers to come up with measures that could ensure students' acceptance of the online library services. Since students' PEOU of online library services is a significant and direct predictor of their actual use of online library services, it is important that students are introduced to these services and briefed about their use and benefits. That would ease the task of getting their acceptance of these services.

Areas of Future Research

This study was a cross-sectional study. Future studies could be longitudinal where they could replicate the conceptual model of this study. Future studies could also use the extended TAM to gain more insights into how students' beliefs and attitudes towards online library services could change overtime while they experience the use of online library services.

REFERENCES

Adams, D. A., Nelson, R. R., & Todd, P. A. (1992). Perceived usefulness, ease of use, and usage of information technology: A replication. *Management Information Systems Quarterly*, *16*(2), 227–247.

Agarwal, R., & Prasad, J. (1999). Are individual differences germane to the acceptance of new information technologies? *Decision Sciences*, *30*, 361–391.

Alajmi, M. A. (2019). The acceptance and use of electronic information resources among faculty of selected Gulf Cooperation Council States universities. *Information Development*, *35*(3), 447–466.

Allen, I. E., & Seaman, J. (2008, November). *Staying the course: Online education in the United States*. Retrieved from Sloan Consortium website: http://www.sloan-c.org/publications/view/index.asp

Allen, M., & Dee, C. (2006). A survey of the usability of digital reference services on academic health science library websites. *Journal of Academic Librarianship*, *32*, 69–78. http://www.elsevier.com

Almaiah, M. A., & Alismaiel, O. A. (2019). Examination of factors influencing the use of mobile learning system: An empirical study. *Education and Information Technologies*, *24*(1), 885–909.

Ameen, N., Willis, R., Abdullah, M. N., & Shah, M. (2019). Towards the successful integration of e-learning systems in higher education in Iraq: A student perspective. *British Journal of Educational Technology*, *50*(3), 1434–1446.

Asabere, N. Y., Acakpovi, A., Agyiri, J., Awuku, M. C., Sakyi, M. A., & Teyewayo, D. A. (2021). Measuring the Constructs That Influence Student and Lecturer Acceptance of an E-Library in Accra Technical University, Ghana. *International Journal of Online Pedagogy and Course Design*, *11*(1), 53–72.

Bandura, A. (1982). Self-efficacy mechanism in human agency. *The American Psychologist*, *37*, 122–147. doi:10.1037/0003-066X.37.2.122

Brandt, S. A. (2008). *Information source selection of traditional and distance students* (Doctoral dissertation). Retrieved from http://etd.fcla.edu/WF/WFE0000098/ Brandt_Sheila_Ann_200805_EdD.pdf

Breeding. (2020). *The Systems Librarian - A Global Crisis May Reshape Library Services*. https://www.infotoday.com/cilmag/may20/Breeding--A-Global-Crisis-May-Reshape-Library-Services.shtml

Cheung, W., & Huang, W. (2005). Proposing a framework to assess Internet usage in university education: An empirical investigation from a student's perspective. *British Journal of Educational Technology*, *36*, 237–253. http://www.wiley.com/bw/ journal.asp?ref=0007-1013

Chung, J. E., Park, N., Wang, H., Fulk, J., & McLaughlin, M. (2010). Age differences in perceptions of online community participation among non-users: An extension of the Technology Acceptance Model. *Computers in Human Behavior, 26*(6), 1674–1684.

Cox. (2020). *Academic libraries will change in significant ways as a result of the pandemic (opinion).* https://www.insidehighered.com/views/2020/06/05/academic-libraries-will-change-significant-ways-result-pandemic-opinion

Davis, F., Bagozzi, R., & Warshaw, R. (1989). User Acceptance of computer technology: A comparison of two theoretical models. *Management Science, 35*, 982–1002.

Davis, F. D. (1986). *A technology acceptance model for empirically testing new enduser information systems: Theory and results* [Unpublished doctoral dissertation]. Massachusetts Institute of Technology.

Davis, F. D. (1989). Perceived usefulness, perceived ease of use, and user acceptance of information technology. *Management Information Systems Quarterly, 13*, 319–339. http://www.jstor.org/stable/249008

Davis, F. D. (1993). User acceptance of information technology: System characteristics, user perceptions and behavior impacts. *International Journal of Man-Machine Studies, 39*, 475–487.

Davis, F. D., Bagozzi, R. P., & Warshaw, P. R. (1989). User acceptance of computer technology: A comparison of two theoretical models. *Management Science, 35*, 982–1003. https://www.jstor.org/stable/2632151

Davis, F. D., Bagozzi, R. P., & Warshaw, P. R. (1989). User acceptance of computer technology: A comparison of two theoretical models. *Management Science, 35*(8), 982–1003.

De Rosa, C., Cantrell, J., Hawk, J., & Wilson, A. (2006). *College students' perceptions of libraries and information resources.* Retrieved from Online Computer Library Center website: https://www.oclc.org/us/en/reports/perceptionscollege.htm

Dilevko, J., & Gottlieb, L. (2002). Print sources in an electronic age: A vital part of the research process for undergraduate students. *Journal of Academic Librarianship, 28*, 381–392.

Fernando, I. D. K. L., & Senevirathna, R. A. P. S. (2020). *Survey on online library services provided during the COVID pandemic situation: With special reference to academic libraries of Sri Lanka.* Academic Press.

Gardner, S., & Eng, S. (2005). What students want: Generation Y and the changing function of the academic library. *Portal (Baltimore, Md.), 5*, 405–420. doi:10.1353/ pla.2005.0034

Ghazal, S., Al-Samarraie, H., & Aldowah, H. (2018). "I am still learning": Modeling LMS critical success factors for promoting students' experience and satisfaction in a blended learning environment. *IEEE Access: Practical Innovations, Open Solutions, 6*, 77179–77201.

Gluck, M. (1996). Exploring the relationship between user satisfaction and relevance in information systems. *Information Processing & Management, 32*(1), 89–104.

Hall-Ellis, S. D. (2006). Cataloging electronic resources and metadata: Employers' expectations as reflected in American libraries and AutoCAT, 2000-2005. *Journal of Education for Library and Information Science, 47*, 38–51. http://vnweb.hwwilsonweb.com/hww/login.jhtml?_requestid=108885

Hinchliffe & Wolff-Eisenberg. (2020, March 24). First This, Now That: A Look at 10-Day Trends in Academic Library Response to COVID19. *Ithaka S+R*. https://sr.ithaka.org/blog/first-this-now-that-a-look-at-10-day-trends-in-academic-library-response-to-covid19/

Hong, W., Thong, J. Y. L., Wong, W.-M., & Tam, K.-Y. (2002). Determinants of user acceptance of digital libraries: An empirical examination of individual differences and system characteristics. *Journal of Management Information Systems, 18*(3), 97–124.

Hu, P. J., Chau, P. Y. K., Sheng, O. R. L., & Tam, K. Y. (1999). Examining the technology acceptance model using physician acceptance of telemedicine technology. *Journal of Management Information Systems, 16*, 91–112.

Hwee, L., & Yew, J. (2018). The constructs that influence students' acceptance of an e-library system in Malaysia. *International Journal of Education and Development Using ICT, 14*(2).

Ilahi, R., Widiaty, I., Wahyudin, D., & Abdullah, A. G. (2019). Digital library as learning resources. *Journal of Physics: Conference Series, 1402*(7), 077044.

Isibika, I. S., & Kavishe, G. F. (2018). *Utilisation of subscribed electronic resources by library users in Mzumbe university library*. Global Knowledge, Memory and Communication.

Jackson, C. M., Chow, S., & Leitch, R. A. (1997). Toward an understanding of the behavioural intentions to use an information system. *Decision Sciences, 28*, 357–389.

Janes, J. W. (1994). Other people's judgments: A comparison of users' and others' judgments of document relevance, topicality, and utility. *Journal of the American Society for Information Science, 45*(3), 160–171.

Johnson, K., Trabelsi, H., & Fabbro, E. (2008). Library support for e-learners: E-resources, e- services, and the human factors. In T. Anderson (Ed.), *The theory and practice of online learning* (2nd ed., pp. 397-418). Retrieved from https://www.aupress.ca/index.php/books/120146

Kelley, K., & Orr, G. (2003). Trends in distant student use of electronic resources. *College & Research Libraries, 64*, 176–191. http://www.ala.org/ala/mgrps/divs/acrl/publications/crljournal/collegeresearch.cfm

Kelly, A., & Columbus, R. (2020). *College in the time of coronavirus: Challenges facing American higher education*. American Enterprise Institute. doi:10.2307/resrep25358

Kennedy, J. (2005). *A collection development policy for digital information resources? In Determining the impact of technological modernization and management capabilities on user satisfaction and trust in library services*. Global Knowledge, Memory and Communication.

Koohang, A. (2004). Students' perceptions toward use of the digital library in weekly web-based distance learning assignments portion of a hybrid programme. *British Journal of Educational Technology, 35*, 617–626. doi:10.1111/j.0007-1013. 2004.00418.x

Koohang, A., & Ondracek, J. (2005). Users' views about the usability of digital libraries. *British Journal of Educational Technology*, *36*, 407–423. http://www.hwwilconweb.com

Koohang, A., & Ondracek, J. (2005). Users' views about the usability of digital libraries. *British Journal of Educational Technology*, *36*(3), 407–423.

Lee, D. Y., & Lehto, M. R. (2013). User acceptance of YouTube for procedural learning: An extension of the Technology Acceptance Model. *Computers & Education*, *61*, 193–208.

Lin, C. A. (1998). Exploring personal computer adoption dynamics. *Journal of Broadcasting & Electronic Media*, *42*(1), 95–112.

Liu, Z., & Yang, Z. Y. (2004). Factors influencing distance education graduate students' use of information sources: A user study. *Journal of Academic Librarianship*, *30*, 24–35. doi:10.1016/j.jal.2003.11.005

Lwoga, E. T., & Sife, A. S. (2018). Impacts of quality antecedents on faculty members' acceptance of electronic resources. *Library Hi Tech*.

Marchionini, G. (2000). Evaluating digital libraries: A longitudinal and multifaceted view. *Library Trends*, *49*(2), 304–333.

Marchionini, G., Dwiggins, S., Katz, A., & Lin, X. (1993). Information seeking in full-text end-user-oriented search systems: The roles of domain and search expertise. *Library & Information Science Research*, *15*, 35–69.

Marchionini, G., & Fox, E. A. (1999). Progress toward digital libraries: Augmentation through integration. *Information Processing & Management*, *35*, 219–225.

Mashroofa, M. M. (2021). Sustainability of library and information services during Covid-19 pandemic: A case of South Eastern University of Sri Lanka (SEUSL) Libraries. Academic Press.

Mohamad Rosman, M. R., Ismail, M. N., & Masrek, M. N. (2021). Investigating the predictors of digital library engagement: A structured literature analysis. *Pakistan Journal of Information Management and Libraries*, *22*, 60–82.

Moncrieff, J., Macauley, P., & Epps, J. (2007). —My universe is here‖: Implications for the future of academic libraries from the results of a survey of teachers. *Australian Academic and Research Libraries*, *38*, 71–83. http://alianet.alia.org.au/

Moore, G. C., & Benbasat, T. (1991). Development of an instrument to measure the perceptions of adopting an information technology innovation. *Information Systems Research*, *2*, 192–222.

Moore, J. (2008). *A synthesis of Sloan-C effective practices*. Retrieved from http://www.sloan- c.org/effective/v12n3_moore-2.pdf

Moyo, L. M. (2004). The virtual patron. *Science & Technology Libraries*, *25*, 185–209. doi:10.1300/J122v25n01_12

Nelson, D. L. (1990). Individual adjustment to information-driven technologies: A critical review. *Management Information Systems Quarterly*, *14*(1), 79–98.

Nguyen, X., Pho, D.-H., & Luong, D.-H., & Xuan-thuc-anh, C. A. O. (2021). Vietnamese students' acceptance of using video conferencing tools in distance learning in COVID-19 pandemic. *Turkish Online Journal of Distance Education, 22*(3), 139–162.

Nicholas, D. (2008). The information seeking behaviour of the virtual scholar: From use to users. *Serials, 21*, 89-92. Retrieved from http://serials.uksg.org

Nicholas, M., & Tomeo, M. (2005). Can you hear me now? Communicating library services to distance education students and faculty. *Online Journal of Distance Learning Administration, 8*(2), 1–8. https://www.westga.edu/~distance/ojdla/ search_results_id.php?id=298

Omotayo, F. O., & Haliru, A. (2020). Perception of task-technology fit of digital library among undergraduates in selected universities in Nigeria. *Journal of Academic Librarianship, 46*(1), 102097.

Online Computer Library Center (OCLC). (2002). *OCLC white paper on the information habits of college students.* Retrieved from Online Computer Library Center website: http://www5.oclc.org/downloads/community/informationhabits.pdf

Park, N., Lee, K. M., & Cheong, P. H. (2007). University instructors' acceptance of electronic courseware: An application of the Technology Acceptance Model. *Journal of Computer-Mediated Communication, 13*(1). http://jcmc.indiana.edu/vol13/issue1/park.html

Park, N., Roman, R., Lee, S., & Chung, J. E. (2009). User acceptance of a digital library system in developing countries: An application of the technology acceptance model. *International Journal of Information Management, 29*, 196–209. doi:10.1016/j.ijinfomgt.2008.07.001

Perera, W. P. G. L., & Suraweera, S. A. D. H. N. (2021). *The Academic Library Support for E-Learning: Students' Perspectives and Web Observation.* Academic Press.

Pinho, C., Franco, M., & Mendes, L. (2020). Exploring the conditions of success in e-libraries in the higher education context through the lens of the social learning theory. *Information & Management, 57*(4), 103208.

Rafique, H., Almagrabi, A. O., Shamim, A., Anwar, F., & Bashir, A. K. (2020). Investigating the acceptance of mobile library applications with an extended technology acceptance model (TAM). *Computers & Education, 145*, 103732.

Rafique, H., Alroobaea, R., Munawar, B. A., Krichen, M., Rubaiee, S., & Bashir, A. K. (2021). Do digital students show an inclination toward continuous use of academic library applications? A case study. *Journal of Academic Librarianship, 47*(2), 102298.

Rafique, H., Anwer, F., Shamim, A., Minaei-Bidgoli, B., Qureshi, M. A., & Shamshirband, S. (2018). Factors affecting acceptance of mobile library applications: Structural equation model. *Libri, 68*(2), 99–112.

Rahman, A. R. A., & Mohezar, S. (2020). Ensuring continued use of a digital library: A qualitative approach. *The Electronic Library, 38*(3), 513–530.

Rivo, K., & Žumer, M. (2022). Academic Libraries and Use of Mobile Devices: Case Study of Slovenia. *Journal of Academic Librarianship, 48*(3), 102507.

Rosman, M. R. M., Ismail, M. N., Masrek, M. N., Branch, K., & Campus, M. (2019). Investigating the determinant and impact of digital library engagement: A conceptual framework. *Journal of Digital Information Management*, *17*(4), 215.

Schamber, L., Eisenberg, M., & Nilan, M. S. (1990). A re-examination of relevance: Toward a dynamic, situational definition, Information Processing and Management. *International Journal (Toronto, Ont.)*, *26*(6), 755–776.

Sharon and Frank. (2020). *Views on Digital Libraries* [PowerPoint slides]. https://u.cs.biu.ac.il/~franka2/download/ird665/ird3-2_lib.ppt

Shih, H.-P. (2004). Extended technology acceptance model of Internet utilization behavior. *Information & Management*, *41*(6), 719–729.

Shivdas, A., Menon, D. G., & Nair, C. S. (2020). *Antecedents of acceptance and use of a digital library system: Experience from a tier 3 Indian city*. The Electronic Library.

Silipigni. (2008). Make room for the Millennials. *NextSpace, 10*, 18-19. Retrieved from https://www.oclc.org/nextspace

Soltani-Nejad, N., Taheri-Azad, F., Zarei-Maram, N., & Saberi, M. K. (2020). Developing a model to identify the antecedents and consequences of user satisfaction with digital libraries. *Aslib Journal of Information Management*.

Spink, A., Greisdorf, H., & Bateman, J. (1998). From highly relevant to not relevant: Examining different regions of relevance. *Information Processing & Management*, *34*(5), 599–621.

Stephan, E., Cheng, D. T., & Young, L. M. (2006). A usability survey at the University of Mississippi libraries for the improvement of the library home page. *Journal of Academic Librarianship*, *32*, 35–51.

Stockham, M., & Turtle, E. (2004). Providing off-campus library services by —Team‖: An assessment. *Journal of Library Administration*, *41*(3/4), 443–452. doi:10.1300/ J111v41n03_09

Teo, T., Doleck, T., Bazelais, P., & Lemay, D. J. (2019). Exploring the drivers of technology acceptance: A study of Nepali school students. *Educational Technology Research and Development*, *67*(2), 495–517.

Thong, J. Y. L., Hong, W., & Tam, K.-Y. (2002). Understanding user acceptance of digital libraries: What are the roles of interface characteristics, organizational context, and individual differences? *International Journal of Human-Computer Studies*, *57*, 215–242.

Tipton, C. J. (2002). *Academic libraries and distance learners: A study of graduate student perceptions of the effectiveness of library support for distance learning* (Doctoral dissertation). Available from ProQuest Dissertations and Theses database. (UMI No. 3060910)

Tyagi, S. K., Sharma, S. K., & Gaur, A. (2022). Determinants of continuous usage of library resources on handheld devices: Findings from PLS-SEM and fuzzy sets (fsQCA). *The Electronic Library,* ahead-of-print.

Vaidyanathan, G., Sabbaghi, A., & Bargellini, M. (2005). User acceptance of digital library: An empirical exploration of individual and system components. *Issues in Information Systems*, *6*(2), 279–285.

Venkatesh, V. (1999). Creation of favorable user perceptions: Exploring the role intrinsic motivation. *Management Information Systems Quarterly*, *23*(2), 239–260.

Venkatesh, V. (2000). Determinants of perceived ease of use: Integrating control, intrinsic motivation, and emotion into the technology acceptance model. *Information Systems Research*, *11*(4), 342–365.

Venkatesh, V., & Davis, F. D. (1996). A model of the antecedents of perceived ease of use: Development and test. *Decision Sciences*, *27*(3), 451–481.

Venkatesh, V., & Davis, F. D. (2000). A theoretical extension of the technology acceptance model: Four longitudinal field studies. *Management Science*, *46*(2), 186–204.

Walters, W. (2004). Criteria for replacing print journals with online journal resources: The importance of sustainable access notes on operations. *Library Resources & Technical Services*, *18*(4), 300–309. http://www.hwwilsonweb.com

Wibowo, M. P. (2019). *Technology Acceptance Models and Theories in Library and Information Science Research*. Seminar in Theory and Foundations of Information Sciences Course at Florida State University.

Williamson, K., Bernath, V., Wright, S., & Sullivan, J. (2007). Research students in the electronic age. *Communications in Information Literacy*, *1*, 47–63. http://www.comminfolit.org/index.php/cil

Wilson, E. J. (2003). *The information revolution and developing countries*. MIT Press.

Wilson, F., & Keys, J. (2004). AskNow! Evaluating an Australian collaborative chat reference service: A project manager's perspective. *Australian Academic and Research Libraries, 35*, 81-95. Retrieved from http://vnweb.hwwilsonweb.com/hww/login.jhtml?_requestid=29758

Yi, M. Y., & Hwang, Y. (2003). Predicting the use of web-based information systems: Self-efficacy, enjoyment, learning goal orientation, and the technology acceptance model. *International Journal of Human-Computer Studies*, *59*(4), 431–449.

Zhang, X. (2016). An analysis of online students' behaviors on course sites and the effect on learning performance: A case study of four LIS online classes. *Journal of Education for Library and Information Science*, *57*(4), 255–270. doi:10.2307/90015229

Zhang, Y., & Estabrook, L. (1998). Accessibility to Internet-based electronic resources and its implications for electronic scholarship. In *Proceedings of the American Society for Information Science Annual Meeting* (pp. 463–473). Academic Press.

Section 4

Social Organizing in the Teeth of an Unfolding Global Pandemic

Chapter 10

Community Awareness and Leadership Among Singapore Youths Amidst a COVID–19 Landscape

Intan Azura Mokhtar

https://orcid.org/0000-0002-9131-8254

Singapore Institute of Technology, Singapore

Yaacob Ibrahim

Singapore Institute of Technology, Singapore

ABSTRACT

The COVID-19 pandemic has changed how businesses operate, how people work, and the way people socialize and interact. The changes that needed to be made were significant and did not happen easily. However, the COVID-19 pandemic also presented opportunities for creativity to flourish, innovations to happen, and kindness and magnanimity to be extended to one another. In Singapore, an island-nation city-state, significant changes had to be implemented to ring-fence the spread of infections and ensure the local economy and healthcare system could cope with the impact of the pandemic. At the forefront of some of these changes were the youths. Young people with creative ideas, boundless energy, and a strong sense of social cause and fairness led initiatives that had significant and positive impact on those most vulnerable. In this chapter, the backdrop of the evolution of a values-based education system in Singapore and its impact on the younger generation of Singaporeans is discussed followed by examples of youth-led initiatives in Singapore amidst a COVID-19 landscape.

DOI: 10.4018/978-1-6684-5934-8.ch010

Copyright © 2023, IGI Global. Copying or distributing in print or electronic forms without written permission of IGI Global is prohibited.

INTRODUCTION

The Covid-19 pandemic that began in December 2019 spread quickly and globally throughout the two years 2020 and 2021. Even as the Covid-19 vaccination programs were rolled out in almost every country in those two years, the way that businesses operate, how people work, and how people socialize and interact, have changed significantly. Constant reminders on personal hygiene, frequent cleaning and sanitizing, safe distancing, and management measures, as well as regular self-administered checks and tests, remain the norm. In many societies, community-centric initiatives and programs were launched to help groups, especially vulnerable groups, better cope with these significant changes to our daily lives. In this chapter, we explore some of these community-centric initiatives and programs in Singapore, a small city-state in Southeast Asia, specifically those that were led by the youths or younger Singaporeans who have increasingly demonstrated a strong advocacy for social causes and social justice. This is done by first dissecting values-based education in the Singapore education system, and how that had paved the way for a more extensive and deeper integration of social innovation projects, or initiatives that generate positive social impact, in the education curricula from primary schools through to universities and other institutes of higher learning. The chapter ends with a discussion of how the social impact of such youth-led projects or initiatives can be evaluated for sustained impact and continuity of efforts.

BACKGROUND OF SINGAPORE

Singapore is a relatively small island nation situated in Southeast Asia, just one degree north of the equator, off the southern tip of peninsular Malaysia. Having gained independence in 1965, this young city-state has grown by leaps and bounds, having progressed from an underdeveloped country to a progressive and advanced nation with impressive achievements in education, healthcare, information technology, scientific research and development, and many other areas.

The Singapore education system, which has garnered sufficient interest and scrutiny from academics, practitioners, and policymakers alike the world over, has, to a large extent, a significant part to play in shaping the mindsets and aspirations of youths in Singapore. The integration of values-based elements in the school curricula was instrumental in developing common core values among Singaporeans – that of *respect, responsibility, resilience, integrity, care,* and *harmony* (or R^{3}ICH, as an acronym) – which form the basis of the framework for 21st century competencies student outcomes that undergird teaching and learning in the Singapore education system. The next section provides a brief overview of the development of a values-based education in the Singapore school curricula.

VALUES-BASED EDUCATION IN SINGAPORE

Not long after Singapore attained independence, the government played an active role in stimulating public discussion on moral and national values that would ensure social cohesion of the new multi-racial and multi-religious city-state. It was alluded that the motive behind this keen interest to articulate and implement a set of shared or common values for the new nation was precipitated by the government's then concern about activities related to the 1970s "hippie" culture of the west (Murray, 1991, p.8). By the early 1980s, a moral education syllabus was introduced for primary and secondary schools, beginning with the primary school levels in 1981, under the *Good Citizen,* and *Being and Becoming* programs. *Religious Knowledge* (RK) was introduced in all secondary schools in 1984 as a compulsory subject (National Library Board, 2014a), focusing on moral values through the study of a religious or ethical system. However, in 1990, RK was made a non-compulsory or elective subject, as the then Ministry of Education felt that the teaching of religious-based values should be the responsibility of parents and families, and not that of schools.

It is also instructive to recognize that *communitarianism* forms the basis of values-based education in the Singapore school curricula (Tan, 2013). To elaborate, values education in Singapore is "…commonly underpinned by an ideology of communitarianism that seeks to promote the needs and interests of 'others' over the 'self'". The focus of a communitarianism approach to values education, is on the greater good, and shaped by equal emphases on moral values, social norms, and cultural attitudes.

Civics and Moral Education (CME) was introduced in 1991, at the primary and secondary school levels, to replace *Religious Knowledge* lessons in schools (National Library Board, 2014a; Tan, 2013). The Ministry of Education proceeded with this move as it felt that it was not appropriate for schools to offer RK in schools as Singapore is a secular state. CME aimed to "…nurture individuals who could put society before self, live harmoniously with one another and contribute effectively to Singapore's multicultural society". With the implementation of the CME syllabi, the six core values as detailed in the R^3ICH acronym, were first introduced. At the pre-university level, *Civics* was introduced (without the terms 'moral education' incorporated in the subject name). The pre-university *Civics* syllabus developed from the CME primary and secondary level syllabi, with a particular emphasis on nurturing students who could "…play an active role in helping to improve the quality of civic life in the community and to take the lead in service to others" (Tan, 2013).

National Education (NE) was introduced in 1996 by the Ministry of Education to foster national cohesion and instill a sense of national identity among students and younger Singaporeans, emphasizing unity in a diverse, multi-racial and multi-religious Singapore (National Library Board, 2014b). NE was not taught as a separate subject but infused in activities and programs in the school such as the daily flag-raising ceremony and oath of allegiance (or national pledge), and visits to key state institutions such as fire stations under the Singapore Civil Defense Force or military museums under the Singapore Armed Forces.

Character and Citizenship Education (CCE) was introduced in 2011, and implemented in the school curricula from 2014, which brought together the foci and contents of CME, NE, and *Civics* (Lee, 2012; Tan, 2013). There were two distinct accents in the CCE syllabus. First, was the involvement of all teachers, and not just the teachers teaching the CCE subject, in the learning, development and demonstration of the six core values identified. Second, was the inclusion of parents and the larger community as partners in inculcating and reinforcing these values through action-oriented and student-centric initiatives such as experiential learning, service-learning or community involvement projects, and perspective-taking.

Even at the institutes of higher learning (IHLs), community service and service-learning initiatives continue to shape the higher education landscape and attract youth participation, despite varying requirements across the different IHLs, which are not always a graduation requirement. For instance, in the Singapore Management University (SMU), the undergraduates are required to serve 80 hours of community service as a graduation requirement, which include local and overseas community service projects (SMU, 2021). Likewise, in the Singapore University of Social Sciences (SUSS), service-learning forms the cornerstone of the undergraduate learning experience and SUSS students are expected to be involved in projects or initiatives that "… engage the community, create social impact in the communities, or address social issues" (SUSS, 2021).

In the National University of Singapore, community service is not a graduation requirement and is largely a student-led initiative, spearheaded by student groups such as NUS Social Impact Catalyse and NUS Rotaract Club (NUS, 2021). In the Singapore Institute of Technology (SIT), projects that create social impact for specific community beneficiaries in society are still elective endeavors for students. However, with the recent SIT curriculum review, this will be a graduation requirement for SIT cohort intakes from academic year 2022.

The integrated and extensive incorporation of citizenship, moral and civics learning and narratives in the education system – from primary school through to the university levels – where "…students are taught to make good on the privilege of education by giving back to the community", have also developed in our youths "…a keen awareness that building a better society would require not only stepping forward to plug gaps in the social sector, but also stepping up to drive or demand more extensive change over the longer term." (Kwek, 2019). As a result, community service, volunteering, social innovation, and community leadership have become central to the psyche of our Singaporean youths.

IMPACT OF COVID-19 ON DIFFERENT DEMOGRAPHIC GROUPS IN SINGAPORE

The Covid-19 global pandemic had a huge impact on Singapore. The first infections were detected in February 2020, and the numbers grew quickly to more than a hundred infection cases, which precipitated a nationwide circuit-breaker, or lockdown, from 7 April to 4 May 2020. For the first time in the nation's short 55-year history, schools were closed *en masse*, and teaching and learning moved to full home-based learning, while workplaces and offices were also shut and employees had to work-from-home, except for workers in essential services such as healthcare, transport, and utilities and sanitation services. This brought about significant impact on the different demographic groups in Singapore.

There was significant impact caused by the closure of schools during the circuit-breaker period on many families in Singapore. With more than 65% of families (i.e., couples with at least one child aged below 21 years old) being dual income families or having both husband and wife working (Ministry of Social and Family Development, 2017, p.5), the demand on parents in managing both their work and childcare commitments was high. Hence, it was not easy for parents to cope with their work demands, taking care of their children and their respective home-based learning needs during the circuit-breaker period (Ng & Panch, 20 May 2020). In addition, there were families that faced other forms of difficulties in meeting the needs of home-based learning or working-from-home. For instance, families that had existing economic struggles found it difficult to afford the necessary information technology (IT) devices and provisions such as laptops, printers or even an Internet connection, so that their school-going children could carry out their home-based learning (HBL) or so that they themselves could work from home (WFH) during the circuit-breaker period, and thereafter. These families had to depend on help from the government, the generosity of donors, and the efforts of volunteers to be able to be HBL- and WFH-ready (Goh, 2020). It was also found that low-income families faced a much more challenging time during the Covid-19 pandemic, and not just during the circuit-breaker period, with the household incomes of these families falling by as much as 69% in 2020 (Menon, 2021). This placed a strain on familial ties and the well-being of these already vulnerable families.

Other than the impact on families, the foreign worker community in Singapore were also significantly affected by the Covid-19 pandemic. Singapore has a substantial foreign worker community – about 1.3 million of the 5.6 million population in Singapore, was made up of foreign workers holding work passes or work permits (Ministry of Manpower, 2021). Because of the high numbers of infections among the foreign workers during the circuit-breaker period (Chang & Tjendro, 2020), severe restrictions were placed on the foreign worker dormitories and the movement of foreign workers outside of these dormitories. There were concerns about the well-being and mental health of the foreign workers who had to be isolated during the circuit-breaker period and through the Covid-19 pandemic, and who faced strict restrictions from their usual routines pre-Covid-19 (Ng, 2020).

The elderly in Singapore was another group that were greatly impacted by the Covid-19 pandemic. Many registered higher levels of dissatisfaction with their lives, confusion with the many changes brought about by safe distancing or safe management measures that were implemented, as well as feelings of social isolation and loneliness (Chua, 2021; Menon, 2021). What was even more worrying was the higher number of suicides that happened in the year 2020, which was at a 29-year high (Chua, 2021).

There were also concerns for another group that was impacted by the Covid-19 pandemic – persons with disabilities (PwDs) and their employment prospects (Goh, 2020). As employers struggled to keep their businesses running and afloat, the inclusive hiring of PwDs were somewhat affected. While government-funded schemes and programs were in place to help employers continue to hire PwDs, more could still be done to ensure both employers and PwDs are ready to work and thrive in a largely remote work environment.

Against these backdrops of the various challenges faced by the different segments of society in Singapore, new ground-up initiatives and programs were launched and introduced by community groups and social service agencies in Singapore, many of which were led by youths, and which were targeted at the most vulnerable groups in the Singapore society.

YOUTH-LED INITIATIVES ARISING OUT OF COVID-19

The Covid-19 pandemic has transformed lives, businesses, and communities globally. Safe distancing, containment, and social interaction measures across many countries have unduly affected less privileged or marginalized communities, such as low-income families with young as well as elderly dependents, individuals with disabilities or special needs, and low-wage or low-skilled workers. In Asia, the impact of Covid-19 is unevenly distributed across populations, falling disproportionately on the most vulnerable individuals and communities (Jurzyk et al., 2020). The post-pandemic world could experience even greater challenges and inequalities unless mitigated by the necessary global, government and social responses (Stiglitz, 2020). One of these responses pointed out by Stiglitz is that of social solidarity and responsiveness, where citizens recognize that their behavior has an impact on others.

In studying social issues and inequalities, Social Innovation (SI) has "...come up as a theme that questions structures and policies which have not been able to eliminate recurrent problems, such as world epidemics, social inequality, hunger and weather changes." (Bittencourt, Figueiro & Schutel, 2017). Considered a relatively novel and empirically under-researched area, a large-scale study found that (i) social needs and societal challenges are the focus and driver of SI; (ii) multiple actors and cross-sector collaborations form the backbone of SI initiatives; and (iii) empowerment of end-users or beneficiaries, as well as end-user or beneficiary engagement and involvement are pivotal to the success of SI initiatives (Howaldt, Kaletka, Schroder, Rehfeld & Terstriep, 2016). Howaldt et al. (2016) also found that "…individuals and groups at the grassroots level is [sic] often at the heart of social innovation. As such a country which promotes, encourages and develops an active civil society and proactive individuals creates an enabling environment for social innovation".

With the unfolding of the Covid-19 pandemic, it was found that many youth-led movements and initiatives – in the social or entrepreneurship sectors – emerged and have made significant impact on communities. For instance, in South Korea, young innovators and entrepreneurs are "…sparking technology-driven innovations to respond to crises" that have arisen and to "…help communities cope with their daily lives" (United Nations Development Program (UNDP), 2021). A survey, involving 410 youths across 18 countries, carried out by UNDP and the Citi Foundation found that "…youth-led enterprises across Asia-Pacific are innovating to support their communities to combat coronavirus and build back better. Youth-led enterprises are fighting misinformation, mobilizing community action to protect the vulnerable, and developing innovative new products and services" (Youth Co:Lab, 2020).

Likewise in Singapore, several youth-led SI initiatives have emerged and made significant social impact, precipitated by the Covid-19 pandemic and its attendant challenges.

Computers Against Covid by Engineering Good, a non-profit organization in Singapore, is another SI initiative that is youth-led. Since April 2020, when Singapore went into its Covid-19 circuit breaker, more than 4,000 computer laptops and notebooks have been donated to the Computers Against Covid initiative, and which are refurbished by youth volunteers of Engineering Good. These refurbished computer laptops and notebooks are then donated to families who "…do not have access to these devices to stay digitally connected. These laptops are used for purposes such as children's home-based learning needs and adults looking for employment to access on-line job databases" (Engineering Good, 2021). This initiative has helped many young people from less privileged families be more digitally ready and digitally connected despite the ongoing Covid-19 pandemic which hampered many physical meetings and interactions.

Another youth-led SI initiative in Singapore is the Covid-19 Migrant Support Coalition (CMSC) campaign started in April 2020 by Ray of Hope, which is a charity registered in Singapore. The CSMC campaign, which is led by a group of youth advocates such as Ms Jewel Yi, "…aimed to meet the immediate supply, mental wellness and learning engagement, as well as casework needs" or migrant workers in Singapore (Ray of Hope, 2019). This is especially critical because of the high numbers of Covid-19 infections in the migrant workers' dormitories in 2020, and the resulting stringent movement and physical interaction restrictions put in place.

Yet another youth-led SI initiative in Singapore is Project DUST – which stands for *Differently-Abled UpSkill Training* by Codesurance, which is a social enterprise registered in Singapore. Project DUST is led by Mr Max Ong and Mr Jayren Teo, who met and became friends when they were undergraduates in the Singapore Institute of Technology (SIT). Project DUST aims to equip persons with disabilities (PwDs) with digital skills to develop or create websites with just a drag and drop application programming interface (API) or low code platforms and creates networking opportunities between the trained PwDs and prospective employers (SIT, 2021). Opportunities for PwDs to work remotely were identified amidst developments arising out of the Covid-19 pandemic. These led to Project DUST's objective of training PwDs in APIs and low code platforms so that they can continue to do technology-based work remotely, despite the restrictions during the pandemic. After a successful pilot of Project DUST, they are now expanding the scope of the initiative and will be launching a bigger roll-out in 2022.

YOUTH-LED INITIATIVES IN A COVID-19 LANDSCAPE IN SIT

In SIT, student- or youth-led social innovation (SI) projects for specific segments of the community form an increasingly important part of the university curriculum. While it is currently an elective, students will have to be involved in an SI project as part of graduation requirements from academic year 2022.

One example of a pilot SI project led by students in SIT was a curriculum-based module-integrated project meant to promote well-being and health among seniors (58 years old and above) in Singapore. Two groups of students reached out to and engaged seniors in a nursing home run by Tsao Foundation, a social service agency in Singapore. As part of understanding how seniors would be using digital tools during the Covid-19 pandemic (after the circuit-breaker period), the students managed to engage and talk to a group of 7 seniors who attended a senior activity center under Tsao Foundation, on a regular basis. Through a survey that was carried out in two face-to-face sessions with the seniors, the students found that social isolation and loneliness were the two most cited concerns the seniors had.

Hence, in order to help these seniors, combat social isolation and loneliness, a workshop on video conferencing was organized (Figures 1 and 2). The 'Zoom' video conferencing platform was chosen because of its wide availability and ease-of-use. The workshop included step-by-step instructions to help the seniors create their own Zoom accounts and use the features on Zoom through their respective mobile phones or computers at home. During the engagement session with the seniors, the students found that the seniors enjoyed singing karaoke together and the safe management and physical distancing measures during the Covid-19 pandemic meant that they missed their regular karaoke sessions. Hence, the students taught the seniors how to log into their Zoom accounts, and how they could have an online karaoke session. A recording of the workshop was done and made available to the seniors so they could refer to it should they forget how to do the online karaoke over Zoom.

Figure 1. Workshop on using Zoom

Figure 2. Features of Zoom explained in Chinese to the seniors who were mostly Chinese speaking

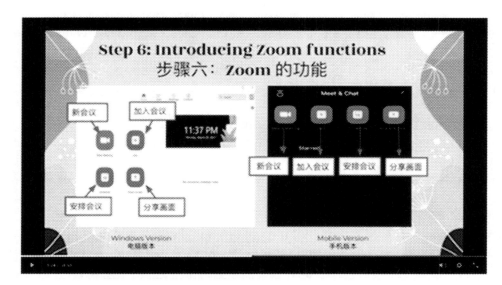

Feedback from the seniors who were involved in the workshop was that they enjoyed it, and that they could now "meet" with their friends and sing karaoke together, even though it was not in person. Students involved in the initiative also shared that it was a good learning experience, and it helped them empathize and better understand what the seniors faced and needed, in order to mitigate loneliness and social isolation.

Another example of a pilot SI project led by students in SIT was a curriculum-based module-integrated project meant to design a prototype of a smart water meter to help low-income households monitor their water usage and thus better manage their water costs, especially when more household members continue to work or study from home during the Covid-19 pandemic. In addition, with plans to scale up the project and aim for deployment of the smart water meters across different households in Singapore, the project would also be an exercise in public education on the importance and need for water sustainability in Singapore.

The motivation for the project was two-pronged. The first prong was that a water consumption survey carried out by Singapore's Public Utilities Board (PUB) in 2018/2019 found that for many households, "…shower, flushing, kitchen and laundry remained as the largest water consuming areas in households, constituting 77% of its total water usage." (PUB, 2020). The findings of this survey did not show improvement in water consumption rates and patterns from the earlier survey carried out in 2016/2017, despite continuous public education on water use and conservation.

The second prong was that even though PUB already had a smart water meter program planned for implementation in 2022 (PUB, 2021), the PUB smart water meters would provide aggregated readings and data of water consumption for the entire household, and not for individual water points within the household. Hence, this project would allow each household to monitor their water usage for each water point such as for showering, laundry (via the washing machine), kitchen sink, flushing, and so on. This would then help each household manage their water consumption behaviors in a more targeted and proactive manner, especially when more household members continue to work or study from home because of the Covid-19 pandemic.

A group of five students in SIT's Mechanical Engineering degree program embarked on this project, led by an Engineering faculty in SIT. The students were brought on a visit to a couple of rental flats for them to take measurements of the water points and to engage with the household members to understand their water consumption habits and patterns (Figures 3 and 4). From the measurements made and information gathered, the students designed their smart water meter and made a few prototypes to test them in 2 locations – a bathroom in one of their own homes, and a public toilet in the University campus (Figure 5).

This project has just completed the prototype testing stage at the time of writing, but there are plans by the faculty lead to scale up the project and expand it to 20 households for the next phase of pilot testing. This would provide substantial data to look at and better understand household water consumption patterns and habits, and subsequently design public education programs. The PUB found out about the project and had expressed interest to learn more and explore possible collaboration with the SIT project team.

Students involved in the project had shared that the opportunity to engage with members of households where they took measurements, helped them to better understand their water consumption habits and patterns of the household residents and some of the possible constraints in the smart water meter design and installation. The students also expressed that the opportunity to engage with the household members helped them develop a sense of empathy for specific members of society, such as towards the elderly or low-income households, and helped them to have a more grounded and user-centric approach in designing their smart water meter prototypes.

Figure 3. Visits to rental flats to engage household members and take measurements of water points

Figure 4. Visits to actual rental flats allowed students to understand space constraints faced by the household members and incorporate these considerations when finalizing the measurements and designs of their smart water meter prototypes

Figure 5. Installation of the smart water meter prototype on campus

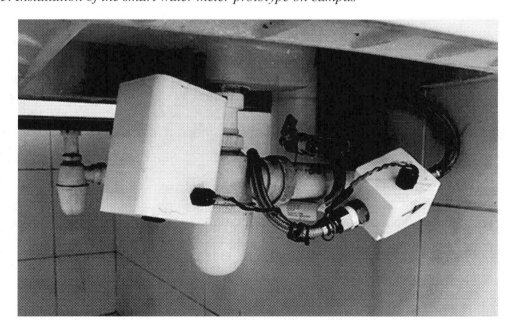

EVALUATING THE SOCIAL IMPACT AND ENSURING SUSTAINABILITY OF THESE INITIATIVES

Despite the heartwarming and inspiring initiatives by youths that have created positive social impact on the different demographic groups in Singapore, there will always be the question of how we evaluate the social impact done by these well-meaning initiatives. Another question that follows is how we ensure the sustainability of these initiatives, particularly when these are youth-led. As such, when the youths have grown older (termed as "aging out") and would have to start assuming more responsibilities at work or in their families (Advocates for Youth, 2009), these same youths who planned and implemented these initiatives, may not be able to continue to do so. Hence, these initiatives may risk discontinuation.

Evaluating Social Impact

For clarity, 'social impact' is "…what has an effect on people, on social existing challenges or social needs" and the "…challenges and needs mainly depend on local contexts, environment and situation" (Marie, Boyer & Collombo, 2020, p.3). 'Social impact' can also be defined as "…beneficial outcomes resulting from prosocial behavior that are enjoyed by the intended targets of that behavior and/or by the broader community of individuals, organizations, and/or environments" (Rawhauser, Cummings & Newbert, 2019, p.83).

The Organization for Economic Co-operation and Development (OECD, 2015, p.3) has defined social impact with reference to four key elements: (i) value created as a result of someone's of some entity's activity; (ii) value experienced by beneficiaries and those affected by the activity; (iii) an impact which includes both positive and negative effects; and (iv) an impact marked against the status quo, if the activity had not taken place.

'Social impact measurement' (or 'social impact evaluation') is used to identify different evaluation items or criteria that when consolidated, create an estimate of the **social value** of activities done on or with a specific group of beneficiaries. Evaluating social impact is shaped by reviewing the objectives or **purpose,** the **outcomes** as well as **relevance** of the initiative implemented (Florman, Klingler-Vidra, & Facada, 2016, p.5; Marie, Boyer & Collombo, 2020, p.6; Rawhauser, Cummings & Newbert, 2019, p.83).

It is recognized that social impact is multi-dimensional and is not focused on just one dimension or measure alone. There are several dimensions to consider especially when evaluating the social impact of an initiative – the economic value creation, the impact on the environment, social returns, societal benefit, democratic ideals or values, and the list goes on (Marie, Boyer & Collombo, 2020, p.10; Rawhauser, Cummings & Newbert, 2019, p.84). It is recognized that there are many social impact measurement dimensions for social innovation, or initiatives with intended social impact (Lee et al., 2019). While no single initiative can strive to measure each and every socially significant dimension, it is important for each initiative implemented to identify clearly what it seeks to achieve (i.e., purpose) and to what extent it is able to do so (i.e. outcomes and relevance).

Researchers have articulated that the intents or purpose of a social innovation, or initiatives with intended social impact, would need to be formalized in the form of a solution, a product, a framework, a new technology, a business model, a piece of legislation or amendments to existing legislation, an intervention, a social movement, or a combination of any of these (Lee et al., 2019).

Community Awareness and Leadership Among Singapore Youths Amidst a COVID-19 Landscape

In measuring the social impact, the outcomes of the social innovation, or initiatives with intended social impact, need to be clearly defined and identified. Researchers have described these outcomes as the social value that is created through changes in processes, routines, structures, practices or even policies (Maas & Liket, 2011) which results in a social need being met, a social problem being addressed, or the overall improvement in either the "quality or quantity of life" (Lee et al., 2019). In essence, the desired social outcomes would be an overall improvement to the well-being of humans, other creatures, or the environment, and that the metrics or indicators used to measure social impact should be linked to the intended purpose and scope of the social innovation, or initiatives with intended social impact, guided by the identified needs of the beneficiaries involved (Lee et al., 2019; Maas & Liket, 2011). There is no single standard, metric, indicator, or report to be benchmarked against. As the OECD suggests, adopting a "measuring process rather than imposing specific metrics or indicators" would be more meaningful for many social innovation projects or social impact initiatives (OECD, 2015 p.5).

The following five-stage process is proposed for all social impact measurements: 1) identify objectives; 2) identify stakeholders; 3) set relevant measurements; 4) measure, validate and value; 5) report, learn and improve. It is added that there is "freedom as to which indicator to use, in order for the measurement to remain appropriate to the intervention and stakeholders' (or beneficiaries') needs" (OECD, 2015 p.5).

Ensuring Sustainability of Youth-led Initiatives

There are some strategies in ensuring the sustainability or continuity of youth-led initiatives where the youths may age out.

One, is to accept the flexibility of the approach and process of carrying out the initiatives implemented, and refrain from imposing traditional methods or approaches of implementing initiatives or activities. Programs that are youth-led usually have a "… completely different approach to project and development itself… much less hierarchical… much more open. They usually engage in a, what we would call, *adaptive programming*. If something is not working, they (will) change it." (Asian Development Bank, February 2019). Many organizations, including non-government organizations or social service agencies, are used to planning and implementing programs or activities in a traditional manner, where structures are more hierarchical, and approaches are more linear. But youths, typically from Generations Y and Z, prefer a less structured and more networked approach to doing things. Allowing this degree of flexibility and freedom will help ensure that it is easier for younger and newer youths to take over and carry out the initiatives in a manner comfortable to and acceptable for them.

Two, follow the *Take Two Principle* (Advocates for Youth, 2009). It is advised that when inviting participants from youth organizations to a meeting with more traditional organizations, at least two of them should be invited: one a more experienced youth member, the other a newer and younger youth member. This *Take Two Principle* will help ensure "… the sharing of knowledge, experience, and capacity building and facilitate the transition process immensely by building new leadership capacity. This approach allows for greater youth participation and inclusion while also facilitating member and staff transitions and organizational development." (Advocates for Youth, 2009).

Third, there must be strong internal systems established, especially in documentation and in managing data related to all the programs and initiatives implemented by these youth participants (Gaughen, Flynn-Khan & Hayes, 2009, p.19). These internal systems allow for transferability and help maintain accountability and quality control. Hence, when the programs or initiatives implemented need to be done in phases and need to be handed over to newer or younger youth leads, the transfer process can be made more seamless, and continuity will be easier.

Fourth, having a sustainability plan helps to articulate and document the vision, objectives, processes or approaches, budgets, and intended outcomes of the program or initiative planned and implemented (Gaughen, Flynn-Khan & Hayes, 2009, p.23). The sustainability plan must "... document these decisions in writing. A written plan provides a record of decisions. It is an on-going reference for short- and long-term operations. It can be the initiative's most important document to persuade funders to invest in the initiative." The sustainability plan helps to ensure continuity of the program or initiative implemented, regardless of the youths leading it.

In SIT, we strive to implement the above four strategies for our youth-led initiatives, and social innovation projects that our students are involved in. However, we remain guided by the need to evaluate the social impact of our projects effectively and purposefully – for the beneficiaries' benefit; for our students' learning and growth; and to ensure the sustainability of these projects. It may not always be easy to ensure adherence to all three expected outcomes, especially during the current global pandemic. Nevertheless, these four strategies help guide the development and implementation of our youth-led community initiatives and projects, as we continuously respond to the changes that happen around us.

FUTURE RESEARCH DIRECTIONS

While the Covid-19 pandemic has, to a large extent, abated and become endemic, its effects are very much widespread and experienced differently across different communities or groups of individuals. Those considered vulnerable would need a longer time to get back on their feet as they reel from the various unforeseen and unintended consequences of the pandemic, that traverse beyond public health or medical challenges alone. However, there were slivers of hope and sparks of courage and optimism that have surfaced, and which have paved the way for socially innovative initiatives or programs that have generated positive social impact on the lives of those most vulnerable among us. In this chapter, we have seen how many of such initiatives were led by youths, with their strong sense of social cause and justice, and the fire in their belly to help those most in need.

While we celebrate these initiatives by our youths, we also must be mindful of the challenges in ensuring the sustainability, continuity, and impact of such initiatives. As discussed in the previous section, there are four strategies identified in ensuring the sustainability or continuity of youth-led initiatives where the youths may age out. In addition, there is also the need to design an evaluation matrix or tool to measure or assess the extent of social impact of these initiatives. Both the strategies and evaluation matrix or tool are important to help us better scope and define socially innovative initiatives or programs, and ensure their sustained and continuous utility and impact, regardless of the crisis in which they are forged. Nevertheless, there remains the challenge of designing and implementing these strategies and evaluation matrix or tool, because unlike laboratory-based experiments, social innovation initiatives or programs are not exact sciences and data that are collected are largely defined by individual perceptions and expectations, cultural contexts and backgrounds, and human interpretations. However, where there are challenges, there are also opportunities. The challenges identified could spur future research opportunities in these areas.

CONCLUSION

Gouthro (2005) explained the importance of *sociological imagination* in education as a "…useful approach to encourage educators to think more deeply about the world around them and their place in it, and it evokes the need for learners to develop the capacity to move between abstract ideas and concrete experience". Gouthro (2005) further explained that sociological imagination is "…a means to emphasize the importance of carefully listening to understand the experiences of others, but at the same time making connections between how individuals make sense of their experience and [the] larger social, political, and economic structures." This experience is particularly useful for students who are embarking on their careers as trained professionals in their respective fields. The experience of having engaged and worked closely with members of the community would have provided them with the ability to empathize, understand and internalize the various needs and expectations of different people, many of whom will be the users of the products of services which these students and new professionals would offer and take to market.

Hence, it is important for higher and continuous education to provide opportunities for this *sociological imagination* to flourish, by creating sufficient opportunities for young people to engage and work with specific community groups or society at large co-design solutions that address current social issues or challenges. It is hoped that despite the challenges and difficulties faced by all living through this Covid-19 pandemic, which is now endemic, the ongoing discourse on how we measure the impact of social innovation or initiatives, or the challenges in ensuring the sustainability or continuity of such initiatives, our youths will continue to rise and lead social innovation and social impact initiatives that can positively change and improve lives as well as the environment in which we live.

"The greatness of a community is most accurately measured by the compassionate actions of its members." – Coretta Scott King

ACKNOWLEDGMENT

This research received no specific grant from any funding agency in the public, commercial, or not-for-profit sectors. However, we convey our appreciation to the sources we consulted and the support from our university.

REFERENCES

Advocates for Youth. (2009). *Youth leadership: Recommendations for sustainability*. https://www.advocatesforyouth.org/wp-content/uploads/storage/advfy/documents/youth_sustainability.pdf

Asian Development Bank. (2019, February 22). *Understanding Youth's Role to Achieving the Sustainable Development Goals.* https://www.adb.org/news/features/understanding-youths-role-achieving-sustainable-development-goals

Bittencourt, B. A., Figueiro, P. S., & Schutel, S. (2017). The impact of social innovation: Benefits and opportunities from Brazilian social business. *Revista Espacios, 38*(26). https://www.revistaespacios.com/a17v38n26/a17v38n26p07.pdf

Chang, N., & Tjendro, J. (2020, April 5-6). Singapore sees record daily spike of 120 COVID-19 cases, 'significant number' linked to worker dormitories. *ChannelNewsAsia.* https://www.channelnewsasia.com/news/singapore/covid19-singapore-record-daily-spike-120-new-cases-workers-dorms-12611132

Chua, N. (2021, July 9). Suicide rate among seniors hits 29-year high last year: SOS. *The New Paper.* https://www.tnp.sg/news/singapore/suicide-rate-among-seniors-hits-29-year-high-last-year-sos

Engineering Good. (2021). *Computers Against Covid.* https://engineeringgood.org/digital-inclusion/cac/

Florman, M., Klingler-Vidra, R., & Facada, M. J. (2016, February). *A critical evaluation of social impact assessment methodologies and a call to measure economic and social impact holistically through the External Rate of Return platform.* LSE Enterprise Working Paper # 1602. http://eprints.lse.ac.uk/id/eprint/65393

Gaughen, K., Flynn-Khan, M., & Hayes, C. D. (2009). *Sustaining Youth Engagement Initiatives: Challenges and Opportunities.* The Finance Project. https://wvsystemofcare.org/wp-content/uploads/2013/10/Sustaining-Youth-Engagement-2009-Finance-Project.pdf

Goh, C. T. (2020, April 8). Volunteers rush to deliver laptops to families in need before full home-based learning kicks in. *ChannelNewsAsia.* https://www.channelnewsasia.com/news/singapore/covid19-home-based-learning-laptops-volunteers-donation-12617146

Goh, Y. H. (2020, July 29). Job support for persons with disabilities to continue despite Covid-19 pandemic: Desmond Lee. *The Straits Times.* https://www.straitstimes.com/singapore/manpower/job-support-for-persons-with-disabilities-to-continue-despite-covid-19-pandemic

Gouthro, P. A. (2005). Understanding local and global contexts: The importance of the Sociological Imagination for Adult Education. *Adult Education Research Conference.* https://newprairiepress.org/aerc/2005/papers/46

Jurzyk, E., Nair, M. M., Pouokam, N., Sedik, T. S., Tan, A., & Yakadina, I. (2020). *COVID-19 and inequality in Asia: Breaking the vicious cycle.* IMF Working Paper, WP/20/217. https://www.imf.org/-/media/Files/Publications/WP/2020/English/wpiea2020217-print-pdf.ashx

Kwek, T. (2019, July 24). How Singapore's youth are changing the social sector by going beyond volunteerism. *TODAYOnline.* https://www.todayonline.com/commentary/how-singapores-youth-are-changing-social-sector-going-beyond-volunteerism

Lee, E. K. M., Lee, H., Kee, C. H., Kwan, C. H., & Ng, C. H. (2019). Social Impact Measurement in Incremental Social Innovation. *Journal of Social Entrepreneurship*, *12*(1), 69–86. doi:10.1080/19420676.2019.1668830

Lee, W. O. (2012). Education for future-oriented citizenship: Implications for the education of 21st century competencies. *Asia Pacific Journal of Education*, *32*(4), 498–517. doi:10.1080/02188791.2012.741057

Maas, K., & Liket, K. (2011). Social impact measurement: Classification of methods. In R. Burritt, S. Schaltegger, M. Bennett, T. Pohjola, & M. Csutora (Eds.), *Environmental Management Accounting and Supply Chain Management: Eco-Efficiency in Industry and Science* (Vol. 27). Springer. doi:10.1007/978-94-007-1390-1_8

Marie, C., Boyer, H., & Collombo, M. G. (2020, June). *ASIS - Guideline #1 - Social impact evaluation and indicators*. http://de.alpine-space.eu/projects/asis/deliverables/wp3/guideline1-final.pdf

Menon, M. (2021, February 9). Household income from work for poor families in Singapore fell 69% last year due to Covid-19: Study. *The Straits Times*. https://www.straitstimes.com/singapore/household-income-from-work-for-poor-families-fell-69-last-year-due-to-covid-19-study-by

Menon, M. (2021, March 4). Fewer elderly residents were satisfied with life during Covid-19 pandemic: SMU survey. *The Straits Times*. https://www.straitstimes.com/singapore/fewer-elderly-residents-were-satisfied-with-life-during-covid-19-pandemic-smu-survey

Ministry of Manpower. (2021, June 24). *Foreign workforce numbers*. https://www.mom.gov.sg/documents-and-publications/foreign-workforce-numbers

Ministry of Social and Family Development. (2017). *Family and Work – Insight Series, 4/2017*. https://www.msf.gov.sg/research-and-data/Research-and-Data-Series/Documents/Family%20and%20Work%20Report.pdf

Murray, T. R. (1991). *The nature of values education in Southeast Asia*. Educational Resources Information Center (ERIC), ED 365 609. https://files.eric.ed.gov/fulltext/ED365609.pdf

National Library Board. (2014a). Civics and Moral Education is introduced. *History SG – An online resource guide*. https://eresources.nlb.gov.sg/history/events/7a63e9a1-c949-41d0-9b6f-d3853d832bb1

National Library Board. (2014b). Launch of National Education. *History SG – An online resource guide*. https://eresources.nlb.gov.sg/history/events/44fa0306-ddfe-41bc-8bde-8778ff198640

National University of Singapore. (2021). *Community Service*. https://nus.edu.sg/osa/student-life/student-organisations-directory/community-service

Ng, D., & Panch, V. (2020, May 20). Facing circuit breaker blues, parents of young kids help each other in chat groups. *ChannelNewsAsia*. https://www.channelnewsasia.com/news/cnainsider/covid19-parents-chat-groups-whatsapp-facebook-12750732

Ng, K. G. (2020, November 6). New task force to tackle mental health issues among migrant workers. *The Straits Times*. https://www.straitstimes.com/singapore/new-task-force-to-tackle-mental-health-issues-among-migrant-workers

Organisation for Economic Co-operation and Development. (2015). *Policy Brief on Social Impact Measurement for Social Enterprises: Policies for Social Entrepreneurship*. Luxembourg: Publications Office of the European Union. https://www.oecd.org/social/PB-SIM-Web_FINAL.pdf

Public Utilities Board. (2020, March 9). *Make Every Drop Count: Continuing Singapore's Water Success - Better appreciation of Singapore's water journey to inspire generations of water users*. Press Release. https://www.pub.gov.sg/news/pressreleases/MakeEveryDropCountContinuingSingaporesWaterSuccess

Public Utilities Board. (2021, April 16). *About the Smart Water Meter Programme*. https://www.pub.gov.sg/smartwatermeterprogramme/about

Rawhauser, H., Cummings, M., & Newbert, S. L. (2019, January). Social impact measurement: Current approaches and future directions for social entrepreneurship research. *Entrepreneurship Theory and Practice, 43*(1), 82–115. doi:10.1177/1042258717727718

Singapore Institute of Technology. (2021, March 5). *Enabling more persons with disabilities for jobs in technology industry*. https://www.singaporetech.edu.sg/sitizen-buzz/project-dust/

Singapore Management University. (2021, March 23). *Community Service*. https://www.smu.edu.sg/campus-life/community-service

Singapore University of Social Sciences. (2021). *Office of Service-Learning & Community Engagement*. https://www.suss.edu.sg/about-suss/college-of-lifelong-experiential-learning/cel/office-of-service-learning-community-engagement

Stiglitz, J. (2020). Conquering the Great Divide: The pandemic has laid bare deep divisions, but it's not too late to change course. *International Monetary Fund – Finance and Development Point of View*. https://www.imf.org/external/pubs/ft/fandd/2020/09/pdf/COVID19-and-global-inequality-joseph-stiglitz.pdf

Tan, C. (2013). For group, (f)or self: Communitarianism, Confucianism and values education in Singapore. *Curriculum Journal, 24*(4), 478–493. doi:10.1080/09585176.2012.744329

United Nations Development Programme. (2021). *Youth-led innovation & entrepreneurship for CO-VID-19: Examples from Republic of Korea*. https://www1.undp.org/content/seoul_policy_center/en/home/presscenter/articles/2020/youth-led-innovation---entrepreneurship-for-covid-19--examples-f.html

Youth Co. Lab. (2020, May 6). *Young entrepreneurs explain how COVID-19 is affecting their businesses*. https://www.youthcolab.org/post/young-entrepreneurs-explain-how-covid-19-is-affecting-their-businesses

KEY TERMS AND DEFINITIONS

Community Engagement: Community engagement can be described as a strategic and well-defined process of reaching out to, interacting, and communicating with identified groups of people (whether they are connected by geographic location, special interest, or affiliation) to identify and address issues affecting their well-being.

Community Leadership: Community leadership is a key aspect of non-profit management. It involves leading and managing a community of individuals, volunteers, supporters, or other stakeholders, who share common goals, objectives, or issues in a specific community that affect members of that community.

Singapore: A cosmopolitan island-nation in Southeast Asia that is only 57 years old at the time of writing. Being a multi-racial and multi-religious society, Singapore is also a highly connected and well-developed nation where English is the lingua franca and working language, while the mother tongue languages (such as Mandarin, Malay, Tamil, among others) are also learnt in school.

Singapore Institute of Technology: The third-largest autonomous university (AU) in Singapore, in terms of student enrolment. The university is one of the youngest AUs in Singapore, being only 13 years old at the time of writing. The university is also known as the university of applied learning.

Social Impact: The Organization for Economic Co-operation and Development (OECD, 2015, p. 3) has defined social impact with reference to four key elements: (i) value created as a result of someone's of some entity's activity; (ii) value experienced by beneficiaries and those affected by the activity; (iii) an impact which includes both positive and negative effects; and (iv) an impact marked against the status quo, if the activity had not taken place.

Social Innovation: According to the Organization of Economic Cooperation and Development (OECD, 2021), "Social innovation refers to the design and implementation of new solutions that imply conceptual, process, product, or organizational change, which ultimately aim to improve the welfare and wellbeing of individuals and communities". There are numerous initiatives and projects undertaken and implemented globally by the social economy and by civil groups, which have proven to be innovative in dealing with socio-economic and environmental problems, while contributing to the economic development of individuals, families, communities and even societies.

Values-Based Education: The incorporation of moral values in the formal school curricula. In the Singapore context, communitarianism forms the basis of values-based education that seeks to promote the needs and interests of 'others' over the 'self'". The focus of a communitarianism approach to values education, is on the greater good, and shaped by equal emphases on moral values, social norms, and cultural attitudes, taking into consideration Singapore's multi-racial and multi-religious context.

Youths: In Singapore, youths are categorized as individuals between the ages of 15 and 34 years old.

Section 5
Working on Inclusion

Chapter 11

Navigating Inequitable (Mis)Treatment and Racist Harassment in Higher Education During the COVID–19 Pandemic:
A Self–Decentered Autoethnographic Case

Shalin Hai-Jew
(ID) https://orcid.org/0000-0002-8863-0175
Kansas State University, USA

ABSTRACT

The SARS-CoV-2/COVID-19 pandemic (late 2019 to the present) brought to the fore latent and externalized forms of racism and bias and xenophobia. The author experienced a range of inequitable mistreatment and racist harassment in her workplace in higher education during this time, including from her direct supervisor who engaged in a racist microassault along with excess work assignments (the work of several individuals or multiple FTEs) during multiple years of the pandemic. This work uses a self-decentered auto-ethnography to explore practical ways to address racism and discrimination in the workplace, through clear documentation, honest in-lane reportage, and other efforts up an escalatory ladder. This work highlights the challenges of working towards a solution in a bureaucracy with a mix of apparently conflicting objectives and foremost to protect the institution against lawsuits and negative publicity.

DOI: 10.4018/978-1-6684-5934-8.ch011

Copyright © 2023, IGI Global. Copying or distributing in print or electronic forms without written permission of IGI Global is prohibited.

INTRODUCTION

For a multiracial pluralistic liberal democracy such as that of the U.S., to function at high efficiency, people need to be able to engage each other with various differences with mutual respect and trust. Without such collaboration and mutual understanding, human organizations will break down, and people will retreat to their respective social groupings. To this end, there has been a lot of work invested into research about racism and its causes, various types of antiracist pedagogies in education, and policy research. There has been work to de-bias language. The thinking is that outright racism is more of a rarity, and those with racist ideas have taken their ideas underground and expressed them more indirectly through microaggressions and microassaults of various types.

The social order though seems to be in constant flux. Humanity will be drawing lessons from the SARS-CoV-2 / COVID-19 pandemic for many years to come. On the social front, the two years (and counting) of the pandemic—with necessary lockdowns and social distancing and masking measures followed by vaccination measures—have taken a toll on people's social relationships. Politicians have emerged to take advantage of the social disarray, with political messaging to differentiate themselves from others and scapegoating particular minorities in order to gain political points (cater to their voter base and encourage their showing up to vote for them in the future). The hyper-suggestible and those with racist sympathies have taken the message as authorization to bully and harass and even attack others. Some of these racial tensions have also spilled into workplaces, with some engaging in microaggressions, microassaults, and other expressions of hate, perhaps influenced by macroaggressions from hate messaging from national leaders in the U.S., a country with its own fraught history of collective racism and intergenerational traumas. Researchers note the effects of such historical challenges.

Experiencing microaggressions may be particularly harmful to people who are members of social group categories (i.e., race, ethnicity/national origin, sexual orientation, gender identity, disability/ability, etc.) with long histories of systemic and legal exclusion, physical marginalization, oppression, and state-sponsored violence or discrimination because they are markers of ongoing systems of oppression and inequalities. The continued normalization and acceptance of microaggressions serve to reinforce existing inequities. (Skinta & Torres-Harding, 2022, p. 3)

Many argue that it is not just the oppressed who are harmed by racism but that the perpetrators of the biases also are harmed because of compromises to their own characters and lives. Reparation is seen as a possible approach to making peoples whole (Klein, 1964, as cited in Rasmussen & Salhani, 2010, p. 505).

A Triggering Personal-professional Event

In September 2021, the author and her supervisor were in a Zoom web conference call discussing the untenability of stacking multiple work positions on the author. In mid-2019, the last of a group of three staff had left the university. The work they supported had slowly accrued to the author, who had been assigned to the task on a ticketing system used by ITS. [In IT, the ticketing system is used as a forcing function at times to monitor work and to force extra work.] Even though the conversation was civil and without tension, on the surface, without warning, the author's supervisor took off his glasses, rubbed his eyes hard with both hands, and then pulled out the outer edges of his eyes into a racist "slant eyes"

Navigating Inequitable (Mis)Treatment and Racist Harassment in Higher Education During COVID-19

or "chink eyes" expression. He held that expression for several seconds, and then he returned to the one-on-one Zoom meeting at hand as if nothing had happened. The derogatory hate-based act itself was unprecedented and unprovoked (from the author's perspective), and she was not even sharing her camera. [As one research study noted, microaggressions show that "the target's racial group is highly visible to the perpetrator" (Kim, Block, & Nguyen, 2019, p. 75).] *The experience was bizarre and unbefitting a supervisor at any level. The facial expression was taken as one of social supremacy based on race, perhaps white supremacy, in a time of intense anti-Asian hatred (due in part to the pandemic) and perhaps due to a roiling historical racial history of the country. It read like a betrayal from a supervisor who could not practically solve problems and who then distracted by playing his version of a race card.*

Such a blatant expression of racism has been rare for the author after childhood, and she had not seen such a facial expression since the schoolyard some 40 years ago. The schoolyard taunts were hurtful during a sensitive developmental age, and that shaped the author's sense of caution and non-trust of people through the years.

The supervisor had already shown signs of irregular supervision, such as trying to police the author's speech about a change of a university's technology system during an instructional design club meeting. Then, he placed himself to "sit" on service tickets which he had assigned to the author even though this was extraneous to her professional role and not described in any part of her work position; he had no role in handling those tickets but apparently wanted to use his position to coerce work. When confronted with his bullying and over-reach, he responded, "I'm your supervisor," as if it was his prerogative to harass and pursue personal harm to a staffer. He would shoulder-surf the author's computer at her cubicle. He would approach her 8 – 9 times a day in person once she returned to work in the office in late April 2021. [He did not engage in such behaviors when another colleague was in the office. The other colleague often telecommuted, however, leaving the office comprised of only the author and the supervisor.] He was making the workspace hostile for the author by bringing his personal needs for social company to the workplace and expecting fulfillment there.

The racist action (the "slant eyes" face) was accompanied by prior and continuing usage of racist and sexist tropes ["you don't belong here" messaging, "you can't take risks" (the idea of Asians being "yellow" or "cowardly"), expressions of xenophobia, denigrations of non-white staff, and other antagonistic actions] and inequitable treatments [assigning multiple "full-time equivalency" (or FTE) of work (doing the work of multiple positions) to the author without any additional staffing support, antagonistic put-downs of the author during a public meeting with a within-university team, various gossip with subordinates, and other negative and harassing actions]. "Other duties as assigned," that antiquated add-on to a list of job tasks, does not and has never meant full additional other professional positions to be stacked on an individual. The office where the author worked was not provisioned for any office supplies even a half-year after her return to in-person work in April 2021. The author had long noticed that the additional workloads were applied to the non-Caucasians in the office, and when these were not accepted by some, the supervisor would gossip and try to trash their reputations among his subordinates. This behavior conveyed the sense that non-whites were lesser and partial persons; they had to justify their value by overwork into the nights and weekends for uncompensated hours.

His racist actions were triggering of traumas for the author, whose family had dealt with generations of racist taunts (by neighbors of different races, not just the mainstream Caucasian neighbors). Even though there were decades between childhood and this racist communications from a supervisor, the author experienced memories of racist childhood taunts.

Whistleblowing is not taken on without some due consideration because the outcomes usually do not benefit the whistleblower. Reporting on a supervisor who is directly in one's hierarchy is illogical, given what is needed to advance one's work (resources, support, and others). One has "known unknowns" and "unknown unknowns." Bureaucracies protect themselves even if they ostensibly have some interest in the individual worker. There is often a price to keep one's soul, character, and integrity. Based on the racist expression, made in a context of racialized hostilities, the author filed a formal complaint through the university hierarchy...starting a necessarily adversarial process given the structure of the bureaucracy and the mixed interests of the various parties—supervisor and employee, among others. At some point, keeping silent perpetuates the hate and biased decision-making. The false luster of leadership continues with the false narratives of competence. Broken trust magnifies.

Still, the author has had very constructive work relationships over the years. The decades of work life have been angst-free and tension-free for decades. This most recent phase was a negative anomaly.

This experience has been traumatizing and difficult, but it has also brought to the fore some observations about how such issues may be addressed more effectively in workplaces. And to be fair, the author has sufficient reserves (in every sense of the word: financial, reputational, emotional, legal, and others) to be able to take this risk.

This work is framed lightly as a self-decentered autoethnography. The work is based on self-reflective, writing, and research, with the goal of engaging wider cultural, political and social meanings and understandings. The author's "version" of events has been corroborated by the direct supervisor who instigated the chain of events with his bullying and racist response to a legitimate request that multiple FTEs of work be addressed appropriately. While the sparking event of this work is a personal and professional one for the author, the main focus is not the personal-professional aspects of this racist microassault and the concomitant biased supervision that accompanied it both prior and post. This work is not about settling scores nor casting aspersions nor leverage to resolve the workplace issue. Whatever professional issues there are being handled within the institution through the university's policies and the judgment of leaders in Information Technology Services and Anderson Hall. No names are used here. However, in this experience, there are various issues that resonate beyond the local. While the microassault above was racial and likely gendered, this work will address more dimensionalities of personhood in the microaggression and microassault context. It is in that spirit that this work has been undertaken.

REVIEW OF THE LITERATURE

The understanding of social relations in the U.S. and elsewhere is a contested space. A "postracial society" is "an illusion" (Rasmussen & Salhani, 2010, p. 491). There are various forms of "subtle racism," such as symbolic (indirect expression of prejudice), ambivalent (the sense of "positive and negative feelings against stigmatized racial groups"), modern (seeing racism as wrong but seeing "racial minorities as

Navigating Inequitable (Mis)Treatment and Racist Harassment in Higher Education During COVID-19

making unfair demands or receiving too many resources"), and aversive (believing in egalitarianism but experiencing "a personal aversion toward racial minorities") (Holmes, 2018, p. 154). Microaggressions may be seen as a moral transgression based on a Kantian framework, with transgressors failing in their ethical "duties of respect" towards others, especially those with oppressed social identities (O'Dowd, 2018, p. 1219).

There are a range of biases based on various dimensions of human identity. Some dimensions of personhood are listed in Table 1.

Table 1. Some dimensionalities of personhood

Some Dimensionalities of Personhood	Elaboration
socioeconomic status (SES), class	
socioeconomic background	
races in U.S. (Hispanic/Latino, American Indian or Alaska Native, Asian, Black or African American, Native Hawaiian or Other Pacific Islander, White, and two or more races.	
ethnicity (Hispanic, non-Hispanic)	
religion / belief system	
work	
gender (male, female, other/nonbinary; cis gender)	
sex (trans)	
age	
culture	
language	
birthplace (nativity)	
nationality	
migrant status (immigrant, emigrant, other)	
marital status (married, never married, divorced/separated, living with partner)	
parental status	
those with chronic health issues (like diabetes)	

continues on following page

Table 1. Continued

Some Dimensionalities of Personhood	Elaboration
education	
military status	
ability, perception (vision, hearing, touch / tactuality, and others and other combinations), mobility	
geolocation	

Figure 1. Differing Dimensions of Identity in the Core versus the Periphery

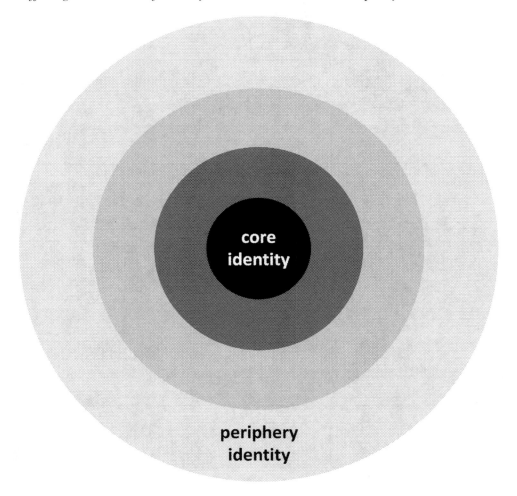

Navigating Inequitable (Mis)Treatment and Racist Harassment in Higher Education During COVID-19

In each person, there may be a variety of dimensions, with several of them related to the dimensions in Table 1. There are different systems to rank the dimensions of identity, with core parts of a person identified as their core personality. Others include core identifiers as age, gender, gender identity(ies), sexual orientation(s), various abilities (physical, cognitive, perceptual, brain processing, and others), race(s), and ethnicity(ies), among others. Further out, there are other dimensions of the individual based on changeable life factors like geographical location, socioeconomic status (SES), education, language, and others. The most diffuse sense includes beliefs, attitudes, values, and other aspects of thinking and feeling. Perhaps for different individuals, they may perceive what belongs in their core identity vs. their periphery identity in different ways. (Figure 1)

There may be crossover dimensions of a person, such as multiple different abilities. Experts in accessibility suggest that many do not claim or announce their disabilities formally. Also, some of the dimensions are more evolutionary than others.

Important Definitions of Some Relevant Terms

Critical race theory (CRT) was originated by Kimberlé Crenshaw in the late 1990s (Crenshaw, 2011), and it is used as an interdisciplinary framework to understand racism and human biases based on race. This framework posits that racism has been endemic in American life, with racist history informing present-day living (Matsuda et al., 1993, p. 6, as cited in Minikel-Lacocque, 2013, pp. 435 - 437). In this conceptualization, racism and other forms of bias have to be combatted for a more just society. CRT draws from "law, sociology, history, ethnic studies, and women's studies" (Solorzano, Ceja, & Yosso, 2000, p. 63). [At the present moment, in the U.S. in 2022, critical race theory is a major point of contention for some voters, who do not want it taught in K-12 or higher education, in some cases. The fervor against CRT is high, in the lead-up to the mid-term elections later in 2022.] Beyond this theory, there are various other understandings underlying human identity, in- and out- groups, and some atavistic biological senses (such as of tribalism).

To add to the complexity, there are intersectional identities, such as a mix of identities such as race, gender, and class. These interweaving's of multiple simultaneous identities may mean different instantiations of bias, based on racism, patriarchy, and class relationships. The originator of the concept of intersectionality writes of an example: "structural intersectionality, the ways in which the location of women of color at the intersection of race and gender makes our actual experience of domestic violence, rape, and remedial reform qualitatively different from that of white women" (Crenshaw, 1991, p. 1242). There is "political intersectionality" to help combat the biasing, such as with feminist and antiracist politics (Crenshaw, 1991, p. 1242). For societies to advance, democracies emphasize the importance of freedom and justice for all…in an indivisible way…for everyone. Inequalities are seen to stem from social constructs from power relations including "racism, class exploitation, sexism, and heterosexism," which are amenable to change (Collins, 2012, p. 442). Intersectionality "provides a distinctive analysis of social inequality, power, and politics" (Collins, 2012, p. 444). A seminal thinker in intersectionality writes about how "individuals and groups are differently positioned in a distinctive matrix of domination, which has implications for how we experience society, including *what we know and can imagine*, and the material realities that accompany this experience" (Collins, 2012, p. 454). This researcher writes:

> *Intersectionality is a newly recognized field of study within the academy whose purpose has been to analyze social inequality, power, and politics. Because not only understanding but challenging social inequality have also been central to the mission of intersectionality, the interrelationships among social inequality, power, and politics have assumed distinctive forms within this knowledge project. (Collins, 2012, p. 449)*

Social inequalities are "multiple, complex, and mutually constructing" (Collins, 2012, p. 455), making these more difficult to address. There may be "dual" marginalization based on race and gender, or ethnicity and accessibility, or other combinations. Intersectionality emerged from "this border space between social movement and academic politics as a term that seemed to best capture the fluidity of this emerging, influential, yet amorphous knowledge project" (Collins, 2012, p. 451). A theme in intersectional scholarship relates to "how intersecting power relations of race/class/gender/sexuality" shape individual and group-based social relations (Collins, 2012, p. 452). Individuals and groups can experience privilege and disadvantage simultaneously (Collins, 2012, p. 454).

In some cases, persons may be rendered invisible (and unrecognized and uncredited) in their work and study and lives; in others, their intersectional identities may mean that they are hyper-visible and treated as a representation of particular social categories. One study of graduate female students of color in STEM (science, technology, engineering, and math) fields found that their "experiences of intersectional invisibility increase the likelihood of being scrutinized, isolated, and marginalized by the dominant group" (Wilkins-Yel, Hyman, & Zounlome, 2019, p. 51). The researchers describe a "chilly STEM climate" and identified four themes: "delegitimization of one's skills and expertise, implicit and explicit messages communicating their lack of belonging in STEM, instances where both their voice and physical presence were ignored, and gendered and racialized encounters" (Wilkins-Yel, Hyman, & Zounlome, 2019, p. 51). In the face of such challenges, the students did well to cultivate communities of support and to internalize "messages of success" (Wilkins-Yel, Hyman, & Zounlome, 2019, p. 51), instead of lapsing into sense of "imposter syndrome." Persons with "complex, intersectional identities" make them "uniquely situated individuals" who are "rooted in the different intersections of our identities" (Hess, 2016, p. 86). One study focuses on black women living with HIV in the U.S. facing "microaggressions based on race, gender, HIV-status, and sexual orientation" (Dale et al., 2021, p. 4000), with a mix of "unique adversities" (p. 4000). Theirs are worlds of mixes of privileges and oppressions.

As one case-in-point, one study examined male-dominated work environments like information technology. In this space, various "inequality regimes" have been identified in terms of how minorities are treated. This study found that "racially dominant (white and Asian) women, who identified as LGBTQ and presented as gender-fluid, reported a greater sense of belonging in their workplace. They are perceived as more competent by male colleagues and avoided microaggressions that were routine among conventionally feminine, heterosexual women" (Alfrey & Twine, 2017, p. 28). This work revealed "a spectrum of belonging" in workplaces "dominated by men" (Alfrey & Twine, 2017, p. 28). The gender fluidity was somewhat nullified by race for those non-white or non-Asian in the IT workspace.

Particular Types of Subtle and Not-so-Subtle Bias and Discrimination

Microaggressions are defined as "commonplace daily verbal, behavioral or environmental slights, whether intentional or unintentional, that communicate hostile, derogatory, or negative attitudes toward stigmatized or culturally marginalized groups" ("Microaggression," Feb. 10, 2022). Microaggressions may

Navigating Inequitable (Mis)Treatment and Racist Harassment in Higher Education During COVID-19

be "verbal, nonverbal, and / or visual" (Solorzano, Ceja, & Yosso, 2000, p. 60). Such communications and actions are "subtle insults, invalidations, or slights that target people due to their association with a marginalized group" (Coalson, et al., 2022, p. 1). They are "verbal or non-verbal communications that invalidate those with non-dominant group identities across all dimensions of human diversity" (Bryant, Godsay, & Nnawulezi, 2021, p. 1). Microaggressions can "happen any day and anywhere" and "come in all *shapes* and *sizes"* and can target anyone based on any dimension of a person (Holmes, 2018, p. 155) or combinations of dimensions through intersectional aspects. Microaggressions "reflect the active manifestation of oppressive worldviews that create, foster, and enforce marginalization" (Wing Sue, 2010, as cited in Holmes, 2018, p. 156).

Microaggressions are "an elusive but toxic bias" (Suárez-Orozco et al., 2015, p. 151). ["Microaggression" is a term coined by Harvard psychiatrist at Harvard Dr. Chester Pierce in 1969. The term was defined in more depth (Sue, et al., 2007), in ways that inform contemporary usage of the term. Various validated scales have been created to measure various aspects of microaggressions in their various forms.] Microinsults are unconscious actions that are meant to cause offense to another, often based on their marginalized group status. Microinvalidations are "communications that exclude, negate, or nullify the thoughts, feelings, or experiential reality of a racial-ethnic minority individual" (Sue et al., 2007, as cited in Keels, Durkee, & Hope, 2017, p. 1318). Microassaults are blatant verbal, behavioral, or environmental slights that are purposefully committed by the aggressor against a member of a marginalized group (Kim, Block, & Nguyen, 2019, p. 75). Environmental microaggressions are those that exist at systemic and institutional levels. Where microaggressions, microinsults, and microinvalidations are generally thought to be unconscious actions, microassaults are thought to be conscious and purposeful ones. Microassaults are committed with the intention to harm the intended victim with explicit racial derogations "through name calling, blatant isolation of the individual, or purposeful discriminatory actions" (Sue et al., 2007, as cited in Keels, Durkee, & Hope, 2017, p. 1318).

Macroaggressions are defined as "large scale or overt aggression toward those of another race, culture, gender, etc." (Wiktionary, as cited in Druery, Young, & Elbert, 2018, p. 75). The Trump presidency (2017 – 2021) is considered by many to be a time of politicized racial politics and abysmal treatment of immigrants and lost children. Specifically: Donald J. Trump has "actually made America racist and sexist again" with his political "Make America Great Again" (MAGA) rhetoric and self-presentation (Druery, Young, & Elbert, 2018, p. 73). The Trump presidency "has been filled with both covert and overt acts of racism, sexism, and intolerance" (Druery, Young, & Elbert, 2018, p. 74) at a macro level. Macroaggression is an "emerging scholarly construct, given more credence in the era of Trump" (Druery, Young, & Elbert, 2018, p. 76).

Especially in times of large-scale hostile actions and rhetoric, how people are ethical *"conscious* and *responsible"* citizens is important (Accilien, 2018, p. 72). Except for anomalous periods, given years of hard work and legislation and education, there has been a decline of "blatant expressions of prejudice" in the past few decades (Williams, 2021, p. 709). People are thought to have suppressed their racism in alignment with the social unacceptability of such discrimination and instead gone to microaggressions, which are pervasive in modern societies, according to the research in the academic literature. Discrimination does rise and fall based on the sense of the social inappropriateness of that behavior, according to an empirical research study (Barr, Lane, & Nosenzo, 2018). Microaggressions have become "the chief vehicle for proracist behaviors" (Pierce et al., 1977, p. 66).

Biases come in many forms. They may be "overvalidation," by attributing to the target individual or group unearned senses of their capabilities based on a limited dimension of the person. Researchers write:

Overvalidation is a microaggression based on positive stereotypes of Asians, such as possessing competence in math or a strong work ethic, both of which are seen as beneficial and advantageous. However, if these stereotypes are positive, why do Asians view being treated on the basis of them as more problematic than Whites who are high on color-blindness? This may be because positive stereotypes are often not interpreted as positively for those on the receiving end. (Kim, Block, & Nguyen, 2019, p. 84)

For some, over-expectations from overvalidation may mean demands for overwork. [Some victims of racial stereotypes go to "compulsive work" as a response (McGee, 2015, as cited in McGee, 2016, p. 1627), which can be self-harming.] Asian Americans are also seen by many to have arrived and so supposedly do not experience racial discrimination in the U.S. That said, positive senses of Asian Americans can help those around them be more sensitive to microaggressions:

As expected, individuals with more positive attitudes toward Asian Americans viewed the blatant microaggressions against Asian Americans as more harmful compared to those who held less positive attitudes. Results also revealed that positive attitudes toward Asian Americans did not influence perceptions of the harmful effects of the subtler microaggressions (overvalidation and microinvalidation). (Kim, Block, & Yu, 2021, p. 1).

"Normalizing chaos" can lead to "cocreated self-violence and trauma under the guise of martyrdom" (Ricks, 2018, p. 343), and these ideas may lead to "overwork, self-neglect, and abuse" (Ricks, 2018, p. 350). There are real risks to people and sub-groups to internalizing abusive messages of the self, by hostile oppressive people.

The various forms of microaggressions and macroaggressions are found to have short- and long-term negative effects on the targets of those attacks. Stereotypes themselves result in detrimental effects, such as stereotype threat.

Stereotypes are specific associations and / or attributions of characteristics with a social identity group, and can be positive, negative, or neutral. Stereotype threat occurs when negative stereotypes about one's group undermine one's ability to perform in an area in which the negative stereotype applies—regardless of whether one has internalized those stereotypes. (Steele, 1997, as cited in Nadal et al., 2021, p. 4).

To the good, there are messages and activities that may be antiracist and anti-discriminatory, too. Allyship refers to the coming alongside a target of discrimination and providing support in various ways. There may be formal attestations in a bureaucratic process. There may be microaffirmations or messages of support to the individual.

Finally, it may help to define "white fragility," which is considered defensiveness by those in the majority when faced with racial issues. This phenomenon is defined as follows:

White people in North America live in a social environment that protects and insulates them from race-based stress. This insulated environment of racial protection builds white expectations for racial comfort while at the same time lowering the ability to tolerate racial stress, leading to what I refer to as White

Fragility. White Fragility is a state in which even a minimum amount of racial stress becomes intoler-able, triggering a range of defensive moves. These moves include the outward display of emotions such as anger, fear, and guilt, and behaviors such as argumentation, silence, and leaving the stress-inducing situation. (DiAngelo, 2010 as cited in Hardimon, 2019, p. 225)

Some in mainstream society view the focus on race as a political ploy to induce societal guilt in order to acquire special treatments and resources (such as "special considerations" like affirmative action, reparations). They view a "political correctness" regime as onerous and superficial. Such messages are not rare on social media, and not only on particular extremist sites.

A later study explored how far "white sensitivities" should be accommodated. For example, when should the term "racism" be used? Should it be held for "the most egregious of racial ills" only? One researcher writes:

If the word 'racism' is restricted to practices such as slavery, genocide, and lynching, most of us are off the hook. The notion that the word should be allowed to range over items such as unconscious racial antipathy, derogation, and indifference, microaggressions, and implicit bias goes with the idea that few of us are altogether off the hook. (Hardimon, 2019, p. 239)

A limited definition of "racism" may leave out *racial indifference*" as racism when "racial indiffer-ence can, and often does, mask racial hostility or derogation" (Hardimon, 2019, p. 227). The researcher elaborates: "Racial indifference itself constitutes race-based refusal of recognition. People who are racially indifferent refuse to recognize individuals belonging to a particular racially designated group as fully human or equally worthy of moral concern. Racial indifference is like racial antipathy and derogation in undermining human self-esteem, but its harms are more insidious and harder to resist" (Hardimon, 2019, p. 228) Racism is a "polysemous" or multi-meaning term (Hardimon, 2019, p. 224). However, does defining it overly broadly dilute its effect?

One study has work to classify different linguistic microaggressions by exploring the following re-search questions: "(i) on what linguistic grounds is a recipient licensed to infer that a microaggression has been committed, and (ii) to what extent can a speaker claim they have been misunderstood and hence deny responsibility for having committed a microaggression?" (Elder, 2021, p. 37)

This is a complicated space with complex multiple framing. One researcher highlights the fact that microaggressions are a form of aggression (lest people miss the point and minimize the impacts of such mistreatment) (Williams, 2021, p. 709).

In social psychology, aggression is most commonly defined as a behavior intended to harm another person who does not wish to be harmed, and violence is aggression that has harm as its goal (Allen & Anderson, 2017; Bushman & Huesmann, 2010).

The aggressions may be expressed in various modalities: verbal, relational, physical, ostracization, and avoidance, among others (Warren et al., 2011, as cited in Williams, 2021, p. 710). Perpetrators of various aggressions tend to be motivated by anger. For example, researchers have found "a significant positive correlation between negative affectivity and the propensity of White participants to commit microaggressions" (Williams, 2021, p. 709). Microaggressions "appear to represent a discrete form of subtle relational aggression" (Williams, 2021, p. 715). Finally, the researcher found that aggressive anger was "more strongly correlated to all four categories of micro-aggressions (negative/hostile attitudes, colorblindness, objectifying, and avoidance), more so than negative affect, although aggressive hostility showed the stronger correlations across microaggression categories" (Williams, 2021, p. 716). "Color blindness," the assertion that the person does not see color (or race, ethnicity), is a power move by the majority against minority persons of color (Holmes, 2018, p. 151).

Micro and Macro-aggressions Against Various Dimensionalities of Human Identity

Microaggressions are defined as "verbal, behavioral, or environmental communications that convey hostility, invalidation, or insult based on an individual's marginalized status in society" (Fisher, Chatterjee, Shapiro, Katz, & Yialamas, 2021, p. 3592). Part of the research literature focuses on particular marginalized groups who have been targeted with various micro- and macro- aggressions.

Gender Identity, Gender Fluidity and Nonbinary Identities, Gender Roles, Sexuality, and Sexual Identity

One study found that "dismissal; mistrust; sexualization; social exclusion; and denial of complexity" as identified microaggression factors seen to afflict bisexual women based on biphobia and other factors (Flanders, LeBreton, & Robinson, 2019, p. 143). As to supports for members of this community, the researchers describe a bisexual microaffirmation scale for women includes four subscales: "Acceptance, which relates to the acceptance of bisexuality as a legitimate sexual identity; Social Support, which communicates the general support individuals give to bisexual people and relationships; Recognition of Bisexuality and Biphobia, which conveys both the recognition of bisexuality as an identity, and also the identification of and resistance to biphobia; Emotional Support, which relates to the emotional support people provide a bisexual individual" (Flanders, LeBreton, & Robinson, 2019, pp. 154 - 155). Another study identified the "prejudicial experiences" for different bisexual groups. They found "bisexual-specific microaggressions include hostility; denial/dismissal; unintelligibility; pressure to change; lesbian, gay, bisexual and transgender legitimacy; dating exclusion; and hypersexuality" (Bostwick & Hequembourg, 2014, p. 488).

Differentiated Abilities

Those with different abilities have experienced various disability microaggressions: ignoring a person's identity other than the disability, minimizing the impact of disability-related experiences, "denial of privacy," treating the targeted individual as helpless, expectations of praise for doing something for the person with a disability ("secondary gain"), a "spread effect" ("expectations about a person are assumed to be due to one specific disability"), infantilization (treating the individual "like a child"), praising the person / people with disability/disabilities (PWD/D) for "almost anything" as a form of patronizing, denying the individual a "right to equality" because "they are bothersome, expensive, and a waste of time, effort, or resources," and "desexualization" by denying any aspect of the person as a sexual being (Keller & Galgay, 2010, pp. 249 – 250, as cited in Coalson et al., 2022, p. 4). Those who have invisible or non-apparent disabilities—cognitive processing, neuro-divergence (vs. neuro-typical), stuttering, dyslexia, traumatic brain injury, and others—also face a wide range of microaggressions.

Navigating Inequitable (Mis)Treatment and Racist Harassment in Higher Education During COVID-19

The research literature addresses a number of constructive ways to accommodate differentiated abilities. Researchers have also studied ableist microaggressions against those with disabilities, such as minimizing disabilities and deriding the need for accommodations; "bystander pushback in response to PWD/D self-advocacy," and other examples (Kattari et al., 2018, pp. 481 – 486, as cited in Coalson, et al., 2022, p. 5). Microaggressions can "degrade quality of life and corroborate negative stereotypes towards persons with disabilities" (Coalson et al., 2022, p. 1). Stuttering "is characterized by atypical blocks, repetitions, and prolongations during speech production" (Coalson et al., 2022, p. 1), and people who stutter are sometimes treated aggressively. Various themes in terms of microaggression behaviors experienced by adults who stutter were found in the research: "patronization, second-class status, perceived helplessness, workplace microaggression, clinical microaggression, denial of privacy" (Coalson et al., 2022, p. 1).

Various studies indicate successful work. One study found that "students with autism in inclusive settings are as accepted, visible, and members of peer groups, as well as both their peers without disabilities and those with other disabilities" (Boutot & Bryant, 2005, p. 14).

In Education: Pre, K-12, and Higher Education

Various prior frameworks of inclusivity in education have focused on marginalized population sub-groups. There are the typical demographics categories, those from diverse cultural groups, the foreign-born, and others. There are "students with exceptionalities" (DeLuca, 2013, p. 305). Inclusion is seen in a multicentric way vs. a "historical unicentric (i.e., dualistic) conception of inclusion" (DeLuca, 2013, p. 316). Inclusion applies to "all groups of difference" (DeLuca, 2013, p. 324).

One researcher proposes an interdisciplinary framework for educational inclusivity. This framework represents "multiple forms of inclusivity to edify historical, existing, and idealistic educational practices and structures for all forms of difference" (DeLuca, 2013, p. 305). Four disciplinary perspectives on educational inclusivity include the following: "(a) special education and disability studies, (b) multiculturalism and anti-racist education, (c) gender and women's education, and (d) queer studies"; further, there are four conceptions of inclusivity: "normative, integrative, dialogical, and transgressive" (DeLuca, 2013, p. 305).

In the sequence, the dominant group is centered in a hub and spoke relationship with other groups (normative). Next, the dominant group is decentered, in a multi-centric setup (integrative). In the next phase, the advanced multicentric one, the dominant group is one of many and less dominant (dialogical); it is engaged with others in connection. Finally, in the concentric phase, the society is represented by overlapping circles, and the dominance of the former group is no longer apparent in the society (transgressive). (DeLuca, 2013, p. 326). There is no dominant group in the final stage but a society of people co-existing in harmony and fairness. The researcher writes: "In a transgressive conception of inclusivity, student diversity is used as a vehicle for the generation of new knowledge and learning experiences. All individuals are regarded as culturally complex who contribute to the learning context" (DeLuca, 2013, p. 334).

Existing systems of oppression in higher education have resulted in disparities in student performance and graduation. Targets of microaggressions have experienced induced imposter syndrome, performance anxiety, and other negative cumulative effects of microaggressions (Nadal et al., 2021, p. 1).

Another case of "peripheral student" syndrome includes mature foreign students attaining a doctorate in education in the UK, based on various needs, including "prestige" (Savva & Nygaard, 2021, p. 154). Peripheral students experience "struggles related to identity, language and / or culture" (Savva & Nygaard, 2021, p. 155). They strive to internalize a scholarly identity even while struggling with social loneliness (Savva & Nygaard, 2021, p. 158), even as they build their social networks. This study found a broad lack of cultural awareness by faculty, from the student view.

- **Graduate teaching assistants:** Various studies have explored microaggressions in the tertiary education space. Racial and gender patterns in microaggressions have been found in predominantly white campuses, with "covert insults towards subordinated groups" (McCabe, 2009, p. 133). One study identified four themes in the microaggressions:

    (a) views of black men as threatening, (b) views of Latinas as sexually available and exotic, (c) the classroom as a particular setting for microaggressions experienced by black women, and, (d) male-dominated academic majors as particular settings for microaggressions experienced by white women. (McCabe, 2009, p. 133)

Persons on majority-white institutions viewed persons as foreign even though they were American-born. They perceived "accents" in the absence of an individual even speaking a language beyond English (McCabe, 2009). Another study found that Black students experienced "race, gender, and class microaggressions" in higher education. They described microaggressive experiences in which they were seen as "exotic, hypersexual and aggressive" as compared to non-Blacks on campus (Morales, 2014, p. 48). They experienced "racial microaggressions are tied to racialized, gendered and classed ideas of low-income Black male and female bodies" (Morales, 2014, p. 48). Some research participants complained that they were forced into roles of playing a "cultural expert" about others assumed to be in the person's social group. The hostilities are not only in actions. One study found a blocking of access and resources to oppressed groups, such as African American faculty (Pittman, 2012, p. 86).

Teaching assistants "from nonmainstream backgrounds in a predominantly white institution (PWI) of U.S. education" have experienced widespread microaggressions, with "subtle challenges to their teaching based on race and ethnicity" and marginalization of their work (Gomez et al., 2011, p. 1189). Those around these graduate students experienced various tactics of "avoidance and slighting," such as silence, "continual questioning of their instructional decisions," and other behaviors (Gomez et al., 2011, p. 1197). These graduate teaching assistants had to disrupt various stereotypes and racist narratives in their work, even as some were discouraged from pursuing teaching as a profession.

The campus racial climate of predominantly white institutions (PWIs) is often hostile for non-whites, who often experience "racialized experiences" (Leath & Chavous, 2018, p. 125). Researchers write:

Overall, Black women experienced a more hostile racial climate and less academic satisfaction than women from other racial/ethnic groups. Black women reported similar levels of academic competence, suggesting their determination to excel despite experiencing race-related challenges to their institutional context. (Leath & Chavous, 2018, p. 125)

Racial stigma is associated with lessened academic motivation, with implications for non-continuance of study. For some students, they take on fighting "institutionalized racism on college campuses" such as predominantly white institutions and working towards changing exclusionary school policies and enabling other institutional reforms (Jones & Reddick, 2017).

- **Minority academic librarians:** Academic librarians of color experienced "subtle, denigrating" messages in their work that were not experienced by non-minority librarians, in another study (Alabi, 2015, p. 47). Here, minority participants in a research study "both experienced and observed racial microaggressions more often than non-minority respondents" (Alabi, 2015, p. 50), suggesting differences in lived professional lives. A later study of the experiences of librarians of color found five themes:

uniqueness and difference, broad range of professional skills; messiness and beauty of the human interaction; working in a web of outside forces; and learning, growth, and change. (VanScoy & Bright, 2017, p. 104)

That librarians of color "have unique experiences of reference and information services work because of microaggressions and discrimination and because of their focus on serving as a role model or mentor" (VanScoy & Bright, 2017, p. 104). Under-represented groups have qualitatively different workplace experiences because of the nature of society.

Defenses (Protective Factors) Against Social Hostilities

"Students' exposure to microaggressions and its effects were conditional on individual and school characteristics" (Keels, Durkee, & Hope, 2017, p. 1316). Many who are targeted for racial microaggressions on campus have their defenses.

One study identified four strategic responses to racial microaggressions by undergraduate Black, Indigenous, and People of Color (BIPOC) groups at a Canadian university: "*using humor to mitigate tension, seeking community and solidarity for support, avoiding or withdrawing for protection* and *confronting perpetrators and challenging stereotypes*" (Houshmand & Spanierman, 2021, pp. 1, 5 - 8). Another protective factor comes from the use of racial microaffirmations as a way to fight everyday systemic racism and racial microaggressions (Huber, Gonzalez, Robles, & Solórzano, 2021, p. 1). For Black and Latino learners engaging in STEM culture, some engage "stereotype management" as a form of self-protection (McGee, 2016, p. 1626). They engage bi-culturally and code-switch as they move between different microcultures (McGee, 2016). A three-year ethnographic study found Native American students sometimes go to silence as a protection, with "silence as a form of critical literacy—or critical silent literacies—in response to racial microaggressions enacted by their peers, their teachers, or a combination of both" (San Pedro, 2015, p. 132). There are counter narratives against educational ideas that "reify dominant, Eurocentric norms" (San Pedro, 2015, p. 144).

People do well to not let others define them. In another study, adult stutterers who were victims of microaggressions "expressed reticence to perceive themselves as a victim, which contributed to PWS/S exonerating their interactants for microaggressive slights" (Coalson et al., 2022, p. 13). ["PWS/S" refers to "person or people who stutter."] Another protective response is to recognize microaggressions for what they are and responding with a healthy anger instead of self-pathologizing and internalizing the damaging ideas of the self (Minikel-Lacocque, 2013, p. 459). Some have observed that in the face of a microaggression, it can be a Catch-22 if they respond or do not respond (Sue, 2010, p. 58, as cited in Minikel-Lacocque, 2013, p. 460). In another study, Black women college students used various ways to cope:

two resistance coping strategies (i.e., Using One's Voice as Power, Resisting Eurocentric Standards), one collective coping strategy (i.e., Leaning on One's Support Network), and two self-protective coping strategies (i.e., Becoming a Black Superwoman, Becoming Desensitized and Escaping). (Lewis et al., 2013, p. 51)

There was a theme of "Picking and Choosing One's Battles" (Lewis et al., 2013, p. 51), which evokes something of the Catch-22 mentioned in another study. How appropriate the various coping mechanisms seem to depend on the complexities of the context. Indeed, energy deployed to dealing with the stresses of microaggressions and then changing the culture and environment has been found to result in "racial battle fatigue" (Smith, Hung, & Franklin, 2011, p. 63). One researcher highlights some important points in responding to microaggressions:

Pierce (1970) advocated that in challenging microaggressions, the first step is to identify the incident and the next is to respond. Kohli and Solórzano (2012) also advocate first identifying and then undertaking a close consideration of response to the incidents, but suggest an additional element, analyzing the effects of microaggressions. Perez Huber and Solórzano (2015) define responses as their psychological and physiological impact. (Pearce, 2019, p. 84)

One work describes the power of school counselors to support African American students, including with spiritual bolstering. School counselors may include culturally relevant spirituality in supporting African American students "in coping with oppression and racism while deriving personal meaning, a sense of hopefulness, and promoting healing within the context of school systems" (Curry, 2010, p. 405).

There are protections against sexual objectifications against gendered and racialized microaggressions. One study found "appearance-contingent self-worth as a mediator between stress related to experiencing sexually objectifying gendered racial microaggressions and body appreciation" (Dunn, Hood, & Owens, 2019, p. 121). A healthy sense of self-worth can be a buffer against hostilities and denigrations. Student "private regard, an internally sponsored affective responses" was an important "identity asset that helped blunt the negative effects of microaggressions on depressive symptoms" (Keels, Durkee, & Hope, 2017, p. 1337). Further, "public regard" for their racial-ethnic group by others also blunted the negative effects of microaggressions (Keels, Durkee, & Hope, 2017, p. 1336). Students and other targets may become more resilient and self-aware and active in their own well-being, in the protection of their academic achievements and mental health. They may engage in encouraging and positive self-talk and surround themselves with supportive others.

Combating Institutional Biases

Workplace discrimination and institutional racism "yielded decreased odds of reporting good health status" for the targets of those hostilities (Oh, 2021, p. 1). One researcher found an association between "racial microaggressions, discrimination, and self-reported health status varied across ethnic subgroup,"

Navigating Inequitable (Mis)Treatment and Racist Harassment in Higher Education During COVID-19

in particular, finding that "verbal aggression score was more predictive for the East Asian group while institutional racism was most harmful to Southeast Asians" (Oh, 2021, p. 1).

Various types of interventions to fight stigma and discrimination exist in the research literature. One narrative review of a selective literature identifies what is effective and what is not. There are limits to one-off contacts, but there are benefits of something longer term and continuing in terms of interventions (Ashton, Gordon, & Reeves, 2018, p. 316). There are benefits to teaching people how to counter stigma and discrimination. There are benefits to open dialogue. Effective public interventions often occur at local levels of communities. There are some empirically effective ways to measure attitude and behavior change (Ashton, Gordon, & Reeves, 2018).

In workplaces, addressing biases and microaggressions may require various interventions, including policy setting, policy enforcement, trainings, employee supports, and microaffirmations. One toolkit to use in a workplace to deal with microaggressions include the following: "Practice microaffirmations, assume best intent, state your take, depersonalize, get curious, repeat/reflect, reframe, redirect, use preference statements, set boundaries, disengage, debrief, and revisit" (Fisher et al., 2021, p. 3594).

There are effective interventions for organizations and workplaces. Effective interventions are possible, such as holding bystander training for faculty, so that they may intervene and disrupt the barriers to entry and advancement for "faculty from traditionally marginalized groups" for more effective inclusion in the academy and work fields (Haynes-Baratz et al., 2021, p. 1). There are innovative ways to confront microaggressions in workplaces (Skinta & Torres-Harding, 2022). Another work describes the value of "honest and open dialogue on race in the military, at all levels of government, and in society at large" (Yeung & Lim, 2021, p. 37), even if the interactions may feel fraught, especially in times of societal unrest. Participants may fear being seen as "ignorant or prejudiced" (Yeung & Lim, 2021, p. 37); they may fear seeing their own racism and privilege and may experience "fear of taking responsibility for ending racism" (Yeung & Lim, 2021, p. 39). Hiding inequities and discrimination can hurt workplace morale and productivity.

One research team has conducted a systematic review of research of workplace interventions as a way of addressing "subtle bias and / or its behavioral manifestations" (Metinyurt, Haynes-Baratz, & Bond, 2021, p. 1). The researchers evaluated "the efficacy of trainings *designed to reduce microaggressions in the workplace,* and / or the efficacy of trainings *designed to reduce other conceptually related constructs of subtle bias and subtle discrimination (even if not microaggressions specifically)*" (Metinyurt, Haynes-Baratz, & Bond, 2021, p. 3). The researchers write:

All evaluations reported some success at increasing explicit awareness of personal subtle biases, which is a critical step to improve attitudes towards marginalized (e.g., women and people of color). Given the variety of approaches to assessing awareness, it is not possible to disentangle genuine changes in individual perceptions of biases from participants' understanding of the material presented. (Metinyurt, Haynes-Baratz, & Bond, 2021, p. 7)

Follow-on evaluations of trainings were not common. Also, they write:

The majority of the evaluations did not collect behavioral measures related to the expression of bias nor did they assess outcomes distal from the training. Even though all of the training examples documented changes in attitude and knowledge in the short term, we know little about whether the trainings created long-lasting effects. Given that biased beliefs and attitudes can be resistant to change, 'one-time' train-ings may fail to create changes that persist over time. (Metinyurt, Haynes-Baratz, & Bond, 2021, p. 7)

Interventions against discriminatory communications and actions are more effective if fully integrated into organizational change and culture. Perhaps the trainings about the relativism of culture may enable those who live in multicultural spaces to lessen their adherence to dominant culture and unthinking glomming on to it.

Debiasing Work in Academia

Academia is not seen as a safe space for diverse persons, given the "pervasiveness of white supremacy within these legitimized spaces of knowledge production" (Levchak, 2018, n.p.). The belief of own-group superiority leads to tensions in the collegiate racial climate (Solorzano, Ceja, & Yosso, 2000, pp. 60 – 61). Various microinsults experienced on a predominantly white campus include the following: "ascription of intelligence, second class citizen (treatment), pathologizing cultural values / communica-tion styles, (and) assumption of criminal status" and various microinvalidations include "alien in own land, color blindness ("pretense that a White person does not see color or races"), myth of meritocracy ("statements which assert that race plays a minor role in life success"), (and) denial of individual racism" (Minikel-Lacocque, 2013, pp. 435 - 436).

One study found common microaggressions in nearly 30% of the community college classrooms ob-served. Instructors were the most common perpetrators (Suárez-Orozco, Casanova, Martin, Katsiaficas, Cuellar, Smith, & Dias, 2015, p. 157), which suggests also the abuse of their power in the classroom, as students were the most common recipients of the microaggressions, in the "toxic classrooms." In another study, Black men in engineering graduate education experienced racial microaggressions in the "advisor-advisee relationship" (Burt, McKen, Burkhart, Hormell, & Knight, 2019, p. 493), with negative impacts on the students' studies and potential future career. Another study suggests that the African American experience "is not important to faculty and the university" (Von Robertson & Chaney, 2017), even as it is known that racial tensions lead to higher risks of dropout. One study found that microaggressions can play a significant role in how Black faculty perceive and experience participation, engagement, retention and advancement" in higher education (Payton, Yarger, & Pinter, 2018, p. 217), resulting in talent loss in a field where Black faculty are severely underrepresented.

There has long been work in decolonizing and anti-biased curriculums. In the academic and other spaces, there is work that may be done to de-bias, even in the face of modern racism. One study involves teaching white students the "skills to be proactive in discussing race, confronting racism, building in-terracial friendships, and acknowledging racism" (Holmes, 2018, p. 173). This study refers to skills to analyze media critically, to manage racial stress, to "honor and respect racial affinity spaces for students of color," to "develop authentic relationships with peers of color and other white students," and to recog-nize "one's racist and antiracist identities" (Holmes, 2018, p. 173). Various de-biasing interventions also include "counter-stereotypic training," exposing people to "counter-stereotypic individuals," increased intergroup contact, education, accountability for people, perspective-taking, and "deliberative process-ing" (Staats, 2014, pp. 20 – 21, as cited in Holmes, 2018, pp. 176-177); individuating people, disrupting class hierarchies (Quintero, 2014b, as cited in Holmes, 2018, p. 177), and other interventions. Student voices are important to enable optimized inclusive education (Andriana & Evans, 2020). Indigenous knowledge has also been used to destabilize "cultural imperialism…in favor of inclusive social education" (Prempeh, 2022, p. 1).

Native American women in doctoral programs were also found to experience that space as racially hostile, isolating, and unwelcoming. The participants of the study were treated as outsiders to their programs and were not invited to social gatherings or rituals. Their presence was not acknowledged. They experienced challenges to their academic abilities and knowledge and belongingness in the program.

Some romanticized Native people based on stereotypes (Shotton, 2017, p. 46). There were assumptions of "homogeneity of Native people" as if they are all of a type ((Shotton, 2017, p. 47).

- **Principal leadership:** Effective principal leadership is needed to support core values of inclusivity, "a data system that monitors student progress," and "a school-based system of learner-centered professional development to improve instruction" in actualizing inclusivity in K12 schools (McLeskey & Waldron, 2015, p. 68).
- **Teacher education:** The "history of educating children with disabilities has been one of exclusion, institutionalization, and segregation," which was countered by "parent and organization advocacy, human rights activists, and statements from international organizations" (Timmons, 2009, p. 95). Preservice teachers engage with diversity, which is defined in many ways. There are risks to the lack of diversity among teachers (Timmons, 2009, p. 98), who could bring richer experiential understandings not brought to the work. A later study found that teachers of courses "focused on diversity perceived microaggressions more negatively and were more likely to respond to the microaggressions than teachers of nondiversity courses. Students believed that teacher responses to microaggressions were effective and ignoring microaggressions was ineffective" (Boysen, 2012, p. 122). This study suggests the importance for trained awareness. New teachers benefit when they learn about microaggressions, so they may challenge discrimination in schools. One study captured various racial microaggressions in learning:

Examples of racial microaggressions may be repeatedly mispronouncing or reassigning someone's name; rejecting the validity of a black classmate's experiences; asking someone where they are really from; assuming a black teacher must be the teaching assistant; having all questions directed at a more junior, white, colleague, though it has been made clear who is in charge. This is just a small sample of the many incidents relayed to me by minority ethnic student teachers and practicing teachers this year. (Pearce, 2019, p. 84)

Often, biases are expressed in coded ways (Pearce, 2019, p. 90).

One study found that mainstreaming had its limits. This study involved participation by both parents and their children with special education needs. The researcher writes:

…current research indicates that actual 'inclusion' (the child experiencing inclusion as well as being placed in a mainstream environment) is not necessarily occurring in practice. As it stands, the conflict is between desires to embrace difference based on a philosophy of 'equal rights' ('inclusive' education) and prioritizing educational performance, structuring it in such a way that it leaves little room for difference and creativity due to the highly structured testing and examination culture. (Rogers, 2007, p. 55)

This study found a lack of positive parent experiences with inclusive education in this study (Rogers, 2007). Another study suggests that inclusive classrooms may not be suitable for all learners and argues for "segregated classrooms" for learners with "mild cognitive disabilities" where they may experience specialized programming in a low-stress environment (Tkachyk, 2013, p. 15).

One meta-analysis studied the relationship between K-12 teacher self-efficacy and their attitudes towards inclusive special education. This study found "a positive sample size weighted correlation between teachers' self-efficacy and attitudes" towards inclusive education, suggesting that "the relationship might be somewhat universal regardless of time, culture, or gender" (Yada, Leskinen, Savolainen, & Schwab, 2022, p. 1). A different study was conducted to evaluate teacher concerns about inclusive education in order to better design interventions for the promotion of inclusions in education (Lozano, Wüthrich, Büchi, & Sharma, 2022).

Another work describes the training of health professions educators to mitigate the experiences of underrepresented students' senses of marginalization (Ackerman-Barger, Bakerjian, & Latimore, 2015, p. 1060).

Applying relevant preservice training and field experiences to teachers is one way to lessen teacher fears of having students with differentiated needs in their classroom. Such trainings improve teacher agency and raise their self-confidence in their ability to support the learning of all their students in inclusive classrooms. Researchers suggest that having only one special education course in a preservice teacher curriculum may be too limited, and it would benefit all to infuse such contents throughout a curriculum (McCray & McHatton, 2011, p. 150) and perhaps include special education certification (p. 151). Inclusion is seen as an important part of the general education classroom, without exception (Obiakor, Harris, Mutua, Rotatori, & Algozzine, 2012).

In terms of accessible instructional design, the Universal Design for Learning (UDL) is seen to align well with inclusive education. One research team writes:

In the model, the UDL approach is presented as an approach of transforming the process of education and strengthening teacher inclusive attitudes, as a prerequisite for the pupil's becoming an expert learner, a means for mobilizing the school community, a tool for reflecting teacher competences, and a new perspective for re-interpreting educational practices. (Galkienė & Monkevičienė, 2021, p. 313)

Ideally, all learners are enabled, and all barriers to learning are absent.

- **Student peers:** Another approach involves setting up peer supports to actualize inclusive education, as part of whole-classroom strategies. There are various methods--class-wide peer tutoring, cross-age tutoring—and other methods at the secondary level (Bond & Castagnera, 2006, p. 224).

Inclusive Education Globally

The concepts and practices of inclusive have extended globally, often based on the UN Convention on the Rights of Persons with Disabilities. UNESCO (2020) pointed to educational, social, and economic justifications for inclusion and equity in education as global priorities (Ydo, 2020, p. 98). There have been international advances in the inclusive education space and effects on various countries around the world (Singal, 2006, p. 239), both developed and developing. Some work involves analysis on how

Navigating Inequitable (Mis)Treatment and Racist Harassment in Higher Education During COVID-19

to advance inclusive education goals in the real (Opertti, Brady, & Duncombe, 2009). Multi-level and multi-faceted strategies and tactics are necessary to support inclusive education (Acedo, 2011).

Participants may be encouraged to take part in inclusive education with future-oriented thinking, which can show inclusive education in positive light for both those with and without disabilities (Maeda, Hashimoto, & Sato, 2021). Local conditions—the staffing, the resources—have effects how the inclusive education: "In inclusive schooling the aim is not to change the student with disabilities to fit into the environment. The aim is to change the environment to accommodate the needs of the student" (Chimedza, 2008, p. 126). In every locality, though, there have to be customizations to integrate the inclusiveness in the education.

Inclusiveness has been broadened beyond education, such as addressing issues of disadvantage like "poverty, ethnicity (minorities) and other challenging conditions" (Schiemer, 2017, p. 175), in a human rights framework (Acedo, 2008). Inclusion has broadened to include various diversities and combinations of diversity in race, social class, ethnicity, religion, gender, sexual orientation, migrant status, and ability" (Ydo, 2020, p. 97). When there is "education for all" at the primary, secondary, and tertiary levels, societies tend to be more equitable, healthier, and richer (Roche, 2016, p. 131).

Technologies and Pedagogies to Aid Inclusion in Learning

Finally, there was a small set of research works highlighting the contributions of information and communication technologies (ICT) and robotics and other technologies to inclusive education. With assistive, ICT, e-learning, and other technologies, teachers are thought to be able to address "the special educational needs of all pupils" (Feyerer, 2002, p. 64). Still, there are gaps in teacher competences in incorporating informatics in their inclusive education work (Jašková, 2006). One work describes the use of "games, exercises, body motions, animations, a quiz and a robot-based system with audio, video and vibro-tactile interfaces" to enhance the education of children with disabilities (hearing impairment, autism, and others) (Hersh, Leporini, & Buzzi, 2020, p. 123).

E-inclusion is critical for learning, so digital divides have to be addressed for teachers and learners to ensure access (Marín-Díaz, 2020, p. 869). Inclusive education is advanced using a mix of tangible interfaces and virtual worlds in high school learning (Mateu, Lasala, & Alamán, 2013); a mixed reality book in high school (Mateu, Lasala Bello, & Alamán, 2014); educational games about science (Marino & Hayes, 2012, p. 945); educational robotics to provision for special needs, socio-economic status, cultural diversity, and gender for inclusive education (and to lower school leaving) (Daniela & Lytras, 2019); an adaptive robotic platform to enable communications for children with autism spectrum disorder inclusive education (Lancheros-Cuesta et al., 2020); Makerspaces ("fablabs" and "hackerspaces") for STEM education where "higher education students…formed multidisciplinary teams to create novel accessible, affordable devices containing inclusive technology to foster inclusive learning environments" (Reynaga-Peña et al., 2020, p. 246), and others. One study explored how people may interact meaningfully with computational systems to enable inclusive education (Hornung, Pereira, & Baranauskas, 2016). One technology tool is a blended learning platform "that addresses the needs of different types of learners and offers accessible and usable materials including movies, television broadcasts, and interactive and multimedia content for students with different prerequisites for learning" (Bosse, 2015, p. 3).

In terms of inclusive education pedagogies, one work describes a problem-solving Olympics, which includes computational thinking and learning informatics (Borchia et al., 2018). Another publication describes the need to make assessments more accessible to all learners, so the inclusive education includes the tests (McConlogue, 2020, p. 137). Another describes content personalization for inclusive education in model-driven engineering (Power & Paige, 2009).

In Various Professional Spaces

One work involves research on microaggressions experienced by music therapists based on sexism and cisgenderism. Those with "marginalized gender identities" include "trans/cis women, trans men, and nonbinary persons." This study identified five themes: "qualities of micro-aggressions, impact of incident, survival tactics, interpersonal dynamics, and gender in music therapy" (McSorley, 2020, p. 1). Some categories of gender microaggressions towards cis women include the following: "sexual objectification, assumptions of inferiority, assumptions of traditional gender roles, use of sexist language, denial of individual sexism, invisibility, denial of the reality of sexism, (and) environmental gender microaggressions" (Nadal, 2010, as cited in McSorley, 2020, p. 2). Categories of gender microaggressions towards trans individuals: "use of transphobic and / or incorrectly gendered terminology, assumptions of universal transgender experience, exoticization, discomfort / disapproval of transgender experience, endorsement of gender normative and binary culture or behaviors, denial of the existence of transphobia, assumption of sexual pathology or abnormality, physical threat or harassment, denial of individual transphobia, denial of personal body privacy, familial microaggression, (and) systemic and environmental microaggressions" (Nadal, et al., 2012, as cited in McSorley, 2020, p. 2). Using inappropriate gender terms in reference to people diminish transgender people's self-respect and cause "microaggressive psychological harms" (Kapusta, 2016, p. 502). Insensitive terminology "...either exclude at least some transgender women, or else they implicitly foster hierarchies among women, marginalizing transgender women in particular" (Kapusta, 2016, p. 502). This suggests the need for additional interventions to avoid enacting of gendered microaggressions in this field.

In human service organizations, microaggressions "may lower therapeutic alliance, reduce retention, and result in negative outcomes" (Bryant, Godsay, & Nnawulezi, 2021, p. 1).

Microaggressions in Public Awareness

Several big data queries were run to infer the amount of social awareness of "microaggressions" in global journalism and also in graduate studies.

In the Global Press

In the global press, there seems to be general awareness of "microaggressions," with common emotions around this term showing "disgust" and "surprise," per a big-data search in ProQuest's TDM Studio (Text and Data Mining Studio). (Figure 2)

A geographical mapping of the articles in this data query show fairly broad global exposures. (Figure 3)

In Graduate Student Research

In terms of graduate student research (mostly doctoral), some 9,720 mentioned microaggressions in the set from Jan. 2014 to Jan. 2022. (Figure 4)

Figure 2. Sentiment Analysis of "Microaggressions in the Global Press" (Dec. 2007 – Jan. 2022) (from ProQuest's TDM Studio)

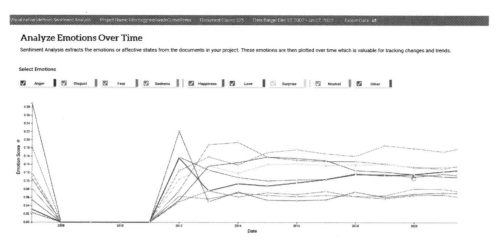

Figure 3. Geographical Mapping of "Microaggressions in the Global Press" (Dec. 2007 – Jan. 2022) (from ProQuest's TDM Studio)

These publications appear to be situated somewhat globally but also with quiet zones where no student publications including this topic appear. (Figure 5)

Finally, in January 2022, the topic modeling of "microaggression" in the global press identified a focus on Asians and Chinese as foci of microaggressions with spikes in 2013 and 2020 onwards. The more recent spike apparently stems from the SARS-CoV-2 / COVID-19 pandemic (Figure 6). Indeed, in the author's university town, it is a liberal island in a sea of conservatism. Experientially, accessing local services like plumbing and electrical work has often resulted in surprisingly large bills with an apparent tax on being a female Asian client. There may have been pressures, too, on the various service providers given rising inflation or perhaps local issues such as the need to "meet bank."

Figure 4. Sentiment Analysis of "Microaggressions in Dissertations and Theses" (Jan. 2014 – Dec. 2023 / actually Jan. 2022) (from ProQuest's TDM Studio)

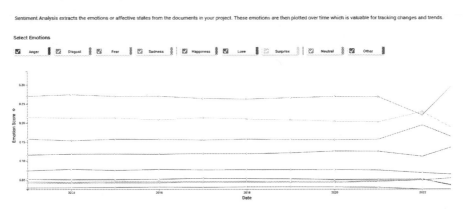

Figure 5. Geographical Mapping of "Microaggressions in Dissertations and Theses" (Jan. 2014 – Dec. 2023 / actually Jan. 2022) (from ProQuest's TDM Studio)

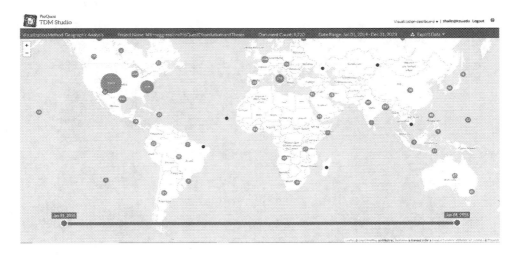

Figure 6. A Focus on Anti-Asian Hate from the "Microaggressions in the Global Press" (Dec. 2007 – Jan. 2022) (Topic Modeling from ProQuest's TDM Studio)

The greater awareness of microaggressions and microassaults and targeted groups may help democratic societies and others self-correct against some of the rampant hatreds afoot, especially in larger society and especially in workplaces.

Navigating Inequitable (Mis)Treatment and Racist Harassment in Higher Education During the COVID-19 Pandemic: A Self-Decentered Autoethnographic Case

Every person was likely shaken by the pandemic to varying degrees. The pandemic was highly disruptive and threatening to human lives and human health. It was threatening to livelihoods. The social fabric, for many, was rent. The stresses caused some to fail in their relationships with others. Many emerged into social interactions with less mental bandwidth to engage and to empathize. For the author, she experienced several remote student rants by posted messages against "Chinese" that were unprovoked. Out of the blue, one student who identified as Hispanic wrote about what she saw as racial animus between Hispanics and Chinese. Another said that some documentation (a manual) she read seemed to be written in "Chinese," and that she "taught Chinese students." She was communicating that she did not understand the technical manual as she cast aspersions on the author. She placed herself socially above her "Chinese students." This verbal attack, too, came out of nowhere. Some students made appointments and never showed up. Some student staff tried to assign the author their own work even though they had no standing to do so, and they also had no funding to pay for the requested work. Some were so committed to this course of action that they reached out multiple times with this request. Students made assumptions based on the author's name of her identity and capabilities. There have been some on-the-street issues, where people have reacted with hostile looks, verbal challenges, erratic driving (a car turning in front of the author onto a driveway and then backing up threateningly as she walked by), and other issues. During a checkup, a phlebotomist asked of the author's nationality (she is native-born American), and when apprised of that, the African American phlebotomist asked, "Where are you really from?" People all require grace in their social interactions. Perhaps they are well-meaning. Perhaps they are working towards being their best selves. Maybe.

The supervisor's actions cannot be separated from the context. In a workplace though, with power relations at play, and a lifetime's investment in work, racist microassaults cannot go unchallenged. Discriminatory biases are distortionary, and they change the perpetrator's sense of the world and of others (even as it may make them feel more self-important). Racism, sexism, and the others, debilitate the holder of the views in a professional sense, not to mention the corrosion to their personal character. The author did try to resolve the issue directly and respectfully first.

The "chink eyes" expression by the supervisor, which emerged unprovoked, broke trust (after 16 years of profession-based interactions between the author and this individual) and basic decorum. When the author mentioned his racist tropes to the supervisor, his response via email was, "Oh my goodness!" This was taken as a patronizing expression of denial and non-responsibility. And he mentioned that Human Resources should be brought in. Then he dropped the issue and tried to bully the author into the monthly meetings again as if nothing had happened. Then, he stopped calling meetings altogether with the author, even as he met weekly with two of his other staff and once a month or every-two-months with a non-white staff member.

When it was clear there would be no personal addressing the issues or stoppage of the intimidation, a few weeks after the initial "slant eyes" expression by the supervisor, the author filed a complaint with the university office and also with the high leader secondarily.

The author documented the incident and complained to the Office of Institutional Equity, which promptly labeled the issue a "microaggression" during the initial half-hour meeting Even if all the assertions were borne out by investigators, it would not likely rise to the level where OIE would have to take action. If the supervisor continued in that harassing and racist / sexist vein, the complaint would reach threshold, and the office would act. They asked if the author wanted the issue to be brought to Employee Relations. At Employee Relations, the issue was sent to the the leader of the unit. The constant refrain was, "Go back to your chain of command because work assignment issues are dealt with there" (in paraphrase). This approach gives the sense of political cover for administrators to engage in negative acts that harm staff, without cost. Indeed, the direct supervisor got a few more swipes in. He threatened the author's employment several times verbally ("we're considering whether instructional design is part of ITS") but did not apparently take additional actual actions; it seemed as if he was trying to intimidate her to not take the issue further. He also said he would just simply change her job description (in the PERS-23 form) and just add the extra FTEs of work. He perhaps did not know what actions had already been taken by the author in terms of formalizing a complaint.

Five months after the initial event, the high leader organized a meeting for issues to be aired, with a focus on the supervisor's anger and abusiveness, the multiple-FTE assignments, and the racist gesture. During the three-person meeting, the direct supervisor admitted to all the issues (surprisingly to the author), and he apologized for the racist gesture although he disavowed the meaning. He said he made the physical gestures without knowing why and respected the author "as a worker" (notably, not as a person). To the author, the "apology" rang false as cheap talk. The high leader also said that it was totally fine for the supervisor to experience "emotions," which was how he characterized the supervisor's outbursts and perhaps even the racist microassault. Or perhaps he was only trying to find some middle ground where everyone felt justified and the issue could be put to rest. The leader said he would notify university leadership of the meeting and what occurred. The perpetrator's admission of the racist action while fully sentient meant that the action could not be attributed to ambiguity. Officially, the "microaggression" moved into the category of purposeful "microassault." The egregious nature of the act of hate was compounded by the cultural focus on unfailing politeness and expressed care for others in the Midwest. Such behaviors may be mere social performances without substance, but on the surface, such are the common practices. [The leader left the impression that he was trying to see if he could just put the issue away first by slow-walking it... It seemed as if he was testing whether the issue would hold or would somehow dissipate on its own.]

Meanwhile, the high leader put into motion the move of the additional multiple FTEs of work to other units on campus. Months afterwards, no progress at hiring for the work has occurred. The author's direct supervisor had to take on the extra work, and the author stopped donating the extra work hours to the causes of the multiple FTEs. The direct supervisor has not engaged in obvious racial harassment since. However, he has continued to try to force extra work into the off-hours.

The author had sensed that nothing would be done about the initial offense if she would have accepted the high leader's inferred offer of a job transfer, but remaining would also have its cost, with a vindictive individual in a position of power over her career and general well-being. How was such racism so-called leadership material? How could such obvious biases not be career-ending? The protections

Navigating Inequitable (Mis)Treatment and Racist Harassment in Higher Education During COVID-19

of Anderson Hall would likely be tested. At some point, everyone involved would have to make a good faith effort to continue with their best work possible, for the sake of the university and its faculty, staff, and students. Individuals would have to keep working on themselves. Perhaps the racialized climate of the pandemic would pass, and people would find new footing. Perhaps people could move beyond living in their heads and feral minds after years of lockdown and social isolation. Certainly, along the way, there were allies and stalwarts against the expression of hate in the workplace. Still, for all the expressions of support, all efforts had limits. The core decisions remained in the work hierarchy, which is top-down. Power in a university is somewhat federated and distributed, but it is also hierarchical. Still, the university has bureaucracies in place to address such issues, and these were hard-won investments in a more equitable workplace. The jury is out as yet as to whether the full issues have been addressed some eight months after the microassault offense and three years after the extra assignments were added on to the author's workload by a prior supervisor who had since retired (and two years after the author first notified leadership of the excess load and its untenability, with concomitant risk to the university of a single point of failure for graduating students).

At this point, there is still healing to be achieved. There is still a reboot in the offing. It is hoped that the sub-unit in ITS can move forward more constructively, but there do not seem to be deeper changes. The top leadership of ITS is supposedly providing some administrative oversight, and more importantly, there is some oversight by university leadership over ITS. The supervisor, in the half-year since the racist microassault, cancelled a scheduled monthly meeting with the author and has not rescheduled since. He has taken on part of the responsibility of the extra ETDR (electronic theses, dissertations, and reports) assignments himself—albeit without training and letting various sundry mistakes by. He often requests help to support the tickets, even though he takes full credit for the tickets. The essentials of the situation have not yet been addressed, some three years after the extra work was assigned. He has maintained an idée fixe on trying to pass back the ETDR portfolio even though the agreement had been to have me transition back to my instructional designer responsibilities, without the extra night and weekend work including the support for graduate students. The promises are many, but actual objective and measurable progress has been short. Seven months after the initial racist gesture, after various efforts at creating a workable professional situation, the author requested a transfer to another part of ITS, where there may be perhaps less hostility, more basic respect for persons, more equal treatment of all employees, and more professional supervision in the real. This request was made when the supervisor escalated an email exchange up to the high leader.

At the initial meeting with the high leader, it became clear that there was nowhere in the structure that he could see a reasonable transfer. He also declined to move the author to a different physical work office even though he acknowledged there was plenty of physical space—because he said that the report structure was the larger issue, and he wanted that resolved first. He would try to solve that one first, which seemed reasonable; however, this was now eight months past the initial offense. At the time of publication, this workplace issue is being worked out. Per the high leader's advice, the author reached out to an executive at the Human Capital Services office, and she went through yet another retelling of the workplace challenges. All prior files and emails and notes are legitimately considered official documents, but it is not clear if those were accessed or read. The author is requesting a re-assignment out of an office with a hostile and racist supervisor to a healthier work condition, perhaps using a different part of her skillset (research). Working within the system matters given that an individual may have a limited and subjective perspective; however, the system is designed to prevail over the individual, unless the individual wants to make a legal fight of it. And even then, systems tend to prevail, and systems tend to exert their own interests.

Months after the racist expression by the supervisor, the overwork has been basically addressed, with both the author and the supervisor taking on pieces of the labor. The author provides trainings about the ETDRs, and the supervisor takes all service tickets. Meanwhile, the IT bureaucracy is trying to make a solution within the bureaucracy, in an environment of steep budget cuts and student enrollment pressures. In the micro context, there seems to be a battle between personal spite vs. shared interests, and it is not yet clear which will prevail, in terms of the supervisor's approaches. For years, he has never yet defined his priorities for staff. His ambition for them to do everything means that he prioritizes nothing. He is perhaps waiting for top leadership to set guidance, per his comments.

There are clearly limits to organizational responses to racist harassments. While there are bureaucratic structures to supposedly address such issues, a certain threshold has to be reached before action can be taken. Until then, the offices seem like they provide window dressing. Perhaps addressing limits to leadership and supervision, malice, ineptitude, or other challenges is harder than it looks.

The damage of expressed biases in the workplace in higher education is all the more corrosive since this is a place for supporting the development of people in their character and abilities; it is the place for collaborations and innovations; it is the place to improve societal functioning. Education is at the heart of the grand living experiment of a multi-ethnic liberal democracy. Optimally, administrative interventions with the target employees would make it very expensive for those in leadership (or any position) to act on their own internal biases in the workplace and in life.

As for allyship, these were expressed in different ways. One neighbor bought some delicious cookies and wrote a nice card. A colleague, who is Chinese-Canadian, continued a campaign of buying tea and maple syrup and other goodies for the supervisor, as a way to get on his good side. He avoided going into the office because he did not want to experience the tensions, even though his presence would have benefitted by infusing a larger sense of normalcy. A colleague reached out to a contact and wrangled a head-hunting offer for a job that would double the author's pay for the company. Another colleague said to ask for a transfer of work to another part of IT.

Ideally, such personnel issues are handled at the local level. Ideally, they should be handled privately. All parties to the issue need to be addressed fairly. Complaints are not without risks. There are min-max ranges of possibilities, and a fair solution is not guaranteed. Such efforts also require inordinate patience since bureaucracies runs slowly in most cases. Still, there has to be hope that a rational solution that protects all sides is possible. On paper, there is not quite a zero-discrimination policy, but something like a sliding scale, a loose negotiation, a suggested policing without solid action until a threshold is reached. Employees are assumed to have the good sense to keep their personal biases out of the workplace and their work. To use a colloquialism, there are "ifs, ands, or buts about it." On the other hand, the mere suggestion of racism triggers a response of varying quality.

Lessons Learned About Dealing with Work-place Exclusions, Denials, Racist Tropes, and Racialized Harassment

In making the decision to file a formal complaint against a supervisor, it may help to set up a back-of-the-napkin backwards design. What are the goals, and what will it take to achieve them? Does the individual need to have the racism acknowledged, apologized for, and totally stopped? Does the individual need a non-hostile workplace? Does the individual need eyes on a situation, so that sabotage and resource denial and other hostilities stop? Does the individual need the unfair multiple-FTE workload to stop? Does the individual need racist tropes to stop? Some aspects are practical as a reasoned workplace request. Some—such as changing a person's heart and mind—may be much less possible, and that is beyond the purview of such a complaint. It helps to reason through what is legally required of higher-level supervisors to do and be reasoned about what is in the realm of the impossible. It is not that people cannot change, but individual change is hard, and people do not arrive at their state-of-being overnight. Changes, too, will require time and effort. The formal filing of a complaint should not be about vengeance or cancelling another person's career. The institution will have to decide fitness to serve, even as change means pulling against the inertial draw of the *status quo*. Those lines of authority are fairly hard-set, at least in the author's narrow context.

Earlier, the author observed the importance of striving to address such issues directly with the perpetrator. If the context does not allow, perhaps one's own unit or their unit may be reached out to. If that fails, then, perhaps, the next step is to reach out to the institution, and so on, in-line along the designed trajectory. In general, the issues would be handled at the lowest possible levels, and each escalatory "raise" has to be considered with care. An escalatory ladder is proposed in Figure 7. Social relationships can be fragile, so escalations have to be considered with care. Balanced against this consideration is the gravitational pull of the organization, with escape velocity needed to push beyond each layer. Some people may be offended that they are brought into the troubles or the fracas. The complainant needs a full knowledge of the law, their own rights and the rights of others, and how to work within bureaucracies. The complainant benefits by following rules, rules of the institution, rules of etiquette. Even as an issue may be escalated into ever larger units, the focus should be on problem-solving to arrive at a state that is fair for all involved. All individuals should feel (and be) safe and respected in the process. Ideally, no one would be unfairly penalized as individuals reach for the power of checks and balances. After all, for all the stacking of power and the concentrated centers of power, even though power usually dominates, perhaps the outcome would not be a foregone conclusion (naïve?). There are reverberations and chain reactions as one escalates.

The problem with handling an issue at the most local level, though, is that the individual often self-justifies their own actions. They have a vested interest in pretending to be an upstanding person in public while the private self is hidden. Then, if their supervisor is covering for them, or has an inaccurate sense of the situation, or applies their own personality forcefield, the dynamics of their relationship (a twist on *folie à deux*) may result in negative workplace dynamics. An escalatory ladder expands the scope of oversight, ideally. It assumes that organizations alone may not be able to be self-policing. It makes the situation less isolated and less isolating. A larger community to work the issue enables a normalizing of civility vs. incivility. The ecosystem itself becomes larger. Keeping such offenses secret compounds the negatives and further enables continuing abuses.

In the less formal spaces, some might argue that it is fair to share information with others for mutual safety and for accountability. Others might say that such talk is uncalled for. The question is how to balance the abuse of power on the one side with the available levers. The judicious sharing of accurate information with trusted others makes sense to me. This does not enable holding others fully accountable, but there should be reasonable information sharing, so people who work with the "toxic" individual can be careful. Such quiet sharing along trust networks will eventually flow out to the larger social spaces and may dissuade those who might want to emulate or feel that they can bring their racism out of the woodwork into the workplace. Abusive workplace practices should never be condoned.

Such workplace issues have the potential of litigation overhanging the dynamics, with all stakeholders at some level of risk. This is where following the law—to the letter, to the spirit—makes sense. It helps not to go off-track where possible. Everything said and done is knowable, and all it takes is a good investigator for it all to be known. Only the very naïve assume that there are secrets in a workplace that may be kept if a process is formalized or if it turns into a legal issue. Going up through the organization means that one has attained an answer from not the individual hierarchy for one's position but from the organization. One sees something of organizational values and culture. Perhaps one sees a circling of the wagons. If the answer there does not address the fundamental issues, the next steps may require going beyond.

This is not about escalation of emotional intensity. Most if not all problems are better solved in logical and cool-headed and principled and legal ways. Most if not all problems are best solved in a context of mutual respect, not anger, not hatred, and never violence in any form.

Figure 7. Escalatory Reporting: From Person/Group to World

Escalatory Reporting: From Person/Group to World

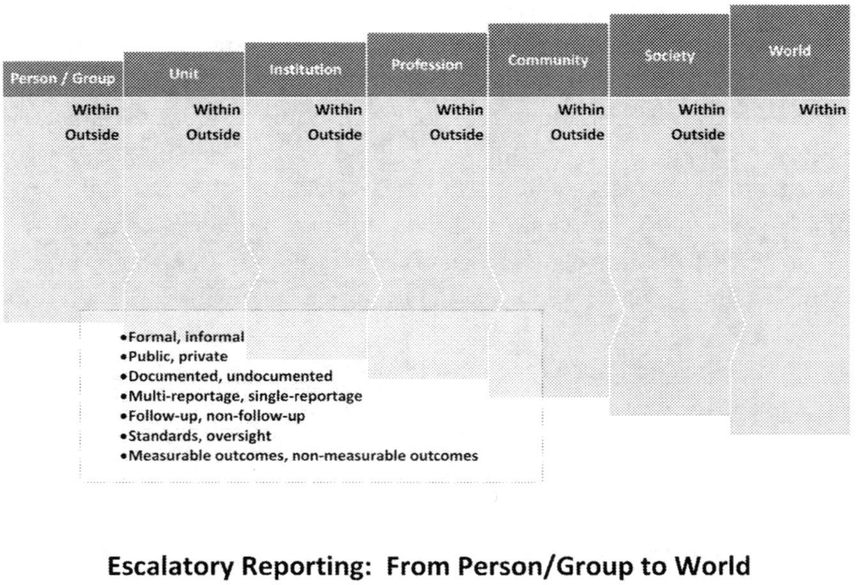

Navigating Inequitable (Mis)Treatment and Racist Harassment in Higher Education During COVID-19

Some core ideas are that there is little benefit in sweeping such offenses under the proverbial rug as that generally does not achieve anything constructive, extenuating circumstances notwithstanding (perhaps). After all, it is important not to normalize workplace aggressions. It makes no sense to enable people who are abusive to remain in a position where they can abuse and harm others (and the institution). A veil of silence makes all who stay silent complicit in the discrimination and abuse. The instinctive excuses-making for the perpetrator compounds the social problems from biased beliefs and actions. Social taboos are created out of mass social discomforts and mass shames and mass cowardice and Machiavellian power plays. People are deserving of their own well-being and dignity; they do not need to internalize their de-valuation by others, especially if it is by a biased supervisor. They should have workplaces where they can grow professionally and exercise their talents and skills. It is important to document completely and accurately, in order to create an accurate and timely record. Facts out. While people may hide parts and pieces, generally behavioral patterns are observable. It is important to notify colleagues and allies, so they have some level of forewarning (while being careful of the gossip circuit). It is important to work up the bureaucracy in order to attain professional relief and protection. It helps to assume blowback from above and laterally and below in a hierarchical context, based on people's points-of-view (people "judge" from where they stand and what they stand to gain). Many people resist the idea that "respectable" folk can be petty, misguided, biased, discriminatory, dishonest, belittling, gossiping, and vengeful behind shiny public masks.

One of my maxims that applies here is the following: Go after truth like your life depended on it because it does. One does not level a charge without grounds and ways to prove as much of it as possible. [While professional investigators can be highly astute and professional, they are only people. Not everything that happens in the world leaves a discernible trail.] Certainly, every assertion made in every document and meeting becomes part of the public record. That record has implications for the present and for the future. For organizational reviews, they may inform on themes and patterns. And each piece had better stand up to scrutiny. In the work, it helps to continue to be respectful unless there are accusations of insubordination. Throughout it is important to work professionally but not put in the prior extra uncompensated work hours during the pandemic, at the risk of the supervisor misunderstanding the employee's professional role and how much can be done within actual work hours. It is important to help the perpetrator experience the felt cost of such unprofessionalism and hate. It helps to use such moments as learning opportunities, for all involved, so all can improve in their treatment and care of others. For the sake of the institution and the students, talk about the negatives in the workplace should be kept to a minimum. It is true that personal and petty gossip does not improve a situation (but this is not that). It is also true that people may get details wrong with second-hand and third-hand information. Expressions of sympathy are fleeting and account for elusive and temporal comfort only.

Another lesson is that it never pays really to work overtime in an uncompensated way. Supervisors assume that the work is free and effortless. Students who are served are not motivated to learn what they need to advance their own learning. The individual walks out with a dead loss overall except for a bit of service and a lot of learning. Even though I had brought up the issue of the overwork from the beginning, it was not addressed until three years in, and the solution left a lot of unhappy folks. Had supervision been professional (and the supervisor actually tried to find an actual and working solution) and had the university decided to fund a necessary service, this difficult outcome would not have come to pass. Volunteerism is important for civil society, but it should not play such a critical role and leave multiple FTE positions unfilled. Even though there are times of need—during a pandemic, in a time of crisis—the cost of bridging gaps in available services can leave a long hangover particularly if there is not reasonable support from supervisors. [Leadership is always in flux, so the leader who is in place one day may well not be there the next.] Similarly, a staffer should not take on the role of making up for unfilled positions, which is an administrative responsibility. Administrators are the ones with the authorities and the budgets. In a time of disarray, it may be tempting to step up and provide extra services to advance the objectives of the unit; however, in the long run, this approach does not get rewarded and can be punished.

In terms of strategy, it is fine to hope for the best, but prepare for the worst. When others provoke (with misinformation, with passive-aggressive actions), it is important not to overreact. Keep reactions muted and comparable to the other side's actions. It helps not to leak details about one's planning or actions, but let the actions speak. Never threaten. Do not rush any escalation. If the other side escalates, that is their prerogative. If one has gone up to the highest administrators early on, then one cannot up that ante when the need arises, and one may be seen as alarmist. At some point, one may have to go outside the local institution (such as if one is let go or given a notice of non-renewal). There are critical events and touchpoints at which certain formal actions have to follow. Focus on overall patterns of behavior to show themes, not one-offs alone, when understanding others' behaviors.

Finally, it could be that people have been so stressed out from the pandemic and two years of inordinate fears and temporal lockdowns and budget constraints that they experience compassion fatigue, a lack of empathy, a lack of trust, and perhaps even a lack of energy to offer others respect. This is not excuses-making, but this is harsh reality in unprecedented history.

DISCUSSION

For those who traffic in hate as a matter-of-course, as a way of daily living, as a casual abusiveness of others, as common rants, intense dislike is not an anomaly. For those, it is common practice, their social right, based on their sense of self-supremacy, their rampaging anger, perhaps their worldview. Empirical research suggests that high in-group identification and concomitant out-group rejection leads to higher senses of *schadenfreude* (pleasure at another's misfortune) and *gluckschmerz* (displeasure at another's good fortune) (Hoogland et al., 2015). Perhaps this is one explanatory thread. Still, personal attacks based on race have not at all been what I have directly experienced in daily life except in childhood growing up in the American Midwest and during the pandemic (2020 – present). There is much work to be done in human societies to ensure equal treatment of peoples. Perhaps there can be a closer reality between public appearances and private hearts, in terms of basic decency and respectability. Perhaps people's mythmaking of themselves and "their folk" can more closely approximate reality. Perhaps love for one's "tribe" can include a "big tent" sense of a tribe with inclusivity at the forefront.

In the "Pyramid of Hate," at the base are "biased attitudes." These include the following: "stereotyping, insensitive remarks, fear of differences, non-inclusive language, microaggressions, justifying biases by seeking out like-minded people, accepting negative or misinformation / screening out positive information." The next layer up includes "acts of bias," which include "bullying, ridicule, name-calling, slurs/ epithets, social avoidance, de-humanization, (and) biased/belittling jokes." The next layer up involves "discrimination": "economic discrimination, political discrimination, educational discrimination, employment discrimination, housing discrimination & segregation, (and) criminal justice disparities." The next layer includes "bias motivated violence" including "murder, rape, assault, arson, terrorism, vandalism, desecration, (and) threats." The top layer involves genocide, including "deliberately and systematically annihilated an entire people" ("Pyramid of Hate," 2018). The pyramid shows the possible escalatory

Navigating Inequitable (Mis)Treatment and Racist Harassment in Higher Education During COVID-19

risks from biased attitudes and hates. Perhaps a "whole of society" approach is necessary to address such challenges in human societies. Addressing and confronting expressions of hate and bias in the workplace are important steps towards building a better society. The issue goes beyond wanting mutual respect, rationality, trust, care, and professional relationships in the workplace. Ignoring the issue or taking a conciliatory approach would only further enable such workplace abuses.

Certainly, the university as a predominantly white institution (PWI). Its leadership is aware that there are social tensions and strife, and they have worked hard to get out ahead of these challenges in prior issues (some of which have made it into public reportage). There seems to be awareness of the need for continuous striving to ensure a Wildcat family atmosphere for all students, staff, faculty, and administrators. There are diverse student clubs and student activities. There are university-wide events to promote social harmonies and understandings. There are bureaucratic structures to partially address discriminatory actions, but these organizational entities are there not only to address the issues but to protect the institution against lawsuits and negative publicity. Employees who are the targets of racial animus do not have their own advocates per se and have to be their own or hire their own (legal representation).

Then, as I have discovered, there is a rules-based order even in a context when it feels chaotic. (Where there is not direct trust in a work situation, going to rules to guide all actions makes a lot of sense. That is something that all employees can focus on. And where people break rules, that is something that can be the focus of remediation.) There are paths for learning and redemption.

Still, the base rate of successful complaints of racially disparate treatment is low, perhaps kept artificially so, based on OIE statistics. The process of complaining can be arduous, with some need for documentation and validation. The official guidance for filing such a complaint is slim, and most of it is from one's own training: do not over-react; do not return in kind; do not threaten; do not go in with a predetermined sense of what the only solution should be. Let the process work, even as it is constrained by legal considerations and by power relationships. In a complex environment, it is hard to know where the antagonisms are coming from: Are there messages from the top that skew the "authorizing environment" to various biases and biased practices? Has the heated political moment led some to practice personal politics in the workplace? Has a particular person lost moorings? Gone rogue? Harnessed hate as a supervisory tool? What is objective, and what is subjective? What are the open secrets, and what are the less obvious ones? Is the academic system evolving too slowly, with everyone aware of legal liabilities and not wanting to move ahead of political and legal cover? Will various conflicts result in individuals washing out or being pushed out, whether fair or not?

Then, for the self, I know that I would not put my well-being into anyone else's hands—at core. I do not let others speak for me because they speak through their own filter and self-deal in virtually all cases. They explain through their own point-of-view. I work hard to give people grace, to assume their best intentions. I avoid high reactance sorts of interpretations, even as I see patterns forming. I do not seek grievance; I do not try to find a pain and escalate it. I am not interested in fomenting bitterness in myself, even as I believe in *realpolitik*. I know people play dirty, and they engage in sabotage and other ugliness even as they aspire to some pretend-nice public face. I've also observed that behaviors that break trust—that maybe did not require much thought, that was an expression of unwarranted work rage—did not occur in a social vacuum, and then return to *ceteris paribus* or all things being equal. There was no snapback to *status quo*. Trust does not magically reconstitute. There is no un-ringing a bell, no unspeaking a slur, no unmaking an ugly face, and no undoing a public expression of a private thought. Certainly, one does not offer one's throat to any person who is obviously malicious and discriminatory. One does not put one's sense of personal value in the hands of another person either.

That said, if one chooses to continue the work relationship, then it has to go on in good faith, with one's own responsibilities, civilities, and ethics. (If the issues cannot be addressed in a healthy way, people should move on.) Of course, only in the playful magic circle of "live improv" is saying "yes" to everything the rule (and then wittily working out how that "yes" should manifest); in all other cases, good sense and judgment should prevail. If a declination is in order, then one should say it, explain the rationale, and work the issue from a sensible space.

This work has enabled a deeper dive into the phenomenon of microaggressions and macroaggressions. I have learned that there are microaggressions even within families against multiracial members, leaving mixed-race family members isolated by other family members, left out of favoritism, deemed inauthentic as a family member, and denied their multiracial identity (Nadal et al., 2013, pp. 195-197), with some feeling like they had not fully explored their own rich heritage given circumstances. The sheer pervasiveness of microaggressive offenses, documented in the research literature, was a second shock after the initial first from the supervisor's squinting eyelid pulls and angry tirades.

On a more local level, should employees take on extra work to "take one for the team"? Certainly. What failed here was not the direct decision or employee actions of support but the failure of leadership—who were notified of the failure of a team being stood up to handle the multiple FTE of work for ETDRs—from the beginning and still took no action. Two years in, it was no longer possible to take on the extra work into the nights and weekends to enable the continuance of the overwork. Additional projects were coming online, and these had to take priority.

FUTURE RESEARCH DIRECTIONS

The problem of discrimination (on any dimension or intersectionality) and its concomitant violence and incivilities have been with humanity for the ages, instantiated in various ways. To resist the negative pull will require continuing efforts, and there are many lapses along the way. In many cases, while the public-facing language has been updated for correctness, the actual follow-through actions may not have followed.

A review of a workplace can surface various issues. For me, the following all occurred, fairly recently:

- A colleague proposes that the local multicultural center should pursue particular grant funds. This colleague works in IT. He has no supervisory experience. He has no direct grant experiences. Yet, he thinks he should go to the multicultural center and supervise them.
- A supervisor in IT automatically uses the "they" pronoun for all non-whites, as a matter of course. He is purposefully and ostentatiously misgendering or multi-gendering as a matter of course, regardless of whatever individuals identify themselves as. He is "othering" them. He is using the practice of optional self-identification in a gendered way as antagonistic social commentary. This is one way some deal with threat.
- A high-level administrator in research expresses her dislike of how "Asian" researchers stack deep reviews of the literature as if they were all a large similar bloc of individuals, with shared approaches to work.
- Another admin described how she was concerned that so many graduate students did not have American-sounding last names. She said she felt that Americans were falling behind in STEM fields.

Navigating Inequitable (Mis)Treatment and Racist Harassment in Higher Education During COVID-19

There are other microaggressions in the workspace, which may not be all that different from other workspaces.

There are open research questions in this space.

- How can institutions of higher education be more welcoming of differences in all their forms instead of just tolerating and patching over hostilities?
- How can institutions of higher education make supports more salient to the targets of discriminations and hatreds?
- How can institutions of higher education take a more central role in creating more socially friction-free societies, even in politically fraught spaces and times?

Certainly, there is room to improve, for all of us. A study of racial minority adolescents found that microaggressions led to depressive and somatic symptoms in these youth. The researcher writes:

Latino adolescents reported more frequent microaggressions that dismiss their realities of discrimination and microaggressions characterized by treatment as a second-class citizen than Asian Americans, but similar levels of microaggressions that highlight differences or foreignness. There were no ethnic differences in the extent to which adolescents were bothered by microaggressions. Moreover, even supposedly innocuous forms of discrimination are associated with elevated levels of anxiety, anger, and stress, which may increase feelings of depression and sickness. (Huynh, 2012, p. 831)

There is no innocuous discrimination. Microaggressions, "similar to overt discrimination, can evoke powerful emotional reactions and may affect mental health" (Huynh, 2012, p. 831). A challenging idea that racially biased people may have includes the "perpetual foreigners" status of those of Asian descent (Huynh, 2012, p. 835). Asians work in spaces where their race and ethnicity are fore fronted, but their contributions to the workplace may seem invisible, in one study (Kim, Block, & Nguyen, 2019, p. 75). In their experiences, they may experience "over-validation" as a "new form of subtle microaggression." Overvalidation occurs "when the perpetrator treats Asians in a seemingly positive way based on stereotypes about Asians (e.g., assigning predominantly quantitative tasks to Asians because they are perceived to be good at math)" (Kim, Block, & Nguyen, 2019, p. 75).

For African American children, historically, educational institutions have labeled their behavior "as dysfunctional or representative of mental disorder" (Curry, 2010, p. 405). For them, too, "…recent scholarship illuminates the connection between oppression, social injustice, racial trauma, and racial microaggressions as the core of stress, depression, and anxiety in African American youth" (Curry, 2010, p. 405). There has long been a "discipline gap" seen between how African American students are suspended and expelled at higher rates than their peers based on teacher misperceptions of their so-called "defiance," responses which the researcher suggests may be a response to classroom microaggressions (Baker, 2019, p. 103).

Institutional academic violence, such as racial and gendered microaggressions in higher education, has been found to lead to various harms, including post-traumatic stress disorder (PTSD) as an outcome (Cueva, 2014, p. 143). One study found that "major experiences of racial discrimination and racial microaggressions" do explain ethnoracial differences in self-reported psychotic experiences (Anglin & Liu, 2021, p. 1). The researchers write:

Results from parallel mediation linear regression models adjusted for immigrant status, age, gender, and family poverty…indicated ethnoracial differences in PE were explained independently by both forms of racism. Specifically, Black young people reported higher mean levels of PE, and distressing PE than both White and Latina/o people and the difference in PE between Black and White and Black and Latino/a young people was significantly explained by both greater exposure to racial microaggressions and major racial discriminatory experiences among Black people. (Anglin & Liu, 2021, p. 1)

Four symptom domains of psychotic experiences include "cognitive disorganization, unusual thinking, perceptual abnormalities, and paranoia/suspiciousness" (Anglin & Liu, 2021, p. 7). There are harmful cumulative effects of microaggressions (O'Dowd, 2018, p. 1219). Sometimes, relationships may be irreparable after a microaggression (Bryant, Godsay, & Nnawulezi, 2021, p. 2). There are physical harms as well to the target of such hostilities, including from self-harm and violence. There are findings of "an association between the frequency of mistreatment and feelings of burnout and suicidal thoughts" (Fisher, Chatterjee, Shapiro, Katz, & Yialamas, 2021, p. 3592). The destructiveness of negative leadership on subordinates and others can be far-reaching, which is why people need to be vigilant against such actions and speak up and act against it. Work contexts do not improve if such issues go unaddressed. A fatalistic approach can end up being self-fulfilling, if employees go passive or just ignore the microattacks and microassaults.

CONCLUSION

The roiling presidential and party politics during the pandemic may have enabled a different "authorizing environment" for racist expression and discrimination, as indicated by crime data and journalistic reportage. Both blatant discrimination and less direct forms came to the fore. Such expressions may be seen as something harmless, perhaps just something transient and part of the culture wars and current politics. Whatever the rationalizations, there is nothing "micro" in the personal hurt from a micro-assault or even a micro-aggression. In the author's case, it is not fair to be stigmatized. There is no point at which one arrives at which point they are safe from hate or harassment. While accomplishments and public reputation and social connections may be somewhat protective, they are not fully so. The colloquial observation goes, "Haters gonna hate." The issue resides in the individual who bears the hatred and perhaps elements of the society in which the individual was nurtured. In the supervisor's case, some 16 years of constructive interactions should not be discarded for one racist slur and some poor supervisory decision-making in terms of stacking multiple FTE of work on one individual and ignoring respectful requests for relief for two-and-a-half to three-years. [Even so, as noted earlier, the author has requested a transfer for a more constructive and productive workplace.] The pain from this sorry workplace episode comes from the broken trust and the lack of character of the supervisor, more than any direct harm from the racist slurring.

The math is telling. Originally, the unit had three instructional designers, and two left, leaving all the central instructional design work in IT to one individual. Then, some 2.5 FTE of non-instructional design work was added to that individual, with no relief. That is impossible math by supervisors (middle and upper management) who should know much better. The question is how to move forward in a way that gives all individuals fair treatment and the institution the optimal value from the employees. Beyond the local, the workplace is not fully integrated nor fully fair. Higher education is not inured from dis-

Navigating Inequitable (Mis)Treatment and Racist Harassment in Higher Education During COVID-19

criminatory depictions and practices, even though the work is high-minded and important, even though the peoples are oftentimes diverse (with scholars and students from all over the world), even though research teams represent many talents, and even though institutions of higher education are so critical to the nation, industry, and peoples. No organization is necessarily safe from staff who go racist and harassing. The self-decentered autoethnography approach is used to not focus on my own wounding through mismanagement, mistreatment, bullying, malice, and hate from a direct supervisor (with major deficits in "leadership" ability) but something bigger and optimally redemptive.

In an ideal world, people would co-exist and co-thrive, with each attaining their highest possibilities based in part on their own self-identities (in full dimensionalities). In a multi-ethnic multi-cultural liberal democracy, ideally, people would treat each other with all due respect and in-depth understanding of each other's full selves, not stereotypes, not caricatures, not racist tropes. In a perfect world, people would police themselves, feel shame at their mistreatment of others, strive for actual strong character and values, and avoid excuses making. Workplaces would be fully inclusive, so that each person can contribute fully to the shared endeavors of the profession. Education would be inclusive, with all members engaged in the "bittersweet labor" of inclusion (Ashton, 1990, p. 33). Ideally, people would be vigilant for oneself and for others. There is no room for going on blithely as if societies were functioning in fair ways. Given that "bias is a human condition," people need to speak up to confront hatred wherever they see it; they need to educate themselves about this phenomenon; they need to push leaders for change ("Ten Ways to Fight Hate," 2017, p. 1). Inclusion in education is supposed to help "develop inclusive societies" (Chimedza, 2008, p. 132). Diversity is "a complex social construct that impacts all members of society" (DeLuca, 2013, p. 325). Individual differences would be "viewed as values and not as problems" (Gallego & Rodriguez, 2007, p. 108, as cited in Marín-Díaz, 2020, p. 868). Biases should not be reinforced. Uncomfortable social histories should not be suppressed. The world is in motion, and it is not in the ideal state desired for human thriving. Perhaps each of us can move the world closer to a more harmonious, inclusive, all-voiced, and fair one. Perhaps we can move away from the politics of personal destruction. Perhaps we all can adapt to a different social reality in a time of social change and flux.

For the author herself, she has to work the workplace to a space of psychological safety. This means keeping authorities apprised of the supervisor's actions. This means engaging in self-care. This means not continuing in the overwork past the fall semester of 2022 and not taking on work that a trainer would do or that an ETDR consultant would do. This means not taking on multiple FTE even in the face of high pressure from the direct supervisor. This means finding workplace and other allies. This means finding narratives of strength and survival by others who have faced similar or dissimilar challenges and triumphed. Finally, there is a responsibility to not engage in overwork because this would encourage further harassment of subordinates into accepting multiple FTEs of work in unpaid labor and continuing abusiveness in the workplace and perhaps beyond. Racist harassment should never be a supervisory tool. This opens up a Pandora's Box of mistrust and interpersonal harms; further, there are secondary damages to professional reputations. Those struggling with racist ideologies and hatreds may reach out for professional help to deal with their own personal problems before anything has to go public, before harms occur to others.

Then the Other Shoe Drops

Finally on August 4, 2022, the high leader (at the vice president level) let the author know that she had a year left of service and that her position would not be renewed. Officially she had been "NNRed" or served with a "notice of nonrenewal". This was described as a budgeting measure given the high inflation and the budget callbacks at the university level. This meant that after some 17 years of work and high professional assessments, the author's career at the institution of higher education would come to an unceremonious end. This meant a professional disenfranchisement after years of investment and overwork. She would not have any of the post-retirement benefits that she would have had had she worked through retirement. The administrator said several times that this action was "not for cause," meaning that it was not anything that the employee had done per se, nothing of her fault. At the same time, the high leader raged that the author had talked about the problems in ITS with another high-level official. He told her not to take on new work (impossible while in the job). He wanted to reserve the author's time for non-instructional design work. There seemed to be an assumption that the author's time was not already assigned with grant projects, faculty requests, ongoing long-term development projects, scheduled trainings, and other work. (The direct supervisor had not scheduled any meetings with the author for the year since he had pulled the "chink eyes" and may not have followed the tickets made for the work.) Perhaps the high leader went with what he thought to be true instead of facts on the ground. He also suggested that the author was experiencing "shock" at the NNR move, but the truth was that the lack of actual solutions in the prior year since the racist gesture indicated that an actual solution would not be coming. The lack of a solution, the lack of political acumen, in a brittle bureaucracy, would mean a less finessed solution, ultimately multiple professional defenestrations.

The author was not the only casualty at the time. Several other staff in the unit were served at the same time. This was done in a context of budgetary duress and dropping student enrollments, particularly from abroad (with high geopolitical tensions between the U.S. and a major source of students from overseas, the P.R.C.). This was also in the context of hundreds of thousands of Americans out of the labor force due to COVID-19's aftermath and long-COVID. This was in the context of a tight job market. One recent job opening in ITS that was opened nationally got only one applicant, from internally. Her supervisor was lowered in the hierarchy, although his position title remained, and he lost all but several staff. And there were whispered plans for several of them to move on to other units. The email announcing the changes did not portray the changes as any demotion. Rather, this was just another re-organization in the sequence. Still, he no longer had a clear path forward to any advancement in the organization when once he had applied for high-level positions. Or so it would seem. [This turn of events reminds one of the colloquial saying, "play stupid games; win stupid prizes." This means that anyone who misfocuses on issues not directly related to actualizing the work will ultimately lose because they will not contribute to the professional organization. The "stupid prizes" here include demotion and likely fairly quick separation from the university.]

The decision arrived after years of no funding for any professional development. This came after years of no allocation of time for learning (which fell to the individual employee to schedule on nights and weekends). This came after a year of supervisory threats and bullying. Such a decision by the lead administrator was within his purview. Perhaps ITS was getting out of the role of "Teaching and Learning" (perhaps, not likely). Perhaps this was a face-saving maneuver. Perhaps the employee's existence as the target of racist harassment from a supervisor was an inconvenient truth, a bad look, a sign of administrative ineptitude, a direct threat to the high leader. Perhaps her removal could save face for the administration. (While some colleagues thought that the move was a surprise one, the author had seen signs of the impending decision, such as the high leader asking the author to perhaps consider working in a part of the university outside of ITS in a meeting some months prior to the career-ending NNR. The act felt like it was informed by anger but planned.) Perhaps this was "costly signaling" (to both the organization and the target employee) against others who might speak out. Perhaps there were a number of reasons, mostly unspoken. The author met with a diversity officer out of the president's office just several weeks after the delivery of the NNR. It should be noted that there is no guaranteed continuing employment for employees under contract. What is problematic is the appearance of potential retaliation from the employee's complaint of the racist harassment by a direct supervisor.

The main takeaways were that the university did a lot of circling the wagons and had a lot of work to do to support diversity. This case was one of many apparently. By the time of this meeting, everything was documented in writing and in emails and others. All the lower offices for whom this might be an issue had been reached out to. The contact likely went into university records. The officer would be reaching out to the principals. And little would happen. One lawyer suggested: Perhaps an outreach could be made to the Equal Employment Opportunity Commission (EEOC)? Or the state's human rights commission? [In this state, apparently, the formal complaint may only be filed at the state level or the federal level. Each one has a different statute of limitations. This means that complaints may be more effective early on in the sequence before further harms have been caused, before the actions become career-ending for the recipient of the hate. The absolute seriousness of the experience may not have been fully observed by the author until the notice of non-renewal.] One lawyer explicitly said he did not want to sue his alma mater. One law firm worked in the same small college town as the main campus and had a conflict of interest. Another law firm in a nearby larger town did not respond (so that is de facto declination).

Then, various individuals involved in the issue started to leave the university or change roles within the university. The problem of possible re-identification started to dissipate and disappear. The researcher changed specific names of identifying roles. I realized that people covering for each other's racism and harassment, in a professional context, served no one even though it may have looked like they had a win early on, that they "got away" with something initially. It is in no one's true interests to let racial animosities reign in a workplace.

Ultimately, such structures do not hold if the majority can uphold democratic values and human rights and social respect of themselves and each other. Social justice may be slow in coming, but if the polity stays the course, together, great things may be achieved. To make a greater union, people all need to step up. This is not to say that people have to be strident or necessarily highly public in the approach. What does need to happen is that there has to be accurate documentation and the outreaches to the proper bureaucratic structures designed to address unfair employment practices, such as overloading of work, racist harassment, and retaliation by nonrenewal of work contract.

Difficult Lessons Learned All Around

Supervisors evaluate their staff, but they are also evaluated back by the "underlings," and the judgment of serving staff is communicated through the grapevine. If the feedback is too negative, the supervisor loses all ability to influence others to do their work effectively and peaceably. If a supervisor loses the ability to accurately read people and set up the right incentives to move them, they cannot collect power and deploy it intelligently for the goals of the institution. Leaders need not only raw power but nuanced application and even intelligent restraint now and again. Another reshuffling occurred within ITS. Ideally, this would solve the issue for the organization. Perhaps ITS has decided not to keep any instructional designers; perhaps they have decided that this belongs to the more academic side of the house. [Any conceptualization or story can be written to follow up decisions. Decisions do harden over time, and these become more difficult to undo once hardened and acted on. Any fallout from a lack of local expertise follows later.] As all organizations, the university would go into defensive mode by following the laws as closely as possible, and they would put a pretty spin on the news. Many suggest that other blasts of layoffs and NNRs will follow given a difficult budgetary and difficult political environment. The leadership mantle is a heavy one.

So, what are some additional macro lessons?

- In the larger environment, the hatreds and social turmoil can reach into an institution and cause havoc in workplaces and leave damage in its wake. On the news airwaves is talk of "white status decline" and resulting fears. Perhaps that may play a role in this local condition.
- Fair workplaces are not about individuals at one level or in one sense; they are about systems— political, legal, economic, social, and others.
- The world is large. It is big enough. There will be opportunities elsewhere. With a historically tight labor market post-pandemic and a need for teachers, perhaps there will be other paths and opportunities forward.

And meso-scale lessons?

- If a festering human resources issue is left unaddressed or weakly addressed, its harm spreads, and often the odds of a workable solution diminish over time. What is left is often more severe reactions for all involved: non-renewals, demotions, and reputational harms.
  - ○ Ideally, workplace issues would be handled locally and reasonably and fairly. This is an elusive ideal.
  - ○ Certainly, every organization has a number of ongoing and present personnel issues at any time.
- Workplaces with toxic work environments have higher reports of employee sick days, lowered workplace productivity, lessened creativity, and poor public relations. Many workplaces also are the target of litigation, with many going to legal remedies for addressing inept or angry administration or staff. (Bagalini, July 14, 2020)
- It is to the strength of the organization that it is somewhat decentralized, with multiple and disparate centers of power. The voices in a university are manifold. Power is not spoken in one voice alone.
- Trust does not return in and of itself to workplace relationships damaged by mistreatment.
- If a skill does not exist in leadership and the leader does not work to acquire those skills, the person will not be able to manage the challenges. The poverty of leadership can be made worse by a tight job market external to the organization…and then the difficult processes of hiring for administrative positions internally. The limited options make it difficult for top leadership to maneuver.
- Taking on trainings against racial bias only apparently go so far. Deep-held hatreds are much harder to address. Pretend is not an effective management strategy. It is important to add actual value. It is not helpful to imagine that others do not see individual shortcomings, in everyone.
- Toxic leadership reverberates, and it creates an authorizing environment in which further harms are enabled. Racism and sexism and other biases are not effective supervisory tools. Ultimately, it is not possible to cause harm to others with impunity. There are harms to the work, to individuals, and also to the self.

- Using the SARS-CoV-2 / COVID-19 pandemic as an excuse for poor leadership is an inappropriate approach. Everyone is under pressure. Poor leadership and myopic decision-making in a disarrayed world only makes the risks worse.
- All people are both winners and losers based on their own personalities. This aligns with that saying that people's strengths are also their weaknesses.
- The university's legal counsel does not enable a magic shield around any staffer if they function outside the scope of their work or if they act illegally.
- The sorry episode is written into the author's personal history. But it also a history in the ITS unit and the university, at least for a time, and at least until other staff move on.
- Organizations do have to close ranks and protect themselves against legal risks and reputational harms. This means removing staff who are identified threats.

More broadly, at global scale, global crises such as the pandemic have ripple effects. They have secondary and tertiary effects. Only some of the effects are able to be anticipated. While most may want to return to a normalcy, recovery, it is turning out, is harder than it looks. Intergroup relations are under strain. The personal attacks based on particular demographic factors is like throwing down a gauntlet, and coming back from that is also challenging perhaps because people may feel justified in their expressions of hate.

What about lessons for the individual, at the micro level?

- The clock is always running, and new stopwatches start with every action of administration and the self. It is important to be aware of the time and to not miss deadlines. Notification of various offices start their clocks. Whether they make or fail is partially in their court.
- If going up the escalatory ladder, individuals should consider all potential consequences, at every level: micro- (self), meso- (organization), and macro- (beyond). The challenge is to avoid public scandal where possible because that causes damage beyond the principals to the context.
- The ideal of escalating is to get a fair hearing, actual neutrality of judgment, and fair outcomes. Sometimes, organizations give the impression of having positions merely to identify "threats" and to neutralize them for the organization. Period.
- Assessing risks involves reading organizations and various likelihood of various actions and reactions.
  - When the fallout hits, there are "allies" who say all the right things but actually have very constrained power to help (without incurring potential backlash on themselves).
  - Allies often suggest that one "go tell" someone else. Each telling is an encumbrance. They may have a "duty to report" about acts of racism and sexism and harassment in the workplace. What most fail to note is that the reports all land at the desk of perhaps one or a few individuals. These individuals make the decisions about whether an issue reaches a threshold or not. And that is a high bar to get past, enabling all sorts of "microaggressions" and "microassaults" to pass with little apparent formal address.
  - Not all those who are told are allies. There is interest from some to elicit information for gossip or other uses.
    - Many who are told do not have helpful advice. Some will offer to bring up the issue to Faculty Senate after one's position has expired (and the information is therefore some-

what more legally and applicably inert). Others will take on actions that are unconstructive. And so on.

- The reality is that the decision has to be made by the individual about how far and how hard they want to push. It is hard to know others' tolerances for pressures.

- Every email is a record. I have always treated emails like a database of records. I know deleting them does not make them disappear from the servers of the email service provider. Everything exists as a record open for discovery, and how people have behaved over time becomes clear.

- When notified of the non-renewal of a work position, one is left with the question of how to best use that remaining contracted time. How should it be used to serve the university with pride but also position the individual for next work phases? How can skills be kept sharp? What about the principles of not taking on extra work beyond normal work hours? Should a person "quiet quit" (in the social lingo of the moment) and not overwork and not take on unpaid labor (and compound further personal harms in the workplace)? [I am a workaholic, and I am not part of any anti-work movement.] Should side projects be continued? What about existing work? [The author was a co-principal investigator on a federal grant, which was awarded a month and a half after the NNR. The awarding was a very positive event, given the 85% or so rejection rate of grant applications for this particular endeavor. She will serve her part in that grant in her remaining time at the university. All other commitments continue, but she has had to filter projects as people propose them so as to stay within the contracted full-time work hours and not excess ones.]

- If one chooses the proverbial "hill to die on," should it be about ensuring safer workplaces for those who come next? What workplace progress was actually made? Were all individuals involved directly and indirectly put on notice about the need for care for each other and the avoidance of microaggressions and microassaults and personal attacks? Is the system more responsive, more protective, more sensitive, and more fair? Or not? Have the principals involved actually learned anything about how people should be treated? Or did the reckoning have outsized impacts on the complainer (the whistleblower, if you will) and not on others in the system? [To be fair: The university has always publicly advocated for fair treatment of all. It has filled administrative positions to this end. It has offered trainings for supervisors on how to fairly treat subordinates and others. For all the efforts, there are still gaps between the ideals and the law…and actual practice…in some cases.]

- If nothing else, this experience has affirmed the importance of maintaining one's values and character and ethics. There may be an illusion of gain in compromising the self, but there is not in the long run. And self-destruction is never the right path. Self-congruity is important for personal well-being, which is one's top responsibility (and no one else's).

- The author will not have the neat work-until-retirement she had wanted after a half-dozen more years of work. She had left tenure to pursue the instructional design work after earning a doctorate, and for all the challenges, that was the right decision then. In the intervening years, many of the ambitions she had have been achieved. There is no way to simulate "what-if" given the complexities of the world. Certainly, other people's challenges and struggles are more dire. The world is not a necessarily fair place, but it is big enough to offer plenty of opportunities. So the author will chance the world again. She will pursue reinvention.

- In terms of the individuals one can trust, those are few. The advice will be mixed. However, as in many issues, researching enough does lead to convergence on some understandings.

Navigating Inequitable (Mis)Treatment and Racist Harassment in Higher Education During COVID-19

- Those who are hateful self-reveal because their perceptions are biased. Their hatred results in sabotaging their own team and other irrational behaviors. Hatred is a parasite on the human mind which leads to harm against others and ultimately also the self. There is no path for redemption in hating. One ultimately shorts oneself. One becomes a lesser potential being.

And yet, there may be other interpretations. Would the individual have taken the actions he did if he could have better handled his stressors? Would the situation turn out more constructively for all involved if he hadn't worked himself into an ugly froth and then gone to hatred? Would the team have benefitted from more informed and enlightened supervisory interventions, to hire staff to do the necessary work instead of overloading staff unthinkingly? Would the sequence of events improve if the various offices had enforced a 0-tolerance policy for racist and sexist actions and made everyone toe-the-line? Would actual expressions of higher character enable better outcomes? Perhaps.

At the individual level, the workplace proposition was the following: Work 3 – 4 FTE of work (ETDR trainings, training provision as extras in addition to the instructional design base work) for the same low wages and no play increases for many years at a time (and with diminishing value given inflation), into the predictable work future, or be forced out essentially. The new roles come with liabilities and hard deadlines. The weekly training schedule (during each semester) would lock in every week, and time with family on the rare vacation would be further constrained. This infeasible proposition was made worse with a supervisor who considered racist harassment and racist tropes appropriate management behavior. In a time of a tight job market, the institution has offered various job descriptions with no takers. At some point, this becomes untenable even if one has a heart for students and faculty and administrators. Sometimes, working in dysfunction is too high a price to pay just to work. The supervisor also never held any workplace meetings with the author after the "chink eyes" debacle, so there was a year without any meetings. The only few conversations were shouted from across the room. The author does not have a clear sense at all why this was his approach, except that maybe he wanted to move her out and was trying to show his hostility without getting into trouble. Was he having difficulty engaging with certain people after the severe social isolation of the pandemic? Was he so committed to his sense of personal animus? Perhaps human frailty may be sufficient to explain that approach.

In separating from the university, the unspoken bargain is to go quietly, even if it leaves in place toxic practices informed by socially ugly inequities. All social systems have their own demands for membership. All systems have spoken and unspoken rules for participation. And perhaps all individuals bend to the forcefield in the organization, with only a sporadic few who can or will withstand the pressures to make any decisions against the local *status quo*. In general, people do not go negative publicly because it adds friction to the situation; it makes the work arguably harder.

This experience has been harrowing and difficult. Perhaps it will take more time to fully process. There is a sense of inevitability about the choices made by all at each phase. Ideally, the individual who caused so much professional harm to others will not be in a position to cause such harm again, but that is not necessarily going to happen. It is hard to know if lessons were learned. And there are limits to knowledge of various professional transgressions due to legal liabilities. Speaking up against bullies and harassers is not without cost but important if people are to be protected and systems to run inclusively for all (not just those who are of preferred race or gender or mix of intersectionality). All workplaces have challenges. One can only try to work the levers of the workplace to make it a space to thrive and advance the work. Ultimately, there is nothing perfect and nothing effortless.

Getting accurate information on a legal record and putting a university on notice for its practices will be satisfying. It will not be about a settlement although that will be important for social justice and fair treatment in the workplace as well. If administrators want to test the boundaries of their power vs. the law, this seems like a fine case for that. Will it be a good look for a supervisor to pile on multiple FTE of work on one person, then threaten and racially harass that person when she asks for relief from the work? What will the various stakeholders think? The oversight board? The faculty? The students? The donors? The general public? That is not a good look. What will come out in discovery?

Separately, were there constructive off-ramps along the way that could have resolved the issues, had the principals been willing? If the leadership had not been so frugal and forced multiple FTE of work on the author, would this issue have arisen? If the larger environment were not one full of political strife, would the issue have emerged this way? If a person had managed his own racial animosities, … But the consideration of these is an intellectual exercise and not a practical one. Even with moving on, autobiographically, there will be challenges and hard work ahead. Still, it is important that the "last word" should not be this ending. Perhaps elsewhere, there can be a context more welcoming and inclusive where professional talents may be expressed.

Finally, there is one more critical lesson here. In every workplace, there are complex interests and social dynamics at play. No one person will see or know everything. Without a full investigation, perhaps, the full facts will not be known. Readers will note that the author worked through systems as accurately as possible. She never went rogue. She never took matters into her own hands. She never made threats. She notified the colleagues who needed to know for their collective protection but did not go to social media or other venues to broadcast the issues. It helps to think through all acts to see what the intentions are…and what the potential impacts may be, intended or unintended.

Note: This is not legal advisement.

REFERENCES

Accilien, C. (2018). Teaching in the Time of "Trumpism": Reflections on Citizenship and Hospitality. *Women, Gender, and Families of Color*, 6(1), 69–72. doi:10.5406/womgenfamcol.6.1.0069

Acedo, C. (2008). Inclusive education: Pushing the boundaries. *Prospects*, 38(1), 5–13. doi:10.100711125-008-9064-z

Acedo, C. (2011). Preparing teachers for inclusive education. *Prospects*, 41(3), 301–302. doi:10.100711125-011-9198-2

Ackerman-Barger, K., Bakerjian, D., & Latimore, D. (2015). How health professions educators can mitigate underrepresented students' experiences of marginalization: Stereotype threat, internalized bias, and microaggressions. *Journal of Best Practices in Health Professions Diversity*, 8(2), 1060–1070.

Alabi, J. (2015). Racial microaggressions in academic libraries: Results of a survey of minority and non-minority librarians. *Journal of Academic Librarianship*, 41(1), 47–53. doi:10.1016/j.acalib.2014.10.008

Alfrey, L., & Twine, F. W. (2017). Gender-fluid geek girls: Negotiating inequality regimes in the tech industry. *Gender & Society*, 31(1), 28–50. doi:10.1177/0891243216680590

Andriana, E., & Evans, D. (2020). Listening to the voices of students on inclusive education: Responses from principals and teachers in Indonesia. *International Journal of Educational Research*, *103*(101644), 1–9. doi:10.1016/j.ijer.2020.101644

Anglin, D. M., & Lui, F. (2021). Racial microaggressions and major discriminatory events explain ethnoracial differences in psychotic experiences. *Schizophrenia Research*, 1–9. doi:10.1016/j.schres.2021.10.014 PMID:34750038

Ashton, L. J., Gordon, S. E., & Reeves, R. A. (2018). Key ingredients—target groups, methods and messages, and evaluation—of local-level, public interventions to counter stigma and discrimination: A lived experience informed selective narrative literature review. *Community Mental Health Journal*, *54*(3), 312–333. doi:10.100710597-017-0189-5 PMID:29185150

Ashton, N. (1990). Inclusive education: Curriculum and pedagogy. *Transformations: The Journal of Inclusive Scholarship and Pedagogy*, *1*(1), 30–35.

Bagalini, A. (2020, July 14). *Systemic racism: 5 ways racism is bad for business—and what we can do about it.* World Economic Forum. Retrieved Sept. 7, 2022, from https://www.weforum.org/agenda/2020/07/racism-bad-for-business-equality-diversity/

Baker, T. L. (2019). Reframing the connections between deficit thinking, microaggressions, and teacher perceptions of defiance. *The Journal of Negro Education*, *88*(2), 103–113. doi:10.7709/jnegroeducation.88.2.0103

Barr, A., Lane, T., & Nosenzo, D. (2018). On the social inappropriateness of discrimination. *Journal of Public Economics*, *164*, 153–164. doi:10.1016/j.jpubeco.2018.06.004

Bond, R., & Castagnera, E. (2006). Peer supports and inclusive education: An underutilized resource. *Theory into Practice*, *45*(3), 224–229. doi:10.120715430421tip4503_4

Borchia, R., Carbonaro, A., Casadei, G., Forlizzi, L., Lodi, M., & Martini, S. (2018, October). Problem Solving Olympics: an inclusive education model for learning Informatics. In *International Conference on Informatics in Schools: Situation, Evolution, and Perspectives* (pp. 319-335). Springer. 10.1007/978-3-030-02750-6_25

Bosse, I. K. (2015, August). Criteria for designing blended learning materials for inclusive education: perspectives of teachers and producers. In *International Conference on Universal Access in Human-Computer Interaction* (pp. 3-14). Springer. 10.1007/978-3-319-20684-4_1

Bostwick, W., & Hequembourg, A. (2014). 'Just a little hint': Bisexual-specific microaggressions and their connection to epistemic injustices. *Culture, Health & Sexuality*, *16*(5), 488–503. doi:10.1080/13691058.2014.889754 PMID:24666221

Boutot, E. A., & Bryant, D. P. (2005). Social integration of students with autism in inclusive settings. *Education and Training in Developmental Disabilities*, 14–23.

Boysen, G. A. (2012). Teacher and student perceptions of microaggressions in college classrooms. *College Teaching*, *60*(3), 122–129. doi:10.1080/87567555.2012.654831

Bryant, L. S., Godsay, S., & Nnawulezi, N. (2021). Envisioning human service organizations free of microaggressions. *New Ideas in Psychology*, *63*(100893), 1–8. doi:10.1016/j.newideapsych.2021.100893

Burt, B. A., McKen, A., Burkhart, J., Hormell, J., & Knight, A. (2019). Black men in engineering graduate education: Experiencing racial microaggressions within the advisor–advisee relationship. *The Journal of Negro Education*, *88*(4), 493–508. doi:10.7709/jnegroeducation.88.4.0493

Chimedza, R. (2008). Disability and inclusive education in Zimbabwe. In *Policy, experience and change: Cross-cultural reflections on inclusive education* (pp. 123–132). Springer. doi:10.1007/978-1-4020-5119-7_9

Coalson, G. A., Crawford, A., Treleaven, S. B., Byrd, C. T., Davis, L., Dang, L., ... Turk, A. (2022). Microaggression and the adult stuttering experience. *Journal of Communication Disorders*, *95*(106180), 1–18. PMID:34954647

Crenshaw, K. (1991). Mapping the margins: Identity politics, intersectionality, and violence against women. *Stanford Law Review*, *43*(6), 1241–1299. doi:10.2307/1229039

Crenshaw, K. (2011). Twenty years of critical race theory: Looking back to move forward. *Connecticut Law Review*, *43*(5), 1253–1354.

Cueva, B. M. (2014). Institutional academic violence: Racial and gendered microaggressions in higher education. *Chicana. Latino Studies*, 142–168.

Curry, J. R. (2010). Addressing the spiritual needs of African American students: Implications for school counselors. *The Journal of Negro Education*, 405–415.

Dale, S. K., Pan, Y., Gardner, N., Saunders, S., Wright, I. A., Nelson, C. M., Liu, J., Phillips, A., Ironson, G. H., Rodriguez, A. E., Alcaide, M. L., Safren, S. A., & Feaster, D. J. (2021). Daily microaggressions and related distress among black women living with HIV during the onset of the COVID-19 pandemic and Black Lives Matter Protests. *AIDS and Behavior*, *25*(12), 4000–4007. doi:10.100710461-021-03321-w PMID:34046762

Daniela, L., & Lytras, M. D. (2019). Educational robotics for inclusive education. *Technology. Knowledge and Learning*, *24*(2), 219–225. doi:10.100710758-018-9397-5

DeLuca, C. (2013). Toward an Interdisciplinary Framework for Educational Inclusivity. *Canadian Journal of Education*, *36*(1), 305–347.

Druery, D. M., Young, J. L., & Elbert, C. (2018). Macroaggressions and civil discourse. *Women, Gender, and Families of Color*, *6*(1), 73–78. doi:10.5406/womgenfamcol.6.1.0073

Dunn, C. E., Hood, K. B., & Owens, B. D. (2019). Loving myself through thick and thin: Appearance contingent self-worth, gendered racial microaggressions and African American women's body appreciation. *Body Image*, *30*, 121–126. doi:10.1016/j.bodyim.2019.06.003 PMID:31238277

Elder, C. H. (2021). Microaggression or misunderstanding? Implicatures, inferences and accountability. *Journal of Pragmatics*, *179*, 37–43. doi:10.1016/j.pragma.2021.04.020

Feyerer, E. (2002, July). Computer and inclusive education. In *International Conference on Computers for Handicapped Persons* (pp. 64-67). Springer.

Fisher, H. N., Chatterjee, P., Shapiro, J., Katz, J. T., & Yialamas, M. A. (2021). "Let's Talk About What Just Happened": A Single-Site Survey Study of a Microaggression Response Workshop for Internal Medicine Residents. *Journal of General Internal Medicine, 36*(11), 3592–3594. doi:10.100711606-020-06576-6 PMID:33479935

Flanders, C. E., LeBreton, M., & Robinson, M. (2019). Bisexual women's experience of microaggressions and microaffirmations: A community-based, mixed-methods scale development project. *Archives of Sexual Behavior, 48*(1), 143–158. doi:10.100710508-017-1135-x PMID:29476410

Galkienė, A., & Monkevičienė, O. (2021). The Model of UDL Implementation enabling the development of inclusive education in different educational contexts: Conclusions. *Improving Inclusive Education through Universal Design for Learning, 5*, 313-323.

Gomez, M. L., Khurshid, A., Freitag, M. B., & Lachuk, A. J. (2011). Microaggressions in graduate students' lives: How they are encountered and their consequences. *Teaching and Teacher Education, 27*(8), 1189–1199. doi:10.1016/j.tate.2011.06.003

Hardimon, M. (2019). should we narrow the scope of "racism" to accommodate white sensitivities? *Critical Philosophy of Race, 7*(2), 223–246. doi:10.5325/critphilrace.7.2.0223

Haynes-Baratz, M. C., Metinyurt, T., Li, Y. L., Gonzales, J., & Bond, M. A. (2021). Bystander training for faculty: A promising approach to tackling microaggressions in the academy. *New Ideas in Psychology, 63*(100882), 1–8. doi:10.1016/j.newideapsych.2021.100882

Hersh, M., Leporini, B., & Buzzi, M. (2020, September). ICT to support inclusive education. In *International Conference on Computers Helping People with Special Needs* (pp. 123-128). Springer. 10.1007/978-3-030-58805-2_15

Hess, J. (2016). "How does that apply to me?" The gross injustice of having to translate. *Bulletin of the Council for Research in Music Education,* (207-208), 81–100. doi:10.5406/bulcouresmusedu.207-208.0081

Holmes, G. G. (2018). Counterpoints: Vol. 149-181. Moving forward: Biasing,(de) biasing, and strategies for change. Academic Press.

Hoogland, C. E., Schurtz, D., Cooper, C. M., Combs, D. J., Brown, E. G., & Smith, R. H. (2015). The joy of pain and the pain of joy: In-group identification predicts schadenfreude and gluckschmerz following rival groups' fortunes. *Motivation and Emotion, 39*(2), 260–281. doi:10.100711031-014-9447-9

Hornung, H., Pereira, R., & Baranauskas, M. C. C. (2016, August). Meaning construction and evolution: A case study of the design-in-use of a system for inclusive education teachers. In *International Conference on Informatics and Semiotics in Organisations* (pp. 181-190). Springer. 10.1007/978-3-319-42102-5_20

Houshmand, S., & Spanierman, L. B. (2021). Mitigating racial microaggressions on campus: Documenting targets' responses. *New Ideas in Psychology, 63*(100894), 1–11. doi:10.1016/j.newideapsych.2021.100894

Huber, L. P., Gonzalez, T., Robles, G., & Solórzano, D. G. (2021). Racial microaffirmations as a response to racial microaggressions: Exploring risk and protective factors. *New Ideas in Psychology*, *63*(100880), 1–9.

Huynh, V. W. (2012). Ethnic microaggressions and the depressive and somatic symptoms of Latino and Asian American adolescents. *Journal of Youth and Adolescence*, *41*(7), 831–846. doi:10.100710964-012-9756-9 PMID:22453294

Jašková, L. U. (2006). Informatics teachers and their competences in inclusive education. *Computers Helping People with Special Needs: 10th International Conference, ICCHP 2006, Linz, Austria, July 11-13, 2006 Proceedings*, *10*, 552–559.

Jones, V. A., & Reddick, R. J. (2017). The heterogeneity of resistance: How Black students utilize engagement and activism to challenge PWI inequalities. *The Journal of Negro Education*, *86*(3), 204–219. doi:10.7709/jnegroeducation.86.3.0204

Kapusta, S. J. (2016). Misgendering and its moral contestability. *Hypatia*, *31*(3), 502–519. doi:10.1111/hypa.12259

Keels, M., Durkee, M., & Hope, E. (2017). The psychological and academic costs of school-based racial and ethnic microaggressions. *American Educational Research Journal*, *54*(6), 1316–1344. doi:10.3102/0002831217722120

Kim, J. Y., Block, C. J., & Yu, H. (2021). Debunking the 'model minority' myth: How positive attitudes toward Asian Americans influence perceptions of racial microaggressions. *Journal of Vocational Behavior*, *131*(103648), 1–14. doi:10.1016/j.jvb.2021.103648

Kim, J. Y. J., Block, C. J., & Nguyen, D. (2019). What's visible is my race, what's invisible is my contribution: Understanding the effects of race and color-blind racial attitudes on the perceived impact of microaggressions toward Asians in the workplace. *Journal of Vocational Behavior*, *113*, 75–87. doi:10.1016/j.jvb.2018.08.011

Lancheros-Cuesta, D., Rangel, J. E., Rubiano, J. L., & Cifuentes, Y. A. (2020). Adaptive robotic platform as an inclusive education aid for children with autism spectrum disorder. In *EUROCAST 2019* (pp. 297–304). Springer. doi:10.1007/978-3-030-45096-0_37

Leath, S., & Chavous, T. (2018). Black women's experiences of campus racial climate and stigma at predominantly white institutions: Insights from a comparative and within-group approach for STEM and non-STEM majors. *The Journal of Negro Education*, *87*(2), 125–139. doi:10.7709/jnegroeducation.87.2.0125

Levchak, C. C. (2018). Microaggressions, Macroaggressions, and Modern Racism. In *Microaggressions and Modern Racism* (pp. 13–69). Palgrave Macmillan.

Lewis, J. A., Mendenhall, R., Harwood, S. A., & Browne Huntt, M. (2013). Coping with gendered racial microaggressions among Black women college students. *Journal of African American Studies*, *17*(1), 51–73. doi:10.100712111-012-9219-0

Lozano, C. S., Wüthrich, S., Büchi, J. S., & Sharma, U. (2022). The concerns about inclusive education scale: Dimensionality, factor structure, and development of a short-form version (CIES-SF). *International Journal of Educational Research*, *111*(101913), 1–12.

Maeda, K., Hashimoto, H., & Sato, K. (2021). Creating a positive perception toward inclusive education with future-oriented thinking. *BMC Research Notes*, *14*(1), 1–4. doi:10.118613104-021-05882-4 PMID:34952632

Marín-Díaz, V. (2020). ICT-based inclusive education. Encyclopedia of Education and Information Technologies, 868 – 1018.

Marino, M. T., & Hayes, M. T. (2012). Promoting inclusive education, civic scientific literacy, and global citizenship with videogames. *Cultural Studies of Science Education*, *7*(4), 945–954. doi:10.100711422-012-9429-8

Mateu, J., Lasala, M. J., & Alamán, X. (2013). Tangible interfaces and virtual worlds: A new environment for inclusive education. In *Ubiquitous Computing and Ambient Intelligence. Context-Awareness and Context-Driven Interaction* (pp. 119–126). Springer. doi:10.1007/978-3-319-03176-7_16

Mateu, J., Lasala Bello, M. J., & Alamán, X. (2014, December). Virtual Touch Book: A Mixed-Reality Book for Inclusive Education. In *International Conference on Ubiquitous Computing and Ambient Intelligence* (pp. 124-127). Springer. 10.1007/978-3-319-13102-3_22

McCabe, J. (2009). Racial and gender microaggressions on a predominantly-White campus: Experiences of Black, Latina/o and White undergraduates. *Race, Gender, & Class*, 133–151.

McConlogue, T. (2020). Developing Inclusive Curriculum and Assessment Practices. *Assessment and Feedback in Higher Education: A Guide for Teachers*, 137-150.

McCray, E. D., & McHatton, P. A. (2011). Less afraid to have them in my classroom": Understanding pre-service general educators' perceptions about inclusion. *Teacher Education Quarterly*, *38*(4), 135–155.

McGee, E. O. (2016). Devalued Black and Latino racial identities: A by-product of STEM college culture? *American Educational Research Journal*, *53*(6), 1626–1662. doi:10.3102/0002831216676572

McLeskey, J., & Waldron, N. L. (2015). Effective leadership makes schools truly inclusive. *Phi Delta Kappan*, *96*(5), 68–73. doi:10.1177/0031721715569474

McSorley, K. (2020). Sexism and cisgenderism in music therapy spaces: An exploration of gender microaggressions experienced by music therapists. *The Arts in Psychotherapy*, *71*(101707), 1–9. doi:10.1016/j.aip.2020.101707

Metinyurt, T., Haynes-Baratz, M. C., & Bond, M. A. (2021). A systematic review of interventions to address workplace bias: What we know, what we don't, and lessons learned. *New Ideas in Psychology*, *63*(100879), 1–9. doi:10.1016/j.newideapsych.2021.100879

Microaggression. (2022, Feb. 10). In *Wikipedia*. Retrieved Feb. 22, 2022, from https://en.wikipedia.org/wiki/Microaggression

Minikel-Lacocque, J. (2013). Racism, college, and the power of words: Racial microaggressions reconsidered. *American Educational Research Journal*, *50*(3), 432–465.

Morales, E. M. (2014). Intersectional impact: Black students and race, gender and class microaggressions in higher education. *Race, Gender, & Class*, 48–66.

Nadal, K. L., King, R., Sissoko, D. G., Floyd, N., & Hines, D. (2021). The legacies of systemic and internalized oppression: Experiences of microaggressions, imposter phenomenon, and stereotype threat on historically marginalized groups. *New Ideas in Psychology*, *63*(100895), 1–9.

Nadal, K. L., Sriken, J., Davidoff, K. C., Wong, Y., & McLean, K. (2013). Microaggressions within families: Experiences of multiracial people. *Family Relations*, *62*(1), 190–201.

O'Dowd, O. (2018). Microaggressions: A Kantian account. *Ethical Theory and Moral Practice*, *21*(5), 1219–1232.

Obiakor, F. E., Harris, M., Mutua, K., Rotatori, A., & Algozzine, B. (2012). Making inclusion work in general education classrooms. *Education & Treatment of Children*, *35*(3), 477–490.

Oh, H. (2021). The Association Between Discriminatory Experiences and Self-Reported Health Status among Asian Americans and Its Subethnic Group Variations. *Journal of Racial and Ethnic Health Disparities*, 1–8.

Opertti, R., Brady, J., & Duncombe, L. (2009). Moving forward: Inclusive education as the core of education for all. *Prospects*, *39*(3), 205–214.

Payton, F. C., Yarger, L. K., & Pinter, A. T. (2018). (Text) mining microaggressions literature: Implications impacting black computing faculty. *The Journal of Negro Education*, *87*(3), 217–229.

Pearce, S. (2019). 'It was the small things': Using the concept of racial microaggressions as a tool for talking to new teachers about racism. *Teaching and Teacher Education*, *79*, 83–92.

Pierce, C. M., Carew, J. V., Pierce-Gonzalez, D., & Wills, D. (1977). An experiment in racism: TV commercials. *Education and Urban Society*, *10*(1), 61–87.

Pittman, C. T. (2012). Racial microaggressions: The narratives of African American faculty at a predominantly White university. *The Journal of Negro Education*, *81*(1), 82–92.

Power, C., & Paige, R. (2009, July). Content personalization for inclusive education through model-driven engineering. In *International Conference on Universal Access in Human-Computer Interaction* (pp. 102-109). Springer.

Prempeh, C. (2022). Polishing the pearls of indigenous knowledge for inclusive social education in Ghana. *Social Sciences & Humanities Open*, *5*(1), 1 - 9.

Pyramid of Hate. (2018). *Anti-Defamation League*. Retrieved May 15, 2022, from https://www.adl.org/sites/default/files/documents/pyramid-of-hate.pdf

Rasmussen, B., & Salhani, D. (2010). A contemporary Kleinian contribution to understanding racism. *The Social Service Review*, *84*(3), 491–513.

Reynaga-Peña, C. G., Myers, C., Fernández-Cárdenas, J. M., Cortés-Capetillo, A. J., Glasserman-Morales, L. D., & Paulos, E. (2020, July). Makerspaces for inclusive education. In *International Conference on Human-Computer Interaction* (pp. 246-255). Springer.

Ricks, S. A. (2018). Normalized Chaos: Black Feminism, Womanism, and the (Re) definition of Trauma and Healing. *Meridians (Middletown, Conn.), 16*(2), 343–350.

Roche, S. (2016). Education for all: Exploring the principle and process of inclusive education. *International Review of Education, 62*(2), 131–137.

Rogers, C. (2007). Experiencing an 'inclusive' education: Parents and their children with 'special educational needs'. *British Journal of Sociology of Education, 28*(1), 55–68.

San Pedro, T. J. (2015). Silence as shields: Agency and resistances among Native American students in the urban Southwest. *Research in the Teaching of English*, 132–153.

Savva, M., & Nygaard, L. P. (2021). The 'Peripheral' Student in Academia: An Analysis. In *Becoming a Scholar: Cross-cultural Reflections on Identity and Agency in an Educational Doctorate* (pp. 154–172). UCL Press.

Schiemer, M. (2017). Inclusive Education and the UN Convention on the Rights of Persons with Disabilities (UNCRPD). In *Education for Children with Disabilities in Addis Ababa, Ethiopia* (pp. 175-186). Springer.

Shotton, H. J. (2017). "I Thought You'd Call Her White Feather": Native Women and Racial Microaggressions in Doctoral Education. *Journal of American Indian Education, 56*(1), 32–54.

Singal, N. (2006). An ecosystemic approach for understanding inclusive education: An Indian case study. *European Journal of Psychology of Education, 21*(3), 239–252.

Skinta, M., & Torres-Harding, S. (2022). Confronting microaggressions: Developing innovative strategies to challenge and prevent harm. *New Ideas in Psychology, 65*(100921), 1–5.

Smith, W. A., Hung, M., & Franklin, J. D. (2011). Racial battle fatigue and the miseducation of Black men: Racial microaggressions, societal problems, and environmental stress. *The Journal of Negro Education*, 63–82.

Solorzano, D., Ceja, M., & Yosso, T. (2000). Critical race theory, racial microaggressions, and campus racial climate: The experiences of African American college students. *The Journal of Negro Education*, 60–73.

Suárez-Orozco, C., Casanova, S., Martin, M., Katsiaficas, D., Cuellar, V., Smith, N. A., & Dias, S. I. (2015). Toxic rain in class: Classroom interpersonal microaggressions. *Educational Researcher, 44*(3), 151–160.

Sue, D. W., Capodilupo, C. M., Torino, G. C., Bucceri, J. M., Holder, A., Nadal, K. L., & Esquilin, M. (2007). Racial microaggressions in everyday life: Implications for clinical practice. *The American Psychologist, 62*(4), 271.

Ten Ways to Fight Hate. (2017). Southern Poverty Law Center.

Timmons, V. (2009). *Overcoming barriers to inclusivity: Preparing preservice teachers for diversity* (Vol. 334). Counterpoints.

Tkachyk, R. E. (2013). Questioning secondary inclusive education: Are inclusive classrooms always best for students? *Interchange, 44*(1), 15–24.

VanScoy, A., & Bright, K. (2017). Including the voices of librarians of color in reference and information services research. *Reference and User Services Quarterly, 57*(2), 104–114.

Von Robertson, R., & Chaney, C. (2017). "I know it [racism] still exists here:" African American males at a predominantly white institution. *Humboldt Journal of Social Relations, 39*, 260–282.

Wilkins-Yel, K. G., Hyman, J., & Zounlome, N. O. (2019). Linking intersectional invisibility and hypervisibility to experiences of microaggressions among graduate women of color in STEM. *Journal of Vocational Behavior, 113*, 51–61.

Williams, M. T. (2021). Microaggressions are a form of aggression. *Behavior Therapy, 52*(3), 709–719.

Yada, A., Leskinen, M., Savolainen, H., & Schwab, S. (2022). Meta-analysis of the relationship between teachers' self-efficacy and attitudes toward inclusive education. *Teaching and Teacher Education, 109*(103521), 1–15.

Ydo, Y. (2020). Inclusive education: Global priority, collective responsibility. *Prospects, 49*(3), 97–101.

Yeung, D., & Lim, N. (2021). Talking about race and diversity. In *Perspectives on Diversity, Equity, and Inclusion in the Department of the Air Force* (pp. 37–42). RAND Corporation.

KEY TERMS AND DEFINITIONS

Allyship: The act of coming alongside a persecuted individual or group and providing effectual support, social association with persecuted others.

Antiracist Pedagogy: The design of learning to combat pervasive racism in order to promote social justice in a democratic (or other) society.

Attributional Ambiguity: A lack of clarity if a microaggression was intentional or unintentional.

Bias: Discriminatory treatment for or against another in a way that seems unfair.

Cisgender: A context where personal sexual identity and birth sex/born-gender align.

Color Blindness: The inability to see color, often used as a metaphor for not seeing others' racial or ethnic or other aspects of social identity and so ideally treating everyone equally; in this concept, a person's racial classification does not affect their social opportunities.

Color Muteness: The inability to discuss race in a particular social context.

Critical Race Theory: An interdisciplinary theory identifying inherent racism institutionalized in societies with potential interventions to address such acculturated biases.

Discrimination: Biased treatment of others based on some dimensions of their identity (age, race, sex, class, religion, sexual identity, or other factors or combination of factors).

Diversity: Difference along one or a number of dimensions.

Ethnicity: Cultural traditions based on different histories, language, practices, beliefs, or ancestry.

Ethnoracial Differences: Ethnicity and racial variations between people groups.

Historical Guilt: Collective or individual senses of guilt over past historical occurrences that may have been perpetrated from those in one's social group.

Inclusion: Equal access to learning opportunities for all.

Inclusive Education: The fair treatment of diverse learners in all learning contexts.

Intersectionality: The interconnections between social identity categorizations such as race, gender, ethnicity, and class, sometimes leading to complex and overlapping discrimination or disadvantage or unfair treatment.

Marginalization: Treating others as peripheral and unimportant.

Microaffirmation: Acts of supporting others, through communications and other actions, such as by validating their opinions and achievements, engaging with them in friendly ways.

Microaggression: A subtle or indirect hostile act or statement against a person of a marginalized group; this social slight may be purposeful or unintentional.

Microassault: A blatant hostile act or statement against a person of a marginalized group that is apparently purposeful.

Neutrality: Impartiality, unbiased, fair.

Overvalidation: A microaggression in which positive stereotypes are applied to a minority group and used as a basis of judgment of individuals from that minority group.

Racism: Antagonism towards another because of their apparent or actual membership in a racial or ethnic group.

Racist Trope: A race-based stereotype or representation of someone, often with negative implications.

Reparations: The paying of money or other resources to right a past injustice or wrong.

Sexism: Discrimination based on a person's gender.

Social Identity: An individual's self-concept from various memberships in different social groups and informed in part by others' treatment of them.

Stereotype Threat: A situation in which an individual is made aware of a derogatory stereotype about themselves that may affect their performance (such as in an academic context).

Stigma: A sense of dishonor or shame based on an attribute, circumstance, behavior, or association.

White Fragility (White Sensitivity): Emotional defensiveness by a person who identifies as white when faced with issues of racial injustice and racial inequality.

White Supremacy: Attributing values to different people or people groups based on their race and concluding with a sense of the inherent superiority of whites to people of color.

APPENDIX

The author initially retracted this work from consideration for publication in an edited book after an initial positive review in mid-2022 because of the potential for this to be used in unintentional ways, the risks of blowback, the risks of triggering vicious cycles (one side takes an action, and the other side escalates, all to the detriment of the respective individuals and context), and the potential trackback to the offending supervisor and the supervisory chain (and concomitant claims of defamation, even though the facts are facts). Perhaps people can be fairly easily re-identified, I thought. There are risks to the incidental tarnishing of reputations. Said another way, there are limits to the benefits of being a "squeaky wheel" beyond a particular point. The world is a small one in a sense, and in a world of online sleuths, re-identifying personages is fairly simple. There is also the matter of protecting the university brand. After all, a majority of university folks are professional and considerate. They work through interpersonal challenges, should anything arise.

An anonymized version would not likely find a publisher, and byline anonymity or the absence of a byline alone would not be enough to de-identify persons to a sufficient level of relative collective and individual safety. [I did submit this work for consideration with one publisher, but they responded by saying that there had to be a clear discipline for this work and a clear way of this changing the field.] Also, anonymizing authorship might implicate innocents, which would be problematic in other ways. The limits of redaction of information would also be a problem. Added ambiguity may mean misunderstandings of who the individual is in the harassment. This work may be less "incendiary" over time and will optimally be published then, when it is less implicating of a known person or known persons. In a litigious environment such as in the U.S., withholding this work from publication is the wiser route. Also, citing an anonymized work would be problematic. Human resources information is also protected, so it should not be shared broadly. Over time, though, the work may be less incendiary and may be shared more broadly. If there is a middle way that might work, it has not yet become apparent. The issues have also not yet been resolved, even some nine months after the initial racist "chink eye" harassment and several years of overwork assignments. The supervisor had agreed to remove the author from the ticket servicing system for ETDR assignments in late March 2022 but secretly put her back in in the new ticketing system to launch in early June 2022. There are many ways to label the work more accurately without assigning it to "instructional design." There was a sense that the supervisor was trying to normalize the work and integrate it into instructional design work, even though this involved multiple FTEs of work outside of the instructional design job description. The same bureaucratic games continue apace, and schemes continue afoot.

Holding fire is not a forever sort of thing. Silence should not be the de facto stance. Not publishing eventually would be self-silencing and compounding of the initial offenses. It would be my colluding with my own disenfranchisement. Perhaps in time, this can be a story of redress and healing and justice. Perhaps this can be a story of hope instead of personal degradation. Perhaps the "managing up" will have some constructive outcome. I have every right to tell my story, contemporaneously, but my story impacts other people, too, so I have to practice due diligence. Perhaps, one day, I can own this story wholly and share it as such, when I cannot be accused of going political or social activist in the professional role. There will be a chance one day to share this fully. As I was mulling this on my drive home from working on a weekend, I was driving behind a sedan with a bumper sticker that read, "Silence is violence." Indeed, the silence will not be forever, only a time. Such transgressions cannot be deemed "unspeakable" even though they are socially ugly. Public face matters, but it should reflect the real. The most important point is to maintain self-respect and honesty and mental health and not let another person's ugly and hatreds define the self—whether one stays or one goes from the workplace. If a healthy state cannot be achieved, I think a person should move on even if that move is unfair to the individual.

Finally, bureaucracies are slow-moving. They are self-dealing. They deal with imperfect staff, and their job is to control the narrative and protect the functioning and face of the organization. They have an interest in keeping stories of "bad apples" quiet: "Nothing to see here." There is nothing heartfelt or personal or supportive about the process. The individual is a cog in the larger machine. This is not how a process should be, in the author's professional opinion. In the next annual contract, the author was offered merit pay along with a cost-of-living raise, rare events in any circumstance, much less coming out of a pandemic. The merit raise, extremely rare in the author's experience, may have been meant to serve multiple purposes.

Four years of working directly with the particular supervisor, he had apparently no formal job description for any of his staff. When the author requested a copy, he had none. He had to request a copy. The latest one was from 13 years ago even though the author had emails indicating that the job descriptions had been updated in 2016 (but these may never have been formalized). The author's tactic is to try to go back to the defined basics, so a supervisor is not rewarded with extra work through hectoring and harassment behaviors. Some healthy rules-based constraints may be beneficial. Perhaps there is something to be said about not attributing to malice what can be explain by ignorance or passivity or disconnection.

Finally, events overtook the decision and led to a decision to actually publish, to reach an academic audience (albeit a typically very small one), to shine bright lights on a reality lived by many who are targets of supervisory hostility based on racial or other types of discriminatory personal animus. Such attention is short-lived. The impacts of publishing can be very limited in terms of effects in the real world. All the actual incentives in a university (and other workplaces) for staff dealing with diversity issues is to minimize risks to the organization, not provide any real support to those harmed. Staff go through the processes because they are generally required to, even as this all feels like going through the motions only. By the time this would be published, there would be sufficient reshuffling and leadership changes and organizational forgetting, perhaps. Regardless, the story is important enough to tell, and there is sufficient documentation for a solid legal defense if needed. There is sufficient documentation for a solid legal offense against the supervisor and institution, if that route is pursued. No names are named, on purpose. Meanwhile, the university puts on a positive public face. Meanwhile, I know from colleagues and friends that biases are rampant in workplaces, and social justice is elusive.

Section 6
Building Back Better...and Better

Chapter 12
Online Education and Student Satisfaction:
Insight From Student Perceptions Towards Online Education Quality

Muteber Tuzcu
https://orcid.org/0000-0001-9528-9158
Yeditepe University, Turkey

ABSTRACT

The phenomenon of online education cannot be accepted as new, but the immediate change from an in-class environment to an online environment is new because of COVID-19 restrictions. The aim of the study is whether students are satisfied with online education during the COVID-19 period to determine the factors that affect students' satisfaction with online education during the period and to find service quality gaps and students' satisfaction based on the gap model. As higher education institutions try to cope with a competitive advantage and maintain service quality, feedback from students is valuable to increase the effectiveness of educational plans and implement future intentions. Students are aware that unusual circumstances bring both advantages and disadvantages. Not being present in the class environment is counted as both a positive and negative thing by students. Overall, students feel satisfied with online education during the lockdown period.

INTRODUCTION

In December 2019, China announced the very first Covid-19 cases. Then, the World Health Organization informed people Covid-19 is a global pandemic rather than an epidemic. Almost every person in every part of the world has been affected by the Covid-19 pandemic. The unique global experience which is the Covid-19 disaster has created remarkable events on social and individual levels so it can be counted as an existential experience (Blustein & Guarino, 2020). In order to slow down and prevent the Covid-19 virus from spreading, many countries started to apply strict rules such as regulations to maintain social

DOI: 10.4018/978-1-6684-5934-8.ch012

Copyright © 2023, IGI Global. Copying or distributing in print or electronic forms without written permission of IGI Global is prohibited.

distance and/or complete lockdown. There were unexpected and huge shifts from the outside to the home. Implementation to stop the viral outbreak involved working from home, closing many institutions such as schools, universities, malls, sports centers, and stores, and/or providing flexible working hours. Online education in Turkish universities was seen as an alternative to traditional learning to sustain education during restriction periods.

The online education system cannot be considered as a new phenomenon. Before the pandemic period, higher education institutions have been willing to develop online education programs because these programs fascinated more students at a lower cost compared to traditional education systems (Green, 2010). Students can reach their courses without being present physically on campuses so they can spend less time and money. Also, they can sustain their work schedule while trying to achieve education goals. However, immediately shifting from an in-class environment to an online environment is not a usual circumstance. Thus, online education during the pandemic period has brought new issues to be handled by all parties including professors, students, and universities. Shifting from school and university environments to homes leads to some problems for students such as technological issues, psychological issues, lack of focus while studying, and lack of interaction with peers or teachers (Kapasia et al.,2020). On the other side, some advantages educated at home are safe, the effectiveness of time and cost, and convenience (Maqableh & Alia, 2021 & Fatani, 2020). In the literature, some researchers find out that students' satisfaction is higher compared to face-to-face learning during the Covid-19 period (Chen et al., 2020). Others claim that students are not satisfied with online learning (Latip et al.,2020, & Cheon et al., 2020). Thus, there is no consensus in the literature.

The research questions of this study are listed below;

Q1: How did the online education system during the Covid-19 period affects students' satisfaction level?
Q2: What were the main gaps affecting student satisfaction with online education during the Covid-19 period?

The main purposes of the study are whether students are satisfied with online education during the Covid-19 period, and to determine the factors that affect students' satisfaction with online education during the period. Also, the research will try to solve problems students are facing in the online education period. Understanding these factors that affect student satisfaction in online education will be useful in order to continue online education programs in the future. Education providers such as universities and colleges would position themselves and differentiate from their competitors. These institutions also would see the result of this study and might correct their lacking point. Used platforms in universities would be aware of their service quality based on the students answers. The unique character of this study would contribute to service marketing and students satisfaction in education literature.

BACKGROUND

Online Education

Information and communication technologies allow for maintaining lectures in a distance environment among students and professors through online courses. (Harsasi & Sutawijaya, 2018). Online education means sustaining education activities in an online environment through web or computer networks

(Harasim, 2020). Online education also can be described as delivering knowledge or skills via electronic devices including smartphones, laptops, and tablets (Singh & Thurman; 2019). Online education can be offered in more than one way. The first one is pure online education or distance education in which every step-in education is delivered in an online environment. Students do not need to visit universities campuses. The second one is blended education which includes a mixed method of online and in-class education. This type of education can be named hybrid education. Individual education is the third option. The education type is offered through the Internet for only certain subjects' courses. The last one is Massive Open Online Courses (MOOCs) which deliver lectures to an unlimited number of students and offered open access lectures through the Internet (Xien et al., 2020).

Xien et al., (2020) have classified positive and negative aspects of online education. Flexibility, information accessibility, global reach, equity, innovation, and efficiency make online education favorable. Despite the bright sides of online learning, network instability and technological constraints, lack of sense of belonging and connectedness, distraction, and lack of engagement create problems for students when they have experienced online education. These authors claimed that online education will become the new normal in the future. Covid-19 has triggered the adaptation of shifting to online education to maintain the long-term survival of universities.

Students Satisfaction and Online Education Quality

Perceived service quality in higher education is not static and it depends on the context in nature (El Alfy & Abukari; 2020). The needs of students and circumstances have changed over time. For example, the need of students in a classroom environment cannot be similar to students who receive online courses during the Covid-19 period. Also, for example, the needs of medical students differ from students in the social sciences area. Mostly, students in medicine have theoretical courses alongside practical courses. However, social sciences courses can be maintained through online education. For this reason, perceived service quality can be changed.

As per Jung (2010), an e-learning quality model from a learners perspective has seven dimensions which are information and publicity, learner support, learning tasks, institutional credibility, institutional quality assurance, interaction, and staff support. The most influential dimensions are staff support, interaction, learner support, and institutional quality assurance, the least influential ones are information and publicity and learning tasks. The most powerful dimension in e-learning is staff support. On the other hand, the least valuable dimension in the study from Korean learners' perspective is information and publicity. The scholar explains the results of the study by learners' characteristics, e-learning design, and culture (Jung, 2010).

Harsasi and Sutawijaya (2018) focus on students' satisfaction with online education. Their model tries to find relationships between dimensions including course structure, online tutorial flexibility, online tutorial quality, technology quality, and students satisfaction. Students' satisfaction is determined by course structure, online tutorial flexibility, and technology quality. While tutorial quality is a dimension that does not influence students' satisfaction (Harsasi & Sutawijaya, 2018).

Chen et al. (2020) have a study in order to determine factors related to users' satisfaction with online education platforms. These scholars use to assemble aback propagation neural network model to predict online platform users' satisfaction. The variables indicated affecting satisfaction are platform ability, the quality of interaction, information quality, system quality, the quality of service, and personal factors. Platform availability, interaction quality, and service quality are the most significant factors in order to determine users' satisfaction among other variables. Also, the research showed that users' satisfaction has a great impact on users' willingness to continue using the platform (Chen et al., 2020)

The research was carried out in China by Chen et al. (2020) who investigate user experience with online education platforms named as Zoom Cloud, Tencent Meeting, MOOC, TIM, WeChat Work, and Chaoxing Learning. The positive and negative sides of these platforms are discussed in terms of platform system characteristics, background customer service support, platform video quality, platform technical quality, and platform teaching support system. Based on the discussion, these authors suggest four possible ways named as improving support service, improving the convenience of interactive communication, optimizing ease of use, and enriching platform resources to eliminate problems related to these platforms (Chen et al., 2020).

Shahzad et al. (2020) pointed out the differences between female students and male students in terms of usage of e-learning platforms in Malaysian Universities. Also, the study examines the impact of system quality, information quality, service quality, and system quality on users' satisfaction and e-learning system use effects on e-learning platforms' success. In this study, information quality and e-service quality are significant to determine female students' satisfaction. In the model, there is a positive relationship between system quality and user satisfaction. On the other side, male students' satisfaction is determined by information quality and system quality. There is also a positive relationship between information quality and users' satisfaction. Moreover, service quality influences students' satisfaction (Shahzad et al., 2020).

Basuony et al. (2020) aim to find out the factors influencing students' satisfaction with online education amidst the Covid-19 pandemic. Their sample consisted of undergraduate students in business schools in Cairo, Egypt. The study exhibits that Internet facilities, the platform used, class time, loss of interest, motivation, and self-motivation, and use of online exams as an assessment affect students' satisfaction in online education during the Covid-19 pandemic period (Basuony et al., 2020).

Another qualitative research to explore students' attitudes toward online learning during Covid-19 was done by Hussein et al. (2020). The sample of the research includes undergraduate studies at a University in Abu Dhabi, United Arab Emirates. These scholars list both positive sides and negative aspects of online learning during the extraordinary period separately. Positive aspects are effectiveness time usage and cost, safety, convenience, and increased participation. On the other hand, distraction and reduced focus, workload, technology, and Internet connectivity, and inadequate support from instructors and colleagues are counted as negative aspects of online learning. According to the study, the most advantageous aspect of online learning is time and cost-effectiveness, and the most problematic aspect is distraction and reduced focus (Hussein et al., 2020).

Another study which is about exploring factors related to e-learning satisfaction was done by Alqahtani et al. (2020). The objective of the study is to sustain and increase nursing students' satisfaction with online education. The scholars point out relationships among e-learning readiness with satisfaction with the teaching subscale, satisfaction with the assessment subscale, generic skills and learning experience subskills, and students' satisfaction. The results of the study show that e-learning readiness correlated with satisfaction with generic skills and learning experience. Nursing students also are satisfied with online learning practices. Moreover, e-learning readiness affects students' satisfaction levels (Alqahtani et al., 2020).

Fatani (2020) researched students' satisfaction with web video conferencing teaching quality amidst the pandemic period. The sample of the study was composed of undergraduate medical students in pediatrics. According to the result of the study, more than 80% of students were satisfied with web video conferencing because lectures were challenging, and instructors encouraged students' participation. Technical issues also are not associated with students' satisfaction. Moreover, teaching quality web-based teaching is about cognitive and social presence instead of technology in the study (Fatani, 2020).

Shim and Lee (2020) listed the sort of variables that cause both students' satisfaction and dissatisfaction during the Covid-19 lockdown period. Comfortable education environments, time utilization, smooth interaction, social distancing, data utilization, academic achievement, physiological stability, and transportation cost reduction can be counted as satisfactory factors for students. On the contrary, network instability, reduced concentration, constraints of practices or experiments, insufficient data provision, dissatisfaction with substitution of assignments, constraints on team projects, reduced academic achievement, unprepared class design, reduced understanding of classes, dissatisfaction with assessments, administrative disassociation, dissatisfaction with relationship formation, and dissatisfaction with educational environments are factors make students dissatisfied to the online classes. These scholars also remark opinions in order to decrease the negative aspects of online learning. These are providing network stabilization, sharing a recorded version of classes, activation of interaction, solving the issue of attendance systems, supporting the systematic environment, reduction in tuition fees, and improving the quality of online classes (Shim and Lee, 2020).

Fidalgo et al. (2020) examined students' perception of distance education at a multinational level including three countries in which Portugal, the United Arab Emirates, and Ukraine. According to this study, students' perceptions of distance education vary based on where they live. Portuguese and Ukrainian students' perceptions are more affirmative compared to students in the United Arab Emirates. Ukrainian students indicate that they had experienced distance learning before the pandemic period. On the other hand, there is a lower rate in experienced in online classes earlier in the Portuguese sample. Thus, in the study, findings show that experiencing online classes before has not affected students' perceptions of online education during Covid-19. The results can be explained by Portuguese students' willingness to accept new technology. Despite differences among these three countries, there are common grounds in students' perceptions. In general, face two face education is favored by students in these three countries because these students run into difficulties in time management, motivation, and English language skills when they have online courses (Fidalgo et al., 2020).

Paudel (2020) has examined research in Nepal. The scholar tried to bring to light the benefits and challenges of online education during the Covid-19 period. Students are mostly satisfied with online education because they are able to connect the practitioners to the global community and gain a huge and authentic resource of knowledge. The downsides of online education are challenges in time-management skills, more freedom for the teachers and learners, and not having reliable internet (Paudel, 2020).

As per Tang et al. (2021); learning motivation, learning readiness, and students' self-efficiency to join online courses during the Covid-19 period were affected by different levels of students' degrees. There are also no significant differences between female students and male students. These authors believed that the Covid-19 pandemic period helped to reduce gender differences in terms of the learning procedure. However, there are significant differences between postgraduate students and undergraduate students in learning readiness regards because students in post-graduate have higher expectations (Tang et al., 2021).

Maqableh and Alia (2021) have comprehensive research including three phases based on academic semesters. The first phase which aims to evaluate the emergency of e-learning shifting and students' satisfaction was carried out between March and April 2020. According to the results of the first phase, students mention that the number of quizzes, exams, and assignments increases compared to normal situations. Also, they highlight teachers and universities are not ready enough for this new education system.

In the second phase, determining of positive and negative aspects of online education, difficulties, and problems faced by students, and student satisfaction are the main objectives. Positive aspects are listed respectively as safety, the effectiveness of time and cost, convenience, and increased participation. On the other hand, workload, destruction, reduced focus, inadequate support, and technology and Internet connectivity are negative sides of online learning during the pandemic period. Students also highlight that their experience with online education does not meet their expectations, and they have issues with mental health, managing time, and learn-life balance. Moreover, the satisfaction levels of students in the second phase decrease compared to the first phase. In the last phase, researchers tried to find out the factors behind students' dissatisfaction. They found that poor interaction with peers and teachers leads to low levels of satisfaction. In addition, the poor interaction issue, destruction, and reduced focus, management, workload, psychological issues, difficulty level, technology and Internet, and inadequate support. Overall research points out these students' expectations were not met by experience, so students were dissatisfied (Maqableh & Alia, 2021).

Yekefallah et al. (2021) aimed to compare the differences between desirable satisfaction and undesirable satisfaction and to find factors related to student's satisfaction with their research. The authors also wanted to investigate the relationships between demographic and background characteristics, and student's satisfaction. The dimensions of this study are educational content and materials, teaching-learning, feedback and evaluation, flexibility, appropriateness and workload, and infrastructure and technology. Almost 60% of students are dissatisfied because of online learning amidst the Covid-19 period. Teaching-learning, feedback and evaluation, flexibility, and appropriateness, and workload influence overall students' satisfaction. Moreover, students who are satisfied with online learning had an online learning experience before the Covid-19 period (Yekefallah et al., 2021).

According to Gopal et al. (2021), the important dimensions affecting students' satisfaction amidst the Covid-19 period are the quality of the instructor, course design, prompt feedback, and expectations of students. Satisfied students also have higher performance compared to others who are not satisfied with online courses (Gopal et al., 2021).

Muthuprasad et al. (2021) carried out research in India about students' satisfaction during the lockdown period. Based on this research, students are willing to participate in online classes during the period. These students use smartphones to attend online classes and preferred recorded courses. Moreover, the flexibility and convenience of online classes make such classes attractive. On the other hand, communication issues with professors, spending more time on assignments, destabilization of internet connection, and data limited, and data speed are seen as the problematic points of online courses (Muthuprasad et al., 2021).

Students' Satisfaction in Turkey

One of the preliminary studies in Turkey is conducted by Karadağ and Yücel (2020). The study is an empirical study and examined undergraduate students' satisfaction regarding the distance education application during the Covid-19 lockdown period in order to determine the problems faced by students during this period. Distance Education Satisfaction Scale was developed for this study. The scale has five dimensions that are satisfied with the Council of Higher Education, satisfaction with the university and faculty management, satisfaction with the digital content/instructional materials, satisfaction with the synchronous/live lessons/video supported lessons, and satisfaction with the technical infrastructure. The Turkish students are most satisfied with the dimension of satisfaction with the Council of Higher Education. On the contrary, students in this study are less satisfied with the university and faculty management and the digital content/instructional materials. In addition, there are no significant differences between female students' satisfaction levels and male students' satisfaction levels. Besides this, there are no significant differences between Turkish students at public universities and Turkish students at private universities (Karadağ and Yücel, 2020.

As per Aslan et al. (2020), Turkish students have high-stress levels like Polish and Saudi Arabian students because of the Covid-19 pandemic. Also, extraordinary circumstances due to covid 19 restrictions have a great impact on students' well-being. Also, stress levels among students are determined by gender and cannot be determined by places where they spend time during the lockdown. Female students have a higher stress level compared to male students. (Aslan et al.,2020).

Avcı and Yıldız (2021) conducted another study in Turkey which determine students' satisfaction. These scholars tried to explain behavioral intentions toward being students in an online learning system within the framework of the Technology Acceptance Model. He found that performance expectations and perceived usefulness affects students' satisfaction and behavioral intentions significantly. The results also showed that nearly 55% of students are dissatisfied with online learning practices (Avcı and Yıldız, 2021).

Doğan (2021) carried out a study to determine the service quality levels of Turkish universities during the Covid-19 period. In order to measure students' service quality, the SERVQUAL method was used as a scale. The results demonstrated that assurance, reliability, and empathy are factors that cause students' dissatisfaction with online learning (Doğan, 2021).

GAP Model

SERVQUAL (Parasuraman et al.,1986) and SERVPERF (Cronin and Taylor; 1992) are antecedent models to measure service quality in the higher education sector. While SERVQUAL aims to compare customers' perceptions with expectations, SERVPERF intent to measure only the performance experienced by customers (Tóth and Surman; 2019). SERVQUAL provides more detailed information compared to SERVPERF (Tóth and Surman; 2019, Voss et al., 2007 and Quester et al., 1995).

SERVQUAL is based on the service quality model by Parasuraman et al. (1985). The model is also named as the gap model The model mainly has two gaps which are the consumer gap and the service provider gap. For the education sector, these gaps are labeled as the learning side's gap and the teaching side's gap (Babiarz et al., 2003). Parasuraman et al., (1985) provide main propositions about the gap model and these propositions define that extensively includes the key concepts, strategies, and decisions in services marketing (Wilson et al., 2012, p.96). Customer gap indicates a discrepancy between customers' perceptions in which judgment of actual service action and expectations in which customers' reference point (Parasuraman et al., 1985). Every customer brings his/her standards to a service experience. These standards should match the actual performances of services.

1. Provider gap 1 occurs when there is a difference between service providers who do not know what service receivers expect.
2. Provider gap 2 occurs when service providers do not select the right service quality design and standards.
3. Provider gap 3 occurs when there is a discrepancy between service delivery and service providers' external communication.
4. Provider gap 4 occurs when customers' expectations are not being met by perceived services (Parasuraman et al., 1985).

In order to have satisfied customers, these gaps should be closed.

RESEARCH METHODOLOGY

Research Design and Sampling

This study is designed as a descriptive qualitative study aiming to find out service quality gaps and students' satisfaction based on the gap model. To gain an insight into different approaches from students, the authors select students from different universities and different degrees. Convenience sampling techniques (Flick, 2009 are used to reach the target interviewees. The sample consists of eight participants (a student in a master's program, three students in a doctoral program, and four undergrad students). All of these participants are students in business administration departments. Students are between 20-32 years old. 4 students are female, and 4 students are male. These students also are educated at universities in İstanbul, Turkey.

Data Collection Method, Data Collection Instrument, and Analysis

The interviews were performed face-to-face from 30.06.2022 and 20.06.2022. A total of 8 structured interviews, lasted between 10 and 25 minutes. The author developed a guide, by reviewing the GAP model and consisting of self-developed questions. The interviews were recorded through audio devices (eight audios) in order to have the transcription of the data.

Findings

Gap 1: Expected Service- Customer Expectations

This gap occurs because service providers do not know what service receivers expect (Parasuraman et al., 1985). For this study, service providers are universities and professors, and students are service receivers. Almost every student indicated that their universities and professors did not inform them about new education systems and producers specifically. However, these students do not think that not being informed did not create an issue because the lockdown period brought an immediate change in their daily routine.

I was not informed by the university and professors before the online education started. Both the university and professors had no other choice to sustain the education. Thus, The Council of Higher Education in Turkey has decided on the new education system and universities should have followed the new regulations (S2).

Gap 2: Customer Driven Service Design-Customer Expectation

Not selecting the right service quality design and standards create the second gap (Parasuraman et al., 1985). Even though most of the students in this sample had not experienced online education, they expected online education to be part of certain standards. 4 undergrad students indicated that the most problematic online lectures were finance and accounting. They believe that course materials in such courses did not meet their expectations. 3 doctoral students mentioned that classes in their programs are suitable for maintaining lectures online.

I expected nothing but I was only concerned about the finance course. So, I had really difficulties when I was studying finance. I did not understand how our professor solved problems when I was studying the lecture by myself. The professor has not clearly explained the solving of the problems during class time, after that he sent us only the answer key to problems. At the end of the semester, I failed the course (S4).

I had to drop the accounting course because I was afraid of failing the course. I have wanted to keep my GPA above 3.00 in order to participate in the Erasmus program. I did not follow my professor when she explained solving problems and I failed the midterm(S2).

I, as a doctoral student, believe that our program had certain standards and was suitable for online education. Our professors only gave basic information at the beginning of the courses. After that, we led the lectures instead of our professor. Explaining my studies and making presentations in an online environment was easier compared in-class environment (S5).

Gap 3: Service Delivery- Customer Driven Service Design

Gap 3 represents the difference between the application of customer-driven service standards and actual service performance by service providers, and professors (Parasuraman et al., 1985). 7 Out of 8 students mentioned that they had not been faced difficulties when they were using online platforms such as Google Meet and Zoom. The most interesting finding about the gap is to be mentioned by all students about the relationship between professors' ages and usage of technology. Students in this study mentioned those older professors were not good at the usage of technology and online education systems. Moreover, most students believed that service recovery in online lectures was more effective compared to face-to-face education.

Older professors could not use online education platforms properly. They could not show presentations on the screen early during online education periods. These professors gave lectures like YouTube videos without showing any presentations because they did not know how to make a presentation on the Zoom platform (S4).

It was easy to complete online lectures with high scores. It was my first year of university. I was concerned about my adaptation period. However, I easily adopted these courses, when they were online (S1).

Actually, I allocated more time both to concentrate on online lectures and study by myself. This is because I cannot fully focus on my lectures from beginning to end. I forced myself to be awake. Also, the class environment had been made me study before the pandemic. I had been participating in lectures actively and studying with my classmates. It had been a way to study for midterms and finals (S3).

Gap 4: Service Delivery-External Communication

The discrepancy between service delivery and service providers' external communication causes gap 4 (Parasuraman et al., 1985). The main communication channels between professors and students were e-mail and WhatsApp messages. Also, syllabuses of the lectures are seen as a contract between students and professors in the education context. Completing syllabuses during terms can be seen as a reliable education service delivered to students.

I never had difficulties when I was trying to reach my lectures. They always answered my question immediately compared to a traditional education environment (S6).

Chapters in our syllabus were not completed at the end of the semester. These chapters were essential parts of our curriculum. However, our professor delivered us extra lectures after the semester, thanks to the online education environment (S8).

I cannot deny that the online education system that we used was problematic at a very early period of online education. However, based on students' and professors' feedback, useful improvements have been made during the semester (S3).

Gap 5: The Customer Gap (Expected Service- Perceived Service)

Gap 5 represents customers' expectations not being met by perceived services (Parasuraman et al., 1985). All students in this study have been not experienced online education in formal training before the pandemic period. For this reason, they had not been had high expectations during this period. However, most of the students in the study feel satisfied with online education services when they had them during the online education period.

Education could have been canceled during the Covid-19 period. Instead of this, we had online education to maintain our training program. Even though I had some problems, I was satisfied with the overall online education experience (S8).

Time is important for doctoral students like me. I felt not satisfied with some of the lectures. Unfortunately, I have no chance to get back to this class time now.

Students Satisfaction

Students in this study highlighted the positive aspects and negative aspects of online education amidst the Covid-19 lockdown period. Depending on the answers from students, the overall satisfaction level is high despite problems in online education.

My home is far away from my university. During the lockdown period, being at home and getting lecturers online helped to save time. Contrary to these benefits, I was used to an in-class environment until that time. So, I felt I lost concentration in most of the lectures because of being away from that environment.

Online Education and Student Satisfaction

I had been trying to concentrate during lectures. In general, I am satisfied with online education during that period. (S3).

I really felt satisfaction during getting an education via online. This is because education could have been interrupted. Instead of that, education had been maintained (S8).

CONCLUSION

The study is designed to delineate students' satisfaction during the online education periods and find out the problematic part of it. For this aim, the students' overall online education experiences are examined based on the gap model (Parasuraman et al., 1985).

Students are aware that unusual circumstances bring both advantages and disadvantages. For example, not being present in-class environment is counted as both a positive and negative thing by students. These students mention that time and money saving, reaching their professors easily, and quick response to unusual circumstances are seen as advantages of online education. On the other hand, older professors who could not use technological devices and online systems effectively, to understand finance, accounting, and math courses, and loss of concentration because of being away from the class environment were stated as disadvantages of the online education period. When the students compared these advantages and disadvantages, they felt satisfied during those periods. The satisfaction can be explained by low or no expectations during those periods. Most of the students in this study had not experienced online education before covid restrictions. Also, quick responses in education have made students satisfied with the new circumstances. Students had been sustaining their education in an online environment without interruption. Chapters written syllabuses had been completed by most of the lecturers. These syllabuses are seen as promises between professors and students in an educational context. Students can develop their expectations based on such promises in both online and offline education environments.

Another reason to explain satisfaction is to have more lectures had been sustaining application same as before online education. Before covid restriction, professors had been using PowerPoint slayts instead of the usage of whiteboards. These applications have been easily maintained in an online environment. However, lectures such as math, finance, and accounting need more practice during class hours. Without the usage of special software programs in the online environment, it becomes difficult to understand such courses in online education.

The main problematic part of online education was caused by the professors who are not able to use electronic devices and online systems effectively and courses that were not designed for online education properly. Education is a pure service that needs value co-creation by students and instructors. Both parties are antecedents of service quality (El Alfy & Abukari, 2019).

Shifting the education system from an in-class environment to online classes fully will not be possible in the future but a hybrid system would be useful for future educational development as a new normal (Muthuprasad et al., 2021). In order to have a sustainable and successful hybrid education system, problems in online education should be solved. Even though students in this research are satisfied with the online education during the lockdown period, they face some problems. In order to develop online education as part of the hybrid system, students experience during the Covid-19 period would be a beneficial guide. First of all, university professors have to be well-educated for the online environment as well. Universities should train their instructors who are able to meet the necessities of online education.

Free workshops about technology usage could be arranged by universities to train professors. Hiring policies in the universities also might be changed and one of the basic criteria could be the effective usage of technology. Secondly, special and user-friendly software programs for mathematics, finance, and accounting lectures could be used for online classes. Last but not least, the duration of online classes could be decreased in order to eliminate students' loss of concentration.

LIMITATIONS AND FUTURE RESEARCH DIRECTIONS

As with any research, this study has certain limitations. The first one is to have an interview with only eight students because of time constraints. Secondly, these students also are educated at universities in the same province in Turkey. There was no chance to interview with students from other parts of Turkey and from other countries. Thirdly, the study only examined students from the business administration department. Last but least, the sample of the study consists of students. This study depends on students' views about online education.

For further studies, the sample size could be enlarged in order to understand issues deeply and to generalize results. Also, upcoming research could compare students from different countries depending on the gap model. As it is mentioned earlier, the study has only one party's point of view. View of the provider gap called the teaching side and universities' management side should be addressed for further research. This is because education as a main service needs the collaboration of service providers and service receivers. In order to eliminate these gaps, the other party's experiences are important. Lastly, students in Turkey have experienced hybrid education. To investigate hybrid education is desirable for further studies. This is because neither online nor face-to-face education can meet students' needs in the modern world. The combination of these two styles is suitable for students in our new normal.

REFERENCES

Alqahtani, N., Innab, A., & Bahari, G. (2020). Virtual education during COVID-19. *Nurse Educator*, *46*(2), E18–E22. Advance online publication. doi:10.1097/NNE.0000000000000954 PMID:33234836

Aslan, I., Ochnik, D., & Çınar, O. (2020). Exploring perceived stress among students in Turkey during the COVID-19 pandemic. *International Journal of Environmental Research and Public Health*, *17*(23), 8961. doi:10.3390/ijerph17238961 PMID:33276520

Avcı, İ., & Yıldız, E. (2021). Examination of the Satisfaction and Behaviors of Students Using Distance Education in the Covid-19 Pandemic Process within the Framework of Technology Acceptance Model [Covid-19 Pandemi Sürecinde Uzaktan Eğitimi Kullanan Öğrencilerin Memnuniyet ve Davranışlarının Teknoloji Kabul Modeli Çerçevesinde İncelenmesi]. *Gümüşhane Üniversitesi Sosyal Bilimler Dergisi*, *12*(3), 814-830. Retrieved from https://dergipark.org.tr/en/pub/gumus/issue/65088/886553

Babiarz, P., Piotrowski, M., & Wawrzynkiewicz, M. (2003). The application of the service quality GAP model to evaluate the quality of blended learning. In *IADIS International Conference e-Society 2003* (pp. 911-915). Academic Press.

Basuony, M. A. K., EmadEldeen, R., Farghaly, M., El-Bassiouny, N., & Mohamed, E. K. A. (2020). The factors affecting student satisfaction with online education during the COVID-19 pandemic: An empirical study of an emerging Muslim country. *Journal of Islamic Marketing*, *12*(3), 631–648. doi:10.1108/JIMA-09-2020-0301

Blustein, D. L., & Guarino, P. A. (2020). Work and unemployment in the time of covid-19: The existential experience of loss and Fear. *Journal of Humanistic Psychology*, *60*(5), 702–709. doi:10.1177/0022167820934229

Chen, T., Peng, L., Jing, B., Wu, C., Yang, J., & Cong, G. (2020). The impact of the COVID-19 pandemic on user experience with online education platforms in China. *Sustainability*, *12*(18), 7329. doi:10.3390u12187329

Chen, T., Peng, L., Yin, X., Rong, J., Yang, J., & Cong, G. (2020). Analysis of user satisfaction with online education platforms in China during the COVID-19 pandemic. *Health Care*, *8*(3), 200. doi:10.3390/healthcare8030200 PMID:32645911

Cheon, S. H., Reeve, J., & Vansteenkiste, M. (2020). When teachers learn how to provide classroom structure in an autonomy-supportive way: Benefits to teachers and their students. *Teaching and Teacher Education*, *90*, 103004. doi:10.1016/j.tate.2019.103004

Cronin, J. J. Jr, & Taylor, S. A. (1992). Measuring Service Quality: A reexamination and extension. *Journal of Marketing*, *56*(3), 55–68. doi:10.1177/002224299205600304

Doğan, A. (2021). *A study to determine the service quality levels of Turkish universities during the Covid-19 pandemic process* [Covid-19 Pandemi Sürecinde, Türk üniversitelerinin Hizmet Kalite Düzeylerini Belirlemeye Yönelik Bir Araştırma]. OPUS Uluslararası Toplum Araştırmaları Dergisi. doi:10.26466/opus.944561

El Alfy, S., & Abukari, A. (2019). Revisiting perceived service quality in higher education: Uncovering Service Quality Dimensions for postgraduate students. *Journal of Marketing for Higher Education*, *30*(1), 1–25. doi:10.1080/08841241.2019.1648360

Fatani, T. H. (2020). Student satisfaction with videoconferencing teaching quality during the COVID-19 pandemic. *BMC Medical Education*, *20*(1), 396. Advance online publication. doi:10.118612909-020-02310-2 PMID:33129295

Fidalgo, P., Thormann, J., Kulyk, O., & Lencastre, J. A. (2020). Students' perceptions on Distance Education: A multinational study. *International Journal of Educational Technology in Higher Education*, *17*(1), 18. Advance online publication. doi:10.118641239-020-00194-2

Fishman, B., Konstantopoulos, S., Kubitskey, B. W., Vath, R., Park, G., Johnson, H., & Edelson, D. C. (2013). Comparing the impact of online and face-to-face professional development in the context of Curriculum Implementation. *Journal of Teacher Education*, *64*(5), 426–438. doi:10.1177/0022487113494413

Flick, U. (2009). *An introduction to qualitative research* (4th ed.). Sage Publications Ltd.

Gopal, R., Singh, V., & Aggarwal, A. (2021). Impact of online classes on the satisfaction and performance of students during the pandemic period of COVID 19. *Education and Information Technologies*, *26*(6), 6923–6947. doi:10.100710639-021-10523-1 PMID:33903795

Green, K. C. (2010). *The Campus Computing Survey*. The Campus Computing Project. Retrieved from https://www.campuscomputing.net/2010-campus-computing-survey

Harasim, L. (2000). Shift happens: Online education as a new paradigm in learning. *The Internet and Higher Education*, *3*(1-2), 41–61. doi:10.1016/S1096-7516(00)00032-4

Harsasi, M., & Sutawijaya, A. (2018). Determinants of student satisfaction in the online tutorial: A study of a distance education institution. *Turkish Online Journal of Distance Education*, *19*(1), 89–99. doi:10.17718/tojde.382732

Hussein, E., Daoud, S., Alrabaiah, H., & Badawi, R. (2020). Exploring undergraduate students' attitudes towards emergency online learning during COVID-19: A case from the UAE. *Children and Youth Services Review*, *119*, 105699. doi:10.1016/j.childyouth.2020.105699

Jung, I. (2010). The dimensions of e-learning quality: From the learner's perspective. *Educational Technology Research and Development*, *59*(4), 445–464. doi:10.100711423-010-9171-4

Kapasia, N., Paul, P., Roy, A., Saha, J., Zaveri, A., Mallick, R., Barman, B., Das, P., & Chouhan, P. (2020). Impact of lockdown on learning status of undergraduate and postgraduate students during COVID-19 pandemic in West Bengal, India. *Children and Youth Services Review*, *116*, 105194. doi:10.1016/j.childyouth.2020.105194 PMID:32834270

Karadağ, E., & Yücel, C. (2020). Distance Education at universities during the novel coronavirus pandemic: An analysis of undergraduate students' perceptions. *Yuksekogretim Dergisi*, *10*(2), 181–192. doi:10.2399/yod.20.730688

Latip, M. S. A., Newaz, F. T., & Ramasamy, R. (2020). Students' perception of lecturers' competency and the effect on institution loyalty: The mediating role of students' satisfaction. *Asian Journal of University Education*, *16*(2), 183. doi:10.24191/ajue.v16i2.9155

Maqableh, M., & Alia, M. (2021). Evaluation online learning of undergraduate students under lockdown amidst COVID-19 pandemic: The online learning experience and students' satisfaction. *Children and Youth Services Review*, *128*, 106160. doi:10.1016/j.childyouth.2021.106160

Muthuprasad, T., Aiswarya, S., Aditya, K. S., & Jha, G. K. (2021). Students' perception and preference for online education in India during covid -19 pandemic. *Social Sciences & Humanities Open*, *3*(1), 100101. doi:10.1016/j.ssaho.2020.100101 PMID:34173507

Parasuraman, A., Zeithaml, V. A., & Berry, L. L. (1985). A conceptual model of service quality and its implications for future research. *Journal of Marketing*, *49*(4), 41–50. doi:10.1177/002224298504900403

Parasuraman, A., Zeithaml, V. A., & Berry, L. L. (1986). *Servqual: A multiple item scale for measuring consumer perceptions of service quality*. Marketing Science Institute.

Paudel, P. (2020). Online education: Benefits, challenges and strategies during and after COVID-19 in higher education. *International Journal on Studies in Education*, *3*(2), 70–85. doi:10.46328/ijonse.32

Quester, P., Wilkinson, J. W., & Romaniuk, S. (1995). *A test of four service quality measurement scales: the case of the Australian advertising industry*. Working Paper 39, Centre de Recherche et d'Etudes Appliquees, Group esc Nantes Atlantique, Graduate School of Management.

Rust, R. T., & Zahorik, A. J. (1993). Customer satisfaction, customer retention, and market share. *Journal of Retailing*, *69*(2), 193–215. doi:10.1016/0022-4359(93)90003-2

Shahzad, A., Hassan, R., Aremu, A. Y., Hussain, A., & Lodhi, R. N. (2021). Effects of COVID-19 in E-learning on higher education institution students: The group comparison between male and female. *Quality & Quantity*, *55*(3), 805–826. doi:10.100711135-020-01028-z PMID:32836471

Shim, T. E., & Lee, S. Y. (2020). College students' experience of emergency remote teaching due to covid-19. *Children and Youth Services Review*, *119*, 105578. doi:10.1016/j.childyouth.2020.105578 PMID:33071405

Singh, V., & Thurman, A. (2019). How many ways can we define online learning? A systematic literature review of definitions of online learning (1988-2018). *American Journal of Distance Education*, *33*(4), 289–306. doi:10.1080/08923647.2019.1663082

Tang, Y. M., Chen, P. C., Law, K. M. Y., Wu, C. H., Lau, Y., Guan, J., He, D., & Ho, G. T. S. (2021). Comparative analysis of student's live online learning readiness during the coronavirus (COVID-19) pandemic in the Higher Education Sector. *Computers & Education*, *168*, 104211. doi:10.1016/j.compedu.2021.104211 PMID:33879955

Tóth, Z. E., & Surman, V. (2019). Listening to the voice of students, developing a service quality measuring and evaluating framework for a special course. *International Journal of Quality and Service Sciences*, *11*(4), 455–472. doi:10.1108/IJQSS-02-2019-0025

Voss, R., Gruber, T., & Szmigin, I. (2007). Service quality in higher education: The role of student expectations. *Journal of Business Research*, *60*(9), 949–959. doi:10.1016/j.jbusres.2007.01.020

Voss, R., Gruber, T., & Szmigin, I. (2007). Service quality in higher education: The role of student expectations. *Journal of Business Research*, *60*(9), 949–959. doi:10.1016/j.jbusres.2007.01.020

Wilson, A. M., Zeithaml, V. A., Bitner, M. J., & Gremler, D. D. (2021). *Services marketing: Integrating customer focus across the firm*. McGraw-Hill.

Xie, X., Siau, K., & Nah, F. F.-H. (2020). Covid-19 pandemic – online education in the New Normal and the next normal. *Journal of Information Technology Case and Application Research*, *22*(3), 175–187. doi:10.1080/15228053.2020.1824884

Yekefallah, L., Namdar, P., Panahi, R., & Dehghankar, L. (2021). Factors related to students' satisfaction with holding e-learning during the covid-19 pandemic based on the dimensions of e-learning. *Heliyon*, *7*(7), e07628. Advance online publication. doi:10.1016/j.heliyon.2021.e07628 PMID:34381894

Chapter 13

From Routine Mode to Emergency Mode and Back:
Reflections on Israeli Online Teaching and Learning in Higher Education After the COVID–19 Period

Hagit Meishar-Tal

Holon Institute of Technology (HIT), Israel

ABSTRACT

This chapter analyses Israeli higher education institutions' transitions from campus learning to online learning due to the COVID-19 pandemic and critically discusses the transition back to routine campus-based learning. The chapter reviews the state of online teaching in pre-COVID-19 academia, the changes required during lockdowns and social distancing restrictions, and the essential difference between routine and emergency online teaching. It also discusses the consequences of returning to campus-based learning and ways to leverage the changes that took place during the COVID-19 period and adapt them to routine mode again.

INTRODUCTION

The COVID-19 breakdown and the quarantines and social distancing restrictions followed, was a shaky and challenging period for higher education institutions (HEIs), which have always been considered a stronghold of conservatism. However, they proved their ability to adapt to the new situation quickly and effectively. Academic institutions in Israel are part of the few public institutions that were not paralyzed during the pandemic. Teaching continued almost uninterrupted, with a rapid and impressive transition from face-to-face to online learning (Donitsa-Schmidt & Ramot, 2020; Cohen & Sabag, 2020). The higher education system has proven that it can address the changing needs of students and be flexible and adaptive to a changing situation. However, the "day after", we will have to address complex dilemmas: how to manage the change in academic teaching and what to preserve and what to improve.

DOI: 10.4018/978-1-6684-5934-8.ch013

Copyright © 2023, IGI Global. Copying or distributing in print or electronic forms without written permission of IGI Global is prohibited.

The State of Online Teaching in Higher Education in Israel Before COVID-19

Integrating online technologies into teaching is not new in higher education worldwide (Perry & Pilati, 2011). Adopting these learning technologies is a recognition of their contribution to improving teaching, learning, and assessment (Goodison, 2001). For many years, HEIs in Israel have been working to integrate tools for online learning in teaching (Cohen & Davidovitch, 2020). Online learning management systems have been commonly used in Israeli HEIs to provide online environments that accompany courses for about two decades (Naveh et al., 2010; Ghilay, 2019). They enable access to study materials, presentations and articles, lesson summaries, and the submission of assignments. However, many studies conducted in academia have shown that these sites do not constitute a significant pedagogical change and that the quality of educational activity in these environments is pretty low (Roth, 2015). While the many attempts to develop meaningful learning based on interaction and knowledge construction in these environments, have yielded some successful examples of student activities (e.g., Anatolievna, 2018; Palahicky & Halcomb-Smith, 2020; Munni & Hasan, 2020; Ng et al., 2020), from a systemic perspective, they did not bring about any significant change in learning in the pre-COVID era (Nichols, 2008). As long as they are accompanied by face-to-face sessions their main advantage was mainly as a repository of learning material for students and asynchronous communication with the lecturers between sessions in question and answer forums (Carvalho et al., 2011; Olmos et al., 2015).

Synchronous learning systems, such as Zoom, which is now in use in every home in Israel following the COVID-19 lockdowns and quarantines, were also used in HEIs before the pandemic as a substitute for face-to-face sessions (Stewart et al., 2011; Warden et al., 2013). Synchronous distance learning enabled immediate communication between students and distant lecturers. It allowed students to get to know each other and communicate during class without meeting physically. Indeed, students participating in these classes reported high levels of involvement during synchronous classes (Falloon, 2011; Hrastinski, 2008; Stein et al., 2009). However, since these systems allow recording of the session and later viewing of the recorded session at the students' convenience, some students took advantage of this option and made no effort to participate in the live sessions (Kear et al., 2012). Moreover, lecturers who taught in synchronous courses indicated a decrease in interaction with the students and an inability to 'feel' the students during the live sessions (Villalón et al., 2012). Another phenomenon in synchronous teaching is the avoidance of students turning on their camera in synchronous classes, thus further reducing their involvement in the class (Bedenlier, 2021; Castelli & Sarvary, 2021).

Another phenomenon that shaped online learning in higher education before COVID-19 was the MOOCs (Massive Open Online Courses). MOOCs are courses designed for the public and developed according to the asynchronous model, allowing self-learning and maximum flexibility in time and space. These courses do not accompany face-to-face courses but stand alone as distance learning courses, when there is usually no lecturer who supports the learners by providing feedback and assessment (Pappano, 2012). The courses are usually based on short videos in which the lecturers are recorded and on interactive activities and/or interaction with other learners (Baturay, 2015). One of the challenges students face in learning with MOOCs is the self-regulation required of the learner and the lack of framework provided by an official academic institution (Onah & Sinclair, 2017; Reparaz et al., 2020). The result is that despite the great attractiveness of these courses, there is a high dropout rate and a lack of perseverance (Aldowah et al., 2020; Feng, 2019; Gitinabard et al., 2018).

At first, it seemed that the MOOCs were threatening to render academia irrelevant as they provided an easily accessible alternative for students to acquire theoretical and practical knowledge in courses without enrolling in full academic studies (Vardi, 2012; Yuan & Powell, 2013). Academia perceived MOOCs as a disruptive innovation, a real threat to its very existence, and enlisted in a war for survival (Flynn, 2013). It has invested resources to developing its own MOOCs (Sandeen, 2013) which are accessible to the general public for free, but without accreditation. Nevertheless, they can be accredited under the management and support of the lecturers who teach them. In this move, HEIs contributed to the accessibility of knowledge to the general public while ensuring their survival.

The Transition from Routine to Emergency

And then came COVID-19. Within a short time, HEIs in Israel and worldwide had to transition to online learning (Khalil et al., 2020; Murphy et al., 2020; Rad, et al., 2021), mainly in synchronous format, based on live sessions in which the lecturers teach frontally. The model that gained the least interest and weight in previous online academic teaching now became the main one.

Choosing the synchronous format as the leading teaching model in the COVID period was justified. For most lecturers, this was their first experience in online teaching, since their readiness for online teaching was low (Moralista & Oducado, 2020; Pandya et al., 2021). Since this format was the closest to classroom teaching, and required very little training, adjustment, and preparation, it enabled a quick and easy transition to online teaching.

Moreover, when all lecturers and students were at home anyway and wanted to maintain a degree of routine during the extreme state of the pandemic, it was possible to hold live sessions according to the original plan and without a break down of the learning framework. Both lecturers and students had a common interest in maintaining the learning time frame. Thus, the absolute necessity of the immediate transition to synchronous learning facilitated an easy and rapid adaptation to online learning and teaching.

But what will happen after the COVID period ends? What will happen to academic teaching? What will happen to synchronous learning and what will happen to the asynchronous models that dominated pre-COVID academic online learning?

We must remember that emergency remote learning is not the same as online learning (Hodges et al., 2020). Some of the experience gained in academia during the pandemic regarding online learning may contribute to the acceptance of the technology even during routine, while some may impair it.

Routine online learning is a planned process, usually applied by choice for both lecturers and students. It is a long, drawn-out process to which adaptation is slow and changes in the learning and teaching can be made gradually and over the long-term. It is usually accompanied by training for the lecturers that imparts the skills needed for the development and operation of online teaching and learning (Hodges et al., 2020).

In routines times, technology is not the only means of learning, as most models of online learning are hybrid and combine face-to-face class meetings with online meetings whether in groups or in private meetings with the lecturers. Wwhereas in emergencies, such as pandemics that require social distancing, the only possible way to sustain learning is online.

Routine online teaching is measured by high pedagogical quality metrics and is compared to the quality of face-to-face learning sessions, aiming to offer added value beyond classroom learning. In contrast, in emergency remote learning and teaching, the transition usually comes as a surprise, without prior warning (Hodges et al., 2020), the only alternative being the suspension of studies altogether. Moreover, there is no time for early assessments in emergency learning as change is rapid. The change is perceived as a temporary and therefore the criteria for assessment are different. In emergencies, the

From Routine Mode to Emergency Mode and Back

very existence of teaching and learning is the goal. The lecturers are required to adapt the pedagogical aspect their work while also address aspects of teaching in an emergency, which requires coping with the resulting emotional states of stress and anxiety (Petillion & McNeil, 2020).

A study conducted among academics during the COVID-19 period found that despite low readiness and the rapid transition, the feelings lecturers developed towards online teaching were positive, and expressed as a sense of success and opportunity, rather than of threat and failure (Author, 2021). This probably stemmed from the survival experience of continuing to function professionally in crisis, and the danger of unpaid leave hovering like a cloud over the heads. As the lockdowns ended, the threat of unemployment decreased, and the sense of survival became less relevant.

In addition, in routine times, students could choose to study online. They compared the pros and cons of online learning versus campus learning, and made a conscious choice to study online, whereas in the pandemic state emergency, there was no choice and no alternative. One of the problematic outcomes of remote learning during the pandemic was the significant decrease in the extent of social connections among the students (Author, submitted). The studying from home was based mainly on self-regulated learning. The social experience that accompanies classroom learning is known for its importance and contribution to student persistence. Students who experience loneliness and lack social interaction are more exposed to the risk of depression, which can lead to a decrease in academic achievement and even to dropping out (Schmits et al., 2021).

The fact that lecturers and students experienced online learning in an emergency also impacted their model for quality online teaching. As mentioned, there is a significant difference between routine and emergency online learning since in the latter, the lecturers had to devote part of their lessons to addressing the emotional need of the students, even at the expense of keeping up with the original teaching plan, assuming that this period may end soon and gaps can be filled. In future routine mode, however, lecturers will have to keep up and adapt their teaching better to the online medium (Schultz & DeMers, 2020). The students' forgiveness of lecturers' poor performance in the unplanned and unprepared emergency transition to online learning will not last for long. Instead, students will expect lecturers to be more professional in online teaching, namely, preparing quality learning materials and utilizing the advanced options provided by the online systems. Table 1 summarizes the differences between emergency learning and routine learning.

Table 1. Differences between emergency learning and routine learning

Emergency	Routine
Unexpected change	Planned change
Change with no choice	Change out of choice
Quick change	Slowly and continual process
Temporary/Short-term change	Long-term change
Knowledge in emergency remote teaching is required	Training in online pedagogy is provided
Technology as the main infrastructure	Technology as another layer
Emphasis on the very existence of instruction	Emphasis on quality of instruction

The Transition from Emergency to Routine

The transition from emergency back to routine is usually accompanied by a natural desire to return to the original state. The demand to return to campus-based studies is ubiquitous (Derry, 2021; Kashti, 2021). But was the previous situation the most desirable one or is it possible to adopt some of the changes that the COVID period introduced to teaching and leverage this change to promote a significant in-depth process of integrating online technologies in teaching in a high-quality, sustainable manner?

It seems impossible to turn back time altogether, because some students who have experienced online learning and recognize its benefits will prefer to continue learning this way. Online learning allows students great flexibility in time and space (Veletsianos & Houlden, 2019), no traffic jams on the way to campus and no searching for parking. They can learn from recorded sessions whenever and from wherever they want. These benefits cannot be replaced by teaching on campus. It is likely that anyone who experienced positive online learning during this period will be open to the option of online distance learning even in routine times. The experience of distance learning during the COVID-19 period contributed significantly to removing barriers and opened a window to an in-depth and planned process of assimilating digital learning technologies in teaching (Author, 2021). This openness of lecturers and students is a real opportunity for the higher education system that has struggled for years with opposition to online teaching especially among lecturers (Bousbahi & Alrazgan, 2015; Wingo et al., 2017). If the HEIs can leverage this opportunity and expand the use of learning technologies in teaching and learning, they will benefit from the crisis.

At the same time, there is no doubt that the synchronous learning model that dominated online learning during the COVID-19 period is not the optimal model for routine studies. Most synchronous sessions were based on Zoom lectures in which the traditional concept of teaching as a one-way transfer of knowledge from the lecturer to the students was maintained. This format was widely perceived even before the COVID-19 period as less suitable for teaching in the 21st century, where knowledge is accessible to learners anywhere and anytime and there is importance in imparting self-learning skills that enable the construction of knowledge, and not just delivering knowledge (Acedo & Hughes, 2014; Scott, 2015).

The Zoom platform enables students to increase their involvement in learning through online discussions, instant messaging (chat), the use of breakout rooms, surveys and more. However, it seems that lecturers' use of these options has been limited (Author, 2020). In the future, lecturers seeking to use Zoom or other synchronous solutions will need to expand instructional strategies and develop lessons that utilize functions that engage learners and produce more collaborative and interactive learning processes.

Beyond the synchronous teaching, the lecturers will have to take better advantage of asynchronous learning, which has been the leader so far in distance learning but became secondary during the pandemic. There are many benefits to asynchronous learning, but there are also many challenges for both students and lecturers. Beyond the flexibility in time, place and pace that asynchronous learning allows, it shifts the responsibility for learning to the students and requires more active learning (Northey et al., 2015). as they interact with the study material. It requires more time and effort, which is not always welcomed by the students, and may even lead to dropout and instability, as indeed happens in the MOOC model we mentioned above (Aldowah et al., 2020; Feng, 2019; Gitinabard et al., 2018).

In this type of teaching, students' learning is not under the lecturers' control, and they may perceive themselves as redundant. However, lecturers play an essential role in managing "behind the scenes" online learning, planning students' learning processes, selecting and evaluating learning materials, creating and assessing assignments, and providing essential additional guidance (Anderson, 2004; Coppola et

From Routine Mode to Emergency Mode and Back

al., 2002; Dabbagh, 2003; Maor, 2003). These tasks require different skills than in in-person learning. These skills that most lecturers have not acquired so far. Therefore, a systemic and comprehensive training process is needed to allow them to professionalize their asynchronous teaching.

Another kind of asynchronous teaching is the collaborative model, in which students do not work alone, but rather constantly interact with a small group of their peers. They are given collaborative tasks that require them to divide up roles, coordinate and synthesize. This type of learning has many cognitive, social, and emotional benefits. It encourages higher-order thinking and greater familiarity with the study material and provides an important opportunity for social connections between students, which is so lacking in remote teaching-learning (Roberts, 2005). The online environment offers many tools for collaborative learning ranging from discussion forums (Camarero et al., 2012), collaborative writing tools such as Google Docs or Wiki (Author, 2008) and various web 2.0 environments for creating and sharing collaborative learning products (Newland & Byles, 2014; Den Exter et al., 2012). For students, these collaobrative processes are often perceived as more difficult, despite their great importance, as they require interpersonal skills of cooperation and mutual trust as well as coordination and synchronization among participants (Donelan & Kear, 2018; Stover & Holland, 2018). For lecturers, they require more complex management and knowledge in developing, supervising, and assessing collaborative learning processes (Author, 2011).

Lecturers' ability of to make effective use of the technology and the pedagogical models of e-learning, can provide tailored solutions to various learning needs according to their goals and contents. All of these, of course, require appropriate training for both lecturers and students.

Another key aspect that will have to be addressed in the expanded inclusion of routine online teaching is the social aspect discussed earlier. During the pandemic, a major weakness of online teaching was the decline in social interaction among students. HEIs will need to find ways to address students' need for social interaction when studying remotely, whether by initiating social events or implementing collaborative learning that generates personal ties among students and contribute to the development of social relationships (Author, 2022).

Another insight emerges from studies conducted among students during the COVID-19 period is that during the emergency, students mostly appreciated their lecturers' sense of empathy and personal attention more than their professionalism and efforts to develop active learning and student involvement (Author, 2021; Bigman & Mitchell, 2020). This finding emphasizes the importance of lecturers' social and emotional presence in distance learning. To bridge the distance between the lecturer and the students, it is important that expressions of empathy, which was understandable and came naturally to lecturers in the emergency, will be maintained, and that lecturers continue to provide emotional support as part of their role.

Table 2 summarizes the main points for preservation (Keep) and improvement (Improve) in the transition from emergency instruction to routine online instruction.

Higher education institutions in Israel are already working to combine on-campus learning with online learning in various hybrid models in an attempt to address all students, both those who prefer online learning and those who prefer face-to-face learning (Gan-El, 2021). Some models are more successful, and some are less. It is especially worth critically examining the hyflex model that combines a live classroom session and simultaneous synchronous broadcasting for students at home as well (Archee et al., 2021). According to Archee et al., 2021) wide adoption of HyFlex is considered problematic except for specific cohorts of students under extreme circumstances. This model preserves all the disadvantages of a frontal session and of an online session and does not optimally utilize the benefits of online learning mentioned above. However, a combination of synchronous sessions, asynchronous assignments, and face-to-face meetings in a blended mode throughout the semester may provide a more pedagogically suitable solution that effectively takes optimal advantage of online learning and will address students demand for flexible learning.

Table 2. 'Keep' and 'improve' in the transition from emergency instruction to routine online instruction

Keep	Improve
Openness to the use of technology and removal of barriers and resistance	Expanding pedagogical variety and tools beyond Zoom
Recognition that technology is a necessary infrastructure for teaching	Training lecturers for online teaching
Giving students the option of distance learning	
Initiating online and offline social activities	
Expressing empathy and personal attention to students	
Implementing social learning pedagogy in online learning	

CONCLUSION

In recent years, even before the pandemic, the academia in Israel has encouraged the transition to online learning but has encountered opposition from lecturers who have not risen to the challenge and were not interested in incorporating technology into teaching.

The barriers to expanding online learning in academia have undoubtedly been breached following the pandemic and the inevitable transition to online teaching, but the model that emerged from the special situation is not exactly the model aimed for by online learning experts. The challenge facing HEIs in the post-COVID era will be to leverage the opportunities created by technologies and lecturers' openness to technology and manage the assimilation and adaptation of online and hybrid teaching models in routine times. HEIs will have to expend the variety of tools used in online learning and develop sustainable pedagogical models for teaching online in routine, especially flexible models based on asynchronous technologies which are more collaborative and student-centered, and train the lecturers to use these models effectively. Researchers in educational technologies in higher education will have to provide more evidence-based models and cases of successful implementation of online technologies that could serve as examples for lecturers worldwide.

REFERENCES

Acedo, C., & Hughes, C. (2014). Principles for learning and competences in the 21-century curriculum. *Prospects*, *44*(4), 503–525. doi:10.100711125-014-9330-1

Aldowah, H., Al-Samarraie, H., Alzahrani, A. I., & Alalwan, N. (2020). Factors affecting student dropout in MOOCs: A cause and effect decision-making model. *Journal of Computing in Higher Education*, *32*(2), 429–454. doi:10.100712528-019-09241-y

Anatolievna, K. S. (2018). The use of LMS Moodle to intensify the independent work of students in teaching a foreign language in a non-linguistic university. *Азимут научных исследований: педагогика и психология, 7*(25).

Anderson, T. (2004). Teaching in an online learning context. *Theory and practice of online learning, 273*.

Archee, R., Dawkins, R., & Gurney, M. (2021). Evaluating HyFlex at Western Sydney University 2021: Considerations for Curriculum and Pedagogy. In T. Bastiaens (Ed.), *Proceedings of Innovate Learning Summit 2021* (pp. 484-492). Association for the Advancement of Computing in Education (AACE). https://www.learntechlib.org/primary/p/220319/

Baturay, M. H. (2015). An overview of the world of MOOCs. *Procedia-Social and Behavioral Sciences, 174*, 427-433. doi:10.1016/j.sbspro.2015.01.685

Bedenlier, S., Wunder, I., Gläser-Zikuda, M., Kammerl, R., Kopp, B., Ziegler, A., & Händel, M. (2021). Generation invisible? Higher Education Students'(Non) Use of Webcams in Synchronous Online Learning. *International Journal of Educational Research Open, 2*, 100068. doi:10.1016/j.ijedro.2021.100068

Bigman, M., & Mitchell, J. C. (2020). Teaching Online in 2020: Experiments, Empathy, Discovery. In 2020 IEEE Learning With MOOCS (LWMOOCS) (pp. 156-161). IEEE.

Bousbahi, F., & Alrazgan, M. S. (2015). Investigating IT faculty resistance to learning management system adoption using latent variables in an acceptance technology model. *TheScientificWorldJournal, 2015*, 2015. doi:10.1155/2015/375651 PMID:26491712

Camarero, C., Rodríguez, J., & San José, R. (2012). An exploratory study of online forums as a collaborative learning tool. *Online Information Review, 36*(6), 568–586. doi:10.1108/14684521211254077

Carvalho, A., Areal, N., & Silva, J. (2011). Students' perceptions of Blackboard and Moodle in a Portuguese university. *British Journal of Educational Technology, 42*(5), 824–841. doi:10.1111/j.1467-8535.2010.01097.x

Castelli, F. R., & Sarvary, M. A. (2021). Why students do not turn on their video cameras during online classes and an equitable and inclusive plan to encourage them to do so. *Ecology and Evolution, 11*(8), 3565–3576. doi:10.1002/ece3.7123 PMID:33898009

Cohen, E., & Davidovitch, N. (2020). The Development of Online Learning in Israeli Higher Education. *Journal of Education and Learning, 9*(5), 15-26. doi:10.5539/jel.v9n5p15

Cohen, S., & Sabag, Z. (2020). The Influence of the COVID-19 Epidemic on Teaching Methods in Higher Education Institutions in Israel. *Journal of Research in Higher Education, 4*(1), 44–71. doi:10.24193/JRHE.2020.1.4

Coppola, N. W., Hiltz, S. R., & Rotter, N. G. (2002). Becoming a virtual professor: Pedagogical roles and asynchronous learning networks. *Journal of Management Information Systems, 18*(4), 169-189. doi:10.1109/HICSS.2001.926183

Dabbagh, N. (2003). Scaffolding: An important teacher competency in online learning. *TechTrends, 47*(2), 39-44. doi:10.1007/BF02763424

Den Exter, K., Rowe, S., Boyd, W., & Lloyd, D. (2012). Using Web 2.0 technologies for collaborative learning in distance education—Case studies from an Australian university. *Future Internet, 4*(1), 216-237. doi:10.3390/fi4010216

Derry, E. (2021, April 19) Students return to the campus! *Maariv Online.* Retrieved from https://www.maariv.co.il/journalists/opinions/Article-834686

Donelan, H., & Kear, K. (2018). Creating and Collaborating: Students' and Tutors' Perceptions of an Online Group Project. *The International Review of Research in Open and Distributed Learning, 19*(2). Advance online publication. doi:10.19173/irrodl.v19i2.3124

Donitsa-Schmidt, S., & Ramot, R. (2020). Opportunities and challenges: teacher education in Israel in the COVID-19 pandemic. *Journal of Education for Teaching, 46*(4), 586-595. doi:10.1080/02607476.2020.1799708

Falloon, G. (2011). Making the connection: Moore's theory of transactional distance and its relevance to the use of a virtual classroom in postgraduate online teacher education. *Journal of Research on Technology in Education, 45*(3), 187–209. doi:10.1080/15391523.2011.10782569

Feng, W., Tang, J., & Liu, T. X. (2019, July). Understanding dropouts in MOOCs. *Proceedings of the AAAI Conference on Artificial Intelligence, 33*(01), 517–524. doi:10.1609/aaai.v33i01.3301517

Flynn, J. T. (2013). MOOCS: Disruptive innovation and the future of higher education. *Christian Education Journal, 10*(1), 149–162. doi:10.1177/073989131301000112

Gan El, A. (2021). Hybrid learning will be the new normal. *Ynet.* https://www.ynet.co.il/digital/technology/article/bywcluyyk

Ghilay, Y. (2019). *Effectiveness of learning management systems in higher education: Views of Lecturers with different levels of activity in LMSs.* Academic Press.

Ghilay, Y. (2019). Effectiveness of Learning Management Systems in Higher Education: Views of Lecturers with Different Levels of Activity in LMSs. https://ssrn.com/abstract=3736748. *Journal of Online Higher Education, 3*(2), 29–50.

Gitinabard, N., Khoshnevisan, F., Lynch, C. F., & Wang, E. Y. (2018). *Your actions or your associates? Predicting certification and dropout in MOOCs with behavioral and social features.* arXiv preprint arXiv:1809.00052.

Goodison, T. A. (2001). The implementation of e-learning in higher education in the United Kingdom: The road ahead. *Higher Education in Europe, 26*(2), 247-262. doi:10.1080/03797720120082642

Hodges, C., Moore, S., Lockee, B., Trust, T., & Bond, A. (2020). The difference between emergency remote teaching and online learning. *Educause.* https://er.educause.edu/articles/2020/3/the-difference-between-emergency-remote-teaching-and-online-learning

Hrastinski, S. (2008). A study of asynchronous and synchronous c-lcarning methods discovered that each supports different purposes. *Educause Quarterly, 4*, 51-55. http:// www.educause.edu/ero/article/asynchronous-and-synchronous-c-leaming

Kashti, A. (2021) The universities will return to hold frontal classes after the Passover holiday. *Haaretz*. https://www.haaretz.co.il/news/education/.premium-1.9641556

Kear, K., Chetwynd, F., Williams, J., & Donelan, H. (2012). Web conferencing for synchronous online tutorials: Perspectives of tutors using a new medium. *Computers & Education, 58*(3), 953-963. doi:10.1016/j.compedu.2011.10.015

Khalil, R., Mansour, A. E., Fadda, W. A., Almisnid, K., Aldamegh, M., Al-Nafeesah, A., ... Al-Wutayd, O. (2020). The sudden transition to synchronized online learning during the COVID-19 pandemic in Saudi Arabia: a qualitative study exploring medical students' perspectives. *BMC Medical Education, 20*(1), 1-10. doi:10.1186/s12909-020-02208-z

Maor, D. (2003). The teacher's role in developing interaction and reflection in an online learning community. *Educational Media International, 40*(1-2), 127-138. doi:10.1080/0952398032000092170

Moralista, R., & Oducado, R. M. (2020). *Faculty perception toward online education in higher education during the coronavirus disease 19 (COVID-19) pandemic*. doi:10.13189/ujer.2020.081044

Munni, B. E., & Hasan, S. M. (2020). Teaching English during COVID-19 Pandemic Using Facebook Group as an LMS: A Study on Undergraduate Students of a University in Bangladesh. *Language in India, 20*(6).

Murphy, L., Eduljee, N. B., & Croteau, K. (2020). College Student Transition to Synchronous Virtual Classes during the COVID-19 Pandemic in Northeastern United States. *Pedagogical Research, 5*(4). doi:10.29333/pr/8485

Naveh, G., Tubin, D., & Pliskin, N. (2010). Student LMS use and satisfaction in academic institutions: The organizational perspective. *The Internet and Higher Education, 13*(3), 127-133. doi:10.1016/j.iheduc.2010.02.004

Newland, B., & Byles, L. (2014). Changing academic teaching with Web 2.0 technologies. *Innovations in Education and Teaching International, 51*(3), 315-325. doi:10.1080/14703297.2013.796727

Ng, J., Lei, L., Iseli-Chan, N., Li, J., Siu, F., Chu, S., & Hu, X. (2020). Non-repository Uses of Learning Management System through Mobile Access. *Journal of Educational Technology Development and Exchange, 13*(1), 1. doi:10.18785/jetde.1301.01

Nichols, M. (2008). Institutional perspectives: The challenges of e-learning diffusion. *British Journal of Educational Technology, 39*(4), 598-609. doi:10.1111/j.1467-8535.2007.00761.x

Northey, G., Bucic, T., Chylinski, M., & Govind, R. (2015). Increasing student engagement using asynchronous learning. *Journal of Marketing Education, 37*(3), 171–180. doi:10.1177/0273475315589814

Olmos, S., Mena, J., Torrecilla, E., & Iglesias, A. (2015). Improving graduate students' learning through the use of Moodle. *Educational Research Review, 10*(5), 604–614. doi:10.5897/ERR2014.2052

Onah, D., & Sinclair, J. (2017). Assessing self-regulation of learning dimensions in a stand-alone MOOC platform. *International Journal of Engineering Pedagogy, 7*(2), 4-21. doi:10.3991/ijep.v7i2.6511

Palahicky, S., & Halcomb-Smith, L. (2020). Utilizing Learning Management System (LMS) Tools to Foster Innovative Teaching. In Handbook of Research on Innovative Pedagogies and Best Practices in Teacher Education (pp. 1-17). IGI Global. doi:10.4018/978-1-5225-9232-7.ch001

Pandya, B., Patterson, L., & Cho, B. (2021). Pedagogical transitions experienced by higher education faculty members – "Pre-COVID to COVID". *Journal of Applied Research in Higher Education*. doi:10.1108/JARHE-01-2021-0028

Pappano, L. (2012). The Year of the MOOC. *The New York Times, 2*(12).

Perry, E. H., & Pilati, M. L. (2011). Online learning. *New Directions for Teaching and Learning, 128,* 95–104.

Petillion, R. J., & McNeil, W. S. (2020). Student experiences of emergency remote teaching: Impacts of instructor practice on student learning, engagement, and well-being. *Journal of Chemical Education, 97*(9), 2486–2493.

Rad, F. A., Otaki, F., Baqain, Z., Zary, N., & Al-Halabi, M. (2021). Rapid transition to distance learning due to COVID-19: Perceptions of postgraduate dental learners and instructors. *PLoS One, 16*(2), e0246584.

Reparaz, C., Aznárez-Sanado, M., & Mendoza, G. (2020). Self-regulation of learning and MOOC retention. *Computers in Human Behavior, 111,* 106423.

Roberts, T. S. (2005). Computer-supported collaborative learning in higher education. In Computer-supported collaborative learning in higher education (pp. 1-18). IGI Global.

Roth, M. (2015). Moodle: Ten Years On. *GSTF Journal on Education, 3*(1).

Sandeen, C. (2013). Integrating MOOCs into traditional higher education: The emerging "MOOC 3.0" era. *Change: The magazine of higher learning, 45*(6), 34-39.

Schmits, E., Dekeyser, S., Klein, O., Luminet, O., Yzerbyt, V., & Glowacz, F. (2021). Psychological Distress among Students in Higher Education: One Year after the Beginning of the COVID-19 Pandemic] . *International Journal of Environmental Research and Public Health, 18*(14), 7445. doi:10.3390/ijerph18147445

Schultz, R. B., & DeMers, M. N. (2020). Transitioning from emergency remote learning to deep online learning experiences in geography education. *The Journal of Geography, 119*(5), 142–146. doi:10.1080/00221341.2020.1813791

Scott, C. L. (2015). *The futures of Learning 3: What kind of pedagogies for the 21st century?* https://unesdoc.unesco.org/images/0024/002431/243126e.pdf

Shisley, S. (2020). Emergency remote learning compared to online learning. *Learning Solutions*. https://learningsolutionsmag.com/articles/emergency-remote-learning-compared-to-online-learning

Stein, D. S., Wanstreet, C. E., Calvin, J., Overtoom, C., & Wheaton, J. E. (2005). Bridging the transactional distance gap in online learning environments. *American Journal of Distance Education, 19*(2), 105–118. https://doi.org/10.1207/s15389286ajde1902_4

Stewart, A. R., Harlow, D. B., & DeBacco, K. (2011). Students' experience of synchronous learning in distributed environments. *Distance Education, 32*(3), 357–381.

Stover, S., & Holland, C. (2018). Student Resistance to Collaborative Learning. *International Journal for the Scholarship of Teaching and Learning, 12*(2), 8.

Vardi, M. Y. (2012). Will MOOCs destroy academia? *Communications of the ACM, 55*(11), 5–5.

Veletsianos, G., & Houlden, S. (2019). An analysis of flexible learning and flexibility over the last 40 years of Distance Education. *Distance Education, 40*(4), 454–468.

Villalón, R., Luna, M., & García-Barrera, A. (2012). What do lecturers say about their use of a synchronous tool in an open university. *Proceedings of ICERI2012 International Conference.*

Warden, C. A., Stanworth, J. O., Ren, J. B., & Warden, A. R. (2013). Synchronous learning best practices: An action research study. *Computers & Education, 63*, 197–207.

Wingo, N. P., Ivankova, N. V., & Moss, J. A. (2017). Faculty perceptions about teaching online: Exploring the literature using the technology acceptance model as an organizing framework. *Online Learning, 21*(1), 15-35. doi:10.10.24059/olj.v21i1.761

Yuan, L., & Powell, S. J. (2013). *MOOCs and open education: Implications for higher education.* doi:10.13140/2.1.5072.8320

Chapter 14
Experiences and Challenges of Indigenous Students in Higher Education During the Pandemic

Ana Arán Sánchez

https://orcid.org/0000-0001-7149-3461

Escuela Normal Rural Ricardo Flores Magón, Mexico

ABSTRACT

This chapter describes and analyzes the experiences of indigenous students of higher education during the COVID-19 pandemic. They are undergraduates of the bachelor's degree of elementary education who attend a public university located in the north of Mexico, as part of an affirmative action policy that began in 2017. Through the phenomenological method, with an interpretative framework and qualitative approach, this research examines the testimonies of 15 key informants using in-depth interviews, in order to convey the academic challenges they went through during the school lockdown and isolation period of the health emergency caused by the SARS-COV-2 virus, including the development of their dissertation to obtain their degree. The chapter reveals the extreme difficulties they experienced due to the lack of suitable computer equipment, internet connection, and absence of an adequate digital competence. For the ones that had to do their thesis report in order to graduate, having to write their theses in a second language meant an additional obstacle as well.

INTRODUCTION

Indigenous population throughout the globe have been historically marginalized in the economic, social and educational realms (Bello and Rangel, 2002); a phenomenon whose repercussions still have an echo in present day. The efforts in different areas through public policies and educational reforms have not had the desired outcome (Horbath and García, 2012), so the need to generate a real and permanent change has become unavoidable. Additionally, circumstances such as the health emergency due to the *SARS-COV-2 virus* has exacerbated the previously vulnerable situation of the indigenous population, due

DOI: 10.4018/978-1-6684-5934-8.ch014

Copyright © 2023, IGI Global. Copying or distributing in print or electronic forms without written permission of IGI Global is prohibited.

to their low socioeconomic level which prevents them from accessing the necessary tools and means to continue their education process in an online setting.

This chapter will examine how indigenous students of a normal rural school[1] located in the north of Mexico, which is an all women boarding school higher education institution, have experienced the pandemic caused by the Covid-19 virus. It will provide first person testimonies about the challenges the students went through during this period of time, their academic experiences (including the process of constructing their thesis report in order to graduate) and how all of these circumstances impacted their emotional wellbeing.

BACKGROUND

Ricardo Flores Magón Rural Normal School (ENRRFM), is located in Saucillo city, which is in the state of Chihuahua, in the north of Mexico. This school was founded in 1931 and it offers two different bachelor's degrees: Elementary Education and Preschool Education. Since the ENRRFM is a rural institution, it functions as a boarding school exclusively for women, with a full schedule from 7:30 a.m. to 7:30 p.m. This Normal School has approximately 400 students between first and fourth grade, most of them from the states of Chihuahua and Durango.

Rural Normal Schools were created after the Mexican Revolution, the first of its kind in Latin America (Salas, 2018) with an important influence of the political ideals to eradicate poverty by schooling: "Education, until then far away from the most impoverished sectors of society, played an important role: the challenge for the rural school was to become the engine for the social transformation" (Elortegui, 2017, p.163). During the 1920s, Regional Normal and Central Agriculture Schools were founded to train students on teaching how to read and write, as well as master new agriculture techniques. Later, when these institutions merged, they changed their name to Peasant Regionals and in 1926 they officially become Rural Normal Schools (Padilla, 2009).

The boarding school modality originated as a way to reduce the inequality that less privileged populations had because students are provided with meals, school supplies, uniform, psychological support, medical and assistance services, as well as tuition fees without any additional cost. It also has a fully equipped computer laboratory with internet connection, where students can use the equipment to do their homework.

That is why "rural Normal Schools were the only way by which farmers could socially ascend" (Padilla, 2009, p.88). Particularly for women, these schools "offered a new life option as gateway to study and work, because when they graduated a permanent position as teacher was granted, but also as a survival mode, because they offered scholarships so students could live in the boarding schools "(Civera, 2010, p. 5).

One peculiarity of the classes in Saucillo's Normal is that, since the 2017-2018 school year, 15 places were opened and reserved exclusively for indigenous students, increasing the enrollment by 20 for the 2019-2020, 2020-2021 and 2021-2022 school year. This type of educational policy is considered an affirmative action, which centers in "the affirmation and acknowledgment of linguistic and cultural diversity and the demands of wide indigenous sectors that claim the end of social inequality and exclusion" (Bermúdez, 2016, p. 81). They are projects implement differential measures to ensure the access, permanence and graduation of indigenous students (Ossola, 2016).

Since the health emergency declaration in March 2020, and the implementation of national precautionary measures, classes at ENRRFM were suspended and the campus resident students were instructed to return to their homes for as long as the contingency lasted. At the beginning, the education authorities extended the two weeks-vacation period to one month, which occurs between March and April, in the belief that the pandemic could be contained and regular school activities would be resumed. However, after that four week break, and due to the high infection levels and the risk of going back to face to face classes, the authorities prolonged social distancing safe distance measures until the end of the school year. Consequently, to continue the work that was being carried out in class and in order to cover the rest of the semester program, it was decided that a virtual teaching strategy should be implemented, from first to third grade (fourth grade students had already finished their curricular credits and were working on their thesis report).

However, in order to take part of a virtual education learning system, students must have at least the basic resources, both technical and internet connection. The students of ENRRFM belong to a low socioeconomic level so they do not have the monetary resources to acquire that equipment. Additionally, they come from isolated and remote communities that do not have internet access and, in some cases, not even telephone service. Most of the institution's students are from rural backgrounds, and according to the latest National Survey about Availability and ICT use in the Homes (2019) conducted by the National Institute of Statistics and Geography (INEGI), only 47.7% of the population rural areas nationwide are frequent internet users. Another drawback for the students when it comes to study form home is the fact they must get a job in order to contribute in the family economy.

The following table, shows the number of indigenous students that have entered this school in each school year, since the affirmative action program was created in 2017. It is worth noting that, although 15 to 20 spaces are exclusive for indigenous undergraduates, the demand is not always as high as to being able to cover that number with potential candidates.

Table 1. Indigenous students per school year

2017-2018	2018-2019	2019-2020	2020-2021	2021-2022
15	13	12	14	20

Source: *(data provided by school administrators)*

In the next chart, the number of students for each school year is showed, according to their indigenous group. It is evident that the largest are the ones that local to the state where the school is located, such as the Tarahumaras and Tepehuanes. Mayo and Pima are located in the nearby state of Sonora. The rest (Náhutal, Mixteco, Zapoteco and Tlapaneco) are from the south of the country.

Finally, table 3 includes the number of indigenous students according to their group and state or origin. Since the normal school is located in the state of Chihuahua, most of the indigenous groups represented are from that state or the ones that are close to it, such as Durango and Sonora.

Experiences and Challenges of Indigenous Students in Higher Education During the Pandemic

Table 2. Students' distribution according to their indigenous group

	Tarahumara	Tepehuan	Mayo	Pima	Náhuatl	Mixteco	Zapoteco	Chinanteco	Tlapaneco
2017	11	4	0	0	0	0	0	0	0
2018	6	6	1	0	0	0	0	0	0
2019	5	4	0	0	0	0	1	1	1
2020	7	5	0	1	0	1	0	0	0
2021	12	1	3	1	3	0	0	0	0
Total	41	20	4	2	3	1	1	1	1

Source: *(data provided by school administrators)*

Table 3. Distribution according to state

Chihuahua		Durango		Sonora		Guerrero		Veracruz		Oaxaca	
Tarahumara	41	Tepehuan	8	Mayo	4	Náhuatl	3	Chinanteco	1	Mixteco	1
Tepehuan	8			Pima	2	Tlapaneco	1			Zapoteco	1
Total:	49			Total:	6	Total:	4			Total:	2

Source: *(data provided by school administrators)*

Theoretical Framework

Online Education

Online learning does not only require the equipment or connectivity, but also the knowledge needed to use those tools or artefacts. According to Svensson and Baelo (2015) the European Commission established in 2006 the definition of digital competence as "the know-how, and is related to attitudes, confidence and critical use of the ICT to ensure the active participation of the citizens in society and the economy" (p. 1527). The term digital literacy is also important and relevant in this area, understood by Coffin and Perez (2014) as a concept built on the principles of "skills and knowledge to access and use a variety of hardware devices and software applications, adeptness to understand and critically analyse digital content and applications and ability to create with digital technology" (p.86).

All this becomes a problem when, in an online learning environment, such as the one that had to be implemented during the recent pandemic, teachers face the fact that that the students do not possess the necessary skills to continue their studies this way (Gallardo-Echenique et al., 2015). Undergraduates' self-perception of their digital competence coincides with this finding, in aspects such as internet browsing and email use (Danner and Pesu, 2013) or general skills needed with digital technologies for learning (Blayone et al., 2018). Ahmad, Karim, Din and Mohd (2013) explain that one cause for this situation is that young adults believe that they have highly developed technological skills because they use the internet every day, so they are less interested in learning how to use search engines in a more critical way.

That is why is important to take into consideration the socioeconomic context of their students and what it allows them to accomplish in terms of online education, in terms of having suitable equipment and an adequate internet connection (Pérez-López, Vázquez and Cambero, 2021). For example, Bonal and González (2020) highlight how the digital divide and differences in access to technological devices among students leaves individuals with fewer options to access online education. Also, Fishbane and Tomer (2020) state that "as the level of poverty increases in the community, the rate of internet accessibilities declined rapidly and by implications, students with no or low socio-economic power to afford broadband connection are most vulnerable to fall behind" (p. 4). Moreover, Godeau et al. (2021), explain that social class disparities also have an impact in online education, since in homes in which parental educational levels are low, the access to digital resources is consequently low too.

Likewise, digital disparity is another phenomenon that increases during situations as the pandemic. According to Beaunoyer, Duperé and Guitton (2020) it refers to the "capacity, knowledge, motivation, and competence to access, process, engage and understand the information needed to obtains benefits from the use of digital technologies, such as computers, Internet, mobiles devices and applications" (p.1). For Esteban-Navarro et al. (2020), it is related to how we approach technological services (mobile telephones, computers and the internet), which in turn generates inequalities in opportunities to satisfy certain needs, such as education in this case. On the other hand, Azubuike, Adegboye and Quadri (2021) propose a similar concept which they name as digital divide, as a "sharp divide between two distinct groups and emphasises physical access to technology in absolute terms" (p. 2).

The Process of Constructing a Thesis Report

There are different researches whose main focus is the construction of a thesis in diverse educational levels, mainly bachelors and master's degree. For example, in his study about the challenges that master students experience in regards to the construction of their thesis, Escalante (2010) finds that the undergraduates feel they lack the necessary skills to create and conduct an investigation. The subjects in his study explain that the development of their thesis is an emotionally demanding task when they consider their personal competences. In addition, Kleijn et al. (2012) highlight the importance of the supervisor role when undergraduates are developing their dissertation, revealing that a close and strong relationship between tutor and student promotes a higher quality of work.

Another research that touches on this topic is the one conducted by Ramírez et al. (2017). They conclude that the process of writing a thesis test the skills, attitudes and knowledge that students assume that they have. Therefore, is a challenging activity for any undergraduate. Specially, to manage the frustration of experiencing difficulties in writing each chapter (particularly at the beginning), due to a lack of inspiration or fear of facing the blank page. Finally, they explain that students lack basic understanding of how to construct a theoretical and methodological framework.

Regarding the methodology and research designs, Donohue et al. (2021) find that data collection was an element of the student's dissertation that was more affected, since interviews and observations with human subjects were not possible to conduct because of the lockdown. Adding "even if data collection protocols could be modified for online delivery, some respondents found their target participants were less available, impacting recruitment and response rates "(p. 540). This is also shared by Alvarado et al. (2021), who state that the major pivot in the research process of many undergraduates was the methodological aspect.

Particularly, in regards to working on a dissertation during the Covid-19 pandemic, López, Pedraza and De León (2021) explain that the isolation measures that were implemented caused a change from face to face to virtual education, which consequently, provoked that problems such as inequality and school dropout to worsen. This new modality also showed the weaknesses in regards to the use and access of information technologies in both teachers and students, as well as in the technological infrastructure.

Likewise, the research and writing that the construction of a thesis involves, entails not only to overcome academic difficulties, but also personal, such as family, work and health issues, which became more complex during the pandemic.

In connection to this phenomenon, Arán (2021), examines, via a case study, the process that two indigenous students experience of creating a thesis to obtain their elementary education degree. It documents the challenges the undergraduates experienced during the Covid-19 pandemic, as well as their own difficulties since they had to write their document in Spanish when their native language is an indigenous one. Although they faced obstacles such as understanding scientific text and writing using a formal language, when this is contrasted with other studies, is evident that these are challenges that all students faced in one way or another, during the bachelor's degree, master and even PhD.

MAIN FOCUS OF THE CHAPTER

Issues, Controversies, Problems

Methodology

This study uses the phenomenological method with an interpretative framework, to document the experiences of the indigenous students during the almost two years that they had of distance learning education, using questionnaires and in-depth interviews with 15 key informants. The purpose of the phenomenological method, is to comprehend the complex experiences that people live, in order to raise awareness towards the meanings of the phenomenon that is being studied (Fuster, 2019). Likewise, the interpretative framework allows the researcher to deepen the analysis of the object of study, with open and emergent designs which can be contextualized (Ricoy, 2006). The analysis of the information is carried out using the steps proposed by Strauss and Corbin (2002) in order to analyze the results, categorize the information and relate it to the theoretical framework.

Participants

The key informants were selected though a convenience sample from the total population of indigenous students in the school during the time period where the study was conducted (35), according to their availability of time for an interview and to participate in the research. The following table shows the characteristics of the students, such as the indigenous group to which they belong, their state of origin and the semester they were studying.

Results

The results of the research will be presented in two categories: experience with online education in general and experience constructing the thesis or dissertation (which is divided in three subcategories: a) the writing process, b) working in an online setting and c) tutoring process)

Table 4. Key informants

Assigned number	Indigenous group	State	Semester
1	Rarámuri	Chihuahua	8th
2	Tepehuan	Durango	8th
3	Tepehuan	Durango	8th
4	Tarahumara	Chihuahua	7th
5	Tarahumara	Chihuahua	8th
6	Tepehuan	Chihuahua	7th
7	Tepehuan	Durango	5th
8	Tepehuan	Chihuahua	5th
9	Zapoteco	Oaxaca	5th
10	Tarahumara	Chihuahua	3rd
11	Tarahumara	Chihuahua	3rd
12	Tarahumara	Chihuahua	5th
13	Tepehuan	Durango	3rd
14	Mayo	Sonora	5th
15	Pima	Sonora	3rd

Source: *(data provided by the key informants)*

Experience with Online Education in General

Students identify few, but important positive aspects of online education, such as learning about different applications and platforms. They also mention that it gave them the opportunity to be more self-educated, by researching classes' topics because they did not have direct access to their teachers. According to one of the students: "I have the opportunity to know new ways of learning, I am more independent because I learned about some topics in an autonomous way" (p. 10). However, this is a sentiment that is not shared by the majority of the future teachers, as one of them explains:

It is a little bit complicated having to be part of distance education because there are topics that are not being understood in that way, and when we are in face to face classes our questions are answered in a direct and accurate way, nevertheless, online I have to research by my own and I do not know if what I find is correct or not, in order words, we go in the blind without a guide (p.8).

Nevertheless, the majority of the key informants cannot pinpoint advantages of online education, they agree that the lack of internet access and an adequate smart phone and computer equipment was an obstacle to continue with their teacher training. As Bonal and González (2020) note, the digital divide and differences in access to technological devices among students, leaves them with fewer options to continue with their education. The lack of understanding and adequate preparation is an area that worries them extremely, because they believe that they did not acquire the necessary skills and concepts needed for their future profession, as one of them expresses: "Essentially, I did not learn anything because my questions lead me to other questions that were never answered, I was more worried about turning in the activities than about learning (p.9)". The experience of this student, showcases how important it is that teachers take into consideration the specific circumstances of their pupils, especially when those conditions affect their performance in an online learning environment (Pérez-López, et al, 2021).

This is because students that live in poor communities not only have limited access to an internet connection, but their social context, such as the low educational parental levels (Godeau et al, 2021) and additional conflicts in their areas, such as violence induced by organized crime, make them more vulnerable to fall behind in their school achievement performance (Fishbane and Tomer, 2020).

During the pandemic I have been spending more time with my family, but I have neglected my education, because I have had many problems related to connectivity and because of not knowing how to use a computer as well as digital platforms where we had to do the activities. It is very hard for us as indigenous students because we live in a village and I have felt stressed because I did not know what to do. Being in my community does not help because there is a lot of organized crime (p. 13).

Besides the struggles they had related to the lack of internet access and appropriate equipment, students expressed feeling inadequate in their digital skills. In this regard, the concept of digital disparity becomes especially relevant, as it has increased during the pandemic, as described by Beaunoyer et. Al (2020). When they were asked about how they acquired their digital competence and knowledge in order to continue with their studies in an online setting, all of them expressed that platforms such as Google Classroom, Meet and Zoom were new for them. Even after one year of taking classes online, they confessed that they do have not mastered these abilities. One of the participants explains it in this way:

It is very hard to study at normal now with the pandemic, I think it has been like this for all universities because for young people, we do not have the knowledge to survive and study in a school that has worked with face-to-face classes for years. With online classes, we have a heavier workload, so we experience more frustration, stress. In some cases, I have even seen emotional crisis (p. 7).

The testimonies of the key informants agree with the conclusions of Gallardo-Echenique et al (2015), about students not possessing the necessary degree of digital competence to continue with their studies in an online learning environment. It also illustrates the concept of digital divide proposed by Azubuike et al (2021), which highlights the differences to physically access technology among the population.

Experience with Thesis Report

The last two syllabuses (2012 and 2018) for the bachelor's degree in elementary education of Normales schools, contemplate the subject thesis report Seminar in the seventh and eight semesters. The objective of this course is that students design and develop a thesis about a topic of their interest related to education, during their fourth and last year as university students. The professional competences that this subject reinforces are the use of different resources in educational research through different technological mediums and research sources, by applying the results that their research shows and by disseminating them (Arán, 2021).

During the 2021-2022 school year, indigenous students in fourth grade had to attend this course on line, since the cautionary measures implemented during the pandemic still continued. This implied that they no longer had access to the computer lab at the school, equipped with internet access and desktop computers in case they don't have a laptop. In this way, Normales Rurales Schools with their boarding school modality, reduce the socioeconomic inequalities of its students, by meeting their academic, health and food requirements. Back home, students did not have those needs covered, so they had to get a job to help maintain their families, this having less time to focus on their studies. When they entered the seventh semester of the 2020-2021 school year, students had to continue with their studies on line including the seminar to construct their thesis.

Writing the Thesis Report

The key informants of the 7th and 8th semester, identify the most difficult challenge in regard to their thesis, the use of formal language in their writing, as well as grammatical and spelling errors. One student explains that "my problem is writing and understanding Spanish, it is not my first language, so I still have a lot to learn and understand" (p. 3). In second place, they explain that is hard for them to understand scientific texts such as the peer reviewed research that they have to read in order to support their thesis, and, consequently, to paraphrase what the authors are proposing. In their own words: "When I started this research, the topic was really difficult for me because writing is hard for me, my language is limited as well and my biggest challenge is to research each author and paraphrase what they say" (p.5). This testimony is linked to the conclusions of Ramírez, et al (2017), who state that students often lack the necessary knowledge to correctly construct the theoretical and methodological framework of their document. Another participant explains:

I had a lot of difficulties, one of them was that, after I researched the concepts I had to explain them, and is a challenge to write using my own words but with formal language, I was really stucked in that, I could not find the words, and I felt pressure because I knew I had to finish, but at the same time do it with a lot of patience and finish the investigation (p.1).

The testimony of this interviewee underlines an important finding of the research conducted by Escalante (2010), since the students feel that they do not have the appropriate skills necessary to develop their thesis report adequately.

Students highlight the importance of the work their teachers do with them during the dissertation seminary, since they had video sessions each week in which the professors gave them feedback about their progress as well as explained the next chapter that they had to work on. The key informants expressed that their tutors used different strategies to attend the difficulties that they experienced, such as giving them examples, using simpler vocabulary words so they could understand them better and providing them with useful texts they could incorporate into their work. The teachers also considered the specific situations that the students were going through during the pandemic; for example, when the internet connection was not adequate they used phone calls or text messages to monitor their work. This finding is connected to what Kleijn et al, (2012) propose about the importance of the role of the supervisor with undergraduate students, and how a close relationship where they have constructive feedback and accompaniment can be a positive force that determines the quality of their research.

Working in the Thesis Report in an Online Setting

One of the things that the key informants comment more often is that, in their homes, they did not have a private space to have an online session with their thesis advisor, which also implied that they did not have a room of their own where they could concentrate and work on their chapters each week, struggling to pay attention to their work because of distractions at home like noises, presence of family members and other activities common to a household routine. This is because the construction of the thesis report during the pandemic, was affected by family, social, work and health issues (López, et al, 2021).

In second place, they explained that they experienced connection problems due to lack of Wi-Fi or a slow internet connection, and that weather conditions, such as the wind and rain affected the electricity at their homes. This situation impacted, not only the online session with their corresponding thesis director, but also the quality of the field work they had to accomplish, as one of them specifies: "I would have liked to see the people I interviewed and be able to talk to them, I struggled a little bit when I did the interviews online because my connection was not good and sometimes I could not hear correctly what they were saying" (p. 3). This shows how the pandemic impacted the methodology aspect of the thesis construction, since the undergraduates had difficulties accessing their interview subjects in order to collect the necessary data (Donohue et. Al, 2021).

Finally, they mentioned that, in some cases, they did not have a computer that worked correctly or a well-equipped cellphone. Also, they noted that, because they were at home, they had to help out with the chores and taking care of family members, and in some cases, find a job to help the family income. One of the testimonies encapsulates all of the mentioned above: "This new modality was very difficult because I live in a rural area and it lacks good cellphone signal and internet connection. It has been really stressful because I also have to work and do well at school" (p.1).

SOLUTIONS AND RECOMMENDATIONS

The pandemic provoked by the SARS-COV-2 virus, has profoundly impacted every aspect of our lives, and the educational area could not be any different. The emergence of this pandemic brought society into questioning different aspects of our everyday life that we used to take for granted: how do we work, how do we socially interact, what do we do with our free time and also how do we buy items; and, particular, how do we teach and learn. Although it can be assumed that all of these activities, including education, were previously permeated by the use of technology, there are segments of our society that have been historically excluded from accessing those tools, and the pandemic has only intensified this situation:

The pandemic could mean a new disadvantage for the education of low, middle low and middle socio-economic sectors of children and teenagers, deepening the inequality in education by presenting bigger limitations to access virtual education, which in some cases means no right to education (Quiroz, 2020, p.4).

Indigenous students are an example of a previously vulnerable group that has been negatively affected by this virus. In fact, Mexico is recognized as a multicultural country because of the numerous indigenous groups that live in it (Schmelkes, 2013). Unfortunately, as many other native communities around the world, they have a social and cultural history of discrimination, racism and exclusion, "in spite of a bigger acknowledgment of their rights (…) they have the highest poverty levels, deficient health and nutritional conditions and less access to education and health services" (Blanco, 2014, p. 22). This translates in five times higher illiteracy levels compared to the rest of the population (Schmelkes, 2013) and low schooling levels, 5.7 years in total (INEGI, 2015).

Affirmative action policies allow the access to higher education for marginalized population (Lloyd, 2016), such as indigenous students. It is a way to compensate the vulnerability of certain group of students, by reinforcing and complementing the differences of conditions in order to continue with their studies (Davinson, 2017). Nevertheless, is not enough to create opportunities for them to study a bachelor's degree in a university, like normal rural schools; actions and programs should be implemented to guarantee their permanence and conclusion of their higher education. The experiences of the students portrayed in this chapter reveal how the social gap between the different socioeconomic levels of our population increases in situations such as this global pandemic, creating more exclusion for social groups that are already vulnerable.

What can be done to mitigate the negative consequences that the pandemic is causing in the public higher educational context of Mexico? In regards to online education, according to Oyarzo (2011), one strategy that could be implemented in the long term, is to strengthen and develop students ICTS (Information and Communication technologies) learning competences as well as teacher's pedagogical digital competence (PDC), understood as the "ability to develop/improve pedagogical work by means of digital technology in a professional context, primarily in web course/online teaching" (p. 47). Beaunoyer, Duperé and Guitton (2020) propose a series of strategies that are focused on individuals" technology use, including increasing the physical access to connected devices and internet as well as developing digital literacy and social support measures. Also, Adedoyin and Soykan (2020) suggest that schools should collaborate with telecommunication industries to subsidize the cost of the internet connection and provide free browsing data. Furthermore, Ala Mutka, Punie and Redecker (2008) quoted in Opoku, Chen and Permadi (2022) suggest that universities should design platforms so students can learn digital skills. Finally, Gordeau et al, (2021) recommend that teachers monitor students in an individualized manner, as well as training sessions so they can become aware of cultural and psychological barriers that working class students face during online education.

Regarding the socioeconomic gap and how it impacts the access to online education, some countries have implemented palliative measures in the form of socio-economic support, such as food items, lower tuition costs, as well as psychological and medical assistance for students (Adedoyin and Soykan, 2020). Gordeau et al, (2021), suggest to concentrate resources on the students that are more deprived, by providing equipment and internet connection for low-income families, as well as gather financial support for remedial courses. Another possible intervention, according to Bono, Reil and Hescox (2020) is to design online accessible interventions to help specifically university students, address stress, depression and wellbeing. Also, Blaskó, Da Costa and Schnepf (2022) stress that schools and teachers need to be prepared for more lockdowns in the future due to another pandemic, and that "education policies need to target directly the most disadvantaged students to decrease the worst effects of learning inequalities deriving from home schooling" (p. 12).

FUTURE RESEARCH DIRECTIONS

First person testimonies of the protagonists of this phenomenon become relevant in order to comprehend their current situation, as it has the potential to contribute to a better understanding of the problem and thus to generate adequate solutions to address it. Consequently, the interpretative framework and phenomenological method offer an ideal path to give them a space to share their voices through the description of their experiences. Another recommended methodology would be the biographical-narrative approach, which enables the creation of knowledge that can transform, thus becoming political action (Schöngut and Pujol, 2015) and are a way to give voice to different subjects in order to emphasize their experiences (Susinos and Parrilla, 2008).

According to Lloyd (2016), structural studies that focus on the tensions and conflicts that surround affirmative action policies are also needed, in regard to public policies. As a future line of research, a study to compare and contrast different universities in the Latin-American context that implement these types of policies with indigenous students would be appropriate, also specifically among the rural normales schools; in order to share successful strategies and implemented programs. Specifically, it would be interesting to address how each institution has managed the health emergency caused by the SARS-COV-2 virus, since, as agreed by Quijada (2021), the affirmative action programs she examined of Brazil, Colombia and Mexico, have not yet designed nor implemented special measures for the students who have been affected by the global pandemic.

In regards to online education and digital disparity, Azubuike et al. (2021) state that there is a need to understand the digital divide as schools reopen, and to examine how "digital skills development during the pandemic for some children may further exacerbate social and educational inequalities" (p. 8). Likewise, Esteban-Navarro et al (2021) propose as a line of research and social intervention, to create and deploy training programs to improve social communication processes in rural areas.

CONCLUSION

Bonal and González (2020) explain that each individual has been affected by the pandemic and the school lockdown in a different way, so an educational emergency plan, that includes both social and educational objectives, should be in place in all educational institutions. One of the outcomes that this research highlights is the argument for the existence of rural normal schools in the context of Mexico's educational system, since they are institutions that perform a fundamental role in diminishing the socioeconomic gap and thus securing access and permanence in higher education for vulnerable populations, such as indigenous students, through affirmative action policies such as the one that has been in place since 2017 in ENRRFM. Nevertheless, unexpected situations such as the worldwide health emergency reveal the necessity to implement different actions and strategies during emergencies such as the one that we are experiencing, in order to stop the socioeconomic gap and digital disparity to continue growing.

Since the undergraduates are part of a vulnerable and often excluded population, the school lockdown and isolation part of the pandemic has been an enormous challenge, due to their lack of suitable computer equipment, internet connection and a poorly developed digital competence. For the ones that had to do their dissertation in order to obtain their bachelor's degree, the above mentioned factors plus the fact that they had to write in a second language meant an added difficulty. Therefore, this document illustrates how necessary it has become to examine, in order to understand, the experiences that graduate and undergraduate students have had during the pandemic, and how it may differ when compared with other time periods (Opoku, Chen and Permadi, 2022).

REFERENCES

Ahmad, M., Karim, A. A., Din, R., & Mohd, I. S. (2013). Assessing ICT Competencies among Postgraduate Students Based on the 21st Century ICT Competency Model. *International Journal of Educational Technology in Higher Education, 15*(37), 2–22. https://doi.org/10.1186/s41239-018-0119-9

Alvarado, C., García, L., Gilliam, N., Minckler, S., & Samay, C. (2021). Pandemic Pivots: The Impact of a Global Health Crisis on the Dissertation in Practice. *Journal of Transforming Professional Practice, 6*(2), 5-10. doi:10.5195/ie.2021.165

Arán, A. (2021). Preparation of a bachelor's thesis in times of pandemic: a case study [Elaboración de una tesis de licenciatura en tiempos de pandemia: un estudio de caso]. In *Un año de pandemia, miradas desde la educación* (299-328). Colofón.

Azubuike, O. B., Adegboye, O., & Quadri, H. (2021). Who gets to learn in a pandemic? Exploring the digital divide in remote learning during the COVID-19 pandemic in Nigeria. *International Journal of Educational Research Open, 2*, 100022. doi:10.1016/j.ijedro.2020.100022 PMID:35059664

Beaunoyer, E., Duperé, S., & Guitton, M. (2020). COVID-19 and digital inequalities: Reciprocal impacts and mitigation strategies. *Computers in Human Behavior, 111*, 1–9. doi:10.1016/j.chb.2020.106424 PMID:32398890

Bello, A., & Rangel, M. (2002). Equity and exclusion of indigenous and Afro-descendant peoples in Latin America and the Caribbean [La equidad y la exclusión de los pueblos indígenas y afrodescendientes en América Latina y el Caribe]. *Revista Cepal, 76*, 39–54. doi:10.18356/61fc0d54-es

Bermúdez, F. M. (2016). Affirmative action, discrimination and denial of linguistic and cultural rights in Mexican higher education [Acción afirmativa, discriminación y negación de derechos lingüísticos y culturales en la educación superior mexicana]. *Revista de Derechos Humanos y Estudios Sociales, 16*, 79-97. http://www.derecho.uaslp.mx/Paginas/REDHES/N%C3%BAmero-16.aspx

Blanco, R. (2014). *Educational inclusion in Latin America: paths traveled and to be traveled. Advances and challenges of inclusive education in Ibero-America* [Inclusión educativa en América Latina: caminos recorridos y por recorrer. Avances y desafíos de la educación inclusiva en Iberoamérica]. Madrid, Spain: Organización de Estados Iberoamericanos. https://www.observatoriodelainfancia.es/oia/esp/documentos_ficha.aspx?id=4275

Blaskó, Z., Da Costa, P., & Schnepf, S. V. (2022). Learning losses and educational inequalities in Europe: Mapping the potential consequences of the COVID-19 crisis. *Journal of European Social Policy, 32*(4), 1–15. doi:10.1177/09589287221091687

Blayone, T., Mykhailenko, O., Kavtaradze, M., Kokhan, M., vanOostveen, R., & Barber, W. (2018). Profiling the digital readiness of higher education students for transformative online learning in the post-soviet nations of Georgia and Ukraine. *International Journal of Educational Technology in Higher Education, 15*(37), 1–22.

Bonal, X., & González, S. (2020). The impact of lockdown on the learning gap: Family and school divisions in times of crisis. *International Review of Education, 66*(5-6), 635–655. doi:10.100711159-020-09860-z PMID:32952208

Bono, G., Reil, K., & Hescox, J. (2020). Stress and wellbeing in college students during the COVID-19 pandemic: Can grit and gratitude help? *International Journal of Wellbeing, 10*(3), 39–57. doi:10.5502/ijw.v10i3.1331

Civera, A. (2010). Women, school and life choices: rural normalista students in Mexico in the fifties [Mujeres, escuela y opciones de vida: las estudiantes normalistas rurales en México en los años cincuenta]. *Naveg@mérica, La Asociación Española de Americanista,* (4), 1-13. https://revistas.um.es/navegamerica/article/view/99881

Coffin, M., & Perez, J. (2014). Unraveling the digital literacy paradox: how high education fails at the fourth literacy. Issues in Informing Science and Information Technology, 11 85-100. https://doi.org/10.28945/1982

Davinson, G. (2017). University Education and Indigenous Peoples1 in Chile: A Program of Affirmative Action [Educación universitaria y pueblos indígenas1 en Chile: Un programa de acción afrimativa]. *Cuadernos del Cordicom, 3,* 137-158. https://repositorio.consejodecomunicacion.gob.ec//handle/CONSEJO_REP/644

Elortegui, M. (2017). A historical tour of the Rural Normal Schools of Mexico: The subversive act of remembering the events against the students of Ayotzinapa [Un recorrido histórico de las Escuelas Normales Rurales de México: el acto subversivo de hacer memoria desde los acontecimientos contra los estudiantes de Ayotzinapa]. *Estudios Latinoamericanos NUEVA ÉPOCA, 40,* 157–178. doi:10.22201/cela.24484946e.2017.40.61600Hi

Escalante, E. (2010). The descriptive and phenomenological analysis of problems in the preparation of master's theses [El análisis descriptivo y fenomenológico de problemas en la elaboración de tesis de maestría]. *Reencuentro, 57,* 38-47. https://www.redalyc.org/articulo.oa?id=34012514006

Esteban-Navarro, M. A., García-Madurga, M. A., Morte-Nadal, T., & Nogales-Bocio, A. I. (2020). The rural digital divide in the face of the COVID-19 pandemic in Europe- Recommendations from a scoping review. *Informatics (MDPI), 7*(54), 1–18. doi:10.3390/informatics7040054

Fishbane, L., & Tomer, A. (2020). *As classes move online during COVID-19, what are disconnected students to do?* Brookings. https://www.brookings.edu/blog/the-avenue/2020/03/20/as-classes-move-online-during-covid-19-whatare-disconnected-students-to-do/

Fuster, D. E. (2019). Qualitative research: Hermeneutic phenomenological method [Investigación cualitativa: Método fenomenológico hermenéutico]. *Propósitos y Representaciones, 7*(1), 201–229. doi:10.20511/pyr2019.v7n1.267

Gallardo, E., De Oliveira, J. M., Marqués-Molias, L., & Esteve-Mon, F. (2015). Digital Competence in the Knowledge Society. *Journal of Online Learning and Teaching / MERLOT, 11*(1), 1–16. https://jolt.merlot.org/vol11no1/abstracts.htm

Goudeau, S., Sanrey, C., Stanczak, A., Manstead, A. & Darnon, c. (2021). Why lockdown and distance learning during the COVID-19 pandemic are likely to increase the social class achievement gap. Nature-Human Behavior, 5, 1273–1281. https://www.nature.com/articles/s41562-021-01212-7

Horbath, J. E., & García, A. (2012) Social backwardness and discrimination of social policy towards indigenous groups in Sonora [Rezago social y discriminación de la política social hacia los grupos indígenas en Sonora]. *Revista de relaciones internacionales, estrategia y seguridad, 7*(1), 173-189. http://www.scielo.org.co/scielo.php?script=sci_abstract&pid=S190930632012000100008&lng=es&nrm=iso&tlng=es

Kleijn, R. A., Mainhard, M. T., Meijer, P. C., Pilot, A., & Brekelmans, M. (2012). Master's thesis supervision: Relations between perceptions of the supervisor–student relationship, final grade, perceived supervisor contribution to learning and student satisfaction. *Studies in Higher Education, 37*(8), 925–939.

Lloyd, M. (2016). A decade of affirmative action policies in Brazilian higher education: Impacts, scope and future [Una década de políticas de acción afirmativa en la educación superior brasileña: impactos, alcances y futuro]. *Revista de la Educación Superior, 45*(178), 17–29. doi:10.1016/j.resu.2016.02.002

López, E., Pedraza, C. A., & De León, D. A. (2019). Research and resilience in times of pandemic [Investigación y resiliencia en tiempos de pandemia]. *Reencuentro: Educación y COVID, 31*(78), 54-72. https://reencuentro.xoc.uam.mx/index.php/reencuentro/article/view/1021

National Institute of Statistics and Geography. (2015). *Intercensal survey 2015* [Encuesta intercensal 2015]. Retrieved July 23rd, 2022 from https://www.inegi.org.mx/programas/intercensal/2015/

National Institute of Statistics and Geography. (2018). *National Survey on Availability and Use of Information Technologies in Households 2018* [Encuesta Nacional sobre Disponibilidad y uso de Tecnologías de la Información en los Hogares 2018]. Retrieved July 23rd, 2022 from www.inegi.org.mx/programas/dutih/2018

Opoku, E. K., Chen, L. H., & Permadi, S. (2022). The dissertation journey during the COVID-19 pandemic: Crisis or opportunity? *Journal of Hospitality, Leisure, Sport & Tourism Education, 30*, 1-9.

Ossola, M. (2016). Indigenous Peoples and Higher Education in Argentina: Emerging Debates [Pueblos indígenas y educación superior en la Argentina: debates emergentes]. *Revista del Cisen Tramas/Maepova, 4*(1), 57-77. http://ppct.caicyt.gov.ar/index.php/cisen/index

Oyarzo, F. (2011). Competencies for the 21st century: Integrating ICT to life, school and economical development. *Procedia: Social and Behavioral Sciences, 28*, 54–57. doi:10.1016/j.sbspro.2011.11.011

Padilla, T. (2009). The Rural Normal Schools: History and nation project [Las Normales Rurales: historia y proyecto de nación]. *El Cotidiano, 154*, 85–93.

Quijada, K. Y. (2021). Affirmative actions for the university inclusion of Afro-descendant and indigenous students in Brazil, Colombia and Mexico [Acciones afirmativas para la inclusión universitaria de estudiantes afrodescendientes e indígenas en Brasil, Colombia y México]. *Ciencia y Cultura, 46,* 135–162. http://www.scielo.org.bo/pdf/rcc/v25n46/v25n46_a07.pdf

Quiroz Reyes, C. (2020). Covid-19 Pandemic and Territorial Inequality: The Aggravation of Educational Inequalities in Chile [Pandemia Covid-19 e Inequidad Territorial: El agravamiento de las Desigualdades Educativas en Chile]. *Revista Internacional de Educación para la Justicia Social, 9*(3), 1–6.

Ramírez García, R. G., Pérez Colunga, B. Y., Soto Bernabé, A. K., Mendoza Tovar, M., Coiffier López, F. Y., Gleason Guevara, K. J., & Flores Zuñiga, J. A. (2017). Disassembling the puzzle around the experience of preparing a master's thesis [Desarmando el rompecabezas en torno a la experiencia de elaboración de una tesis de maestría]. *Perfiles educativos, 39*(155), 68-86.

Ricoy, C. (2006). Contribution on research paradigms [Contribución sobre los paradigmas de investigación]. *Revista do Centro Educação, 31*(1), 11–11.

Salas, L. (2018). The educational policy of the Mexican state in relation to the initial training of teachers in rural normal schools [La política educativa del estado mexicano en relación a la formación inicial del profesorado de las escuelas normales rurales]. *Didácticas Específicas, 4,* 77–95.

Schmelkes, S. (2013). Education and indigenous peoples: Measurement problems [Educación y pueblos indígenas: problemas de medición]. *Realidad, Datos y Espacio: Revista Internacional de Estadistica y Geografia, 4*(1), 5–13.

Schöngut, N., & Pujol, J. (2015). Methodological stories: Diffracting narrative experiences of research [Relatos metodológicos: difractando experiencias narrativas de investigación]. *Forum Qualitative Social Research, 16*(2), 24.

Strauss, A., & Corbin, J. (2002). *Bases of qualitative research. Techniques and procedures to develop grounded theory* [Bases de la investigación cualitativa. Técnicas y procedimientos para desarrollar la teoría fundamentada]. Universidad de Antioquía.

Susinos, T., & Parrilla, A. (2008). Give voice in inclusive research. Debates on inclusion and exclusion from a biographical-narrative approach [Dar la voz en la investigación inclusiva. Debates sobre inclusión y exclusión desde un enfoque biográfico-narrativo]. *Revista Electrónica Iberoamericana sobre Calidad, Eficacia y Cambio en Educación, 6*(2), 151–171.

Svenson, M., & Baelo, R. (2015). Teacher Students' Perceptions of their Digital Competence. *Procedia: Social and Behavioral Sciences, 180*(5), 1527–1534. doi:10.1016/j.sbspro.2015.02.302

Trejo-Quintana, J. (2020). The lack of access to and use of means and technologies: two deudas of education in Mexico [La falta de acceso y aprovechamiento de los medios y las tecnologías: dos deudas de la educación en México]. In *Educación y pandemia: una visión académica* (pp. 122-129). Universidad Nacional Autónoma de México, Instituto de Investigaciones sobre la Universidad y la Educación. https://www.iisue.unam.mx/nosotros/covid/educacion-y-pandemia

KEY TERMS AND DEFINITIONS

Affirmative Action: Policy in the higher educational level to include a particular group of students based on a specific characteristic. In the case of this study, the affiliation to an indigenous group.

Mayo: Or Yoreme, they live in the states of Sonora and Sinaloa. The origin of their name comes from the Mayo river.

Mixteco: Also known as the Mixtecs, they live in Oaxaca and Puebla. Is one of the most important group of the Mesoamerican era of the history of Mexico.

Náhuatl: Is the largest indigenous group in Mexico, and its language has many variants. They live in the central part of Mexico.

Normal Rural School: Public Mexican universities in Latin America that educate students to become preschool and elementary school teachers.

Pima: Indigenous group located in Mexico in the state of Chihuahua and Sonora, their name means "river people".

Tarahumara: Or Raramuri, a group of indigenous people that live in the state of Chihuahua, Mexico. Their name means "runners by feet".

Tepehuan: Group of indigenous people that live in the northwestern of Mexico, specifically the state of Chihuahua and Durango. They are divided in Ódami (Northern Tepehuán) and O'dam (Southeastern Tepehuan).

Zapoteco: An indigenous group mainly located in the state of Oaxaca, Mexico. One of the most developed civilization during the Mesoamerican period.

ENDNOTE

[1] Public Mexican universities in Latin America that educate students to become preschool and elementary school teachers.

Chapter 15

What to Keep, What to Discard:
Remaking an Instructional Design Service Post Pandemic

Shalin Hai-Jew
iD https://orcid.org/0000-0002-8863-0175
Kansas State University, USA

ABSTRACT

As humanity seems to be moving ahead from the novel SARS-CoV-2/COVID-19 pandemic, people are reckoning with the changes adopted during the high-stress period, of unprecedented threats to lives and health, lockdowns and reopenings, social tensions, and political strife. Instructional design (ID) work at a university also underwent some seminal changes. This work explores what changes to keep and what to discard, based on a SWOT (strengths, weaknesses, opportunities, and threats) analysis and a grounding of some 17 years of ID work and decades of prior college and university teaching work.

INTRODUCTION

The advent of SARS-CoV-2, as a human-transmissible pathogen, forced humanity into social distancing and lockdowns for the better part of two years from 2000 onwards. With varying outbreaks through the present and incomplete immunizations, the lockdowns have continued through the present. During the pandemic, some 1.5 billion students experienced learning disruptions, and a percentage of these shifted to online learning (where infrastructure was available). Teachers, too, had to shift to virtuality, along with administrators and staff. Instructional designers found their roles shifting.

Instructional design, broadly speaking, is defined as "the iterative, systematic design of effective learning experiences by following a coherent process that gives measurable results" (Bart & Shaffer, 2016, p. 240). In the SARS-CoV-2 / COVID-19 pandemic (2020 – present), instructional designers had to support the emergency remote teaching. One study found that "their role shift focused on building relationships within the university community" and "gathering, organizing, and distributing resources,

DOI: 10.4018/978-1-6684-5934-8.ch015

Copyright © 2023, IGI Global. Copying or distributing in print or electronic forms without written permission of IGI Global is prohibited.

designing faculty course development workshops, providing technology support, and advocating for students and for their profession" (Xie & Rice, 2021, p. 70).

With advances in medicine and healthcare, government policies, workplace hygiene, humanity is moving slowly away from the pandemic and its restrictions. There is now more space to consider adaptations made during the acute phases of the pandemic (late-2019 to mid-2022) and to see what to keep and what to discard. The particular position, in the years leading up to the pandemic and through the pandemic, has been used to fulfill various needs for weekly trainings (on various office and research and online learning technologies), to support graduate students in their theses and dissertations, to support research, to support usage of a range of technologies, to pursue grant funds, and other endeavors. This work explores the remaking of an ID position "post-pandemic". Based on a SWOT (strengths, weaknesses, opportunities, and threats) analysis of the larger world post-pandemic, the realm of higher education, and the particular university, what makes sense to strategically advance and to retract.

The interrelated research questions include the following:

- What was the state of instructional design services at the Midwestern university prior to the pandemic?
- How did the service menu change during the pandemic?
- What standards should be applied to assessing the instructional design service?
- What service menu changes are worth keeping, and which should be discarded? Why?

This work offers some initial insights.

REVIEW OF THE LITERATURE

Instructional design may be achieved through a range of different frameworks or theories. These methods may be applied to complete new learning builds or to existing ones (for further refinement). A training course was developed on how to plan and create courses for distance learning for quality, for use in multiple countries in a region (Neto, Nolan, & Mendes, 2021, p. 201). There are pedagogical frameworks and approaches shared transnationally (Granić, Mifsud, & Ćukušić, 2009, p. 1057).

Transcoding courses from face-to-face to online learning courses is no easy feat. One research work involves transcoding active-learning based courses into "e-active" courses online (Belcadhi & Ghannouchi, 2013, p. 119). Hybrid instruction, which combines face-to-face (F2F) and online learning, may be designed for higher quality learning outcomes (Wood, Bonakdarian, & Whittaker, 2012, p. 6). One research team suggests that a social constructivist approach to designing learning may be based on the ICAP (Identity, Community, Activity, and Personal) design framework (Chen & Hung, 2007, p. 127), for more effective communities of practice. One work explores a method for the design of learning in resource-constrained environments, through functional design. Here, the instructional designer applies various layers to the design, with each layer informed by their own theory; the layers enable a systematized orderliness in decision making. Here, "instructional conversations" are divided into various functions: representational, messaging, user control, content, strategic (in a pedagogic sense), data management, and "media-logic" functions (Gibbons, 2009, pp. 2 - 3). A more recent work suggests that design conflicts may be resolved in interactive learning environments (ILEs) by setting and following goal hierarchies,

What to Keep, What to Discard

conducting "parameter experiments" and "cross-iteration studies" as controlled experiments, so as to use method and empirical findings to inform design decisions (Rau et al., 2013, p. 114).

Universal instructional design involves the use of "inclusive instructional strategies that benefit the broadest range of learners" in terms of learning styles (Rutherfoord & Rutherfoord, 2008, 2009, p. 1), and these principled approaches have been applied broadly (Rutherfoord & Rutherfoord, 2008, p. 45), including to learning in virtual worlds (Rutherfoord & Rutherfoord, 2007, p. 141). Multicultural instructional design, based on integrated multicultural instructional design (IMID), enables social inclusions to benefit the learning for all (Schultz & Higbee, 2011). Various "ethno" curriculums harness the informal and nonformal learning from homes and communities to benefit complex formal learning.

Novice instructional designers apply various types of judgment in their work, based on the particulars of their context and their working case. The various judgments may include the following: "framing judgment, default judgment, off-hand judgment, appreciative judgment, appearance judgment, quality judgment, instrumental judgments, navigational judgment, compositional judgment, connective judgment, core judgment, (and) mediative judgment" (Nelson & Stolterman, 2012, as cited in Zhu, Basdogan, & Bonk, 2020, pp. 4-5). With the acquisition of more experiences, more knowledge, training, more of the decisions become pro forma.

Contemporary instructional design uses learner data in various ways. One approach harnesses learner data from a learning platform in order to ultimately improve the instructional design of the course (Molina-Carmona et al., 2017, p. 1).

Users of the learning have come to the fore in various design approaches. One work suggests a needs analysis to ensure that learners can use the created contents and technologies (Murphy, Teng, & Matusky, 2014). If e-learning is held back by the fact that technologies are "still limited to just being online repositories," there may be benefits from personalization and customization of the learning based on information about the learners (Teo & Gay, 2006, p. 1).

How learners respond to the teaching and learning offers other sources of information data-driven design. One work involves the tracking of student eye fixation patterns and clustering their behaviors into different types of learners. The researchers were able to identify three main patterns and then to associate the respective patterns to learning performance. They found the benefit of learners understanding the fundamentals of the various tasks and then applying their learning to solve the problems instead of just going to the hints and rushing to an answer (The & Mavrikis, 2016, p. 411). Learners do better when they engage in the learning, for learning achievement.

Another approach harnesses "the instructional power of multiple conceptions," instead of merely conveying direct knowledge to learners. Here, constructivism is used to let students create the knowledge themselves. By comparing multiple conceptions of a learning topic, based on the "multiple conceptions theory," learners are better able to capture a more nuanced sense of the topic. There are various forms of incorrect conceptions, with various features, such as incompleteness ("missing knowledge"), erroneous information, misconceptions from "the misapplication of prior knowledge to a new concept," and / or some combination of the prior (Margulieux, Denny, Cunningham, Deutsch, & Shapiro, 2021, p. 185). There are a range of techniques for comparing the multiple conceptions: "test-enhanced learning, erroneous examples, analogical reasoning, refutation texts, productive failure, ambitious pedagogy, problem-based learning, inquiry/discovery learning," and various combinations (Margulieux, Denny, Cunningham, Deutsch, & Shapiro, 2021, pp. 186-189). These multiple conceptions approach involves using various instructional techniques, including "test-enhanced learning, erroneous examples, analogical reasoning, refutation texts, productive failure, ambitious pedagogy, problem-based learning, (and) inquiry learning" (Margulieux et al., 2021, p. 191).

The research literature includes particular case-based works, with a variety of pedagogical methods. One uses a small project-based teaching mode (Wang, Wu, & Li, 2018, p. 12). Another described mobile apps for language learning (Safonov et al., 2021, p. 89). Another case involved the design of an embodied interaction design. Here, a "bodily-syntonic" experience was designed to promote "both mathematics learning and physical exercise" (Charoenying, 2013, p. 495), for real-space learning. One work describes an ambitious curricular design: supporting students in engaging in novel research design in an international context (Damian et al., 2012). Another approach strives to train skills that are "flexible, adaptive and creative" rather than mere "technical and procedural skills" given "an uncertain and variable environment" (Field et al., 2011, p. 27) in the field of crisis management. To understand the complexity of trainee exercises, a "variable uncertainty framework" was created and applied (Field et al., 2011, p. 34).

The focus on learner retention has led to gamifying particular courses. Indeed, game design is seen to inform instructional design, and vice versa (Bayliss & Schwartz, 2009, p. 10). Instructional design features have been integrated into game design tools (Ahmad, Law, & Moseley, 2020). Learners benefit from effective feedback systems to enhance their learning experience. Some instructional designs focus on particular learner groups and their particular needs (Orth & Bastiaens, 2008). There are methods to understand how learners are facing complexity (and high cognitive load) in the particular learning tasks and to design to their experience (Duran, 2018). In some cases, learners or users of the learning contents are brought into the participatory design process (Correia & Yusop, 2008). There are efforts to integrate social media and the Social Web into particular learning objectives (Celik, Torre, & Torsani, 2017, p. 19).

Identifying relevant multimedia for learning involves a process that is "a complex and interdisciplinary problem characterized by uncertainty, dynamics, explicit and implicit knowledge and constraints, and involvement of different stakeholders" (Abdelhakim & Shirmohammadi, 2007, p. 27). To help teachers identify relevant educational multimedia, one research team has created a Web-based group decision support system.

What to Keep, What to Discard: Remaking Instructional Design Post-Pandemic

Traditionally, instructional design (ID) is focused on the design, development, and deployment of teaching and learning experiences. This work involved the following: direct one-on-one and small-group consultations with faculty, analyses of online courses and digital learning objects, the design and development of various courses (from research to design to development to deployment), educational research, and others. The distributed nature of teaching and learning on a university campus, and the variance between disciplines, has always resulted in variability in terms of client needs on various projects. The instructional designs tend to be "boutique" ones, even as there are e-learning quality rubrics and checklists widely distributed on the campus. There are also course redesigns and retrofits, to update the learning. All instructional designs fall under a raft of laws for privacy protections, intellectual property protections, mass media laws, accessibility requirements, and others. The courses may be face-to-face (F2F) ones, some fully online, and some blended / hybrid (involving both some face-to-face and some fully online learning). In terms of virtuality, the technologies may be learning management systems (LMSes), content management systems (CMSes), social media platforms, virtual worlds, game worlds, and other technologies.

What to Keep, What to Discard

There are side projects, such as supporting faculty with editing and research for book projects. There is also committee work on campus, such as supporting open-access book publishing, hiring committees, training committees, and so on. And there are external projects, such as supporting non-profit professional organizations.

During the pandemic, the workload doubled or even quadrupled given the resignations, the furloughs, and the non-continuation of contracts. "Supervision" in some cases dwindled to the occasional Zoom meeting. Technologies started to age out, without replacement. People are under stress and duress, given the threat to lives, livelihoods, health, finances, and other challenges. To set a basic context, some observations about the local instructional design context have been recorded. (Table 1)

This research is based on four interrelated research questions. A summary of those findings may be seen in Table 2.

Table 1. Local instructional design during pre-pandemic, during pandemic, and post-pandemic phases

	Pre-Pandemic	**During Pandemic**	**Post-Pandemic**
Complimentary Work	Trainings (for the university, particular units, courses, one-on-one, projects, student clubs, and others) Initial analytics	Trainings (for the university, particular units, courses, one-on-one, projects, student clubs, and others) Initial analytics	Trainings (for the university, particular units, courses, one-on-one, projects, student clubs, and others) Initial analytics
Paid Projects	Research Pedagogical analysis Data analytics Data visualization Digital content creation IP / copyright pursuit Survey creation Design, development, and deployment Documentation Assessment creation Grant writing	Research Pedagogical analysis Data analytics Data visualization Digital content creation IP / copyright pursuit Survey creation Design, development, and deployment Documentation Assessment creation Grant writing	Research Pedagogical analysis Data analytics Data visualization Digital content creation IP / copyright pursuit Survey creation Design, development, and deployment Documentation Assessment creation Grant writing
Extra-Instructional Design Work	Graduate student ETDRs (electronic theses, dissertations, and reports) Support and troubleshooting for survey support system Support for the campus LMS Others	Graduate student ETDRs (electronic theses, dissertations, and reports) Support and troubleshooting for survey support system Support for the campus LMS Others	Support and troubleshooting for survey support system Support for the campus LMS Others

Table 2. Four interrelated research questions

Four Research Questions	Initial Answers
• What was the state of instructional design services at the Midwestern university prior to the pandemic?	Light presence on campus Paid for under a university rate card Involving a range of services, both *gratis* and for pay Often negotiated politically between individuals
• How did the service menu change during the pandemic?	More support for faculty transitioning from F2F and hybrid to fully online teaching and learning (in a context of duress) Onboarding of extra ETDR services Onboarding of extra hours
• What standards should be applied to assessing the instructional design service?	Variable valuing of need based on various dimensions (legacy commitments, source of the request, political clout, payment or non-payment, ITS or not, and other factors)
• What service menu changes are worth keeping, and which should be discarded? Why?	Continuance of prior services (ID, training, support, and others) Pursuit of grant funds Discontinuance of non-ID work (such as ETDRs)

SWOT Analysis

A general strengths, weaknesses, opportunities, and threats (SWOT) approach looks at the "opportunities" and "threats" in the larger macro environment, and then it sees how the organization can be most adaptive and strategic in terms of its own "strengths" and "weaknesses." The macro environment informs the meso and micro, where "macro" is global, where "meso" is organizational and "micro" is individual. Table 3 highlights the analysis. At the macro level, the SARS-CoV-2 / COVID-19 pandemic is in a transition to endemicity from the acute phases. Geopolitically, the existing world order is under military challenge with the Russian invasion of Ukraine. In the U.S., inflation is somewhat runaway at 8.5%, and the job market itself is very tight, with many who had stepped out of the job market hesitating to return. Public salaries have fallen sharply in real value, given the widespread inflation. At the meso level, institutions of higher education in the U.S. are under pressure, with severe drops in student enrollments, thinned staffing, tight budgets, and stressed leadership. The learning curve on the various technologies are high, and IT is constantly changing (Helps, 2011, p. 323), which makes trainings about IT difficult.

The return to work to the physical office in April 2021 ended up being a traumatizing experience for the author, who experienced racial harassment by her then-supervisor as he kept insisting that she maintain multiple FTE of work, with tasks well outside her instructional designer role. She realized that her taking on of extra unpaid hours throughout the pandemic, into nights and weekends, served students and faculty and the university but were ultimately thankless. Back in the office, she had to insist in order to acquire basic equipment. Perhaps the year-and-a-half of relative isolation and great fear changed essential workplace relationships and personalities. Part of her effort to educate administration about ID work involved the making of the following 1-0 decision tree. The path would flow to 1's in most cases. If there is competition between a project on-campus or off, the preference is for on-campus work. If there is a choice between paid or unpaid work, the preference is towards paid work. If there is work requested that is ITS-based or non-ITS-based, the preference is toward ITS. Legacy commitments also affect commitments, with a preference for continuance of legacies. [This explains continuing work for multi-state community organizations.] There is preference for work that will enhance instructional designer capabilities. The work has to be doable, with the available or purchase-able technologies. The

Table 3. Strengths, weaknesses, opportunities, threats (SWOT) for a local instructional design office (matrix)

	Strengths (internal)	**Weaknesses (internal)**
	• Draw of university to major fields in veterinary medicine, political science, and other areas (macro, meso) • Experiences with online learning (macro, meso) • Experiences with blended and hybrid learning (macro, meso) • Need for an educated workforce (macro, meso) • Awareness of instructional design (macro, meso) • Broad experiences with federal and state and local grants (meso, micro) • Broad experiences with academic research (meso, micro) • Broad experiences with data analytics and analysis (meso, macro) • Broad experiences with educational publishing (meso, macro)	• Centralized funding for instructional design (but rate cards for the university) (micro) • Faculty considered to have a teaching and instructional design skillset even without the formal training (meso, micro) • Access to limited technologies (meso, micro) • Gaps in staffing, gaps in skillsets (meso, micro) • Gaps in accessibility tools (meso, micro) • Limited access to research resources given expenses (meso, micro)
Opportunities (external) • New administration to online learning due to the pandemic (macro, meso) • New faculty to online learning due to the pandemic (macro, meso) • New students to online learning ◦ Popularization of online courses (macro, meso) ◦ Popularization of blended and hybrid courses (macro, meso) ◦ Openness to open-source learning resources post-pandemic (macro, meso, micro) ◦ Wide range of technologies to distribute open-source learning resources	**SOs (Strengths and Opportunities)** • Trainings (continuing) for a variety of basic technologies needed in the academic space (Adobe Creative Cloud, Microsoft Office Suite, data analytics software, and others; support for ETDRs) (micro) • Support (continuing) for policies at the university level to ensure higher quality learning (micro) • Partnering with faculty to work on instructional designs from various disciplines (for custom or boutique solutions) (meso, micro) • Known individuals and personalities (micro) • Supporting grant applications early on, seat at the table when decisions are made (micro) • Engaging learning analytics (meso, micro) • Engaging academic publishing (meso, micro) • Engaging the development of ruggedized open-source learning resources (for in-house expertise building, for organizational publicity) (micro) Requiring • Publicity about instructional design resources (meso, micro) • Brokering of projects (meso, micro) • Proper usage of professional time (meso, micro)	**WOs (Weaknesses and Opportunities)** • Learning opportunities with each new instructional design project (meso, micro) • Some campus-wide training opportunities for andragogy and relevant technologies (meso, micro) • Acquiring relevant technologies with different funded projects (also writing into grants) (meso, micro) • Access to library-subscribed databases for research information (meso, micro) • Access to a text-and-data-mining resource (meso, micro) Requiring • Free hours for first five hours of consultation (micro) • Training design and training delivery (meso, micro)
Threats (external) • Mass social trauma from pandemic (macro, meso, micro) • Losing student enrollments (down some 8% since the beginning of the pandemic); reliance on a falling population of learners in feeder schools (meso) • Unknown overseas student demand, given restrictions to travel, given geopolitics (macro) • Lower levels of preparedness of learners to learning (macro, meso) • Indigenous role of instructional design in information technology services (ITS) under question vs. in academic realm (macro, meso, micro)	**STs (Strengths and Threats)** • Ensuring the learning experiences in critical courses for all learners (through participatory design, information gathering, and other efforts) (meso, micro) • Offering cognitive scaffolding of learning for course sequences, for pre- and post- formal learning (micro) • Ensuring accessibility for learning experience through universal design (and legal cover) (micro) • Integrating student-created works into digital learning objects for internal and external usage (micro) Requiring • Collaboration with faculty and students (meso, micro)	**WTs (Weaknesses and Threats)** • Stepping back from projects due to limited staffing and limited resources (micro) • Breaking collegiality due to social strifes (micro) • Ending of multiple FTEs of extra unpaid responsibilities (and unpaid overtime, during the years of the pandemic) for administrative address (addressing potential single points of failure given thin staffing) (meso, micro) Requiring • Working with the university bureaucracy to address staffing shortfalls and mistreatment of staff (meso, micro)

client has to be a trusted entity, who follows professional practice (otherwise, the work will create legal liabilities). Finally, the decision tree does seem somewhat *ad hoc* because in some ways it is. Supervisors who oversee instructional design have a set of political considerations that also affect their decision-making. (Figure 1)

Figure 1. Defining Instructional Design Work through a 1-0 Decision Tree

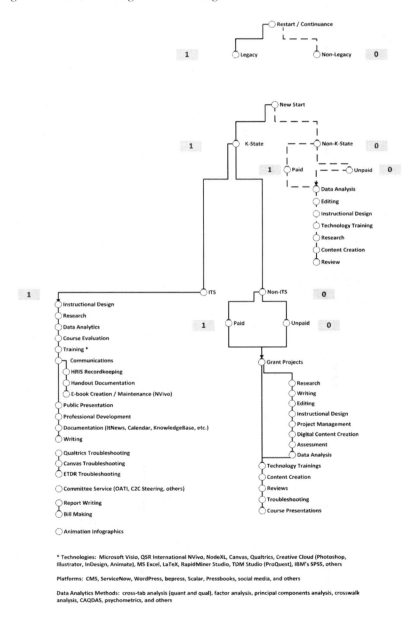

What to Keep, What to Discard

To be clear, the economy on a campus is to try to get free work as much as possible. Faculty and administration are willing to pay for work if they can take full credit for the work during conferences and in publications. Many dangles publication credit in order to try to trade for free labor. Some promise credit and then fail to follow through. Somehow, attention is seen as something with value, so there can be irrationalities, such as turning away work if someone else is seen as benefitting from some attention from the work.

Discussion

This initial analysis of instructional design does suggest a way forward, involving both a mix of policy goals, outreach to other entities on campus, and the most pressing needs. There is also a clear need to carve out time to be able to accept grant projects, given the over-assignment of hours.

FUTURE RESEARCH DIRECTIONS

In the world, different countries have different levels of development in terms of online education design and foci (Li, Wang, & Shi, 2021, p. 276). Additional assessments may be conducted at global to regional to national to institutional levels.

Future research may harness insights from other stakeholders to instructional design in this context: administrators, faculty, staff, and learners. Perhaps the SWOT (strengths, weaknesses, opportunities, and threats) approach may be harnessed in surveys to elicit insights. The findings may inform the shape of the instructional design service, and perhaps additional staff may be added. It would be important to avoid so-called "single points of failure" in terms of thin staffing. A more formal service mapping may be done to understand institutional needs, given the distributed existing of instructional designers in various colleges within the university, all with varying roles.

Instructional design engages ill-structured problems, for which there may be a range of possible answers. The skillset itself is a complex one, including pedagogical knowledge, educational psychology, research, writing, documentation, communications, digital content creation, legal knowledge, and others. Perhaps there can be some input from central academics (provost's office) for curricular coherence (while protecting academic freedoms of instructors). There are quality rubrics and checklists for e-learning already, and various interventions do reduce degrees of freedom as a tradeoff for learning quality and legality. Some departments use design templates for courses as a kind of instructional design structure. One researcher suggests the importance of considering how learners will engage the knowledge in the actual learning context as an important consideration (Walwema, 2012). Certainly, inherited guides should not be used unthinkingly but as part of instructional design thinking. One government has used a framework to strengthen teachers' abilities in critical thinking to improve teaching and learning (AlMarwani, 2020, p. 1). One research team has observed: "Strong autonomy of teacher design teams may result in discontinuous IL (information literacy)-learning-teaching trajectories that hamper student learning" (Wopereis, Frerejean, & Brand-Gruwel, 2016, p. 685). Data may be captured using live course data as part of formative evaluation to improve the course design for teaching and learning (Richards

& DeVries, 2011, p. 157) and design reflection based on observed learner and digital object behavior (Howard, Johnson, & Neitzel, 2010).

Identifying learner mistakes can be another path for instructional design refinement (Gusukuma et al., 2018). It may help for learners to understand that it is effortful work to teach online (Okamoto et al., 2009, p. 219), even as the popular sense among learners in the emergency online learning context that their instructors seem disengaged and not present. Perhaps new approaches to assessing current courses may be applied, such as through the lens of the learner experience; through the lens of sociality and group work; through learning assessments; through accessibility; and others. How learners engage with particular learning contents—such as animated video lectures—is also an important area of study, with both subjective self-reported inputs and biological indicators, such as facial temperatures captured with thermal imaging cameras for more objective measures (Srivastava et al., 2020, p. 250).

This assessment also brought up a question of how the instructional designer role itself should change, given the many and disparate professional roles that ended up combined in the position. With the winnowing out of tasks, there may be a concomitant adding on of other tasks, albeit to a full-time position only and not beyond. In the position, perhaps there can be creative time for "blue sky" thinking. There should be more time to take on new technologies, online learning ecosystems, pedagogical methods and models and theories, new ways of thinking and doing, and fresh domain knowledge. This way, the full capabilities and interests of the individual may be applied. Perhaps there can be centralized trainings about how to harness open-source learning materials and then how to contribute. Not only are there piecemeal digital learning objects and modules but also whole learning labs, such as an open-source networking lab (Yuan & Zhong, 2009, p. 37). There are also collaboratively created open books for open education (Rodés et al., 2014).

CONCLUSION

This work describes the state of instructional design services at a Midwestern university prior to the pandemic as a fairly flexible one, with work supporting a number of objectives for the local ITS office and then the greater university. The service menu changed during the pandemic in terms of the provision of more support for faculty transitioning to the learning management system (LMS) and online learning. There was also the taking on of non-instructional design work, given the lack of administrative interest in funding the prior related positions (with the retiring of an administrator). This work broadly suggests a refocus on instructional design for the ID role and some playing by ear of what ID services to keep based on grant funding pursuits and perceived local needs.

REFERENCES

Abdelhakim, M. N. A., & Shirmohammadei, S. (2007). A web-based group decision support system for the selection and evaluation of educational multimedia. Proceedings of EMME '07. doi:10.1145/1290144.1290150

Ahmad, A., Law, E. L., & Moseley, A. (2020, October). Integrating instructional design principles in serious games authoring tools: Insights from systematic literature review. In *Proceedings of the 11th Nordic Conference on Human-Computer Interaction: Shaping Experiences, Shaping Society* (pp. 1-12). 10.1145/3419249.3420133

AlMarwani, M. (2020). Pedagogical potential of SWOT analysis: An approach to teaching critical thinking. *Thinking Skills and Creativity, 38*(100741), 1–6. doi:10.1016/j.tsc.2020.100741

Bart, A. C., & Shaffer, C. A. (2016, February). Instructional design is to teaching as software engineering is to programming. In *Proceedings of the 47th ACM Technical Symposium on Computing Science Education* (pp. 240-241). 10.1145/2839509.2844674

Bayliss, J. D., & Schwartz, D. I. (2009, April). Instructional design as game design. In *Proceedings of the 4th International Conference on Foundations of Digital Games* (pp. 10-17). 10.1145/1536513.1536526

Belcadhi, L. C., & Ghannouchi, S. A. (2013, November). An instructional design approach for e-active courses. In *Proceedings of the First International Conference on Technological Ecosystem for Enhancing Multiculturality* (pp. 119-126). 10.1145/2536536.2536555

Celik, I., Torre, I., & Torsani, S. (2017, March). Integrating social media into an instructional design support system. In *Proceedings of the 2017 ACM Workshop on Intelligent Interfaces for Ubiquitous and Smart Learning* (pp. 19-24). 10.1145/3038535.3038544

Charoenying, T. (2013, June). Graph hopping: learning through physical interaction quantification. In *Proceedings of the 12th International Conference on Interaction Design and Children* (pp. 495-498). 10.1145/2485760.2485850

Chen, D-T. V., & Hung, D. W.L. (2007). Towards a community incubator: The ICAP design framework for social constructivist educational designers. *Proceedings of the CSCL 2007*, 127 – 130.

Correia, A. P., & Yusop, F. D. (2008, October). "I don't want to be empowered" the challenge of involving real-world clients in instructional design experiences. In *Proceedings of the Tenth Anniversary Conference on Participatory Design 2008* (pp. 214-216). Academic Press.

Damian, D., Petre, M., Miller, M., & Hadwin, A. F. (2012, May). Instructional strategies in the EGRET course: an international graduate forum on becoming a researcher. In *Proceedings of the Seventeenth Western Canadian Conference on Computing Education* (pp. 41-45). 10.1145/2247569.2247583

Duran, R. (2018, August). Towards an instructional design of complex learning in introductory programming courses. In *Proceedings of the 2018 ACM Conference on International Computing Education Research* (pp. 262-263). 10.1145/3230977.3231007

Field, J., Rankin, A., Van der Pal, J., Eriksson, H., & Wong, W. (2011, August). Variable uncertainty: Scenario design for training adaptive and flexible skills. In *Proceedings of the 29th Annual European Conference on Cognitive Ergonomics* (pp. 27-34). 10.1145/2074712.2074719

Gibbons, A. S. (2009, May). A theory-based alternative for the design of instruction: functional design. In *Proceedings of the 4th International Conference on Design Science Research in Information Systems and Technology* (pp. 1-5). 10.1145/1555619.1555633

Granić, A., Mifsud, C., & Ćukušić, M. (2009). Design, implementation and validation of a Europe-wide pedagogical framework for e-learning. *Computers & Education, 53*(4), 1052–1081. doi:10.1016/j.compedu.2009.05.018

Gusukuma, L., Bart, A. C., Kafura, D., Ernst, J., & Cennamo, K. (2018, February). Instructional design+ knowledge components: A systematic method for refining instruction. In *Proceedings of the 49th ACM Technical Symposium on Computer Science Education* (pp. 338-343). 10.1145/3159450.3159478

Helps, R. G. (2011). A domain model to improve IT course design. *Proceedings of SIGITE '11*, 323 – 324.

Howard, L., Johnson, J., & Neitzel, C. (2010, June). Reflecting on online learning designs using observed behavior. In *Proceedings of the fifteenth annual conference on Innovation and technology in computer science education* (pp. 179-183). 10.1145/1822090.1822142

Li, Z., Wang, J., & Shi, S. (2021, October). Bibliometric analysis of instructional design in online education based on Citespace. In *2021 13th International Conference on Education Technology and Computers* (pp. 276-283). 10.1145/3498765.3498808

Margulieux, L., Denny, P., Cunningham, K., Deutsch, M., & Shapiro, B. R. (2021, August). When wrong is right: The instructional power of multiple conceptions. In *Proceedings of the 17th ACM Conference on International Computing Education Research* (pp. 184-197). 10.1145/3446871.3469750

Molina-Carmona, R., Villagrá-Arnedo, C., Gallego-Durán, F., & Llorens-Largo, F. (2017). Analytics-driven redesign of an instructional course. *Proceedings of TEEM 2017*, 1 – 7.

Murphy, T. M., Teng, J., & Matusky, R. (2014, November). Needs analysis for instructional technology projects. In *Proceedings of the 42nd annual ACM SIGUCCS conference on User services* (pp. 23-28). 10.1145/2661172.2661183

Neto, J., Nolan, S., & Mendes, A. (2021, June). Planning and developing courses in distance learning environments: A training course for HiEdTec Project. In *International Conference on Computer Systems and Technologies' 21* (pp. 201-206). 10.1145/3472410.3472440

Okamoto, T., Anma, F., Nagata, N., & Kayama, M. (2009, September). The organizational knowledge circulated management on e-learning practices in universities-through the case study in UEC. In *2009 IEEE/WIC/ACM International Joint Conference on Web Intelligence and Intelligent Agent Technology* (Vol. 3, pp. 219-222). IEEE. 10.1109/WI-IAT.2009.267

Orth, C., & Bastiaens, T. (2008, June). Situated multimedia learning for older adults: Exploring the benefits of age-specific instructional design. In EdMedia+ Innovate Learning (pp. 3864-3879). Association for the Advancement of Computing in Education (AACE).

Rau, M. A., Aleven, V., Rummel, N., & Rohrbach, S. (2013, April). Why interactive learning environments can have it all: resolving design conflicts between competing goals. In *Proceedings of the SIGCHI Conference on Human Factors in Computing Systems* (pp. 109-118). 10.1145/2470654.2470670

Richards, G., & DeVries, I. (2011, February). Revisiting formative evaluation: dynamic monitoring for the improvement of learning activity design and delivery. In *Proceedings of the 1st international conference on learning analytics and knowledge* (pp. 157-162). 10.1145/2090116.2090141

What to Keep, What to Discard

Rodés, V., Mustaro, P. N., Silveira, I. F., Omar, N., & Ochôa, X. (2014, September). Instructional design models to support collaborative open books for open education. In *Proceedings of the XV International Conference on Human Computer Interaction* (pp. 1-7). 10.1145/2662253.2662346

Rutherfoord, R. H., & Rutherfoord, J. K. (2007). Universal instructional design for learning how to apply in a virtual world. *Proceedings of SIGITE '07*, 141 - 146. 10.1145/1324302.1324332

Rutherfoord, R. H., & Rutherfoord, J. K. (2008). Exploring teaching methods for on-line course delivery—Using universal instructional design. *Proceedings of SIGITE '08*, 45 – 50.

Rutherfoord, R. H., & Rutherfoord, J. K. (2008-2009). Universal instructional design – An approach to designing & delivering on-line and hybrid courses. *Methods (San Diego, Calif.)*, *1*, 2.

Safonov, M. A., Usov, S. S., Arkhipov, S. V., & Sorokina, L. P. (2021, January). SWOT analysis of mobile applications in the high education e-learning of the Chinese language. In *2021 12th International Conference on E-Education, E-Business, E-Management, and E-Learning* (pp. 89-94). 10.1145/3450148.3450208

Schultz, J. L., & Higbee, J. L. (2011). Implementing integrated multicultural instructional design in management education. *American Journal of Business Education*, *4*(12), 13–22. doi:10.19030/ajbe.v4i12.6609

Srivastava, N., Nawaz, S., Lodge, J. M., Velloso, E., Erfani, S., & Bailey, J. (2020, March). Exploring the usage of thermal imaging for understanding video lecture designs and students' experiences. In *Proceedings of the Tenth International Conference on Learning Analytics & Knowledge* (pp. 250-259). 10.1145/3375462.3375514

Teo, C. B., & Gay, R. K. L. (2006). A knowledge-driven model to personalize e-learning. *Journal of Educational Resources in Computing*, *6*(1), 1–15. doi:10.1145/1217862.1217865

The, B., & Mavrikis, M. (2016, April). A study on eye fixation patterns of students in higher education using an online learning system. In *Proceedings of the Sixth International Conference on Learning Analytics & Knowledge* (pp. 408-416). 10.1145/2883851.2883871

Walwema, J. N. (2012, October). Design templates in instructional design. In *Proceedings of the 30th ACM International Conference on Design of Communication* (pp. 17-22). Academic Press.

Wang, W., Wu, X., & Li, J. (2018, October). The practice of small project-based mode in the teaching of SCM course. In *Proceedings of the 10th International Conference on Education Technology and Computers* (pp. 12-16). 10.1145/3290511.3290513

Wood, R., Bonakdarian, E., & Whittaker, T. (2012). Designing courses for hybrid instruction: Principles and practice. Consortium for Computing Sciences in Colleges. *Journal of Computing Sciences in Colleges*, *27*(4), 6–14.

Wopereis, I., Frerejean, J., & Brand-Gruwel, S. (2016, October). Teacher perspectives on whole-task information literacy instruction. In *European Conference on Information Literacy* (pp. 678-687). Springer. 10.1007/978-3-319-52162-6_66

Xie, J. A. G., & Rice, M. F. (2021). Instructional designers' roles in emergency remote teaching during COVID-19. *Distance Education*, *42*(1), 70–87. doi:10.1080/01587919.2020.1869526

Yuan, D., & Zhong, J. (2009, October). An instructional design of open source networking laboratory and curriculum. In *Proceedings of the 10th ACM conference on SIG-information technology education* (pp. 37-42). 10.1145/1631728.1631742

Zhu, M., Basdogan, M., & Bonk, C. J. (2020). A case study of the design practices and judgments of novice instructional designers. *Contemporary Educational Technology*, *12*(2), 1–19. doi:10.30935/cedtech/7829

KEY TERMS AND DEFINITIONS

Instructional Design: Various systematic ways to create effective learning experiences.

SWOT Analysis (Strengths, Weaknesses, Opportunities, and Threats): A systematic review of an organization's context that involves the analysis of opportunities and threats in the larger ecosystem and the strengths and weaknesses of the organization within that larger context (with results often presented in a matrix format).

Section 7

Harnessing Motion for More Effective Applied Learning

Chapter 16
Infographics for Information Conveyance:
A Light History From Early Days (Stasis) to Today (Motion, Interactive, Immersive)

Shalin Hai-Jew
https://orcid.org/0000-0002-8863-0175
Kansas State University, USA

ABSTRACT

To help the world emerge from the COVID-19 pandemic, an older tool has come back to the fore: analog and digital informational graphics. Infographics (information + graphics) have been used for many decades to convey data, knowledge, information, and learning. In the latest phase, there are now motion (animated) and interactive and immersive infographics that offer richer ways. This work explores the basic mechanisms of information conveyance in infographics from early days through the contemporaneous moment with the richer. Finally, a summary graphic captures the general sequence in the design, development, and deployment of modern motion, interactive, and/or immersive infographics.

INTRODUCTION

For higher education recovery from long-term challenges, such as the multiple years of the SARS-CoV-2 / COVID-19 pandemic, it helps to maximize opportunities for learning. This means learning materials that are used in real time and those that are digital leave-behinds for formal, informal, and nonformal learning. [Formal learning refers to accredited learning managed by formal agencies with oversight; informal learning refers to learning that is a byproduct of non-learning activities, and nonformal learning refers to course-based learning that is not credit-based.] Infographics have long been used to enhance learning. While they are not considered glamorous, theirs is an approach that would benefit learners as they strive to address learning loss from 2020 – 2023 as the world emerges from the pandemic.

DOI: 10.4018/978-1-6684-5934-8.ch016

Copyright © 2023, IGI Global. Copying or distributing in print or electronic forms without written permission of IGI Global is prohibited.

Infographics for Information Conveyance

An informational graphic or "infographic" [an amalgam of information + graphic] refers to static "visual representations of information" (Andry et al., 2021, p. 1; Bigelow et al., 2014, p. 17) or data, concepts, and knowledge (Nhan & Yen, 2021b, p. 85). Said eloquently: an infographic is a "visual translation of data" (Bradshaw & Porter, 2017, p. 57). An infographic contains "verbal, pictorial and schematic components" (de Castro Andrade & Spinillo, 2018, p. 187). Information graphics "combine elements of data visualization with design" (Harrison, Reinecke, & Chang, 2015, p. 1187). Infographics offer overviews of a topic (Szoltysik, 2016). They are "a form of knowledge assemblage" (Featherstone, 2014, p. 147). Through "a fusion of data and graphical elements," infographics tell an information story (Lu, et al., 2020, p. 1). Infographics are often "self-contained pictorials" (Balkac & Ergun, 2018, p. 2514), which means that they can exist in a stand-alone fashion with full details. [One researcher writes: "An ideal in infographics might be something like a self-interpreting artifact" (Rosenberg, 2015, p. 40).] There are assumed efficiencies of infographics. Infographics offer "a way of delivering the maximum amount of content in the least amount of space while still being precise and clear" to "tell a story, show relationships, and reveal structure" (Dunlap & Lowenthal, 2016, p. 42). Another definition asserts that an infographic is "a highly effective visualization tool, which allows (creators) to present organized and structured information about any event, fact, object or phenomenon in a graphical form" (Tarkhova & Tarkhov, 2020, p. 66). Infographics can serve as "instructional materials" (Yildirim, 2016, p. 109). Digital (and digitized) infographics "rarely fit on one screen, the reader usually has to scroll (and sometimes zoom in) to read them in full" (Veszelszki, 2014, p. 100). At least one definition suggests that infographics are necessarily web-based:

a web-based image that takes a large amount of information in text or numerical form and condenses it into a combination of images and text with a goal of making the information presentable and digestible to an audience (Albers, 2015, p. 2).

Another also focuses on the online versions of infographics. Infographics take on many forms, but are most commonly found as "online posters…and short animated videos (usually less than five minutes)" (Bellato, 2013, p. 1). Developers of infographics pre-filter learning contents and so get "straight to the point" (Bellato, 2013, p. 3.

Another definition reads: "a complex compilation of connected images that convey an idea" (Hsiao et al., 2019, p. 26). The feature of having a core central idea is similar to that of essays with a core idea as an organizing principle.

A "motion infographic" is a 2d (Hai-Jew, Aug. 5 – 7, 2020, Slide 3) or 3d information-carrying visual that contains motion (4d) or animation. The visual may be accompanied by text or voiceover or other multimedia content. Another form of a motion infographic involves "animated maps," first created in 1940 (Peterson, 1995, as cited in Griffin, MacEachren, Hardisty, Steiner, & Li, 2006, p. 740). Animated maps show various phenomena over geographical space. Infographics as "animated videos" may include "music, voiceover, and animation" (Bellato, 2013, p. 1). "Animated infographics" are also known as "data videos" (Doukianou, Daylamani-Zad, & O'Loingsigh, 2021; Amini, Riche, Lee, Leboe-McGowan, & Irani, 2018, p. 1). A "video infographic" has also been described as "a visualization that is achieved with short videos combined with visual images, illustrations and text" (Damyanov & Tsankov, 2018, p. 84). An "interactive infographic" provides mechanisms for users to engage with the data based on their own preferences and at their own pace; they are often able to change various parameters of the data, such as time spans, locales, and other information). Users may run queries against the data in some cases. Immersive infographics include those that place users in three-dimensional space, such as through augmented reality (AR) or virtual reality (VR) or mixed reality (MR). These spaces often not only include 3d but movement or 4d (changes over time). Infographics have been "popular media" for decades (Krum, 2013, as cited in Kanthawala, 2019, p. 73), in various forms.

In terms of various styles of sub-categories of infographics, one is "data comics," defined as "a relatively new and unexplored format" with the information presented in sequential panels. Data comics are informed by the "tradition of comics" combined with "infographics, data visualization, journalism, and other formats of visual explanations" (Wang, et al., 2019, p. 2) Another new type involves "geo-infographics" (He, Tang, & Huang, 2011, p. 1), including the uses of infographics to augment maps and forms such as "cartograms, schematic maps, topological maps, concept maps, grid maps, etc." (He, Tang, & Huang, 2011, p. 1) to enhance the expression of spatial data. A fairly recent form is the digital political infographic, or "hybrid political forms" for political messaging and influence (Amit-Danhi & Shifman, 2018). Such messaging may spotlight political issues and political candidates, and social injustices (Amit-Danhi & Shifman, 2018). So-called "instructional infographics" emerging in 2014 (Alrwele, 2017, p. 106), and these have diversified into many forms for usage in the instructional context.

This chapter offers a light history of infographics and then explores the present-day ones that include 2d and 3d, motion (4d) and interactivity. The through-line for this review involves technological enablements and practices around those capabilities. The works analyzed include a scraping of "motion" infographics and "interactive" infographics from the Social Web (through Google Images). These image types were also explored from a social art-sharing site (DeviantArt). And some were sampled as hosted contents in the wild from a variety of websites.

Then, there were indirect samples as well. A related tags network of "infographics" was extracted from a mega social image-sharing site (Flickr). Also, a social network graph was pulled around #infographics on a large-scale microblogging site (Netlytics as applied to Twitter). A graph was made of "infographics" on a shadow dataset (Google Books Ngram Viewer). This work provides an early exploration of the topic in the current slice-in-time.

REVIEW OF THE LITERATURE

Infographics are thought to have re-emerged into the broad public given the high flows of available data in the information age. Humanity needs to make sense of massive amounts of unprocessed data (Dur, 2014a, p. 39), including through the use of designed infographics. Data have to be made meaningful to be potentially useful. One insight about science-based research advancement and innovation:

Infographers observe that as quantities increase, patterns emerge, then patterns become more complex, subject areas emerge, become complex, and merge eventually into a new field or new technology. The organizing principle (patterns) tends to be relational rather than axiomatic (Williams, 2002, p. 5).

Auto-generated infographics have also been harnessed to represent Twitter microblogging data, along various dimensions: "spatial, chronological, quantitative, hierarchical, and contextual or, as is usually the case, a combination of all five" (López-Ornelas & Hernández, 2016, p. 25). Data visualizations help "amplify cognition" and make certain data patterns more salient.

Infographics for Information Conveyance

A review of the extant literature around infographics provides insights about the characteristics of infographics in the wild, applied purposes of infographics, and then how they are designed.

Characteristics of Infographics in the Wild

Infographics exist in many forms in the wild. They are seen as in part a response to the generation of so much public information. They are seen as a critical part of the offline and online communications ecosystem. In some contexts, infographics are not to "impose interpretations" but to make transparent and to reveal patterns in data (Rosenberg, 2015, p. 39). In other perspectives, there is an inherent selectivity of data in infographics, framing, and built-in "bias" and in the shaping of user perceptions of the content (Arum, 2017, p. 5).

Infographics have become more like articles or speeches than charts. Their purpose can be categorized into the same three objectives as public speaking: to inform, entertain, or persuade the audience. (Arum, 2017, p. 1).

Another work suggests that such visuals are designed to provide "the percipient with new insights and a quick overview on complex facts on subjects like politics, science, technology, and nature that are hard to understand just using text-based information" (Zwinger & Zeiller, 2016, p. 2). The most common of the topics in interactive infographics were "politics" and "economics" (Zwinger & Zeiller, 2016, p. 8). A historical review of infographics harkens back to the 1700s and through the present, with various seminal works.

Different Typographies of Infographics

Infographics are categorized in different ways. One research work describes three types of infographics: "principle representations, cartographic infographics, (and) statistics chart" (Zwinger & Zeiller, 2016, p. 2), based on the core underlying contents. Another work suggests that there are five types: presentation infographic, mnemonic infographic, specialized infographic, directive infographic, and cartographic infographic (Tarkhova & Tarkhov, 2020, pp. 66-67). The prior seems to be based on purposive designed usage. There is a diversity of infographics, with "icons, images, embellishments, or text" (Lu, et al., 2020, p. 1). Another system classifies infographics based on bottom-up coding and measures various variables to predict the infographic's class (Purchase, et al., 2018). The seven categories are the following: "bar charts, geographical, units, area-as-quantity, single circle, proportion-as-quantity, (and) flags" based on data presentation forms, primary shapes, quantity of data in graphical representations, and mixed features (Purchase, et al., 2018, p. 2). Another categorization of infographics is the following: "statistical-based, timeline-based, process-based, (and) location-based" (Cui, et al., 2019, p. 908). None of the categorization of infographic types is fully comprehensive as yet.

Motion infographics may include those communicating weather and other types of data-informed phenomena. They may be animations. They may be video-based motion.

Interactive infographics are enabled by various "technical systems," but the interactivity elements "have to be recognized and utilized by users" to enable value-added (Zwinger & Zeiller, 2016, p. 2). The broadly available infographics have levels of interactivity understood at various levels, from low to medium to high (Weber & Wenzel, 2013, as cited in Zwinger & Zeiller, 2016, p. 3). Most of the studied published interactive infographics were "nonlinear" in terms of their actions (Zwinger & Zeiller, 2016, p. 6). In terms of frequency counts of types, one study found the following:

The majority of interactive infographics, i.e., 43.11%, shows a low degree of interactivity. 38.77% of the analyzed infographics have a medium degree of interactivity, whereas only 18.12% of the analyzed infographics offer a high degree of interactivity. (Zwinger & Zeiller, 2016, p. 6)

Another study examined the visual information flows (VIFs) of public infographics in a "high-level analysis" (Lu, et al., 2020, p. 1). The VIF refers to "the underlying semantic structure that links the graphical data elements to convey the information and story to the user, as a means to understand visual organization of stories" (Lu, et al., 2020, p. 1). Two main element types are used for this taxonomy: a backbone shape, and content placement. The researchers label a "backbone shape" as "the line that most visual groups in the narrative are aligned with," typically circular (along a circle around an object) or linear (in various lines. The circular ones may be full circles such as "clock" or "star," and there are partial circles in arcs, which they term "bowl, dome, left-wing, (and) right-wing"; the linear ones may show the objects aligned along a straight line or a curved one and may be horizontal linear or vertical linear...and up-ladder or down-ladder (Lu, et al., 2020, p. 7). "Content placement" refers to how the visuals are "arranged along the information flow in relation to the backbone shape," such as if the objects are "placed inside or outside of the backbone" or on the same side as the linear backbone flow or alternating on various sides around it and others (Lu, et al., 2020, p. 7). The backbone shape shows the main flow of the visual elements, and the content placement focuses on how the visual groups are laid out in relation to the backbone. From this setup, the researchers identified 12 different design patterns: landscape, portrait; clock, star; spiral, pulse; bowl, dome; down-ladder, up-ladder; left-wing, and right-wing (Lu, et al., 2020, p. 8). The VIF patterns are not exhaustive, with the researchers even finding counterexamples. However, their research captures perhaps a majority of the patterns of infographic types based on a skim of the public infographics online and elsewhere.

Immersive infographics may be those that exist in immersive virtual worlds and full-surround digital games. They may be those that use augmentations to reality.

Computational Engagement with Infographics

Infographics have become such a critical part of the information space that there are programs being developed to use computer vision to interpret infographics. One enables the capture of smaller visual elements (often including text) known as icons. Icon detection may be used for future applications like "automatic captioning, summarization, search, and question-answering" (Madan et al., 2021, p. 31). Parsing out the components of an informational graphic and interpreting them enables full automatic infographic understanding, even in cases of low spatial resolution. Another program uses machine vision to find infographics with similar visual styles to inform a tool for searching for infographics (Saleh et al., 2015, p. 1). The thinking is that those who learn better with particular setups of infographics would benefit by being able to find similar ones. Another system involves methods to enable the retrieval of informational graphics based on user queries using natural language (Li et al., 2014). Still another team has created a technology system to enable the identification of icons that may be parts of infographics, by identifying "text tags and visual hashtags that are textually and visually representative of the infographic's topics" with fidelity (Madan et al., 2018, p. 1). One work describes a computational system

Infographics for Information Conveyance

for automatically extracting information from raster-based infographics, including both the extraction of graphical symbols and text capture and interpretation (Huang & Tan, 2007, p. 9).

Professionals in various disciplines are encouraged to learn how to create and deploy infographics. For example, healthcare professionals are training to use infographics to spark interest and sharing of the messages more widely (Scott, Fawkner, Oliver, & Murray, 2016, p. 1104). Researchers are studying the power of "information design" in the healthcare space" (Balkac & Ergun, 2018, p. 2514). Some of the best practices for infographic design in the medical sciences includes the following: targeting the audience based on facts, using "a compelling title," creating a clear narrative, emphasizing key messages, offering a balance of "images, charts and text," limiting the number of fonts and colors, and other factors (Murray et al., 2017, p. 620).

Applied Purposes of Infographic Usage

To explore various purposes of infographic usage, this section explores five main topics:

- Communicating with the public (1)
- Outreach in data journalism (2)
- Expanding learning: andragogical and pedagogical applications (3)
- Reception of infographics: How infographics are consumed (4), and
- Design of infographics (of various types) (5)

Communicating with the Public

One general public is thought to be more receptive to informational graphics for information consumption than various amounts of complex reading. Many journalistic articles come with indicators about how long the article would take to read. Surveys are written to the 5th grade level, which is below that of journalistic articles, which are often pegged to the 8th grade level. A contemporaneous topic has been public health communications around SARS-CoV-2 / COVID-19 during the pandemic (November 2019 – present). Public health professionals have coordinated to create and disperse infographics to fight COVID-19 vaccine hesitancy and rampant misinformation about the pathogen and pandemic. Their communications outreach work has resulted in powerful impressions on Twitter, the major microblogging site (Rotolo, et al., 2021, p. 1). Another endeavor has involved COVID-19 risk infographics, to help people better understand risk in the context of the COVID-19 pandemic and the benefits of viral infection mitigations (Kemp, King, Upshaw, Mackert, & Jensen, 2021). Infographics were created to help people maintain physical fitness through exercise during the pandemic and under conditions of lockdown and social distancing (Fitzpatrick, Castricum, Seward, Tulloh, & Dawson, 2020, p. 1360). Those who are less fit are at high risk of bad outcomes with SARS-CoV-2 / COVID-19 infection. Another health infographic helped with decision making for when athletes may return to competition or "play" in the time of COVID-19 based on clinical recommendations (Löllgen, et al., 2021, p. 344). In public health education, a small-group assignment "facilitated learning about accessing and translating data" in the public health information space to non-expert audiences (Shanks, Izumi, Sun, Martin, & Byker Shanks, 2017, p. 1). Infographics may have detrimental effects on "risk perception/comprehension" about cardiovascular disease risk, especially for those with less education about the topic (Damman et al., 2018).

Infographics for Information Conveyance

Researchers, in a scoping review (including grey literature), have explored the use of health infographics for knowledge translation (Mc Sween-Cadieux, Chabot, Fillol, Saha, & Dagenais, 2021). A "video infographic" was used to convey public safety messaging about not driving through floodwaters (Hamilton, Peden, Keech, & Hagger, 2017).

Various governmental agencies and groups also use infographics to communicate about projects: an upcoming transportation project (Terabe & Tanno, 2020), terror threats (Lonsdale, Baxter, Graham, Kanafani, Li, & Peng, 2019), and other topics.

Infographics are also used for social advocacy. One work describes the placement of various data infographics about the larger neighborhood and community in various urban spaces, as a way of placing "problems out in the open" (Claes & Moere, 2013, p. 137) and inviting the public to explore further and perhaps contribute to solutions. Infographics provide opportunities for "urban visualization" (Claes & Moere, 2013, p. 138), with the combination of "the physical, social, visual and content features of an urban, physical environment and its identity, captured by data" (Claes & Moere, 2013, p. 138).

There is a call to action at the end of some infographics (Arum, 2017, p. 1). Some infographics are designed for behavior change, such as those promoting nutrition and "healthy eating" (Wilkinson, Strickling, Payne, Jensen, & West, 2016, p. 1), lessening food waste in the home (Wharton, Vizcaino, Berardy, Opejin, 2021), or updating antivirus protection software (Zhang-Kennedy, Chiasson, & Biddle, 2014). One group of researchers studied whether behavior change theory was integrated in a set of public infographics on Pinterest, a social pinning website. They found few with such factors for health behavior change, and they suggest that such infographics would benefit by the integration of more such factors. Another area for advocacy through infographics involves environmentalism (Tuncali, 2016). Addressing various issues of social injustices may be achieved with "infoadvocacy" through infographics (Yearta, Kelly, Kissel, & Schonhar, 2018), which requires advocates to harness various multiple literacies to be effective. In the same way that design elements help guide viewer eyes, those who create infographics also guide human imagination through visual rhetoric in animated infographics, to inform and change behaviors (Lengler & Moore, 2009). In yet another example, privacy policies on public sites were conveyed either by animated video or text: this study found animated video was more effectual at promoting "user engagement, delivery of content, and comprehensibility of information" as compared to textual information (Nivas, Gokul, Banahatti, & Lodha, 2021, p. 732).

Another team engaged in participatory design of infographics to improve health for community members, who have varying levels of health literacy. They learned about the target population through structured or semi-structured elicitations. They write:

Contrary to the design dictum that 'less is more,' we discovered that when it comes to health information, sometimes more is more. Low health literacy implies potential difficulty interpreting health information, not a diminished desire for information. Efforts to make health messages more accessible via simplification run the risk of stripping away valuable meaning. (Arcia, et al., 2016, p. 180)

Another team went full global and crowd-sourced infographics in a competition about antimicrobial resistance (Kpokin et al., 2021). Another work involved figuring out how to communicate physical activity evidence visually (Reid et al., 2017, p. 764), to help people acquire self-awareness of their activity and to plan their own fitness regimens. One study found video more compelling than infographics in one study about critical health messaging (Occa & Suggs, 2016). Certainly, the video modality is much more common and familiar than infographics per se.

Infographics for Information Conveyance

Environmental messaging has also harnessed infographics. One study of pro-environment communication using infographics that found that "…individuals engage in greater levels of issue-relevant thinking when shown infographics compared to messages that rely just on text or just on illustration, with learning preferences and visual literacy as moderators" (to that effect) (Lazard & Atkinson, 2015, p. 6). They found that the persuasive power of infographics "holds true across different audiences, regardless of learning preferences or visual literacy. Individuals who report a preference for verbal learning styles as well as individuals who score lower on visual literacy scales actually elaborate more after exposure to infographic messages than they do with text-based messages" (Lazard & Atkinson, 2015, p. 26).

Academic researchers also use infographics to publicize their work on social media, to reach a broader audience and to burnish their "altmetrics" (alternative metrics, to include social media platforms) of reach. Indeed, social media are harnessed to disseminate infographics communicating science research to both lay and professional audiences (Lochner, Swenson, & Martinson, 2021; Murray, et al., 2018). Consumers of data were found to prefer "infographic summaries" to represent medical literature (Martin, et al., 2019). In other cases, infographics are used to make structural equation modeling (SEM) studies more easily understood and effective to a broader audience (Ashman & Patterson, 2015, p. 613). Representing quantitative data analytics techniques as visuals can make them more interpretable by users (Ashman & Patterson, 2015, p. 622), without a need to over-simplify too much.

Outreach in Data Journalism

One study examined how receptive readers of online newspapers were to interactive infographics. This survey study found that "the offering of interactive infographics is highly accepted among users with all levels (of) user experience" although many do not recognize control tools on interactive infographics as such and so leave many features unused or only partially used (Zwinger, Langer, & Zeiller, 2017, p. 181). These controls include those for data sorting and filtering and re-visualization. To encourage the uses of such features, those who design interactive infographics need to communicate clearly about those functions to encourage their usage. Infographics in web journalism have to be designed correctly to avoid communication distortions or risk confusion (Pinto, 2017, p. 428). Such visual communications products are both enabled and constrained based on the available technologies and skillsets, but there is a sense of promise with such electronic infographics (Pinto, 2017).

In digital journalism, interactive infographics are created to engage their readers. Such infographics are informed by "news values and working practices" (Dick, 2014, p. 490). Because of the costs of creating such infographics, the editorial leadership in a newsroom have to make hard decisions about what infographics get made and published: "Interactives are more suited to some news stories than to others, on account of narrative type and the dynamics involved" (Dick, 2014, p. 504). One example mentioned was personalized calculators offering people the ability to extract "news you can use" (Dick, 2014, p. 504).

What of published health infographics with animations? One study found that "the health infographics of the selected sample do not follow the recommendations of prior literature, leading us to question the positive effect of interaction when merged with animation and the negative effect of on-screen text combined with animation or static images" (de Castro Andrade & Spinillo, 2018, p. 187). Animations may contribute to communication in different ways, to meet different functions: "decorative, attentional, motivational, presentation and elucidation functions" (de Castro Andrade & Spinillo, 2018, p. 189). This study harnessed the principles of cognitive theory of multimedia learning including practices such as "coherence, signaling, redundancy, spatial contiguity, temporal contiguity, segmenting, pre-training, modality, multimedia, personalization, voice, and image" (Mayer, 2005, as cited in de Castro Andrade & Spinillo, 2018, p. 191), based on empirical research. The researchers focused on various components of the infographics:

In general, animation was employed to convey the main health contents of the infographics, drawings style was used to depict the human body and sectional views to show internal parts of the body. The combined use of sectional views and drawings is typical in anatomy illustrations, as those in the medical atlases. The menus were mainly located inside the infographics, showing verbal elements, such as buttons displaying words to indicate different stages of the content of the infographic. The menus also employed schematic elements for narrative control (e.g., arrows, small squares). In addition, schematic elements (lines, arrows) were used to link images to their referring texts (captions, labels). Color was predominantly used to emphasize certain parts of the images/animations to call viewers/users (sic) attention. (de Castro Andrade & Spinillo, 2018, p. 192)

The health infographics samples used animation "with elucidation function" to make visible "parts / elements which would not be possible for a naked eye" through pullouts. And some used animation for decorative functions (de Castro Andrade & Spinillo, 2018, p. 192).

Limited Interactions

Interaction tended to be used in "a limited way" for "narrative controls" such as forwarding and backwarding and multimedia controls" (de Castro Andrade & Spinillo, 2018, p. 194). They observe: "…interaction as an aid to learning/understanding" is generally "neglected in the design of newspaper animated health infographics" (de Castro Andrade & Spinillo, 2018, p. 194). Perhaps the sophistication of animations has not yet been arrived at in these early days.

Interactive infographics do have an effect on learning from online news. One research found "a negative impact of interactive infographics on news consumers' memory" (Greussing & Boomgaarden, 2021, p. 3336). In theory, interactive features are thought to provide users with some agency. This work found "significant negative relative *direct* effects of the clickable and the slide-based infographic on learning" (Greussing & Boomgaarden, 2021, p. 3346), with the interactivity impairing "news consumers' ability to understand and remember the content of a news story" (Greussing & Boomgaarden, 2021, p. 3347). The researchers do note that other types of interactivities may have salutary effects, such as clicking hotspots to access more information.

Infographics serve as both "design elements" and as ways to convey data in newspapers (Pasternack & Utt, 1990, p. 28). In early uses of infographics in newspapers, there was a sense that they were there for the graphical features; of late, they are considered present more for informational purposes newspapers (Pasternack & Utt, 1990). Developing countries follow some similar trajectories in terms of their news organization development. In India, for example, infographics were initially used for statistical and data information sharing but have broadened to include "news and information content" (Ghode, 2012, p. 35).

Mixed Effects of Infographics and Hyperlinks

A user-based study found that adding infographics to the news encouraged readers to "process the news story more actively and engage in higher message elaboration" but only among a part of the news reader population (Lee & Kim, 2016, p. 1592).

…heightened the extent to which they engaged in news elaboration, albeit only among those with higher issue involvement. However, in-text hyperlinks hindered information recall among those with less prior knowledge, creating an information acquisition gap between more and less resourceful individuals. The graphical representation of news appeared to have heuristic appeals to those less involved in and less knowledgeable about the news topic, leading to more favorable news evaluation. (Lee & Kim, 2016, p. 1479)

Interactivity in the form of hyperlinks were found to be distractive to those who require more cognition to process other parts of the story: "Interestingly, the negative effect of interactivity that hampers news acquisition dissipated when the news was presented in graphs. Although graphical representation of the news did not enhance information acquisition, it attenuated the memory-impairing influence of interactivity" (Lee & Kim, 2016, p. 1594). This work found mixed effects of the infographics and hyperlinks.

Expanding Learning: Andragogical and Pedagogical Applications

Instructional infographics can "adapt to a range of research projects and curriculum designs, including stand-alone assignments or scaffolded research projects" (Mendenhall & Summers, 2015, p. 359). They can heighten the "metacognitive awareness" of the learning. Instructional infographics are used for children and adults, and in various types of learning contexts (formal/accredited, non-formal/unaccredited, and informal/incidental learning), infographics are being harnessed. They are created by the teachers and subject matter experts / content experts. They are also created by learners in K-12 and higher education. They are also auto created as parts of data dashboards. Infographics, in their various forms (static, motion, and interactive), have come to the fore for pedagogical applications. A review has been conducted on infographics design from various disciplines in order to capture knowledge about infographics for the education space. The researchers write:

Infographics can be used when the students want to get across a big idea or make a point to learners. Concepts that are tricky for learners might lend themselves well to infographics. Or, if they have facts that are hard to learn, the researcher might investigate how they might be turned into infographics. Infographics can be broadly categorized into the following: comparison, flow chart, timeline, process, image-based, data, narrative, metaphor, combination, and other. Many of the infographics can be considered background reading for the course and may be helpful as the students complete their future assignments. (Naparin & Saad, 2017, p. 16)

Infographics may help bridge learners to understanding more difficult lessons and course content in a technological age (Naparin & Saad, 2017, p. 24). Another "use case" is to harness infographics for cognitive modeling (conceptualizing various aspects of the world) in education (Damyanov & Tsankov, 2018). The design of infographics in this context includes tasks such as modeling, "transcoding information from one model to another," classifying, comparing, generalizing, and evaluating (Damyanov & Tsankov, 2018, pp. 89-90).

Instructional infographics are those created with often familiar components but presented in newer ways (Yildirim, 2016, p. 99). This study suggests that the factors that affect the educational value of infographics include the following: information-visual adaptation, information quality, quality of the visualization, quality of the visuals and design approach" (Yildirim, 2016, p. 105). Further, learners have higher confidence levels in the infographics "if the person or entity, who prepared the infographic, is known by the reader" (Yildirim, 2016, p. 108). The authorship of such works, then, matter. Another research team emphasizes the importance of investing the time and expertise "to get an infographic right" (Murray, et al., 2017, p. 619).

Some researchers suggest that infographics may be used in lieu of traditional lectures, such as for teaching statistical reasoning in anatomy (Ozdamli et al., 2016, p. 370), in a shift well received by students (p. 377). In an introductory curriculum course, researchers studied the effect of using instructional infographics over nine learning sessions of two hours each, followed by achievement tests and a questionnaire. The results of this quasi-experimental design found "significantly higher achievement in the experimental group than in the control group" (Alrwele, 2017, p. 104). Further, 90% of participants in the experimental group self-reported that the infographics "had a positive impact on their intellectual, life skills, and affective development" (Alrwele, 2017, p. 104).

Instructional infographics are used in instructional materials in geography, with one researcher writing:

Infographics can be effectively and widely used in geography lessons in different grade levels and learning areas when visual and information are to be given together. It is also suggested to use infographics in cases where achievement and attitudes of students in geography lesson is (sic) low. (Çifçi, 2016, p. 154)

The geography lessons using infographics have to fit the learners' developmental level (Çifçi, 2016, p. 155). The "visuals, videos, sounds, animations or information are to be attracting" (Çifçi, 2016, p. 155). The study found improved performance in the experimental group in the post-test scores in a 10th grade geography class (Çifçi, 2016, p. 163). There were also improvements in attitudes towards geography in the some of the experimental groups over the control ones (Çifçi, 2016, p. 163).

Informational graphics are seen as foundational as a five-paragraph essay for 8th graders in STEM (science, technology, engineering, and math) fields who used infographics as "a leading form of information display and communication" (Kos & Sims, 2014, p. 1). The assignment was for learners to create an infographic around a particular career field of interest, and the work as appealing to learners because of their interest in infographics, interest in researching a career, and triggered interests in particular careers that were researched (Kos & Sims, 2014, p. 3). The work was "more enjoyable than an essay" although students found limitations to the free software used for their work (Kos & Sims, 2014, p. 4).

Another work includes the identification of seminal infographics in history that have affected the field. This work includes an exploration of interactive infographics online to see how they're used for the transfer of "comprehensible information" (Dur, 2014b, p. 1). In education, infographics are "a contracted multi-level polysemantic thing" (Bystrova, 2019, p. 152). What makes them effective for learning? One researcher suggests the following features: "scalability, structure-based, focusing on the key points, visual simplicity, emphasis on the relationship between elements" (Bystrova, 2019, p. 152).

Some use the ADDIE model (common in instructional design) to design infographics creation. ADDIE refers to "analysis, design, development, implementation, and evaluation" in a cyclical sequence.

Infographics for Information Conveyance

This study found positive experiences for teachers and students in their usage of infographics for learning literacies (Ozdamli & Ozdal, 2018, p. 1197).

One work identified five purposes of harnessing infographics for instruction:

1. organizing ideas and coherent manners (sic) in a useful way;
2. illustrating biographical, scientific, art and design, historical, and social studies concepts in a visual way;
3. comparing information in an effective way;
4. making data meaningful by providing analogies, examples, and themes; plain data can be transformed into meaningful information;
5. telling a story to convey the ideas with visuals and words in an exciting way rather than using only words…" (Lamb & Johnson, 2014, as cited in Nhan & Yen, 2021b, p. 87)

In one research work, infographics are used to mediate knowledge between "older generations and present-day students of art and design" to fight the "amnesia" that could otherwise without the bridge between generations. Here, interactive infographic re-inscribe "artistic and creative legacies" from older generations of artists and designers to upcoming generations of students (Martins et al., 2020, p. 213). Certainly, such sharing of knowledge between generations applies well beyond creative fields.

Informational graphics have been harnessed to improve the reading comprehension skills of learners. They have been used to help learners engage in applied demonstration of language skills (Cupita & Franco, 2019). English as a Foreign Language (EFL) learners have used infographics for grammar retention in what has been termed "infographics instruction" (Nhan & Yen, 2021a, p. 225). Infographics are used in foreign languages learning at the high school level to raise the communicative competence of the learners (Pisarenko & Bondarev, 2016).

Infographics have been used to help students regulate their own learning based on course performance data at various times in a learning term (Ott, Robins, & Shephard, 2014). Infographics have been harnessed to teach computer ethics lessons (Alabdulqader, 2013). Those teaching in the STEM (Science, Technology, Engineering, and Mathematics) fields are seen to benefit with technical communications pedagogy, including digital storytelling through infographics. One tactic is to use a question to set up the suspense for the digital storytelling, with the appeal of the unknown. There are requisite skills in using author voice, pacing the story, and other elements of narration (Hill & Grinnell, 2014), with infographics in the story flow. Infographics are used as learning aids and materials for nursing education (Bradshaw & Porter, 2017).

Infographics are used to increase undergraduate student engagement in health economics. In this case, the teachers conduct research, synthesize information, and then tell a visual story:

Infographics are composed of five components: a skeleton and flowchart, a color scheme, graphics, research and data, and knowledge. In our view, the core of an infographic is composed of three parts: the visual, which provides the color, graphics, and reference icons; the content, which provides the timeframe, facts, statistics, and sources; and finally the knowledge, which includes the answer to the research question(s), deductions, and possible recommendations. (VanderMolen & Spivey, 2017, p. 199)

Employing infographics for teaching and learning requires the harnessing of various teaching strategies and approaches.

One work describes the using of motion-based augmented reality (AR) infographics for a high school biology course (Dehghani et al., 2020, p. 1). This "infographic with AR" condition showed significant positive effects on the learning. More specifically, there were benefits of "visualizing the data, infographic illustration with 3D AR representation, the use of organizer images and, at the same time, reducing the complexity of AR with the help of infographic visualization" for a superior teaching and learning approach (Dehghani et al., 2020, p. 1). Another described the harnessing of infographics to teach the evidence analysis process to senior undergraduate students (Hsiao, Loquatra, Johnson, & Smolic, 2019, p. 26).

Some studies have not found an advantage of informational graphics over other communications modalities. For example, a comparison between the usage of the informational graphic vs. plain text in controlled studies did not find a significant difference in learner performance (Buljan, et al., 2018). A study comparing "graphic + text" vs. infographics for learning value did not find a statistically significant difference in performance for robust learning (Lyra, et al., 2016, p. 370). A comparison between summary modalities between infographics and critical appraisals (which appear to be text-only or text-heavy) resulted in the finding of equal preferences for in a study of professionals who work to harness knowledge "to improve emergency care for children" (Crick & Hartling, 2015, p. 1). Different features were appreciated with the different formats. The infographic was "preferred for aesthetic appeal" and being "visually engaging" and "easy to read while capturing a lot of information"; the critical appraisal format "was preferred in terms of clarity and was found to be directive, professional, and concise" (Crick & Hartling, 2015, p. 6). The infographic as more useful "to patients and their caregivers, the public and the media, while the critical appraisal format was believed to be more appropriate for researchers and research funders" (Crick & Hartling, 2015, p. 6).

Another study in the STEM and visual arts teaching context explored whether static or animated formatting of the infographics had a learning effect. The researcher found that animated infographics were not necessarily more effective than static ones; rather, both were found to be effective "in increasing the knowledge and comprehension of the subject for both groups A and B" (Hassan, 2016, p. 94), in this doctoral dissertation research.

One study examined the role of infographics for the scientific inscription purposes, to assess their quality. The team found five super-ordinate categories of the science infographics that informed their analysis: "purpose/message, audience, organization and design, representation, and data and sources" (Polman & Gebre, 2015, p. 878). This work highlights both effective and non-effective examples in the genre. Infographics have been used in high school science courses as a way of mainstreaming data and making data more understandable (Lamb, Polman, Newman, & Smith, 2014, p. 25).

Infographics and Language Learning

Infographics have been found to benefit the study of language. They are used in the teaching of linguistics and semantics of English as a Foreign Language in the Arab world (Dahmash, Al-Hamid, & Alrajhi, 2017). They may "contain personalized information, specifically examples from the participants' native language" (Dahmash, Al-Hamid, & Alrajhi, 2017, p. 436). The infographics benefit learners in various ways:

59.7% of them suggested that saving and revisiting their data at their convenience is the most important advantage of using infographic-creating software as well as websites. 51.6% of the participants agreed that working on infographics gave them an opportunity to have interactive and dynamic discussions

Infographics for Information Conveyance

with the members of their group…76.9% agreed that infographics helped them analyze information, and 68.8% of them believed that infographics helped them summarize the material efficiently. (Dahmash, Al-Hamid, & Alrajhi, 2017, p. 437)

Researchers have found that infographic instruction is effective for Iranian EFL learners and grammar learning (Rezaei & Sayadian, 2015). Infographics can "significantly" raise EFL learner motivations for learning grammar (Nhan & Yen, 2021b, pp. 85, 96).

Interactivity, seen as intrinsic in the digital age, enables ways to build "empathy" with the users of infographics (Martins, Penedos-Santiago, Lima, Barreto, & Salado, 2020, p. 62). At the present time, the "interactive infographic" is a "relatively new concept" (Martins et al., 2020, p. 62). Even though infographics have been used in "education in general and English language teaching in particular," some teachers are reluctant to engage in "multimedia or infographics" in particular contexts (Khan, 2021, p. 1).

A study found that infographics may benefit "independent learning for English learning in the secondary level context" (Dewantari, Utami, & Santosa, 2021, p. 250). These learning materials may be designed such that they "can provide a complete learning focus in each material" (Dewantari, Utami, & Santosa, 2021, p. 250). This requires the teachers to use their knowledge of the discipline and technology skills and pedagogical skills to help independent learners "explore more" (Dewantari, Utami, & Santosa, 2021, p. 264). The infographics benefit by having experts review them for learning quality.

Another study explored the effects of infographics in "presentations, mnemonic diagrams, instructions" (Tarkhova & Tarkhov, 2020, p. 63). They found more accessible learning for students with different language backgrounds or for whom the language of the teaching is not their primary language (Tarkhova & Tarkhov, 2020, p. 63). The "mnemonic diagrams" enhanced memory (Tarkhova & Tarkhov, 2020, p. 63).

Infographics have been found to be effective in conveying mathematical phenomena, principles, and laws, to make math learning more accessible through visualization as augmentation. A study of how such infographics were received in an undergraduate mathematics course found that a majority of students benefitted (Sudakov, Bellsky, Usenyuk, & Polyakova, 2016, p. 19). Another study found benefits of using infographics for those with math learning difficulties (Bağlama, Yucesoy, Uzunboylu, & Özcan, 2017), based on a literature review.

Student-created Infographics for Learning

The conceptualization and creation of infographics in a learning context have also been useful for learning, according to the research. One study found that "an infographic creation-based training process has a significant effect on academic achievement and metacognitive skills, especially on facilitating the management of the learning process" in a postgraduate course (Yuruk, Yilmaz, & Bilici, 2019, p. 495). The making of infographics was helpful for summarizing information and aided comprehension and recall (Yuruk, Yilmaz, & Bilici, 2019, p. 510). Infographics can be used as an alternative assessment method (Yuruk, Yilmaz, & Bilici, 2019, p. 510). Students generated infographics in a sophomore analytical chemistry course to increase their research and informational literacy and communications skills (Mitchell, Morris, Meredith, & Bishop, 2017, p. 113).

Student-created infographics are used for the training of those working in graphic design and digital media fields, to blend "data with design" (Noh, Fauzi, Jing, & Ilias, 2017, p. 59). Researchers suggest that there is an important middle space between too little guidance and too much guidance in the student work (Noh, Fauzi, Jing, & Ilias, 2017, p. 58). Students learn how to create informational graphics, so they may communicate the "visual legacies" of their work beyond the initial contemporaneous moment (Thompson, 2015, p. 91).

Students in social work have created infographics to build their digital skills. A study found that the students said that "it improved their engagement and learning and offered opportunities for creativity and decision making" (Jones, Sage, & Hitchcock, 2019, p. 1). In business communications, one researcher proposes the teaching of infographics, with ideas for an analytical assignment and another on students producing an actual infographic (Toth, 2013), given their prevalence in the world. Another case involved using infographics in an online college classroom as "a research-based graphic design assignment," which was found to enhance multimodal digital literacies (Matrix & Hodson, 2014, p. 1). Another approach in online courses involves using infographics as weekly course content summaries, with students seeing infographics as "valuable" for their learning (Yarbrough, 2019, p. 1). One work describes a collaboration across disciplines for the creation of infographics for interdisciplinary learning online. These were instructor-created summary infographics capturing key learning objectives and contents in graphical form. Would these be helpful in an online learning environment? Students participating in this study said such infographic summaries were "useful and appealing for retaining, clarifying and understanding learning concepts" in the massive online learning environment (Gallagher, et al., 2017, p. 129). These summary infographics at the end of each module were effective in helping learners understand key points in the learning, according to some 91% of student respondents (Gallagher, et al., 2017, p. 137), and they aided in retention or improved memory of the learning (p. 141).

Teachers who would use student-created infographics in learning need to help learners explain data and information visually. They have to apply strategic uses of visual materials (Taspolat, Kaya, Sapanca, Beheshti, & Ozdamli. 2017), with a clear learning focus.

Another study found that there were typical mistakes made by students when they created infographics since the work required drawing on various skillsets around which learners had low or no competence" (Tarkhova & Tarkhov, 2020).

Secondary school students have also learned by creating infographics. They acquire hands-on learning about representing scientific data in multiple ways. The study explored "how infographics can serve as process-oriented cognitive tools for learning and instruction of science literacy in classroom contexts" (Gebre, 2018, p. 1). Creating an infographic is "a knowledge construction process" enabling learners to engage data sources, visuals, and then the composited "holistic" layer of the infographic (Gebre, 2018, p. 16). The researcher advocates for the benefits of ensuring that the assignments are "open-ended," so that students "make active decisions" (Gebre, 2018, p. 15). There are social aspects to the learning, such as collaboration around infographic creation and feedback.

Infographics and e-Books

Digital educational publishing has also incorporated digital infographics, given the capabilities of e-readers. The making of animation "even with modern software...is slow work" (Lievemaa, 2017, p. 27); it is a demanding craft to create animated infographics that are effective.

Infographics in K-12 Learning

Infographics are also used in K-12 learning. One study examined the effect of infographics on four areas of courses for fifth grade learners, with the finding that infographics "had a positive impact on

Infographics for Information Conveyance

the academic success" in four courses and learning retention in three of the studied courses (Özdal, & Ozdamli, 2017, p. 1256).

During the pandemic, students were encouraged to create green chemistry infographics given the inability to run the organic chemistry labs under lockdown to protect human health (Grieger & Leontyev, 2021, p. 2881).

One study explored how receptive undergraduate students are to the uses of infographics in education or the "teaching by infographics" (Bicen & Beheshti, 2017, p. 99). The approach is as follows:

In education, the infographics are used to illustrate the complex information in a compact form. This feature enables teachers to make ready various learning activities, comprises warm-up lectures and summaries of the unit in order to engage students with the course contents and make more chances for interaction. (Vanichvasin, 2013, as cited in Bicen & Beheshti, 2017, p. 101)

Learning using infographics is seen as "very efficient" by students and apparently "enhances students' creativity, knowledge, motivation, imagination, and communication skills" (Bicen & Beheshti, 2017, p. 105).

Infographic Trainings

Influencing people to take on new learning and change their behaviors can be challenging. One area of focus that has received an infographic educational treatment is debt literacy. Particular capabilities of the learners affected the efficacy of the training. For example, numeracy played an important role in mediating the relationship between the initial and final debt literacy (Porzak, Cwynar, & Cwynar, 2021, p. 10). The researchers write:

...infographics-based education may be effective, at least in the short run. The scale of debt literacy growth of 2/3 of the entry level in the experimental group after exposition to a series of 4 simple infographics is very promising, suggesting the high potential of using infographics in debt education. (Porzak, Cwynar, & Cwynar, 2021, p. 11)

This and other studies apply critical empirical methods to understanding the relative efficacy of the infographics-based trainings.

RECEPTION OF INFOGRAPHICS: HOW INFOGRAPHICS ARE CONSUMED

At a basic level, infographics require both visual perception (or equivalent perceptual channels, based on accessibility mitigations) and cognitive processing to consume. Part of the design of infographics involves visuocognitive design for human learning; this ensures that the infographic maps to human cognitive processes (Gay et al., 2019).

There are some external referents to the infographics, in many cases, even as the visuals are supposed to be stand-alone. The motion and interactivity aspects introduce "transience," which requires higher cognitive load to consume effectively. At the simplest level, infographics may mean that users take a longer look, a second look, and invest longer attention to the messages of the infographic. One central debate about how infographics should be designed has been represented as Tufte vs. Holmes. Edward Tufte has suggested that infographics should be sparse, with the mere data and little else, while Nigel Holmes advocates for having "ample amounts of graphics and design elements in information design (Won, 2017, p. 59). The more dense an infographic, the less function it is perceived to be by users (generally) (Locoro, Cabitza, Actis-Grosso, & Batini, 2017, p. 34). However, given modern changes and the sophistication of data consumers, many infographics today contain various layers and dimensions of complex information.

One cited study suggests that user comprehension does not suffer in terms of decorative vs. minimal graphs; however, the decorative one "received a higher score…in recollection after two to three weeks. Moreover, the participants preferred the decorative graph" (Bateman, et al., 2010, as cited in Won, 2017, p. 59). Perhaps there is a fine line between sufficient simplicity and sufficient complexity. Design-wise, infographics range from minimalism to "elaborately decorated, or embellished" (with storytelling on this end) (Andry, Hurter, Lambotte, Fastrez, & Telea, 2021, p. 1). The multisource-based research, involving questionnaires, interviews, and eye-tracking data, resulting in the following finding:

We found that, within bounds, embellishments have a positive effect on how users get engaged in understanding an infographic, with very limited downside (Andry et al., 2021, p. 1).

Embellishments like icons especially "have a positive impact on reading a visualization, by (1) reducing the adverse feeling of effort needed to read the data and (2) engaging the reader with the visualization topic" (Andry et al., 2021, p. 11). They write: "Our analysis showed that embellishment reduces the user's feeling of effort and produces more engagement…and only marginally decreases understandability" (Andry et al., 2021, p. 13). Perhaps some contexts benefit more from embellishments and others, less.

Perceptions of Changes in Space-time Clusters

One work explored human perception of changes in space-time clusters (that "move over space and through time") shown on animated maps (Griffin et al., 2006, p. 740). These works found that "animation pace, cluster coherence, and gender" were factors in the perception (Griffin et al., 2006, p. 740). One finding was that "map readers answer more quickly and identify more patterns correctly when using animated maps than when using static small-multiple maps" (Griffin et al., 2006, p. 740). Participants in the research had difficulty seeing "subtle moving clusters" (Griffin et al., 2006, p. 747). "Strong" clusters were easier to perceive than "subtle" ones. This work found clear advantages to animation:

…our results show that the animated representation enabled users to more often correctly identify whether a particular type of pattern was present than did the static small-multiple representation. Participants were also able to come to a conclusion about what they saw more quickly while viewing an animated representation. (Griffin et al., 2006, p. 749)

This study also cast doubt on the idea that animations require higher levels of cognitive processing. The researchers write: "It may be that the cognitive load associated with visually identifying moving clusters is relatively light, and those factors that influence the map reader's perceptual capabilities are more important for successfully completing this task" (Griffin et al., p. 749).

Infographics for Information Conveyance

Other stories have explored the effects of color—hue, saturation, lightness—on short-term memory. One study found that four colors were most correlated with recall: "magenta, red, yellow, and cyan" (Kang, 2016, p. 145). This researcher found "significant correlations between color and short-term memory" (Kang, 2016, p. 145).

The top four recalled colors feature with high lightness and wavelength. The brightness and wavelength of the line could have an arousing effect, be able to catch more attention, and therefore might cause enough arousal to trigger better short-term memory. The results of the experiment also show that 41 percent of people like bright colors. 63 percent of people have their favorite colors. 65 percent of people prefer theirs (sic) favorite color items. (Kang, 2016, p. 145).

Another study examined how the symmetric concept in Gestalt ideas of visuals could be improved for human perception and memory, by sharpening and intensifying select edges of visuals to emphasize existing symmetries to help direct human attention to local regions of interest (Yasuda, Takahashi, & Wu, 2016, p. 35).

Benefits of Animation

The designing and creating of animated infographics require "tremendous effort" (Wang, Gao, Huang, Cui, Zhang, & Zhang, June 2021, p. 507). There are cost considerations. Many use precise storyboards with "shot-by-shot specifications representing and correlating the graphics, text, animation, voiceover and sound effects" (Bellei, Welch, Pryor, & Ketheesan, 2016, p. 477). The input of discipline experts is important for accuracy (Bellei, Welch, Pryor, & Ketheesan, 2016, p. 477). The individual or team that creates the motion visual has to follow conventions in the displaying of data, such as with main layouts: linear, radial, segmented, and "fiveform" (Wang, Gao, Huang, Cui, Zhang, & Zhang, June 2021, p. 510). There are temporal considerations. This research work suggests that there are three types: concurrently (where the animation is applied globally to the entire structure and "shown all at once"); by repeating units (where the animation is applied to units "one by one and the elements in a unit tend to appear together"), and finally by element groups (where the animation applies to similar elements together, such as titles first, and then descriptions next) (Wang, Gao, Huang, Cui, Zhang, & Zhang, June 2021, p. 510). There are three styles of animation pacing: one-by-one, all-at-once, and staggering (with different start times) (Wang, Gao, Huang, Cui, Zhang, & Zhang, June 2021, p. 511).

One study found that both "animation" and "pictographs" in data videos have "an effect on viewer engagement" (Amini, Riche, Lee, Leboe-McGowan, & Irani, 2018, p. 1), with animation that "significantly improved viewer engagement" (p. 7). This work explored how to use visual and motion elements in a way that supports the message instead of detracting from it. In part, the researchers used a questionnaire designed to understand factors that affect viewer engagement with data videos. They identified five factors that influence user engagement: "(1) affective involvement, (2) enjoyment, (3) aesthetics, (4), focused attention, and (5) cognitive involvement" (Amini, Riche, Lee, Leboe-McGowan, & Irani, 2018, p. 1). This study also found a preference for "pictographic representations" of standard charts (Amini, Riche, Lee, Leboe-McGowan, & Irani, 2018, p. 7) which are able to "provoke emotions" (p. 8). From this work, they researchers offer some advice about the making of data videos:

When the information being communicated through data videos requires focused attention from the viewers, we suggest incorporation of setup animation to avoid attention drift. Gradual building of the visualization scene in data clips showed to also help viewers comprehend the information better. (Amini et al., 2018, p. 8)

Other studies do not identify a benefit to animations per se. One work about the uses of infographics for terror messaging from governments to protect citizens resulted in the finding of "no significant difference between communicating information via an infographic or motion graphics" in "situations where information needs to be assimilated as a crescendo (i.e., levels of severity) or as a series of steps to be followed (action in an emergency)" (Lonsdale et al., 2019, p. 37).

Even as those creating infographics consider human factors, others are designing adaptive systems to align with human needs, to take into account user metacognition and user motivations and adapt accordingly (Germanakos et al., 2019, p. 331). Researchers point to preferred technologies for the creation of infographics, such as scalable vector graphics vs. raster:

SVG infographics can be personalized or visually customized for different demographic groups, cultures, aesthetical preferences or users with special needs. SVG content can be dynamically generated based on the existing information and the end user can interactively choose how that information will be shown. (Pavazza & Pap, 2012, p. 53)

Some consider infographics to be manual creations, "handcrafted to effectively communicate messages about complex and often abstract topics" (Madan, et al., 2018, p. 1). Some interactive infographics require programming (Dur, 2014a, p. 47). There are also automated systems that can output infographics to dashboards or the Web or other contexts. One automatic infographics generator is based on "machine learning algorithms / user-defined rules and visual embellishments" and is informed by data (Zhu et al., 2020, p. 24). Machine learning was harnessed to form algorithms and programs to achieve the outputs. The researchers observe the need to get the balance right between "creativity and automation" (Zhu et al., 2020, p. 38), and automatic annotations are common to help users consume the displayed data and visualizations (p. 27). Another work describes a technological technique for creating designed infographics (Tymchenko et al., 2019). Yet another describes the automated creating of an extensible timeline (Chen, Wang, Wang, Wang, & Qu, 2019).

Then, there are the familiar algorithms that render text frequency counts to visualizations, such as area charts (treemap diagrams, sunburst diagrams, and others) and word clouds. One work describes the automatic generation of infographics from proportion related natural language statements based on various patterns (Cui et al., 2019, p. 906). Automated creation of proportion-based infographics (Qian et al., 2020) also enable building various data-based resources.

Data Comics or Infographics

A comparative study about user preferences for either data comics or infographics found a preference for "data comics in terms of enjoyment, focus, and overall engagement" and further that data comics improved "understanding and recall of information in the stories" as compared to infographics (Wang et al., 2019, p. 1). In general, comics are "highly accessible to a large audience, compatible with many different media" and able to be consumed at the user's own pace (Wang et al., 2019, p. 2). Data comics

Infographics for Information Conveyance

are presented as a sequence of panels. Having a large distance between the text and the picture "impairs understanding and increases cognitive load" (Wang et al., 2019, p. 9). This study found some strengths to infographics, too:

Infographics are well-suited to represent spatial content and are good at delivering both overview and detail. Participants liked the way they allow for comparison, and were more likely to want to share their discoveries with other viewers. (Wang et al., 2019, p. 10)

This work suggests effective design features for data comics, including "balancing repetition and highlighting," "balancing sequence and overview," "using the layout to structure information," "reducing visual complexity," and other insights (Wang et al., 2019, p. 10). This work suggests the use of selected "techniques from data comics and infographics…" in a "seamlessly integrated way" for effective data messaging (Wang et al., 2019, p. 10)

Mixed Findings About Infographics and Multimedia Effects on People

Another work offers mixed findings related to multimedia and cognition and learning in the study of health infographics. This study found limited uses of interactions, usually for "simple narrative controls… which only allowed forwarding and/or backwarding the content sequence"; specifically, interactions were not so often used as "an aid to learning/understanding" in terms of health-based infographics in newspapers in one study (de Castro Andrade & Spinillo, 2018, p. 194). One question the researchers asked related to the use of on-screen text—whether it aided comprehension or detracted and incurred a cognitive load price. They write:

The versions presenting on-screen text showed better results on comprehension than those without text, except the version in which on-screen text was presented with interaction and animation (IAT). This version showed the lowest rate in comprehension, whereas interaction employed with static images produced the highest rate (IST). These unexpected results may lead to question: (a) the positive effect of interaction employed together with animation; and (b) the negative effect of on-screen text employed together with animation or static images. (de Castro Andrade & Spinillo, 2018, p. 197)

Another study focused on game-based infographics. This research explored "how to embed meaningful visual analytic interactions into game mechanics that in turn impact user behavior around a data-driven graphic" (Diakopoulos, Kivran-Swaine, & Naaman, 2011, p. 1717) in a gamified experience. This work explored how to encourage people to engage "playable data" used at various points in the game-based story.

There are complex findings in another work. Here, students were broken out into reflective and impulsive ones, in terms of cognitive style.

The findings showed that interactive infographics are more effective than static infographics in improving academic achievement. Reflective students outperformed impulsive students in terms of academic achievement, and there was a significant interaction between interactive infographics and reflective students. (Ismaeel & Al Mulhim, 2021, p. 147)

This would suggest benefits of creating various infographics with informational equivalencies for different learners, to align with their preferences, where possible.

Handling of Deceptive Infographics

How do consumers of data respond to deceptive infographic, when paired with deceptive vs. non-deceptive explanatory text? One study found "...deceptive techniques in data visualizations caused participants to misinterpret the information in the deceptive data visualizations even when they were accompanied by accurate explanatory text" (O'Brien & Lauer, 2018, p. 1). They found that certain demographic portions of the population affected susceptibility to the deceptive techniques. The level of comfort with particular data chart types were also a factor in susceptibility to deceptive infographics (there is a benefit to having some prior experience).

Infographics may also affect issues of credibility, such as trust in science. In one study, the researchers asked how people could increase trust in science through particular design features in competing infographics. How could infographics convey "oppositional interpretation" in some of the messaging given how science is conducted (Agley et al., 2021, p. 5)?

Another factor for data credibility involves the fact of mixed citations of sources for infographics. One researcher observes:

Although most infographics indicate its sources and start points (e.g. as a collection of URLs in small print at the bottom of the image), however, it is usually impossible to track back the source of information (and the reliability of each source). For this reason, repeatability and verifiability, source criticism, the reliability of the data, and thus the risk of manipulation and methods to avoid it remain salient issues in this field. (Veszelszki, 2014, p. 109)

Clearer tracking of data sources in infographics may improve trust in infographics.

Another work explored how science-based information was evaluated based on various infographic designs, with the finding that "viewers tend to rely on preexisting levels of trust and peripheral cues, such as source attribution, to judge the credibility of shown data, whereas their comprehension level did not relate to perception of data credibility" (Li et al., 2018, p. 1). The predisposition of users was also seen to have an effect, including in areas such as "graph efficacy," "numeracy skills," and "domain knowledge" (Li et al., 2018, p. 7). This suggests the importance of knowing the target users of the planned infographics, such as their backgrounds and "cognitive needs" in order to shape the infographic (Li et al., 2018, p. 20).

Interactivity Along Various Dimensions

One research study differentiates between the functional and emotional categories of expressions in interactive infographics. Functional expressions work "by accentuating and adding information; emotional ones entertain "users and invite(s) their participation" (Won, 2017, p. 62). The researcher explains:

Functional expressions of interactive infographics included functional elements such as adding or subtracting information, accentuating necessary information through interaction, presenting relationships between multiple graphs, and providing selected information in detail through movements or changes in

Infographics for Information Conveyance

chart types. Emotional expressions included elements such as showing colorful animations—for example, tables put together—and presenting interesting movements without changing the provided information as users interact with them. (Won, 2017, p. 62)

This study found that "infographics with interactions generated more positive evaluations than those without interactions in the aspects of entertainment, reliability, and informativeness" (Won, 2017, p. 68).

Also: "Emotional interactions recorded the highest scores for entertainment, while functional interactions received high scores in informativeness and reliability" (Won, 2017, p. 68). The study highlighted the importance of both reliability and entertainment on the "perceived cognitive effects of infographics" (Won, 2017, p. 68). In terms of user acceptance, this was informed by both entertainment and informativeness (Won, 2017, p. 68). This study suggests that the entertainment value of infographics is an important factor affecting user responses. The researcher writes:

When we looked at the influence of interaction design types on the value assessment of infographics, infographics with interactions generated more positive evaluations than those without interactions in the aspects of entertainment, reliability, and informativeness. Reliability and entertainment showed meaningful influences on the attitude towards and perceived cognitive effects of infographics, while informativeness showed minimal influence on attitude and showed no influence on cognitive effects. In the case of acceptance intentions, entertainment and informativeness showed meaningful influence but reliability itself did not influence acceptance intentions. Overall, entertainment showed the greatest influence. And entertainment especially showed a very high correlation with perceived cognitive effects. (Won, 2017, p. 57)

Interactions may be considered integral parts of infographics as an information type, in some contexts.

Quality Standards in Infographics

"Good design is a lot like clear thinking made visual" -- Edward Tufte

There are particular standards for infographics in general (although not with full consensus) but also specific quality standards for particular applications of infographics in various use contexts. There are variances, too, in terms of quality standards for motion infographics and interactive ones, based on features of their modality, and human perceptions and cognitive processing. Public critiques of various public infographics for not meeting particular quality standards are rife (Featherstone, 2014, p. 148).

Designers identified various features as critical to the quality of the infographics: information-visual consistency, visual quality, information quality, level of information visualization, typographical features, resources, and "designer person / organization" (Yildirim, 2017, p. 269). They preferred to go with visuals instead of data tables for designers of infographics (Yildirim, 2017, p. 269). They tended towards warmer colors for shapes and cooler colors for text and numbers (also for definition) (Yildirim, 2017, p. 275).

Various attributes have been identified in different research works for quality infographics. Quality standards for infographics emerged during the second half of the 19th century (Dick, 2017, p. 3). One work maps out quality approaches in four discourses: "functionalist-idealist," "pragmatist-realist," "expressionist-aesthete," and "didactic-persuasive" (Dick, 2017, p. 4). The data underlying the infographic

341

should be accurately represented. The various standards are also informed by the practical usage of the infographic by the target audiences and others.

Quality in Static Infographics

The component parts of an infographic include the following: data, design, story, and visibility. The data has to be "reliable and timely"; the design including complementary fonts and colors set up in a legible way; story that focuses on "a single message," and visibility in terms of social exposure on social media or prime locations in print. (Evans, 2016, p. 4)

Some works describe quality layout practices for the elements of an infographic. "In practice, seven grouping principles are usually listed as the Gestalt laws: proximity, similarity, continuity, closure, area (figure and ground), common fate, and symmetry" (Yasuda, Takahashi, & Wu, 2016, p. 35). ["Common fate" involves objects moving together in the same direction or at the same rate of movement being seen as a group that shares a "common fate."] Based on color and contrast and shape, certain features emerge as conspicuous based on features of human vision. Designers can direct the "instant visual attention" in people through design (Yasuda, Takahashi, & Wu, 2016, p. 35). One approach involves finding image edges that contribute to "symmetry saliency" and augmenting the image gradient to create an edge which can be picked up on visually (Yasuda, Takahashi, & Wu, 2016, p. 35).

Another work suggests that the quality of infographics is based on two main factors: "content and visual appeal" (Joshi & Gupta, 2021, p. 1). The information content has to be "concise, understandable and self-explanatory," and the visual presentation has to be achieved without "over or under crowding" (Joshi & Gupta, 2021, p. 4). There has to be a reasoned color scheme aligned with the human visual system. The design itself has to be consistent.

In the health infographics space, clarity of messaging and credibility of the underlying data sources are critical. One study involved the exploration of several health infographics to understand what elements supported the trust in the infographics. The researcher summarizes the research: "...the structure of the health infographic did indeed play a role in its message credibility determination. The importance of this structure is discussed through the lens of its importance in creating a narrative for the health infographic. Message exaggeration was also found to have an effect on message credibility, thus indicating the possible effect of having unbiased or opinionated visual messages. The moderating effect of prior assumptions about manipulated content were also found" (Kanthawala, 2019, p. 1). Purposeful communication has to be carefully designed since it may inform decisions that follow that have effects on people. Some infographics themselves may be direct decision aids.

Quality in Motion Infographics

Another work suggests that with motion in infographics, there are rules related to sequencing, montages and process montages, the *Kuleshov-Effect* (Lengler & Moere, 2009, p. 587), and other factors. Generally consecutive sequences are thought to be related.

Quality in Interactive Infographics

One study involved the creation of an exploratory model "to assess the overall quality of static and interactive infographics, based on information, interaction and design quality dimensions" (Locoro et al.,

Infographics for Information Conveyance

2017, p. 1). Here, quality dimensions of infographics include the following: sinteticity, clarity, informativity, intuitivity, elegance, attractiveness, usability, and ease of use (Locoro et al., 2017, pp. 4-7). More specifically, "sinteticity" refers to "the capability of representing the aspects of the reality of interest with the minimal use of informative resources" with expressions of both "minimality and essentiality" (p. 7). "Clarity" refers to how readable the information is and how comprehensible. "Informativity" refers to how the "relevant aspects of the reality of interest" are fully conveyed. "Intuitivity: focuses on "the organization of information in terms of context" for at-a-glance consumption. "Elegance" points to the look-and-feel of the infographic. "Attractiveness" refers to the "aesthetic pleasure of visualizing information" that may affect user engagement. (Locoro et al., 2017, p. 8). "Usability" refers to a range of user use cases with various goals, and is described as the level of "effectiveness, efficiency and satisfaction in a specified context of use" (as based on the ISO-9241-11). Lastly, "ease of use" refers to the user-friendliness of the experience when using the infographic (Locoro et al., 2017, p. 9). This work uses a user-centered user-experience model to assess quality.

Other works have also used usability studies to ensure that they are designed effectively for the target audience, such as those consumers of online newspapers. One study explored the effects of interactive infographics to communicate complexity and spark user excitement. This work involved assessing for suitability of the infographic for achieving various tasks, conformity with user expectations, self-descriptiveness of the interactive infographics, and controllability (Langer & Zeiller, 2017).

One study found a gender difference in terms of the efficacy of static infographics vs. animated infographics (AI), with static ones having "a greater effect on female student learning while AI was found more effective for male student learning" (Ibrahem & Alamro, 2021, p. 907).

Another work describes the effective use of interactive augmented reality (AR) for business presentations for audience engagement and presentation effects. The novelty of such AR approaches captured audience attention positively given the boredom with "traditional slideshows" (Doukianou, Daylamani-Zad, & O'Loingsigh, 2021). Certainly, there are rules for effective AR motion design and interactivity.

Communicating Uncertainty

There are particular aspects that are considered for infographic quality, such as visual and other methods to convey uncertainty about the future (using probabilities). Some common strategies include "cones of uncertainty," such as those used to project paths of hurricanes and tornadoes. Some use text size. Others use color and icons and text and verbals. The tips about handling probabilistic uncertainty are from one research work:

- "Use multiple formats, because no single representation suits all members of an audience.
- Illuminate graphics with words and numbers.
- Design graphics to allow part-to-whole comparisons, and choose an appropriate scale, possibly with magnification for small probabilities.
- To avoid framing bias, provide percentages or frequencies both with and without the outcome, using frequencies with a clearly defined denominator of constant size.
- Helpful narrative labels are important. Compare magnitudes through tick marks, and clearly label comparators and differences.
- Use narratives, images, and metaphors that are sufficiently vivid to gain and retain attention, but which do not arouse undue emotion. It is important to be aware of affective responses.

Infographics for Information Conveyance

- Assume low numeracy of a general public audience and adopt a less-is-more approach by reducing the need for inferences, making clear and explicit comparisons, and providing optional additional detail.
- Interactivity and animations provide opportunities for adapting graphics to user needs and capabilities.
- Acknowledge the limitations of the information conveyed in its quality and relevance. The visualization may communicate only a restricted part of a whole picture.
- Avoid chart junk, such as three-dimensional bar charts, and obvious manipulation through misleading use of area to represent magnitude.
- Most important, assess the needs of the audience, experiment, and test and iterate toward a final design." (Spiegelhalter, Pearson, & Short, 2011, p. 1399)

Learning from Infographic Designers to Enhance Technologies

One observational study explored how designers plan data visualizations in order to improve the tools that they use to enable such works. Designers often draw out "high-level elements of their design such as the layout and axes, followed by a sketching in of data points based on their perceived ideas of data behavior" (Bigelow et al., 2014, p. 19). Further: "…while the designers frequently refined the nondata visual elements of their designs, such as color and font choices, the design of their data encodings remained unchanged until assumptions about data behavior were shown to be incorrect" (Bigelow et al., 2014, p. 20). This study emerged with four themes to inform the design of such technologies:

First, manual encoding is acceptable when the tradeoff is flexibility, and is a form of data exploration. Second, designers prefer to place data on existing graphics instead of generating graphics directly from data. Third, to support flexibility, operations should be commutative. Finally, tool creators should be aware of designers' struggles to define and modify data abstractions. These themes have interesting implications for two known challenges in the visualization community: the challenge of creating tools that support defining and modifying the data abstraction; and the challenge of creating flexible yet efficient tools for producing visual representations of data. (Bigelow et al., 2014, p. 21)

Aesthetics Appeal of Infographics

"Infographics are not art displays, but are tools to communicate information" reads one observation (Albers, 2015, p. 1), which indirectly alludes to the high aesthetic quality of some infographics. (Some infographics are so complex and alluring that they have been included in museum displays.)

Still, in general, infographics are usually purposefully designed for particular strategic and tactical communications. There are ties between clear design, aesthetics, and learning value in infographics: "Visual metaphors and quality designs that have deep connections with their content support the subject and make it more attractive, which helps in recollection of the information" (Won, 2017, p. 59). Design is often function-based, to help users work through visual complexity to better understand the data and to help them focus on salient information (Albers, 2015). Some groups use style guides to tailor infographics to particular standards and aesthetics, such as one for electronic health data (Arcia, Velez, & Bakken, 2015).

Infographics for Information Conveyance

The designed beauty or aesthetics of infographics are seen based on a "mere exposure effect" in less than a second (within the first 500 milliseconds of viewing) (Harrison, Reinecke, & Chang, 2015, pp. 1187 - 1188) and affect how that infographic is interacted with by people (how they engage, how memorable the information is, and what is learned from the infographic). The appeal is based on "colorfulness and visual complexity" (Harrison, Reinecke, & Chang, 2015, p. 1187). Demographic factors such as "age, gender, and education level" affect the level of color and complexity preferred (Harrison, Reinecke, & Chang, 2015, p. 1187). Interestingly, though, infographics were not universally seen as attractive or unattractive. The researchers write:

Some infographics appeal broadly, but the majority produced controversial judgements. Although people are consistent in their judgements, they have strong, diverse opinions about the infographics they like/dislike. (Harrison, Reinecke, & Chang, 2015, p. 1188)

The quality assessment of infographics seems to be more socio-culturally based and local than universal. One research team writes:

Acquired codes leverage a user's experience to understand the meaning of a visualization. They range from figurative visualizations which rely on the reader's recognition of shapes, to conventional arrangements of graphic elements which represent particular subjects. (Byrne, Angus, & Wiles, 2015, p. 509).

The context informs how the perceptual shape primitives are viewed. Various works also engage "hybrid representations" (Byrne, Angus, & Wiles, 2015, p. 511), which introduce even more complexity. Infographics are "grounded in a tradition of narrative" (Byrne, Angus, & Wiles, 2015, p. 515), which requires learning to be read into those traditions. Various visualization conventions are based on "an evolving community of practice" (Byrne, Angus, & Wiles, 2015, p. 517). A study of a dataset of infographics suggests that "the supposed ideal of graphic purity is not adhered to by data visualization designers" (Byrne, Angus, & Wiles, 2015, p. 517).

One research team selected the *aesthetic learning experience framework* (Parrish, 2009, as cited in Dunlap & Lowenthal, 2016, p. 46) as a basis to study what makes for a "good infographic." They identify the import of creating a direct connection of the learners to the content ("immediacy," with "a sense of urgency or excitement") to be effective (Dunlap & Lowenthal, 2016, p. 47). The messaging has to be sufficiently "malleable" so that users can "determine personal meaning and relevance" so as to be "co-owners/co-creators of the experience" (Dunlap & Lowenthal, 2016, p. 47), and it has to be coherent in terms of "logic, clarity and consistency" (p. 48). The content has to be compelling to capture learner interest. Also, the informational graphic has to be "resonant" to be able to create a "lasting relevant effect" (Dunlap & Lowenthal, 2016, p. 48). Visuals should be informative foremost and not decorative (Dunlap & Lowenthal, 2016).

DESIGN OF INFOGRAPHICS (OF VARIOUS TYPES)

Those who create infographics "tend to be graphic designers, visual journalists, bloggers, cartographers, artists, or urban planners" (Klein, 2014, p. 28). In the present moment, infographics are considered such a central part of communications that their creation is considered part of the technical writer toolkit writers (Bursi-Amba, Gaullier, & Santidrian, 2016). Technical writers are expected to be able to engage the literal or metaphorical conveyance of information using data and visualizations and text. The skills of "content curation, mapping, and visualization" for the making of infographics are also suggested for those in the visual arts (Klein, 2014, p. 25). Other works here mention programmers as well. Regardless, there is a mix of complex skills required.

It has been suggested that those who create infographics are sometimes creating novel ideas. For example, those who use fresh metaphors in their infographics are creating new knowledge (Lengler & Moere, 2009, p. 588). For their work to be appreciated, though, the audience has to be familiar with the metaphor target, on which the visual comparison is made.

There has been a call for the need for more research and clearer guidelines about how to create effective infographics (Albers, 2014, p. 1).

Various research works describe a variety of different approaches in designing, developing, and deploying infographics for various purposes. A general approach has been depicted as a cross-functional diagram in Figure 1. Often, in Phase 1: Design, the process begins with either conceptualization or research (each, informing the other). A design is formulated across a variety of dimensions (layout, pedagogy, motion, interactivity, aesthetics, accessibility, and others). The work is paper-prototyped and vetted. Once approved, the development work proceeds in Phase 2. The development includes creating the artwork, the layout, the motion, the interactivity, and so on. The infographic is alpha- and beta- tested. Alpha testing involves testing for all relevant standards based on the design. The beta testing involves bringing in live users from outside the organization for usability and other assessments. Necessary revisions are made, and then the deployment proceeds in Phase 3.

The summary cross-functional diagram is fairly generic. The research literature can shed some light on others' approaches. The diagram suggests three phases: design, development, and deployment. A different team suggests that there are three phases: Design, development, and evaluation of the infographic (Dewantari, Utami, & Santosa, 2021, p. 260).

Other Approaches and Sequences

One of the infographics from the "motion" set summarized a design sequence: script, storyboard, graphics, voiceover and music, first pass, and final pass. Several works here use instructional design frameworks for the design of infographics (Ozdamli & Ozdal, 2018, p. 1197; Dyjur & Li, 2015, p. 62). One researcher describes the design and sequence as beginning with research of the subject. Then, there is preparation of the "presentation scenario," deciding the core components of the design, "identification of information importance level," creating methods for attracting reader attention, setting up relationships between the information, preparing the text, making the visualizations, creating a slogan, and the compositing the design components, based on feedback from those who design infographics (Yildirim, 2017, p. 268).

Another research describes a different set of steps:

1. Analyzing and data preparation
2. Choosing the appropriate tools
3. Determining the leitmotif
4. Determining the form of the data presentation
5. Developing of content corresponding to the theme of infographics
6. Determining the order of data presentation

Infographics for Information Conveyance

7. Finalization of the project (Szoltysik, 2016, p. 172)

Another lesson involving "planning, researching, drafting, revising, and publishing" (Yearta, Kelly, Kissel, & Schonhar, 2018, p. 57), in terms of a high-level sequence. One work mentioned the importance of knowledge of "copyright, publicity, references, design preferences, production environments and production processes" (Yildirim, 2017, p. 248), which evokes some of the underlying complexities. Legal considerations such as copyright are important (Fadzil, 2018, p. 11). One research team emphasizes the importance of the judicious use of infographic history in the design and deployment of infographics today (Burgio & Moretti, 2017). Their point is that stylistic choices do not exist in a vacuum.

There is meaningfulness beyond information in infographics. A question is posited: "What is the boundary between useless decoration, narrative illustration and helpful visual metaphors?" (Burgio & Moretti, 2017, p. 1) Perhaps such a question may help direct the design, development and deployment of infographics.

Figure 1. Basic Steps to Creating a Motion and Interactive Infographic for Learning (a cross functional diagram)

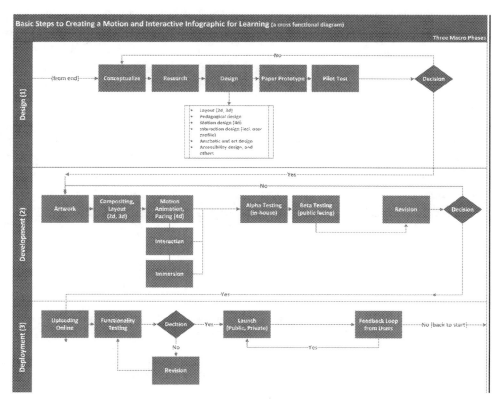

INFOGRAPHICS FOR INFORMATION CONVEYANCE: A LIGHT HISTORY FROM EARLY DAYS (STASIS) TO TODAY (MOTION, INTERACTIVE, IMMERSIVE)

This work uses both direct and indirect approaches to learn about infographics, including "motion" and "interactive" infographics. There are direct ways to access infographics on the Social Web and Internet by downloading the informational visuals. Then there are less direct ways to look at infographics on the Social Web: a related tags network from a large social image-sharing site, a social network graph around the hashtag network #infographics on a major microblogging site, an "infographics" shadow dataset from the world's largest collection of digitized and digital books. Other sorts of approaches may be taken, but perhaps, those may be set for a follow-on work.

Capturing still images related to various aspects of modern infographics—motion, interactive, and immersive—is similar to capturing information from the informal gray literature. These are popular examples in the real world.

Motion Infographics

A "motion infographics" search on Google Images resulted in 1,145 images. The tags used for filtering were the following: "projectile, simple, force, law, newton, gif, interactive, after effects motion, animated gif, interactive infographic design, infographic examples, graphic designer, visual communication, motion designer, infographic video, interactive animation, cartoon, graphics examples, (and) illustration," which may give a sense of the initial contents of the imageset. Tags are usually all in lower case, so that is how they are represented here. (Figure 2) The visuals were downloaded as thumbnails (using a third-party web browser add-on on Chrome) and were analyzed, albeit many without the designed motion (which require other technological dependencies to play).

Some were animated gifs. Some showed scrolling through visual and textual information. Some showed numerical data rising or falling. There were some motion accentuations to bring human attention to particular data points. A few were clever uses of visuals in mini-Rube Goldberg machine-like sequences. There were some pinball-based motions, with virtual balls rolling down ramps. Some were so busy that they would likely trigger annoyance. Most were still images (some with dotted lines to indicate implied motion, some using left-to-right panels indicating sequentially). One work was an advertisement for moving text as "animation," such as "wiggly text." There were many depictions of data graphs ("data is fuel"), including some with moving sliders. Some of the visuals were decorative, something to draw attention. In terms of shapes, there were both abstract forms (in area charts) and figurative shapes. A few referred to particle motion.

One visual advertising the advantages of motion graphics as the following: "cost and time effective, attractive, different effects, easily shareable, (and) elegant style." Another pointed to the power of visual aids for "motivation, clarification, increased vocabulary, save time, avoid dullness, (and) direct experience." Another ad argued about why to use infographics: "educate viewers, demonstrate authority, use across platforms."

Some of the visuals in this set were advertisements for services and technologies related to motion infographics and messaging. Several point to benefits of brand promotion using motion visuals and infographics. One highlights motion as a special effect. Another contrasted motion infographics against "flat infographics." Several of the visuals spotlighted the work and personalities of "motion graphic artists." Only very few of the works are apparently for education, such as one text-heavy poster about

Infographics for Information Conveyance

Galileo. A few were "how-to's" about how to create various types of infographics, including motion. Several advertised the use of augmented reality in the home.

Several technologies enabling motion design were mentioned, including a mainline one included in a major suite of tools, a new 3d rendering tool with special materials surfacing, a stand-alone technology, and freeware in a few cases. Several advertised tutorials for this work.

A general impression is that motion infographics are still in nascent stages, with some level of sophistication required.

Figure 2. Collected Social Imagery from "Motion Infographics" Search on Google Image Search

Interactive Infographics

A complementary imageset of "interactive infographics" was similarly captured from Google Image search, with a resulting set of 1,036 visuals. The tags for this "interactive infographics" imageset were the following: "design, interactive map, animated, timeline, creative, amazing, cool, interesting, music, html 5, javascript, powerpoint, training, data, product, list, website, guide, wall, elearning industry, management, space, geographic, new, chart, media, instructional, smart, gif, (and) animated gif." (Figure 3) These thumbnails were also analyzed, without the interactivity (because those also require other technological dependencies).

The interactivity here may be seen in various visual depictions: gameplay, video games (as social-based entertainment), mobile apps, and others. There are common data visualization types, like bar graphs, funnel charts, pie charts, circle graphs (or ring lattice graphs), intensity matrices, and others. Some visuals show choropleth maps. Others show maps where areas may be selected for more information. Some of the visuals point to some innovations, such as puzzles with interactivity, "interactive theatre," and data-driven storytelling. Some show screens where avatar characters may be developed with different visual characteristics. This set of "interactive infographics" shows more substantive issues instead of self-promotion as compared to the "motion infographics" imageset.

The topical resources show focuses on the following (Table 1).

Infographics for Information Conveyance

Table 1. Top-level topics and subtopics in the "interactive infographic" social imageset

Top-level Topics (in alphabetical order)	Subtopics
business	a B2B buyer's journey (for business-to-business work); a corporate annual report's highlights;
children's education	children's education
consumer	buying a mobile phone; coffee;
cultural analysis	analysis of The Beatles; a particular part of a city known as billionaires' row; contemporary authors; the number of unique words used within a hip hop artist's first 35,000 lyrics (interesting factoids); the challenges of remote work; common modern myths; musician John Coltrane;
economics	the car sharing phenomenon in the sharing economy; Brexit; nursing as a career; the male-female pay gaps; disparities between wealthiest and the regular citizen in terms of earnings and wealth;
entertainment-education	the life of Spartacus; different types of cocktails;
environmental concerns	saving water (to protect the environment); power usage in cities; alternate energy sources; Earth Day; Butterflies of North America;
geopolitics	the U.S. vs. the U.K.; Brexit; a bombing in Damascus, Syria; social protests in Kazahkstan; women's political rights around the world;
global cities	a tourist guide to London; Tokyo; the Tokyo Olympics;
historical	the famous Charles Minard data visualization map (created in 1869) of Napoleon's Russian Campaign of 1812
human health	mental health issues in a population; how rheumatoid arthritis affects the body; alcohol consumption in particular populations; how the cerebellum works in the human brain; the global spread of the Zika virus; HIV/AIDS; jow a ventilator works for a person with severe COVID-19; coronavirus infection and other numbers; how to safeguard on-site employees against the spread of SARS-CoV-2; a dot map of the U.S. of "gun deaths since Sandy Hook"; a map of recent mass shootings in the U.S.; the risks of a sedentary life; dentistry; how the Omicron variant of SARS-CoV-2 compares to other ones;
humor	A b/w image of a person pointing to a visual about the varying sizes of doughnut holes from 1927, 1937, and 1948; then, the 2017 commentary: "I bet the people in the post were wise, cultured people" (in a contrastive humor post from social media apparently); overrated dog breeds;
industry	technology giants in the industry; entrepreneurship and new businesses; how a hybrid car works; biofuels; how boomer women affect buying decisions;
information technology	cloud computing; data breaches; information security; cyber-based fraud; world's largest data breaches;
road safety	rockfall risks on particular stretches of road
science and technology	new technologies in sunglasses; "what the Internet thinks about"; how a flat panel display works; how a car engine works;
social justice	a map of the geography of hate;
sports competitions	FIFA World Cup; NCAA football;

That is not to say that there are not some sales images, such as those that promise higher "conversion" rates through animated and interactive videos ["Conversion" here refers to turning a non-customer into a customer, a non-subscriber to a subscriber.] Another advertises interactive "line infographics." Another describes methods for experience design through digital means. Beyond marketing businesses and infographic creative shops, others who are advertising in the scraped visuals include museums, architecture firms, dessert makers, shirt-makers, tourist destination sites, a motor speedway, a bank, an automotive tire company, and others. Other areas focused on besides international cities are places like Tennessee, Atlanta, and others.

Figure 3. Collected Social Imagery from "Interactive Infographics" Search on Google Image Search

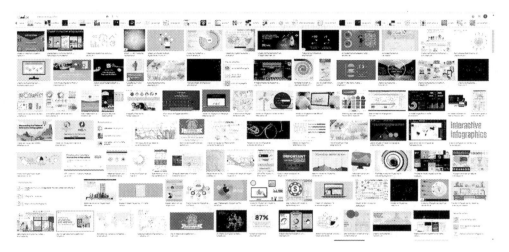

Immersive Infographics

A search for "immersive infographics" in Google Image Search resulted in 911 images. (Figure 4). The tags for these images include the following: interactive, simulation, interactive infographic examples, artificial intelligence, training, virtual reality, screen based simulation, dreamstime, infographic interface, microsoft, triage, immersive exercises, learning, immersive technologies, augmented reality, (and) hologram". This "immersive infographics" set contains some images not seen in the "motion" or "interactive" social imagesets, such as virtual reality headsets, references to various AR/VR/MR (augmented reality, virtual reality, mixed reality) technologies, robotics, haptics technologies, and others. There are icons of buttons and sliders. One infographic compares AR vs. VR trends from 2016 – 2017. Another summarizes the evolution of virtual reality (VR). One work mentions at-home "video walls". There are various ads for "mobile AR" and VR advertising. One describes low-code or no-code ways to create immersive experiences. Then, too, there is "immersive music" and "surround sound." Several refer to artificial intelligence (AI). There are immersive augmented reality "picture books." One visual makes the case for using AR and MR to enhance field service for construction and electrical workers.

Only one of the images shows true physical immersion, of a museum-goer entering an art installation that involves glowing blue lights in a darkened room. Several refer to industrial "immersion cooling." Some point to VR technologies (so immersion from the outside, not the inside). One shows mobile network systems, so other parts of the infrastructure that enable immersive informational graphics. Several visions refer to gaming devices, gaming platforms, various digital gaming peripherals, and even particular games. Two of the visuals referred to software engineering "immersive" experiences, which involve trainings for this work. One visual focuses on women in technology serving as mentors. One is about youth camping in real space.

The visuals engage issues of human health, such as post-exercise cooling; weight loss methods; atrial fibrillation; tips for working in cold temperatures; and others. Some focus on human learning: the bilingual brain; learning Spanish, and such. One visual shows how interactive (vs. immersive) video may be used for experiential learning. One visual shows immersive online learning. One infographic is about the uses of haptics to trigger emotions, so the "immersive" infographics set includes more sensory approaches. Immersive sound techniques and technologies are also addressed.

One visual shares a method for finding and purchasing the best kitchen blender, another about how to find the best gaming laptop. One describes supporting brand ambassadors of a product. Another highlights research behind the study of weightlessness and gravity. One is about COVID-19's impact on corporate planning. One is a stylized sideview slice of the world, including a layer for coal and oil extraction in the strata. Locations mentioned include Yukon in one, and New Brunswick in another, and Alberta in yet another. One is a rating chart for reference. One is a customer journey map. One infographic explores the state of the real estate market in a locality. One referred to a professional boxing match.

There are the typical marketing companies advertising as in the other two social imagesets. There is a screenshot of a newscast. There are some environmental messages, such as about how to lower water usage, the need to fight ocean plastic, protecting rivers from harm during "festivities," and others. Some of the visuals are brand logos. One visual is for a company that sells stock imagery.

Figure 4. Collected Social Imagery from "Immersive Infographics" Search on Google Image Search

These image types, "motion infographics" and "interactive infographics" and "immersive infographics" were also explored from a social art-sharing site (DeviantArt). The motion infographics set showed complex visuals; the interactive infographics set was sparse and seemed to show stock images; the interactive infographics set showed three posters about immersive learning.

Some instructional infographics were sampled from other sites and platforms.

Then there are less direct ways to look at infographics on the Social Web,

Infographics for Information Conveyance

Figure 5. "Infographic" Related Tags Network on Flickr Social Image-Sharing Site (1.5 deg)

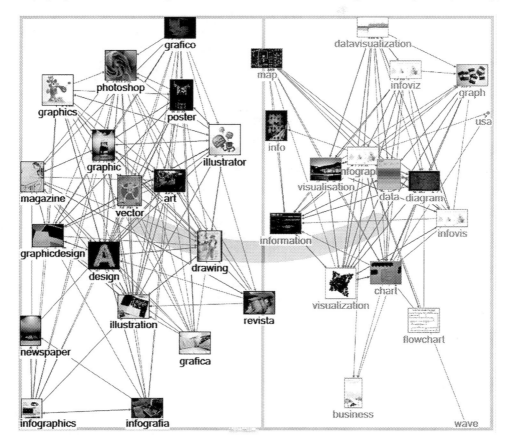

On a Social Image Sharing Site

A related tags network around "infographic" (as the seeding term) was captured from the Flickr social image sharing site. The related tags show the interrelatedness of ideas based on co-occurrence of the tags with shared images labeled "infographic." The network was captured at 1.5 degrees. Two groups of tags were extracted based on the Clauset-Newman-Moore clustering algorithm in NodeXL. The group on the left shows various publications that use infographics, like magazines and newspapers, and posters. Various technologies are also cited. The work of design and graphicdesign are also cited. The group at the right focuses on various types of contents in infographics, such as graphs, diagrams, data, charts, flowcharts, and others. [The more complex "motion" and "interactive" infographics are too specific to be used as query terms.] The visual does show an international sense of infographics as well, with mentioned countries and multiple languages used in the tagging. (Figure 5)

Table 2 is the complement to Figure 5. The graph here is a fairly small one, with only 35 vertices and 357 unique edges. The size is not unusual for this type of network graph though given the threshold to be included in a related tags network.

Table 2. Graph metrics from the "infographic" related tags network on Flickr social image-sharing site (1.5 deg)

Graph Metrics	Values
Graph Type	Directed
Vertices	35
Unique Edges	357
Edges With Duplicates	0
Total Edges	357
Self-Loops	0
Reciprocated Vertex Pair Ratio	0.317343173
Reciprocated Edge Ratio	0.481792717
Connected Components	1
Single-Vertex Connected Components	0
Maximum Vertices in a Connected Component	35
Maximum Edges in a Connected Component	357
Maximum Geodesic Distance (Diameter)	2
Average Geodesic Distance	1.500408
Graph Density	0.3
Modularity	Not Applicable
NodeXL Version	1.0.1.336

On a Microblogging site

Microblogging sites are a destination for some of the infographics, given the broad reach of such platforms. The Netlytic platform was used to capture the mentions of "infographics" in a keyword search on Twitter. This resulted in the capture of 2,397 Tweets. Figure 6 shows that the social networks around "infographics" as a keyword is comprised of a few central clusters and many smaller groups and motifs.

To capture the gist of some of the short conversations around "infographics," the extracted messaging was analyzed in NVivo. The word cloud in Figure 7 shows the frequency of various one-grams in the text set. Of special interest are various hashtag campaigns around #infosec (information security) and #informationsecurity and #blockchain. Then, too, there are various @ accounts which are particularly active and commonly referenced in the "infographics" keyword network on Twitter. Particular topics emerge: writing, healthcare, academics, and other aspects. Poems are a genre in infographics.

Infographics for Information Conveyance

Figure 6. "Infographics" Tweetset on Twitter via Netlytics

Figure 7. Word Cloud of "Infographics" Tweetset on Twitter via Netlytics

355

From the "infographics" keyword tweetset, a word tree was created around the term "infographic." A full review of the word tree shows a variety of topics but also various URLs to websites, highlighting the referential usage of Twitter and Tweets, in many cases (to point to other contents, to drive traffic). (Figure 8)

Figure 8. Partial View of Word Tree of "Infographics" Tweetset on Twitter via Netlytics

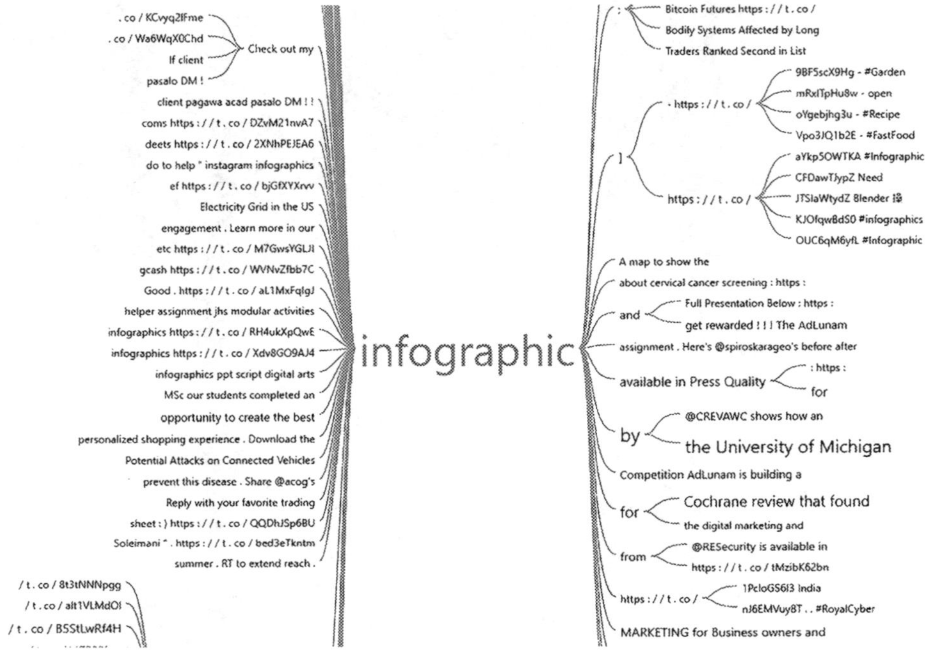

On Google Books Ngram Viewer

In the formal book publishing space, the Google Books project has some 40 million titles (Google Books, Jan. 14, 2022). A search of "infographics" on this viewer shows that the concept started gaining momentum in the 1980s and really only took off past the 2000s (Figure 8), in terms of presence in formal books at larger scale.

Discussion

This work provides an exploration of "infographics" as they manifest on the World Wide Web, the Social Web, and the Internet. This work found that there are a range of practical uses of infographics online and offline in various contexts.

Infographics for Information Conveyance

Figure 9. "Infographics" on Google Books Ngram Viewer

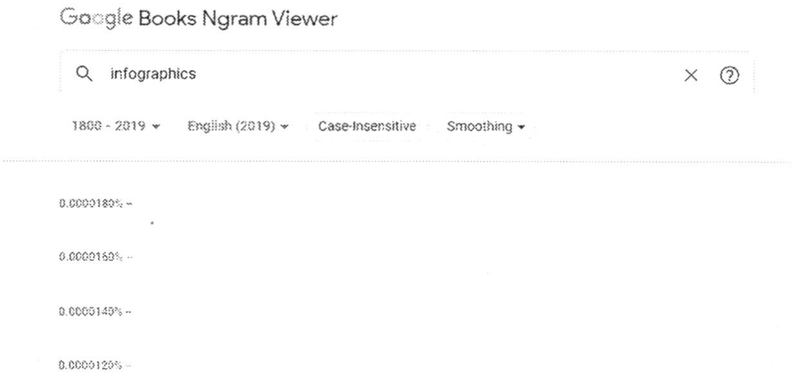

FUTURE RESEARCH DIRECTIONS

A core part of this project involved kanual coding conducted on over 3,000 combined thumbnail images from the "motion," "interactive," and "immersive" social imagesets. In the future, as the technologies improve for machine vision and icon extraction, perhaps more reproducible sorts of research work may be done, and finer insights may be extracted.

Given the different instantiations of infographics in so many contexts, it would be helpful to map different categories of infographics by some selection of dimensions: data, content, messaging, visuals, design aesthetics, and other aspects.

In terms of style, what are some ways to identify distinctive design "hands" of various creatives? Creative teams? One start to answering this may be found in one of the works, which describes different sensibilities of designers, which may be seen in "design concept, design process, readability level, sharing and contribution to the personal development, visual components, colours, information sources, themes and quality perception" (Yildirim, 2017, p. 248).

CONCLUSION

Infographics are lauded as the communications tools of the Digital Age with so many technological enablements (Siricharoen, 2013, p. 169). With advances in technologies and concomitant complex uses of this form, infographics have emerged from stasis into motion and interactivity and immersion. This work provides a light review of infographics in the recent past and into the present in terms of practical usages.

REFERENCES

Agley, J., Xiao, Y., Thompson, E. E., & Golzarri-Arroyo, L. (2021). Using infographics to improve trust in science: A randomized pilot test. *BMC Research Notes*, *14*(1), 1–6. doi:10.118613104-021-05626-4 PMID:34051823

Alabdulqader, E. (2013, July). Visualizing computer ethics using infographics. In *Proceedings of the 18th ACM conference on Innovation and technology in computer science education* (pp. 355-355). ACM.

Albers, M. J. (2014, October). Infographics: Horrid chartjunk or quality communication. In *2014 IEEE International Professional Communication Conference (IPCC)* (pp. 1-4). IEEE.

Albers, M. J. (2015, July). Infographics and communicating complex information. *Proceedings of the International Conference of Design, User Experience, and Usability*, 267 – 276.

Alrwele, N. S. (2017). Effects of infographics on student achievement and students' perceptions of the impacts of infographics. *Journal of Education and Human Development, 6*(3), 104-117.

Amini, F., Riche, N. H., Lee, B., Leboe-McGowan, J., & Irani, P. (2018, May). Hooked on data videos: assessing the effect of animation and pictographs on viewer engagement. In *Proceedings of the 2018 International Conference on Advanced Visual Interfaces* (pp. 1-9). 10.1145/3206505.3206552

Amit-Danhi, E. R., & Shifman, L. (2018). Digital political infographics: A rhetorical palette of an emergent genre. *New Media & Society, 20*(10), 3540–3559. doi:10.1177/1461444817750565

Andry, T., Hurter, C., Lambotte, F., Fastrez, P., & Telea, A. (2021, May). Interpreting the effect of embellishment on chart visualizations. In *Proceedings of the 2021 CHI Conference on Human Factors in Computing Systems* (pp. 1-15). 10.1145/3411764.3445739

Arcia, A., Suero-Tejeda, N., Bales, M. E., Merrill, J. A., Yoon, S., Woollen, J., & Bakken, S. (2016). Sometimes more is more: Iterative participatory design of infographics for engagement of community members with varying levels of health literacy. *Journal of the American Medical Informatics Association: JAMIA, 23*(1), 174–183. doi:10.1093/jamia/ocv079 PMID:26174865

Arcia, A., Velez, M., & Bakken, S. (2015). Style guide: An interdisciplinary communication tool to support the process of generating tailored infographics from electronic health data using EnTICE3. *EGEMS (Washington, DC), 3*(1), 1–10. doi:10.13063/2327-9214.1120 PMID:25848634

Arum, N. S. (2017). *Infographic: Not just a beautiful visualisation.* Obtenido de https://www. academia. edu/31903865/Infographic_Not_Just_a_Beautiful_Visualisation

Ashman, R., & Patterson, A. (2015). Seeing the big picture in services marketing research: Infographics, SEM and data visualisation. *Journal of Services Marketing, 29*(6/7), 613–621. doi:10.1108/JSM-01-2015-0024

Balkac, M., & Ergun, E. (2018). Role of infographics in healthcare. *Chinese Medical Journal, 131*(20), 2514–2517. doi:10.4103/0366-6999.243569 PMID:30334544

Bellato, N. (2013). Infographics: A visual link to learning. *ELearn, 2013*(12), 1–4. doi:10.1145/2556598.2556269

Bellei, M., Welch, P., Pryor, S., & Ketheesan, N. (2016). A cost-effective approach to producing animated infographics for immunology teaching. *Journal of Microbiology & Biology Education, 17*(3), 477–479. doi:10.1128/jmbe.v17i3.1146 PMID:28101279

Bicen, H., & Beheshti, M. (2017). The psychological impact of infographics in education. *BRAIN. Broad Research in Artificial Intelligence and Neuroscience, 8*(4), 99–108.

Bigelow, A., Drucker, S., Fisher, D., & Meyer, M. (2014, May). Reflections on how designers design with data. In *Proceedings of the 2014 International Working Conference on Advanced Visual Interfaces* (pp. 17-24). 10.1145/2598153.2598175

Bradshaw, M. J., & Porter, S. (2017). Infographics: A new tool for the nursing classroom. *Nurse Educator, 42*(2), 57–59. doi:10.1097/NNE.0000000000000316 PMID:27532677

Buljan, I., Malički, M., Wager, E., Puljak, L., Hren, D., Kellie, F., West, H., Alfirević, Z., & Marušić, A. (2018). No difference in knowledge obtained from infographic or plain language summary of a Cochrane systematic review: Three randomized controlled trials. *Journal of Clinical Epidemiology, 97*, 86–94. doi:10.1016/j.jclinepi.2017.12.003 PMID:29269021

Burgio, V., & Moretti, M. (2017). Infographics as images: Meaningfulness beyond information. In Multidisciplinary Digital Publishing Institute Proceedings (Vol. 1, No. 9, p. 891). Academic Press.

Bursi-Amba, A., Gaullier, A., & Santidrian, M. (2016). Infographics: A toolbox for technical writers. *Ufr D'etudes Interculturelles De Langues Appliquees*, 1-13.

Bylinskii, Z., Alsheikh, S., Madan, S., Recasens, A., Zhong, K., Pfister, H., . . . Oliva, A. (2017). *Understanding infographics through textual and visual tag prediction.* arXiv preprint arXiv:1709.09215.

Byrne, L., Angus, D., & Wiles, J. (2015). Acquired codes of meaning in data visualization and infographics: Beyond perceptual primitives. *IEEE Transactions on Visualization and Computer Graphics, 22*(1), 509–518. doi:10.1109/TVCG.2015.2467321 PMID:26529716

Bystrova, T. (2020). Infographics as a tool for improving effectiveness of education. *KnE Social Sciences*, 152-158.

Chen, Z., Wang, Y., Wang, Q., Wang, Y., & Qu, H. (2019). Towards automated infographic design: Deep learning-based auto-extraction of extensible timeline. *IEEE Transactions on Visualization and Computer Graphics*, 1–10. doi:10.1109/TVCG.2019.2934810 PMID:31443028

Çifçi, T. (2016). Effects of infographics on students (sic) achievement and attitude towards geography lessons. *Journal of Education and Learning, 5*(1), 154–166. doi:10.5539/jel.v5n1p154

Claes, S., & Vande Moere, A. (2013, June). Street infographics: Raising awareness of local issues through a situated urban visualization. In *Proceedings of the 2nd ACM International Symposium on Pervasive Displays* (pp. 133-138). 10.1145/2491568.2491597

Crick, K., & Hartling, L. (2015). Preferences of knowledge users for two formats of summarizing results from systematic reviews: Infographics and critical appraisals. *PloS One, 10*(10), 1 - 8.

Cui, W., Zhang, X., Wang, Y., Huang, H., Chen, B., Fang, L., Zhang, H., Lou, J.-G., & Zhang, D. (2019). Text-to-viz: Automatic generation of infographics from proportion-related natural language statements. *IEEE Transactions on Visualization and Computer Graphics, 26*(1), 906–916. doi:10.1109/TVCG.2019.2934785 PMID:31478860

Cupita, L. A. L., & Franco, L. M. P. (2019). The use of infographics to enhance reading comprehension skills among learners. *Colombian Applied Linguistics Journal*, *21*(2), 230–242. doi:10.14483/22487085.12963

Dahmash, A. B., Al-Hamid, A., & Alrajhi, M. (2017). Using infographics in the teaching of linguistics. *Arab World English Journal*, *8*(4), 430–443. doi:10.24093/awej/vol8no4.29

Damman, O. C., Vonk, S. I., Van den Haak, M. J., van Hooijdonk, C. M., & Timmermans, D. R. (2018). The effects of infographics and several quantitative versus qualitative formats for cardiovascular disease risk, including heart age, on people's risk understanding. *Patient Education and Counseling*, *101*(8), 1410–1418. doi:10.1016/j.pec.2018.03.015 PMID:29559200

Damyanov, I., & Tsankov, N. (2018). The role of infographics for the development of skills for cognitive modeling in education. *International Journal of Emerging Technologies in Learning*, *13*(1), 82–92. doi:10.3991/ijet.v13i01.7541

de Castro Andrade, R., & Spinillo, C. G. (2018, July). Interaction and animation in health infographics: A study of graphic presentation and content comprehension. In *International Conference of Design, User Experience, and Usability* (pp. 187-199). Springer. 10.1007/978-3-319-91803-7_14

Dehghani, M., Mohammadhasani, N., Hoseinzade Ghalevandi, M., & Azimi, E. (2020). Applying AR-based infographics to enhance learning of the heart and cardiac cycle in biology class. *Interactive Learning Environments*, 1–16. doi:10.1080/10494820.2020.1765394

Dewantari, F., Utami, I. G. A. L. P., & Santosa, M. H. (2021). Infographics and independent learning for English learning in the secondary level context. *Journal on English as a Foreign Language*, *11*(2), 250–274. doi:10.23971/jefl.v11i2.2784

Diakopoulos, N., Kivran-Swaine, F., & Naaman, M. (2011, May). Playable data: characterizing the design space of game-y infographics. In *Proceedings of the SIGCHI Conference on Human Factors in Computing Systems* (pp. 1717-1726). 10.1145/1978942.1979193

Dick, M. (2014). Interactive infographics and news values. *Digital Journalism*, *2*(4), 490–506. doi:10. 1080/21670811.2013.841368

Dick, M. (2017). Developments in infographics. *The Routledge Companion to Digital Journalism Studies*, 1 – 12.

Doukianou, S., Daylamani-Zad, D., & O'Loingsigh, K. (2021). Implementing an augmented reality and animated infographics application for presentations: Effect on audience engagement and efficacy of communication. *Multimedia Tools and Applications*, *80*(20), 1–23. doi:10.100711042-021-10963-4

Dunlap, J. C., & Lowenthal, P. R. (2016). Getting graphic about infographics: Design lessons learned from popular infographics. *Journal of Visual Literacy*, *35*(1), 42–59. doi:10.1080/1051144X.2016.1205832

Dur, B. I. U. (2014a). Data visualization and infographics in visual communication design education at the age of information. *Journal of Arts and Humanities*, *3*(5), 39–50.

Dur, B. I. U. (2014b). Interactive infographics on the Internet. *Online Journal of Art and Design*, *2*(4), 1–14.

Dyjur, P., & Li, L. (2015). Learning 21st century skills by engaging in an infographics assessment. Proceedings of the IDEAS: Designing Responsive Pedagogy Conference, 62 - 71.

Evans, R. S. (2016). *Infographics on the brain.* Articles, Chapters and Online Publications. Digital Commons at the University of Georgia School of Law.

Fadzil, H. M. (2018). Designing infographics for the educational technology course: Perspectives of pre-service science teachers. *Journal of Baltic Science Education, 17*(1), 8–18. doi:10.33225/jbse/18.17.08

Featherstone, R. (2014). Visual research data: An infographics primer. *JCHLA/JABSC, 35,* 147 - 150.

Fitzpatrick, J., Castricum, A., Seward, H., Tulloh, L., & Dawson, E. (2020). Infographic. COFIT-19: Let's get moving through the COVID-19 pandemic! *British Journal of Sports Medicine, 54*(22), 1360–1361. doi:10.1136/bjsports-2020-102661 PMID:32561519

Gallagher, S. E., O'Dulain, M., O'Mahony, N., Kehoe, C., McCarthy, F., & Morgan, G. (2017). Instructor-provided summary infographics to support online learning. *Educational Media International, 54*(2), 129–147. doi:10.1080/09523987.2017.1362795

Gay, J., Simms, V., Bond, R., Finlay, D., & Purchase, H. (2019, September). An audit tool for assessing the visuocognitive design of infographics. In *Proceedings of the 31st European Conference on Cognitive Ergonomics* (pp. 1-5). 10.1145/3335082.3335117

Gebre, E. (2018). Learning with multiple representations: Infographics as cognitive tools for authentic learning in science literacy. *Canadian Journal of Learning and Technology/La revue canadienne de l'apprentissage et de la technologie, 44*(1), 1 - 24.

Germanakos, P., Kasinidou, M., Constantinides, M., & Samaras, G. (2019, June). A metacognitive perspective of InfoVis in education. In *Adjunct Publication of the 27th Conference on User Modeling, Adaptation and Personalization* (pp. 331-336). Academic Press.

Ghode, R. (2012). Infographics in news presentation: A study of its effective use in Times of India and Indian Express the two leading newspapers in India. *Journal of Business Management & Social Sciences Research, 1*(1), 35-43.

Google Books. (2022, Jan. 14). In *Wikipedia.* Retrieved Jan. 17, 2022, from https://en.wikipedia.org/wiki/Google_Books

Greussing, E., & Boomgaarden, H. G. (2021). Promises and pitfalls: Taking a closer look at how interactive infographics affect learning from news. *International Journal of Communication, 15*(22), 3336–3357.

Grieger, K., & Leontyev, A. (2021). Student-generated infographics for learning green chemistry and developing professional skills. *Journal of Chemical Education, 98*(9), 2881–2891.

Griffin, A. L., MacEachren, A. M., Hardisty, F., Steiner, E., & Li, B. (2006). A comparison of animated maps with static small-multiple maps for visually identifying space-time clusters. *Annals of the Association of American Geographers, 96*(4), 740–753.

Hai-Jew, S. (2020, Aug. 5 – 7). Creating a motion infographic for learning. In *Virtual SIDLIT 2020*. Colleague 2 Colleague. Retrieved Dec. 30, 2021, from https://www.slideshare.net/ShalinHaiJew/creating-a-motion-infographic-for-learning-236203316

Hamilton, K., Peden, A. E., Keech, J. J., & Hagger, M. S. (2017). Changing people's attitudes and beliefs toward driving through floodwaters: Evaluation of a video infographic. *Transportation Research Part F: Traffic Psychology and Behaviour, 53*, 50–60.

Harrison, L., Reinecke, K., & Chang, R. (2015). *Infographic aesthetics: Designing for the first impression. In the proceedings of CHI 2015*. Crossings.

Hassan, H. G. (2016). *Designing Infographics to support teaching complex science subject: A comparison between static and animated Infographics* [Doctoral dissertation]. Iowa State University.

He, M., Tang, X., & Huang, Y. (2011, June). To visualize spatial data using thematic maps combined with infographics. In *2011 19th International Conference on Geoinformatics* (pp. 1-5). IEEE.

Hill, S., & Grinnell, C. (2014, October). Using digital storytelling with infographics in STEM professional writing pedagogy. In *2014 IEEE International Professional Communication Conference (IPCC)* (pp. 1-7). IEEE.

Hsiao, P. Y., Loquatro, I., Johnson, R. M., & Smolic, C. E. (2019). Using infographics to teach the evidence analysis process to senior undergraduate students. *Journal of the Academy of Nutrition and Dietetics*, 26–30.

Huang, W., & Tan, C. L. (2007, August). A system for understanding imaged infographics and its applications. In *Proceedings of the 2007 ACM Symposium on Document Engineering* (pp. 9-18). ACM.

Ibrahem, U. M., & Alamro, A. R. (2021). Effects of Infographics on Developing Computer Knowledge, Skills and Achievement Motivation among Hail University Students. *International Journal of Instruction, 14*(1), 907–926.

Ismaeel, D., & Al Mulhim, E. (2021). The influence of interactive and static infographics on the academic achievement of reflective and impulsive students. *Australasian Journal of Educational Technology, 37*(1), 147–162.

Jones, N. P., Sage, M., & Hitchcock, L. (2019). Infographics as an assignment to build digital skills in the social work classroom. *Journal of Technology in Human Services, 37*(2-3), 1–22.

Joshi, M., & Gupta, L. (2021). Preparing infographics for post-publication promotion of research on social media. *Journal of Korean Medical Science, 36*(5), 1–16.

Kang, X. (2016, September). The effect of color on short-term memory in information visualization. In *Proceedings of the 9th International Symposium on Visual Information Communication and Interaction* (pp. 144-145). Academic Press.

Kanthawala, S. (2019). Credibility of health infographics: Effects of message structure and message exaggeration. Michigan State University.

Kemp, D., King, A. J., Upshaw, S. J., Mackert, M., & Jensen, J. D. (2021). Applying harm reduction to COVID-19 prevention: The influence of moderation messages and risk infographics. *Patient Education and Counseling*, 1–8.

Khan, I. A. (2021). Psychology of color, integration of local culture and effect of infographics on English language learning. *PSU Research Review*, 1 - 18.

Klein, S. R. (2014). Making sense of data in the changing landscape of visual art education. *Visual Arts Research*, *40*(2), 25–33.

Kos, B. A., & Sims, E. (2014). Infographics: The new 5-paragraph essay. *Rocky Mountain Celebration of Women in Computing*, 1 – 5.

Kpokiri, E., John, R., Wu, D., Fongwen, N., Budak, J., Chang, C., ... Tucker, J. (2021). Crowdsourcing to Develop Open-Access Learning Resources on Antimicrobial Resistance. *BMC Infectious Diseases*, 1–7.

Lamb, G., Polman, J. L., Newman, A., & Smith, C. G. (2014). Science news infographics. *Science Teacher (Normal, Ill.)*, *81*(3), 25–30.

Langer, J., & Zeiller, M. (2017, November). Evaluation of the User Experience of Interactive Infographics in Online Newspapers. *Forum Media Technology*, 1 - 10.

Lazard, A., & Atkinson, L. (2015). Putting environmental infographics center stage: The role of visuals at the elaboration likelihood model's critical point of persuasion. *Science Communication*, *37*(1), 6–33.

Lee, E. J., & Kim, Y. W. (2016). Effects of infographics on news elaboration, acquisition, and evaluation: Prior knowledge and issue involvement as moderators. *New Media & Society*, *18*(8), 1579–1598.

Lengler, R., & Moere, A. V. (2009, July). Guiding the viewer's imagination: How visual rhetorical figures create meaning in animated infographics. In *2009 13th International Conference Information Visualisation* (pp. 585-591). IEEE.

Li, N., Brossard, D., Scheufele, D., Wilson, P. H., & Rose, K. M. (2018). Communicating data: interactive infographics, scientific data and credibility. *Journal of Science Communication, 17*(2), 1 – 20.

Li, Z., Carberry, S., Fang, H., McCoy, K. F., & Peterson, K. (2014, June). Infographics retrieval: A new methodology. In *International Conference on Applications of Natural Language to Data Bases/Information Systems* (pp. 101-113). Springer.

Lievemaa, J. (2017). *Animated infographics in digital educational publishing: Case study of educational animated infographics*. Academic Press.

Lochner, H., Swenson, R., & Martinson, K. (2021). 120 Disseminating equine science with infographics on social media. *Journal of Equine Veterinary Science*, *100*, 103583.

Locoro, A., Cabitza, F., Actis-Grosso, R., & Batini, C. (2017). Static and interactive infographics in daily tasks: A value-in-use and quality of interaction user study. *Computers in Human Behavior*, *71*, 1–51.

Löllgen, H., Bachl, N., Papadopoulou, T., Shafik, A., Holloway, G., Vonbank, K., ... Pitsiladis, Y. P. (2021). Infographic. Clinical recommendations for return to play during the COVID-19 pandemic. *British Journal of Sports Medicine*, *55*(6), 344–345.

Lonsdale, M. D. S., David, L., Baxter, M., Graham, R., Kanafani, A., Li, A., & Peng, C. (2019). Visualizing the terror threat. The impact of communicating security information to the general public using infographics and motion graphics. *Visible Language*, *53*(2), 37–71.

López-Ornelas, E., & Hernández, S. H. S. (2016, July). Using infographics to represent meaning on social media. *In International Conference on Social Computing and Social Media* (pp. 25-33). Springer.

Lu, M., Wang, C., Lanir, J., Zhao, N., Pfister, H., Cohen-Or, D., & Huang, H. (2020, April). Exploring visual information flows in infographics. In *Proceedings of the 2020 CHI Conference on Human Factors in Computing Systems* (pp. 1-12). ACM.

Lyra, K. T., Isotani, S., Reis, R. C., Marques, L. B., Pedro, L. Z., Jaques, P. A., & Bitencourt, I. I. (2016, July). Infographics or graphics+ text: Which material is best for robust learning? In *2016 IEEE 16th International Conference on Advanced Learning Technologies (ICALT)* (pp. 366-370). IEEE.

Madan, S., Bylinskii, Z., Nobre, C., Tancik, M., Recasens, A., Zhong, K., Alsheikh, S., Oliva, A., Durand, F., & Pfister, H. (2021). Parsing and summarizing infographics with synthetically trained icon detection. *Proceedings of the 2021 IEEE 14*th *Pacfici Visualization Symposium (PacificVis)*. 31 – 40.

Madan, S., Bylinskii, Z., Tancik, M., Recasens, A., Zhong, K., Alsheikh, S., . . . Durand, F. (2018). *Synthetically trained icon proposals for parsing and summarizing infographics*. arXiv preprint arXiv:1807.10441.

Martin, L. J., Turnquist, A., Groot, B., Huang, S. Y. M., Kok, E., Thoma, B., & van Merriënboer, J. J. G. (2019). Exploring the role of infographics for summarizing medical literature. *Health Profession Education*, *5*, 48–57.

Martins, N., Alvelos, H., Chatterjee, A., Calado, I., & Quintela, M. (2020, July). Multimedia as mediator of knowledge between older generations and present-day students of art and design. In *2020 The 4th International Conference on Education and Multimedia Technology* (pp. 213-218). Academic Press.

Martins, N., Penedos-Santiago, E., Lima, C., Barreto, S., & Calado, I. (2020, November). Infographics of Wisdom: Study on the individual legacies of retired academics in art and design higher education and research. In *2020 The 4th International Conference on Education and E-Learning* (pp. 62-67). Academic Press.

Matrix, S., & Hodson, J. (2014). *Teaching with infographics: Practising new digital competencies and visual literacies*. Academic Press.

Mc Sween-Cadieux, E., Chabot, C., Fillol, A., Saha, T., & Dagenais, C. (2021). Use of infographics as a health-related knowledge translation tool: Protocol for a scoping review. *BMJ Open*, *11*(6), 1 – 7.

Mendenhall, S., & Summers, S. (2015). Designing research: Using infographics to teach design thinking. composition. *Journal of Global Literacies, Technologies and Emerging Pedagogies*, *3*(1), 359–371.

Mitchell, D. G., Morris, J. A., Meredith, J. M., & Bishop, N. (2017). Chemistry infographics: Experimenting with creativity and information literacy. In *Liberal arts strategies for the chemistry classroom* (pp. 113–131). American Chemical Society.

Murray, A. D., Barton, C. J., Archibald, D., Glover, D., Murray, I. R., Barker, K., & Hawkes, R. A. (2018). Infographics and digital resources: An international consensus on golf and health. Business Journal of Sports Medicine. *BMJ (Clinical Research Ed.)*, *57*(22), 1421–1424.

Murray, I. R., Murray, A. D., Wordie, S. J., Oliver, C. W., Murray, A. W., & Simpson, A. H. R. W. (2017). Maximising the impact of your work using infographics. *Bone & Joint Research*, *6*(11), 619–620.

Naparin, H., & Saad, A. B. (2017). Infographics in education: Review on infographics design. *The International Journal of Multimedia & its Applications, 9*(4), 5, 15 – 24.

Nhan, L. K., & Yen, P. H. (2021a). The effects of using infographics-based learning on EFL learners' grammar retention. *International Journal of Science and Management Studies*, *4*(I4), 225–265.

Nhan, L. K., & Yen, P. H. (2021b). The impact of using infographics to teach grammar on EFL students' learning motivation. *European Journal of Foreign Language Teaching*, *5*(5), 85–102.

Nivas, S., Gokul, C. J., Banahatti, V., & Lodha, S. (2021, August). Visuals Triumph in a Curious Case of Privacy Policy. *In IFIP Conference on Human-Computer Interaction* (pp. 732-741). Springer.

Noh, M. A. M., Fauzi, M. S. H. M., Jing, H. F., & Ilias, M. F. (2017). Infographics: Teaching and learning tool. *Malaysian Online Journal of Education*, *1*(1), 58–63.

O'Brien, S., & Lauer, C. (2018, August). Testing the susceptibility of users to deceptive data visualizations when paired with explanatory text. In *Proceedings of the 36th ACM International Conference on the Design of Communication* (pp. 1-8). ACM.

Occa, A., & Suggs, L. S. (2016). Communicating breast cancer screening with young women: An experimental test of didactic and narrative messages using video and infographics. *Journal of Health Communication*, *21*(1), 1–11.

Ott, C., Robins, A., & Shephard, K. (2014, November). An infographic to support students' self-regulated learning. In *Proceedings of the 14th Koli Calling International Conference on Computing Education Research* (pp. 177-178). Academic Press.

Özdal, H., & Ozdamli, F. (2017). The Effect of Infographics in Mobile Learning: Case Study in Primary School. *Journal of Universal Computer Science*, *23*(12), 1256–1275.

Ozdamlı, F., Kocakoyun, S., Sahin, T., & Akdag, S. (2016). Statistical reasoning of impact of infographics on education. *Procedia Computer Science*, *102*, 370–377.

Ozdamli, F., & Ozdal, H. (2018). Developing an instructional design for the design of infographics and the evaluation of infographic usage in teaching based on teacher and student opinions. *Eurasia Journal of Mathematics, Science and Technology Education*, *14*(4), 1197–1219.

Pasternack, S., & Utt, S. H. (1990). Reader use & understanding of newspaper infographics. *Newspaper Research Journal*, *11*(2), 28–41.

Pavazza, S., & Pap, K. (2012). The alternative way of creating infographics using SVG technology. *Acta graphica: znanstveni časopis za tiskarstvo i grafičke komunikacije, 23*(1-2), 45-56.

Pinto, J. C. (2017). The relevance of digital infographics in online newspapers. *Proceedings of the 5th Mediterranean Interdisciplinary Forum on Social Sciences and Humanities*, 428 – 434.

Pisarenko, V., & Bondarev, M. (2016). Infographics use in teaching foreign languages for specific purposes. *Recent Patents on Computer Science*, *9*(2), 1–9.

Porzak, R., Cwynar, A., & Cwynar, W. (2021). Improving debt literacy by 2/3 through four simple infographics requires numeracy and not focusing on negatives of debt. *Frontiers in Psychology*, *12*(621312), 1–19.

Purchase, H. C., Isaacs, K., Bueti, T., Hastings, B., Kassam, A., Kim, A., & van Hoesen, S. (2018, June). A classification of infographics. In *International Conference on Theory and Application of Diagrams* (pp. 1 - 8). Springer.

Qian, C., Sun, S., Cui, W., Lou, J. G., Zhang, H., & Zhang, D. (2020). Retrieve-then-adapt: Example-based automatic generation for proportion-related infographics. *IEEE Transactions on Visualization and Computer Graphics*, *27*(2), 443–452.

Reid, H., Milton, K., Bownes, G., & Foster, C. (2017). Making physical activity evidence accessible: Are these infographics the answer? *British Journal of Sports Medicine*, *51*(10), 764–766.

Rezaei, N., & Sayadian, S. (2015). The impact of infographics on Iranian EFL learners' grammar learning. *Journal of Applied Linguistics and Language Research*, *2*(1), 78–85.

Rosenberg, D. (2015). Against infographics. *Art Journal*, *74*(4), 38–57.

Rotolo, S. M., Jain, S., Dhaon, S., Dokhanchi, J. K., Kalata, E., Shah, T., ... Arora, V. M. (2021). (Preprint). A coordinated strategy to develop and distribute infographics addressing COVID-19 vaccine hesitancy and misinformation. *Journal of the American Pharmacists Association*, 1–8.

Saleh, B., Dontcheva, M., Hertzmann, A., & Liu, Z. (2015). *Learning style similarity for searching infographics.* arXiv preprint arXiv:1505.01214.

Scott, H., Fawkner, S., Oliver, C., & Murray, A. (2016). Why healthcare professionals should know a little about infographics. *British Journal of Sports Medicine*, *50*(18), 1104–1105.

Shanks, J. D., Izumi, B., Sun, C., Martin, A., & Byker Shanks, C. (2017). Teaching undergraduate students to visualize and communicate public health data with infographics. *Frontiers in Public Health*, *5*(315), 1–6.

Siricharoen, W. V. (2013, May). Infographics: the new communication tools in digital age. In *The International Conference on E-technologies and Business on the Web* (pp. 169-174). Academic Press.

Spiegelhalter, D., Pearson, M., & Short, I. (2011). Visualizing uncertainty about the future. *Science*, *333*(6048), 1393-1400.

Sudakov, I., Bellsky, T., Usenyuk, S., & Polyakova, V. V. (2016). Infographics and mathematics: A mechanism for effective learning in the classroom. *PRIMUS (Terre Haute, Ind.)*, *26*(2), 1–22.

Szołtysik, M. (2017). Processes of creating infographics for data visualization. In *Complexity in Information Systems Development* (pp. 167–184). Springer.

Tarkhova, L., Tarkhov, S., Nafikov, M., Akhmetyanov, I., Gusev, D., & Akhmarov, R. (2020). Infographics and their application in the educational process. *International Journal of Emerging Technologies in Learning*, *15*(13), 63–80.

Taspolat, A., Kaya, O. S., Sapanca, H. F., Beheshti, M., & Ozdamli, F. (2017). An investigation toward advantages, design principles and steps of infographics in education. *Il Ponte*, *73*(7), 157–166.

Terabe, S., Tanno, K., Yaginuma, H., & Kang, N. (2020). The Impact of Flyer with Infographics on Public Awareness and Interest to Transportation Project. *Transportation Research Procedia*, *48*, 2378–2384.

Thompson, C. M. (2015). Creating "visual legacies": Infographics as a means of interpreting and sharing research. *Communication Teacher*, *29*(2), 91–101.

Toth, C. (2013). Revisiting a genre: Teaching infographics in business and professional communication courses. *Business Communication Quarterly*, *76*(4), 446–457.

Tuncali, E. (2016). The infographics which are designed for environmental issues. *Global Journal on Humanities & Social Sciences*, 14 – 19.

Tymchenko, O., Vasiuta, S., Khamula, O., Sosnovska, O., & Dudzik, M. (2019, May). Using the method of pairwise comparisons for the multifactor selection of infographics design alternatives. In *2019 20th International Conference on Research and Education in Mechatronics (REM)* (pp. 1-6). IEEE.

VanderMolen, J., & Spivey, C. (2017). Creating infographics to enhance student engagement and communication in health economics. *The Journal of Economic Education*, *48*(3), 198–205.

Veszelszki, A. (2014). Information visualization: Infographics from a linguistic point of view. *The Power of the Image,* 99-109.

Wang, Y., Gao, Y., Huang, R., Cui, W., Zhang, H., & Zhang, D. (2021, June). Animated presentation of static infographics with InfoMotion. *Computer Graphics Forum*, *40*(3), 507–518.

Wang, Z., Wang, S., Farinella, M., Murray-Rust, D., Henry Riche, N., & Bach, B. (2019, May). Comparing effectiveness and engagement of data comics and infographics. In *Proceedings of the 2019 CHI Conference on Human Factors in Computing Systems* (pp. 1-12). ACM.

Wharton, C., Vizcaino, M., Berardy, A., & Opejin, A. (2021). Waste watchers: A food waste reduction intervention among households in Arizona. *Resources, Conservation and Recycling*, *164*, 105109.

Wilkinson, J. L., Strickling, K., Payne, H. E., Jensen, K. C., & West, J. H. (2016). Evaluation of diet-related infographics on Pinterest for use of behavior change theories: A content analysis. *JMIR mHealth and uHealth*, *4*(4), e6367.

Williams, F. M. (2002). *Diversity, thinking styles, and infographics*. Academic Press.

Won, J. (2017). Interactive infographics and delivery of information: The value assessment of infographics and their relation to user response. *Archives of Design Research*, *31*(1), 57–69.

Yarbrough, J. R. (2019). Infographics: In support of online visual learning. *Academy of Educational Leadership Journal*, *23*(2), 1–15.

Yasuda, K., Takahashi, S., & Wu, H. Y. (2016, September). Enhancing infographics based on symmetry saliency. In *Proceedings of the 9th International Symposium on Visual Information Communication and Interaction* (pp. 35-42). Academic Press.

Yearta, L., Kelly, K. S., Kissel, B., & Schonhar, M. (2018). Infoadvocacy: Writers engage in social justice through infographics. *Voices from the Middle*, *25*(4), 54.

Yildirim, S. (2016). Infographics for educational purposes: Their structure, properties and reader approaches. *Turkish Online Journal of Educational Technology-TOJET*, *15*(3), 98–110.

Yildirim, S. (2017). Approaches of designers in the developed educational purposes of infographics' design processes. *European Journal of Education Studies*, 248 - 284.

Yuruk, S. E., Yilmaz, R. M., & Bilici, S. (2019). An examination of postgraduate students' use of infographic design, metacognitive strategies and academic achievement. *Journal of Computing in Higher Education*, *31*(3), 495–513.

Zhang-Kennedy, L., Chiasson, S., & Biddle, R. (2014). Stop clicking on 'update later': Persuading users they need up-to-date antivirus protection. In *International Conference on Persuasive Technology* (pp. 302-322). Springer.

Zhu, S., Sun, G., Jiang, Q., Zha, M., & Liang, R. (2020). A survey on automatic infographics and visualization recommendations. *Visual Informatics*, *4*(3), 24–40.

Zwinger, S., Langer, J., & Zeiller, M. (2017, July). Acceptance and usability of interactive infographics in online newspapers. In *2017 21st International Conference Information Visualisation (IV)* (pp. 176-181). IEEE.

Zwinger, S., & Zeiller, M. (2016, November). Interactive infographics in German online newspapers. In Forum Media Technology. St. Pölten University of Applied Sciences, Institute of CreativenMedia/Technologies.

ADDITIONAL READING

Hai-Jew, S. (2020, Aug. 5 – 7). Creating a motion infographic for learning. In *Virtual SIDLIT 2020*. Colleague 2 Colleague. Retrieved Dec. 30, 2021, from https://www.slideshare.net/ShalinHaiJew/creating-a-motion-infographic-for-learning-236203316

KEY TERMS AND DEFINITIONS

Interactive Infographic: A 2D or 3D visual with mechanisms for users to interact with the data (such as changing various parameters, time spans, locales, and other information). Users may run queries against the data in some cases.

Motion Infographic: A 2D or 3D information-carrying visual that contains motion (4D) or animation.

Chapter 17
Going Through the Motions:
A Partial Survey of Public Online Multimodal Motion Infographics for Higher Ed

Shalin Hai-Jew
iD https://orcid.org/0000-0002-8863-0175
Kansas State University, USA

ABSTRACT

With the learning slippage that occurred in the aftermath of the SARS-CoV-2/COVID-19 pandemic, learning advantages that may be achieved are a topic of special interest. The popularization of online learning has riveted focus to digital learning methods and contents. In formal higher education, various contemporary digital infographics are in use: static, motion, interactive, and immersive. This work explores some of the publicly available and open infographics used in formal learning in higher education to better understand these digital contents. The search for "infographics" is based on a popular referatory for web-hosted digital learning resources, but with a new search feature that goes beyond the curated and peer-reviewed contents that captures the newest relevant contents from the web. The works are analyzed for modalities, topics, pedagogical value, and design for transience to protect against cognitive overload. This is an exploratory research work.

INTRODUCTION

With the learning slippage that occurred in the aftermath of the SARS-CoV-2 / COVID-19 pandemic, learning advantages that may be achieved are a topic of special interest. The popularization of online learning has riveted focus to digital learning methods and contents. In the Information Age, with so much available data, many who communicate to the public like governments and companies and organizations use informational graphics as succinct communications objects. In the higher education space, infographics are used, too, for various purposes:

DOI: 10.4018/978-1-6684-5934-8.ch017

Copyright © 2023, IGI Global. Copying or distributing in print or electronic forms without written permission of IGI Global is prohibited.

- to publicize issues,
- to publicize events,
- to punctuate certain learning points,
- to serve as learning prompts,
- to summarize learning,
- to enable and consolidate learning,
- and other applications.

Many instructors and students use desktop software and online Web tools to create learning infographics. This work involves an exploration of infographics made publicly available on the MERLOT (Multimedia Educational Resource for Learning and Online Teaching) referatory and on the Web [per the Smart Search capabilities enabling a federated search (MERLOT Smart Search, 2022)]. The use of a central referatory may benefit given that the respective curated learning resources are hosted on external systems and are pointed to by MERLOT, a cloud-based tool. A pointing feature enables the resources to be hosted on websites, virtual world platforms, online libraries, and other spaces. This might suggest that a search for "infographics" might result in static, motion, interactive, immersive, and combined infographics.

The works are categorized based on general infographic modality: static, motion, interactive, immersive, and combined. "Static infographics" are defined as "still analog or digital visuals that communicate information through text, data, data visualizations, images, and other designed elements (and user experiences)." "Motion infographics" are those that "communicate information through animation (or video), text, data, data visualizations, images, and other designed elements (and user experiences)." "Interactive infographics" are digital visuals that "may be triggered or changed based on user inputs to communicate information through text, data, data visualizations, images, and other designed elements (and user experiences)." "Immersive infographics" refer to "digital visuals in immersive virtual worlds or augmented reality or mixed reality to communicate information through text, data, data visualizations, images, and other designed elements (and user experiences)." And finally, "combined" ones are those infographics that include "motion and interactive" features, "motion and immersive," "interactive and immersive," and so on, on the one screen or slide or object. Also, the formal educational infographics are also categorized based on the topic and inclusion in particular disciplines. Some pedagogical analyses are included.

REVIEW OF THE LITERATURE

Learning is generally broken out into three areas: formal (accredited and regulated credit-based learning), nonformal (non-accredited course learning, such as in training applications), and informal (learning as a byproduct of life activities that are not specifically designed for learning). Infographics are used in all three spaces. The academic literature includes various works about the usage of infographics mostly in the nonformal spaces, particularly in healthcare. There are also works that describe infographics in data journalism.

Some works focus on formal learning, such as that in higher education, where infographics are seen to contribute to students' "knowledge, skills, and attitudes" (KSAs) (Al-Dairy & Al-Rabaani, 2017, p. 1), which evokes a bridge to work competencies. Various academic studies have targeted the uses of infographics in academic learning, according to a systematic analysis of the literature, with the "national applications of infographics" in the following geographical spaces: U.S., Turkey, Egypt, Saudi Arabia, Canada, Holland, Oman, Australia, Jordan, S. Korea, Malaysia, and Palestine (Al-Dairy & Al-Rabaani, 2017, p. 2).

One type of educational infographic is called a summarizing infographic. These involve the capture of main learning per period of time, such as per each week…or per unit, such as per module. Such summarizing infographics were used in a software engineering management online course (Heimbürger, Keto, & Isomöttönen, 2020, p. 1), for example.

Various Applications of Educational Infographics

Infographics have been used for school-based mental health support during the COVID-19 pandemic crisis. Infographics, videos, and guidebooks were used in "multiple training webinars on studying and coping skills during social distancing periods for students, classroom consultation skills for teachers" and others (Hanh, Nam, & Vinh, 2022, p. 321). A library reports an effective outreach to the faculty using infographics to ultimately ensure that the collection is used more and more effectively (Bohstedt, 2017). In another case, infographics were used to teach about visual literacy (Kibar & Akkoyunlu, 2014, p. 456). Teachers improved their clinical teaching skills through blogs, podcasts, and infographics, in a continuing education professional development program for faculty (Dowhos, Sherbino, Chan, & Nagji, 2021, p. 390). In a systems analysis and design course, an interactive infographic about systems theory was used in lieu of "91 slides" (Steyn, Botha, Coetzee, & de Villiers, 2021, p. 171). Supplementing the learning with an interactive infographic "made students engage far better with the content, thus, creating a more in-depth learning experience" (Steyn, Botha, Coetzee, & de Villiers, 2021, p. 171).

Ensuring Quality in Educational Infographics

"A strong infographic depicts multiple layers of related information and data, often densely, displaying deep interrelationships among variables and ideas," reads one work (Lamb, Polman, Newman, & Smith, 2014, p. 27). Various researchers have argued for the criticality of teachers developing information and communication technology (ICT) skills, including with the support of educational infographics (Khaydaraliyevna, 2021). Ensuring quality is seen as a central concern. One work harnessed a business modeling method enabling the making of well-planned educational animations (Battaiola, Alves, & Paulin, 2014).

Learner Preferences Related to Educational Infographics

One work describes a study of teenagers and their preferences for online video consumption found preferences for "relaxed or comic approaches" to the educational videos and "short duration, fast editing," and the inclusion of infographics (Almeida & Almeida, 2016, p. 65). This work suggests that design of learning for upcoming generations of learners in higher education would benefit from well-designed videos with infographics, as one element.

In terms of receptivity by learners, various studies have found that students respond positively to educational infographics. For example, one study finds that overwhelming majorities of students in higher education who took part in their study feel positively about the uses of infographics in knowledge transfer of "quantitative information," "scientific information," "professional information," and "historical information" with min-max ranges from 80 – 90% (Papić & Sušilović, 2018, p. 577). They also saw benefit in having some learning about how to learn from infographics (Papić & Sušilović, 2018, p. 577), instead of just presenting the infographic materials without additional learning support. The research team summarizes: "Students would prefer from their teachers to use infographics within their presentations (85%), textbooks or manuals (39%), tasks (30%), and tests (25%)" (Papić & Sušilović, 2018, p. 578).

Fast Capture of Infographic Aesthetics

One study examined how effective a designed series of infographics were for the teaching about lighting and photography for postgraduate students. This research found a learning advantage in the experimental group vs. the control (Albarrak & Shalto, 2015, p. 465).

Another study explored how quickly people formed a first impression of an infographic's aesthetics, which are seen as motivation to further engage with the informational content. They write: "Our results establish that: 1) people form a reliable first impression of the appeal of an infographic based on a mere exposure effect…largely based on colorfulness and visual complexity" (Harrison, Reinecke, & Chang, 2015, p. 1187). The first 500 milliseconds, then, are critical for user engagement, which has implications for the aesthetic design of infographics.

Enabling Behavior Change

For many, the "holy grail" of messaging involves learning and then behavior change, both of which are challenging for people. One study found that designed infographics had a constructive effect on research participants' willingness to wear facemasks during the COVID-19 pandemic (Egan, et al., 2021, p. 1). Infographics informed decision making in a complex and contested space. The infographics improved "recall, sentiment, and willingness" (Egan, et al., 2021) around the topic of masking to lessen the spread of the pathogenic coronavirus.

Learner-created Educational Infographics

In some cases, learners create infographics as part of their learning, often including the need for research, visual thinking, visual design, data analytics, and other skills. Student creation of their own infographics expand learning along various dimensions (Lamb, Polman, Newman, & Smith, 2014). In classes, info-graphics have been used to promote more inclusive student-centered discussions for "genuine inquiry" and diversities of opinions (Barker, Ponzio, & Matthusen, 2018, p. 123). In another course, students created infographics related to the environmental impacts of electronics during their manufacturing and their end-of-life life cycle (Schibuk, 2020, p 54). Here, infographics created by students offered them opportunities to "both showcase and synthesize their learning journey" (Schibuk, 2020, p 61), and their works were socially engaged in a "gallery walk" at the end of the course. In a computing course, stu-dents expanded their sense of "the social and environmental impact of technological evolution and the responsibility for its use and development," based on an ethics construct, in a computing course (Savini, Gasull, & Gimeno, 2019, p. 1). In a requirement engineering online course, infographics were used as a reflective assignment. This study found that learners "can, using infographics, concentrate on essential topics, distill information, and develop their skills for visual literacy and conceptualization" (Heimbürger & Isomöttönen, 2019, p. 1). Prior it was thought that only linear texts enabled such levels of analysis.

Sharing Academic Issues on Social Media

Academic-related infographics have been shared on social media to promote rheumatology messaging for education, broadcast messaging, and "support" for those with this health issue (Bhatia, Gaur, Zimba, Chatterjee, Nikiphorou, & Gupta, 2021, p. 1) and also for nephrology medicine (Diniz & Melilli, 2020, p. 597). Infographics have been used to cybersecurity behaviors by having strong passwords by using infographic posters vs. online educational comics to see which is more efficacious for learning (Zhang-Kennedy, Chiasson, & Riddle, 2013, p. 1). Infographics play an important role in a nuclear power plant safety course (Volman & Kormilicyn, 2018). Infographics are used in utility-university partnership messaging, such as for "potable reuse" of recycled wastewater water for conservation (Eidson, 2015, p. 54).

Several works address ways to create quality infographics and avoid so-called "horrid chartjunk," which occurs when there is an over-focus on the artfulness of an infographic while failing to present information clearly to a target audience (Albers, 2014). This researcher identifies four types of infographics: "bullet list equivalent, snapshot with graphic needs, flat information with graphic needs, and information flow / process" (Albers, 2014, p. 1). A bullet list infographic contains "a collection of facts that typically lack a clear audience and have no implicit visual component" and can be presented as "a bullet list" (Albers, 2014, p. 3). A snapshot infographic presents information "that lacks a sequence for reading, is static, and typically does not need to be compared" (Albers, 2014, p. 3). A "flat information with graphic needs" infographic offers content without an implicit reading sequence "but supports comparing different data points." The "information flow/process" type offers information with "some sort of flow or process" and a designed reading sequence (Albers, 2014, p. 3). The first type, the bullet list, is not conducive to re-expression as an educational infographic. A scoring rubric is used in some cases to ensure quality of the infographics (Kibar & Akkoyunlu, 2014, p. 462). One work describes low-cost and free resources for the making of static infographics (Salim, Saad, & Nor, 2021, p. 23).

GOING THROUGH THE MOTIONS: A PARTIAL SURVEY OF PUBLIC ONLINE INFOGRAPHICS FOR FORMAL LEARNING IN HIGHER EDUCATION

For an overview of educational infographics, a data query for "educational and infographics" was run over mass-scale academic research and journalistic articles through ProQuest's TDM Studio (for "text-and-data mining"). The resulting shadow dataset enabled some extracted data and visuals, for more diffuse insights. The data was captured from Dec. 10, 2009 to Dec. 31, 2022. The data was extracted from the following global resources: ProQuest Dissertations and Theses, The Times of India, The Guardian, Wall Street Journal, Chicago Tribune, Los Angeles Times, New York Times, Sydney Morning Herald, (and) The Washington Post. The search query "educational and infographics" resulted in 2,491 documents. The geographical locations mentioned may be seen in Figure 1.

These articles were analyzed using computational topic modeling (Table 1). The foci include a range of practical uses for learning across a range of topics.

An emotion analysis was run over the articles over time, and the results may be seen in the linegraph (Figure 2). There are time variations but also a general trend-line of consistency across the various respective emotions. As to the varying auto-coded emotions, as close to the present as possible (far right on the line graph), the top emotions to the bottom ones were as follows: neutral, surprise, happiness, disgust, other, anger, fear, sadness, (and) love.

Figure 1. "Educational and Infographics" Documents Mapped Geographically in ProQuest TDM Studio

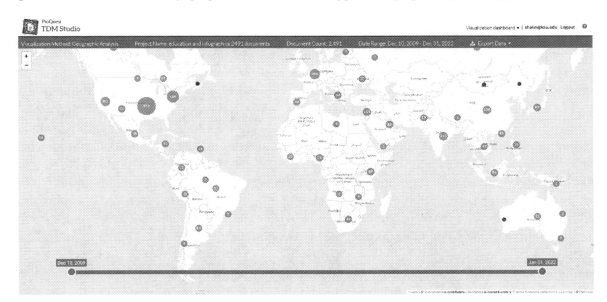

Table 1. Topic modeling of "educational and infographics" documents in ProQuest TDM Studio

Topics	Subtopics
Topic 1	learning, study, design, technology, research, development, data, online, professional, participants...
Topic 2	social, research, data, study, media, use, information, public, business, management...
Topic 3	study, significant, self, participants, results, group, intervention, research, relationship, use...
Topic 4	media, dissertation, social, new, work, news, project, black, ways, studies...
Topic 5	students, study, student, college, education, international, academic, research, university, community...
Topic 6	policy, state, global, political, new, education, chapter, dissertation, research, analysis...
Topic 7	health, care, women, patients, patient, risk, use, healthcare, children, hiv...
Topic 8	school, teachers, students, teacher, study, education, writing, teaching, classroom, research...
Topic 9	information, data, media, design, visual, visualization, text, content, reading, based...
Topic 10	mental, study, leadership, media, military, experiences, social, health, climate, women...

On MERLOT

In late January 2022, "infographics" was used as the seeding search term in the MERLOT Smart Search text window. There were only 49 in the Multimedia Educational Resource for Learning and Online Teaching curated collection (https://www.merlot.org/merlot/). In "Other Libraries," some 100 sites were shared; in "The Web," another 100 sites were shared, with many professional and general topics (without clear application to higher education).

This exploratory research, based on the MERLOT content, is based on the following five questions:

Figure 2. Emotion Analysis of the "Educational and Infographics" Documents in ProQuest TDM Studio Over Time

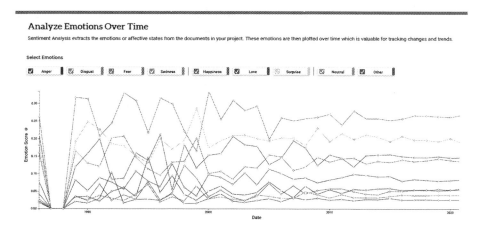

RQ1: In terms of widely available infographics used in higher education, what is the distribution based on the following: static, motion, interactive, immersive, and combined?

RQ2: What are the most common to least common topics addressed in the infographics, in terms of general discipline categories?

RQ3: What are apparent pedagogical strengths to learning with the publicly available infographics used in higher education?

RQ4: What are apparent pedagogical weaknesses to learning with the publicly available infographics used in higher education?

RQ5: For the informational infographics that are transient (due to motion), what are some ways to ensure that these do not result in cognitive overload? What design factors may be brought into play to enable accurate understandings of the underlying data and messaging?

RESEARCH QUESTIONS

RQ1: In terms of widely available infographics used in higher education, what is the distribution based on the following: static, motion, interactive, immersive, and combined?

In terms of modality types, then, static infographics (244) were the most common, followed by combined modalities (30) (based on one sophisticated source that included both stills and videos surrounding statistical analyses). Then, motion infographics (3) and interactive (1) infographics were fairly rare (Figure 3). And no immersive ones were found in this "infographics" search in the MERLOT referatory. This is not to say that the unlogged resources do not exist, but they were not referenced in this web-facing referatory.

More details about the topics along with the modalities may be seen in Table 2.

Many of the curated links, however, did not go to infographics. One link went to a college website that may have offered multimedia courses on how to create infographics. Another went to a web page with curated links to various topics related to infographics. Another went to a website that offered downloadable syllabus templates with placeholders for visuals. Two links went to free online (web-facing) infographics makers. Several resulted in "404 not found" messages. A dead (decayed) link went to an infographic that is supposedly about research contrasting primary and secondary sources. One link redirected to a bank. One website sold access to promised infographics on statistics. (8)

Figure 3. Frequencies of Observed Modalities of Educational Infographics in Higher Education

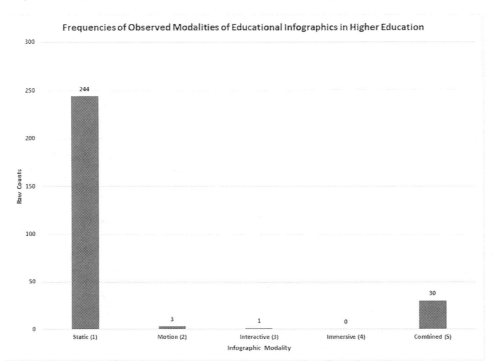

Table 2. Typographies of publicly available infographics for formal higher education (from MERLOT Referatory)

	Static (1)	Motion (2)	Interactive (3)	Immersive (4)	Combined (5)
MERLOT	40 (marketing) 9 (educational) 1 (health) 120 (environmental) 1 (power of badges or micro-credentialing) 1 (chemistry) 1 (mobile device management) 66 (World AIDS Day 2013 collection) 1 (instructional design trends) 1 (fire safety) 1 (online university courses 2019) 1 (COVID-19 impacts on ASEAN households) 1 (chart of history)	5 (chemistry / video)	1 (environmental sustainability)	(none)	30 (statistical analysis)

Going Through the Motions

Several of the links went to various web logs (blogs). One innovation design blog offered information about infographics. There was another about science illustration. One blog focused on learning theories. Another blog lauds information (but felt dated). (5)

Some sites addressed the interests of particular groups in academia. For example, a website targeted to librarians encouraged them to create infographics using publicly available tools, which were duly listed. Some sites focused on teachers. For example, one link went to a slideshow about social teaching using social media tools. A website offered strategies to humanize learning. One site went to a .pdf field guide about fake news and how to discern that. Several of the sources offered open-source books, usually used by teachers and students. One was an open-source book on the Pressbooks platform about "contemporary families." Another was an open textbook about growing plants and biology. Another featured a book on American government on the OpenStax platform. One link went to a futurism publication. (8)

Sales were a main feature on some linked-to sites. One was a website advertising an e-book about pedagogies of care. Another went to a company that creates marketing about other companies' sustainability efforts for good public relations. A study site offered to help students pass pharmacy exams as a commercial service. There was a link to a literacy foundation website. One site shared information about business software. Several sites pointed to apps: a world atlas on iOS, a museum app on iOS, and a presentation software on the iPad. (8)

It seemed that many use the site to drive traffic, and so used broad folk-labeling in the tagging area. Perhaps the Smart Search was set up for broad or "fuzzy" discoveries, on the off-chance that peripheral interest may lead to additional discoveries. MERLOT also enabled the contents to be categorized by general academic disciplines, but this information was not directly used given the level of generality and the fact that these were only applied to some of the curated resources.

RQ2: What are the most common to least common topics addressed in the infographics, in terms of general discipline categories?

The respective infographics, when available, were individually explored and then manually coded. (Table 3)

Table 3. Extracted topics from publicly available infographics for formal higher education (from MERLOT Referatory)

Topic	Count
African American history and culture	1
Automobile history	1
Badging / micro-credentialing	2 (and how badges work; what badging is)
Beer drinks	2 (history of beer, best beer in U.S.)
Chemistry	1 (video)
Coffee drinks	1 (different types of coffee drinks)
Consumer behaviors	2 (consumer savings behaviors; "pissing off the financial world"; consumer spending trends in India)
Counterfeit Credentials (identifying in higher ed)	1 (identifying counterfeit credentials in higher ed)

continues on following page

377

Table 3. Continued

Topic	Count
COVID-19 impacts on ASEAN households	1
Crime	1 (internet piracy pyramid)
Culture	1 (1950s household)
Disneyland footprint	1
Drug consumption	1
Environmentalism	1 (anatomy of an energy-efficient home; a set of 120 hosted on a website on a variety of environmental / sustainability topics)
Fast food franchises	1 (distribution of McDonald's and Starbucks globally)
Fire safety	1
Global financial crisis	3 (2008, "where did all the money go?"; inflation and how it is calculated)
Global trade	3 (in tobacco, consumer spending, US-China trade relations)
Global warming	1
Health	1 (chronic obstructive pulmonary disease or COPD)
Instructional design trends	1
Insurance	1
Internet traffic (global)	2 (activity on the Internet; 50 most influential websites)
Librarian Design Share	1
Mail	1 (what customers get in their regular "mailstream" or mail service)
Mobile device management	1
Motor vehicle fuel consumption	1
Online university courses 2019	1
Population in U.S.	2 (immigration to U.S., population distribution in U.S. on a map)
Popular movies	1 (which ones most pirated)
Social networks	1 (social networks on Flickr, a social image sharing site)
Street vendors in urban USA	1
Student budget	1
Swine flu	1 (history of swine flu from 1976)
Typefaces, font families	1
UX design	1 (user experience design)
War history	3 (1993 Black Hawk Down incident; war fatalities in Iraq; social tensions around competition for water)
World AIDS Day (2013)	66 (one page with many)

In Figure 4, the Pareto chart shows that most of the topics are in the "long tail" as niche topics. Those that are highly frequent were infographics based on a particular event with broad invitations for submittals of infographics according to the event themes. In many ways, the infographics were fairly dated, based on the time when the works were created. Many work as historical objects, perhaps, but may lack direct relevance on the particular issues today.

Figure 4. Identified Topics of the Educational Infographics Set (Pareto chart)

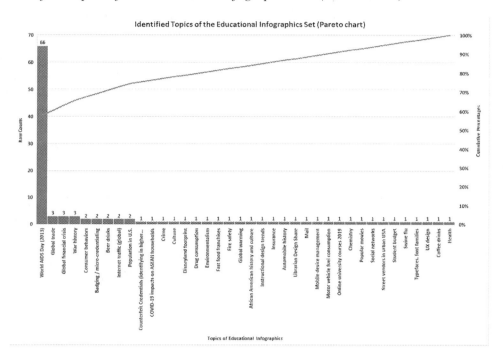

RQ3: What are apparent pedagogical strengths to learning with the publicly available infographics used in higher education?

The learning value of the respective works varied. Per the academic research literature, how the respective infographics as digital learning objects are used will depend on the pedagogical setup. There are different teaching and learning strategies for how to integrate infographics into high school science courses (Lamb, Polman, Newman, & Smith, 2014).

The respective infographics were generally pithy and focused. Many were titled, but they were not identified by author or authoring team. Few stood out as deeply original. Few stood out as designed aesthetically; rather, the focus seemed to be on function.

RQ4: What are apparent pedagogical weaknesses to learning with the publicly available infographics used in higher education?

Many of the infographics were fairly superficial and light in terms of information.

In terms of academic usage, many lacked the features of academic objects. The sources of data were rarely cited in the infographics. The infographics were not often dated within the infographic, but some dates could be ascertained based on the website "surround." Many of the infographics were not sufficiently comprehensive to be "stand-alone." Perhaps there is information in the metadata, but many of the works did not have metadata that accompanied the object.

RQ5: For the informational infographics that are transient (due to motion), what are some ways to ensure that these do not result in cognitive overload? What design factors may be brought into play to enable accurate understandings of the underlying data and messaging?

The chemistry videos were well paced. The motion was not superficial but related to both the person making the presentation with lively facial expressions and movements, but also the animations depicting various phenomena. The videos could be paused. They could be slowed or speeded up. They could be scrubbed through. The user controls meant that the speed of the transient could be slowed. And then, there was instant replay if desired. Beyond that, the videos were on YouTube, which enables full transcription (with machine-generated transcripts, human editability, and translation into a number of foreign languages as desired).

Discussion

This exploration of educational infographics from the respected MERLOT site resulted in only 49 sources, and 29 of these links led to other-than-infographics. Only about 40% of the links went to infographics or infographic collections. The five questions in this work focused on formal educational infographics in higher education and the following points: their modalities (static, motion, interactive, immersive, and combined); their common topics and discipline categories; pedagogical strengths; pedagogical weaknesses; and then methods for how to ensure that motion infographics do not result in cognitive overload but result in actual learning. This work resulted in some general observations.

Higher education would benefit from more effectively designed information graphics that stand the test of time and can be inherited (with heritable features). Researchers in developing countries point to the adoption of mobile technologies in learning and predict the promise of educational infographics and other digital learning objects in developing countries (Johri & Misra, 2017). Ensuring that such digital objects may be used in all web-based contexts would be powerful. The optimal infographics may be designed in ways that can be cited by users in research and in teaching and learning. It would help if there was more mapping of educational infographics from MERLOT to useful resources, given the many apparent gaps in the curation. For example, there are many data visualizations in Second Life (as an immersive virtual world) available through SLURLs, but there were none in the referatory.

FUTURE RESEARCH DIRECTIONS

Additional exploration in the respective areas, using the five research questions, may be conducted based on different sets of infographics. Analysis may be done based on infographics in particular fields, like chemistry, like math, and like statistics, since these seem to be fields in which there are some rich infographic designs. Infographics are said to be relevant in micro-learning opportunities and IT-enabled "fragmented learning, mobile learning and lifelong learning (Hao, Liu, & Zhai, 2018, p. 79), and that angle may be explored. There has already been early work done in studying the efficacy of various educational infographics in different learning contexts, and the field of educational research would benefit from additional insights.

1. How much learning can educational infographics contain?

Going Through the Motions

2. In terms of Combined types of infographics—those that include "motion and interactive" features, "motion and immersive," "interactive and immersive," and others—how can these types of optimized for attention capture, retention, low cognitive load consumption, accessibility, and learning?
3. What are some types of authorship signature identification in infographic analysis?
4. What are some effective ways to harness infographics not designed specifically for educational applications?
5. What are some pedagogical and andragogical methodologies that may be applied to the usage of educational infographics?
6. What about full typologies of educational infographics?
7. How can extant infographics be designed for global usage beyond the local, with considerations for cultures, languages, geographical variances, and other factors?
8. What are various analog and digital content in which educational infographics are used? Print and digital books? Educational kits? Handbooks, guidebooks? Analog kits? And others?
9. What are ways to ensure accessibility of infographics for universal accessibility?
10. What are constructing consensus-based standards for educational infographics?

There are other approaches, too, that may apply to future research related to educational infographics.

CONCLUSION

At present, it does seem as if the full harnessing of the potentials of educational infographics has not been constructively exploited. Rather, in many cases, academia has been going through the motions only, with simplified works with color dazzle but insufficient substance. Overall, there is room for improvement for a very promising digital communications and educational technology modality.

With dropping infection rates for COVID-19 globally, now is the time to advance learning, such as through motion infographics in digital formats for global learners in higher education, and perhaps K-12 and even pre-school learning.

REFERENCES

Al-Dairy, H. M., & Al-Rabaani, A. H. (2017, December). An analytical study of research orientations for infographics applications in education. In *2017 6th International Conference on Information and Communication Technology and Accessibility (ICTA)* (pp. 1-5). IEEE.

Albarrak, S., & Shalto, M. (2015). The effect of electronic educational infographic design on the development of skills in dealing with the lighting in photography by the postgraduate students. *Proceedings of the 2015 Fifth International Conference on e-Learning*, 465 – 485.

Albers, M. J. (2014, October). Infographics: Horrid chartjunk or quality communication. In *2014 IEEE International Professional Communication Conference (IPCC)* (pp. 1-4). IEEE.

Almeida, C., & Almeida, P. (2016, November). Online educational videos: The teenagers' preferences. In *Iberoamerican Conference on Applications and Usability of Interactive TV* (pp. 65-76). Springer.

Barker, L. M., Ponzio, C. M., & Matthusen, A. (2018). Under Discussion: Teaching Speaking and Listening: Promoting Student-Centered Discussion with Digital Tools and Infographics. *English Journal*, *107*(3), 123–126.

Battaiola, A. L., Alves, M. M., & Paulin, R. E. (2014, June). Canvas to improve the design process of educational animation. In *International Conference on Learning and Collaboration Technologies* (pp. 13-24). Springer. 10.1007/978-3-319-07482-5_2

Bhatia, A., Gaur, P. S., Zimba, O., Chatterjee, T., Nikiphorou, E., & Gupta, L. (2021). The untapped potential of Instagram to facilitate rheumatology academia. *Clinical Rheumatology*, 1–7. PMID:34601652

Bohstedt, B. D. (2017). *An Infographic Is Worth a Thousand Words: Using Data Visualization to Engage Faculty in Collection Strategies*. Academic Press.

Diniz, H., & Melilli, E. (2020). The rise of #SocialMedia in the Nephrology world. *Nefrologia*, *40*(6), 597–607. doi:10.1016/j.nefro.2020.02.003 PMID:32386925

Dowhos, K., Sherbino, J., Chan, T. M., & Nagji, A. (2021). Infographics, podcasts, and blogs: A multi-channel, asynchronous, digital faculty experience to improve clinical teaching (MAX FacDev). *Canadian Journal of Emergency Medical Care*, *23*(3), 390–393. doi:10.100743678-020-00069-5 PMID:33788176

Egan, M., Acharya, A., Sounderajah, V., Xu, Y., Mottershaw, A., Phillips, R., Ashrafian, H., & Darzi, A. (2021). Evaluating the effect of infographics on public recall, sentiment and willingness to use face masks during the COVID-19 pandemic: A randomised internet-based questionnaire study. *BMC Public Health*, *21*(1), 1–10. doi:10.118612889-021-10356-0 PMID:33596857

Eidson, B. (2015). Testing potable reuse messages with a utility–university partnership. *Journal - American Water Works Association*, *107*(11), 54–57. doi:10.5942/jawwa.2015.107.0167

Hanh, H. P., Nam, T. T., & Vinh, L. A. (2022). Initiatives to Promote School-Based Mental Health Support by Department of Educational Sciences, University of Education Under Vietnam National University. In *University and School Collaborations during a Pandemic* (pp. 321–331). Springer. doi:10.1007/978-3-030-82159-3_21

Hao, Y., Liu, Q., & Zhai, H. (2018, May). Design and development of educational information processing micro-curriculum in the era of educational informationization. In *Proceedings of the 2018 International Conference on Distance Education and Learning* (pp. 79-83). 10.1145/3231848.3231869

Harrison, L., Reinecke, K., & Chang, R. (2015). *Infographic aesthetics: Designing for the first impression. In the proceedings of CHI 2015*. Crossings. doi:10.1145/2702123.2702545

Heimbürger, A., & Isomöttönen, V. (2019, October). Infographics as a Reflective Assignment Method in Requirements Engineering e-Course? In *2019 IEEE Frontiers in Education Conference (FIE)* (pp. 1-5). IEEE.

Heimbürger, A., Keto, H., & Isomöttönen, V. (2020, October). Learning via Summarizing Infographics Assignment in Software Engineering Management e-Course? In 2020 IEEE Frontiers in Education Conference (FIE) (pp. 1-5). IEEE. doi:10.1109/FIE44824.2020.9274229

Going Through the Motions

Johri, P., & Misra, A. (2017, August). Digital technology in classroom: Changing the face of education infographic. In *2017 International Conference On Smart Technologies For Smart Nation (SmartTechCon)* (pp. 405-406). IEEE. 10.1109/SmartTechCon.2017.8358405

Khaydaraliyevna, P. S. (2021, November). Development of ICT Creativity of Teachers of HEU' With Helping Infographics. In *2021 International Conference on Information Science and Communications Technologies (ICISCT)* (pp. 1-3). IEEE.

Kibar, P. N., & Akkoyunlu, B. (2014, October). A new approach to equip students with visual literacy skills: Use of infographics in education. In *European Conference on Information Literacy* (pp. 456-465). Springer.

Lamb, G., Polman, J. L., Newman, A., & Smith, C. G. (2014). Science news infographics. *Science Teacher*, *81*(3), 25–30. doi:10.2505/4/tst14_081_03_25

MERLOT Smart Search. (2022). *MERLOT*. Retrieved January 26, 2022, from https://info.merlot.org/merlothelp/MERLOT_Smart_Search.htm

Papić, A., & Sušilović, S. (2018, May). Students' preferences regarding the transfer of information and knowledge through infographics tools. In *2018 41st International Convention on Information and Communication Technology, Electronics and Microelectronics (MIPRO)* (pp. 574-579). IEEE.

Salim, M. S., Saad, M. N., & Nor, B. M. (2021, August). Comparative Study of Low-Cost Tools to Create Effective Educational Infographics Content. In *2021 11th IEEE International Conference on Control System, Computing and Engineering (ICCSCE)* (pp. 23-28). IEEE. 10.1109/ICCSCE52189.2021.9530848

Savini, C. A., Gasull, V. L., & Gimeno, P. B. (2019, March). Infographics. A way to increase competences. In *2019 IEEE World Conference on Engineering Education (EDUNINE)* (pp. 1-6). IEEE.

Schibuk, E. (2020). Visualizing the environmental effects of electronics. *Science Scope*, *43*(5), 52–61. doi:10.2505/4s20_043_05_52

Steyn, A. A., Botha, A. J., Coetzee, D., & Villiers, M. D. (2020, July). Interactive Learning: Introducing a First-Year Systems' Analysis and Design Course. *In Annual Conference of the Southern African Computer Lecturers' Association* (pp. 171-186). Springer.

Volman, M., & Kormilicyn, D. (2018, October). Infographics in "Safety of Nuclear Power Plants" Course. In *2018 IV International Conference on Information Technologies in Engineering Education (Inforino)* (pp. 1-4). IEEE. 10.1109/INFORINO.2018.8581744

Zhang-Kennedy, L., Chiasson, S., & Biddle, R. (2013, September). *Password advice shouldn't be boring: Visualizing password guessing attacks. In 2013 APWG eCrime Researchers Summit*. IEEE.

KEY TERMS AND DEFINITIONS

Immersive Infographics: Digital visuals in immersive virtual worlds or augmented reality or mixed reality to communicate information through text, data, data visualizations, images, and other designed elements (and user experiences).

Interactive Infographics: Digital visuals that may be triggered or changed based on user inputs to communicate information through text, data, data visualizations, images, and other designed elements (and user experiences).

Motion Infographics: Motion digital visuals that communicate information through animation (or video), text, data, data visualizations, images, and other designed elements (and user experiences).

Static Infographics: Still analog or digital visuals that communicate information through text, data, data visualizations, images, and other designed elements (and user experiences).

Chapter 18

Using Motion Infographics to Teach Computer Programming Concepts

Apostolos Syropoulos

https://orcid.org/0000-0002-9625-1482

Greek Molecular Computing Group, Greece

ABSTRACT

Although programming languages are expressive tools, their expressive power is quite limited. A direct consequence of this is that novice users have difficulty grasping the basic programming constructs mainly because there is a discrepancy between natural languages and programming languages (e.g., How do we express common human tasks in Python?). A relatively easy way to tackle this discrepancy is to use motion infographics. However, when pupils and students are familiar with abstraction, a basic idea of computational thinking, then one can use motion infographics that show familiar objects and/or ideas that should be used to teach the corresponding programming constructs. The author has used this approach to create motion infographics that explain conditional and repetitive constructs. However, this does not really work with recursion as one has to resort to the use of trees to explain this programming concept. All the motion infographics presented here have been produced with XeLaTeX, an open source tool that can be used to produce excellent printed/electronic documents.

INTRODUCTION

At the time this chapter was written, I was working on a book whose goal was to teach programming to everyone with practically no previous knowledge. I have to say that writing a textbook about programming is by no means an easy task, although many think quite the opposite. Experience shows that when one introduces new concepts and ideas, drawings that visualize them are extremely helpful. This happens mainly because humans comprehend images, pictures, and drawings easier than oral or written descriptions. Thus, when one speaks about variables, she should use visual aids to make the idea of a variable more accessible. For example, the idea that a variable is a container that holds numbers and/

DOI: 10.4018/978-1-6684-5934-8.ch018

Copyright © 2023, IGI Global. Copying or distributing in print or electronic forms without written permission of IGI Global is prohibited.

or character strings is quite instructive. However, single pictures are not sufficient for other commands, because most of them involve some change to the state of a computer and/or the values of some variables. In this case, it is far more instructive to use a series of images and/or drawings or, even better, some sort of short animations that will visualize all the action that takes place when a specific command is executed. Naturally, animations are useful in all kinds of presentations and eBooks. Unfortunately, authors of traditional books on programming have no choice but to use series of images and/or drawings.

Once one has decided what each animation should include, it is necessary to also decide how to realize the idea. Since I am a proponent of Open-Source software, I have opted to realize my creations as Animated PNG (*APNG*) files. The frames of my APNG motion infographic should be simple Portable Network Graphic (*PNG*) files that I had to create somehow. Since I am an *amateur* programmer, I prefer to write code that creates my frames. For this reason, I have opted to use tools from the company of TeX and its friends.

Computational thinking was introduced by Jeannette Marie Wing (Wing, 2008) [see also (Pollak & Ebner, 2019) for a more recent overview of computational thinking; and also (Neumann et al., 2021) for a guide on how to teach computational thinking]. One could define computational thinking as a problem-solving methodology that makes use of the fundamental notions of informatics. Computer programming and computational thinking are not the same thing but knowing how to program helps people to apply computational thinking in many and different kinds of problems. This means that if one provides learners with motion infographics that easily allow them to understand and, consequently, generalize the ideas presented by them, then learning would be much easier. I call the process of generating such motion infographics *inverse computational thinking*. Thus, my aim is to show how to generate motion infographics with open-source tools and to explain how to apply inverse computational thinking to create them.

Python[1] is a widely used programming language that was designed by Guido van Rossum, a Dutch programmer. The language is quite popular[2] and, based on my own experience as a computer science teacher, it has an *increasing-returns* learning curve, which means that learners progress slowly at the beginning but their skills rise over time until full proficiency is obtained. In addition, Python is widely available, and one can use it on smartphones, tablets, desktop computers, etc. In addition, one can run Python programs using a web browser since there are some web pages that provide this ability.

Plan of the Chapter

First of all, I will describe how to generate drawings and animations using Open Source tools. In particular, I will explain what steps are needed in order to create an APNG file. But I will not give a recipe describing how to create any drawing. Instead, I will just describe the tools that I have used to create my own drawings. Then, I will discuss what kind of drawings and animations can be used to teach basic computational constructs—conditional and repetition commands. Next, I will discuss how one can use infographics to allow learners to get an understanding of recursion, which is a powerful yet not so obvious programming technique. The chapter will conclude with the customary conclusions section.

Creating Infographics Using Open-Source Tools

I am sure that there are proprietary tools that can be used to construct infographics, however, I am in favor of open-source tools for two reasons. First of all, such tools can be improved by contacting the author and asking him/her to include a new feature that will increase their functionality. In most cases, authors

Using Motion Infographics to Teach Computer Programming Concepts

respond positively and do the updates quite quickly. The second reason is that these tools are free of charge, and they can be used on almost any computer platform without problems. For many independent researchers and scholars like me, paying for computer programs and operating systems is not an option and so I have to resort to open-source tools. Thus, in what follows I will present the open-source tools that I am using to create infographics.

Usually, when I have to prepare a document that will be eventually printed, I use the XeLaTeX document preparation system[3] (a Unicode-aware version of LaTeX that can also handle OpenType fonts). In addition, I use this tool to create drawings, graphs, etc. In particular, I use the PGF/Ti*k*Z languages[4] for producing vector graphics. These languages were developed by Till Tantau and now they are further developed by Till Tantau and Christian Feuersänger. In a nutshell PGF/Ti*k*Z is a *package* (i.e., something quite similar to modules that most programming languages allow users to use and create) that one loads in a XeLaTeX document so to create pictures. Alternatively, one can create standalone images from single XeLaTeX documents that can be included in a document. The latter approach is much better since it allows one to use whatever resources (e.g., other packages) one may need and, at the same time, one does not have to worry about any computer constraints (e.g., memory or speed), which would possibly make processing the whole document much slower and in certain cases much more difficult. A minimal example that produces the image in Figure 1 is shown below.

```
\documentclass{standalone}
%\documentclass[a4paper,landscape]{article}
\usepackage{xltxtra}
\usepackage{tikz}
\begin{document}
\setmainfont[Mapping=tex-text,Ligatures=Common]{Minion Pro}
\begin{tikzpicture}
\draw[gray, thick] (-1,2) coordinate(A) -- (2,-1) coordinate (B);
\draw[gray, thick] (-1,-1) coordinate(C) -- (2,2) coordinate (D);
\node[red,scale=3,label={Intersection point}]
at (intersection of  A--B and C--D){.};
\end{tikzpicture}
%\thispagestyle{empty}
\end{document}
```

The code is presented only as a demonstration, and I will not make any attempt to explain what it does. There are many freely available online resources about PGF/Ti*k*Z programming and the manual of PGF/Ti*k*Z is very detailed and well written. The manual is freely available, and it is a PDF document that has 1321 pages! However, it is necessary to say that sometimes the **standalone** LaTeX document class (i.e., a general template that allows users to create specific documents, here a standalone image) fails to correctly compute the bounding box of an image-only PDF. This means that image-only PDF files that should have had the same width and height differ slightly. Thus, it is not possible to create animations, as the software that creates APNGs expects images to have the same width and height. To avoid this problem one should comment out the first line of the file [i.e., put an percent sign (%) before the backslash (\)] and uncomment the lines that are commented out. In this case, we have to make one more step—we need to remove the white space around the image. This can easily be done with **pdfcrop**.

Figure 1. A sample drawing created with PGF/TikZ.

The PDF file of the image shown in Figure 1 was transformed into a PNG file using the following command:

```
$ gs -sDEVICE=png256 -r600 -o Fig1.png Fig1.pdf
```

Note that the commands should be entered in a Unix terminal or the equivalent in your own operating system. Here **gs** is Ghostscript[5], an interpreter for the PostScript® language and PDF files.

In some cases, I have borrowed images created with PGF/TikZ but their orientation was "wrong" (e.g., the image of a train, that I have used in my motion infographics, was in the opposite direction from what I wanted). In situation like these, the following command solved my problem:

```
$ gs -o outFile.pdf -sDEVICE=pdfwrite -c \
>"<</Install {-1 1 scale -width 0 translate}>> setpagedevice"\
```

Using Motion Infographics to Teach Computer Programming Concepts

```
>  -f inFile.pdf
$ pdfcrop outFile.pdf
```

Note that the backslash indicates that the command continues on the next line. Now, the first command flips horizontally an image-only PDF file. The parameter *–width* is the width of the image negated and it should be expressed in PostScript points, which are also known as big points or just bp (72 bp = 1 inch = 2.54 cm). The second command crops the unnecessary white space that is produced. If one wants to flip vertically an image-only PDF file, then she has to use the following commands:

```
$ gs -o outFile.pdf -sDEVICE=pdfwrite -c \
>"<</Install {1 -1 scale 0 -height translate}>> setpagedevice" \
> -f inFile.pdf
$ pdfcrop outFile.pdf
```

Here *-height* is the height of the image negated. In both cases, the final output file will be called **outFile-crop.pdf**. Although PDF files are quite useful for the creation of documents that will eventually be printed, these files cannot directly be used for the creation of motion infographics. However, one can easily generate a raster image from a PDF file using Ghostscript.

```
$ gs -sDEVICE=png16m -r600 -o outFile.png inFile.pdf
```

This command creates a PNG file that can have up to 16 million colors and whose resolution is 600 dpi. Clearly by changing 600 to, say, 1200 we will get a PNG file whose resolution will be 1200 dpi. Once we have the frames we can assemble them to build an APNG file. There are many freely available tools that can be used to create APNG files. The program **apngasm**[6] is an excellent command line tool (CLI) that comes with a graphical user interface (GUI) for Windows users. Another tool that can generate APNG files is **FFmpeg**[7] which is a ``complete, cross-platform solution to record, convert and stream audio and video.'' However, for reasons of simplicity I will only explain how one can use **apngasm** to build APNG files. In the simplest case we use a command like the following one:

```
$ pngasm ANIM.apng IMAGE1.png IMAGE2.png IMAGE3.png IMAGE4.png 6
```

Here the number 6 corresponds to the frame delay and in this case it is 6/10 sec. The default value is 1/10 sec. The following HTML5 code snipped shows how one can embed the resulting image in an HTML5 document.

```
<picture>
<source srcset="ANIM.apng" type="image/apng">
<img src="IMAGE1.png">
</picture>
```

Since a few browsers do not support APNG files, the whole tag includes a fail-safe feature. Naturally, one could add some text explaining the problem but there is no reason to elaborate on this matter here.

Teaching Basic Computational Constructs

Computational thinking is a teaching methodology that employs the fundamental ideas of programming to teaching. One of these ideas is *abstraction*, that is, "the process of generalizing from specific instances" (Lee et al., 2011). When teaching programming, this means that one should create examples that will allow students to easily abstract out the basic functionality of a programming construct or the basic principles related to data structure, etc.

It is known that any programming language is considered complete if it includes assignment statements, conditional and repetition commands (Michaelson, 2020). Thus, I will give some examples of how one can create motion infographics of these constructs using inverse computational thinking. Let me start with the Python conditional command.

In the simplest case a conditional evaluates a logical expression and if the expression is true, then some other commands are executed. Otherwise, nothing happens, and the interpreter continues with the execution of the remaining commands. We can visualize the situation by thinking that the interpreter is a vehicle (e.g., a train) and the various commands to be executed are just stops on the path of the vehicle. A simple conditional is like a rail junction where the train can move to one of the two rail routes, and this depends on the railroad signals. If the conditional is true, then it moves into the first rail route as the series of drawings in Figure 2 show.

Figure 2. Drawings that explain the functionality of a simple conditional command when the condition is true.

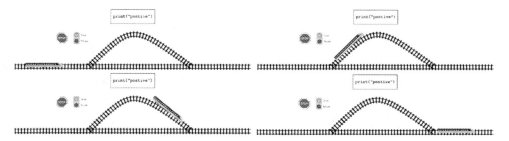

The stop sign indicates that the condition is evaluated at this point. To make the drawings even more useful, one could add a diamond with the condition inside it just above the light. Now, if the conditional is false, then the train moves to the second route as the drawings in Figure 3 show. The reader should notice that now **FALSE** has the green light on (i.e., the condition is false now).

These two sets of drawings can be used to create a simple motion infographic as was described in the previous section. If the animation is not smooth enough, then we can add more "frames" and make it a better animation. Of course, one can add one more "stop" before the rail junction (e.g., an input command) to visualize a program that reads an integer and prints "positive" when the integer is positive.

Based on these ideas, one can visualize a conditional command that checks a condition and if it is true, it executes the first branch and if it is false, it executes the second branch. The set of drawings in Figure 4 show how one could visualize the case that the condition is true.

Using Motion Infographics to Teach Computer Programming Concepts

Figure 3. Drawings that explain the functionality of a simple conditional command when the condition is false.

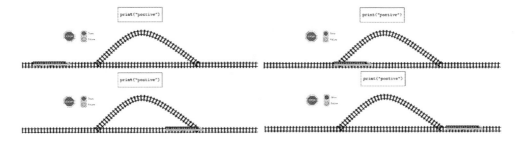

Figure 4. Visualization of an if-then-else command when the condition is true.

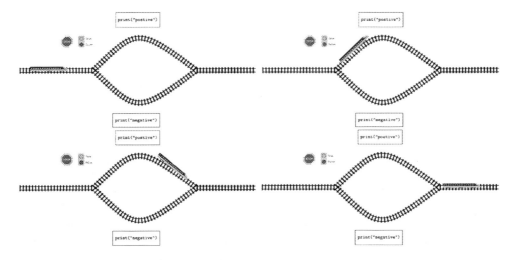

Figure 5. Visualization of an if-then-else command when the condition is false.

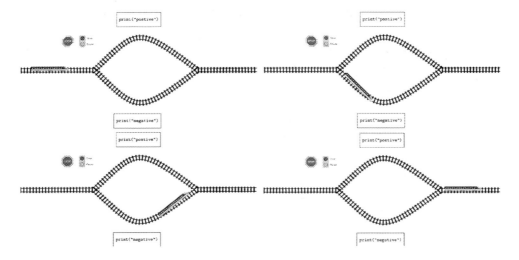

As expected, a "reflection" of this image would be a visualization of the case when the condition is false. Indeed, the drawings in Figure 5 show how this can be realized.

Recently, the Python language creator Guido van Rossum and a number of other contributors have proposed a new syntactic construct that realizes a functionality similar to that of the C/C++ **switch/case** construct. This proposal has been accepted for Python 3.10 and is called *structural pattern matching*. Since this command is quite new I would like to say a few things about it. Suppose one wants to write a simple program that inputs a number, which is a numerical judgment of the song, and prints a phrase that corresponds to this number. The following code solves this "problem" in Python.

```
decision = int(input ("Judge the song!\n? "))
match decision:
case 1:
print ("awful song")
case 2:
        print ("very bad song")
. . . . . . . . . . . . . . . . . . . . . . . . . . . .
case 10:
print ("wonderful song")
case _:
print ("I have no opinion!")
```

It should be clear that this command examines the value of variable **decision** and if it is equal to one, then it executes the command that follows. Unlike the C/C++ **switch** command, the **match** command stops after the execution of the **print** command. Now if the variable's value is equal to two, then it executes the second **case**, etc. The last case is executed when and if the value of the variable, or more generally the expression, next to the **match** keyword, is not included in the various cases that follow.

Structural pattern matching can be visualized by using special traffic light when for each **case** there is light that can be either green or red. Clearly, one light will be green and all other lights will be red. In addition, we need to have as many rails in the rail junction as the number of cases in the **match** command. For example, the **match** command presented above has 11 **case**s, thus we need eleven rails that start from the rail junction. Obviously, when teaching programming one uses relatively simple examples that will have 3-4 different **case**s. Figure 6 shows how one could visualize the **match** command using the train concept I have used so far. Note that the traffic light is bit more involved now. The blue arrows indicate where the command should be. Now let us turn attention to loops.

Basically, there are two kinds of repetition commands: Commands where we specify from the beginning the number of repetitions and commands where the final number of repetitions is unknown and depends on some condition. As expected, Python supports both kinds of commands. Typically, for command uses a variable to traverse a range of commands. For example, the following code prints the integers for 1 to 5 using a for-loop:

```
for i in range(1,6):
        print(i)
```

Figure 6. Visualizing a match command.

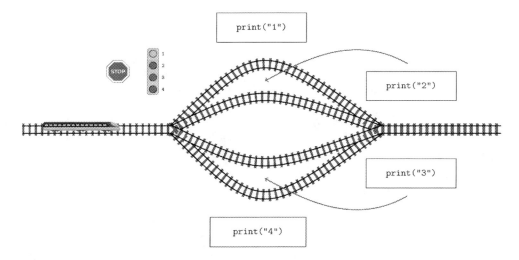

Function **range** creates an *iterable* object, that is, an object that can return its members one at a time thus permitting it to be iterated over in a for-loop. The first argument specifies the beginning of the sequence of numbers and the second the number where the sequence should stop. So, the second element is produced from the first element by adding one to it, the third element is produced from the second by adding one to it, etc. However, it is more instructive to think that, at each iteration, the value of the variable that actually traverses the iterable object is actually incremented at each loop. In addition, we can think that just before each loop, the command checks whether the value of the variable is less than the value of the second argument of function **range**. Figure 7 depicts how these ideas can be visualized. The check and its result are depicted in Figure 8. Note that here I have included two drawings that show what happens when the check fails. Using a series of such images, one can create a really useful motion infographic that will allow pupils to better understand how **for** command works. Thus they will be able to make the next step, that is, to abstract from the concrete and completely understand how the command works.

The **while**-loop is an example of a repetition command of the second kind. Obviously, the previous series of drawings can be used to visualize the following command:

```
i = 1
while i < 6:
        print(i)
        i = i + 1
```

The only difference here is that the command that increments the value of variable **i** is a real command. Thus, it should appear in a normal rectangle and not in a dashed one.

Figure 7. Visualizing one iteration of a for-loop. The normal dashed box shows a "hidden" operation while the dashed box with thick dashes shows the value of the variable using a true condition. Finally, the diamond shows a condition that is checked by Python in order to determine whether one more loop should be performed.

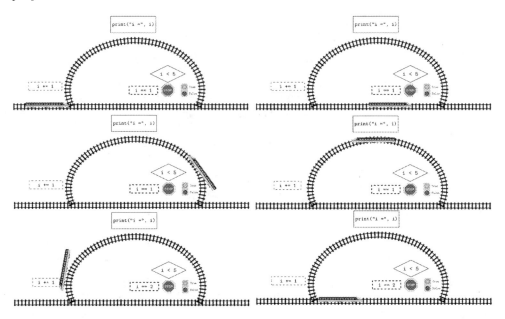

Figure 8. In top two images, the condition is actually checked and found true thus on more loop is performed. However, in the bottom drawings depict the case where the condition is false.

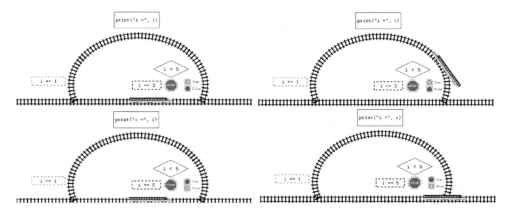

TEACHING RECURSION

Recursion is programming technique and a problem-solving method [see (Barron, 1968) for an overview] that can vaguely be described by showing an image of a camera that points to its live feed monitor (see Figure 9). Trying to explain this image is a good starting point for an informal introduction to recursion. The only problem with this "setup" is that it is infinite. An interesting problem that can be used to introduce recursion is the famous *Towers of Hanoi* problem.[8] Here is an informal description of the problem:

Using Motion Infographics to Teach Computer Programming Concepts

Figure 9. A picture showing the basic idea of recursion. The photograph was shoot by @cottonbro at https://www.pexels.com (the photo is free to use).

In the great temple of Brahma in Benares, on a brass plate under the dome that marks the center of the world, there are 64 disks of pure gold that the priests carry one at a time between these diamond needles according to Brahma's immutable law: No disk may be placed on a smaller disk. In the begging of the world all 64 disks formed the Tower of Brahma on one needle. Now, however, the process of transfer of the tower from one needle to another is in mid course. When the last disk is finally in place, once again forming the Tower of Brahma but on a different needle, then will come the end of the world and all will turn to dust.

Assuming that the tower has n disks, a recursive solution is this: First, move a tower of height $n-1$ from the first needle to the third, then move the remaining disk from the first needle to the second, and, finally, move the tower of height $n-1$ from the third needle to the second one. This means that we have reduced the problem of moving a tower of height n to that of moving a tower of height $n-1$. Clearly, one can use these ideas to explain how to solve the problem. In addition, a simple motion infographic made of the images in Figure 10 can be of great help to any instructor.

For simplicity, I have used a slightly modified version of the LaTeX file created by Takayuki Yato[9] to generate a PDF file where each page of the file contains shows one step of the solution. Then I used the following BASH script to automatically generate the motion infographic:

```
for i in {1..8};
do
pdfextract.sh $i $i TowersOfHanoi.pdf TowersOfHanoi${i}.pdf ;
pdfcrop TowersOfHanoi${i}.pdf;
```

```
gs -sDEVICE=png16m -r300 -o TowersOfHanoi${i}.png \
   TowersOfHanoi${i}-crop.pdf
done
```

Figure 10. Solving the "Towers of Hanoi" problem when the height of the tower is 3.

The script **pdfextract.sh** uses Ghostscript to extract a range of pages from a PDF document. Although this problem is very interesting, it is better to explain recursive function calls using a simpler problem. Then, one can easily generalize. Here I have opted to start from a recursive definition of summation:

```
def s(x):
    if x == 0:
        return 0
    else:
        return x + s(x-1)
```

For obvious reasons, it is quite common to use trees to visualize recursion. For example, Bishal Sarangkoti[10] created a github project that can be used to visualize recursion trees for any recursive function. In addition, each run of the program creates a motion infographic. Also, there is a site[11] that operates similarly to Sarangkoti's program. However, in my own opinion, the visual result produced by both applications needs some improvement. As expected, I have used PGF/Ti*k*Z to create my own version of the infographics shown in Figure 11.

The images in Figure 11 were not created automatically, but it would be possible to create an application that would read the definition of a recursive function and a specific function call and from this it would create a motion infographic.

Self-Evaluation of the Motion Infographics

These motion infographics and some more have been used in an introductory programming lesson for first year pupils in a typical Greek middle school. Although some of the pupils were quite interested in programming, they did not have the chance to learn anything in elementary school. However, some had some experience with Scratch programming, still I do not consider Scratch a real programming language, mainly because no one uses it in real world programming. This was the first time I used these motion infographics in a classroom. I have asked pupils to answer a very simple questionnaire and their responses are quite encouraging. Thus, I believe the work that I described here served it goal.

Figure 11. Infographics that visualize a recursive function call.

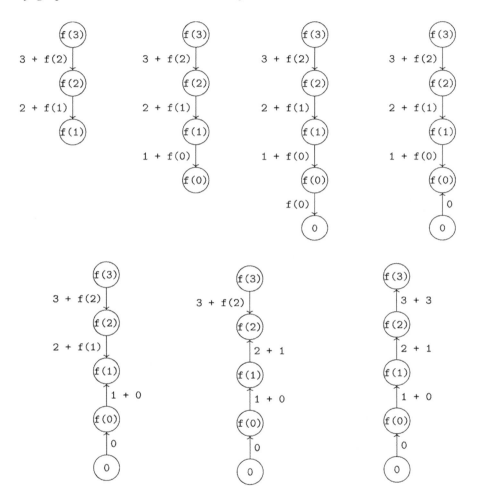

CONCLUSION

Creating motion infographics for computer programming classes is not an easy task. One must find a way to visualize a concept or a construct with something that is quite familiar to her students. Then, one must produce a series of such infographics and "join" then to produce a motion infographic, which will explain the functionality of the concept or the construct. I have used trains and how they move on railways to visualize both conditional and repetitive commands. All people in Europe are quite familiar with trains and many people use them very frequently. Thus, if one has a class of European students, she will not have any problem to introduce students to the relevant ideas when using this approach. However, one can use cars or any kind of vehicle and its motion on the road to describe the same ideas. Since recursion is quite special, it is not easy to improvise and most people teach it by using trees, which have annotations on the arrows that connect the nodes that explain what is going on.

As I have already stated, I was working on a book that introduces programming and I was using the infographics described here in my book. At the same time, I am using parts of the book as some sort of hand-outs for my students, and I am using motion infographics generated from the infographics to teach and explain the relevant ideas. Most students are satisfied with their lessons and admit that they actually learn. This means that one can use this experience to easily reconstruct the teaching method used in programming classes. In my own opinion, adopting motion infographics in any class will make both the teaching and the learning experience particularly joyful. Of course, if a teacher has some artistic background, then she can create infographics that are funny yet really useful. Obviously, this would be particularly appealing to students that enter a class after a crisis that has forced them to stay at home for a long time.

REFERENCES

Barron, D. W. (1968). *Recursive Techniques in Programming*. Macdonald & Co.

Lee, I., Martin, F., Denner, J., Coulter, B., Allan, W., Erickson, J., Malyn-Smith, J., & Werner, L. (2011). Computational Thinking for Youth in Practice. *ACM Inroads, 2*(1), 32–37. doi:10.1145/1929887.1929902

Michaelson, G. (2020). Programming Paradigms, Turing Completeness and Computational Thinking. *The Art, Science, and Engineering of Programming, 4*(3).

Neumann, M. D., Dion, L., & Snapp, R. (2021). *Teaching Computational Thinking: An Integrative Approach for Middle and High School Learning*. The MIT Press. doi:10.7551/mitpress/11209.001.0001

Pollak, M. & Ebner, M. (2019). The Missing Link to Computational Thinking. *Future Internet, 11*(12).

Wing, J. M. (2008). Computational thinking and thinking about computing. *Philosophical Transactions of the Royal Society A, 366*(1881), 3717–3725. doi:10.1098/rsta.2008.0118 PMID:18672462

ENDNOTES

[1]   See https://www.python.org/ for more information about the language.

[2]   For example, see https://distantjob.com/blog/programming-languages-rank/.

[3]   In some cases, I have to use other tools because some publishers do not use this tool but opt to use tools like LibreOffice Write or Microsoft Word. However, in such cases the final typeset document is always of inferior quality when compared to what XeLaTeX would produce.

[4]   See https://github.com/pgf-tikz/pgf for details.

[5]   See https://www.ghostscript.com/

[6]   See https://github.com/apngasm/apngasm.

[7]   See https://ffmpeg.org/

Using Motion Infographics to Teach Computer Programming Concepts

[8]   See https://asyropoulos.eu/TowersOfHanoi/index.html and the references therein for an overview of the problem.

[9]   See https://gist.github.com/zr-tex8r/1753619

[10]   Recursion Tree Visualizer available from https://github.com/Bishalsarang/Recursion-Tree-Visualizer

[11]   See https://recursion.vercel.app/

Chapter 19
Motion Infographics for Stakeholder Engagement:
A Content–Marketing Perspective

Angel Perez Vila
University of North Florida, USA

Rana Soleimani
University of North Florida, USA

Justin Zuopeng Zhang
iD https://orcid.org/0000-0002-4074-9505
University of North Florida, USA

ABSTRACT

This chapter aims to summarize the design considerations of motion infographics to engage stakeholders from the perspective of content marketing. Specifically, the authors synthesize and illustrate the role of motion infographics in facilitating content marketing and promoting stakeholder engagement. This research fills the gap by proposing a multidisciplinary area by exploring the relationships between motion infographics, content marketing, and stakeholder engagement. It provides valuable guidelines for practitioners to design and implement motion infographics in these relevant contexts.

INTRODUCTION

Infographics have become a valuable instrument in clarifying concepts, distributing information, and promoting awareness (Adi & Setiautami, 2021; Mansour, 2021). Based on data visualization techniques, infographics integrate images, illustrations, charts, text, and other elements in a consolidated presentation to visualize a specific topic and present it to the audience (Ismaeel & Al Mulhim, 2021).

DOI: 10.4018/978-1-6684-5934-8.ch019

Motion Infographics for Stakeholder Engagement

Primarily used in an explanatory way, infographics are traditionally designed, developed, and distributed in a static format. The recent advancement in technologies has made it possible to animate various components of infographics (Wang et al., 2021). Besides, the audiences have become increasingly sophisticated, demanding more engaging, appealing formats of digital content. Therefore, incorporating motions in infographics as a new dimension has become an inevitable trend in design considerations of infographics (Doukianou, Daylamani-Zad, & O'Loingsigh, 2021).

Infographics have been applied in marketing settings to help effectively develop the content and deliver it to the relevant recipients (Siricharoen, 2013). In particular, infographics prove to be a powerful tool for content marketing (Gamble, 2016). Digital content in content marketing exhibits the following major characteristics: "information recombination, accessibility, navigation interaction, speed, and essentially zero cost" (Koiso-Kanttila, 2004). Infographics techniques enrich these characteristics to facilitate the design of digital content and its presentation to the stakeholders, enhancing the efficacy of content marketing (Dalton & Design, 2014). Adding motions to infographics further improves the efficiency of content marketing, as animated content can grab the stakeholders' attention and improve their engagement (Baxter, Lonsdale, & Westland, 2021).

Stakeholder engagement, an important area that originated from project management (Pedrini & Ferri, 2019), has seen its critical values in many different contexts, such as corporate social responsibility (O'Riordan & Fairbrass, 2014), supply chain management (Camilleri, 2017), and sustainability (Perrini & Tencati, 2006). Stakeholders are people that are related to organizations in terms of their various responsibilities and rights, such as employees, customers, suppliers, business partners, shareholders, sponsors, government agencies, and beyond (Aksoy et al., 2021). Content marketing supports stakeholder engagement through a process that includes a series of activities such as content planning, creation, optimization, distribution, measurement, and repurposing (Naseri & Noruzi, 2018).

Although infographics play an important role in content marketing for stakeholder engagement, very few studies have explored the mutual interactive connections between infographics, content marketing, and stakeholder engagement. There lacks a holistic framework to systemize the content marketing activities to engage different types of stakeholders with the help of infographics. Furthermore, the role of the animated features of motion infographics in stakeholder engagement needs to be investigated from a content marketing perspective.

This chapter proposes to fill the research gap by developing a design framework of motion infographics to engage stakeholders from the perspective of content marketing. Specifically, we synthesize and illustrate the specific steps and considerations to strengthen the role of motion infographics in facilitating content marketing and promoting stakeholder engagement. Through this work, we hope to advance future research in the multidisciplinary area between motion infographics, content marketing, and stakeholder engagement. This research also provides valuable guidelines for practitioners to design and implement motion infographics in these relevant contexts.

LITERATURE REVIEW

Infographics

Static infographics allow viewers the option to voluntarily navigate the graphics back and forth to access the information all at once (Mayer et al., 2005; Peters, 2013). In contrast, motion infographics unite the features of ongoing images and simplify data, concepts, and theories, offsetting the drawbacks of content in static infographics by strengthening viewers' impressions, thereby enhancing learning outcomes (Tsai, Huang, & Chang, 2020).

There are three types of motion infographics: emotive, explanatory, and promotional. The emotive motion infographics intend to provoke a powerful, emotional response from the audience and then guide them to take specific actions. The explanatory motion infographics aim to clarify complex concepts, methods, processes, phenomena, and theories by distilling their essence into pictures and texts with animated features. The promotional motion infographics motivate viewers' purchasing decisions by providing relevant information about products and services. Videos are a special type of motion infographics where information is delivered to the viewers in a sequential manner. Although viewers could play, pause, stop, and repeat the video, most of them only watch it once if the information presented in the video is not meaningful and engaging. In conclusion, the animated format in motion infographics can address the deficiency in static infographics by continually offering the viewers a graphical solution from a rich set of perspectives (Hassan, 2016).

Content Marketing

Content marketing is a specific type of marketing that aims to stimulate the interest of potential customers in certain products and services by developing and sharing online materials (Rowley, 2008; Xie & Lou, 2020). From a process perspective, content marketing includes the following major elements: content strategy, content creation, content optimization, content distribution, content repurposing, and content maintenance (Koob, 2021). Although all steps are critical to ensure the success of content marketing, content creation is the most crucial step as it is time-consuming to develop effective content to keep the viewers engaged and stimulated (Müller & Christandl, 2019). As a wide range of choices is accessible to consumers, content providers find it more and more challenging to promote their content online through original ways of marketing formats. Marketers are striving to produce content with innovative methods such as short video clips (Liu et al., 2018).

Among all the content marketing tools, infographics have been recognized as an effective instrument to deliver content in an intuitive and clean manner. Infographics help digital marketers tell a story, grab attention, raise brand awareness, simplify complex data and information, reinforce existing content, and increase online traffic (Gamble, 2016).

Stakeholder Engagement

Mitchell et al. (2022, p. 77) define stakeholder engagement as "the interaction among a firm and its stakeholders that address knowledge problems to improve correspondence in understanding between managers and stakeholders, thereby assisting in resolving ethical challenges."

There are three components of stakeholder engagement: moral, strategic, and pragmatic (Kujala et al., 2022). The moral component requires organizations to engage in reciprocal, voluntary management styles with good intentions. The strategic component strives to motivate stakeholders to involve in co-creating business values. The pragmatic component focuses on practical action and problem-solving and their outcomes for improving the stakeholders' way of life. Prior research has explored the connections between content marketing and stakeholder engagement. For instance, Viglia, Pera, and Bigné (2018)

Motion Infographics for Stakeholder Engagement

developed a framework to propose that stakeholders engagement in a digital context is the outcome of the interactions between stakeholders, which relies on the intellectual understanding of relevant content.

In summary, prior research has identified the role of infographics in content marketing and the relationship between content marketing and stakeholder engagement, very few studies have explored the mutual interactive connections between infographics, content marketing, and stakeholder engagement. There lacks a holistic framework to systemize the design considerations of motion infographics to engage stakeholders from the perspective of content marketing, which is the focus of this book chapter.

METHODOLOGY

Case Method

To research the use of motion infographics for content marketing in practice, our study adopts the qualitative case study research methodology. Yin (2017) defines a case study as an empirical method that examines a contemporary problem based on real-life evidence and context. The case study research method enables researchers to concentrate on the details in a case or multiple cases and find how something can be done. It has been commonly employed in modern social science studies and practical research (Yin, 2017). Many scholars in the business field have favorably applied the case study research approach to investigate real business situations (Eriksson & Kovalainen, 2015). In particular, similar approaches have been employed in recent studies. Thus, the case study research method is used for this study. While case studies do not offer generalizable statistical findings, they are widely used for theory development and theory building (Dubois & Gadde, 2002; Eisenhardt, 1989).

Selection of Cases

To identify the cases to support our study, we comprehensively search the best practices of motion infographics, content marketing, and stakeholder engagement in businesses. All authors conduct individual searches from various sources for relevant cases in these categories and then meet weekly to compare notes to ensure consistency. Our findings indicate that although there exist numerous successful cases of motion infographics, content marketing, and stakeholder engagement, there is a lack of specific cases documenting the integration of these three pieces. We identify the most relevant case in each of these categories: Car Engine for motion infographics, Microsoft for content marketing, and PepsiCo for stakeholder engagement. We also find Spotify as the most representative case of using motion infographics for content marketing to maximize stakeholder engagement. Figure 1 summarizes the framework of individual cases, which we discuss in detail in the following section.

CASE ANALYSIS

This section discusses the case identified for each of the three categories: Car Engine for motion infographics, Microsoft for content marketing, and PepsiCo for stakeholder engagement. As these cases may not involve the elements from all three categories: motion infographics, content marketing, and stakeholder engagement, we discuss how motion infographics can be applied to facilitate content marketing

Figure 1. The framework of individual cases

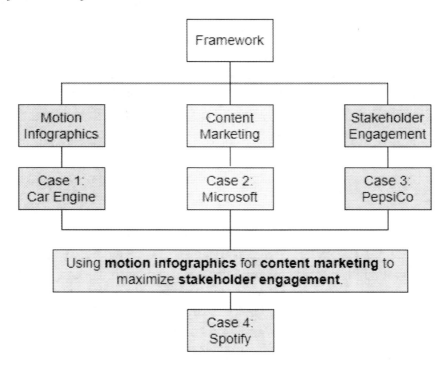

or stakeholder engagement initiatives. Finally, Spotify is illustrated as the most representative case of using motion infographics for content marketing to maximize stakeholder engagement.

Motion Infographics: Car Engine

There are many great examples of motion infographics covering a variety of topics, from car engines to cryptocurrency. We found that motion infographics are simply being used to transmit information without necessarily looking to maximize stakeholder engagement through content marketing. This presents an opportunity for companies or organizations to leverage the high effectiveness of motion infographics in transmitting information to produce quality content marketing and engage stakeholders.

To illustrate the existing value of using motion infographics for content marketing and stakeholder engagement, we have selected an example of existing motion infographics and hypothesized how a company in a topic-related industry could use it as content marketing to maximize stakeholder engagement.

The motion infographic selected for Case 1 in Figure 1 is "How a car engine works." O'Neal (2021) developed this fascinating infographic and presented it in two formats: one in a video (Figure 2) and the other in a motion infographic (Figure 3). They use animations to vividly illustrate the major components of an engine system, the stroke cycle, engine configurations, and other complex concepts and processes related to a car engine. One of the main reasons a motion infographic is an effective tool to display this content is because the information is process-based, which means that there is a sequence that the infographic can easily illustrate the motion aspect. A car company could use a motion infographic similar to this one to increase the visibility of their processes, especially with the introduction of new technologies

Motion Infographics for Stakeholder Engagement

such as electric cars. A motion infographic could also be used to highlight a product's best features and how it differs from competitors. Overall, motion infographics are very effective at illustrating processes, so they can be easily and effectively applied in any scenario involving sequences.

Figure 2. How a car engine works with video format (O'Neal, 2021)

Figure 3. How a car engine works with motion infographics (O'Neal, 2021)

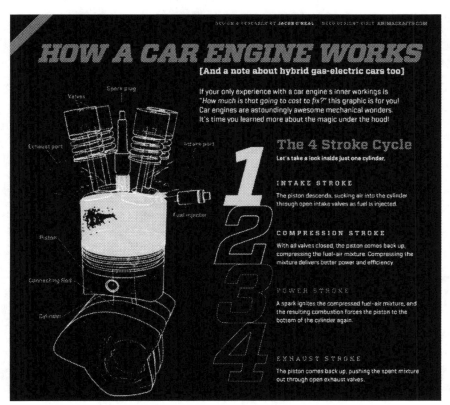

405

Content Marketing: Microsoft

Microsoft is a world-leading technology corporation with millions of consumers that use its products daily. One of their recent initiatives, "Explanimators"—part of Microsoft's Story Labs, is a great example of quality content marketing to engage stakeholders. Figures 4 and 5 demonstrate two examples in Microsoft's Story Labs: the first one shows an animated guide to the decarbonization process (Microsoft, 2021) and the second one demonstrates how Microsoft Garage is hacking creative culture on a global scale (Kohnstamm, 2021), which are good examples of content marketing (Case 2 in Figure 1).

Figure 4. Explanimators—The animated guide to decarbonization (Microsoft, 2021)

Figure 5. Room to dream—How The Microsoft Garage is hacking creative culture on a global scale (Kohnstamm, 2021)

Microsoft's Story Labs is a platform designed to showcase "stories" of Microsoft employees from every department through videos, blog posts, and interviews. Although the content often features Microsoft's products and services in a positive way, they are not necessarily the focus of the platform. The goal is to produce quality content that is interesting for consumers by leveraging Microsoft's internal talent and success stories. This is a great way to generate valuable content that attracts consumers while also maximizing engagement with internal stakeholders.

"Explanimators" is a slightly different section within Microsoft's Story Labs. This initiative focuses on providing informational content about some of the most relevant topics of the moment. Examples include blockchain, decarbonization, and quantum computing. The method chosen is short, animated videos with a different design for each topic in an attempt to maximize engagement with viewers.

Motion infographics are a great tool to display large amounts of information in a small space. The informational nature of the content covered in the "Explanimators" videos makes it ideal for the motion infographics format. Although a user's experience of watching an animated video cannot be replicated in a motion infographic, the latter can act as a complement that showcases the key points described in the video. Motion infographics can quickly get a user's attention without requiring the user to take any action (such as playing a video). The infographics can also be easily shared on social media, which is a useful way to promote existing content marketing, ultimately increasing stakeholder engagement.

Stakeholder Engagement: PepsiCo

PepsiCo is an American multinational food, snack, and beverage company that owns some of the most recognizable food brands in the market: Frito-Lay, Gatorade, and Pepsi. A major component of PepsiCo's sustained success has been its strong ability in stakeholder engagement so as to adapt to the changing demands of the business environment and serve the needs of stakeholders (see Figure 6). PepsiCo develops an effective and comprehensive framework for stakeholder engagement (Case 3 in Figure 1).

Figure 6. Stakeholder engagement (PepsiCo, 2022)

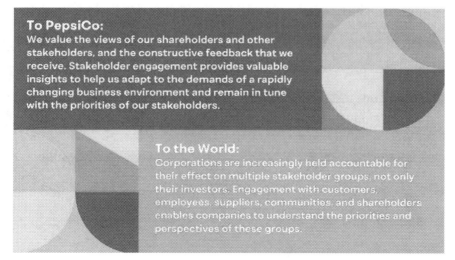

PepsiCo divides stakeholders into eight groups: (1) investors, (2) NGOs, (3) Consumers, (4) Customers, (5) Suppliers, (6) Governments, (7) Employees, and (8) Communities. Although there are significant differences in the way that PepsiCo maximizes engagement for each stakeholder category, a common theme recurrent in every group is clear communication.

Motion infographics can be a valuable tool for organizations that want to communicate clearly with stakeholders while maximizing engagement. Although they are useful tools to communicate key major insights about the company as a whole, motion infographics can also be customized to match the needs of each stakeholder group.

A major part of PepsiCo's efforts to engage with consumers is sustainability reporting (i.e., actions that PepsiCo is taking in order to become a more sustainable company). Motion infographics can help illustrate these actions and results, not just with words but also with images and animated text features, making the user more likely to engage with the content. This is just a specific example of how motion infographics can support stakeholder engagement in a given scenario, but they are flexible tools that can be used and adapted depending on the circumstances.

Motion Infographics, Content Marketing, and Stakeholder Engagement: Spotify

Spotify is one of the leading music streaming platforms, with over 422 million monthly active users worldwide. At the end of every year, Spotify releases a customized "Year in Review" or "Wrapped" summary for each customer, containing the amount of listening time, top artists, favorite genres, most played songs, etc. All the information is presented in an interactive infographic, with animated transitions and motion elements that enhance engagement with stakeholders. Figures 7 and 8 show the infographics released by Spotify that highlight the top songs, artists, playlists, and podcasts in 2019 and those in the previous decade. Spotify is the most successful case of using motion infographics for content marketing in stakeholder engagement (Case 4 in Figure 1).

Users can access this content directly from the Spotify app. Although it varies from year to year, the information is generally presented in a "story" format, in which all the insights are divided into several categories (genres, artists, songs, albums, etc.). This allows users to easily navigate the content sequentially while giving them the freedom to stop and examine the insights most relevant to them.

The design of the infographic also adds to its marketability; it is clear and visually appealing, which are essential components for social media content marketing. In addition to the design, the unique nature of the information included in the infographic is also a key factor that encourages users to share the content (i.e., it is tailored to each individual, and social media is a platform for them to express their uniqueness).

Finally, this is also a great example of handling consumer data. In an era where customers' privacy and data usage are increasingly important issues, Spotify has managed to use the information collected on each user in a way that adds value to their experience as a customer. This, in turn, has resulted in higher stakeholder engagement and positive feedback, in addition to the already mentioned benefit of users sharing the content on social media.

Figure 7. Top songs, artists, playlists, and podcasts in 2019 (Spotify, 2019)

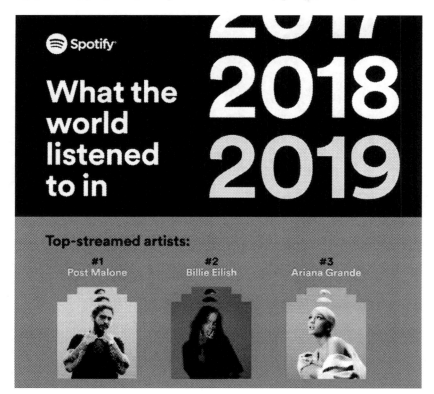

DESIGN CONSIDERATIONS

Motion infographics are an effective tool to engage stakeholders from the content marketing perspective. Many successful content marketing materials have been created in the format of motion infographics to accommodate the story-telling format for any topic. The specific elements in motion infographics allow the audiences to discover and absorb information with high levels of engagement.

Motion Content Scope and Plan

It is important to understand the goals of the motion infographics to identify appropriate motion content and the formats to use to accomplish such goals. This step is indispensable to get all the stakeholders involved, such as customers, employees, suppliers, managers, in-house developers, sponsors, and designers, to discuss major objectives, similar to the requirement collection stage in project management and system development (Kasauli et al., 2021). The traditional methods, including interviews, observations, and document analysis, can generally be used to analyze the clients' needs and determine their goals. Modern approaches such as the joint application design that facilitates face-to-face interactions during in-person meetings can help collect and exchange information (Sensuse et al., 2020). The final plan for developing the motion infographic will include the audience, the topic, types of motion elements and content, navigation, and guidelines for its usage. Besides, the plan will consist of a prototype or demonstration of how the motion content will flow from the viewers' perspective.

Figure 8. Spotify, 2019

Motion Scripts and Scenes

Motion content and storylines are the most important components of any motion infographics. Therefore, it is necessary to document the scripts that need to be displayed on motion infographics at different stages. The scripts and scene directions can also be developed collaboratively in a joint-application-design team with the stakeholders who can be involved to provide feedback during the process. Many factors determine the scripts and scenes of motion infographics, including a budget, timeline, story complexity, production process, and staff availability (Buehring & Vittachi, 2020).

Motion Content Storyboarding

After the scripts and scenes are approved, the next step is to work on the storyboarding, bringing to life the proposed plan for design, development, and execution. In this stage, the main motion elements, such as colors, fonts, themes, images, and illustration styles, are proposed in the storyboard based on the approved plan, scripts, and scenes, which establishes the visual representation of the motion infographic for the stakeholders to respond to (Delil, 2017). This ensures that the entire plan and the scenes are fully embodied to deliver the message to the ultimate audience. As different stakeholders may have different preferences when viewing the storyboard, the motion infographics should collectively resonate with the stakeholders. The storyboard needs to be revised continuously to obtain feedback to ensure it is on the right track for final production. If there is not so much feedback from the stakeholders, the team can move directly to the subsequent stage and incorporate the feedback in a later stage.

Animation Design

Developing the animation for motion infographics is time-consuming but the most crucial stage. The same set of factors of the storyboard designs determines the animations and artwork of the motion infographics. Many types of methods for developing animations can be employed as long as it is well communicated and remains transparent to all the stakeholders. Once the motion infographics enter the stage of animations, the potential changes requested from the stakeholders' feedback will entail a lengthy stage of editing artwork and animation, which may delay the production and impair the budget. Therefore, it is crucial to develop animations to make sure they meet the benchmarks for success. Visuals may not be the only elements in motion infographics. Voices are commonly used to enhance user experience and engage stakeholders. It is critical to select the voice artists to tailor the storyboard, match the animation, and appeal to the target audience. One of the frequently adopted elements in motion infographics is character animation, which also needs to be compatible with the chosen storyboard, styles, and scenes (Freeman, 2015). Finally, it is essential to remain updated with the animators to be informed of the scope of the animation, characters, and voices to ensure the motion infographics are within the timeline and budget.

Motion Content Development

The final stage of developing motion infographics is to integrate all the completed elements and finalize the infographics with the help of the developers and designers. Upon completing this final stage, the motion infographics should have prudently constructed scripts and scenes, custom-built animations, and distinctive artwork to engage stakeholders.

CONCLUSION

Infographics have been employed as an effective tool in content marketing to help develop content and grab viewers' attention. Adding motions to infographics further improves the efficiency of content marketing to engage stakeholders. Although infographics play an important role in content marketing for stakeholder engagement, very few studies have explored the mutual interactive connections between infographics, content marketing, and stakeholder engagement. Prior studies have not specified the role of motion infographics in stakeholder engagement from a content marketing perspective.

This study addresses the research gap by identifying the design considerations of motion infographics to engage stakeholders from the perspective of content marketing. Specifically, we synthesize and illustrate the specific elements that can be animated to strengthen the role of motion infographics in facilitating content marketing and promoting stakeholder engagement. Through this work, we hope to advance future research in the multidisciplinary area between motion infographics, content marketing, and stakeholder engagement. This research also provides valuable guidelines for practitioners to design and implement motion infographics in these relevant contexts.

REFERENCES

Adi, D., & Setiautami, D. (2021, April). Distributing information through infographic on tempodotco to build understanding and awareness about COVID-19 virus outbreak in Indonesia. In *IOP Conference Series: Earth and Environmental Science* (Vol. 729, No. 1, p. 012109). IOP Publishing. 10.1088/1755-1315/729/1/012109

Aksoy, L., Banda, S., Harmeling, C., Keiningham, T. L., & Pansari, A. (2021). Marketing's role in multi-stakeholder engagement. *International Journal of Research in Marketing.*

Baxter, M., Lonsdale, M. D. S., & Westland, S. (2021). Utilising design principles to improve the perception and effectiveness of public health infographics. *Information Design Journal, 26*(2), 124–156. doi:10.1075/idj.20017.bax

Buehring, J., & Vittachi, N. (2020). Transmedia storytelling: Addressing futures communication challenges with video animation. *Journal of Futures Studies, 25*(1), 65–78.

Camilleri, M. A. (2017). The rationale for responsible supply chain management and stakeholder engagement. *Journal of Global Responsibility, 8*(1), 111–126. doi:10.1108/JGR-02-2017-0007

Dalton, J., & Design, W. (2014). *A Brief Guide to Producing Compelling Infographics.* London School of Public Relations.

Delil, S. (2017). The impact of infographic animation videos on data visualization. *International Journal of Social Sciences and Education Research, 3*(4), 1178–1183. doi:10.24289/ijsser.312933

Doukianou, S., Daylamani-Zad, D., & O'Loingsigh, K. (2021). Implementing an augmented reality and animated infographics application for presentations: Effect on audience engagement and efficacy of communication. *Multimedia Tools and Applications, 80*(20), 30969–30991. doi:10.100711042-021-10963-4

Dubois, A., & Gadde, L.-E. (2002). Systematic combining: An adductive approach to case research. *Journal of Business Research, 55*(7), 553–560. doi:10.1016/S0148-2963(00)00195-8

Eisenhardt, K. M. (1989). Building Theories from Case Study Research. *Academy of Management Review, 14*(4), 532–550. doi:10.2307/258557

Eriksson, P., & Kovalainen, A. (2015). Qualitative methods in business research: A practical guide to social research. *Sage (Atlanta, Ga.).*

Freeman, H. D. (2015). *The Moving Image Workshop: Introducing animation, motion graphics and visual effects in 45 practical projects.* Bloomsbury Publishing.

Gamble, S. (2016). *Visual content marketing: leveraging infographics, video, and interactive media to attract and engage customers.* John Wiley & Sons.

Hassan, H. G. (2016). *Designing Infographics to support teaching complex science subject: A comparison between static and animated Infographics* [Doctoral dissertation]. Iowa State University.

Ismaeel, D., & Al Mulhim, E. (2021). The influence of interactive and static infographics on the academic achievement of reflective and impulsive students. *Australasian Journal of Educational Technology*, *37*(1), 147–162. doi:10.14742/ajet.6138

Kasauli, R., Knauss, E., Horkoff, J., Liebel, G., & de Oliveira Neto, F. G. (2021). Requirements engineering challenges and practices in large-scale agile system development. *Journal of Systems and Software*, *172*, 110851. doi:10.1016/j.jss.2020.110851

Kohnstamm, T. (2021). *Room to Dream-How The Microsoft Garage is hacking creative culture on a global scale.* Available at https://news.microsoft.com/stories/microsoft-garage/

Koiso-Kanttila, N. (2004). Digital content marketing: A literature synthesis. *Journal of Marketing Management*, *20*(1-2), 45–65. doi:10.1362/026725704773041122

Koob, C. (2021). Determinants of content marketing effectiveness: Conceptual framework and empirical findings from a managerial perspective. *PLoS One*, *16*(4), e0249457. doi:10.1371/journal.pone.0249457 PMID:33793631

Kujala, J., Sachs, S., Leinonen, H., Heikkinen, A., & Laude, D. (2022). Stakeholder engagement: Past, present, and future. *Business & Society*.

Liu, X., Shi, S. W., Teixeira, T., & Wedel, M. (2018). Video content marketing: The making of clips. *Journal of Marketing*, *82*(4), 86–101. doi:10.1509/jm.16.0048

Mansour, E. (2021). Use of infographics as a technology-based information dissemination tool: The perspective of Egyptian public university libraries library staff. *Library Hi Tech*. Advance online publication. doi:10.1108/LHT-03-2021-0084

Mayer, R. E., Hegarty, M., Mayer, S., & Campbell, J. (2005). When static media promote active learning: Annotated illustrations versus narrated animations in multimedia instruction. *Journal of Experimental Psychology. Applied*, *11*(4), 256–265. doi:10.1037/1076-898X.11.4.256 PMID:16393035

Microsoft. (2021). *Decarbonization. Explanimators-Episode 11.* Available at https://news.microsoft.com/stories/explanimators/decarbonization/

Mitchell, J. R., Mitchell, R. K., Hunt, R. A., Townsend, D. M., & Lee, J. H. (2020). Stakeholder engagement, knowledge problems and ethical challenges. *Journal of Business Ethics*, 1–20.

Müller, J., & Christandl, F. (2019). Content is king–But who is the king of kings? The effect of content marketing, sponsored content & user-generated content on brand responses. *Computers in Human Behavior*, *96*, 46–55. doi:10.1016/j.chb.2019.02.006

Naseri, Z., & Noruzi, A. (2018). Content marketing process model: A meta-synthesis of the literature. *Webology*, *15*(1), 8–18.

O'Neal, J. (2021). *How a Car Engine Works.* Available at https://animagraffs.com/how-a-car-engine-works/

O'Riordan, L., & Fairbrass, J. (2014). Managing CSR stakeholder engagement: A new conceptual framework. *Journal of Business Ethics*, *125*(1), 121–145. doi:10.100710551-013-1913-x

Pedrini, M., & Ferri, L. M. (2019). Stakeholder management: A systematic literature review. *Corporate Governance: The International Journal of Business in Society*, *19*(1), 44–59. doi:10.1108/CG-08-2017-0172

PepsiCo. (2022). *Stakeholder Engagement*. Available at https://www.pepsico.com/our-impact/esg-topics-a-z/stakeholder-engagement

Perrini, F., & Tencati, A. (2006). Sustainability and stakeholder management: The need for new corporate performance evaluation and reporting systems. *Business Strategy and the Environment*, *15*(5), 296–308. doi:10.1002/bse.538

Peters, D. (2013). *Interface design for learning: Design strategies for learning experiences*. Pearson Education.

Rowley, J. (2008). Understanding digital content marketing. *Journal of Marketing Management*, *24*(5-6), 517–540. doi:10.1362/026725708X325977

Sensuse, D. I., Rochman, H. N., Al Hakim, S., & Winarni, W. (2020). Knowledge management system design method with joint application design (JAD) adoption. *VINE Journal of Information and Knowledge Management Systems*, *51*(1), 27–46. doi:10.1108/VJIKMS-10-2018-0083

Siricharoen, W. V. (2013). Infographics: An approach of innovative communication tool for e-entrepreneurship marketing. *International Journal of E-Entrepreneurship and Innovation*, *4*(2), 54–71. doi:10.4018/ijeei.2013040104

Spotify. (2019). *The Top Songs, Artists, Playlists, and Podcasts of 2019—and the Last Decade*. Available at https://newsroom.spotify.com/2019-12-03/the-top-songs-artists-playlists-and-podcasts-of-2019-and-the-last-decade/

Tsai, S. T., Huang, H. Y., & Chang, T. W. (2020). Developing a Motion Infographic-Based Learning System for Effective Learning. *Education in Science*, *10*(9), 247. doi:10.3390/educsci10090247

Viglia, G., Pera, R., & Bigné, E. (2018). The determinants of stakeholder engagement in digital platforms. *Journal of Business Research*, *89*, 404–410. doi:10.1016/j.jbusres.2017.12.029

Wang, Y., Gao, Y., Huang, R., Cui, W., Zhang, H., & Zhang, D. (2021, June). Animated Presentation of Static Infographics with InfoMotion. *Computer Graphics Forum*, *40*(3), 507–518. doi:10.1111/cgf.14325

Xie, Q., & Lou, C. (2020). Curating Luxe experiences online? Explicating the mechanisms of luxury content marketing in cultivating brand loyalty. *Journal of Interactive Advertising*, *20*(3), 209–224. doi:10.1080/15252019.2020.1811177

Yin, R. K. (2017). *Case study research and applications: Design and methods*. Sage publications.

Conclusion

Handbook of Research on Revisioning and Reconstructing Higher Education After Global Crises features researchers and authors / co-authors from around the world. The works are diverse and insightful. They are a product of the present pandemic moment.

Global crises are disruptive in ways imaginable and unimaginable. They exist at the micro, meso, and macro scales simultaneously. So, too, with this slice-in-time.

This book may be my last edited one given certain changes that have occurred in my life and career. I am leaving after a long track record of achievements, even as I am a co-principal investigator on a federal grant that just got awarded in September 2022. I am leaving after having worked with so many professionals who have been kind and caring.

As I have written and spoken, the world is big enough. We all have the ability to adapt and change. We are all able to make our own changes to better fit our lives, personalities, talents, and interests.

Let us do our best for each other!

Shalin Hai-Jew
Kansas State University, USA
October 2022

Compilation of References

Abdelhakim, M. N. A., & Shirmohammadei, S. (2007). A web-based group decision support system for the selection and evaluation of educational multimedia. *Proceedings of EMME '07.* doi:10.1145/1290144.1290150

Abdullah, M. (2020, April 30). Dipu Moni: Private universities can conduct exams, admissions online. *Dhaka Tribune.* https://archive.dhakatribune.com/bangladesh/education/2020/04/30/dipu-moni-students-need-to-be-kept-engaged-to-prevent-depression

Accilien, C. (2018). Teaching in the Time of "Trumpism": Reflections on Citizenship and Hospitality. *Women, Gender, and Families of Color, 6*(1), 69–72. doi:10.5406/womgenfamcol.6.1.0069

Acedo, C. (2008). Inclusive education: Pushing the boundaries. *Prospects, 38*(1), 5–13. doi:10.100711125-008-9064-z

Acedo, C. (2011). Preparing teachers for inclusive education. *Prospects, 41*(3), 301–302. doi:10.100711125-011-9198-2

Acedo, C., & Hughes, C. (2014). Principles for learning and competences in the 21-century curriculum. *Prospects, 44*(4), 503–525. doi:10.100711125-014-9330-1

Ackerman-Barger, K., Bakerjian, D., & Latimore, D. (2015). How health professions educators can mitigate underrepresented students' experiences of marginalization: Stereotype threat, internalized bias, and microaggressions. *Journal of Best Practices in Health Professions Diversity, 8*(2), 1060–1070.

Adams, D. A., Nelson, R. R., & Todd, P. A. (1992). Perceived usefulness, ease of use, and usage of information technology: A replication. *Management Information Systems Quarterly, 16*(2), 227–247.

ADEA, AU/CIEFFA, & APHRC (2021). *Financing Education in Africa during the COVID-19 Pandemic.* ADEA, AU/CIEFFA, APHRC.

Adedoyin, O. B., & Soykan, E. (2020). Covid-19 pandemic and online learning: The challenges and opportunities. *Interactive Learning Environments*, 1–13. doi:10.1080/10494820.2020.1813180

Adi, D., & Setiautami, D. (2021, April). Distributing information through infographic on tempodotco to build understanding and awareness about COVID-19 virus outbreak in Indonesia. In *IOP Conference Series: Earth and Environmental Science* (Vol. 729, No. 1, p. 012109). IOP Publishing. 10.1088/1755-1315/729/1/012109

Advocates for Youth. (2009). *Youth leadership: Recommendations for sustainability.* https://www.advocatesforyouth.org/wp-content/uploads/storage/advfy/documents/youth_sustainability.pdf

Agarwal, R., & Prasad, J. (1999). Are individual differences germane to the acceptance of new information technologies? *Decision Sciences, 30*, 361–391.

Agley, J., Xiao, Y., Thompson, E. E., & Golzarri-Arroyo, L. (2021). Using infographics to improve trust in science: A randomized pilot test. *BMC Research Notes, 14*(1), 1–6. doi:10.118613104-021-05626-4 PMID:34051823

Compilation of References

Aguilar, S. J., Karabenick, S. A., Teasley, S. D., & Baek, C. (2021). Associations between learning analytics dashboard exposure and motivation and self-regulated learning. *Computers & Education*, *162*(104085), 1–11. doi:10.1016/j.compedu.2020.104085

Aguilera-Hermida, A. P. (2020). College students' use and acceptance of emergency online learning due to COVID-19. *International Journal of Educational Research Open*, *1*(100011), 1–8. doi:10.1016/j.ijedro.2020.100011 PMID:35059662

Ahmad, A., Law, E. L., & Moseley, A. (2020, October). Integrating instructional design principles in serious games authoring tools: Insights from systematic literature review. In *Proceedings of the 11th Nordic Conference on Human-Computer Interaction: Shaping Experiences, Shaping Society* (pp. 1-12). 10.1145/3419249.3420133

Ahmad, M., Karim, A. A., Din, R., & Mohd, I. S. (2013). Assessing ICT Competencies among Postgraduate Students Based on the 21st Century ICT Competency Model. *International Journal of Educational Technology in Higher Education*, *15*(37), 2–22. https://doi.org/10.1186/s41239-018-0119-9

Ahmed, S. M. Z. (2013). A survey of students' use of and satisfaction with university subscribed online resources in two specialised universities in a developing country. *Library Hi Tech News*, *30*(3), 6–8. doi:10.1108/LHTN-02-2013-0010

Aji, W. K., Ardin, H., & Arifin, M. A. (2020). Blended learning during pandemic CoronaVirus: Teachers' and students' perceptions. *IDEAS: Journal on English Language Teaching and Learning, Linguistics and Literature*, *8*(2), 632–646. doi:10.24256/ideas.v8i2.1696

Aka, A. M. (2021, February 18). Time for a radical rethinking of our education system. *The Daily Star*. https://www.thedailystar.net/opinion/news/time-radical-rethinking-our-education-system-2046741

Akçayır, G., & Akçayır, M. (2018). The flipped classroom: A review of its advantages and challenges. *Computers & Education*, *126*, 334–345. doi:10.1016/j.compedu.2018.07.021

Aksoy, L., Banda, S., Harmeling, C., Keiningham, T. L., & Pansari, A. (2021). Marketing's role in multi-stakeholder engagement. *International Journal of Research in Marketing*.

Al Mamun, M. A., Lawrie, G., & Wright, T. (2022). Exploration of learner-content interactions and learning approaches: The role of guided inquiry in the self-directed online environments. *Computers & Education*, *178*(104398), 1–22. doi:10.1016/j.compedu.2021.104398

Alabdulkarim, L. (2021). University Health Sciences students rating for a blended learning course framework. *Saudi Journal of Biological Sciences*, *28*(9), 5379–5385. doi:10.1016/j.sjbs.2021.05.059 PMID:34466118

Alabdulqader, E. (2013, July). Visualizing computer ethics using infographics. In *Proceedings of the 18th ACM conference on Innovation and technology in computer science education* (pp. 355-355). ACM.

Alabi, J. (2015). Racial microaggressions in academic libraries: Results of a survey of minority and non-minority librarians. *Journal of Academic Librarianship*, *41*(1), 47–53. doi:10.1016/j.acalib.2014.10.008

Alajmi, M. A. (2019). The acceptance and use of electronic information resources among faculty of selected Gulf Cooperation Council States universities. *Information Development*, *35*(3), 447–466.

Al-Amin, M., Zubayer, A. A., Deb, B., & Hasan, M. (2021). Status of tertiary level online class in Bangladesh: Students' response on preparedness, participation and classroom activities. *Heliyon*, *7*(1), e05943. doi:10.1016/j.heliyon.2021.e05943 PMID:33506126

Alammary, A., Sheard, J., & Carbone, A. (2014). Blended learning in higher education: Three different design approaches. *Australasian Journal of Educational Technology*, *30*(4). Advance online publication. doi:10.14742/ajet.693

Al-Ayed, S. I., & Al-Tit, A. A. (2021). Factors affecting the adoption of blended learning strategy. *International Journal of Data and Network Science*, 267–274. doi:10.5267/j.ijdns.2021.6.007

Albarrak, S., & Shalto, M. (2015). The effect of electronic educational infographic design on the development of skills in dealing with the lighting in photography by the postgraduate students. *Proceedings of the 2015 Fifth International Conference on e-Learning*, 465 – 485.

Albers, M. J. (2015, July). Infographics and communicating complex information. *Proceedings of the International Conference of Design, User Experience, and Usability*, 267 – 276.

Albers, M. J. (2014, October). Infographics: Horrid chartjunk or quality communication. In *2014 IEEE International Professional Communication Conference (IPCC)* (pp. 1-4). IEEE.

Al-Dairy, H. M., & Al-Rabaani, A. H. (2017, December). An analytical study of research orientations for infographics applications in education. In *2017 6th International Conference on Information and Communication Technology and Accessibility (ICTA)* (pp. 1-5). IEEE.

Aldowah, H., Al-Samarraie, H., Alzahrani, A. I., & Alalwan, N. (2020). Factors affecting student dropout in MOOCs: A cause and effect decision-making model. *Journal of Computing in Higher Education*, 32(2), 429–454. doi:10.100712528-019-09241-y

Alfrey, L., & Twine, F. W. (2017). Gender-fluid geek girls: Negotiating inequality regimes in the tech industry. *Gender & Society*, 31(1), 28–50. doi:10.1177/0891243216680590

Alger, M., & Eyckmans, J. (2022). "I took physical lessons for granted": A case study exploring students' interpersonal interactions in online synchronous lessons during the outbreak of COVID-19. *System*, 102716, 1–18. doi:10.1016/j.system.2021.102716

Alijani, G., Kwun, O., & Yu, Y. (2014). *Effectiveness of blended learning in KIPP New Orleans' Schools*. https://www.semanticscholar.org/paper/Effectiveness-of-Blended-Learning-in-KIPP-New-Alijani-Kwun/7b8b10d66fcb218465510 6a16a8df23a46ac7cdf

Ali, W. (2020). Online and Remote Learning in Higher Education Institutes. A Necessity in Light of COVID-19 Pandemic. *Higher Education Studies*, 10(3), 16–25. doi:10.5539/hes.v10n3p16

Allen, I. E., & Seaman, J. (2008, November). *Staying the course: Online education in the United States*. Retrieved from Sloan Consortium website: http://www.sloan-c.org/publications/view/index.asp

Allen, I., Seaman, J., & Garrett, R. (2007). *Blending in: The extent and promise of blended education in the United States*. Sloan Consortium.

Allen, M., & Dee, C. (2006). A survey of the usability of digital reference services on academic health science library websites. *Journal of Academic Librarianship*, 32, 69–78. http://www.elsevier.com

Almaiah, M. A., & Alismaiel, O. A. (2019). Examination of factors influencing the use of mobile learning system: An empirical study. *Education and Information Technologies*, 24(1), 885–909.

AlMarwani, M. (2020). Pedagogical potential of SWOT analysis: An approach to teaching critical thinking. *Thinking Skills and Creativity*, 38(100741), 1–6. doi:10.1016/j.tsc.2020.100741

Almeida, C., & Almeida, P. (2016, November). Online educational videos: The teenagers' preferences. In *Iberoamerican Conference on Applications and Usability of Interactive TV* (pp. 65-76). Springer.

Compilation of References

Al-Nasa'h, M., Awwad, F. M, & Ahmad, I. (2021). Estimating students' online learning satisfaction during COVID-19: A discriminant analysis. *Heliyon, 7*(12), 1 - 7.

Alpert, W., Couch, K., & Harmon, O. (2016). A randomized assessment of online learning. *The American Economic Review, 106*(5), 378–382. doi:10.1257/aer.p20161057

Alqahtani, N., Innab, A., & Bahari, G. (2020). Virtual education during COVID-19. *Nurse Educator, 46*(2), E18–E22. Advance online publication. doi:10.1097/NNE.0000000000000954 PMID:33234836

Alrwele, N. S. (2017). Effects of infographics on student achievement and students' perceptions of the impacts of infographics. *Journal of Education and Human Development, 6*(3), 104-117.

Alvarado, C., García, L., Gilliam, N., Minckler, S., & Samay, C. (2021). Pandemic Pivots: The Impact of a Global Health Crisis on the Dissertation in Practice. *Journal of Transforming Professional Practice, 6*(2), 5-10. doi:10.5195/ie.2021.165

Ameen, N., Willis, R., Abdullah, M. N., & Shah, M. (2019). Towards the successful integration of e-learning systems in higher education in Iraq: A student perspective. *British Journal of Educational Technology, 50*(3), 1434–1446.

American Association of Community Colleges. (2019). *Community college enrollment crisis? Historical trends in community college enrollment.* Retrieved from https://www.aacc.nche.edu/wp-content/uploads/2019/08/Crisis-in-Enrollment-2019.pdf

Amini, F., Riche, N. H., Lee, B., Leboe-McGowan, J., & Irani, P. (2018, May). Hooked on data videos: assessing the effect of animation and pictographs on viewer engagement. In *Proceedings of the 2018 International Conference on Advanced Visual Interfaces* (pp. 1-9). 10.1145/3206505.3206552

Amit-Danhi, E. R., & Shifman, L. (2018). Digital political infographics: A rhetorical palette of an emergent genre. *New Media & Society, 20*(10), 3540–3559. doi:10.1177/1461444817750565

Anatolievna, K. S. (2018). The use of LMS Moodle to intensify the independent work of students in teaching a foreign language in a non-linguistic university. *Азимут научных исследований: педагогика и психология, 7*(25).

Anderson, G. (2020, September 16). *More pandemic consequences for underrepresented students.* Inside Higher Ed. https://www.insidehighered.com/news/2020/09/16/low-income-and-students-color-greatest-need-pandemic-relief

Anderson, T. (2004). Teaching in an online learning context. *Theory and practice of online learning, 273*.

Anderson, B., & Simpson, M. (2012). History and heritage in distance education. *Journal of Open. Flexible and Distance Learning, 16*(2), 1–10.

Andriana, E., & Evans, D. (2020). Listening to the voices of students on inclusive education: Responses from principals and teachers in Indonesia. *International Journal of Educational Research, 103*(101644), 1–9. doi:10.1016/j.ijer.2020.101644

Andry, T., Hurter, C., Lambotte, F., Fastrez, P., & Telea, A. (2021, May). Interpreting the effect of embellishment on chart visualizations. In *Proceedings of the 2021 CHI Conference on Human Factors in Computing Systems* (pp. 1-15). 10.1145/3411764.3445739

Anglin, D. M., & Lui, F. (2021). Racial microaggressions and major discriminatory events explain ethnoracial differences in psychotic experiences. *Schizophrenia Research*, 1–9. doi:10.1016/j.schres.2021.10.014 PMID:34750038

Ankit, A., & El-Sakran, T. (2020). Corporate Social Responsibility: Reflections on Universities in the United Arab Emirates. In E. Sengupta, P. Blessinger, & C. Mahoney (Eds.), *Civil Society and Social Responsibility in Higher Education: International Perspectives on Leadership and Strategies* (pp. 15–32). Emarald Publishing Ltd. doi:10.1108/S2055-364120200000024004

Aragon, S., & Johnson, E. (2004). *Factors influencing completion and non-completion of community college online courses*. https://www.learntechlib.org/primary/p/12019/

Arán, A. (2021). Preparation of a bachelor's thesis in times of pandemic: a case study [Elaboración de una tesis de licenciatura en tiempos de pandemia: un estudio de caso]. In *Un año de pandemia, miradas desde la educación* (299-328). Colofón.

Archee, R., Dawkins, R., & Gurney, M. (2021). Evaluating HyFlex at Western Sydney University 2021: Considerations for Curriculum and Pedagogy. In T. Bastiaens (Ed.), *Proceedings of Innovate Learning Summit 2021* (pp. 484-492). Association for the Advancement of Computing in Education (AACE). https://www.learntechlib.org/primary/p/220319/

Arcia, A., Suero-Tejeda, N., Bales, M. E., Merrill, J. A., Yoon, S., Woollen, J., & Bakken, S. (2016). Sometimes more is more: Iterative participatory design of infographics for engagement of community members with varying levels of health literacy. *Journal of the American Medical Informatics Association: JAMIA*, *23*(1), 174–183. doi:10.1093/jamia/ocv079 PMID:26174865

Arcia, A., Velez, M., & Bakken, S. (2015). Style guide: An interdisciplinary communication tool to support the process of generating tailored infographics from electronic health data using EnTICE3. *EGEMS (Washington, DC)*, *3*(1), 1–10. doi:10.13063/2327-9214.1120 PMID:25848634

Artino, A. R. Jr, & Stephens, J. M. (2009). Academic motivation and self-regulation: A comparative analysis of undergraduate and graduate students learning online. *The Internet and Higher Education*, *12*(3-4), 146–151. doi:10.1016/j.iheduc.2009.02.001

Arum, N. S. (2017). *Infographic: Not just a beautiful visualisation*. Obtenido de https://www. academia. edu/31903865/Infographic_Not_Just_a_Beautiful_Visualisation

Asabere, N. Y., Acakpovi, A., Agyiri, J., Awuku, M. C., Sakyi, M. A., & Teyewayo, D. A. (2021). Measuring the Constructs That Influence Student and Lecturer Acceptance of an E-Library in Accra Technical University, Ghana. *International Journal of Online Pedagogy and Course Design*, *11*(1), 53–72.

Ashman, R., & Patterson, A. (2015). Seeing the big picture in services marketing research: Infographics, SEM and data visualisation. *Journal of Services Marketing*, *29*(6/7), 613–621. doi:10.1108/JSM-01-2015-0024

Ashton, L. J., Gordon, S. E., & Reeves, R. A. (2018). Key ingredients—target groups, methods and messages, and evaluation—of local-level, public interventions to counter stigma and discrimination: A lived experience informed selective narrative literature review. *Community Mental Health Journal*, *54*(3), 312–333. doi:10.100710597-017-0189-5 PMID:29185150

Ashton, N. (1990). Inclusive education: Curriculum and pedagogy. *Transformations: The Journal of Inclusive Scholarship and Pedagogy*, *1*(1), 30–35.

Asian Development Bank. (2019, February 22). *Understanding Youth's Role to Achieving the Sustainable Development Goals*. https://www.adb.org/news/features/understanding-youths-role-achieving-sustainable-development-goals

Aslan, I., Ochnik, D., & Çınar, O. (2020). Exploring perceived stress among students in Turkey during the COVID-19 pandemic. *International Journal of Environmental Research and Public Health*, *17*(23), 8961. doi:10.3390/ijerph17238961 PMID:33276520

Aucejo, E., French, J., Araya, M., & Zafar, B. (2020). The impact of COVID-19 on student experiences and expectations: Evidence from a survey. *Journal of Public Economics*, *191*, 104271. Advance online publication. doi:10.1016/j.jpubeco.2020.104271 PMID:32873994

Compilation of References

Audet, É. C., Levine, S. L., Metin, E., Koestner, S., & Barcan, S. (2021). Zooming their way through university: Which Big 5 traits facilitated students' adjustment to online courses during the COVID-19 pandemic. *Personality and Individual Differences, 180*(110969), 1–5. doi:10.1016/j.paid.2021.110969

Auxier, B., & Anderson, M. (2020). *As schools close due to the coronavirus, some U.S. students face a digital 'homework gap.'* Retrieved from https://www.pewresearch.org/fact-tank/2020/03/16/as-schools-close-due-to-the-coronavirus-some-u-s-students-face-a-digital-homework-gap/

Avcı, İ., & Yıldız, E. (2021). Examination of the Satisfaction and Behaviors of Students Using Distance Education in the Covid-19 Pandemic Process within the Framework of Technology Acceptance Model [Covid-19 Pandemi Sürecinde Uzaktan Eğitimi Kullanan Öğrencilerin Memnuniyet ve Davranışlarının Teknoloji Kabul Modeli Çerçevesinde İncelenmesi]. *Gümüşhane Üniversitesi Sosyal Bilimler Dergisi, 12*(3), 814-830. Retrieved from https://dergipark.org.tr/en/pub/gumus/issue/65088/886553

Ayala, J., Drolet, J., Fulton, A., Hewson, J., Letkemann, L., Baynton, M., Elliott, G., Judge-Stasiak, A., Blaug, C., Gérard Tétreault, A., & Schweizer, E. (2018). Field education in crisis: Experiences of field education coordinators in Canada. *Social Work Education, 37*(3), 281–293. doi:10.1080/02615479.2017.1397109

Ayouni, S., Hajjej, F., Maddeh, M., & Alotaibi, S. (2021). Innovations of materials for student engagement in online environment: An ontology. *Materials Today: Proceedings*, 1–7. doi:10.1016/j.matpr.2021.03.636

Azevedo, J. P., Hasan, A., Goldemberg, D., Geven, K., & Iqbal, S. A. (2021). Simulating the potential impacts of COVID-19 school closures on schooling and learning outcomes: A set of global estimates. *The World Bank Research Observer, 36*(1), 1–40.

Azubuike, O. B., Adegboye, O., & Quadri, H. (2021). Who gets to learn in a pandemic? Exploring the digital divide in remote learning during the COVID-19 pandemic in Nigeria. *International Journal of Educational Research Open, 2*, 100022. doi:10.1016/j.ijedro.2020.100022 PMID:35059664

Babb, S., Rufino, K., & Johnson, R. (2022). Assessing the effects of the COVID-19 pandemic on nontraditional students' mental health and well-being. *Adult Education Quarterly, 72*(2), 140–157. doi:10.1177/07417136211027508 PMID:35520881

Baber, H. (2020). Determinants of students' perceived learning outcome and satisfaction in online learning during the pandemic of COVID19. *Journal of Education and e-learning Research, 7*(3), 285-292. doi:10.20448/journal.509.2020.73.285.292

Babiarz, P., Piotrowski, M., & Wawrzynkiewicz, M. (2003). The application of the service quality GAP model to evaluate the quality of blended learning. In *IADIS International Conference e-Society 2003* (pp. 911-915). Academic Press.

Bagalini, A. (2020, July 14). *Systemic racism: 5 ways racism is bad for business—and what we can do about it.* World Economic Forum. Retrieved Sept. 7, 2022, from https://www.weforum.org/agenda/2020/07/racism-bad-for-business-equality-diversity/

Bai, S., Hew, K. F., Sailer, M., & Jia, C. (2021). From top to bottom: How positions on different types of leaderboard may affect fully online student learning performance, intrinsic motivation, and course engagement. *Computers & Education, 173*, 104297. doi:10.1016/j.compedu.2021.104297

Baker, T. L. (2019). Reframing the connections between deficit thinking, microaggressions, and teacher perceptions of defiance. *The Journal of Negro Education, 88*(2), 103–113. doi:10.7709/jnegroeducation.88.2.0103

Balkac, M., & Ergun, E. (2018). Role of infographics in healthcare. *Chinese Medical Journal, 131*(20), 2514–2517. doi:10.4103/0366-6999.243569 PMID:30334544

Ballotpedia. (2020). *The Republican Party Platform, 2020*. Retrieved from https://ballotpedia.org/The_Republican_Party_Platform,_2020

Bandura, A. (1982). Self-efficacy mechanism in human agency. *The American Psychologist, 37*, 122–147. doi:10.1037/0003-066X.37.2.122

Bank of Zambia. (2022). *Daily ZMW/USD exchange rates*. https://www.boz.zm/historical-series-of-daily-zmw-usd-exchange-rates-zmw.htm

Banu, F. A. L., Roy, G., & Shafiq, S. (2018). Analysing bottlenecks to equal participation in primary education in Bangladesh: An equity perspective. In R. Chowdhury, M. Sarkar, F. Mojumdar, & R. M. Moninoor (Eds.), *Engaging in educational research: Revisiting policy and practice in Bangladesh* (pp. 39–64). Springer Singapore. doi:10.1007/978-981-13-0708-9_3

Bardach, L., Klassen, R. M., Durksen, T. L., Rushby, J. V., Bostwick, K. C., & Sheridan, L. (2021). The power of feedback and reflection: Testing an online scenario-based learning intervention for student teachers. *Computers & Education, 169*(104194), 1–17. doi:10.1016/j.compedu.2021.104194

Barker, L. M., Ponzio, C. M., & Matthusen, A. (2018). Under Discussion: Teaching Speaking and Listening: Promoting Student-Centered Discussion with Digital Tools and Infographics. *English Journal, 107*(3), 123–126.

Barr, A., Lane, T., & Nosenzo, D. (2018). On the social inappropriateness of discrimination. *Journal of Public Economics, 164*, 153–164. doi:10.1016/j.jpubeco.2018.06.004

Barragan, E., & Nusbaum, E. (2017). Perceptions of disability on a postsecondary campus: Implications for oppression and human love. *Negotiating disability: Disclosure and higher education*, 39-56.

Barratt, J. M., & Duran, F. (2021). Does psychological capital and social support impact engagement and burnout in online distance learning students? *The Internet and Higher Education, 100821*, 1–9. doi:10.1016/j.iheduc.2021.100821

Barrilleux, C. (2000). Party strength, party change, and policy making in the American states. *Party Politics, 6*(1), 61–73. doi:10.1177/1354068800006001004

Barron, D. W. (1968). *Recursive Techniques in Programming*. Macdonald & Co.

Bart, A. C., & Shaffer, C. A. (2016, February). Instructional design is to teaching as software engineering is to programming. In *Proceedings of the 47th ACM Technical Symposium on Computing Science Education* (pp. 240-241). 10.1145/2839509.2844674

Basilaia, G., & Kvavadze, D. (2020). Transition to online education in schools during a SARS-CoV-2 coronavirus (COVID-19) pandemic in Georgia. *Pedagogical Research, 5*(4), 10. doi:10.29333/pr/7937

Basuony, M. A. K., EmadEldeen, R., Farghaly, M., El-Bassiouny, N., & Mohamed, E. K. A. (2020). The factors affecting student satisfaction with online education during the COVID-19 pandemic: An empirical study of an emerging Muslim country. *Journal of Islamic Marketing, 12*(3), 631–648. doi:10.1108/JIMA-09-2020-0301

Basu-Ray, I., Adeboye, A., & Soos, M. P. (2022). Cardiac manifestations of coronavirus (COVID-19). StatPearls Publishing.

Battaiola, A. L., Alves, M. M., & Paulin, R. E. (2014, June). Canvas to improve the design process of educational animation. In *International Conference on Learning and Collaboration Technologies* (pp. 13-24). Springer. 10.1007/978-3-319-07482-5_2

Baturay, M. H. (2015). An overview of the world of MOOCs. *Procedia-Social and Behavioral Sciences, 174*, 427-433. doi:10.1016/j.sbspro.2015.01.685

Compilation of References

Bauman, D. (April 28, 2022). *3 things we learned from the latest federal employment and enrollment report*. Retrieved from https://www.chronicle.com/article/3-things-we-learned-from-the-latest-federal-employment-and-enrollment-report

Baxter, M., Lonsdale, M. D. S., & Westland, S. (2021). Utilising design principles to improve the perception and effectiveness of public health infographics. *Information Design Journal, 26*(2), 124–156. doi:10.1075/idj.20017.bax

Bayliss, J. D., & Schwartz, D. I. (2009, April). Instructional design as game design. In *Proceedings of the 4th International Conference on Foundations of Digital Games* (pp. 10-17). 10.1145/1536513.1536526

Beaunoyer, E., Duperé, S., & Guitton, M. (2020). COVID-19 and digital inequalities: Reciprocal impacts and mitigation strategies. *Computers in Human Behavior, 111*, 1–9. doi:10.1016/j.chb.2020.106424 PMID:32398890

Becker, G. (1964). *Human Capital*. Columbia University Press.

Bedenlier, S., Wunder, I., Gläser-Zikuda, M., Kammerl, R., Kopp, B., Ziegler, A., & Händel, M. (2021). Generation invisible? Higher Education Students'(Non) Use of Webcams in Synchronous Online Learning. *International Journal of Educational Research Open, 2*, 100068. doi:10.1016/j.ijedro.2021.100068

Belcadhi, L. C., & Ghannouchi, S. A. (2013, November). An instructional design approach for e-active courses. In *Proceedings of the First International Conference on Technological Ecosystem for Enhancing Multiculturality* (pp. 119-126). 10.1145/2536536.2536555

Bellato, N. (2013). Infographics: A visual link to learning. *ELearn, 2013*(12), 1–4. doi:10.1145/2556598.2556269

Bellei, M., Welch, P., Pryor, S., & Ketheesan, N. (2016). A cost-effective approach to producing animated infographics for immunology teaching. *Journal of Microbiology & Biology Education, 17*(3), 477–479. doi:10.1128/jmbe.v17i3.1146 PMID:28101279

Bello, A., & Rangel, M. (2002). Equity and exclusion of indigenous and Afro-descendant peoples in Latin America and the Caribbean [La equidad y la exclusión de los pueblos indígenas y afrodescendientes en América Latina y el Caribe]. *Revista Cepal, 76*, 39–54. doi:10.18356/61fc0d54-es

Bermúdez, F. M. (2016). Affirmative action, discrimination and denial of linguistic and cultural rights in Mexican higher education [Acción afirmativa, discriminación y negación de derechos lingüísticos y culturales en la educación superior mexicana]. *Revista de Derechos Humanos y Estudios Sociales, 16*, 79-97. http://www.derecho.uaslp.mx/Paginas/REDHES/N%C3%BAmero-16.aspx

Berube, M. (2022). Cut students some slack already. *The Chronicle of Higher Education*. https://www-chronicle-com.wv-o-ursus-proxy01.ursus.maine.edu/article/cut-students-some-slack-already

Berweger, B., Born, S., & Dietrich, J. (2022). Expectancy-value appraisals and achievement emotions in an online learning environment: Within-and between-person relationships. *Learning and Instruction, 77*(101546), 1–9. doi:10.1016/j.learninstruc.2021.101546

Bhatia, A., Gaur, P. S., Zimba, O., Chatterjee, T., Nikiphorou, E., & Gupta, L. (2021). The untapped potential of Instagram to facilitate rheumatology academia. *Clinical Rheumatology*, 1–7. PMID:34601652

Bicen, H., & Beheshti, M. (2017). The psychological impact of infographics in education. *BRAIN. Broad Research in Artificial Intelligence and Neuroscience, 8*(4), 99–108.

Bigelow, A., Drucker, S., Fisher, D., & Meyer, M. (2014, May). Reflections on how designers design with data. In *Proceedings of the 2014 International Working Conference on Advanced Visual Interfaces* (pp. 17-24). 10.1145/2598153.2598175

Bigman, M., & Mitchell, J. C. (2020). Teaching Online in 2020: Experiments, Empathy, Discovery. In 2020 IEEE Learning With MOOCS (LWMOOCS) (pp. 156-161). IEEE]

Binali, T., Tsai, C. C., & Chang, H. Y. (2021). University students' profiles of online learning and their relation to online metacognitive regulation and internet-specific epistemic justification. *Computers & Education, 175*(104315), 1–16. doi:10.1016/j.compedu.2021.104315

Bittencourt, B. A., Figueiro, P. S., & Schutel, S. (2017). The impact of social innovation: Benefits and opportunities from Brazilian social business. *Revista Espacios, 38*(26). https://www.revistaespacios.com/a17v38n26/a17v38n26p07.pdf

Blanco, R. (2014). *Educational inclusion in Latin America: paths traveled and to be traveled. Advances and challenges of inclusive education in Ibero-America* [Inclusión educativa en América Latina: caminos recorridos y por recorrer. Avances y desafíos de la educación inclusiva en Iberoamérica]. Madrid, Spain: Organización de Estados Iberoamericanos. https://www.observatoriodelainfancia.es/oia/esp/documentos_ficha.aspx?id=4275

Blaskó, Z., Da Costa, P., & Schnepf, S. V. (2022). Learning losses and educational inequalities in Europe: Mapping the potential consequences of the COVID-19 crisis. *Journal of European Social Policy, 32*(4), 1–15. doi:10.1177/09589287221091687

Blayone, T., Mykhailenko, O., Kavtaradze, M., Kokhan, M., vanOostveen, R., & Barber, W. (2018). Profiling the digital readiness of higher education students for transformative online learning in the post-soviet nations of Georgia and Ukraine. *International Journal of Educational Technology in Higher Education, 15*(37), 1–22.

Blustein, D. L., & Guarino, P. A. (2020). Work and unemployment in the time of covid-19: The existential experience of loss and Fear. *Journal of Humanistic Psychology, 60*(5), 702–709. doi:10.1177/0022167820934229

Boelens, R., Van Laer, S., De Wever, B., & Elen, J. (2015). *Blended learning in adult education: Towards a definition of blended learning.* https://biblio.ugent.be/publication/6905076/file/6905079.pdf

Bohstedt, B. D. (2017). *An Infographic Is Worth a Thousand Words: Using Data Visualization to Engage Faculty in Collection Strategies.* Academic Press.

Boling, E. C., Hough, M., Krinsky, H., Saleem, H., & Stevens, M. (2012). Cutting the distance in distance education: Perspectives on what promotes positive, online learning experiences. *Internet and Higher Education, 15*(2), 118–126. doi:10.1016/j.iheduc.2011.11.006

Bolliger, D. U., Supanakorn, S., & Boggs, C. (2010). Impact of podcasting on student motivation in the online learning environment. *Computers & Education, 55*(2), 714–722. doi:10.1016/j.compedu.2010.03.004

Bolt, D. (2017). Introduction: Avoidance, the academy, and activism. In Disability, Avoidance and the Academy (pp. 1-8). Routledge.

Bonal, X., & González, S. (2020). The impact of lockdown on the learning gap: Family and school divisions in times of crisis. *International Review of Education, 66*(5-6), 635–655. doi:10.100711159-020-09860-z PMID:32952208

Bond, R., & Castagnera, E. (2006). Peer supports and inclusive education: An underutilized resource. *Theory into Practice, 45*(3), 224–229. doi:10.120715430421tip4503_4

Bono, G., Reil, K., & Hescox, J. (2020). Stress and wellbeing in college students during the COVID-19 pandemic: Can grit and gratitude help? *International Journal of Wellbeing, 10*(3), 39–57. doi:10.5502/ijw.v10i3.1331

Boothe, K. A., Lohmann, M. J., Donnell, K. A., & Hall, D. D. (2018). Applying the principles of universal design for learning (UDL) in the college classroom. *The Journal of Special Education Apprenticeship, 7*(3). Retrieved June 29, 2022, from https://scholarworks.lib.csusb.edu/josea/vol7/iss3/2/

Compilation of References

Borchia, R., Carbonaro, A., Casadei, G., Forlizzi, L., Lodi, M., & Martini, S. (2018, October). Problem Solving Olympics: an inclusive education model for learning Informatics. In *International Conference on Informatics in Schools: Situation, Evolution, and Perspectives* (pp. 319-335). Springer. 10.1007/978-3-030-02750-6_25

Bosch, E., Seifried, E., & Spinath, B. (2021). What successful students do: Evidence-based learning activities matter for students' performance in higher education beyond prior knowledge, motivation, and prior achievement. *Learning and Individual Differences*, *91*(102056), 1–12. doi:10.1016/j.lindif.2021.102056

Bosse, I. K. (2015, August). Criteria for designing blended learning materials for inclusive education: perspectives of teachers and producers. In *International Conference on Universal Access in Human-Computer Interaction* (pp. 3-14). Springer. 10.1007/978-3-319-20684-4_1

Boston Medical Center. (2022). *RECOVER long COVID study*. Retrieved from https://www.bmc.org/infectious-diseases/recover-long-covid-study

Bostwick, W., & Hequembourg, A. (2014). 'Just a little hint': Bisexual-specific microaggressions and their connection to epistemic injustices. *Culture, Health & Sexuality*, *16*(5), 488–503. doi:10.1080/13691058.2014.889754 PMID:24666221

Bousbahi, F., & Alrazgan, M. S. (2015). Investigating IT faculty resistance to learning management system adoption using latent variables in an acceptance technology model. *TheScientificWorldJournal*, *2015*, 2015. doi:10.1155/2015/375651 PMID:26491712

Boutot, E. A., & Bryant, D. P. (2005). Social integration of students with autism in inclusive settings. *Education and Training in Developmental Disabilities*, 14–23.

Bower, M., Dalgarno, B., Kennedy, G. E., Lee, M. J. W., & Kenney, J. (2015). Design and implementation factors in blended synchronous learning environments: Outcomes from a cross-case analysis. *Computers & Education*, *86*, 1–17. doi:10.1016/j.compedu.2015.03.006

Boysen, G. A. (2012). Teacher and student perceptions of microaggressions in college classrooms. *College Teaching*, *60*(3), 122–129. doi:10.1080/87567555.2012.654831

Bradshaw, M. J., & Porter, S. (2017). Infographics: A new tool for the nursing classroom. *Nurse Educator*, *42*(2), 57–59. doi:10.1097/NNE.0000000000000316 PMID:27532677

Brandt, S. A. (2008). *Information source selection of traditional and distance students* (Doctoral dissertation). Retrieved from http://etd.fcla.edu/WF/WFE0000098/ Brandt_Sheila_Ann_200805_EdD.pdf

Braun, V., & Clarke, V. (2006). Using thematic analysis in psychology. *Qualitative Research in Psychology*, *3*(2), 77–101. doi:10.1191/1478088706qp063oa

Breeding. (2020). *The Systems Librarian - A Global Crisis May Reshape Library Services*. https://www.infotoday.com/cilmag/may20/Breeding--A-Global-Crisis-May-Reshape-Library-Services.shtml

Brigham and Women's Hospital. (2022). *Long-term neurological complications of COVID-19*. https://www.brighamandwomens.org/campaigns/physicians/understanding-long-term-effects-of-covid-19

Broton, K. M. (2020). A review of estimates of housing insecurity and homelessness among students in U.S. higher education. *Journal of Social Distress and the Homeless*, *29*(1), 25–38. doi:10.1080/10530789.2020.1677009

Brown, M. (2016). Blended instructional practice: A review of the empirical literature on instructors' adoption and use of online tools in face-to-face teaching. *The Internet and Higher Education*, *31*, 1–10. Advance online publication. doi:10.1016/j.iheduc.2016.05.001

Bryant, L. S., Godsay, S., & Nnawulezi, N. (2021). Envisioning human service organizations free of microaggressions. *New Ideas in Psychology*, *63*(100893), 1–8. doi:10.1016/j.newideapsych.2021.100893

Bryman, A. (2016). *Social research methods*. Oxford University Press.

Bryson, J. R., & Andres, L. (2020). Covid-19 and rapid adoption and improvisation of online teaching: Curating resources for extensive versus intensive online learning experiences. *Journal of Geography in Higher Education*, *44*(4), 608–623. doi:10.1080/03098265.2020.1807478

Buchanan, C. S., & Bailey-Belafonte, S. J. (2021). Challenges in adapting Field placement during a Pandemic: A Jamaican Perspective. *International Social Work*, *64*(2), 285–288. doi:10.1177/0020872820976738

Buehring, J., & Vittachi, N. (2020). Transmedia storytelling: Addressing futures communication challenges with video animation. *Journal of Futures Studies*, *25*(1), 65–78.

Buljan, I., Malički, M., Wager, E., Puljak, L., Hren, D., Kellie, F., West, H., Alfirević, Z., & Marušić, A. (2018). No difference in knowledge obtained from infographic or plain language summary of a Cochrane systematic review: Three randomized controlled trials. *Journal of Clinical Epidemiology*, *97*, 86–94. doi:10.1016/j.jclinepi.2017.12.003 PMID:29269021

Bureau of Economic Analysis. (2021). *GDP by state*. Retrieved from https://www.bea.gov/data/gdp/gdp-state

Burgio, V., & Moretti, M. (2017). Infographics as images: Meaningfulness beyond information. In Multidisciplinary Digital Publishing Institute Proceedings (Vol. 1, No. 9, p. 891). Academic Press.

Burgstahler, S. (2022). *Universal design as a framework for diversity, equity, and inclusion initiatives in higher education*. Disabilities, Opportunities, Internetworking, and Technology. https://www.washington.edu/doit/universal-design-framework-diversity-equity-and-inclusion-initiatives-higher-education

Bursi-Amba, A., Gaullier, A., & Santidrian, M. (2016). Infographics: A toolbox for technical writers. *Ufr D'etudes Interculturelles De Langues Appliquees*, 1-13.

Burt, B. A., McKen, A., Burkhart, J., Hormell, J., & Knight, A. (2019). Black men in engineering graduate education: Experiencing racial microaggressions within the advisor–advisee relationship. *The Journal of Negro Education*, *88*(4), 493–508. doi:10.7709/jnegroeducation.88.4.0493

Bylinskii, Z., Alsheikh, S., Madan, S., Recasens, A., Zhong, K., Pfister, H., . . . Oliva, A. (2017). *Understanding infographics through textual and visual tag prediction*. arXiv preprint arXiv:1709.09215.

Byrne, L., Angus, D., & Wiles, J. (2015). Acquired codes of meaning in data visualization and infographics: Beyond perceptual primitives. *IEEE Transactions on Visualization and Computer Graphics*, *22*(1), 509–518. doi:10.1109/TVCG.2015.2467321 PMID:26529716

Bystrova, T. (2020). Infographics as a tool for improving effectiveness of education. *KnE Social Sciences*, 152-158.

California Legislature. (2022). *California Assembly Bill 288*. 2021-2022 Regular Session.

Camarero, C., Rodríguez, J., & San José, R. (2012). An exploratory study of online forums as a collaborative learning tool. *Online Information Review*, *36*(6), 568–586. doi:10.1108/14684521211254077

Camilleri, M. A. (2017). The rationale for responsible supply chain management and stakeholder engagement. *Journal of Global Responsibility*, *8*(1), 111–126. doi:10.1108/JGR-02-2017-0007

Carbonell, K. B., Dailey-Hebert, A., & Gijselaers, W. (2013). Unleashing the creative potential of faculty to create blended learning. *The Internet and Higher Education*, *18*, 29–37. doi:10.1016/j.iheduc.2012.10.004

Compilation of References

Carvalho, A., Areal, N., & Silva, J. (2011). Students' perceptions of Blackboard and Moodle in a Portuguese university. *British Journal of Educational Technology, 42*(5), 824–841. doi:10.1111/j.1467-8535.2010.01097.x

Casey, D. M. (2008). The historical development of distance education through technology. *TechTrends, 52*(2), 45–51. doi:10.100711528-008-0135-z

Castelli, F. R., & Sarvary, M. A. (2021). Why students do not turn on their video cameras during online classes and an equitable and inclusive plan to encourage them to do so. *Ecology and Evolution, 11*(8), 3565–3576. doi:10.1002/ece3.7123 PMID:33898009

Castleman, B., & Meyer, K. (2019). Financial constraints & collegiate student learning: A behavioral economics perspective. *Daedalus, 148*(4), 195–216. doi:10.1162/daed_a_01767

Celik, I., Torre, I., & Torsani, S. (2017, March). Integrating social media into an instructional design support system. In *Proceedings of the 2017 ACM Workshop on Intelligent Interfaces for Ubiquitous and Smart Learning* (pp. 19-24). 10.1145/3038535.3038544

Cellini, S. (2021, August 13). *How does virtual learning impact students in higher education?* Brookings. https://www.brookings.edu/blog/brown-center-chalkboard/2021/08/13/how-does-virtual-learning-impact-students-in-higher-education/

Cellini, S., & Grueso, H. (2021). Student learning in online college programs. *American Educational Research Association Open, 1*(7), 1–18. 10.1177%2F23328584211008105

Center for American Women and Politics. (2021). *State-by-state information.* Retrieved from https://cawp.rutgers.edu/facts/state-state-information

Chandrasiri, N. R., & Weerakoon, B. S. (2021). Online learning during the COVID-19 pandemic: Perceptions of Allied Health Sciences undergraduates. *Radiography,* 1–5. PMID:34893435

Chang, N., & Tjendro, J. (2020, April 5-6). Singapore sees record daily spike of 120 COVID-19 cases, 'significant number' linked to worker dormitories. *ChannelNewsAsia.* https://www.channelnewsasia.com/news/singapore/covid19-singapore-record-daily-spike-120-new-cases-workers-dorms-12611132

Chang, T. S., Teng, Y. K., Chien, S. Y., & Tzeng, Y. L. (2021). Use of an interactive multimedia e-book to improve nursing students' sexual harassment prevention knowledge, prevention strategies, coping behavior, and learning motivation: A randomized controlled study. *Nurse Education Today, 104883,* 1–7. doi:10.1016/j.nedt.2021.104883 PMID:34218069

Charoenying, T. (2013, June). Graph hopping: learning through physical interaction quantification. In *Proceedings of the 12th International Conference on Interaction Design and Children* (pp. 495-498). 10.1145/2485760.2485850

Chase, S. E. (2005). Narrative inquiry: Multiple lenses, approaches, voices. In N. K. Denzin & Y. S. Lincoln (Eds.), *The SAGE Handbook of Qualitative Research* (pp. 651–679). SAGE.

Chen, D-T. V., & Hung, D. W.L. (2007). Towards a community incubator: The ICAP design framework for social constructivist educational designers. *Proceedings of the CSCL 2007,* 127 – 130.

Cheng, S. L., & Xie, K. (2021). Why college students procrastinate in online courses: A self-regulated learning perspective. *The Internet and Higher Education, 50,* 100807. doi:10.1016/j.iheduc.2021.100807

Chen, K. C., & Jang, S. J. (2010). Motivation in online learning: Testing a model of self-determination theory. *Computers in Human Behavior, 26*(4), 741–752. doi:10.1016/j.chb.2010.01.011

Chen, T., Peng, L., Jing, B., Wu, C., Yang, J., & Cong, G. (2020). The impact of the COVID-19 pandemic on user experience with online education platforms in China. *Sustainability, 12*(18), 7329. doi:10.3390u12187329

Chen, T., Peng, L., Yin, X., Rong, J., Yang, J., & Cong, G. (2020). Analysis of user satisfaction with online education platforms in China during the COVID-19 pandemic. *Health Care*, 8(3), 200. doi:10.3390/healthcare8030200 PMID:32645911

Chen, Z., Wang, Y., Wang, Q., Wang, Y., & Qu, H. (2019). Towards automated infographic design: Deep learning-based auto-extraction of extensible timeline. *IEEE Transactions on Visualization and Computer Graphics*, 1–10. doi:10.1109/TVCG.2019.2934810 PMID:31443028

Cheon, S. H., Reeve, J., & Vansteenkiste, M. (2020). When teachers learn how to provide classroom structure in an autonomy-supportive way: Benefits to teachers and their students. *Teaching and Teacher Education*, *90*, 103004. doi:10.1016/j.tate.2019.103004

Cheung, W., & Huang, W. (2005). Proposing a framework to assess Internet usage in university education: An empirical investigation from a student's perspective. *British Journal of Educational Technology*, *36*, 237–253. http://www.wiley.com/bw/ journal.asp?ref=0007-1013

Chimedza, R. (2008). Disability and inclusive education in Zimbabwe. In *Policy, experience and change: Cross-cultural reflections on inclusive education* (pp. 123–132). Springer. doi:10.1007/978-1-4020-5119-7_9

Chola, R., Kasimba, P., George, R., & Rajan, R. (2020). Covid-19 and e-learning: Perception of freshmen level physics students at Lusaka apex medical university. *International Journal of Academic Research and Development*, *15*(19), 67–76.

Chowdhury, M. K., & Behak, F. B. (2022). Online higher education in Bangladesh during Covid-19: It is challenges and prospects. *Journal of Ultimate Research and Trends in Education*. https://www.semanticscholar.org/paper/Online-Higher-Education-in-Bangladesh-during-It-is-Chowdhury-Behak/ab48203efc4528ae39d3e4c97ca874cb27dd6fee

Chua, N. (2021, July 9). Suicide rate among seniors hits 29-year high last year: SOS. *The New Paper*. https://www.tnp.sg/news/singapore/suicide-rate-among-seniors-hits-29-year-high-last-year-sos

Chung, J. E., Park, N., Wang, H., Fulk, J., & McLaughlin, M. (2010). Age differences in perceptions of online community participation among non-users: An extension of the Technology Acceptance Model. *Computers in Human Behavior*, *26*(6), 1674–1684.

Çifçi, T. (2016). Effects of infographics on students (sic) achievement and attitude towards geography lessons. *Journal of Education and Learning*, *5*(1), 154–166. doi:10.5539/jel.v5n1p154

Civera, A. (2010). Women, school and life choices: rural normalista students in Mexico in the fifties [Mujeres, escuela y opciones de vida: las estudiantes normalistas rurales en México en los años cincuenta]. *Naveg@mérica, La Asociación Española de Americanista,* (4), 1-13. https://revistas.um.es/navegamerica/article/view/99881

Claes, S., & Vande Moere, A. (2013, June). Street infographics: Raising awareness of local issues through a situated urban visualization. In *Proceedings of the 2nd ACM International Symposium on Pervasive Displays* (pp. 133-138). 10.1145/2491568.2491597

Clark, M. (2013). *Student success and retention: Critical factors for success in the online environment* (Publication No. 444) [Doctoral dissertation, University of North Florida]. University of North Florida Digital Commons.

Cleveland-Innes, M., & Wilton, D. (2018). *Guide to blended learning*. Commonwealth of Learning (COL). https://oasis.col.org/handle/11599/3095

Coalson, G. A., Crawford, A., Treleaven, S. B., Byrd, C. T., Davis, L., Dang, L., ... Turk, A. (2022). Microaggression and the adult stuttering experience. *Journal of Communication Disorders*, *95*(106180), 1–18. PMID:34954647

Coffin, M., & Perez, J. (2014). Unraveling the digital literacy paradox: how high education fails at the fourth literacy. Issues in Informing Science and Information Technology, 11 85-100. https://doi.org/10.28945/1982

Compilation of References

Cohen, E., & Davidovitch, N. (2020). The Development of Online Learning in Israeli Higher Education. *Journal of Education and Learning, 9*(5), 15-26. doi:10.5539/jel.v9n5p15

Cohen, L., Manion, L., & Morrison, K. (2011). *Research methods in education* (7th ed.). Routledge.

Cohen, S., & Sabag, Z. (2020). The Influence of the COVID-19 Epidemic on Teaching Methods in Higher Education Institutions in Israel. *Journal of Research in Higher Education, 4*(1), 44–71. doi:10.24193/JRHE.2020.1.4

College Board. (2016). *Trends in college pricing, 2016.* Retrieved from https://research.collegeboard.org/media/pdf/trends-college-pricing-2016-full-report.pdf

College Board. (2021). *Trends in college pricing and student aid, 2021.* Retrieved from https://research.collegeboard.org/media/pdf/trends-college-pricing-student-aid-2021.pdf

Coppola, N. W., Hiltz, S. R., & Rotter, N. G. (2002). Becoming a virtual professor: Pedagogical roles and asynchronous learning networks. *Journal of Management Information Systems, 18*(4), 169-189. doi:10.1109/HICSS.2001.926183

Correia, A. P., & Yusop, F. D. (2008, October). "I don't want to be empowered" the challenge of involving real-world clients in instructional design experiences. In *Proceedings of the Tenth Anniversary Conference on Participatory Design 2008* (pp. 214-216). Academic Press.

Council of Social Work Education. (2008). *Educational Policy and Accreditation Standards.*

Cox. (2020). *Academic libraries will change in significant ways as a result of the pandemic (opinion).* https://www.insidehighered.com/views/2020/06/05/academic-libraries-will-change-significant-ways-result-pandemic-opinion

Cremin, L. (1970). *American education: The colonial experience, 1607-1783.* Harper & Row.

Crenshaw, K. (1991). Mapping the margins: Identity politics, intersectionality, and violence against women. *Stanford Law Review, 43*(6), 1241–1299. doi:10.2307/1229039

Crenshaw, K. (2011). Twenty years of critical race theory: Looking back to move forward. *Connecticut Law Review, 43*(5), 1253–1354.

Crick, K., & Hartling, L. (2015). Preferences of knowledge users for two formats of summarizing results from systematic reviews: Infographics and critical appraisals. *PloS One, 10*(10), 1 - 8.

Cronin, J. J. Jr, & Taylor, S. A. (1992). Measuring Service Quality: A reexamination and extension. *Journal of Marketing, 56*(3), 55–68. doi:10.1177/002224299205600304

Cueva, B. M. (2014). Institutional academic violence: Racial and gendered microaggressions in higher education. *Chicana. Latino Studies,* 142–168.

Cui, W., Zhang, X., Wang, Y., Huang, H., Chen, B., Fang, L., Zhang, H., Lou, J.-G., & Zhang, D. (2019). Text-to-viz: Automatic generation of infographics from proportion-related natural language statements. *IEEE Transactions on Visualization and Computer Graphics, 26*(1), 906–916. doi:10.1109/TVCG.2019.2934785 PMID:31478860

Cupita, L. A. L., & Franco, L. M. P. (2019). The use of infographics to enhance reading comprehension skills among learners. *Colombian Applied Linguistics Journal, 21*(2), 230–242. doi:10.14483/22487085.12963

Curry, J. R. (2010). Addressing the spiritual needs of African American students: Implications for school counselors. *The Journal of Negro Education,* 405–415.

Dabbagh, N. (2003). Scaffolding: An important teacher competency in online learning. *TechTrends, 47*(2), 39-44. doi:10.1007/BF02763424

Dahmash, A. B., Al-Hamid, A., & Alrajhi, M. (2017). Using infographics in the teaching of linguistics. *Arab World English Journal*, *8*(4), 430–443. doi:10.24093/awej/vol8no4.29

Daiute, C., & Lightfoot, C. (Eds.). (2004). *Narrative analysis: Studying the development of individuals in society*. SAGE. doi:10.4135/9781412985246

Dale, S. K., Pan, Y., Gardner, N., Saunders, S., Wright, I. A., Nelson, C. M., Liu, J., Phillips, A., Ironson, G. H., Rodriguez, A. E., Alcaide, M. L., Safren, S. A., & Feaster, D. J. (2021). Daily microaggressions and related distress among black women living with HIV during the onset of the COVID-19 pandemic and Black Lives Matter Protests. *AIDS and Behavior*, *25*(12), 4000–4007. doi:10.100710461-021-03321-w PMID:34046762

Dalton, J., & Design, W. (2014). *A Brief Guide to Producing Compelling Infographics*. London School of Public Relations.

Damian, D., Petre, M., Miller, M., & Hadwin, A. F. (2012, May). Instructional strategies in the EGRET course: an international graduate forum on becoming a researcher. In *Proceedings of the Seventeenth Western Canadian Conference on Computing Education* (pp. 41-45). 10.1145/2247569.2247583

Damman, O. C., Vonk, S. I., Van den Haak, M. J., van Hooijdonk, C. M., & Timmermans, D. R. (2018). The effects of infographics and several quantitative versus qualitative formats for cardiovascular disease risk, including heart age, on people's risk understanding. *Patient Education and Counseling*, *101*(8), 1410–1418. doi:10.1016/j.pec.2018.03.015 PMID:29559200

Damyanov, I., & Tsankov, N. (2018). The role of infographics for the development of skills for cognitive modeling in education. *International Journal of Emerging Technologies in Learning*, *13*(1), 82–92. doi:10.3991/ijet.v13i01.7541

Daniela, L., & Lytras, M. D. (2019). Educational robotics for inclusive education. *Technology. Knowledge and Learning*, *24*(2), 219–225. doi:10.100710758-018-9397-5

Daumiller, M., Rinas, R., Hein, J., Janke, S., Dickhäuser, O., & Dresel, M. (2021). Shifting from face-to-face to online teaching during COVID-19: The role of university faculty achievement goals for attitudes towards this sudden change, and their relevance for burnout/engagement and student evaluations of teaching quality. *Computers in Human Behavior*, *118*(106677), 1–10. doi:10.1016/j.chb.2020.106677

Davinson, G. (2017). University Education and Indigenous Peoples1 in Chile: A Program of Affirmative Action [Educación universitaria y pueblos indígenas1 en Chile: Un programa de acción afirmativa]. *Cuadernos del Cordicom*, *3*, 137-158. https://repositorio.consejodecomunicacion.gob.ec//handle/CONSEJO_REP/644

Davis, F. D. (1986). *A technology acceptance model for empirically testing new enduser information systems: Theory and results* [Unpublished doctoral dissertation]. Massachusetts Institute of Technology.

Davis, F. D. (1989). Perceived usefulness, perceived ease of use, and user acceptance of information technology. *Management Information Systems Quarterly*, *13*, 319–339. http://www.jstor.org/ stable/249008

Davis, F. D. (1993). User acceptance of information technology: System characteristics, user perceptions and behavior impacts. *International Journal of Man-Machine Studies*, *39*, 475–487.

Davis, F. D., Bagozzi, R. P., & Warshaw, P. R. (1989). User acceptance of computer technology: A comparison of two theoretical models. *Management Science*, *35*, 982–1003. https://www.jstor.org/stable/2632151

Davis, F. D., Bagozzi, R. P., & Warshaw, P. R. (1989). User acceptance of computer technology:Acomparison of two theoretical models. *Management Science*, *35*(8), 982–1003.

Davis, F., Bagozzi, R., & Warshaw, R. (1989). User Acceptance of computer technology: A comparison of two theoretical models. *Management Science*, *35*, 982–1002.

Compilation of References

Davis, L., Sun, Q., Lone, T., Levi, A., & Xu, P. (2022). In the storm of COVID-19: College students' perceived challenges with virtual learning. *Journal of Higher Education Theory and Practice*, *22*(1), 66–82. doi:10.33423/jhetp.v22i1.4964

De Backer, L., Van Keer, H., De Smedt, F., Merchie, E., & Valcke, M. (2021). Identifying regulation profiles during computer-supported collaborative learning and examining their relation with students' performance, motivation, and self-efficacy for learning. *Computers & Education*, 104421.

de Castro Andrade, R., & Spinillo, C. G. (2018, July). Interaction and animation in health infographics: A study of graphic presentation and content comprehension. In *International Conference of Design, User Experience, and Usability* (pp. 187-199). Springer. 10.1007/978-3-319-91803-7_14

De Rosa, C., Cantrell, J., Hawk, J., & Wilson, A. (2006). *College students' perceptions of libraries and information resources*. Retrieved from Online Computer Library Center website: https://www.oclc.org/us/en/reports/perceptionscollege.htm

Dečman, M. (2015). Modeling the acceptance of e-learning in mandatory environments of higher education: The influence of previous education and gender. *Computers in Human Behavior*, *49*, 272–281. doi:10.1016/j.chb.2015.03.022

Dehghani, M., Mohammadhasani, N., Hoseinzade Ghalevandi, M., & Azimi, E. (2020). Applying AR-based infographics to enhance learning of the heart and cardiac cycle in biology class. *Interactive Learning Environments*, 1–16. doi:1 0.1080/10494820.2020.1765394

Delaney, J. A. (2014). The Role of state policy in promoting college affordability. *The Annals of the American Academy of Political and Social Science*, *655*(1), 56–78. doi:10.1177/0002716214535898

Delil, S. (2017). The impact of infographic animation videos on data visualization. *International Journal of Social Sciences and Education Research*, *3*(4), 1178–1183. doi:10.24289/ijsser.312933

DeLuca, C. (2013). Toward an Interdisciplinary Framework for Educational Inclusivity. *Canadian Journal of Education*, *36*(1), 305–347.

DeMatthews, D., Knight, D., Reyes, P., Benedict, A., & Callahan, R. (2020). From the field: Education research during a pandemic. *Educational Researcher*, *49*(6), 398–402. doi:10.3102/0013189X20938761

Democratic Party. (2020). *Where we stand: Providing world-class education in every zip code*. Retrieved from https://democrats.org/where-we-stand/party-platform/providing-a-world-class-education-in-every-zip-code/

Den Exter, K., Rowe, S., Boyd, W., & Lloyd, D. (2012). Using Web 2.0 technologies for collaborative learning in distance education—Case studies from an Australian university. *Future Internet, 4*(1), 216-237. doi:10.3390/fi4010216

Denison, E. (1962). *Sources of economic growth in America*. Committee for Economic Development.

Derry, E. (2021, April 19) Students return to the campus! *Maariv Online*. Retrieved from https://www.maariv.co.il/journalists/opinions/Article-834686

Dewantari, F., Utami, I. G. A. L. P., & Santosa, M. H. (2021). Infographics and independent learning for English learning in the secondary level context. *Journal on English as a Foreign Language*, *11*(2), 250–274. doi:10.23971/jefl.v11i2.2784

Dhawan, S. (2020). Online Learning a Panacea in the Time of COVID-19 Crisis. *Journal of Education Technology*, *49*(1), 5–22.

Di Malta, G., Bond, J., Conroy, D., Smith, K., & Moller, N. (2022). Distance education students' mental health, connectedness and academic performance during COVID-19: A mixed-methods study. *Distance Education*, *43*(1), 97–118. doi:10.1080/01587919.2022.2029352

Diakopoulos, N., Kivran-Swaine, F., & Naaman, M. (2011, May). Playable data: characterizing the design space of game-y infographics. In *Proceedings of the SIGCHI Conference on Human Factors in Computing Systems* (pp. 1717-1726). 10.1145/1978942.1979193

Dick, M. (2017). Developments in infographics. *The Routledge Companion to Digital Journalism Studies*, 1 – 12.

Dick, M. (2014). Interactive infographics and news values. *Digital Journalism*, *2*(4), 490–506. doi:10.1080/21670811 .2013.841368

Dietrich, J., Greiner, F., Weber-Liel, D., Berweger, B., Kämpfe, N., & Kracke, B. (2021). Does an individualized learning design improve university student online learning? A randomized field experiment. *Computers in Human Behavior*, *122*, 106819. doi:10.1016/j.chb.2021.106819

Dilevko, J., & Gottlieb, L. (2002). Print sources in an electronic age: A vital part of the research process for undergraduate students. *Journal of Academic Librarianship*, *28*, 381–392.

Diniz, H., & Melilli, E. (2020). The rise of #SocialMedia in the Nephrology world. *Nefrologia*, *40*(6), 597–607. doi:10.1016/j.nefro.2020.02.003 PMID:32386925

Dlamini, S. (2020). 261 Teenage Pregnancies during Lockdown. Mbabane: Eswatini Observer.

Doğan, A. (2021). *A study to determine the service quality levels of Turkish universities during the Covid-19 pandemic process* [Covid-19 Pandemi Sürecinde, Türk üniversitelerinin Hizmet Kalite Düzeylerini Belirlemeye Yönelik Bir Araştırma]. OPUS Uluslararası Toplum Araştırmaları Dergisi. doi:10.26466/opus.944561

Dolmage, J. T. (2017). *Academic ableism: Disability and higher education*. University of Michigan Press.

Domingues-Montanari, S. (2017). Clinical and psychological effects of excessive screen time on children. *Journal of Paediatrics and Child Health*, *53*(4), 333–338. doi:10.1111/jpc.13462 PMID:28168778

Donelan, H., & Kear, K. (2018). Creating and Collaborating: Students' and Tutors' Perceptions of an Online Group Project. *The International Review of Research in Open and Distributed Learning*, *19*(2). Advance online publication. doi:10.19173/irrodl.v19i2.3124

Donitsa-Schmidt, S., & Ramot, R. (2020). Opportunities and challenges: teacher education in Israel in the COVID-19 pandemic. *Journal of Education for Teaching, 46*(4), 586-595. doi:10.1080/02607476.2020.1799708

Donnermann, M., Lein, M., Messingschlager, T., Riedmann, A., Schaper, P., Steinhaeusser, S., & Lugrin, B. (2021). Social robots and gamification for technology supported learning: An empirical study on engagement and motivation. *Computers in Human Behavior*, *121*(106792), 1–9. doi:10.1016/j.chb.2021.106792

Dorko, A. (2021). How students use the 'see similar example' feature in online mathematics homework. *The Journal of Mathematical Behavior*, *63*(100894), 1–25. doi:10.1016/j.jmathb.2021.100894

Doucet, A., Netolicky, D., Timmers, K., & Tuscano, F. J. (2020). *Thinking about pedagogy in an unfolding pandemic: An Independent Report on Approaches to Distance Learning during COVID-19 School Closure*. Academic Press.

Doukianou, S., Daylamani-Zad, D., & O'Loingsigh, K. (2021). Implementing an augmented reality and animated infographics application for presentations: Effect on audience engagement and efficacy of communication. *Multimedia Tools and Applications*, *80*(20), 1–23. doi:10.100711042-021-10963-4

Dowhos, K., Sherbino, J., Chan, T. M., & Nagji, A. (2021). Infographics, podcasts, and blogs: A multi-channel, asynchronous, digital faculty experience to improve clinical teaching (MAX FacDev). *Canadian Journal of Emergency Medical Care*, *23*(3), 390–393. doi:10.100743678-020-00069-5 PMID:33788176

Compilation of References

Doyle, W. R. (2007). Public opinion, partisan identification, and higher education policy. *The Journal of Higher Education*, *78*(4), 369–401. doi:10.1353/jhe.2007.0021

DRA versus University of California Berkeley. (2013). https://www.sdbor.edu/administrative-offices/academics/aac/Documents/5.BSettlementbetweentheUniversityofCalifornia-BerkeleyandDisabilityRightsAdvocatesAAC0613.pdf

Driscoll, M. (2002). *Blended learning: Let's get beyond the hype*. IBM Global Services.http://www-07.ibm.com/services/pdf/blended_learning.pdf

Druery, D. M., Young, J. L., & Elbert, C. (2018). Macroaggressions and civil discourse. *Women, Gender, and Families of Color*, *6*(1), 73–78. doi:10.5406/womgenfamcol.6.1.0073

Dubey, M., & Sinha, K. (2021). Role Of Information Communication Technology In Higher Education In Ranchi. *Elementary Education Online*, *20*(6), 1074–1074.

Dubey, P., & Pandey, D. (2020). Distance learning in higher education during pandemic: Challenges and opportunities. *International Journal of Indian Psychology*, *8*(2), 43–46.

Dubois, A., & Gadde, L.-E. (2002). Systematic combining: An adductive approach to case research. *Journal of Business Research*, *55*(7), 553–560. doi:10.1016/S0148-2963(00)00195-8

Dunlap, J. C., & Lowenthal, P. R. (2016). Getting graphic about infographics: Design lessons learned from popular infographics. *Journal of Visual Literacy*, *35*(1), 42–59. doi:10.1080/1051144X.2016.1205832

Dunn, C. E., Hood, K. B., & Owens, B. D. (2019). Loving myself through thick and thin: Appearance contingent self-worth, gendered racial microaggressions and African American women's body appreciation. *Body Image*, *30*, 121–126. doi:10.1016/j.bodyim.2019.06.003 PMID:31238277

Dunn, T. J., & Kennedy, M. (2019). Technology Enhanced Learning in higher education; motivations, engagement and academic achievement. *Computers & Education*, *137*, 104–113. doi:10.1016/j.compedu.2019.04.004

Duran, R. (2018, August). Towards an instructional design of complex learning in introductory programming courses. In *Proceedings of the 2018 ACM Conference on International Computing Education Research* (pp. 262-263). 10.1145/3230977.3231007

Dur, B. I. U. (2014a). Data visualization and infographics in visual communication design education at the age of information. *Journal of Arts and Humanities*, *3*(5), 39–50.

Dur, B. I. U. (2014b). Interactive infographics on the Internet. *Online Journal of Art and Design*, *2*(4), 1–14.

Dyjur, P., & Li, L. (2015). Learning 21st century skills by engaging in an infographics assessment. Proceedings of the IDEAS: Designing Responsive Pedagogy Conference, 62 - 71.

Dziuban, C., Picciano, A. G., Graham, C. R., & Moskal, P. D. (2016). *Conducting research in online and blended learning environments: New pedagogical frontiers*. Routledge, Taylor & Francis Group.

Ebben, M., & Blewett, L. (2021). Post-pandemic anxiety: Teaching and learning for student mental wellness in communication. In J. Valenzano (Ed.), *Post-pandemic pedagogy: Predicting the change to come* (pp. 129–147). Rowman and Littlefield.

Eberle, J., & Hobrecht, J. (2021). The lonely struggle with autonomy: A case study of first-year university students' experiences during emergency online teaching. *Computers in Human Behavior*, *121*(106804), 1–11. doi:10.1016/j.chb.2021.106804

Egan, M., Acharya, A., Sounderajah, V., Xu, Y., Mottershaw, A., Phillips, R., Ashrafian, H., & Darzi, A. (2021). Evaluating the effect of infographics on public recall, sentiment and willingness to use face masks during the COVID-19 pandemic: A randomised internet-based questionnaire study. *BMC Public Health*, *21*(1), 1–10. doi:10.118612889-021-10356-0 PMID:33596857

Eidson, B. (2015). Testing potable reuse messages with a utility–university partnership. *Journal - American Water Works Association*, *107*(11), 54–57. doi:10.5942/jawwa.2015.107.0167

Eisenhardt, K. M. (1989). Building Theories from Case Study Research. *Academy of Management Review*, *14*(4), 532–550. doi:10.2307/258557

El Alfy, S., & Abukari, A. (2019). Revisiting perceived service quality in higher education: Uncovering Service Quality Dimensions for postgraduate students. *Journal of Marketing for Higher Education*, *30*(1), 1–25. doi:10.1080/0884124 1.2019.1648360

Elazar, D. J. (1984). *American federalism: A view from the states* (3rd ed.). Harper and Row.

Elder, C. H. (2021). Microaggression or misunderstanding? Implicatures, inferences and accountability. *Journal of Pragmatics*, *179*, 37–43. doi:10.1016/j.pragma.2021.04.020

El-Ghalayini, H., & El-Khalili, N. (2011). An approach to designing and evaluating blended courses. *Education and Information Technologies*. Advance online publication. doi:10.100710639-011-9167-7

Elharake, J. A., Akbar, F., Malik, A. A., Gilliam, W., & Omer, S. B. (2022). Mental health impact of COVID-19 among children and college students: A systematic review. *Child Psychiatry and Human Development*. Advance online publication. doi:10.100710578-021-01297-1 PMID:35013847

Ellis, R. (2009). Task-based Language Teaching: Sorting out the Misunderstandings. *International Journal of Applied Linguistics*, *19*(3), 221–246. doi:10.1111/j.1473-4192.2009.00231.x

Elortegui, M. (2017). A historical tour of the Rural Normal Schools of Mexico: The subversive act of remembering the events against the students of Ayotzinapa [Un recorrido histórico de las Escuelas Normales Rurales de México: el acto subversivo de hacer memoria desde los acontecimientos contra los estudiantes de Ayotzinapa]. *Estudios Latinoamericanos NUEVA ÉPOCA*, *40*, 157–178. doi:10.22201/cela.24484946e.2017.40.61600Hi

Elshami, W., Taha, M. H., Abdalla, M. E., Abuzaid, M., Saravanan, C., & Al Kawas, S. (2022). Factors that affect student engagement in online learning in health professions education. *Nurse Education Today*, *110*, 105261. doi:10.1016/j. nedt.2021.105261 PMID:35152148

Engineering Good. (2021). *Computers Against Covid*. https://engineeringgood.org/digital-inclusion/cac/

Eriksson, P., & Kovalainen, A. (2015). Qualitative methods in business research: A practical guide to social research. *Sage (Atlanta, Ga.)*.

Escalante, E. (2010). The descriptive and phenomenological analysis of problems in the preparation of master's theses [El análisis descriptivo y fenomenológico de problemas en la elaboración de tesis de maestría]. *Reencuentro*, *57*, 38-47. https://www.redalyc.org/articulo.oa?id=34012514006

Esteban-Navarro, M. A., García-Madurga, M. A., Morte-Nadal, T., & Nogales-Bocio, A. I. (2020). The rural digital divide in the face of the COVID-19 pandemic in Europe- Recommendations from a scoping review. *Informatics (MDPI)*, *7*(54), 1–18. doi:10.3390/informatics7040054

Evans, R. S. (2016). *Infographics on the brain*. Articles, Chapters and Online Publications. Digital Commons at the University of Georgia School of Law.

Compilation of References

Everett, S. (Ed.). (2021). Editor's introduction. In S. Everett (Ed.), *Trauma-informed teaching: Cultivating healing-centered ELA classrooms* (pp. 9-12). National Council of Teachers of English. https://ncte.org/wp-content/uploads/2022/06/Trauma-Informed-Teaching-.pdf

Fadzil, H. M. (2018). Designing infographics for the educational technology course: Perspectives of pre-service science teachers. *Journal of Baltic Science Education, 17*(1), 8–18. doi:10.33225/jbse/18.17.08

Falloon, G. (2011). Making the connection: Moore's theory of transactional distance and its relevance to the use of a virtual classroom in postgraduate online teacher education. *Journal of Research on Technology in Education, 45*(3), 187–209. doi:10.1080/15391523.2011.10782569

Fandiño, F. G. E., & Velandia, A. J. S. (2020). How an online tutor motivates E-learning English. *Heliyon, 6*(8), 1 - 7.

Fatani, T. H. (2020). Student satisfaction with videoconferencing teaching quality during the COVID-19 pandemic. *BMC Medical Education, 20*(1), 396. Advance online publication. doi:10.118612909-020-02310-2 PMID:33129295

Fawns, T., & O'Shea, C. (2018, May). Distributed learning and isolated testing: tensions in traditional assessment practices. In *Proceedings of the 2018 Networked Learning Conference* (pp. 132-139). Academic Press.

Featherstone, R. (2014). Visual research data: An infographics primer. *JCHLA/JABSC, 35*, 147 - 150.

Feenberg, A. (2017). The online education controversy and the future of the university. *Foundations of Science, 22*(2), 363–371. doi:10.100710699-015-9444-9

Felton, P., & Lambert, L. (2020). *Relationship-Rich Education: How Human Connections Drive Success in College.* Johns Hopkins University Press.

Feng, W., Tang, J., & Liu, T. X. (2019, July). Understanding dropouts in MOOCs. *Proceedings of the AAAI Conference on Artificial Intelligence, 33*(01), 517–524. doi:10.1609/aaai.v33i01.3301517

Fernando, I. D. K. L., & Senevirathna, R. A. P. S. (2020). *Survey on online library services provided during the COVID pandemic situation: With special reference to academic libraries of Sri Lanka.* Academic Press.

Ferreira-Meyers, K., Biswalo, P., Maduna, S., Ngcobo, L., & Dlamini-Zwane, N. (2020). Selected case studies from Eswatini: dealing with the COVID-19 pandemic in the education sectors. In *Digital 2020 online* (pp. 255 – 276). https://www.researchgate.net/profile/Upasana-Singh/publication/348355099_digiTAL_2020_proceedings/

Feyerer, E. (2002, July). Computer and inclusive education. In *International Conference on Computers for Handicapped Persons* (pp. 64-67). Springer.

Fidalgo, P., Thormann, J., Kulyk, O., & Lencastre, J. A. (2020). Students' perceptions on Distance Education: A multinational study. *International Journal of Educational Technology in Higher Education, 17*(1), 18. Advance online publication. doi:10.118641239-020-00194-2

Field, J., Rankin, A., Van der Pal, J., Eriksson, H., & Wong, W. (2011, August). Variable uncertainty: Scenario design for training adaptive and flexible skills. In *Proceedings of the 29th Annual European Conference on Cognitive Ergonomics* (pp. 27-34). 10.1145/2074712.2074719

Fishbane, L., & Tomer, A. (2020). *As classes move online during COVID-19, what are disconnected students to do?* Brookings. https://www.brookings.edu/blog/the-avenue/2020/03/20/as-classes-move-online-during-covid-19-whatare-disconnected-students-to-do/

Fisher, H. N., Chatterjee, P., Shapiro, J., Katz, J. T., & Yialamas, M. A. (2021). "Let's Talk About What Just Happened": A Single-Site Survey Study of a Microaggression Response Workshop for Internal Medicine Residents. *Journal of General Internal Medicine*, *36*(11), 3592–3594. doi:10.100711606-020-06576-6 PMID:33479935

Fishman, B., Konstantopoulos, S., Kubitskey, B. W., Vath, R., Park, G., Johnson, H., & Edelson, D. C. (2013). Comparing the impact of online and face-to-face professional development in the context of Curriculum Implementation. *Journal of Teacher Education*, *64*(5), 426–438. doi:10.1177/0022487113494413

Fitzpatrick, J., Castricum, A., Seward, H., Tulloh, L., & Dawson, E. (2020). Infographic. COFIT-19: Let's get moving through the COVID-19 pandemic! *British Journal of Sports Medicine*, *54*(22), 1360–1361. doi:10.1136/bjsports-2020-102661 PMID:32561519

Flanders, C. E., LeBreton, M., & Robinson, M. (2019). Bisexual women's experience of microaggressions and microaffirmations: A community-based, mixed-methods scale development project. *Archives of Sexual Behavior*, *48*(1), 143–158. doi:10.100710508-017-1135-x PMID:29476410

Flanigan, A. E., Akcaoglu, M., & Ray, E. (2022). Initiating and maintaining student-instructor rapport in online classes. *The Internet and Higher Education*, *53*(100844), 1–11.

Flick, U. (2009). *An introduction to qualitative research* (4th ed.). Sage Publications Ltd.

Florman, M., Klingler-Vidra, R., & Facada, M. J. (2016, February). *A critical evaluation of social impact assessment methodologies and a call to measure economic and social impact holistically through the External Rate of Return platform.* LSE Enterprise Working Paper # 1602. http://eprints.lse.ac.uk/id/eprint/65393

Flynn, J. T. (2013). MOOCS: Disruptive innovation and the future of higher education. *Christian Education Journal*, *10*(1), 149–162. doi:10.1177/073989131301000112

Frank, J., Salsbury, M., McKelvey, H., & McLain, R. (2021). Digital equity & inclusion strategies for libraries: Promoting student success for all learners. *The International Journal of Information, Diversity, & Inclusion*, *5*(3), 185–205.

Fraser, M., Agdamag, A. C. C., Maharaj, V. R., Mutschler, M., Charpentier, V., Chowdhury, M., & Alexy, T. (2022). COVID-19-Associated Myocarditis: An Evolving Concern in Cardiology and Beyond. *Biology (Basel)*, *11*(4), 520. doi:10.3390/biology11040520 PMID:35453718

Freeman, H. D. (2015). *The Moving Image Workshop: Introducing animation, motion graphics and visual effects in 45 practical projects.* Bloomsbury Publishing.

Friedman, Z. (February 3, 2020). *Student loan debt statistics in 2020: A record $1.6 trillion.* Retrieved from https://www.forbs.com/sites/zackfriedman/2020/02/03/student-loan-debt-statistics/#4bb54987281f

Fryer, L. K., & Bovee, H. N. (2016). Supporting students' motivation for e-learning: Teachers matter on and offline. *The Internet and Higher Education*, *30*, 21–29. doi:10.1016/j.iheduc.2016.03.003

Fuster, D. E. (2019). Qualitative research: Hermeneutic phenomenological method [Investigación cualitativa: Método fenomenológico hermenéutico]. *Propósitos y Representaciones*, *7*(1), 201–229. doi:10.20511/pyr2019.v7n1.267

Galkienė, A., & Monkevičienė, O. (2021). The Model of UDL Implementation enabling the development of inclusive education in different educational contexts: Conclusions. *Improving Inclusive Education through Universal Design for Learning*, *5*, 313-323.

Gallagher, S. E., O'Dulain, M., O'Mahony, N., Kehoe, C., McCarthy, F., & Morgan, G. (2017). Instructor-provided summary infographics to support online learning. *Educational Media International*, *54*(2), 129–147. doi:10.1080/09523987.2017.1362795

Compilation of References

Gallardo, E., De Oliveira, J. M., Marqués-Molias, L., & Esteve-Mon, F. (2015). Digital Competence in the Knowledge Society. *Journal of Online Learning and Teaching / MERLOT*, *11*(1), 1–16. https://jolt.merlot.org/vol11no1/abstracts.htm

Gamble, S. (2016). *Visual content marketing: leveraging infographics, video, and interactive media to attract and engage customers*. John Wiley & Sons.

Gan El, A. (2021). Hybrid learning will be the new normal. *Ynet.* https://www.ynet.co.il/digital/technology/article/bywcluyyk

Garand, J. (1985). Partisan change and shifting expenditure priorities in the American states, 1945-1978. *American Politics Quarterly*, *13*(4), 355–391. doi:10.1177/1532673X8501300401

Gardner, S., & Eng, S. (2005). What students want: Generation Y and the changing function of the academic library. *Portal (Baltimore, Md.)*, *5*, 405–420. doi:10.1353/ pla.2005.0034

Garn, A. C., & Morin, A. J. (2021). University students' use of motivational regulation during one semester. *Learning and Instruction*, *74*(101436), 1–10. doi:10.1016/j.learninstruc.2020.101436

Garnham, C., & Kaleta, R. (2002). Introduction to hybrid courses. *Teaching with Technology Today, 8*(6), 5. https://hccelearning.files.wordpress.com/2010/09/introduction-to-hybrid-course1.pdf

Garrison, D. R. (2006). Online collaboration principles. *Journal of Asynchronous Learning Networks*, *10*(1), 25–34. doi:10.24059/olj.v10i1.1768

Garrison, D. R., & Kanuka, H. (2004). Blended learning: Uncovering its transformative potential in higher education. *The Internet and Higher Education*, *7*(2), 95–105. doi:10.1016/j.iheduc.2004.02.001

Garrison, D. R., & Vaughan, N. D. (2008). *Blended learning in higher education: Framework, principles, and guidelines*. Jossey-Bass/Wiley.

Gaughen, K., Flynn-Khan, M., & Hayes, C. D. (2009). *Sustaining Youth Engagement Initiatives: Challenges and Opportunities*. The Finance Project. https://wvsystemofcare.org/wp-content/uploads/2013/10/Sustaining-Youth-Engagement-2009-Finance-Project.pdf

Gay, J., Simms, V., Bond, R., Finlay, D., & Purchase, H. (2019, September). An audit tool for assessing the visuocognitive design of infographics. In *Proceedings of the 31st European Conference on Cognitive Ergonomics* (pp. 1-5). 10.1145/3335082.3335117

Gebre, E. (2018). Learning with multiple representations: Infographics as cognitive tools for authentic learning in science literacy. *Canadian Journal of Learning and Technology/La revue canadienne de l'apprentissage et de la technologie*, *44*(1), 1 - 24.

Geng, L. N., Verghese, A., & Tilburt, J. C. (2021). Consultative medicine-an emerging specialty for patients with perplexing conditions. *The New England Journal of Medicine*, *385*(26), 2478–2484. doi:10.1056/NEJMms2111017 PMID:34936744

Gering, C. S., Sheppard, D. K., Adams, B. L., Renes, S. L., & Morotti, A. A. (2018). Strengths-based analysis of student success in online courses. *Online Learning*, *22*(3), 55–85. doi:10.24059/olj.v22i3.1464

Germanakos, P., Kasinidou, M., Constantinides, M., & Samaras, G. (2019, June). A metacognitive perspective of InfoVis in education. In *Adjunct Publication of the 27th Conference on User Modeling, Adaptation and Personalization* (pp. 331-336). Academic Press.

Ghazal, S., Al-Samarraie, H., & Aldowah, H. (2018). "I am still learning": Modeling LMS critical success factors for promoting students' experience and satisfaction in a blended learning environment. *IEEE Access: Practical Innovations, Open Solutions, 6*, 77179–77201.

Ghazal, S., Al-Samarraie, H., & Aldowah, H. (2018). "I am Still Learning": Modeling LMS critical success factors for promoting students' experience and satisfaction in a blended learning environment. *IEEE Access: Practical Innovations, Open Solutions, 6*, 77201. doi:10.1109/ACCESS.2018.2879677

Ghilay, Y. (2019). *Effectiveness of learning management systems in higher education: Views of Lecturers with different levels of activity in LMSs*. Academic Press.

Ghilay, Y. (2019). Effectiveness of Learning Management Systems in Higher Education: Views of Lecturers with Different Levels of Activity in LMSs. https://ssrn.com/abstract=3736748. *Journal of Online Higher Education, 3*(2), 29–50.

Ghode, R. (2012). Infographics in news presentation: A study of its effective use in Times of India and Indian Express the two leading newspapers in India. *Journal of Business Management & Social Sciences Research, 1*(1), 35-43.

Gibbons, A. S. (2009, May). A theory-based alternative for the design of instruction: functional design. In *Proceedings of the 4th International Conference on Design Science Research in Information Systems and Technology* (pp. 1-5). 10.1145/1555619.1555633

Gillis, A., & Krull, L. (2020). COVID-19 Remote Learning Transition in Spring 2020: Class Structures, Student Perceptions, and Inequality in College Courses. *Teaching Sociology, 48*(4), 283–299. doi:10.1177/0092055X20954263

Gitinabard, N., Khoshnevisan, F., Lynch, C. F., & Wang, E. Y. (2018). *Your actions or your associates? Predicting certification and dropout in MOOCs with behavioral and social features.* arXiv preprint arXiv:1809.00052.

Giusti, L., Mammarella, S., Salza, A., Del Vecchio, S., Ussorio, D., Casacchia, M., & Roncone, R. (2021). Predictors of academic performance during the covid-19 outbreak: Impact of distance education on mental health, social cognition and memory abilities in an Italian university student sample. *BMC Psychology, 9*(1), 1–17. doi:10.118640359-021-00649-9 PMID:34526153

Glazer, F. S. (2012). *Blended learning: Across the disciplines, across the academy.* Stylus Sterling. https://styluspub.presswarehouse.com/browse/book/9781579223243/Blended%20Learning

Gluck, M. (1996). Exploring the relationship between user satisfaction and relevance in information systems. *Information Processing & Management, 32*(1), 89–104.

Goh, C. T. (2020, April 8). Volunteers rush to deliver laptops to families in need before full home-based learning kicks in. *ChannelNewsAsia.* https://www.channelnewsasia.com/news/singapore/covid19-home-based-learning-laptops-volunteers-donation-12617146

Goh, Y. H. (2020, July 29). Job support for persons with disabilities to continue despite Covid-19 pandemic: Desmond Lee. *The Straits Times.* https://www.straitstimes.com/singapore/manpower/job-support-for-persons-with-disabilities-to-continue-despite-covid-19-pandemic

Goldberg, R. (2022). *New NTIA data show barriers to closing the digital divide, achieving digital equality.* Retrieved from https://www.ntia.doc.gov/blog/2022/new-ntia-data-show-enduring-barriers-closing-digital-divide-achieving-digital-equity

Gomez, M. L., Khurshid, A., Freitag, M. B., & Lachuk, A. J. (2011). Microaggressions in graduate students' lives: How they are encountered and their consequences. *Teaching and Teacher Education, 27*(8), 1189–1199. doi:10.1016/j.tate.2011.06.003

Compilation of References

Goodison, T. A. (2001). The implementation of e-learning in higher education in the United Kingdom: The road ahead. *Higher Education in Europe, 26*(2), 247-262. doi:10.1080/03797720120082642

Google Books. (2022, Jan. 14). In *Wikipedia*. Retrieved Jan. 17, 2022, from https://en.wikipedia.org/wiki/Google_Books

Gopal, R., Singh, V., & Aggarwal, A. (2021). Impact of online classes on the satisfaction and performance of students during the pandemic period of COVID 19. *Education and Information Technologies, 26*(6), 6923–6947. doi:10.100710639-021-10523-1 PMID:33903795

Goudeau, S., Sanrey, C., Stanczak, A., Manstead, A. & Darnon, c. (2021). Why lockdown and distance learning during the COVID-19 pandemic are likely to increase the social class achievement gap. Nature-Human Behavior, 5, 1273–1281. https://www.nature.com/articles/s41562-021-01212-7

Gouthro, P. A. (2005). Understanding local and global contexts: The importance of the Sociological Imagination for Adult Education. *Adult Education Research Conference*. https://newprairiepress.org/aerc/2005/papers/46

Government of the Republic of Zambia. (2013). *Higher Education Act No. 4 of 2013*. Government Printers.

Graham, C. (2013). Emerging practice and research in blended learning. In Handbook of Distance Education (pp. 333–350). doi:10.4324/9780203803738.ch21

Graham, C. R. (2006). Blended learning systems: Definition, current trends, and future directions. In C. J. Bonk & C. R. Graham (Eds.), *Handbook of Blended Learning: Global Perspectives, Local Designs* (pp. 3–21). Pfeiffer Publishing.

Granić, A., Mifsud, C., & Ćukušić, M. (2009). Design, implementation and validation of a Europe-wide pedagogical framework for e-learning. *Computers & Education, 53*(4), 1052–1081. doi:10.1016/j.compedu.2009.05.018

Gray, V. (1973). Innovations in the states: A diffusion study. *The American Political Science Review, 67*(4), 1174–1185. doi:10.2307/1956539

Greene, J. A., Duke, R. F., Freed, R., Dragnić-Cindrić, D., & Cartiff, B. M. (2022). Effects of an ego-depletion intervention upon online learning. *Computers & Education, 177*(104362), 1–14. doi:10.1016/j.compedu.2021.104362

Green, K. C. (2010). *The Campus Computing Survey*. The Campus Computing Project. Retrieved from https://www.campuscomputing.net/2010-campus-computing-survey

Greussing, E., & Boomgaarden, H. G. (2021). Promises and pitfalls: Taking a closer look at how interactive infographics affect learning from news. *International Journal of Communication, 15*(22), 3336–3357.

Grieger, K., & Leontyev, A. (2021). Student-generated infographics for learning green chemistry and developing professional skills. *Journal of Chemical Education, 98*(9), 2881–2891.

Griffin, A. L., MacEachren, A. M., Hardisty, F., Steiner, E., & Li, B. (2006). A comparison of animated maps with static small-multiple maps for visually identifying space-time clusters. *Annals of the Association of American Geographers, 96*(4), 740–753.

Grimus, M. (2000, August). ICT and multimedia in the primary school. In *16th conference on educational uses of information and communication technologies, Beijing, China* (pp. 21-25). Academic Press.

Gumede, L., & Badriparsad, N. (2022). Online teaching and learning through the students' eyes–Uncertainty through the COVID-19 lockdown: A qualitative case study in Gauteng province, South Africa. *Radiography, 28*(1), 193–198. doi:10.1016/j.radi.2021.10.018 PMID:34785145

Gusukuma, L., Bart, A. C., Kafura, D., Ernst, J., & Cennamo, K. (2018, February). Instructional design+ knowledge components: A systematic method for refining instruction. In *Proceedings of the 49th ACM Technical Symposium on Computer Science Education* (pp. 338-343). 10.1145/3159450.3159478

Hai-Jew, S. (2020, Aug. 5 – 7). Creating a motion infographic for learning. In *Virtual SIDLIT 2020*. Colleague 2 Colleague. Retrieved Dec. 30, 2021, from https://www.slideshare.net/ShalinHaiJew/creating-a-motion-infographic-for-learning-236203316

Haijian, C., Hexiao, H., Wang, L., Chen, W., & Kunru, J. (2011). Research and application of blended learning in distance education and teaching reform. *I.J. Education and Management Engineering, 3*, 67-72. https://www.mecs-press.org/ijeme/ijeme-v1-n3/IJEME-V1-N3-10.pdf

Hall-Ellis, S. D. (2006). Cataloging electronic resources and metadata: Employers' expectations as reflected in American libraries and AutoCAT, 2000-2005. *Journal of Education for Library and Information Science, 47*, 38–51. http://vnweb.hwwilsonweb.com/hww/login.jhtml?_requestid=108885

Hamilton, K., Peden, A. E., Keech, J. J., & Hagger, M. S. (2017). Changing people's attitudes and beliefs toward driving through floodwaters: Evaluation of a video infographic. *Transportation Research Part F: Traffic Psychology and Behaviour, 53*, 50–60.

Händel, M., Stephan, M., Gläser-Zikuda, M., Kopp, B., Bedenlier, S., & Ziegler, A. (2020). Digital readiness and its effects on higher education students' socio-emotional perceptions in the context of the COVID-19 pandemic. *Journal of Research on Technology in Education*, 1–13.

Hanh, H. P., Nam, T. T., & Vinh, L. A. (2022). Initiatives to Promote School-Based Mental Health Support by Department of Educational Sciences, University of Education Under Vietnam National University. In *University and School Collaborations during a Pandemic* (pp. 321–331). Springer. doi:10.1007/978-3-030-82159-3_21

Hao, Y., Liu, Q., & Zhai, H. (2018, May). Design and development of educational information processing micro-curriculum in the era of educational informationization. In *Proceedings of the 2018 International Conference on Distance Education and Learning* (pp. 79-83). 10.1145/3231848.3231869

Harasim, L. (2000). Shift happens: Online education as a new paradigm in learning. *The Internet and Higher Education, 3*(1-2), 41–61. doi:10.1016/S1096-7516(00)00032-4

Hardimon, M. (2019). should we narrow the scope of "racism" to accommodate white sensitivities? *Critical Philosophy of Race, 7*(2), 223–246. doi:10.5325/critphilrace.7.2.0223

Hardy, C. (1983). *Organizations: Rational*. Natural and Open Systems.

Harper, J., & Widodo, H. P. (2018). Perceptual mismatches in the interpretation of task-based ELT materials: A micro-evaluation of a task-based English lesson. *Innovation in Language Learning and Teaching*. Advance online publication. doi:10.1080/17501229.2018.1502773

Harrison, L., Reinecke, K., & Chang, R. (2015). *Infographic aesthetics: Designing for the first impression. In the proceedings of CHI 2015*. Crossings.

Harsasi, M., & Sutawijaya, A. (2018). Determinants of student satisfaction in the online tutorial: A study of a distance education institution. *Turkish Online Journal of Distance Education, 19*(1), 89–99. doi:10.17718/tojde.382732

Hassan, H. G. (2016). *Designing Infographics to support teaching complex science subject: A comparison between static and animated Infographics* [Doctoral dissertation]. Iowa State University.

Compilation of References

Haynes-Baratz, M. C., Metinyurt, T., Li, Y. L., Gonzales, J., & Bond, M. A. (2021). Bystander training for faculty: A promising approach to tackling microaggressions in the academy. *New Ideas in Psychology, 63*(100882), 1–8. doi:10.1016/j.newideapsych.2021.100882

He, M., Tang, X., & Huang, Y. (2011, June). To visualize spatial data using thematic maps combined with infographics. In *2011 19th International Conference on Geoinformatics* (pp. 1-5). IEEE.

Heimbürger, A., & Isomöttönen, V. (2019, October). Infographics as a Reflective Assignment Method in Requirements Engineering e-Course? In *2019 IEEE Frontiers in Education Conference (FIE)* (pp. 1-5). IEEE.

Heimbürger, A., Keto, H., & Isomöttönen, V. (2020, October). Learning via Summarizing Infographics Assignment in Software Engineering Management e-Course? In 2020 IEEE Frontiers in Education Conference (FIE) (pp. 1-5). IEEE. doi:10.1109/FIE44824.2020.9274229

Helps, R. G. (2011). A domain model to improve IT course design. *Proceedings of SIGITE '11*, 323 – 324.

Hergüner, B. (2021). Rethinking public administration education in the period of pandemic: Reflections of public administration students on online education through a SWOT analysis: Rethinking public administration education. *Thinking Skills and Creativity, 100863*, 1–8. doi:10.1016/j.tsc.2021.100863

Hersh, M., Leporini, B., & Buzzi, M. (2020, September). ICT to support inclusive education. In *International Conference on Computers Helping People with Special Needs* (pp. 123-128). Springer. 10.1007/978-3-030-58805-2_15

Hess, J. (2016). "How does that apply to me?" The gross injustice of having to translate. *Bulletin of the Council for Research in Music Education*, (207-208), 81–100. doi:10.5406/bulcouresmusedu.207-208.0081

Higher Education Authority. (2022). *State of Higher Education in Zambia, 2021 Report*. Author.

Hill, S., & Grinnell, C. (2014, October). Using digital storytelling with infographics in STEM professional writing pedagogy. In *2014 IEEE International Professional Communication Conference (IPCC)* (pp. 1-7). IEEE.

Hiltz, S. R. (1994). *The virtual classroom: Learning without limits via computer networks*. Intellect Books.

Hinchliffe & Wolff-Eisenberg. (2020, March 24). First This, Now That: A Look at 10-Day Trends in Academic Library Response to COVID19. *Ithaka S+R*. https://sr.ithaka.org/blog/first-this-now-that-a-look-at-10-day-trends-in-academic-library-response-to-covid19/

Hodges, C., Moore, S., Lockee, B., Trust, T., & Bond, A. (2020). The difference between emergency remote teaching and online learning. *Educause*. https://er.educause.edu/articles/2020/3/the-difference-between-emergency-remote-teaching-and-online-learning

Holmes, G. G. (2018). Counterpoints: Vol. 149-181. Moving forward: Biasing,(de) biasing, and strategies for change. Academic Press.

Hong, J. C., Hsiao, H. S., Chen, P. H., Lu, C. C., Tai, K. H., & Tsai, C. R. (2021). Critical attitude and ability associated with students' self-confidence and attitude toward "predict-observe-explain" online science inquiry learning. *Computers & Education, 166*(104172), 1–14. doi:10.1016/j.compedu.2021.104172

Hong, J. C., Lee, Y. F., & Ye, J. H. (2021). Procrastination predicts online self-regulated learning and online learning ineffectiveness during the coronavirus lockdown. *Personality and Individual Differences, 174*(110673), 1–8. doi:10.1016/j.paid.2021.110673 PMID:33551531

Hong, W., Thong, J. Y. L., Wong, W.-M., & Tam, K.-Y. (2002). Determinants of user acceptance of digital libraries: An empirical examination of individual differences and system characteristics. *Journal of Management Information Systems, 18*(3), 97–124.

Hoogland, C. E., Schurtz, D., Cooper, C. M., Combs, D. J., Brown, E. G., & Smith, R. H. (2015). The joy of pain and the pain of joy: In-group identification predicts schadenfreude and gluckschmerz following rival groups' fortunes. *Motivation and Emotion, 39*(2), 260–281. doi:10.100711031-014-9447-9

Horbath, J. E., & García, A. (2012) Social backwardness and discrimination of social policy towards indigenous groups in Sonora [Rezago social y discriminación de la política social hacia los grupos indígenas en Sonora]. *Revista de relaciones internacionales, estrategia y seguridad, 7*(1), 173-189. http://www.scielo.org.co/scielo.php?script=sci_abstract&pid=S1909306320120001000008&lng=es&nrm=iso&tlng=es

Hornung, H., Pereira, R., & Baranauskas, M. C. C. (2016, August). Meaning construction and evolution: A case study of the design-in-use of a system for inclusive education teachers. In *International Conference on Informatics and Semiotics in Organisations* (pp. 181-190). Springer. 10.1007/978-3-319-42102-5_20

Hosen, M., Ogbeibu, S., Giridharan, B., Cham, T. H., Lim, W. M., & Paul, J. (2021). Individual motivation and social media influence on student knowledge sharing and learning performance: Evidence from an emerging economy. *Computers & Education, 104262*, 1–18. doi:10.1016/j.compedu.2021.104262

House of Representatives 5380. (2021). *Helping Students Plan for College Act of 2021.* 117th Congress (2021-2022).

Houshmand, S., & Spanierman, L. B. (2021). Mitigating racial microaggressions on campus: Documenting targets' responses. *New Ideas in Psychology, 63*(100894), 1–11. doi:10.1016/j.newideapsych.2021.100894

Howard, L., Johnson, J., & Neitzel, C. (2010, June). Reflecting on online learning designs using observed behavior. In *Proceedings of the fifteenth annual conference on Innovation and technology in computer science education* (pp. 179-183). 10.1145/1822090.1822142

Hrastinski, S. (2008). A study of asynchronous and synchronous e-learning methods discovered that each supports different purposes. *Educause Quarterly, 4*, 51-55. http://www.educause.edu/ero/article/asynchronous-and-synchronous-e-learning

Hrastinski, S. (2019). What do we mean by blended learning? *TechTrends, 63*(5), 564–569. doi:10.100711528-019-00375-5

Hsia, L. H., Huang, I., & Hwang, G. J. (2016). Effects of different online peer-feedback approaches on students' performance skills, motivation and self-efficacy in a dance course. *Computers & Education, 96*, 55–71. doi:10.1016/j.compedu.2016.02.004

Hsiao, P. Y., Loquatro, I., Johnson, R. M., & Smolic, C. E. (2019). Using infographics to teach the evidence analysis process to senior undergraduate students. *Journal of the Academy of Nutrition and Dietetics*, 26–30.

Huang, C. Q., Han, Z. M., Li, M. X., Jong, M. S. Y., & Tsai, C. C. (2019). Investigating students' interaction patterns and dynamic learning sentiments in online discussions. *Computers & Education, 140*(103589), 1–18. doi:10.1016/j.compedu.2019.05.015

Huang, W., & Tan, C. L. (2007, August). A system for understanding imaged infographics and its applications. In *Proceedings of the 2007 ACM Symposium on Document Engineering* (pp. 9-18). ACM.

Huang, X., Mayer, R. E., & Usher, E. L. (2020). Better together: Effects of four self-efficacy-building strategies on online statistical learning. *Contemporary Educational Psychology, 63*(101924), 1–14. doi:10.1016/j.cedpsych.2020.101924 PMID:33041461

Compilation of References

Huber, L. P., Gonzalez, T., Robles, G., & Solórzano, D. G. (2021). Racial microaffirmations as a response to racial microaggressions: Exploring risk and protective factors. *New Ideas in Psychology, 63*(100880), 1–9.

Hung, M. L., & Chou, C. (2015). Students' perceptions of instructors' roles in blended and online learning environments: A comparative study. *Computers & Education, 81*, 315–325. doi:10.1016/j.compedu.2014.10.022

Hu, P. J., Chau, P. Y. K., Sheng, O. R. L., & Tam, K. Y. (1999). Examining the technology acceptance model using physician acceptance of telemedicine technology. *Journal of Management Information Systems, 16*, 91–112.

Hussein, E., Daoud, S., Alrabaiah, H., & Badawi, R. (2020). Exploring undergraduate students' attitudes towards emergency online learning during COVID-19: A case from the UAE. *Children and Youth Services Review, 119*(105699), 1–7. doi:10.1016/j.childyouth.2020.105699

Huynh, V. W. (2012). Ethnic microaggressions and the depressive and somatic symptoms of Latino and Asian American adolescents. *Journal of Youth and Adolescence, 41*(7), 831–846. doi:10.100710964-012-9756-9 PMID:22453294

Hwang, G. J., Wang, S. Y., & Lai, C. L. (2021). Effects of a social regulation-based online learning framework on students' learning achievements and behaviors in mathematics. *Computers & Education, 160*(104031), 1–19. doi:10.1016/j.compedu.2020.104031

Hwang, S., & Grey, V. (1991). External limits and internal determinates of state public policy. *Political Research Policy, 44*(2), 277–299.

Hwee, L., & Yew, J. (2018). The constructs that influence students' acceptance of an e-library system in Malaysia. *International Journal of Education and Development Using ICT, 14*(2).

Ibrahem, U. M., & Alamro, A. R. (2021). Effects of Infographics on Developing Computer Knowledge, Skills and Achievement Motivation among Hail University Students. *International Journal of Instruction, 14*(1), 907–926.

Ilahi, R., Widiaty, I., Wahyudin, D., & Abdullah, A. G. (2019). Digital library as learning resources. *Journal of Physics: Conference Series, 1402*(7), 077044.

International Monetary Fund. (2020). *IMF Executive Board Approves US $ 110.4 Million in Emergency Support to The Kingdom of Eswatini to Address the COVID-19 Pandemic.* Press Release NO. 20/274. IMF.

Iowa Community Indicators Program. (2022). *Urban Percentage of Population for States, Historical.* Retrieved from https://www.icip.iastate.edu/tables/population/urban-pct-states#:~:text=Urban%20Percentage%20of%20the%20Population%20for%20States%2C%20Historical,%20%2087.5%20%2048%20more%20rows%20

Isibika, I. S., & Kavishe, G. F. (2018). *Utilisation of subscribed electronic resources by library users in Mzumbe university library.* Global Knowledge, Memory and Communication.

Islam, D. M. S., Tanvir, K., Salman, M., & Amin, D. M. (2020). *Online classes for university students in Bangladesh during the Covid-19 pandemic- is it feasible?* https://www.tbsnews.net/thoughts/online-classes-university-students-bangladesh-during-covid-19-pandemic-it-feasible-87454

Islam, M. T., & Habib, T. (2022). Barriers of adopting online learning among the university students in Bangladesh during Covid-19. *Indonesian Journal on Learning and Advanced Education, 04*(1), 71–91. doi:10.23917/ijolae.v4i1.15215

Ismaeel, D., & Al Mulhim, E. (2021). The influence of interactive and static infographics on the academic achievement of reflective and impulsive students. *Australasian Journal of Educational Technology, 37*(1), 147–162.

Ivery, C. (2022, March 18). *Pandemic and racial reckoning reframe equity imperative for community colleges.* Diverse Issues in Higher Education. https://www.diverseeducation.com/opinion/article/15289683/pandemic-and-racial-reckoning-reframe-equity-imperative-for-community-colleges

Jackson, C. M., Chow, S., & Leitch, R. A. (1997). Toward an understanding of the behavioural intentions to use an information system. *Decision Sciences, 28,* 357–389.

Jackson, D. O. (2022). *Task-Based Language Teaching.* Cambridge University Press. doi:10.1017/9781009067973

Jaffee, D. (1997). Asynchronous learning: Technology and pedagogical strategy in a distance learning course. *Teaching Sociology, 25*(4), 262–277. doi:10.2307/1319295

Jalili-Grenier, F., & Chase, M. (1997). Retention of nursing students with English as a second language. *Journal of Advanced Nursing, 25*(1), 199–203. doi:10.1046/j.1365-2648.1997.1997025199.x PMID:9004030

Janes, J. W. (1994). Other people's judgments: A comparison of users' and others' judgments of document relevance, topicality, and utility. *Journal of the American Society for Information Science, 45*(3), 160–171.

Jankowski, N. A. (2020). *Assessment during a crisis: Responding to a global pandemic.* National Institute for Learning Outcomes Assessment. https://www.learningoutcomesassessment.org/wp-content/uploads/2020/08/2020-COVID-Survey.pdf

Jaschik, J. (2022). *Decline in male, Black, and Latino students planning on college.* Retrieved from https://www.insidehighered.com/admissions/article/2022/05/23/male-black-and-latino-high-school-students-may-not-be-college-bound?v2

Jašková, L. U. (2006). Informatics teachers and their competences in inclusive education. *Computers Helping People with Special Needs: 10th International Conference, ICCHP 2006, Linz, Austria, July 11-13, 2006 Proceedings, 10,* 552–559.

Jencks, C., & Riesman, D. (1968). *The academic revolution.* University of Chicago Press.

Jensen, L. X., Bearman, M., & Boud, D. (2021). Understanding feedback in online learning–A critical review and metaphor analysis. *Computers & Education, 173*(104271), 1–12. doi:10.1016/j.compedu.2021.104271

Jnr, B. A., Kamaludin, A., Romli, A. M., Raffei, A. F. M., Phon, D. N. E., Abdullah, A., Ming, G., Shukor, N. A., Nordin, M. S., & Baba, S. (2019). Exploring the role of blended learning for teaching and learning effectiveness in institutions of higher learning: An empirical investigation. *Education and Information Technologies.* Advance online publication. doi:10.100710639-019-09941-z

Johnson, K., Trabelsi, H., & Fabbro, E. (2008). Library support for e-learners: E-resources, e- services, and the human factors. In T. Anderson (Ed.), *The theory and practice of online learning* (2nd ed., pp. 397-418). Retrieved from https://www.aupress.ca/index.php/books/120146

Johnson, N., Veletsianos, G., & Seaman, J. (2020). US Faculty and Administrators' Experiences and Approaches in the Early Weeks of the COVID-19 Pandemic. *Online Learning, 24*(2), 6–21. doi:10.24059/olj.v24i2.2285

Johri, P., & Misra, A. (2017, August). Digital technology in classroom: Changing the face of education infographic. In *2017 International Conference On Smart Technologies For Smart Nation (SmartTechCon)* (pp. 405-406). IEEE. 10.1109/SmartTechCon.2017.8358405

Jones, B. D., Krost, K., & Jones, M. W. (2021). Relationships between students' course perceptions, effort, and achievement in an online course. *Computers and Education Open, 2*(100051), 1–10. doi:10.1016/j.caeo.2021.100051

Jones, N. P., Sage, M., & Hitchcock, L. (2019). Infographics as an assignment to build digital skills in the social work classroom. *Journal of Technology in Human Services, 37*(2-3), 1–22.

Compilation of References

Jones, V. A., & Reddick, R. J. (2017). The heterogeneity of resistance: How Black students utilize engagement and activism to challenge PWI inequalities. *The Journal of Negro Education, 86*(3), 204–219. doi:10.7709/jnegroeducation.86.3.0204

Joshi, M., & Gupta, L. (2021). Preparing infographics for post-publication promotion of research on social media. *Journal of Korean Medical Science, 36*(5), 1–16.

Jovanović, J., Saqr, M., Joksimović, S., & Gašević, D. (2021). Students matter the most in learning analytics: The effects of internal and instructional conditions in predicting academic success. *Computers & Education, 104251*, 1–13. doi:10.1016/j.compedu.2021.104251

June, A. (2020, June 8). *Did the scramble to remote learning work? Here's what higher ed thinks.* The Chronicle of Higher Education. https://www.chronicle.com/article/did-the-scramble-to-remote-learning-work-heres-what-higher-ed-thinks

June, A. W. (2020). *Congress gave colleges billions. Who got what?* Retrieved from https://www.chronicle.com/article/congress-gave-colleges-billions-who-got-what

Jung, I. (2010). The dimensions of e-learning quality: From the learner's perspective. *Educational Technology Research and Development, 59*(4), 445–464. doi:10.100711423-010-9171-4

Jurzyk, E., Nair, M. M., Pouokam, N., Sedik, T. S., Tan, A., & Yakadina, I. (2020). *COVID-19 and inequality in Asia: Breaking the vicious cycle.* IMF Working Paper, WP/20/217. https://www.imf.org/-/media/Files/Publications/WP/2020/English/wpiea2020217-print-pdf.ashx

Kaleta, R., Skibba, K., & Joosten, T. (2007). Discovering, designing, and delivering hybrid courses. In A. G. Picciano, & C. Dzuiban (Eds.), *Blended Learning Research Perspectives.* The Sloan Consortium. Retrieved January 10, 2022, from https://www.scirp.org/%28S%28351jmbntvnsjt1aadkposzje%29%29/reference/referencespapers.aspx?referenceid=1427102

Kang, X. (2016, September). The effect of color on short-term memory in information visualization. In *Proceedings of the 9th International Symposium on Visual Information Communication and Interaction* (pp. 144-145). Academic Press.

Kanthawala, S. (2019). Credibility of health infographics: Effects of message structure and message exaggeration. Michigan State University.

Kapasia, N., Paul, P., Roy, A., Saha, J., Zaveri, A., Mallick, R., Barman, B., Das, P., & Chouhan, P. (2020). Impact of lockdown on learning status of undergraduate and postgraduate students during COVID-19 pandemic in West Bengal, India. *Children and Youth Services Review, 116*, 105194. doi:10.1016/j.childyouth.2020.105194 PMID:32834270

Kaplan, A. M., & Haenlein, M. (2016). Higher Education and the Digital Revolution: About MOOCs, SPOCs, Social Media, and the Cookie Monster. *Business Horizons, 59*(4), 441–450. doi:10.1016/j.bushor.2016.03.008

Kapusta, S. J. (2016). Misgendering and its moral contestability. *Hypatia, 31*(3), 502–519. doi:10.1111/hypa.12259

Karadağ, E., & Yücel, C. (2020). Distance Education at universities during the novel coronavirus pandemic: An analysis of undergraduate students' perceptions. *Yuksekogretim Dergisi, 10*(2), 181–192. doi:10.2399/yod.20.730688

Kasauli, R., Knauss, E., Horkoff, J., Liebel, G., & de Oliveira Neto, F. G. (2021). Requirements engineering challenges and practices in large-scale agile system development. *Journal of Systems and Software, 172*, 110851. doi:10.1016/j.jss.2020.110851

Kashti, A. (2021) The universities will return to hold frontal classes after the Passover holiday. *Haaretz.* https://www.haaretz.co.il/news/education/.premium-1.9641556

Kaur, D. P., Mantri, A., & Horan, B. (2020). Enhancing student motivation with use of augmented reality for interactive learning in engineering education. *Procedia Computer Science, 172*, 881–885. doi:10.1016/j.procs.2020.05.127

Kaur, P., Kumar, H., & Kaushal, S. (2021). Affective state and learning environment based analysis of students' performance in online assessment. *International Journal of Cognitive Computing in Engineering, 2*, 12–20. doi:10.1016/j.ijcce.2020.12.003

Kear, K., Chetwynd, F., Williams, J., & Donelan, H. (2012). Web conferencing for synchronous online tutorials: Perspectives of tutors using a new medium. *Computers & Education, 58*(3), 953-963. doi:10.1016/j.compedu.2011.10.015

Kee, C. (2021). The impact of COVID-19: Graduate students' emotional and psychological experiences. *Journal of Human Behavior in the Social Environment, 31*(1-4), 476–488. doi:10.1080/10911359.2020.1855285

Keels, M., Durkee, M., & Hope, E. (2017). The psychological and academic costs of school-based racial and ethnic microaggressions. *American Educational Research Journal, 54*(6), 1316–1344. doi:10.3102/0002831217722120

Keller, C. (2007). *Virtual learning environments in higher education: A study of user acceptance.* Institutionen för ekonomisk och industriell utveckling.

Kelley, K., & Orr, G. (2003). Trends in distant student use of electronic resources. *College & Research Libraries, 64*, 176–191. http://www.ala.org/ala/mgrps/divs/acrl/ publications/crljournal/collegeresearch.cfm

Kelly, A., & Columbus, R. (2020). *College in the time of coronavirus: Challenges facing American higher education.* American Enterprise Institute. doi:10.2307/resrep25358

Kemp, D., King, A. J., Upshaw, S. J., Mackert, M., & Jensen, J. D. (2021). Applying harm reduction to COVID-19 prevention: The influence of moderation messages and risk infographics. *Patient Education and Counseling*, 1–8.

Kennedy, J. (2005). *A collection development policy for digital information resources? In Determining the impact of technological modernization and management capabilities on user satisfaction and trust in library services.* Global Knowledge, Memory and Communication.

Kenney, J., & Newcombe, E. (2011). Adopting a blended learning approach: Challenges encountered and lessons learned in an action research study. *Online Learning, 15*(1). Advance online publication. doi:10.24059/olj.v15i1.182

Kerschbaum, S. L., Eisenman, L. T., & Jones, J. M. (Eds.). (2017). *Negotiating disability: Disclosure and higher education.* University of Michigan Press. doi:10.3998/mpub.9426902

Khalil, R., Mansour, A. E., Fadda, W. A., Almisnid, K., Aldamegh, M., Al-Nafeesah, A., ... Al-Wutayd, O. (2020). The sudden transition to synchronized online learning during the COVID-19 pandemic in Saudi Arabia: a qualitative study exploring medical students' perspectives. *BMC Medical Education, 20*(1), 1-10. doi:10.1186/s12909-020-02208-z

Khan, I. A. (2021). Psychology of color, integration of local culture and effect of infographics on English language learning. *PSU Research Review*, 1 - 18.

Khaydaraliyevna, P. S. (2021, November). Development of ICT Creativity of Teachers of HEU' With Helping Infographics. In *2021 International Conference on Information Science and Communications Technologies (ICISCT)* (pp. 1-3). IEEE.

Kibar, P. N., & Akkoyunlu, B. (2014, October). A new approach to equip students with visual literacy skills: Use of infographics in education. In *European Conference on Information Literacy* (pp. 456-465). Springer.

Kibby, M. D. (2007). *Hybrid teaching and learning: Pedagogy versus pragmatism.* https://scholar.google.com.au/citations?view_op=view_citation&hl=th&user=qKa3xU4AAAAJ&citation_for_view=qKa3xU4AAAAJ:u5HHmVD_uO8C

Compilation of References

Kim, D., Lee, Y., Leite, W. L., & Huggins-Manley, A. C. (2020). Exploring student and teacher usage patterns associated with student attrition in an open educational resource-supported online learning platform. *Computers & Education, 156*, 103961. doi:10.1016/j.compedu.2020.103961

Kim, J. Y. J., Block, C. J., & Nguyen, D. (2019). What's visible is my race, what's invisible is my contribution: Understanding the effects of race and color-blind racial attitudes on the perceived impact of microaggressions toward Asians in the workplace. *Journal of Vocational Behavior, 113*, 75–87. doi:10.1016/j.jvb.2018.08.011

Kim, J. Y., Block, C. J., & Yu, H. (2021). Debunking the 'model minority' myth: How positive attitudes toward Asian Americans influence perceptions of racial microaggressions. *Journal of Vocational Behavior, 131*(103648), 1–14. doi:10.1016/j.jvb.2021.103648

King, S. E., & Arnold, K. C. (2012). Blended learning environments in higher education: A case study of how professors make it happen. *Mid-Western Educational Researcher, 25*(1), 44–59. https://www.mwera.org/MWER/volumes/v25/issue1-2/v25n1-2-King-Arnold-GRADUATE-STUDENT-SECTION.pdf

Kizi, T. M. Y., & Ferdinantovna, M. H. (2022). What is blended learning? What are the benefits of blended learning? *Theory and Analytical Aspects of Recent Research, 1*(5), 735–738.

Klass, B. (2003, May 30). *Streaming media in higher education: Possibilities and pitfalls.* Campus Technology. https://campustechnology.com/articles/2003/05/streaming-media-in-higher-education-possibilities-and-pitfalls.aspx

Kleijn, R. A., Mainhard, M. T., Meijer, P. C., Pilot, A., & Brekelmans, M. (2012). Master's thesis supervision: Relations between perceptions of the supervisor–student relationship, final grade, perceived supervisor contribution to learning and student satisfaction. *Studies in Higher Education, 37*(8), 925–939.

Klein, S. R. (2014). Making sense of data in the changing landscape of visual art education. *Visual Arts Research, 40*(2), 25–33.

Klimova, B. (2021). An insight into online foreign language learning and teaching in the era of COVID-19 pandemic. *Procedia Computer Science, 192*, 1787–1794. doi:10.1016/j.procs.2021.08.183 PMID:34630743

Klopfer, E., Sheldon, J., Perry, J., & Chen, V. H. (2012). Ubiquitous games for learning (UbiqGames): Weatherlings, a worked example. *Journal of Computer Assisted Learning, 28*(5), 465–476. doi:10.1111/j.1365-2729.2011.00456.x

Kocaleva, M., Stojanovic, I., & Zdravev, Z. (2014). *Research on UTAUT application in higher education institutions.* Academic Press.

Kohnstamm, T. (2021). *Room to Dream-How The Microsoft Garage is hacking creative culture on a global scale.* Available at https://news.microsoft.com/stories/microsoft-garage/

Koiso-Kanttila, N. (2004). Digital content marketing: A literature synthesis. *Journal of Marketing Management, 20*(1-2), 45–65. doi:10.1362/026725704773041122

Kombe, C. L., & Mtonga, D. E. (2021). Challenges and Interventions of e-learning for Under- resourced Students amid Covid-19 Lockdown: A Case of a Zambian Public University. *Journal of Student Affairs in Africa, 9*(1), 23–39. doi:10.24085/jsaa.v9i1.1426

Koob, C. (2021). Determinants of content marketing effectiveness: Conceptual framework and empirical findings from a managerial perspective. *PLoS One, 16*(4), e0249457. doi:10.1371/journal.pone.0249457 PMID:33793631

Koohang, A. (2004). Students' perceptions toward use of the digital library in weekly web-based distance learning assignments portion of a hybrid programme. *British Journal of Educational Technology, 35*, 617–626. doi:10.1111/j.0007-1013.2004.00418.x

Koohang, A., & Ondracek, J. (2005). Users' views about the usability of digital libraries. *British Journal of Educational Technology*, *36*, 407–423. http://www.hwwilconweb.com

Kos, B. A., & Sims, E. (2014). Infographics: The new 5-paragraph essay. *Rocky Mountain Celebration of Women in Computing*, 1 – 5.

Kousser, T. (2005). *Term limits and the dismantling of state legislative professionalism.* Cambridge University Press.

Ko, Y., Issenberg, S. B., & Roh, Y. S. (2022). Effects of peer learning on nursing students' learning outcomes in electrocardiogram education. *Nurse Education Today*, *108*(105182), 1–6. doi:10.1016/j.nedt.2021.105182 PMID:34741917

Kpokiri, E., John, R., Wu, D., Fongwen, N., Budak, J., Chang, C., ... Tucker, J. (2021). Crowdsourcing to Develop Open-Access Learning Resources on Antimicrobial Resistance. *BMC Infectious Diseases*, 1–7.

Krause, G., & Melusky, B. (2012). Concentrated power: Unilateral executive authority and fiscal policymaking in the American states. *The Journal of Politics*, *74*(1), 98–112. doi:10.1017/S0022381611001149

Kujala, J., Sachs, S., Leinonen, H., Heikkinen, A., & Laude, D. (2022). Stakeholder engagement: Past, present, and future. *Business & Society.*

Kuo, T. M. L., Tsai, C. C., & Wang, J. C. (2021). Linking web-based learning self-efficacy and learning engagement in MOOCs: The role of online academic hardiness. *The Internet and Higher Education*, *100819*, 1–15. doi:10.1016/j.iheduc.2021.100819

Kwek, T. (2019, July 24). How Singapore's youth are changing the social sector by going beyond volunteerism. *TODAY-Online.* https://www.todayonline.com/commentary/how-singapores-youth-are-changing-social-sector-going-beyond-volunteerism

Kyewski, E., & Krämer, N. C. (2018). To gamify or not to gamify? An experimental field study of the influence of badges on motivation, activity, and performance in an online learning course. *Computers & Education*, *118*, 25–37. doi:10.1016/j.compedu.2017.11.006

Lalima, & Dangwal, K. L. (2017). Blended learning: An innovative approach. *Universal Journal of Educational Research*, *5*(1). https://eric.ed.gov/?id=EJ1124666

Lamb, G., Polman, J. L., Newman, A., & Smith, C. G. (2014). Science news infographics. *Science Teacher (Normal, Ill.)*, *81*(3), 25–30.

Lamb, G., Polman, J. L., Newman, A., & Smith, C. G. (2014). Science news infographics. *Science Teacher*, *81*(3), 25–30. doi:10.2505/4/tst14_081_03_25

Lancheros-Cuesta, D., Rangel, J. E., Rubiano, J. L., & Cifuentes, Y. A. (2020). Adaptive robotic platform as an inclusive education aid for children with autism spectrum disorder. In *EUROCAST 2019* (pp. 297–304). Springer. doi:10.1007/978-3-030-45096-0_37

Langer, J., & Zeiller, M. (2017, November). Evaluation of the User Experience of Interactive Infographics in Online Newspapers. *Forum Media Technology*, 1 - 10.

Lan, Y. J., Sung, Y. T., & Chang, K. E. (2007). A mobile-device-supported peer-assisted learning system for collaborative early EFL reading. *Language Learning & Technology*, *11*(3), 130–151.

Lapitan, L. D. Jr, Tiangco, C. E., Sumalinog, D. A. G., Sabarillo, N. S., & Diaz, J. M. (2021). An effective blended online teaching and learning strategy during the COVID-19 pandemic. *Education for Chemical Engineers*, *35*, 116–131. doi:10.1016/j.ece.2021.01.012

Latip, M. S. A., Newaz, F. T., & Ramasamy, R. (2020). Students' perception of lecturers' competency and the effect on institution loyalty: The mediating role of students' satisfaction. *Asian Journal of University Education*, *16*(2), 183. doi:10.24191/ajue.v16i2.9155

Law, K. M., Geng, S., & Li, T. (2019). Student enrollment, motivation and learning performance in a blended learning environment: The mediating effects of social, teaching, and cognitive presence. *Computers & Education*, *136*, 1–12. doi:10.1016/j.compedu.2019.02.021

Lazard, A., & Atkinson, L. (2015). Putting environmental infographics center stage: The role of visuals at the elaboration likelihood model's critical point of persuasion. *Science Communication*, *37*(1), 6–33.

Leath, S., & Chavous, T. (2018). Black women's experiences of campus racial climate and stigma at predominantly white institutions: Insights from a comparative and within-group approach for STEM and non-STEM majors. *The Journal of Negro Education*, *87*(2), 125–139. doi:10.7709/jnegroeducation.87.2.0125

Lederman, D. (2020, April 22). *How teaching changed in the (forced) shift to remote learning*. Inside Higher Education. https://www.insidehighered.com/digital-learning/article/2020/04/22/how-professors-changed-their-teaching-springs-shift-remote

Lee, Y. H., & Yeung, C. (2021). Incentives for learning: How free offers help or hinder motivation. *International Journal of Research in Marketing*. 1 - 16.

Lee, D. Y., & Lehto, M. R. (2013). User acceptance of YouTube for procedural learning: An extension of the Technology Acceptance Model. *Computers & Education*, *61*, 193–208.

Lee, E. J., & Kim, Y. W. (2016). Effects of infographics on news elaboration, acquisition, and evaluation: Prior knowledge and issue involvement as moderators. *New Media & Society*, *18*(8), 1579–1598.

Lee, E. K. M., Lee, H., Kee, C. H., Kwan, C. H., & Ng, C. H. (2019). Social Impact Measurement in Incremental Social Innovation. *Journal of Social Entrepreneurship*, *12*(1), 69–86. doi:10.1080/19420676.2019.1668830

Lee, I., Martin, F., Denner, J., Coulter, B., Allan, W., Erickson, J., Malyn-Smith, J., & Werner, L. (2011). Computational Thinking for Youth in Practice. *ACM Inroads*, *2*(1), 32–37. doi:10.1145/1929887.1929902

Lee, W. O. (2012). Education for future-oriented citizenship: Implications for the education of 21st century competencies. *Asia Pacific Journal of Education*, *32*(4), 498–517. doi:10.1080/02188791.2012.741057

Lempres, D. (2022, May 12). *Is hybrid learning here to stay in higher ed?* EdSurge. https://www.edsurge.com/news/2022-05-12-is-hybrid-learning-here-to-stay-in-higher-ed

Lengler, R., & Moere, A. V. (2009, July). Guiding the viewer's imagination: How visual rhetorical figures create meaning in animated infographics. In *2009 13th International Conference Information Visualisation* (pp. 585-591). IEEE.

Levchak, C. C. (2018). Microaggressions, Macroaggressions, and Modern Racism. In *Microaggressions and Modern Racism* (pp. 13–69). Palgrave Macmillan.

Lewis, J. A., Mendenhall, R., Harwood, S. A., & Browne Huntt, M. (2013). Coping with gendered racial microaggressions among Black women college students. *Journal of African American Studies*, *17*(1), 51–73. doi:10.100712111-012-9219-0

Li, N., Brossard, D., Scheufele, D., Wilson, P. H., & Rose, K. M. (2018). Communicating data: interactive infographics, scientific data and credibility. *Journal of Science Communication*, *17*(2), 1 – 20.

Li, Z., Wang, J., & Shi, S. (2021, October). Bibliometric analysis of instructional design in online education based on Citespace. In *2021 13th International Conference on Education Technology and Computers* (pp. 276-283). 10.1145/3498765.3498808

Lievemaa, J. (2017). *Animated infographics in digital educational publishing: Case study of educational animated infographics.* Academic Press.

Li, H., Majumdar, R., Chen, M. R. A., & Ogata, H. (2021). Goal-oriented active learning (GOAL) system to promote reading engagement, self-directed learning behavior, and motivation in extensive reading. *Computers & Education, 104239*, 1–11. doi:10.1016/j.compedu.2021.104239

Li, J., & Mak, L. (2022). The effects of using an online collaboration tool on college students' learning of academic writing skills. *System, 102712*, 1–14. doi:10.1016/j.system.2021.102712

Li, L. Y., & Tsai, C. C. (2017). Accessing online learning material: Quantitative behavior patterns and their effects on motivation and learning performance. *Computers & Education, 114*, 286–297. doi:10.1016/j.compedu.2017.07.007

Lim, C. (2019). *Driving, sustaining and scaling up blended learning practices in higher education institutions: A proposed framework.* https://www.researchgate.net/publication/337068663_Driving_sustaining_and_scaling_up_blended_learning_practices_in_higher_education_institutions_a_proposed_framework

Lin, O. (2014). Student views of hybrid learning. *Journal of Computing in Teacher Education, 25*(2), 57-66. .10784610 doi:10.1080/10402454.2008

Lin, C. A. (1998). Exploring personal computer adoption dynamics. *Journal of Broadcasting & Electronic Media, 42*(1), 95–112.

Lin, C. H., Zhang, Y., & Zheng, B. (2017). The roles of learning strategies and motivation in online language learning: A structural equation modeling analysis. *Computers & Education, 113*, 75–85. doi:10.1016/j.compedu.2017.05.014

Linder, K. E. (2016). *The blended course design workbook: A practical guide.* Stylus Publishing, LLC.

Lin, H. C., Hwang, G. J., Chang, S. C., & Hsu, Y. D. (2021). Facilitating critical thinking in decision making-based professional training: An online interactive peer-review approach in a flipped learning context. *Computers & Education, 173*(104266), 1–25. doi:10.1016/j.compedu.2021.104266

Lin, Y. N., Hsia, L. H., & Hwang, G. J. (2021). Promoting pre-class guidance and in-class reflection: A SQIRC-based mobile flipped learning approach to promoting students' billiards skills, strategies, motivation and self-efficacy. *Computers & Education, 160*(104035), 1–18. doi:10.1016/j.compedu.2020.104035

Liptak, K. (2022). *Treasury Secretary concedes she was wrong on 'path inflation would take'.* Retrieved from https://www.msn.com/en-us/news/politics/treasury-secretary-concedes-she-was-wrong-on- path-that-inflation-would-take/ar-AAXWmGD?ocid=uxbndlbing

Liu, T. C., Lin, Y. C., Tsai, M. J., & Paas, F. (2012). Split-attention and redundancy effects on mobile learning in physical environments. *Computers & Education, 58*(1), 172–180. doi:10.1016/j.compedu.2011.08.007

Liu, X., Shi, S. W., Teixeira, T., & Wedel, M. (2018). Video content marketing: The making of clips. *Journal of Marketing, 82*(4), 86–101. doi:10.1509/jm.16.0048

Liu, Z., & Yang, Z. Y. (2004). Factors influencing distance education graduate students' use of information sources: A user study. *Journal of Academic Librarianship, 30*, 24–35. doi:10.1016/j.jal.2003.11.005

Compilation of References

Li, Z., Carberry, S., Fang, H., McCoy, K. F., & Peterson, K. (2014, June). Infographics retrieval: A new methodology. In *International Conference on Applications of Natural Language to Data Bases/Information Systems* (pp. 101-113). Springer.

Lloyd, M. (2016). A decade of affirmative action policies in Brazilian higher education: Impacts, scope and future [Una década de políticas de acción afirmativa en la educación superior brasileña: impactos, alcances y futuro]. *Revista de la Educación Superior, 45*(178), 17–29. doi:10.1016/j.resu.2016.02.002

Lochner, H., Swenson, R., & Martinson, K. (2021). 120 Disseminating equine science with infographics on social media. *Journal of Equine Veterinary Science, 100,* 103583.

Locoro, A., Cabitza, F., Actis-Grosso, R., & Batini, C. (2017). Static and interactive infographics in daily tasks: A value-in-use and quality of interaction user study. *Computers in Human Behavior, 71,* 1–51.

Löllgen, H., Bachl, N., Papadopoulou, T., Shafik, A., Holloway, G., Vonbank, K., ... Pitsiladis, Y. P. (2021). Infographic. Clinical recommendations for return to play during the COVID-19 pandemic. *British Journal of Sports Medicine, 55*(6), 344–345.

Lonsdale, M. D. S., David, L., Baxter, M., Graham, R., Kanafani, A., Li, A., & Peng, C. (2019). Visualizing the terror threat. The impact of communicating security information to the general public using infographics and motion graphics. *Visible Language, 53*(2), 37–71.

López, E., Pedraza, C. A., & De León, D. A. (2019). Research and resilience in times of pandemic [Investigación y resiliencia en tiempos de pandemia]. *Reencuentro: Educación y COVID, 31*(78), 54-72. https://reencuentro.xoc.uam.mx/index.php/reencuentro/article/view/1021

López-Fernández, D., Ezquerro, J. M., Rodríguez, J., Porter, J., & Lapuerta, V. (2019). Motivational impact of active learning methods in aerospace engineering students. *Acta Astronautica, 165,* 344–354. doi:10.1016/j.actaastro.2019.09.026

Lopez-Leon, S., Wegman-Ostrosky, T., Perelman, C., Sepulveda, R., Rebolledo, P. A., Cuapio, A., & Villapol, S. (2021). More than 50 long-term effects of COVID-19: A systematic review and meta-analysis. *Scientific Reports, 11*(1), 1–12. doi:10.103841598-021-95565-8 PMID:34373540

López-Ornelas, E., & Hernández, S. H. S. (2016, July). Using infographics to represent meaning on social media. *In International Conference on Social Computing and Social Media* (pp. 25-33). Springer.

Lorenza, L., & Carter, D. (2021). Emergency online teaching during COVID-19: A case study of Australian tertiary students in teacher education and creative arts. *International Journal of Educational Research Open, 2*(100057), 1–8. doi:10.1016/j.ijedro.2021.100057 PMID:35059667

Lowi, T. (1964). American business, public policy, case studies, and political theory. *World Politics, 16*(4), 677–715. doi:10.2307/2009452

Lozano, C. S., Wüthrich, S., Büchi, J. S., & Sharma, U. (2022). The concerns about inclusive education scale: Dimensionality, factor structure, and development of a short-form version (CIES-SF). *International Journal of Educational Research, 111*(101913), 1–12.

Lufungulo, E., Mwila, K., Mudenda, S., Kampamba, M., Chulu, M., & Hikaambo, C. (2021). Online Teaching during COVID-19 Pandemic in Zambian Universities: Unpacking Lecturers' Experiences and the Implications for Incorporating Online Teaching in the University Pedagogy. *Creative Education, 12*(12), 2886–2904. doi:10.4236/ce.2021.1212216

Lu, M., Wang, C., Lanir, J., Zhao, N., Pfister, H., Cohen-Or, D., & Huang, H. (2020, April). Exploring visual information flows in infographics. In *Proceedings of the 2020 CHI Conference on Human Factors in Computing Systems* (pp. 1-12). ACM.

Lwoga, E. T., & Sife, A. S. (2018). Impacts of quality antecedents on faculty members' acceptance of electronic resources. *Library Hi Tech*.

Lyra, K. T., Isotani, S., Reis, R. C., Marques, L. B., Pedro, L. Z., Jaques, P. A., & Bitencourt, I. I. (2016, July). Infographics or graphics+ text: Which material is best for robust learning? In *2016 IEEE 16th International Conference on Advanced Learning Technologies (ICALT)* (pp. 366-370). IEEE.

Maas, K., & Liket, K. (2011). Social impact measurement: Classification of methods. In R. Burritt, S. Schaltegger, M. Bennett, T. Pohjola, & M. Csutora (Eds.), *Environmental Management Accounting and Supply Chain Management: Eco-Efficiency in Industry and Science* (Vol. 27). Springer. doi:10.1007/978-94-007-1390-1_8

Madan, S., Bylinskii, Z., Nobre, C., Tancik, M., Recasens, A., Zhong, K., Alsheikh, S., Oliva, A., Durand, F., & Pfister, H. (2021). Parsing and summarizing infographics with synthetically trained icon detection. *Proceedings of the 2021 IEEE 14th Pacfici Visualization Symposium (PacificVis)*. 31 – 40.

Madan, S., Bylinskii, Z., Tancik, M., Recasens, A., Zhong, K., Alsheikh, S., . . . Durand, F. (2018). *Synthetically trained icon proposals for parsing and summarizing infographics*. arXiv preprint arXiv:1807.10441.

Maeda, K., Hashimoto, H., & Sato, K. (2021). Creating a positive perception toward inclusive education with future-oriented thinking. *BMC Research Notes*, *14*(1), 1–4. doi:10.118613104-021-05882-4 PMID:34952632

Mahmood, S., Lodhi, H., & Fatima, Q. (2022). Transition to blended learning: Teachers' pedagogical beliefs, practices and challenges. *Harf-O-Sukhan, 6*(2), 253-270. Retrieved from https://harf-o-sukhan.com/index.php/Harf-o-sukhan/article/view/506

Mansour, E. (2021). Use of infographics as a technology-based information dissemination tool: The perspective of Egyptian public university libraries library staff. *Library Hi Tech*. Advance online publication. doi:10.1108/LHT-03-2021-0084

Maor, D. (2003). The teacher's role in developing interaction and reflection in an online learning community. *Educational Media International, 40*(1-2), 127-138. doi:10.1080/0952398032000092170

Maqableh, M., & Alia, M. (2021). Evaluation online learning of undergraduate students under lockdown amidst COVID-19 pandemic: The online learning experience and students' satisfaction. *Children and Youth Services Review*, *128*(106160), 1–11. doi:10.1016/j.childyouth.2021.106160

Marchionini, G. (2000). Evaluating digital libraries: A longitudinal and multifaceted view. *Library Trends*, *49*(2), 304–333.

Marchionini, G., Dwiggins, S., Katz, A., & Lin, X. (1993). Information seeking in full-text end-user-oriented search systems: The roles of domain and search expertise. *Library & Information Science Research*, *15*, 35–69.

Marchionini, G., & Fox, E. A. (1999). Progress toward digital libraries: Augmentation through integration. *Information Processing & Management*, *35*, 219–225.

Margulieux, L., Denny, P., Cunningham, K., Deutsch, M., & Shapiro, B. R. (2021, August). When wrong is right: The instructional power of multiple conceptions. In *Proceedings of the 17th ACM Conference on International Computing Education Research* (pp. 184-197). 10.1145/3446871.3469750

Marie, C., Boyer, H., & Collombo, M. G. (2020, June). *ASIS - Guideline #1 - Social impact evaluation and indicators*. http://de.alpine-space.eu/projects/asis/deliverables/wp3/guideline1-final.pdf

Marín-Díaz, V. (2020). ICT-based inclusive education. Encyclopedia of Education and Information Technologies, 868 – 1018.

Compilation of References

Marino, M. T., & Hayes, M. T. (2012). Promoting inclusive education, civic scientific literacy, and global citizenship with videogames. *Cultural Studies of Science Education*, 7(4), 945–954. doi:10.100711422-012-9429-8

Marinoni, G., vant Land, H., & Jenssen, T. (2020). The Impact of COVID-19 on Higher Education around the World: IAU Global survey report. Paris: International Association of Universities (IAU).

Martin, F., Ritzhaupt, A., Jumar, S., & Budhrani, K. (2019). Award-winning faculty online teaching practices: Course design, assessment and evaluation, and facilitation. *The Internet and Higher Education*, 42, 34–43. doi:10.1016/j.iheduc.2019.04.001

Martin, L. J., Turnquist, A., Groot, B., Huang, S. Y. M., Kok, E., Thoma, B., & van Merriënboer, J. J. G. (2019). Exploring the role of infographics for summarizing medical literature. *Health Profession Education*, 5, 48–57.

Martins, N., Alvelos, H., Chatterjee, A., Calado, I., & Quintela, M. (2020, July). Multimedia as mediator of knowledge between older generations and present-day students of art and design. In *2020 The 4th International Conference on Education and Multimedia Technology* (pp. 213-218). Academic Press.

Martins, N., Penedos-Santiago, E., Lima, C., Barreto, S., & Calado, I. (2020, November). Infographics of Wisdom: Study on the individual legacies of retired academics in art and design higher education and research. In *2020 The 4th International Conference on Education and E-Learning* (pp. 62-67). Academic Press.

Martín-Sómer, M., Moreira, J., & Casado, C. (2021). Use of Kahoot! to keep students' motivation during online classes in the lockdown period caused by Covid 19. *Education for Chemical Engineers*, 36, 154–159. doi:10.1016/j.ece.2021.05.005

Marzano, A., & Miranda, S. (2021). Online learning environments to stimulate in students the processes of mutual interaction between digital and analog artefacts to enhance student learning. *MethodsX*, 8(101440), 1–9. doi:10.1016/j.mex.2021.101440 PMID:34430329

Masadeh, T. S. Y. (2021). Blended learning: Issues related to successful implementation. *International Journal of Scientific Research and Management*, 9(10), 1897–1907. doi:10.18535/ijsrm/v9i10.el02

Mashroofa, M. M. (2021). Sustainability of library and information services during Covid-19 pandemic: A case of South Eastern University of Sri Lanka (SEUSL) Libraries. Academic Press.

Mateu, J., Lasala Bello, M. J., & Alamán, X. (2014, December). Virtual Touch Book: A Mixed-Reality Book for Inclusive Education. In *International Conference on Ubiquitous Computing and Ambient Intelligence* (pp. 124-127). Springer. 10.1007/978-3-319-13102-3_22

Mateu, J., Lasala, M. J., & Alamán, X. (2013). Tangible interfaces and virtual worlds: A new environment for inclusive education. In *Ubiquitous Computing and Ambient Intelligence. Context-Awareness and Context-Driven Interaction* (pp. 119–126). Springer. doi:10.1007/978-3-319-03176-7_16

Matrix, S., & Hodson, J. (2014). *Teaching with infographics: Practising new digital competencies and visual literacies.* Academic Press.

Matters, Q. (n.d.). *Specific review standards from the QM Higher Education Rubric* (6th ed.). https://www.qualitymatters.org/sites/default/files/PDFs/StandardsfromtheQMHigherEducationRubric.pdf

Mayer, R. E. (2002). Multimedia learning. *Psychology of Learning and Motivation*, 41, 85–139. doi:10.1016/S0079-7421(02)80005-6

Mayer, R. E., Hegarty, M., Mayer, S., & Campbell, J. (2005). When static media promote active learning: Annotated illustrations versus narrated animations in multimedia instruction. *Journal of Experimental Psychology. Applied*, 11(4), 256–265. doi:10.1037/1076-898X.11.4.256 PMID:16393035

Mbodila, M., & Muhandji, K. (2012, July). The use of ICT in Education: a comparison of traditional pedagogy and emerging pedagogy enabled by ICTs. *Proceedings of the 11th International Conference on Fontier in Education.*

Mc Sween-Cadieux, E., Chabot, C., Fillol, A., Saha, T., & Dagenais, C. (2021). Use of infographics as a health-related knowledge translation tool: Protocol for a scoping review. *BMJ Open, 11*(6), 1 – 7.

McCabe, J. (2009). Racial and gender microaggressions on a predominantly-White campus: Experiences of Black, Latina/o and White undergraduates. *Race, Gender, & Class,* 133–151.

McConlogue, T. (2020). Developing Inclusive Curriculum and Assessment Practices. *Assessment and Feedback in Higher Education: A Guide for Teachers,* 137-150.

McCray, E. D., & McHatton, P. A. (2011). Less afraid to have them in my classroom": Understanding pre-service general educators' perceptions about inclusion. *Teacher Education Quarterly, 38*(4), 135–155.

McDonald, J., & Postle, G. (1999). Teaching online: Challenge to a reinterpretation of traditional instructional models. AusWeb99, Lismore, NSW.

McGee, E. O. (2016). Devalued Black and Latino racial identities: A by-product of STEM college culture? *American Educational Research Journal, 53*(6), 1626–1662. doi:10.3102/0002831216676572

McGuire, S. Y. (2018). *Teach yourself how to learn: Strategies you can use to ace any course at any level.* Stylus Publishing, LLC.

McLeskey, J., & Waldron, N. L. (2015). Effective leadership makes schools truly inclusive. *Phi Delta Kappan, 96*(5), 68–73. doi:10.1177/0031721715569474

McPartlan, P., Rutherford, T., Rodriguez, F., Shaffer, J. F., & Holton, A. (2021). Modality motivation: Selection effects and motivational differences in students who choose to take courses online. *The Internet and Higher Education, 49*(100793), 1–14. doi:10.1016/j.iheduc.2021.100793

McSorley, K. (2020). Sexism and cisgenderism in music therapy spaces: An exploration of gender microaggressions experienced by music therapists. *The Arts in Psychotherapy, 71*(101707), 1–9. doi:10.1016/j.aip.2020.101707

Means, B., Bakia, M., & Murphy, R. (2014). *Learning online: What research tells us about whether, when and how.* Routledge. doi:10.4324/9780203095959

Meier, K. (1994). *The politics of sin: drugs, alcohol, and public policy.* Sharpe.

Melgaard, J., Monir, R., Lasrado, L. A., & Fagerstrøm, A. (2022). Academic procrastination and online learning during the COVID-19 pandemic. *Procedia Computer Science, 196,* 117–124. doi:10.1016/j.procs.2021.11.080 PMID:35035617

Memmer, M. K., & Worth, C. C. (1991). Retention of English-as-a-second-language (ESL) students: Approaches used by 21 generic baccalaureate nursing programs. *The Journal of Nursing Education, 30*(9), 389–396. doi:10.3928/0148-4834-19911101-04 PMID:1663540

Mendenhall, S., & Summers, S. (2015). Designing research: Using infographics to teach design thinking. composition. *Journal of Global Literacies, Technologies and Emerging Pedagogies, 3*(1), 359–371.

Menon, M. (2021, February 9). Household income from work for poor families in Singapore fell 69% last year due to Covid-19: Study. *The Straits Times.* https://www.straitstimes.com/singapore/household-income-from-work-for-poor-families-fell-69-last-year-due-to-covid-19-study-by

Compilation of References

Menon, M. (2021, March 4). Fewer elderly residents were satisfied with life during Covid-19 pandemic: SMU survey. *The Straits Times*. https://www.straitstimes.com/singapore/fewer-elderly-residents-were-satisfied-with-life-during-covid-19-pandemic-smu-survey

MERLOT Smart Search. (2022). *MERLOT*. Retrieved January 26, 2022, from https://info.merlot.org/merlothelp/MERLOT_Smart_Search.htm

Merriam, S. B., & Caffarella, R. S. (1999). *Learning in Adulthood: A Comprehensive Guide* (2nd ed.). Jossey-Bass Publishers.

Metinyurt, T., Haynes-Baratz, M. C., & Bond, M. A. (2021). A systematic review of interventions to address workplace bias: What we know, what we don't, and lessons learned. *New Ideas in Psychology, 63*(100879), 1–9. doi:10.1016/j.newideapsych.2021.100879

Michaelson, G. (2020). Programming Paradigms, Turing Completeness and Computational Thinking. *The Art, Science, and Engineering of Programming, 4*(3).

Microaggression. (2022, Feb. 10). In *Wikipedia*. Retrieved Feb. 22, 2022, from https://en.wikipedia.org/wiki/Microaggression

Microsoft. (2021). *Decarbonization. Explanimators-Episode 11*. Available at https://news.microsoft.com/stories/explanimators/decarbonization/

Miller, J. (2022, May 19). BLOG: UK online principles, priorities, wild possibilities. *University of Kentucky News*. https://uknow.uky.edu/campus-news/blog-uk-online-principles-priorities-wild-possibilities

Minikel-Lacocque, J. (2013). Racism, college, and the power of words: Racial microaggressions reconsidered. *American Educational Research Journal, 50*(3), 432–465.

Ministry of Health. (2022). *COVID-19: Daily Information updated, 21st July 2022*. Ministry of Health.

Ministry of Manpower. (2021, June 24). *Foreign workforce numbers*. https://www.mom.gov.sg/documents-and-publications/foreign-workforce-numbers

Ministry of Social and Family Development. (2017). *Family and Work – Insight Series, 4/2017*. https://www.msf.gov.sg/research-and-data/Research-and-Data-Series/Documents/Family%20and%20Work%20Report.pdf

Mishra, L., Gupta, T., & Shree, A. (2020). Online teaching-learning in higher education during the lockdown period of the COVID-19 pandemic. *International Journal of Educational Research Open, 1*, 100012. doi:10.1016/j.ijedro.2020.100012 PMID:35059663

Mississippi Legislature. (2022). *Mississippi House Bill 147*. 2022 Regular Session.

Mitchell, D. G., Morris, J. A., Meredith, J. M., & Bishop, N. (2017). Chemistry infographics: Experimenting with creativity and information literacy. In *Liberal arts strategies for the chemistry classroom* (pp. 113–131). American Chemical Society.

Mitchell, J. R., Mitchell, R. K., Hunt, R. A., Townsend, D. M., & Lee, J. H. (2020). Stakeholder engagement, knowledge problems and ethical challenges. *Journal of Business Ethics*, 1–20.

Mkhala, T., (2022). *Government allocates Faith's K65M to Students' bursaries*. Lusaka: News Diggers.

Mkhonta, N. (2022, Aug.). 5200 Children Orphaned by COVID-19 Pandemic. *Eswatini Times*.

Mohamad Rosman, M. R., Ismail, M. N., & Masrek, M. N. (2021). Investigating the predictors of digital library engagement: A structured literature analysis. *Pakistan Journal of Information Management and Libraries, 22*, 60–82.

Molina-Carmona, R., Villagrá-Arnedo, C., Gallego-Durán, F., & Llorens-Largo, F. (2017). Analytics-driven redesign of an instructional course. *Proceedings of TEEM 2017*, 1 – 7.

Moncrieff, J., Macauley, P., & Epps, J. (2007). ―My universe is here‖: Implications for the future of academic libraries from the results of a survey of teachers. *Australian Academic and Research Libraries*, *38*, 71–83. http://alianet.alia.org.au/

Moody, J. (2022). *A 5th straight semester of enrollment declines*. Retrieved from https://www.insidehighered.com/news/2022/05/26/nsc-report-shows-total-enrollment-down-41-percent?v2

Mooney, C., & Lee, M. (1995). Legislating morality in the American states: The case of pre-Roe abortion regulation reform. *American Journal of Political Science*, *39*(3), 599–627. doi:10.2307/2111646

Mooney, C., & Lee, M. (2000). The influence of values on consensus and contentious morality policy: U.S. death penalty reform, 1956-82. *The Journal of Politics*, *62*(1), 223–239. doi:10.1111/0022-3816.00011

Moonga, F. (2020). Civil Society Organisations, Higher Education Institutions, and Corporate Social Responsibility in Zambia. In Leadership Strategies for Promoting Social Responsibility in Higher Education (pp. 33-44). Emerald Publishing.

Moonga, F., Mabundza, L., & Hlatshwayo, P. (2022). Post COVID-19 Reforms in Higher Education in Eswatini. In Education reform in the Aftermath of the COVID-19 Pandemic (pp. 158-175). IGI Global.

Moonga, F. (2022). Africa's University Landscape: Embracing Digital Transformation. In A. Kaplan (Ed.), *Digital Transformation and Disruption of Higher Education* (pp. 60–72). doi:10.1017/9781108979146.008

Moore, J. (2008). *A synthesis of Sloan-C effective practices*. Retrieved from http://www.sloan- c.org/effective/v12n3_moore-2.pdf

Moore, G. C., & Benbasat, T. (1991). Development of an instrument to measure the perceptions of adopting an information technology innovation. *Information Systems Research*, *2*, 192–222.

Morales, E. M. (2014). Intersectional impact: Black students and race, gender and class microaggressions in higher education. *Race, Gender, & Class*, 48–66.

Moralista, R., & Oducado, R. M. (2020). *Faculty perception toward online education in higher education during the coronavirus disease 19 (COVID-19) pandemic*. doi:10.13189/ujer.2020.081044

Morris, M., Kuehn, K., Brown, J., Nurius, P., Zhang, H., Sefidgar, Y., Xu, X., Riskin, E., Dey, A., Consolvo, S., & Mankoff, J. (2021). College from home during COVID-19: A mixed-methods study of heterogeneous experiences. *PLoS One*, *16*(6), e0251580. Advance online publication. doi:10.1371/journal.pone.0251580 PMID:34181650

Moskal, P., Dziuban, C., & Hartman, J. (2013). Blended learning: A dangerous idea? *The Internet and Higher Education*, *18*, 15–23. doi:10.1016/j.iheduc.2012.12.001

Moyo, L. M. (2004). The virtual patron. *Science & Technology Libraries*, *25*, 185–209. doi:10.1300/J122v25n01_12

Mphahlele, R. S. (2020). Online learning support in a ubiquitous learning environment. In Managing and designing online courses in ubiquitous learning environments (pp. 1-18). IGI Global. doi:10.4018/978-1-5225-9779-7.ch001

Mthembu, M. V. (2021). Pro-Democracy protests in the Kingdom of Eswatini 2018-2019. In E. R. Sanches (Ed.), *Popular Protest, Political Opportunities and Change in Africa* (pp. 200–217). Routledge.

Muflih, S., Abuhammad, S., Al-Azzam, S., Alzoubi, K. H., Muflih, M., & Karasneh, R. (2021). Online learning for undergraduate health professional education during COVID-19: Jordanian medical students' attitudes and perceptions. *Heliyon*, *7*(9), e08031. doi:10.1016/j.heliyon.2021.e08031 PMID:34568607

Compilation of References

Muleya, G., Simui, F., Mundende, K., Kakana, F., Mwewa, G., & Namangala, B. (2019). Exploring learning cultures of digital immigrants in technologically mediated postgraduate distance learning mode at the University of Zambia. *Zambia ICT Journal, 3*(3), 1–10. doi:10.33260/zictjournal.v3i2.83

Müller, J., & Christandl, F. (2019). Content is king–But who is the king of kings? The effect of content marketing, sponsored content & user-generated content on brand responses. *Computers in Human Behavior, 96*, 46–55. doi:10.1016/j.chb.2019.02.006

Mulyono, H., Suryoputro, G., & Jamil, S. R. (2021). The application of WhatsApp to support online learning during the COVID-19 pandemic in Indonesia. *Heliyon, 7*(8), 1 - 8.

Munni, B. E., & Hasan, S. M. (2020). Teaching English during COVID-19 Pandemic Using Facebook Group as an LMS: A Study on Undergraduate Students of a University in Bangladesh. *Language in India, 20*(6).

Murakami, K. (2021). *Billions in Aid Head to Colleges.* Retrieved from https://www.insidehighered.com/news/2021/01/15/education-department-releases-billions-aid-colleges#:~:text=The%20U.S.%20Education%20Department%20on,through%20emergency%20student%20grants%20again

Murphy, L., Eduljee, N. B., & Croteau, K. (2020). College Student Transition to Synchronous Virtual Classes during the COVID-19 Pandemic in Northeastern United States. *Pedagogical Research, 5*(4). doi:10.29333/pr/8485

Murphy, T. M., Teng, J., & Matusky, R. (2014, November). Needs analysis for instructional technology projects. In *Proceedings of the 42nd annual ACM SIGUCCS conference on User services* (pp. 23-28). 10.1145/2661172.2661183

Murray, T. R. (1991). *The nature of values education in Southeast Asia.* Educational Resources Information Center (ERIC), ED 365 609. https://files.eric.ed.gov/fulltext/ED365609.pdf

Murray, A. D., Barton, C. J., Archibald, D., Glover, D., Murray, I. R., Barker, K., & Hawkes, R. A. (2018). Infographics and digital resources: An international consensus on golf and health. Business Journal of Sports Medicine. *BMJ (Clinical Research Ed.), 57*(22), 1421–1424.

Murray, I. R., Murray, A. D., Wordie, S. J., Oliver, C. W., Murray, A. W., & Simpson, A. H. R. W. (2017). Maximising the impact of your work using infographics. *Bone & Joint Research, 6*(11), 619–620.

Muthuprasad, T., Aiswarya, S., Aditya, K. S., & Jha, G. K. (2021). Students' perception and preference for online education in India during COVID-19 pandemic. *Social Sciences & Humanities Open, 3*(1), 1 - 11.

Muthuprasad, T., Aiswarya, S., Aditya, K. S., & Jha, G. K. (2021). Students' perception and preference for online education in India during covid -19 pandemic. *Social Sciences & Humanities Open, 3*(1), 100101. doi:10.1016/j.ssaho.2020.100101 PMID:34173507

Mwale, N., & Chita, J. (2020). Higher education and programme delivery in the context of COVID-19 and institutional closures: Student responses to the adoption of e-Learning at a public university in Zambia. In Technology-based teaching and learning in higher education during the time of COVID-19 (pp. 9-33). CSSALL Publishers (Pty) Ltd.

Nadal, K. L., King, R., Sissoko, D. G., Floyd, N., & Hines, D. (2021). The legacies of systemic and internalized oppression: Experiences of microaggressions, imposter phenomenon, and stereotype threat on historically marginalized groups. *New Ideas in Psychology, 63*(100895), 1–9.

Nadal, K. L., Sriken, J., Davidoff, K. C., Wong, Y., & McLean, K. (2013). Microaggressions within families: Experiences of multiracial people. *Family Relations, 62*(1), 190–201.

Naparin, H., & Saad, A. B. (2017). Infographics in education: Review on infographics design. *The International Journal of Multimedia & its Applications, 9*(4), 5, 15 – 24.

Naseri, Z., & Noruzi, A. (2018). Content marketing process model: A meta-synthesis of the literature. *Webology*, *15*(1), 8–18.

Nath, S. R., Roy, G., Rahman, M. H., Ahmed, K. S., & Chowdhury, A. M. R. (2014). New Vision Old Challenges: The State of Pre-primary Education in Bangladesh. In M. Mohsin, M. G. Mostafa & A. Begum (Eds.), Campaign for Popular Education (CAMPE). Academic Press.

National Archives. (2022*). Servicemen's Readjustment Act*. Retrieved from https://www.archives.gov/milestone-documents/servicemens-readjustment-act

National Association of Student Financial Aid Administrators. (2022a). *NASFAA higher education emergency relief reference page*. Retrieved from https://www.nasfaa.org/covid19_heerf

National Association of Student Financial Aid Administrators. (2022b). *NASFAA higher education emergency relief fund ii (HEEF II) reference page*. Retrieved from https://www.nasfaa.org/heerf_ii

National Association of Student Financial Aid Administrators. (2022c). *NASFAA higher education emergency relief fund iii (HEEF III) reference page*. Retrieved from https://www.nasfaa.org/heerf_iii

National Association of the Deaf v. Harvard and MIT. (2015). Retrieved from https://www.nad.org/2015/02/17/nad-sues-harvard-and-mit-for-discrimination-in-public-online-content/

National Center for Education Statistics. (2022). *College enrollment rates*. Retrieved from https://nces.ed.gov/programs/coe/indicator/cpb

National Center for Education Statistics. (n.d.). *Nontraditional undergraduates/Highlights*. https://nces.ed.gov/pubs/web/97578a.asp#:~:text=A%20nontraditional%20student%20was%20identified,or%20did%20not%20obtain%20a

National Conference of State Legislatures. (2021). *Full-and-part-time legislatures*. https://www.ncsl.org/research/about-state-legislatures/full-and-part-time-legislatures.aspx

National Conference of State Legislatures. (2022). *Postsecondary Bill Tracking Database*. Retrieved from https://www.ncsl.org/research/education/postsecondary-bill-tracking-database.aspx

National Institute of Statistics and Geography. (2015). *Intercensal survey 2015* [Encuesta intercensal 2015]. Retrieved July 23rd, 2022 from https://www.inegi.org.mx/programas/intercensal/2015/

National Institute of Statistics and Geography. (2018). *National Survey on Availability and Use of Information Technologies in Households 2018* [Encuesta Nacional sobre Disponibilidad y uso de Tecnologías de la Información en los Hogares 2018]. Retrieved July 23rd, 2022 from www.inegi.org.mx/programas/dutih/2018

National Institutes of Health. (2022). *Recover: Researching COVID to enhance recovery*. Retrieved from https://recovercovid.org/

National Library Board. (2014a). Civics and Moral Education is introduced. *History SG – An online resource guide*. https://eresources.nlb.gov.sg/history/events/7a63e9a1-c949-41d0-9b6f-d3853d832bb1

National Library Board. (2014b). Launch of National Education. *History SG – An online resource guide*. https://eresources.nlb.gov.sg/history/events/44fa0306-ddfe-41bc-8bde-8778ff198640

National Telecommunications and Information Administration. (2022). *Biden Administration announces more than $10 million in grants to expand high-speed Internet to minority-serving colleges and universities*. Retrieved from https://www.internetforall.gov/sites/default/files/2022-07/DOC-NTIA-CMC-Award-Announcement-Press-Release-7.22.22.pdf

Compilation of References

National University of Singapore. (2021). *Community Service*. https://nus.edu.sg/osa/student-life/student-organisations-directory/community-service

Naveh, G., Tubin, D., & Pliskin, N. (2010). Student LMS use and satisfaction in academic institutions: The organizational perspective. *The Internet and Higher Education, 13*(3), 127-133. doi:10.1016/j.iheduc.2010.02.004

Nebraska Legislature. (2021) *Nebraska Legislative Bill 200*. 107th Legislature.

Nelson, D. L. (1990). Individual adjustment to information-driven technologies: A critical review. *Management Information Systems Quarterly, 14*(1), 79–98.

Neto, J., Nolan, S., & Mendes, A. (2021, June). Planning and developing courses in distance learning environments: A training course for HiEdTec Project. In *International Conference on Computer Systems and Technologies' 21* (pp. 201-206). 10.1145/3472410.3472440

Neumann, M. D., Dion, L., & Snapp, R. (2021). *Teaching Computational Thinking: An Integrative Approach for Middle and High School Learning*. The MIT Press. doi:10.7551/mitpress/11209.001.0001

Newland, B., & Byles, L. (2014). Changing academic teaching with Web 2.0 technologies. *Innovations in Education and Teaching International, 51*(3), 315-325. doi:10.1080/14703297.2013.796727

Ng, D., & Panch, V. (2020, May 20). Facing circuit breaker blues, parents of young kids help each other in chat groups. *ChannelNewsAsia*. https://www.channelnewsasia.com/news/cnainsider/covid19-parents-chat-groups-whatsapp-facebook-12750732

Ng, J., Lei, L., Iseli-Chan, N., Li, J., Siu, F., Chu, S., & Hu, X. (2020). Non-repository Uses of Learning Management System through Mobile Access. *Journal of Educational Technology Development and Exchange, 13*(1), 1. doi:10.18785/jetde.1301.01

Ng, K. G. (2020, November 6). New task force to tackle mental health issues among migrant workers. *The Straits Times*. https://www.straitstimes.com/singapore/new-task-force-to-tackle-mental-health-issues-among-migrant-workers

Nguyen, X., Pho, D.-H., & Luong, D.-H., & Xuan-thuc-anh, C. A. O. (2021). Vietnamese students' acceptance of using video conferencing tools in distance learning in COVID-19 pandemic. *Turkish Online Journal of Distance Education, 22*(3), 139–162.

Nhan, L. K., & Yen, P. H. (2021a). The effects of using infographics-based learning on EFL learners' grammar retention. *International Journal of Science and Management Studies, 4*(I4), 225–265.

Nhan, L. K., & Yen, P. H. (2021b). The impact of using infographics to teach grammar on EFL students' learning motivation. *European Journal of Foreign Language Teaching, 5*(5), 85–102.

Nicholas, D. (2008). The information seeking behaviour of the virtual scholar: From use to users. *Serials, 21*, 89-92. Retrieved from http://serials.uksg.org

Nicholas, M., & Tomeo, M. (2005). Can you hear me now? Communicating library services to distance education students and faculty. *Online Journal of Distance Learning Administration, 8*(2), 1–8. https://www.westga.edu/~distance/ojdla/ search_results_id.php?id=298

Nichols, M. (2008). Institutional perspectives: The challenges of e-learning diffusion. *British Journal of Educational Technology, 39*(4), 598-609. doi:10.1111/j.1467-8535.2007.00761.x

Nilson, L. B., & Goodson, L. A. (2018). *Online teaching at its best: Merging instructional design with teaching and learning research*. Jossey-Bass.

Nivas, S., Gokul, C. J., Banahatti, V., & Lodha, S. (2021, August). Visuals Triumph in a Curious Case of Privacy Policy. *In IFIP Conference on Human-Computer Interaction* (pp. 732-741). Springer.

Nkosi, L. (2020). *Ministry of Health Press statement COVID-19 Update, 17th April, 2020.* Ministry of Health.

Noh, M. A. M., Fauzi, M. S. H. M., Jing, H. F., & Ilias, M. F. (2017). Infographics: Teaching and learning tool. *Malaysian Online Journal of Education, 1*(1), 58–63.

Noori, A. Q. (2021). The impact of COVID-19 pandemic on students' learning in higher education in Afghanistan. *Heliyon, 7*(10), 1 - 9.

Norberg, A., Dziuban, C., & Moskal, P. (2011). A time based blended learning model. *On the Horizon, 19*(3), 207–216. doi:10.1108/10748121111163913

Nordahl-Pedersen, H., & Heggholmen, K. (2022). What promotes motivation and learning in project management students? *Procedia Computer Science, 196,* 791–799. doi:10.1016/j.procs.2021.12.077

North Carolina General Assembly. (2021). *North Carolina Senate Bill 706.* Session 2021.

Northey, G., Bucic, T., Chylinski, M., & Govind, R. (2015). Increasing student engagement using asynchronous learning. *Journal of Marketing Education, 37*(3), 171–180. doi:10.1177/0273475315589814

Nortvig, A. M., Petersen, A. K., & Balle, S. (2018). *A literature review of the factors influencing e-learning and blended learning in relation to learning outcome, student satisfaction and engagement.* https://www.semanticscholar.org/paper/A-literature-review-of-the-factors-influencing-and-Nortvig-Petersen/1462df81936e74422d9d365b851c769a72784222

Novak, K. (2022). *UDL Now! A teacher's guide to applying universal design for learning in today's classrooms* (3rd ed.). CAST, Inc.

O'Brien, S., & Lauer, C. (2018, August). Testing the susceptibility of users to deceptive data visualizations when paired with explanatory text. In *Proceedings of the 36th ACM International Conference on the Design of Communication* (pp. 1-8). ACM.

O'Dowd, O. (2018). Microaggressions: A Kantian account. *Ethical Theory and Moral Practice, 21*(5), 1219–1232.

O'Neal, J. (2021). *How a Car Engine Works.* Available at https://animagraffs.com/how-a-car-engine-works/

O'Riordan, L., & Fairbrass, J. (2014). Managing CSR stakeholder engagement: A new conceptual framework. *Journal of Business Ethics, 125*(1), 121–145. doi:10.100710551-013-1913-x

Obiakor, F. E., Harris, M., Mutua, K., Rotatori, A., & Algozzine, B. (2012). Making inclusion work in general education classrooms. *Education & Treatment of Children, 35*(3), 477–490.

Occa, A., & Suggs, L. S. (2016). Communicating breast cancer screening with young women: An experimental test of didactic and narrative messages using video and infographics. *Journal of Health Communication, 21*(1), 1–11.

OECD. (2019). *Education at a Glance 2019: OECD Indicators.* OECD. doi:10.1787/f8d7880d-

Office of Postsecondary Education. (2021). *Cares Act: Higher education emergency relief fund.* Retrieved from https://www2.ed.gov/about/offices/list/ope/caresact.html#:~:text=This%20bill%20allotted%20%242.2%20trillion,Emergency%20Relief%20Fund%2C%20or%20HEERF

Oh, H. (2021). The Association Between Discriminatory Experiences and Self-Reported Health Status among Asian Americans and Its Subethnic Group Variations. *Journal of Racial and Ethnic Health Disparities,* 1–8.

Compilation of References

Okamoto, T., Anma, F., Nagata, N., & Kayama, M. (2009, September). The organizational knowledge circulated management on e-learning practices in universities-through the case study in UEC. In *2009 IEEE/WIC/ACM International Joint Conference on Web Intelligence and Intelligent Agent Technology* (Vol. 3, pp. 219-222). IEEE. 10.1109/WI-IAT.2009.267

Oliver, M., & Trigwell, K. (2005). Can 'Blended Learning' be redeemed? *E-Learning and Digital Media, 2*(1), 17–26. doi:10.2304/elea.2005.2.1.17

Olmos, S., Mena, J., Torrecilla, E., & Iglesias, A. (2015). Improving graduate students' learning through the use of Moodle. *Educational Research Review, 10*(5), 604–614. doi:10.5897/ERR2014.2052

Olson-Morrison, D., Radohl, T., & Dickey, G. (2019). Strengthening Field Education: An Integrated Model for Signature Pedagogy in Social Work. *InSight: A Journal of Scholarly Teaching, 14*, 55-73.

Omotayo, F. O., & Haliru, A. (2020). Perception of task-technology fit of digital library among undergraduates in selected universities in Nigeria. *Journal of Academic Librarianship, 46*(1), 102097.

Onah, D., & Sinclair, J. (2017). Assessing self-regulation of learning dimensions in a stand-alone MOOC platform. *International Journal of Engineering Pedagogy, 7*(2), 4-21. doi:10.3991/ijep.v7i2.6511

Online Computer Library Center (OCLC). (2002). *OCLC white paper on the information habits of college students.* Retrieved from Online Computer Library Center website: http://www5.oclc.org/downloads/community/informationhabits.pdf

Opertti, R., Brady, J., & Duncombe, L. (2009). Moving forward: Inclusive education as the core of education for all. *Prospects, 39*(3), 205–214.

Opoku, E. K., Chen, L. H., & Permadi, S. (2022). The dissertation journey during the COVID-19 pandemic: Crisis or opportunity? *Journal of Hospitality, Leisure, Sport & Tourism Education, 30*, 1-9.

Orey, B., Smooth, W., Adams, K., & Harris-Clark, K. (2006). Race and gender matter: Refining models of legislative policy making in state legislatures. *Journal of Women, Politics & Policy, 28*(3-4), 97–119. doi:10.1300/J501v28n03_05

Organisation for Economic Co-operation and Development. (2015). *Policy Brief on Social Impact Measurement for Social Enterprises: Policies for Social Entrepreneurship.* Luxembourg: Publications Office of the European Union. https://www.oecd.org/social/PB-SIM-Web_FINAL.pdf

Orth, C., & Bastiaens, T. (2008, June). Situated multimedia learning for older adults: Exploring the benefits of age-specific instructional design. In EdMedia+ Innovate Learning (pp. 3864-3879). Association for the Advancement of Computing in Education (AACE).

Ossola, M. (2016). Indigenous Peoples and Higher Education in Argentina: Emerging Debates [Pueblos indígenas y educación superior en la Argentina: debates emergentes]. *Revista del Cisen Tramas/Maepova, 4*(1), 57-77. http://ppct.caicyt.gov.ar/index.php/cisen/index

Ott, C., Robins, A., & Shephard, K. (2014, November). An infographic to support students' self-regulated learning. In *Proceedings of the 14th Koli Calling International Conference on Computing Education Research* (pp. 177-178). Academic Press.

Owston, R., York, D., & Malhotra, T. (2018). Blended learning in large enrolment courses: Student perceptions across four different instructional models. *Australasian Journal of Educational Technology.* Advance online publication. doi:10.14742/ajet.4310

Oyarzo, F. (2011). Competencies for the 21st century: Integrating ICT to life, school and economical development. *Procedia: Social and Behavioral Sciences, 28*, 54–57. doi:10.1016/j.sbspro.2011.11.011

Özdal, H., & Ozdamli, F. (2017). The Effect of Infographics in Mobile Learning: Case Study in Primary School. *Journal of Universal Computer Science*, *23*(12), 1256–1275.

Ozdamlı, F., Kocakoyun, S., Sahin, T., & Akdag, S. (2016). Statistical reasoning of impact of infographics on education. *Procedia Computer Science*, *102*, 370–377.

Ozdamli, F., & Ozdal, H. (2018). Developing an instructional design for the design of infographics and the evaluation of infographic usage in teaching based on teacher and student opinions. *Eurasia Journal of Mathematics, Science and Technology Education*, *14*(4), 1197–1219.

Padilla, T. (2009). The Rural Normal Schools: History and nation project [Las Normales Rurales: historia y proyecto de nación]. *El Cotidiano*, *154*, 85–93.

Palahicky, S., & Halcomb-Smith, L. (2020). Utilizing Learning Management System (LMS) Tools to Foster Innovative Teaching. In Handbook of Research on Innovative Pedagogies and Best Practices in Teacher Education (pp. 1-17). IGI Global. doi:10.4018/978-1-5225-9232-7.ch001

Panday, P. K. (2020, September 2). Online classes and lack of interactiveness. *Daily Sun*. https://www.daily-sun.com/printversion/details/502935

Pandya, B., Patterson, L., & Cho, B. (2021). Pedagogical transitions experienced by higher education faculty members – "Pre-COVID to COVID". *Journal of Applied Research in Higher Education*. doi:10.1108/JARHE-01-2021-0028

Papić, A., & Sušilović, S. (2018, May). Students' preferences regarding the transfer of information and knowledge through infographics tools. In *2018 41st International Convention on Information and Communication Technology, Electronics and Microelectronics (MIPRO)* (pp. 574-579). IEEE.

Pappano, L. (2012). The Year of the MOOC. *The New York Times, 2*(12).

Parasuraman, A., Zeithaml, V. A., & Berry, L. L. (1985). A conceptual model of service quality and its implications for future research. *Journal of Marketing*, *49*(4), 41–50. doi:10.1177/002224298504900403

Parasuraman, A., Zeithaml, V. A., & Berry, L. L. (1986). *Servqual: A multiple item scale for measuring consumer perceptions of service quality*. Marketing Science Institute.

Park, J., & Seo, M. (2021). Influencing factors on nursing students' learning flow during the COVID-19 pandemic: A mixed method research. *Asian Nursing Research*, 1 - 10.

Parker, K. (2021). *What's behind the growing gap between men and women in college completion?* Retrieved from https://www.pewresearch.org/fact-tank/2021/11/08/whats-behind-the-growing-gap-between-men-and-women-in-college-completion/

Parker, P. C., Perry, R. P., Hamm, J. M., Chipperfield, J. G., Pekrun, R., Dryden, R. P., Daniels, L. M., & Tze, V. M. (2021). A motivation perspective on achievement appraisals, emotions, and performance in an online learning environment. *International Journal of Educational Research*, *108*(101772), 1–16. doi:10.1016/j.ijer.2021.101772

Park, N., Lee, K. M., & Cheong, P. H. (2007). University instructors' acceptance of electronic courseware: An application of the Technology Acceptance Model. *Journal of Computer-Mediated Communication*, *13*(1). http://jcmc.indiana.edu/vol13/issue1/park.html

Park, N., Roman, R., Lee, S., & Chung, J. E. (2009). User acceptance of a digital library system in developing countries: An application of the technology acceptance model. *International Journal of Information Management*, *29*, 196–209. doi:10.1016/j.ijinfomgt.2008.07.001

Compilation of References

Partner Relations Team. (2020). *Update on the Impact of COVID-19 to Eswatini*. Bulembu Ministries.

Pasternack, S., & Utt, S. H. (1990). Reader use & understanding of newspaper infographics. *Newspaper Research Journal*, *11*(2), 28–41.

Paudel, P. (2020). Online education: Benefits, challenges and strategies during and after COVID-19 in higher education. *International Journal on Studies in Education*, *3*(2), 70–85. doi:10.46328/ijonse.32

Paul, B. V., Finn, A., Chaudhary, S., Mayer Gukovas, R., & Sundaram, R. (2021). *COVID-19, Poverty, and Social Safety Net Response in Zambia*. Policy Research Working Paper, 9571. Washington, DC: The World Bank.

Pavazza, S., & Pap, K. (2012). The alternative way of creating infographics using SVG technology. *Acta graphica: znanstveni časopis za tiskarstvo i grafičke komunikacije, 23*(1-2), 45-56.

Payton, F. C., Yarger, L. K., & Pinter, A. T. (2018). (Text) mining microaggressions literature: Implications impacting black computing faculty. *The Journal of Negro Education*, *87*(3), 217–229.

Pearce, S. (2019). 'It was the small things': Using the concept of racial microaggressions as a tool for talking to new teachers about racism. *Teaching and Teacher Education*, *79*, 83–92.

Pedrini, M., & Ferri, L. M. (2019). Stakeholder management: A systematic literature review. *Corporate Governance: The International Journal of Business in Society*, *19*(1), 44–59. doi:10.1108/CG-08-2017-0172

PepsiCo. (2022). *Stakeholder Engagement*. Available at https://www.pepsico.com/our-impact/esg-topics-a-z/stakeholder-engagement

Perera, W. P. G. L., & Suraweera, S. A. D. H. N. (2021). *The Academic Library Support for E-Learning: Students' Perspectives and Web Observation*. Academic Press.

Perrini, F., & Tencati, A. (2006). Sustainability and stakeholder management: The need for new corporate performance evaluation and reporting systems. *Business Strategy and the Environment*, *15*(5), 296–308. doi:10.1002/bse.538

Perry, E. H., & Pilati, M. L. (2011). Online learning. *New Directions for Teaching and Learning*, *128*, 95–104.

Peters, D. (2013). *Interface design for learning: Design strategies for learning experiences*. Pearson Education.

Petillion, R. J., & McNeil, W. S. (2020). Student experiences of emergency remote teaching: Impacts of instructor practice on student learning, engagement, and well-being. *Journal of Chemical Education*, *97*(9), 2486–2493.

Petrovskaya, A., Pavlenko, D., Feofanov, K., & Klimov, V. (2020). Computerization of learning management process as a means of improving the quality of the educational process and student motivation. *Procedia Computer Science*, *169*, 656–661. doi:10.1016/j.procs.2020.02.194

Phuong, A. E., Nguyen, J., & Marie, D. (2017). Evaluating an adaptive equity-oriented pedagogy: A study of its impacts in higher education. *The Journal of Effective Teaching*, *17*(2), 5–44. Retrieved June 29, 2022, from https://uncw.edu/jet/articles/vol17_2/phuong.html

Picciano, A. (2006). Blended learning: Implications for growth and access. *Journal of Asynchronous Learning Networks*, *10*(3). Advance online publication. doi:10.24059/olj.v10i3.1758

Pierce, C. M., Carew, J. V., Pierce-Gonzalez, D., & Wills, D. (1977). An experiment in racism: TV commercials. *Education and Urban Society*, *10*(1), 61–87.

Pinho, C., Franco, M., & Mendes, L. (2020). Exploring the conditions of success in e-libraries in the higher education context through the lens of the social learning theory. *Information & Management*, *57*(4), 103208.

Pinto, J. C. (2017). The relevance of digital infographics in online newspapers. *Proceedings of the 5th Mediterranean Interdisciplinary Forum on Social Sciences and Humanities*, 428 – 434.

Piper, T. H. (2010). *What policy changes do experts recommend K-12 instructional leaders enact to support the implementation of online instruction and learning?* (Doctoral Dissertation). https://www.proquest.com/openview/591508c7 8e9964e2168c757ae82abab8/1?pq-origsite=gscholar&cbl=18750&diss=y

Pisarenko, V., & Bondarev, M. (2016). Infographics use in teaching foreign languages for specific purposes. *Recent Patents on Computer Science, 9*(2), 1–9.

Pittman, C. T. (2012). Racial microaggressions: The narratives of African American faculty at a predominantly White university. *The Journal of Negro Education, 81*(1), 82–92.

Pollak, M. & Ebner, M. (2019). The Missing Link to Computational Thinking. *Future Internet, 11*(12).

Poon, J. (2012). Use of blended learning to enhance the student learning experience and engagement in property education. *Property Management, 30*(2), 129–156. Advance online publication. doi:10.1108/02637471211213398

Poon, J. (2013). Blended learning: An institutional approach for enhancing students' learning experiences. *Journal of Online Learning and Teaching, 9*(2), 271–288. https://dro.deakin.edu.au/view/DU:30057995

Porzak, R., Cwynar, A., & Cwynar, W. (2021). Improving debt literacy by 2/3 through four simple infographics requires numeracy and not focusing on negatives of debt. *Frontiers in Psychology, 12*(621312), 1–19.

Power, C., & Paige, R. (2009, July). Content personalization for inclusive education through model-driven engineering. In *International Conference on Universal Access in Human-Computer Interaction* (pp. 102-109). Springer.

Prempeh, C. (2022). Polishing the pearls of indigenous knowledge for inclusive social education in Ghana. *Social Sciences & Humanities Open, 5*(1), 1 - 9.

Pressley, J. (2022, May 25). *Online learning can help minimize racism and ableism in and out of the classroom.* EdTech. https://edtechmagazine.com/higher/article/2022/05/online-learning-can-help-minimize-racism-and-ableism-and-out classroom

Public Law 116-136 (2020). *Coronavirus, Aid, Relief, and Economic Security Act.*

Public Law 78-346 (1944). *Servicemen's Readjustment Act.*

Public Law 85-864 (1958). *National Defense Education Act.*

Public Law 89-329 (1965). *Higher Education Act of 1965.*

Public Utilities Board. (2020, March 9). *Make Every Drop Count: Continuing Singapore's Water Success - Better appreciation of Singapore's water journey to inspire generations of water users.* Press Release. https://www.pub.gov.sg/news/pressreleases/MakeEveryDropCountContinuingSingaporesWaterSuccess

Public Utilities Board. (2021, April 16). *About the Smart Water Meter Programme.* https://www.pub.gov.sg/smartwatermeterprogramme/about

Purchase, H. C., Isaacs, K., Bueti, T., Hastings, B., Kassam, A., Kim, A., & van Hoesen, S. (2018, June). A classification of infographics. In *International Conference on Theory and Application of Diagrams* (pp. 1 - 8). Springer.

Purnama, S., Ulfah, M., Machali, I., Wibowo, A., & Narmaditya, B. S. (2021). Does digital literacy influence students' online risk? Evidence from Covid-19. *Heliyon, 7*(6), 1 - 6.

Compilation of References

Pyramid of Hate. (2018). *Anti-Defamation League*. Retrieved May 15, 2022, from https://www.adl.org/sites/default/files/documents/pyramid-of-hate.pdf

Qian, C., Sun, S., Cui, W., Lou, J. G., Zhang, H., & Zhang, D. (2020). Retrieve-then-adapt: Example-based automatic generation for proportion-related infographics. *IEEE Transactions on Visualization and Computer Graphics, 27*(2), 443–452.

Quayyum, M. A., & Chowdhury, O. M. A. (2016, September 4). Natural disasters and uninterrupted education. *The Daily Star*. https://www.thedailystar.net/op-ed/natural-disasters-and-uninterrupted-education-1280044

Quester, P., Wilkinson, J. W., & Romaniuk, S. (1995). *A test of four service quality measurement scales: the case of the Australian advertising industry*. Working Paper 39, Centre de Recherche et d'Etudes Appliquees, Group esc Nantes Atlantique, Graduate School of Management.

Quijada, K. Y. (2021). Affirmative actions for the university inclusion of Afro-descendant and indigenous students in Brazil, Colombia and Mexico [Acciones afirmativas para la inclusión universitaria de estudiantes afrodescendientes e indígenas en Brasil, Colombia y México]. *Ciencia y Cultura, 46*, 135–162. http://www.scielo.org.bo/pdf/rcc/v25n46/v25n46_a07.pdf

Quiroz Reyes, C. (2020). Covid-19 Pandemic and Territorial Inequality: The Aggravation of Educational Inequalities in Chile [Pandemia Covid-19 e Inequidad Territorial: El agravamiento de las Desigualdades Educativas en Chile]. *Revista Internacional de Educación para la Justicia Social, 9*(3), 1–6.

Rad, F. A., Otaki, F., Baqain, Z., Zary, N., & Al-Halabi, M. (2021). Rapid transition to distance learning due to COVID-19: Perceptions of postgraduate dental learners and instructors.] *PLoS One, 16*(2), e0246584.

Rafique, G. M., Mahmood, K., Warraich, N. F., & Rehman, S. U. (2021). Readiness for Online Learning during COVID-19 pandemic: A survey of Pakistani LIS students. *The Journal of Academic Librarianship, 47*(3), 1 - 10.

Rafique, H., Almagrabi, A. O., Shamim, A., Anwar, F., & Bashir, A. K. (2020). Investigating the acceptance of mobile library applications with an extended technology acceptance model (TAM). *Computers & Education, 145*, 103732.

Rafique, H., Alroobaea, R., Munawar, B. A., Krichen, M., Rubaiee, S., & Bashir, A. K. (2021). Do digital students show an inclination toward continuous use of academic library applications? A case study. *Journal of Academic Librarianship, 47*(2), 102298.

Rafique, H., Anwer, F., Shamim, A., Minaei-Bidgoli, B., Qureshi, M. A., & Shamshirband, S. (2018). Factors affecting acceptance of mobile library applications: Structural equation model. *Libri, 68*(2), 99–112.

Rahiem, M. D. (2021). Remaining motivated despite the limitations: University students' learning propensity during the COVID-19 pandemic. *Children and Youth Services Review, 120*(105802), 1–14. doi:10.1016/j.childyouth.2020.105802 PMID:33318719

Rahman, A. R. A., & Mohezar, S. (2020). Ensuring continued use of a digital library: A qualitative approach. *The Electronic Library, 38*(3), 513–530.

Ramírez García, R. G., Pérez Colunga, B. Y., Soto Bernabé, A. K., Mendoza Tovar, M., Coiffier López, F. Y., Gleason Guevara, K. J., & Flores Zuñiga, J. A. (2017). Disassembling the puzzle around the experience of preparing a master's thesis [Desarmando el rompecabezas en torno a la experiencia de elaboración de una tesis de maestría]. *Perfiles educativos, 39*(155), 68-86.

Rasmitadila, R., Widyasari, W., Humaira, M., Tambunan, A., Rachmadtullah, R., & Samsudin, A. (2020). Using blended learning approach (BLA) in inclusive education course: A study investigating teacher students' perception. *International Journal of Emerging Technologies in Learning, 15*(2), 72–85. doi:10.3991/ijet.v15i02.9285

Rasmussen, B., Hutchinson, A., Lowe, G., Wynter, K., Redley, B., Holton, S., Manias, E., Phillips, N., McDonall, J., McTier, L., & Kerr, D. (2022). The impact of COVID-19 on psychosocial well-being and learning for Australian nursing and midwifery undergraduate students: A cross-sectional survey. *Nurse Education in Practice*, *58*(103275), 1–9. doi:10.1016/j.nepr.2021.103275 PMID:34922092

Rasmussen, B., & Salhani, D. (2010). A contemporary Kleinian contribution to understanding racism. *The Social Service Review*, *84*(3), 491–513.

Rau, M. A., Aleven, V., Rummel, N., & Rohrbach, S. (2013, April). Why interactive learning environments can have it all: resolving design conflicts between competing goals. In *Proceedings of the SIGCHI Conference on Human Factors in Computing Systems* (pp. 109-118). 10.1145/2470654.2470670

Rawhauser, H., Cummings, M., & Newbert, S. L. (2019, January). Social impact measurement: Current approaches and future directions for social entrepreneurship research. *Entrepreneurship Theory and Practice*, *43*(1), 82–115. doi:10.1177/1042258717727718

Razak, R. A., & See, Y. C. (2010). Improving academic achievement and motivation through online peer learning. *Proceedings of WCLTA 2010, 358 – 352.*

Reid, H., Milton, K., Bownes, G., & Foster, C. (2017). Making physical activity evidence accessible: Are these infographics the answer? *British Journal of Sports Medicine*, *51*(10), 764–766.

Reiken, S., Sittenfeld, L., Dridi, H., Liu, Y., Liu, X., & Marks, A. R. (2022). Alzheimer's-like signaling in brains of COVID-19 patients. *Alzheimer's & Dementia*, *18*(5), 955–965. doi:10.1002/alz.12558 PMID:35112786

Reinhold, F., Schons, C., Scheuerer, S., Gritzmann, P., Richter-Gebert, J., & Reiss, K. (2021). Students' coping with the self-regulatory demand of crisis-driven digitalization in university mathematics instruction: Do motivational and emotional orientations make a difference? *Computers in Human Behavior*, *120*(106732), 1–10. doi:10.1016/j.chb.2021.106732

Reiser, R. A. (2001). A history of instructional design and technology: Part I: A history of instructional media. *Educational Technology Research and Development*, *49*(1), 53–64. doi:10.1007/BF02504506

Remuzzi, A., & Remuzzi, G. (2020). COVID-19 and Italy: What next? *Lancet*, *395*(10231), 1225–1228. doi:10.1016/S0140-6736(20)30627-9 PMID:32178769

Reparaz, C., Aznárez-Sanado, M., & Mendoza, G. (2020). Self-regulation of learning and MOOC retention. *Computers in Human Behavior*, *111*, 106423.

Republik Indonesia. (2020, December 3). Kementerian Pendidikan dan Kebudayaan » Republik Indonesia. Retrieved September 30, 2022, from https://www.kemdikbud.go.id/main/blog/2020/12/perkuliahan-dapat-dilakukan-secara-tatap-muka-dan-dalam-jaringan-tahun-2021

Resolution Agreement. (2015). *National Federation of the Blind*. Retrieved from https://nfb.org/images/nfb/documents/pdf/higher-ed-toolkit/sou-agreement.pdf

Resolution Agreement. (2016). *National Federation of the Blind*. Retrieved from https://www.wichita.edu/services/mrc/access/_documents/wichita-state-agreement-redacted.pdf

Reynaga-Peña, C. G., Myers, C., Fernández-Cárdenas, J. M., Cortés-Capetillo, A. J., Glasserman-Morales, L. D., & Paulos, E. (2020, July). Makerspaces for inclusive education. In *International Conference on Human-Computer Interaction* (pp. 246-255). Springer.

Rezaei, N., & Sayadian, S. (2015). The impact of infographics on Iranian EFL learners' grammar learning. *Journal of Applied Linguistics and Language Research*, *2*(1), 78–85.

Compilation of References

Richards, G., & DeVries, I. (2011, February). Revisiting formative evaluation: dynamic monitoring for the improvement of learning activity design and delivery. In *Proceedings of the 1st international conference on learning analytics and knowledge* (pp. 157-162). 10.1145/2090116.2090141

Richardson, J. T. (2015). Coursework versus examinations in end-of-module assessment: A literature review. *Assessment & Evaluation in Higher Education, 40*(3), 439–455. doi:10.1080/02602938.2014.919628

Ricks, S. A. (2018). Normalized Chaos: Black Feminism, Womanism, and the (Re) definition of Trauma and Healing. *Meridians (Middletown, Conn.), 16*(2), 343–350.

Ricoy, C. (2006). Contribution on research paradigms [Contribución sobre los paradigmas de investigación]. *Revista do Centro Educação, 31*(1), 11–11.

Rivo, K., & Žumer, M. (2022). Academic Libraries and Use of Mobile Devices: Case Study of Slovenia. *Journal of Academic Librarianship, 48*(3), 102507.

Roberts, T. S. (2005). Computer-supported collaborative learning in higher education. In Computer-supported collaborative learning in higher education (pp. 1-18). IGI Global.

Rochefort, D. A., & Cobb, R. W. (1994). *The politics of problem definition.* University Press.

Roche, S. (2016). Education for all: Exploring the principle and process of inclusive education. *International Review of Education, 62*(2), 131–137.

Rodés, V., Mustaro, P. N., Silveira, I. F., Omar, N., & Ochôa, X. (2014, September). Instructional design models to support collaborative open books for open education. In *Proceedings of the XV International Conference on Human Computer Interaction* (pp. 1-7). 10.1145/2662253.2662346

Rogers, C. (2007). Experiencing an 'inclusive' education: Parents and their children with 'special educational needs'. *British Journal of Sociology of Education, 28*(1), 55–68.

Roschelle, J., Rafanan, K., Bhanot, R., Estrella, G., Penuel, B., Nussbaum, M., & Claro, S. (2010). Scaffolding group explanation and feedback with handheld technology: Impact on students' mathematics learning. *Educational Technology Research and Development, 58*(4), 399–419. doi:10.100711423-009-9142-9

Rose, E. (2017). Cause for optimism: Engaging in a vital conversation about online learning. *Foundations of Science, 22*(2), 373–376. doi:10.100710699-015-9445-8

Rosenberg, D. (2015). Against infographics. *Art Journal, 74*(4), 38–57.

Rosman, M. R. M., Ismail, M. N., Masrek, M. N., Branch, K., & Campus, M. (2019). Investigating the determinant and impact of digital library engagement: A conceptual framework. *Journal of Digital Information Management, 17*(4), 215.

Ross, B., & Gage, K. (2006). Blended learning: Global perspectives from WebCT and our customers in higher education. In C. J. Bonk & C. R. Graham (Eds.), *Handbook of blended learning: Global perspectives, local designs* (pp. 155–168). Pfeiffer.

Roth, M. (2015). Moodle: Ten Years On. *GSTF Journal on Education, 3*(1).

Rotolo, S. M., Jain, S., Dhaon, S., Dokhanchi, J. K., Kalata, E., Shah, T., ... Arora, V. M. (2021). (Preprint). A coordinated strategy to develop and distribute infographics addressing COVID-19 vaccine hesitancy and misinformation. *Journal of the American Pharmacists Association*, 1–8.

Rowley, J. (2008). Understanding digital content marketing. *Journal of Marketing Management, 24*(5-6), 517–540. doi:10.1362/026725708X325977

Roy, G. (2018). *Massive open online courses among Bengali-speaking people: Participation patterns, motivations and challenges about data analysis* [Master's thesis, University of Twente]. Student Theses. https://essay.utwente.nl/76043/

Roy, G., Babu, R., Kalam, M. A., Yasmin, N., Zafar, T., & Nath, S. R. (2021). *Response, readiness and challenges of online teaching amid COVID-19 pandemic: the case of higher education in Bangladesh.* Educational and Developmental Psychologist. doi:10.1080/20590776.2021.1997066

Rusli, R., Rahman, A., & Abdullah, H. (2020). Student perception data on online learning using heutagogy approach in the Faculty of Mathematics and Natural Sciences of Universitas Negeri Makassar, Indonesia. *Data in Brief, 29*(105152), 1–6. doi:10.1016/j.dib.2020.105152 PMID:32025542

Rust, R. T., & Zahorik, A. J. (1993). Customer satisfaction, customer retention, and market share. *Journal of Retailing, 69*(2), 193–215. doi:10.1016/0022-4359(93)90003-2

Rutherfoord, R. H., & Rutherfoord, J. K. (2007). Universal instructional design for learning how to apply in a virtual world. *Proceedings of SIGITE '07*, 141 - 146. 10.1145/1324302.1324332

Rutherfoord, R. H., & Rutherfoord, J. K. (2008). Exploring teaching methods for on-line course delivery—Using universal instructional design. *Proceedings of SIGITE '08*, 45 – 50.

Rutherfoord, R. H., & Rutherfoord, J. K. (2008-2009). Universal instructional design – An approach to designing & delivering on-line and hybrid courses. *Methods (San Diego, Calif.), 1*, 2.

Safi'i, A., Muttaqin, I., Hamzah, N., Chotimah, C., Junaris, I., & Rifa'i, M. K. (2021). The effect of the adversity quotient on student performance, student learning autonomy and student achievement in the COVID-19 pandemic era: evidence from Indonesia. *Heliyon, 7*(12), 1 – 8.

Safonov, M. A., Usov, S. S., Arkhipov, S. V., & Sorokina, L. P. (2021, January). SWOT analysis of mobile applications in the high education e-learning of the Chinese language. In *2021 12th International Conference on E-Education, E-Business, E-Management, and E-Learning* (pp. 89-94). 10.1145/3450148.3450208

Salas, L. (2018). The educational policy of the Mexican state in relation to the initial training of teachers in rural normal schools [La política educativa del estado mexicano en relación a la formación inicial del profesorado de las escuelas normales rurales]. *Didácticas Específicas, 4*, 77–95.

Saleem, N., Al-Suqri, M., & Ahmed, S. (2016). Acceptance of Moodle as a teaching/learning tool by the faculty of the department of Information Studies at Sultan Qaboos University, Oman based on UTAUT. *International Journal of Knowledge Content Development and Technology, 6*(2), 5–27. doi:10.5865/IJKCT.2016.6.2.005

Saleh, B., Dontcheva, M., Hertzmann, A., & Liu, Z. (2015). *Learning style similarity for searching infographics.* arXiv preprint arXiv:1505.01214.

Salim, M. S., Saad, M. N., & Nor, B. M. (2021, August). Comparative Study of Low-Cost Tools to Create Effective Educational Infographics Content. In *2021 11th IEEE International Conference on Control System, Computing and Engineering (ICCSCE)* (pp. 23-28). IEEE. 10.1109/ICCSCE52189.2021.9530848

Salis, F., & Rodhes, B. (2021). Trauma informed care during a global pandemic: Synergies and multidisciplinary boundaries for working with childhood, adolescence, senility and disability. *Education Sciences & Society-Open Access, 12*(1), 149–163. Advance online publication. doi:10.3280/ess1-2021oa11822

Samuels, C., & Prothero, A. (July 29, 2020). *Could the 'Pandemic Pod' be a lifeline to parents or a threat to equality?* Retrieved from https://www.edweek.org/ew/articles/2020/07/29/could-the-pandemic-pod-be-a-lifeline.html

Compilation of References

San Pedro, T. J. (2015). Silence as shields: Agency and resistances among Native American students in the urban Southwest. *Research in the Teaching of English*, 132–153.

Sanchez, R. (2017). Doing disability with others. *Negotiating disability: Disclosure and higher education*, 211-225.

Sandeen, C. (2013). Integrating MOOCs into traditional higher education: The emerging "MOOC 3.0" era. *Change: The magazine of higher learning, 45*(6), 34-39.

Sandulache, S. (2019, October 13). *Natural disaster in Bangladesh*. Adrabangladesh. https://www.adrabangladesh.org/single-post/2019/10/13/natural-disaster-in-bangladesh

Sansone, C., Smith, J. L., Thoman, D. B., & MacNamara, A. (2012). Regulating interest when learning online: Potential motivation and performance trade-offs. *The Internet and Higher Education, 15*(3), 141–149. doi:10.1016/j.iheduc.2011.10.004

Savage, R. (1978). Policy innovativeness as a trait of American states. *The Journal of Politics, 40*(1), 212–219. doi:10.2307/2129985

Savini, C. A., Gasull, V. L., & Gimeno, P. B. (2019, March). Infographics. A way to increase competences. In *2019 IEEE World Conference on Engineering Education (EDUNINE)* (pp. 1-6). IEEE.

Savva, M., & Nygaard, L. P. (2021). The 'Peripheral' Student in Academia: An Analysis. In *Becoming a Scholar: Cross-cultural Reflections on Identity and Agency in an Educational Doctorate* (pp. 154–172). UCL Press.

Schamber, L., Eisenberg, M., & Nilan, M. S. (1990). A re-examination of relevance: Toward a dynamic, situational definition, Information Processing and Management. *International Journal (Toronto, Ont.), 26*(6), 755–776.

Schibuk, E. (2020). Visualizing the environmental effects of electronics. *Science Scope, 43*(5), 52–61. doi:10.2505/4s20_043_05_52

Schiemer, M. (2017). Inclusive Education and the UN Convention on the Rights of Persons with Disabilities (UNCRPD). In *Education for Children with Disabilities in Addis Ababa, Ethiopia* (pp. 175-186). Springer.

Schmelkes, S. (2013). Education and indigenous peoples: Measurement problems [Educación y pueblos indígenas: problemas de medición]. *Realidad, Datos y Espacio: Revista Internacional de Estadistica y Geografia, 4*(1), 5–13.

Schmits, E., Dekeyser, S., Klein, O., Luminet, O., Yzerbyt, V., & Glowacz, F. (2021). Psychological Distress among Students in Higher Education: One Year after the Beginning of the COVID-19 Pandemic]. *International Journal of Environmental Research and Public Health, 18*(14), 7445. doi:10.3390/ijerph18147445

Schöngut, N., & Pujol, J. (2015). Methodological stories: Diffracting narrative experiences of research [Relatos metodológicos: difractando experiencias narrativas de investigación]. *Forum Qualitative Social Research, 16*(2), 24.

Schultz, J. L., & Higbee, J. L. (2011). Implementing integrated multicultural instructional design in management education. *American Journal of Business Education, 4*(12), 13–22. doi:10.19030/ajbe.v4i12.6609

Schultz, R. B., & DeMers, M. N. (2020). Transitioning from emergency remote learning to deep online learning experiences in geography education]. *The Journal of Geography, 119*(5), 142–146. doi:10.1080/00221341.2020.1813791

Schumacher, C., & Ifenthaler, D. (2021). Investigating prompts for supporting students' self-regulation–A remaining challenge for learning analytics approaches? *The Internet and Higher Education, 49*(100791), 1–12. doi:10.1016/j.iheduc.2020.100791

Scott, C. L. (2015). *The futures of Learning 3: What kind of pedagogies for the 21st century?* https://unesdoc.unesco.org/images/0024/002431/243126e.pdf

Scott, H., Fawkner, S., Oliver, C., & Murray, A. (2016). Why healthcare professionals should know a little about infographics. *British Journal of Sports Medicine*, *50*(18), 1104–1105.

Selvaraj, A., Radhin, V., Nithin, K. A., Benson, N., & Mathew, A. J. (2021). Effect of pandemic based online education on teaching and learning system. *International Journal of Educational Development*, *85*(102444), 1–11. doi:10.1016/j.ijedudev.2021.102444 PMID:34518732

Sengupta, E., Blessinger, P., & Mahoney, C. (2020). Introduction to Leadership Strategies for promoting Social Responsibility in Higher Education. In E. Sengupta, P. Blessinger, & C. Mahoney (Eds.), *Civil Society and Social Responsibility in Higher Education: International Perspectives on Leadership and Strategies* (pp. 3–13). Emarald Publishing Ltd. doi:10.1108/S2055-364120200000024003

Senn, G. J. (2008). *Comparison of face-to-face and hybrid delivery of a course that requires technology skills development.* https://www.researchgate.net/publication/220590646_Comparison_of_Face-To-Face_and_Hybrid_Delivery_of_a_Course_that_Requires_Technology_Skills_Development

Sensuse, D. I., Rochman, H. N., Al Hakim, S., & Winarni, W. (2020). Knowledge management system design method with joint application design (JAD) adoption. *VINE Journal of Information and Knowledge Management Systems*, *51*(1), 27–46. doi:10.1108/VJIKMS-10-2018-0083

Shahriar, S. H. B., Arafat, S., Sultana, N., Akter, S., Khan, M. M. R., Nur, J. E. H., & Khan, S. I. (2021). The transformation of education during the corona pandemic: Exploring the perspective of the private university students in Bangladesh. *Asian Association of Open Universities Journal, 16*(2), 161-176. https://www.emerald.com/insight/content/doi/10.1108/AAOUJ-02-2021-0025/full/html

Shahzad, A., Hassan, R., Aremu, A. Y., Hussain, A., & Lodhi, R. N. (2021). Effects of COVID-19 in E-learning on higher education institution students: The group comparison between male and female. *Quality & Quantity*, *55*(3), 805–826. doi:10.100711135-020-01028-z PMID:32836471

Shalubala, C. (2022). Successful Teacher Recruitment Excites Government. Lusaka: News Diggers.

Shanks, J. D., Izumi, B., Sun, C., Martin, A., & Byker Shanks, C. (2017). Teaching undergraduate students to visualize and communicate public health data with infographics. *Frontiers in Public Health*, *5*(315), 1–6.

Shapiro, H. B., Lee, C. H., Roth, N. E. W., Li, K., Çetinkaya-Rundel, M., & Canelas, D. A. (2017). Understanding the massive open online course (MOOC) student experience: An examination of attitudes, motivations, and barriers. *Computers & Education*, *110*, 35–50. doi:10.1016/j.compedu.2017.03.003

Sharon and Frank. (2020). *Views on Digital Libraries* [PowerPoint slides]. https://u.cs.biu.ac.il/~franka2/download/ird665/ird3-2_lib.ppt

Shih, H. F., Chen, S. H. E., Chen, S. C., & Wey, S. C. (2013). The relationship among tertiary level EFL students' personality, online learning motivation and online learning satisfaction. *Procedia: Social and Behavioral Sciences*, *103*, 1152–1160. doi:10.1016/j.sbspro.2013.10.442

Shih, H.-P. (2004). Extended technology acceptance model of Internet utilization behavior. *Information & Management*, *41*(6), 719–729.

Shim, T. E., & Lee, S. Y. (2020). College students' experience of emergency remote teaching due to covid-19. *Children and Youth Services Review*, *119*, 105578. doi:10.1016/j.childyouth.2020.105578 PMID:33071405

Shin, T. S., Ranellucci, J., & Roseth, C. J. (2017). Effects of peer and instructor rationales on online students' motivation and achievement. *International Journal of Educational Research*, *82*, 184–199. doi:10.1016/j.ijer.2017.02.001

Compilation of References

Shisley, S. (2020). Emergency remote learning compared to online learning. *Learning Solutions.* https://learningsolutionsmag.com/articles/emergency-remote-learning-compared-to-online-learning

Shivdas, A., Menon, D. G., & Nair, C. S. (2020). *Antecedents of acceptance and use of a digital library system: Experience from a tier 3 Indian city.* The Electronic Library.

Shi, Y., Tong, M., & Long, T. (2021). Investigating relationships among blended synchronous learning environments, students' motivation, and cognitive engagement: A mixed methods study. *Computers & Education, 168*(104193), 1–15. doi:10.1016/j.compedu.2021.104193

Shotton, H. J. (2017). "I Thought You'd Call Her White Feather": Native Women and Racial Microaggressions in Doctoral Education. *Journal of American Indian Education, 56*(1), 32–54.

Silipigni. (2008). Make room for the Millennials. *NextSpace, 10*, 18-19. Retrieved from https://www.oclc.org/nextspace

Singal, N. (2006). An ecosystemic approach for understanding inclusive education: An Indian case study. *European Journal of Psychology of Education, 21*(3), 239–252.

Singapore Institute of Technology. (2021, March 5). *Enabling more persons with disabilities for jobs in technology industry.* https://www.singaporetech.edu.sg/sitizen-buzz/project-dust/

Singapore Management University. (2021, March 23). *Community Service.* https://www.smu.edu.sg/campus-life/community-service

Singapore University of Social Sciences. (2021). *Office of Service-Learning & Community Engagement.* https://www.suss.edu.sg/about-suss/college-of-lifelong-experiential-learning/cel/office-of-service-learning-community-engagement

Singh, J., Singh, L., & Matthees, B. (2022). Establishing Social, Cognitive, and Teaching Presence in Online Learning—A Panacea in COVID-19 Pandemic, Post Vaccine and Post Pandemic Times. *Journal of Educational Technology Systems, 51*(1), 28–45. Advance online publication. doi:10.1177/00472395221095169

Singh, V., & Thurman, A. (2019). How many ways can we define online learning? A systematic literature review of definitions of online learning (1988-2018). *American Journal of Distance Education, 33*(4), 289–306. doi:10.1080/08923647.2019.1663082

Siricharoen, W. V. (2013, May). Infographics: the new communication tools in digital age. In *The International Conference on E-technologies and Business on the Web* (pp. 169-174). Academic Press.

Siricharoen, W. V. (2013). Infographics: An approach of innovative communication tool for e-entrepreneurship marketing. *International Journal of E-Entrepreneurship and Innovation, 4*(2), 54–71. doi:10.4018/ijeei.2013040104

Skinta, M., & Torres-Harding, S. (2022). Confronting microaggressions: Developing innovative strategies to challenge and prevent harm. *New Ideas in Psychology, 65*(100921), 1–5.

Slade, C., Lawrie, G., Taptamat, N., Browne, E., Sheppard, K., & Matthews, K. E. (2021). Insights into how academics reframed their assessment during a pandemic: Disciplinary variation and assessment as afterthought. *Assessment & Evaluation in Higher Education, 47*(4), 588–605. doi:10.1080/02602938.2021.1933379

Smalley, A. (2022). *Legislative preview: Affordability, free speech among trends in higher education.* Retrieved from https://www.ncsl.org/research/education/legislative-preview-affordability-free-speech-among-trends-in-higher-education-magazine2022.aspx

Smith, K., & Hill, J. (2019). Defining the nature of blended learning through its depiction in current research. *Higher Education Research & Development, 38*(2), 383–397. doi:10.1080/07294360.2018.1517732

Smith, W. A., Hung, M., & Franklin, J. D. (2011). Racial battle fatigue and the miseducation of Black men: Racial microaggressions, societal problems, and environmental stress. *The Journal of Negro Education*, 63–82.

Smyth, S., Houghton, C., Cooney, A., & Casey, D. (2012). Students' experiences of blended learning across a range of postgraduate programmes. *Nurse Education Today*, *32*(4), 464–468. doi:10.1016/j.nedt.2011.05.014 PMID:21645947

Snow, M. A., & Brinton, D. M. (1988). Content-based language instruction: Investigating the effectiveness of the adjunct model. *TESOL Quarterly*, *22*(4), 553–574. doi:10.2307/3587256

Sohail, E. (2018, January 26). A digital education for a digital Bangladesh? *Dhaka Tribune*. https://archive.dhakatribune.com/opinion/2018/01/26/digital-education-digital-bangladesh

Solorzano, D., Ceja, M., & Yosso, T. (2000). Critical race theory, racial microaggressions, and campus racial climate: The experiences of African American college students. *The Journal of Negro Education*, 60–73.

Soltani-Nejad, N., Taheri-Azad, F., Zarei-Maram, N., & Saberi, M. K. (2020). Developing a model to identify the antecedents and consequences of user satisfaction with digital libraries. *Aslib Journal of Information Management*.

Song, Y., Lee, Y., & Lee, J. (2022). Mediating effects of self-directed learning on the relationship between critical thinking and problem-solving in student nurses attending online classes: A cross-sectional descriptive study. *Nurse Education Today*, *109*(105227), 1–5. doi:10.1016/j.nedt.2021.105227 PMID:34972030

Spiegelhalter, D., Pearson, M., & Short, I. (2011). Visualizing uncertainty about the future. *Science, 333*(6048), 1393-1400.

Spink, A., Greisdorf, H., & Bateman, J. (1998). From highly relevant to not relevant: Examining different regions of relevance. *Information Processing & Management*, *34*(5), 599–621.

Spitzer, M. W. H., Gutsfeld, R., Wirzberger, M., & Moeller, K. (2021). Evaluating students' engagement with an online learning environment during and after COVID-19 related school closures: A survival analysis approach. *Trends in Neuroscience and Education*, *25*(100168), 1–8. doi:10.1016/j.tine.2021.100168 PMID:34844697

Spotify. (2019). *The Top Songs, Artists, Playlists, and Podcasts of 2019—and the Last Decade*. Available at https://newsroom.spotify.com/2019-12-03/the-top-songs-artists-playlists-and-podcasts-of-2019-and-the-last-decade/

Srivastava, N., Nawaz, S., Lodge, J. M., Velloso, E., Erfani, S., & Bailey, J. (2020, March). Exploring the usage of thermal imaging for understanding video lecture designs and students' experiences. In *Proceedings of the Tenth International Conference on Learning Analytics & Knowledge* (pp. 250-259). 10.1145/3375462.3375514

Staff, R. (2020). Zambia Records First Coronavirus Death. *Reuters*, (April), 2.

Starr, J. P. (2020). Public school priorities in a political year: The 52nd Annual PDK Poll of the Public's Attitudes Toward the Public Schools. *Phi Delta Kappan*, *102*(1), K1–K16. doi:10.1177/0031721720956844

State Higher Education Executive Officers Association. (2021). State Higher Education Finance: FY 2020. Author.

State of Illinois. (2022). *Illinois House 5311*. 102nd General Assembly.

State of New York. (2021). *New York A 361*. 2021-2022 Regular Sessions.

Stein, D. S., Wanstreet, C. E., Calvin, J., Overtoom, C., & Wheaton, J. E. (2005). Bridging the transactional distance gap in online learning environments. *American Journal of Distance Education*, *19*(2), 105–118. https://doi.org/10.1207/s15389286ajde1902_4

Stephan, E., Cheng, D. T., & Young, L. M. (2006). A usability survey at the University of Mississippi libraries for the improvement of the library home page. *Journal of Academic Librarianship*, *32*, 35–51.

Compilation of References

Stevick, E. (1996). *Memory, meaning and method*. Newbury House.

Stewart, A. R., Harlow, D. B., & DeBacco, K. (2011). Students' experience of synchronous learning in distributed environments. *Distance Education*, *32*(3), 357–381.

Stewart, M. K. (2021). Social presence in online writing instruction: Distinguishing between presence, comfort, attitudes, and learning. *Computers and Composition*, *62*, 102669. doi:10.1016/j.compcom.2021.102669

Steyn, A. A., Botha, A. J., Coetzee, D., & Villiers, M. D. (2020, July). Interactive Learning: Introducing a First-Year Systems' Analysis and Design Course. *In Annual Conference of the Southern African Computer Lecturers' Association* (pp. 171-186). Springer.

Stiglitz, J. (2020). Conquering the Great Divide: The pandemic has laid bare deep divisions, but it's not too late to change course. *International Monetary Fund – Finance and Development Point of View*. https://www.imf.org/external/pubs/ft/fandd/2020/09/pdf/COVID19-and-global-inequality-joseph-stiglitz.pdf

Stockham, M., & Turtle, E. (2004). Providing off-campus library services by —Team‖: An assessment. *Journal of Library Administration*, *41*(3/4), 443–452. doi:10.1300/ J111v41n03_09

Storevik, M. (2015). *A study of vocationalisation of English in Norwegian upper secondary schools. "Why do I need Norwegian and English? I'm training to become a carpenter"* [Master thesis]. Retrieved from https://bora.uib.no/bora-xmlui/handle/1956/10611

Stover, S., & Holland, C. (2018). Student Resistance to Collaborative Learning. *International Journal for the Scholarship of Teaching and Learning*, *12*(2), 8.

Strauss, A., & Corbin, J. (2002). *Bases of qualitative research. Techniques and procedures to develop grounded theory* [Bases de la investigación cualitativa. Técnicas y procedimientos para desarrollar la teoría fundamentada]. Universidad de Antioquía.

Suárez-Orozco, C., Casanova, S., Martin, M., Katsiaficas, D., Cuellar, V., Smith, N. A., & Dias, S. I. (2015). Toxic rain in class: Classroom interpersonal microaggressions. *Educational Researcher*, *44*(3), 151–160.

Subedi, S., Nayaju, S., Subedi, S., Shah, S. K., & Shah, J. M. (2020). Impact of e-learning during COVID-19 pandemic among nurshing students and teachers of Nepal. *International Journal of Science and Healthcare Research*, *5*(3), 68–76.

Sudakov, I., Bellsky, T., Usenyuk, S., & Polyakova, V. V. (2016). Infographics and mathematics: A mechanism for effective learning in the classroom. *PRIMUS (Terre Haute, Ind.)*, *26*(2), 1–22.

Sue, D. W., Capodilupo, C. M., Torino, G. C., Bucceri, J. M., Holder, A., Nadal, K. L., & Esquilin, M. (2007). Racial microaggressions in everyday life: Implications for clinical practice. *The American Psychologist*, *62*(4), 271.

Suneeth, B. G., Kashyap, S., Reddy, G. M., & Kaushal, V. (2021). Resilience adaptations in tourism education for the post-COVID-19 era - a study of India. In *Tourism Destination Management in a Post-Pandemic Context* (pp. 291–302). Emerald Publishing Limited. doi:10.1108/978-1-80071-511-020211020

Supiano, B. (2022, January 20). The attendance conundrum: Students find policies inconsistent and confusing. They have a point. *The Chronicle of Higher Education*. https://www.chronicle.com/article/the-attendance-conundrum

Susinos, T., & Parrilla, A. (2008). Give voice in inclusive research. Debates on inclusion and exclusion from a biographical-narrative approach [Dar la voz en la investigación inclusiva. Debates sobre inclusión y exclusión desde un enfoque biográfico-narrativo]. *Revista Electrónica Iberoamericana sobre Calidad, Eficacia y Cambio en Educación*, *6*(2), 151–171.

Svenson, M., & Baelo, R. (2015). Teacher Students' Perceptions of their Digital Competence. *Procedia: Social and Behavioral Sciences*, *180*(5), 1527–1534. doi:10.1016/j.sbspro.2015.02.302

Szadziewska, A., & Kujawski, J. (2017). *Advantages and disadvantages of the blended-learning method used in the educational process at the faculty of management at the University of GDANSK, in the opinion of undergraduate students.* doi:10.21125/iceri.2017.1051

Szołtysik, M. (2017). Processes of creating infographics for data visualization. In *Complexity in Information Systems Development* (pp. 167–184). Springer.

Szopiński, T., & Bachnik, K. (2022). Student evaluation of online learning during the COVID-19 pandemic. *Technological Forecasting and Social Change*, *174*, 121203. doi:10.1016/j.techfore.2021.121203 PMID:34531617

Tamez-Robledo, N., Koenig, R., & Young, J. (2022, May 17). *The pandemic's lasting lessons for colleges, from academic innovation leaders.* EdSurge. https://www.edsurge.com/news/2022-05-17-the-pandemic-s-lasting-lessons-for-colleges-from-academic-innovation-leaders

Tan, C. (2013). For group, (f)or self: Communitarianism, Confucianism and values education in Singapore. *Curriculum Journal*, *24*(4), 478–493. doi:10.1080/09585176.2012.744329

Tan, D. Y., & Cheah, C. W. (2021). Developing a gamified AI-enabled online learning application to improve students' perception of university physics. *Computers and Education: Artificial Intelligence*, *2*(100032), 1–10. doi:10.1016/j.caeai.2021.100032

Tang, Y. M., Chen, P. C., Law, K. M., Wu, C. H., Lau, Y. Y., Guan, J., He, D., & Ho, G. T. (2021). Comparative analysis of Student's live online learning readiness during the coronavirus (COVID-19) pandemic in the higher education sector. *Computers & Education*, *168*(104211), 1–17. doi:10.1016/j.compedu.2021.104211 PMID:33879955

Taquet, M., Sillett, R., Zhu, L., Mendel, J., Camplisson, I., Dercon, Q., & Harrison, P. J. (2022). Neurological and psychiatric risk trajectories after SARS-CoV-2 infection: An analysis of 2-year retrospective cohort studies including 1 284 437 patients. *The Lancet. Psychiatry*, *9*(10), 815–827. doi:10.1016/S2215-0366(22)00260-7 PMID:35987197

Tarkhova, L., Tarkhov, S., Nafikov, M., Akhmetyanov, I., Gusev, D., & Akhmarov, R. (2020). Infographics and their application in the educational process. *International Journal of Emerging Technologies in Learning*, *15*(13), 63–80.

Taspolat, A., Kaya, O. S., Sapanca, H. F., Beheshti, M., & Ozdamli, F. (2017). An investigation toward advantages, design principles and steps of infographics in education. *Il Ponte*, *73*(7), 157–166.

Ten Ways to Fight Hate. (2017). Southern Poverty Law Center.

Teo, C. B., & Gay, R. K. L. (2006). A knowledge-driven model to personalize e-learning. *Journal of Educational Resources in Computing*, *6*(1), 1–15. doi:10.1145/1217862.1217865

Teo, T., Doleck, T., Bazelais, P., & Lemay, D. J. (2019). Exploring the drivers of technology acceptance: A study of Nepali school students. *Educational Technology Research and Development*, *67*(2), 495–517.

Terabe, S., Tanno, K., Yaginuma, H., & Kang, N. (2020). The Impact of Flyer with Infographics on Public Awareness and Interest to Transportation Project. *Transportation Research Procedia*, *48*, 2378–2384.

The Daily Star. (2020a). Conduct academic activities online during closure: UGC to universities. *The Daily Star*. https://www.thedailystar.net/country/news/conduct-academic-activities-online-during-closure-ugc-universities-1884748

The Daily Star. (2020b). UGC urges univs to continue classes online. *The Daily Star*. https://www.thedailystar.net/city/news/ugc-urges-univs-continue-classes-online-1885063

Compilation of References

The Financial Express. (2020). *UGC suggests universities introducing online education.* The Financial Express. https://thefinancialexpress.com.bd/national/ugc-suggests-universities-introducing-online-education-1584975932

The Financial Express. (2022). *UGC directs implementation of blended learning.* The Financial Express. https://thefinancialexpress.com.bd/education/ugc-directs-implementation-of-blended-learning-1655035062

The Kalamazoo Promise. (n.d.) *The Kalamazoo Promise.* Retrieved from https://www.kalamazoopromise.com

The Kingdom of Eswatini. (2013). *Higher Education Act, 2013.* Author.

The Kingdom of Eswatini. (2018). *National Education and Training Sector Policy.* Author.

The Kingdom of Eswatini. (2020). The Disaster Management (Coronavirus-COVID-19) Regulations 2020. Author.

The Scottish Government. (2015). *Literature Review on the Impact of Digital Technology on Learning and Teaching.* ICF Consulting Services Ltd.

The, B., & Mavrikis, M. (2016, April). A study on eye fixation patterns of students in higher education using an online learning system. In *Proceedings of the Sixth International Conference on Learning Analytics & Knowledge* (pp. 408-416). 10.1145/2883851.2883871

Theobald, M. (2021). Self-regulated learning training programs enhance university students' academic performance, self-regulated learning strategies, and motivation: A meta-analysis. *Contemporary Educational Psychology, 66*(101976), 1–19. doi:10.1016/j.cedpsych.2021.101976

Thepwongsa, I., Sripa, P., Muthukumar, R., Jenwitheesuk, K., Virasiri, S., & Nonjui, P. (2021). The effects of a newly established online learning management system: The perspectives of Thai medical students in a public medical school. *Heliyon, 7*(10), 1 - 7.

Thibodeau, T. (2021, June 6). *The science and research behind the UDL framework.* Novak Education. https://www.novakeducation.com/blog/the-science-and-research-behind-the-udl-framework#:~:text=The%20Introduction%20of%20Universal%20Design,Center%20for%20Applied%20Specialized%20Technology

Thomas, C., & La Raja, J. (2012). Parties and elections. In V. Gray, R. Hanson, & T. Kousser (Eds.), *Politics in the American states: A comparative analysis* (10th ed., pp. 63–104). CQ Press.

Thompson, C. M. (2015). Creating "visual legacies": Infographics as a means of interpreting and sharing research. *Communication Teacher, 29*(2), 91–101.

Thong, J. Y. L., Hong, W., & Tam, K.-Y. (2002). Understanding user acceptance of digital libraries: What are the roles of interface characteristics, organizational context, and individual differences? *International Journal of Human-Computer Studies, 57*, 215–242.

Tiedt, J. A., Owens, J. M., & Boysen, S. (2021). The effects of online course duration on graduate nurse educator student engagement in the community of inquiry. *Nurse Education in Practice, 55*(103164), 1–8. doi:10.1016/j.nepr.2021.103164 PMID:34371480

Timmons, V. (2009). *Overcoming barriers to inclusivity: Preparing preservice teachers for diversity* (Vol. 334). Counterpoints.

Tipton, C. J. (2002). *Academic libraries and distance learners: A study of graduate student perceptions of the effectiveness of library support for distance learning* (Doctoral dissertation). Available from ProQuest Dissertations and Theses database. (UMI No. 3060910)

Tithi, N. (2021, September 26). Blended learning is what we will need in the coming days. *The Daily Star*. https://www.thedailystar.net/opinion/interviews/news/blended-learning-what-we-will-need-the-coming-days-2183941

Tkachyk, R. E. (2013). Questioning secondary inclusive education: Are inclusive classrooms always best for students? *Interchange, 44*(1), 15–24.

Topîrceanu, A. (2017). Gamified learning: A role-playing approach to increase student in-class motivation. *Procedia Computer Science, 112*, 41–50. doi:10.1016/j.procs.2017.08.017

Toth, C. (2013). Revisiting a genre: Teaching infographics in business and professional communication courses. *Business Communication Quarterly, 76*(4), 446–457.

Tóth, Z. E., & Surman, V. (2019). Listening to the voice of students, developing a service quality measuring and evaluating framework for a special course. *International Journal of Quality and Service Sciences, 11*(4), 455–472. doi:10.1108/IJQSS-02-2019-0025

Trejo-Quintana, J. (2020). The lack of access to and use of means and technologies: two deudas of education in Mexico [La falta de acceso y aprovechamiento de los medios y las tecnologías: dos deudas de la educación en México]. In *Educación y pandemia: una visión académica* (pp. 122-129). Universidad Nacional Autónoma de México, Instituto de Investigaciones sobre la Universidad y la Educación. https://www.iisue.unam.mx/nosotros/covid/educacion-y-pandemia

Trines, S. (2019, January 8). *Education in Bangladesh*. https://wenr.wes.org/2019/08/education-in-bangladesh

Tsai, M. N., Liao, Y. F., Chang, Y. L., & Chen, H. C. (2020). A brainstorming flipped classroom approach for improving students' learning performance, motivation, teacher-student interaction and creativity in a civics education class. *Thinking Skills and Creativity, 38*(100747), 1–11. doi:10.1016/j.tsc.2020.100747

Tsai, P. S., & Liao, H. C. (2021). Students' progressive behavioral learning patterns in using machine translation systems– A structural equation modeling analysis. *System, 101*(102594), 1–13. doi:10.1016/j.system.2021.102594

Tsai, S. T., Huang, H. Y., & Chang, T. W. (2020). Developing a Motion Infographic-Based Learning System for Effective Learning. *Education in Science, 10*(9), 247. doi:10.3390/educsci10090247

Tseng, H., Yi, X., & Yeh, H. T. (2019). Learning-related soft skills among online business students in higher education: Grade level and managerial role differences in self-regulation, motivation, and social skill. *Computers in Human Behavior, 95*, 179–186. doi:10.1016/j.chb.2018.11.035

Tseng, S. C., & Tsai, C. C. (2010). Taiwan college students' self-efficacy and motivation of learning in online peer assessment environments. *The Internet and Higher Education, 13*(3), 164–169. doi:10.1016/j.iheduc.2010.01.001

Tshabalala, M., Ndeya-Ndereya, C., & Merwe, T. (2014). Implementing blended learning at a developing university: Obstacles in the way. *Electronic Journal of E-Learning, 12*, 101–110. https://eric.ed.gov/?id=EJ1020735

Tuncali, E. (2016). The infographics which are designed for environmental issues. *Global Journal on Humanities & Social Sciences*, 14 – 19.

Turk, M., Heddy, B. C., & Danielson, R. W. (2022). Teaching and social presences supporting basic needs satisfaction in online learning environments: How can presences and basic needs happily meet online? *Computers & Education, 104432*, 1–15. doi:10.1016/j.compedu.2022.104432

Tyagi, S. K., Sharma, S. K., & Gaur, A. (2022). Determinants of continuous usage of library resources on handheld devices: Findings from PLS-SEM and fuzzy sets (fsQCA). *The Electronic Library,* ahead-of-print.

Compilation of References

Tymchenko, O., Vasiuta, S., Khamula, O., Sosnovska, O., & Dudzik, M. (2019, May). Using the method of pairwise comparisons for the multifactor selection of infographics design alternatives. In *2019 20th International Conference on Research and Education in Mechatronics (REM)* (pp. 1-6). IEEE.

U.S. Access Board. (n.d.). *Guidance Documents*. https://www.access-board.gov/guidance.html

U.S. Department of Education. (2021). *CARES Act: Higher education emergency relief fund*. Retrieved from https://www2.ed.gov/about/offices/list/ope/caresact.html

U.S. Department of Justice. (n.d.). *A Guide to Disability Rights Law*. https://www.ada.gov/cguide.htm

UNFPA. (2020). *Eswatini Population projections report, 2017-2038*. https://eswatini.unfpa.org/sites/default/files/pub-pdf/eswatini_population_projections_report_2017-2038.pdf

UNICEF. (2021). *Responding to COVID-19: UNICEF annual report 2020*. UNICEF.

United Nations Development Programme. (2020). *A Rapid Socioeconomic Assessment of COVID-19 in Eswatini*. UNDP.

United Nations Development Programme. (2021). *Youth-led innovation & entrepreneurship for COVID-19: Examples from Republic of Korea*. https://www1.undp.org/content/seoul_policy_center/en/home/presscenter/articles/2020/youth-led-innovation---entrepreneurship-for-covid-19--examples-f.html

United Nations. (2015). *Sustainable Development Goals (SDGs): The 2030 Agenda for Sustainable Development*. United Nations.

United Nations. (2020). *Shared Responsibility, Global Solidarity: Responding to the socioeconomic impacts of COVID-19*. United Nations.

United States District Court for the District of New Jersey. (2015). *Consent Decree*. http://www.atlantic.edu/documents/nfb_lanzailotti_atlantic_cape_consent_decree.pdf

Usher, M., Barak, M., & Haick, H. (2021). Online vs. on-campus higher education: Exploring innovation in students' self-reports and students' learning products. *Thinking Skills and Creativity, 42*(100965), 1–10. doi:10.1016/j.tsc.2021.100965

Vaidyanathan, G., Sabbaghi, A., & Bargellini, M. (2005). User acceptance of digital library: An empirical exploration of individual and system components. *Issues in Information Systems, 6*(2), 279–285.

Valdez, J. P. M., Datu, J. A. D., & Chu, S. K. W. (2022). Gratitude intervention optimizes effective learning outcomes in Filipino high school students: A mixed-methods study. *Computers & Education, 176*(104268), 1–16. doi:10.1016/j.compedu.2021.104268

Valle, N., Antonenko, P., Valle, D., Dawson, K., Huggins-Manley, A. C., & Baiser, B. (2021). The influence of task-value scaffolding in a predictive learning analytics dashboard on learners' statistics anxiety, motivation, and performance. *Computers & Education, 173*, 104288. doi:10.1016/j.compedu.2021.104288

van Alten, D. C., Phielix, C., Janssen, J., & Kester, L. (2021). Secondary students' online self-regulated learning during flipped learning: A latent profile analysis. *Computers in Human Behavior, 118*(106676), 1–13. doi:10.1016/j.chb.2020.106676

van der Hoorn, B., & Killen, C. P. (2021). Stop sanitizing project management education: Embracing Desirable Difficulties to enhance practice-relevant online learning. *Project Leadership and Society, 2*(100027), 1–9. doi:10.1016/j.plas.2021.100027

Van Nguyen, S., & Habók, A. (2021). Vietnamese non-English-major students' motivation to learn English: from activity theory perspective. *Heliyon, 7*(4), 1 - 11.

VanderMolen, J., & Spivey, C. (2017). Creating infographics to enhance student engagement and communication in health economics. *The Journal of Economic Education*, *48*(3), 198–205.

VanScoy, A., & Bright, K. (2017). Including the voices of librarians of color in reference and information services research. *Reference and User Services Quarterly*, *57*(2), 104–114.

Vanslambrouck, S., Zhu, C., Lombaerts, K., Philipsen, B., & Tondeur, J. (2018). Students' motivation and subjective task value of participating in online and blended learning environments. *The Internet and Higher Education*, *36*, 33–40. doi:10.1016/j.iheduc.2017.09.002

Vanslambrouck, S., Zhu, C., Pynoo, B., Lombaerts, K., Tondeur, J., & Scherer, R. (2019). A latent profile analysis of adult students' online self-regulation in blended learning environments. *Computers in Human Behavior*, *99*, 126–136. doi:10.1016/j.chb.2019.05.021

Vardi, M. Y. (2012). Will MOOCs destroy academia? *Communications of the ACM*, *55*(11), 5–5.

Vaughan, N. (2007). Perspectives on blended learning in higher education. *International Journal on E-Learning*, *6*(1), 81–94. https://www.learntechlib.org/index.cfm?fuseaction=Reader.ViewAbstract&paper_id=6310

Veletsianos, G., & Houlden, S. (2019). An analysis of flexible learning and flexibility over the last 40 years of Distance Education. *Distance Education*, *40*(4), 454–468.

Venkatesh, V. (1999). Creation of favorable user perceptions: Exploring the role intrinsic motivation. *Management Information Systems Quarterly*, *23*(2), 239–260.

Venkatesh, V. (2000). Determinants of perceived ease of use: Integrating control, intrinsic motivation, and emotion into the technology acceptance model. *Information Systems Research*, *11*(4), 342–365.

Venkatesh, V., & Davis, F. D. (1996). A model of the antecedents of perceived ease of use: Development and test. *Decision Sciences*, *27*(3), 451–481.

Venkatesh, V., & Davis, F. D. (2000). A theoretical extension of the technology acceptance model: Four longitudinal field studies. *Management Science*, *46*(2), 186–204.

Veszelszki, A. (2014). Information visualization: Infographics from a linguistic point of view. *The Power of the Image*, 99-109.

Viglia, G., Pera, R., & Bigné, E. (2018). The determinants of stakeholder engagement in digital platforms. *Journal of Business Research*, *89*, 404–410. doi:10.1016/j.jbusres.2017.12.029

Villalón, R., Luna, M., & García-Barrera, A. (2012). What do lecturers say about their use of a synchronous tool in an open university. *Proceedings of ICERI2012 International Conference.*

Villasenor, J. (2022, February 10). *Online college classes can be better than in-person ones. The implications for higher ed are profound.* Brookings. https://www.brookings.edu/blog/techtank/2022/02/10/online-college-classes-can-be-better-than-in-person-ones-the-implications-for-higher-ed-are-profound/

Volman, M., & Kormilicyn, D. (2018, October). Infographics in "Safety of Nuclear Power Plants" Course. In *2018 IV International Conference on Information Technologies in Engineering Education (Inforino)* (pp. 1-4). IEEE. 10.1109/INFORINO.2018.8581744

von Keyserlingk, L., Yamaguchi-Pedroza, K., Arum, R., & Eccles, J. (2022). Stress of university students before and after campus closure in response to COVID-19. *Journal of Community Psychology*, *50*(1), 285–301. doi:10.1002/jcop.22561 PMID:33786864

Compilation of References

Von Robertson, R., & Chaney, C. (2017). "I know it [racism] still exists here:" African American males at a predominantly white institution. *Humboldt Journal of Social Relations*, *39*, 260–282.

Voss, R., Gruber, T., & Szmigin, I. (2007). Service quality in higher education: The role of student expectations. *Journal of Business Research*, *60*(9), 949–959. doi:10.1016/j.jbusres.2007.01.020

W3C. (n.d.). *Web Content Accessibility Guidelines 2.0*. https://www.w3.org/TR/WCAG20/

Walker, J. (1969). The diffusion of innovation among the American states. *The American Political Science Review*, *63*(3), 880–899. doi:10.2307/1954434

Walters, W. (2004). Criteria for replacing print journals with online journal resources: The importance of sustainable access notes on operations. *Library Resources & Technical Services*, *18*(4), 300–309. http://www.hwwilsonweb.com

Walwema, J. N. (2012, October). Design templates in instructional design. In *Proceedings of the 30th ACM International Conference on Design of Communication* (pp. 17-22). Academic Press.

Wang, C., Hsu, H. C. K., Bonem, E. M., Moss, J. D., Yu, S., Nelson, D. B., & Levesque-Bristol, C. (2019). Need satisfaction and need dissatisfaction: A comparative study of online and face-to-face learning contexts. *Computers in Human Behavior*, *95*, 114–125. doi:10.1016/j.chb.2019.01.034

Wang, H., Wang, L., & Zhu, J. (2022). Moderated mediation model of the impact of autonomous motivation on postgraduate students' creativity. *Thinking Skills and Creativity*, *100997*, 1–11. doi:10.1016/j.tsc.2021.100997

Wang, W., Wu, X., & Li, J. (2018, October). The practice of small project-based mode in the teaching of SCM course. In *Proceedings of the 10th International Conference on Education Technology and Computers* (pp. 12-16). 10.1145/3290511.3290513

Wang, X., Liu, T., Wang, J., & Tian, J. (2021). Understanding Learner Continuance Intention: A Comparison of Live Video Learning, Pre-Recorded Video Learning and Hybrid Video Learning in COVID-19 Pandemic. *International Journal of Human-Computer Interaction*. Advance online publication. doi:10.1080/10447318.2021.1938389

Wang, Y., Gao, Y., Huang, R., Cui, W., Zhang, H., & Zhang, D. (2021, June). Animated presentation of static infographics with InfoMotion. *Computer Graphics Forum*, *40*(3), 507–518.

Wang, Y., Gao, Y., Huang, R., Cui, W., Zhang, H., & Zhang, D. (2021, June). Animated Presentation of Static Infographics with InfoMotion. *Computer Graphics Forum*, *40*(3), 507–518. doi:10.1111/cgf.14325

Wang, Z., Wang, S., Farinella, M., Murray-Rust, D., Henry Riche, N., & Bach, B. (2019, May). Comparing effectiveness and engagement of data comics and infographics. In *Proceedings of the 2019 CHI Conference on Human Factors in Computing Systems* (pp. 1-12). ACM.

Warden, C. A., Stanworth, J. O., Ren, J. B., & Warden, A. R. (2013). Synchronous learning best practices: An action research study] *Computers & Education*, *63*, 197–207.

Wardoyo, C., Satrio, Y. D., Narmaditya, B. S., & Wibowo, A. (2021). Do technological knowledge and game-based learning promote students achievement: Lesson from Indonesia. *Heliyon*, *7*(11), 1 - 8.

Warschauer, M. (2007). The Paradoxical Future of Digital Learning. *Learning Inquiry*, *1*, 41–49.

Warshawsk, S. (2022). Academic self-efficacy, resilience and social support among first-year Israeli nursing students learning in online environments during COVID-19 pandemic. *Nurse Education Today*, *105267*, 1–6. doi:10.1016/j.nedt.2022.105267

Wayne, J., Bogo, M., & Raskin, M. (2010). Field education as the signature pedagogy of social work education. *Journal of Social Work Education*, *46*(3), 327–339. doi:10.5175/JSWE.2010.200900043

Wharton, C., Vizcaino, M., Berardy, A., & Opejin, A. (2021). Waste watchers: A food waste reduction intervention among households in Arizona. *Resources, Conservation and Recycling*, *164*, 105109.

Wibowo, M. P. (2019). *Technology Acceptance Models and Theories in Library and Information Science Research*. Seminar in Theory and Foundations of Information Sciences Course at Florida State University.

Wilkinson, J. L., Strickling, K., Payne, H. E., Jensen, K. C., & West, J. H. (2016). Evaluation of diet-related infographics on Pinterest for use of behavior change theories: A content analysis. *JMIR mHealth and uHealth*, *4*(4), e6367.

Wilkins-Yel, K. G., Hyman, J., & Zounlome, N. O. (2019). Linking intersectional invisibility and hypervisibility to experiences of microaggressions among graduate women of color in STEM. *Journal of Vocational Behavior*, *113*, 51–61.

Williams, F. M. (2002). *Diversity, thinking styles, and infographics*. Academic Press.

Williams, M. T. (2021). Microaggressions are a form of aggression. *Behavior Therapy*, *52*(3), 709–719.

Williamson, K., Bernath, V., Wright, S., & Sullivan, J. (2007). Research students in the electronic age. *Communications in Information Literacy*, *1*, 47–63. http://www.comminfolit.org/index.php/cil

Wilson, F., & Keys, J. (2004). AskNow! Evaluating an Australian collaborative chat reference service: A project manager's perspective. *Australian Academic and Research Libraries*, *35*, 81-95. Retrieved from http://vnweb.hwwilsonweb.com/hww/login.jhtml?_requestid=29758

Wilson, A. M., Zeithaml, V. A., Bitner, M. J., & Gremler, D. D. (2021). *Services marketing: Integrating customer focus across the firm*. McGraw-Hill.

Wilson, E. J. (2003). *The information revolution and developing countries*. MIT Press.

Wing, J. M. (2008). Computational thinking and thinking about computing. *Philosophical Transactions of the Royal Society A*, *366*(1881), 3717–3725. doi:10.1098/rsta.2008.0118 PMID:18672462

Wingo, N. P., Ivankova, N. V., & Moss, J. A. (2017). Faculty perceptions about teaching online: Exploring the literature using the technology acceptance model as an organizing framework. *Online Learning, 21*(1), 15-35. doi:10.10.24059/olj.v21i1.761

Wong, I. H., & Wong, T. T. (2021). Exploring the relationship between intellectual humility and academic performance among post-secondary students: The mediating roles of learning motivation and receptivity to feedback. *Learning and Individual Differences*, *88*(102012), 1–8. doi:10.1016/j.lindif.2021.102012

Wong, J., Baars, M., He, M., de Koning, B. B., & Paas, F. (2021). Facilitating goal setting and planning to enhance online self-regulation of learning. *Computers in Human Behavior*, *106913*, 1–15. doi:10.1016/j.chb.2021.106913

Wong, L., Tatnall, A., & Burgess, S. (2014). A framework for investigating blended learning effectiveness. *Education + Training*, *56*(2/3), 233–251. Advance online publication. doi:10.1108/ET-04-2013-0049

Won, J. (2017). Interactive infographics and delivery of information: The value assessment of infographics and their relation to user response. *Archives of Design Research*, *31*(1), 57–69.

Wood, R., Bonakdarian, E., & Whittaker, T. (2012). Designing courses for hybrid instruction: Principles and practice. Consortium for Computing Sciences in Colleges. *Journal of Computing Sciences in Colleges*, *27*(4), 6–14.

Compilation of References

Woodworth, P., & Applin, A. A. (2007). *A hybrid structure for the introductory computers and information technology course.* Semantic Scholar. https://www.semanticscholar.org/paper/A-hybrid-structure-for-the-introductory-computers-Woodworth-Applin/780faf868da6760f9f915602a3b37acad1703d2a

Wopereis, I., Frerejean, J., & Brand-Gruwel, S. (2016, October). Teacher perspectives on whole-task information literacy instruction. In *European Conference on Information Literacy* (pp. 678-687). Springer. 10.1007/978-3-319-52162-6_66

World Bank. (2022). *Inflation, consumer prices (annual %) - Zambia.* Author.

World Bank. (2022). *Overview.* World Bank. https://www.worldbank.org/en/country/bangladesh/overview

Wu, G., Zheng, J., & Zhai, J. (2021). Individualized learning evaluation model based on hybrid teaching. *International Journal of Electrical Engineering Education*, 1–15. doi:10.1177/0020720920983999

Xie, J. A. G., & Rice, M. F. (2021). Instructional designers' roles in emergency remote teaching during COVID-19. *Distance Education*, *42*(1), 70–87. doi:10.1080/01587919.2020.1869526

Xie, Q., & Lou, C. (2020). Curating Luxe experiences online? Explicating the mechanisms of luxury content marketing in cultivating brand loyalty. *Journal of Interactive Advertising*, *20*(3), 209–224. doi:10.1080/15252019.2020.1811177

Xie, X., Siau, K., & Nah, F. F.-H. (2020). Covid-19 pandemic – online education in the New Normal and the next normal. *Journal of Information Technology Case and Application Research*, *22*(3), 175–187. doi:10.1080/15228053.2020.1824884

Xu, J. (2022). A profile analysis of online assignment motivation: Combining achievement goal and expectancy-value perspectives. *Computers & Education*, *177*(104367), 1–17. doi:10.1016/j.compedu.2021.104367

Xu, J., Lio, A., Dhaliwal, H., Andrei, S., Balakrishnan, S., Nagani, U., & Samadder, S. (2021). Psychological interventions of virtual gamification within academic intrinsic motivation: A systematic review. *Journal of Affective Disorders*, *293*, 444–465. doi:10.1016/j.jad.2021.06.070 PMID:34252688

Yada, A., Leskinen, M., Savolainen, H., & Schwab, S. (2022). Meta-analysis of the relationship between teachers' self-efficacy and attitudes toward inclusive education. *Teaching and Teacher Education*, *109*(103521), 1–15.

Yang, C. C., Tsai, I. C., Kim, B., Cho, M. H., & Laffey, J. M. (2006). Exploring the relationships between students' academic motivation and social ability in online learning environments. *The Internet and Higher Education*, *9*(4), 277–286. doi:10.1016/j.iheduc.2006.08.002

Yang, J., Zhang, Y., Pi, Z., & Xie, Y. (2021). Students' achievement motivation moderates the effects of interpolated pre-questions on attention and learning from video lectures. *Learning and Individual Differences*, *91*(102055), 1–9. doi:10.1016/j.lindif.2021.102055

Yarbrough, J. R. (2019). Infographics: In support of online visual learning. *Academy of Educational Leadership Journal*, *23*(2), 1–15.

Yasuda, K., Takahashi, S., & Wu, H. Y. (2016, September). Enhancing infographics based on symmetry saliency. In *Proceedings of the 9th International Symposium on Visual Information Communication and Interaction* (pp. 35-42). Academic Press.

Ydo, Y. (2020). Inclusive education: Global priority, collective responsibility. *Prospects*, *49*(3), 97–101.

Yearta, L., Kelly, K. S., Kissel, B., & Schonhar, M. (2018). Infoadvocacy: Writers engage in social justice through infographics. *Voices from the Middle*, *25*(4), 54.

Yekefallah, L., Namdar, P., Panahi, R., & Dehghankar, L. (2021). Factors related to students' satisfaction with holding e-learning during the Covid-19 pandemic based on the dimensions of e-learning. *Heliyon*, *7*(7), 1 - 6.

Yekefallah, L., Namdar, P., Panahi, R., & Dehghankar, L. (2021). Factors related to students' satisfaction with holding e-learning during the covid-19 pandemic based on the dimensions of e-learning. *Heliyon*, *7*(7), e07628. Advance online publication. doi:10.1016/j.heliyon.2021.e07628 PMID:34381894

Yelland, N. (2005). The future is now: A review of the literature on the use of computers in early childhood education (1994-2004). *AACE Review*, *13*(3), 201–232.

Yeung, D., & Lim, N. (2021). Talking about race and diversity. In *Perspectives on Diversity, Equity, and Inclusion in the Department of the Air Force* (pp. 37–42). RAND Corporation.

Yildirim, S. (2017). Approaches of designers in the developed educational purposes of infographics' design processes. *European Journal of Education Studies*, 248 - 284.

Yildirim, S. (2016). Infographics for educational purposes: Their structure, properties and reader approaches. *Turkish Online Journal of Educational Technology-TOJET*, *15*(3), 98–110.

Yilmaz, R. (2017). Exploring the role of e-learning readiness on student satisfaction and motivation in flipped classroom. *Computers in Human Behavior*, *70*, 251–260. doi:10.1016/j.chb.2016.12.085

Yi, M. Y., & Hwang, Y. (2003). Predicting the use of web-based information systems: Self-efficacy, enjoyment, learning goal orientation, and the technology acceptance model. *International Journal of Human-Computer Studies*, *59*(4), 431–449.

Yin, R. K. (2017). *Case study research and applications: Design and methods*. Sage publications.

Youth Co. Lab. (2020, May 6). *Young entrepreneurs explain how COVID-19 is affecting their businesses*. https://www.youthcolab.org/post/young-entrepreneurs-explain-how-covid-19-is-affecting-their-businesses

Yuan, L., & Powell, S. J. (2013). *MOOCs and open education: Implications for higher education.* doi:10.13140/2.1.5072.8320

Yuan, D., & Zhong, J. (2009, October). An instructional design of open source networking laboratory and curriculum. In *Proceedings of the 10th ACM conference on SIG-information technology education* (pp. 37-42). 10.1145/1631728.1631742

Yuruk, S. E., Yilmaz, R. M., & Bilici, S. (2019). An examination of postgraduate students' use of infographic design, metacognitive strategies and academic achievement. *Journal of Computing in Higher Education*, *31*(3), 495–513.

Zainuddin, Z. (2018). Students' learning performance and perceived motivation in gamified flipped-class instruction. *Computers & Education*, *126*, 75–88. doi:10.1016/j.compedu.2018.07.003

Zakrajsek, T. D. (2022). *The New Science of Learning: How to Learn in Harmony With Your Brain*. Stylus Publishing, LLC.

Zaman, F. (2014, November 27). "Student Politics" in Bangladesh. *The Daily Star*. https://www.thedailystar.net/student-politics-in-bangladesh-52187

Zhang, Y., & Estabrook, L. (1998). Accessibility to Internet-based electronic resources and its implications for electronic scholarship. In *Proceedings of the American Society for Information Science Annual Meeting* (pp. 463–473). Academic Press.

Zhang-Kennedy, L., Chiasson, S., & Biddle, R. (2013, September). *Password advice shouldn't be boring: Visualizing password guessing attacks. In 2013 APWG eCrime Researchers Summit*. IEEE.

Zhang-Kennedy, L., Chiasson, S., & Biddle, R. (2014). Stop clicking on 'update later': Persuading users they need up-to-date antivirus protection. In *International Conference on Persuasive Technology* (pp. 302-322). Springer.

Compilation of References

Zhang, S., & Liu, Q. (2019). Investigating the relationships among teachers' motivational beliefs, motivational regulation, and their learning engagement in online professional learning communities. *Computers & Education*, *134*, 145–155. doi:10.1016/j.compedu.2019.02.013

Zhang, X. (2016). An analysis of online students' behaviors on course sites and the effect on learning performance: A case study of four LIS online classes. *Journal of Education for Library and Information Science*, *57*(4), 255–270. doi:10.2307/90015229

Zhang, Y., Zhao, G., & Zhou, B. (2021). Does learning longer improve student achievement? Evidence from online education of graduating students in a high school during COVID-19 period. *China Economic Review*, *70*, 101691. doi:10.1016/j.chieco.2021.101691

Zhao, L., Cao, C., Li, Y., & Li, Y. (2021). Determinants of the digital outcome divide in E-learning between rural and urban students: Empirical evidence from the COVID-19 pandemic based on capital theory. *Computers in Human Behavior*, *107177*, 1–15.

Zheng, C., Liang, J. C., Li, M., & Tsai, C. C. (2018). The relationship between English language learners' motivation and online self-regulation: A structural equation modelling approach. *System*, *76*, 144–157. doi:10.1016/j.system.2018.05.003

Zhu, M., Basdogan, M., & Bonk, C. J. (2020). A case study of the design practices and judgments of novice instructional designers. *Contemporary Educational Technology*, *12*(2), 1–19. doi:10.30935/cedtech/7829

Zhu, S., Sun, G., Jiang, Q., Zha, M., & Liang, R. (2020). A survey on automatic infographics and visualization recommendations. *Visual Informatics*, *4*(3), 24–40.

Zurita, G., Hasbun, B., Baloian, N., & Jerez, O. (2015). A blended learning environment for enhancing meaningful learning using 21st century skills. In G. Chen, V. Kumar, Kinshuk, R. Huang, & S. C. Kong (Eds.), Emerging Issues in Smart Learning (pp. 1–8). Springer. doi:10.1007/978-3-662-44188-6_1

Zwinger, S., & Zeiller, M. (2016, November). Interactive infographics in German online newspapers. In Forum Media Technology. St. Pölten University of Applied Sciences, Institute of CreativenMedia/Technologies.

Zwinger, S., Langer, J., & Zeiller, M. (2017, July). Acceptance and usability of interactive infographics in online newspapers. In *2017 21st International Conference Information Visualisation (IV)* (pp. 176-181). IEEE.

About the Contributors

Shalin Hai-Jew works as an instructional designer at Kansas State University (K-State). She has taught at the university and college levels for many years (including four years in the People's Republic of China) and was tenured at Shoreline Community College but left tenure to pursue instructional design work. She has Bachelor's degrees in English and psychology, a Master's degree in Creative Writing from the University of Washington (Hugh Paradise Scholar), and an Ed.D in Educational Leadership with a focus on public administration from Seattle University (Morford Scholar). She tested into the University of Washington at 14. She reviews for several publishers and publications. She has worked on a number of instructional design projects, including public health, biosecurity, One Health, mental health, PTSD, grain science, turfgrass management, social justice, and others. She has authored and edited a number of books. Hai-Jew was born in Huntsville, Alabama, in the U.S. Currently, she is working on multiple projects. She uses educational technologies daily in her work for the design, development, and deployment of teaching and learning resources. She also uses CAQDAS and other data analysis tool types in her work, including those with machine learning capabilities. She works on both internal and external work teams.

* * *

Md. Minhazul Abdin is a postgraduate student from the Institute of Education and Research at the University of Rajshahi, Rajshahi, Bangladesh. He has been actively involved in several community services, and he is a passionate, recognised professional, contributing tirelessly towards achieving sustainable development, shared prosperity and peace within society and the world. As a student of education and research, he dreams of conducting research that leads him to contribute to the education sector of Bangladesh. He has some experience as a research assistant with several organisations.

Ana Arán Sánchez has a bachelor's degree in Psychology, a master's degree in Psychopedagogy and is currently a PhD candidate for Educational Sciences. She is a full-time professor at a public university in the north of Mexico and a researcher as well, specializing in issues such as indigenous students and higher education, as well as English as a second language.

Carolyn Arcand, Ph.D. (University of Massachusetts Boston), is a Senior Lecturer in Public Administration and Public Policy at the University of New Hampshire's Carsey School of Public Policy. Her research focuses on the impact of public policy on women's labor and care work. Dr. Arcand's peer-reviewed work can be found in publications including Labor Studies Journal, The International Journal of Care and Caring, and Community College Journal of Research and Practice.

About the Contributors

Shayantani Banerjee is an Assistant Professor of English in Amity University Jharkhand. She completed her Doctorate in 2018. Her research interests focus on the presentation of subalterns in Indian English novels. She has 11 years of teaching experience while working in institutions like Nirmala College, BIT Extn. and T.I.M.E. She has also worked as an Assistant Commissioning Editor – Journals in Sage Publications, New Delhi. She has published book chapters and research papers in various journals. She is also a part of the UGC STRIDE funded Major Project in the capacity of Co-Investigator. Her work focuses on teaching literature, language and communication skills.

Lisa Dotterweich Bryan, Ph.D., completed her M.A. and Ph.D. in Public Policy at Kent State University. Her research interests include education policy and the role of social media in U.S. elections. She works in Institutional Research at Western Iowa Tech Community College in Sioux City, IA.

Jessica A. Cannon, Ph.D., is an Associate Professor of History at the University of Central Missouri. She has also completed graduate coursework in instructional design and earned a certificate in Assistive Technologies.

Sheilas K. Chilala is a researcher and lecturer in the School of Social Sciences at Mulungushi University in Kabwe, Zambia. Prior to joining Mulungushi University, Chilala worked for National College for Management and Development Studies (NCMDS) as a lecturer. She holds a master's degree in social work, University of Botswana and bachelor's degree in social work, the University of Zambia. Her scholarly interests are in social development, gender and policy related matters.

Maureen Ebben, Ph.D. (University of Illinois at Urbana-Champaign), is an Associate Professor in the Department of Communication and Media Studies at the University of Southern Maine, Portland. An award-winning scholar and teacher, her work focuses on pedagogy, digital communication and everyday life, particularly in the wake of the COVID-19 pandemic. Dr. Ebben's recent scholarship appears in the volumes Post-Pandemic Pedagogy: A Paradigm Shift (2021), Career Re-Invention in the Post-Pandemic Era (2022), Common Visual Art in a Social Digital Age (2022), Badass Feminist Politics: Exploring Radical Edges of Feminist Theory, Communication, and Activism (2022), and the journal Learning, Media, and Technology (2022).

Eky Hapsari is a passionate lecturer and researcher with 17+ years of experience in the field of Japanese linguistics, Japanese language education, Japanese language teaching, and many others. Experienced in teaching undergraduate students.

Hastowohadi is currently teaching English for vocational purposes in the Department of Flight Operation Officer at Akademi Penerbang Indonesia (API) Banyuwangi, East Java, Indonesia. He completed his Master's degree in English Education at Universitas Islam Malang (UNISMA). His research interests lie in language materials development, task-based language teaching, and English for Vocational Purposes.

Yaacob Ibrahim is currently an Advisor, Office of the President, Singapore Institute of Technology (SIT), as well as Director, Community Leadership and Social Innovation Centre (CLASIC), SIT, where he oversees the University's efforts in community-related projects and initiatives, and the nurturing of social advocate leaders who are grounded in research and community development. Prior to his current positions at SIT, Prof Yaacob served as a Minister in the Ministries of Communications and Information (2011 – 2018), Environment and Water Resources (2004 – 2011) and Community Development and Sports (2002 – 2004). Throughout the 16 years as a Minister, he was also Minister-in-charge of Muslim Affairs. Prof Yaacob started his political career as a Member of Parliament in Jalan Besar GRC on 2 January 1997, and held several political appointments before becoming a Minister in 2002. Prof Yaacob graduated from the University of Singapore with a degree in Civil Engineering in 1980. He worked as a structural engineer with a multinational engineering consulting firm from 1980 to 1984. He pursued his PhD at Stanford University from 1984 and graduated in 1989. He spent two years as a post-doctoral fellow at Cornell University. He joined the National University of Singapore (NUS) as a faculty member in 1990 where he became a tenured member. He took a leave of absence from NUS from July 1998 till his resignation from NUS in August 2018. Prof Yaacob sits on the board of several private companies and unions. He is Chairman of the Governing Board for the Earth Observatory of Singapore (EOS). He is on the Board of Trustees for the Building Construction and Timber Industries Employees' Union (BATU), and is a Board Member of Surbana Jurong Group and Singapore Power. He is also an independent director of Chip Eng Seng Corporation Limited. Prof Yaacob was most recently appointed non-executive independent director for Oceanus Group Limited on 1 September 2020. He also serves as Advisor, AI Singapore, a national Artificial Intelligence (AI) programme launched by the National Research Foundation to catalyse Singapore's AI capabilities.

Nilesh Kumar is an Academic Coordinator at Amity University Jharkhand. He is Pursuing his Ph.D. in management domain from Ranchi University, Ranchi. His research interests focus on the Marketing and Retail formats. She has more than 5 years of teaching experience. He has published book chapters and research papers in various journals. His work focuses on retail and marketing strategies.

Navinandan Kumar Singh is an Assistant Professor at Amity University Jharkhand, Ranchi in the department of Foreign Languages (French). He has a teaching experience of more than five years. He has done his graduation and post-graduation in French from Banaras Hindu University, Varanasi. His areas of interest include French and Francophone Literature, Language acquisition and Translation Studies.

Amir Manzoor holds a PhD in Management Sciences. He is a graduate of NED University, Pakistan, Lahore University of Management Sciences (LUMS), Pakistan and Bangor University, United Kingdom. He has more than 20 years of diverse professional and teaching experience working at many renowned national and internal organizations and higher education institutions. His research interests include E-commerce, Strategic Management, Enterprise Resource Planning (ERP), Project Management,Supply Chain Management, Data Analysis, and Technology applications.

Ramona McNeal is an Associate Professor in the Department of Political Science at the University of Northern Iowa. Her chief research interests include e-government, telehealth, campaign finance reform and telecommunications policy. She also studies the impact of technology on participation, including its relationship to voting, elections, and public opinion. She has published work in a number of journals including Journal of Information Technology & Politics, Social Science Quarterly, Policy Studies Journal, Public Administration Review, Political Research Quarterly and State Politics and Policy Quarterly. She is a co-author of Digital Citizenship: The Internet, Society and Participation (MIT Press, 2007) with Karen Mossberger and Caroline Tolbert.

About the Contributors

Hagit Meishar-Tal (PhD) is a senior lecturer and the former head of Instructional Technologies BA Program in Holon Institute of Technology (HIT) in Israel. Her main fields of research are collaborative learning, mobile learning, game-based learning, Social media as learning environments and distance learning. She has published many papers in prestigious peer reviewed journals, as well as chapters in academic books and in international conferences proceedings.

Intan Azura Mokhtar is Associate Professor in the Business, Communication and Design Cluster, and Deputy Director of the Community Leadership and Social Innovation Centre (CLASIC) in the Singapore Institute of Technology, which is Singapore's 5th autonomous university that is focused on applied learning. Intan has more than 20 years of teaching experience, fifteen years of which are at the university level. Intan has taught courses related to social context and change management, social innovation and community leadership, school and change leadership, educational technology, and information science for both Undergraduate and Masters degree programmes. Intan has published widely on the above topics and has more than 50 publications to her name. Intan has been extensively involved in public policy making in Singapore, having been a legislator in the Singapore parliament, and Deputy Chairperson of the Singapore Government Parliamentary Committee (GPC) for Education, as well as member of the GPCs for Manpower and Transport, from 2011-2020.

Fred Moonga is a Lecturer at the University Eswatini, in Eswatini, formerly Swaziland. Previously, he was Lecturer and Head of Department at Mulungushi University in Zambia. He has also worked in international non-Governmental organizations and the Government of the Republic of Zambia. He holds a PhD in Social work from Stellenbosch University, South Africa; MSc, Global Aging and policy, University of Southampton, UK; MSc, International Social Work, Gothenburg University, Sweden; and BSW, University of Zambia. His research interests are in gerontology, social protection, eco-social work, migration, poverty and vulnerability, and child welfare.

Ireen Moonga is a Lecturer and Researcher at Mulungushi University in the Department of Literature and Languages. She obtained a master's Degree in Literacy and Learning from the University of Zambia and currently studying for a master's degree in Linguistic Sciences. Previously, she worked as a tutor at the University of Zambia and as a part-time lecturer for three years at Kwame Nkrumah University. Ireen also served as a secondary school teacher specializing in English language and Religious Education in the Ministry of General Education for about 17 years before joining Mulungushi University. Her research interests are in language development and implementation, educational leadership and management, religion, and moral values in higher education. Ireen Moonga has undertaken research and consultancy projects with local women groups. She has published articles in renowned Journals.

Audrey Muyuni Phiri is a Lecturer in the Department of religious studies at Mulungushi University in Zambia. She has a Bachelor of Arts in Education and Religous Studies and a Diploma in Religious Studies, Primary and Early Childhood teaching. She previously worked at University of Zambia, Eden University, Cavendish University and Blessing University of Excellence. Her research interest is in religious studies and moral values in higher education. She has published many journal articles and book chapters. She has also undertaken consultancies and research projects in Zambia and participated in many international conferences.

Angel Perez is a Graduate Student at the University of North Florida.

Goutam Roy is working as an Associate Professor in Education at the Institute of Education and Research, University of Rajshahi, Rajshahi, Bangladesh. Mr Roy is mainly responsible for teaching courses on research methods and evaluation at undergraduate and postgraduate levels in his current role. His research interests include early childhood and primary education, community participation in schools, assessment of student learning, teaching-learning activities, science and online education. During his career in teaching and research, Mr Roy has presented several academic papers on some of the abovementioned areas at different national and international conferences. He has also contributed to several books, book chapters and journal articles. Before starting his career in academia, he worked for two international NGOs in which he carried out several research projects on primary education, teaching and learning process, learning achievement of students, and program evaluation on school improvement and program effectiveness. Mr Roy was also involved with some nationwide surveys on pre-primary and primary education in Bangladesh. He also has experience in doing collaborative work with some non-governmental organisations (NGOs) and different government bodies.

Mary Schmeida is a public policy expert who has served in several key research positions. She received her Ph.D. in Political Science, Public Policy Analysis and Design, from Kent State University, Ohio, USA. She has held several faculty appointments in public and private Universities. Her works are published in books and academic journals, including Government Information Quarterly, Administration and Policy in Mental Health and Mental Health Services Research, and Journal of Health Policy and Technology. She is a co-author of Cyber Harassment and Policy Reform in the Digital Age: Emerging Research and Opportunities, with Ramona McNeal and Susan Kunkle (IGI Global, 2018).

Glorianne C. Schott, MS, MSE, is a part-time Lecturer in the Department of Communication and Media Studies at the University of Southern Maine, Portland, and an online Instructor at Iowa Central Community College. Schott earned an M.S.E. in Higher Education from Drake University and an M.S. in Communication Studies from Fort Hays State University.

Apostolos Syropoulos holds a B.Sc. in Physics, an M.Sc. in Computer Science, and a Ph.D. in Theoretical Computer Science. His research interests focus on theory of computation, category theory, fuzzy set theory, and digital typography. Lately, he is also interested in educational tools and methodologies. He has authored or co-authored 12 books, over 60 papers and articles, and co-edited 2 books.

Judith Tupper, D.H.Ed., CHES, CPPS, is the Director of Population Health at the Catherine Cutler Institute, University of Southern Maine. Dr. Tupper teaches quality improvement, patient safety, and health literacy courses in the Graduate Program in Public Health and quality improvement for the School of Nursing graduate program. Her applied research portfolio includes federally funded initiatives in workforce training, infection prevention, and culture of safety. Credentialed as a Master Certified Health Education Specialist and a Certified Professional in Patient Safety, she is enthusiastically engaged in interprofessional education and international online learning collaboration.

About the Contributors

Justin Zhang is a faculty member in the Department of Management at Coggin College of Business in University of North Florida. He received his Ph.D. in Business Administration with a concentration on Management Science and Information Systems from Pennsylvania State University, University Park. His research interests include economics of information systems, knowledge management, electronic business, business process management, information security, and social networking. He has published research articles in various scholarly journals, books, and conference proceedings. He is the editor-in-chief of the Journal of Global Information Management. He also serves as an associate editor and an editorial board member for several other journals.

Ayushi Zina is an Assistant Professor at Amity University Jharkhand, Ranchi. She has been teaching for the past five years. She has four books to her credit. She has done her graduation and post-graduation in English literature from St. Xavier's College, Ranchi. She is pursuing her PhD from RU on the topic; 'Mythology in Popular Fiction: A Study of Select Works of Amish Tripathi and Ashwin Sanghi'. Her research areas include, mythological studies, feminism, popular literature, gender studies. She is an avid reader and a dynamic speaker. She is a soft-skills expert and has been called as a soft-skills trainer by many prestigious institutions. She has been felicitated by the National Council of Educational Research and Training for securing the highest marks in English all over India in her 10th Board examination.

Index

A

Ableism 11, 19-20, 27, 29, 32
Administrators' Perception 122
Affirmative Action 215, 288-290, 298-302, 304
Allyship 214, 232, 256
Animation 143, 321, 327-328, 334, 336-339, 348, 358, 360, 368, 370, 382, 384, 386, 390, 400, 411-412
Anti-Asian Hatred 207
Antiracist Pedagogy 256
APNG 385-386, 389
Attributional Ambiguity 256
Authentic Learning 1, 3, 16, 20, 57, 361
Authentic Teaching and Learning 1
Autonomous 37, 39, 48, 50, 65-67, 82, 85-86, 92-93, 96, 203, 294

B

Balance Wheel Model 109-111, 113-114, 120
Bangladesh 122, 124-128, 132-133, 135-143, 285
Best Practices 1, 3-6, 16, 29, 31, 248, 286-287, 325, 403
Bias 205, 211-213, 215, 221, 236-237, 241, 244, 248, 253, 256, 323, 343
Blended Learning 37, 41, 46, 50, 61, 63, 73, 77, 82, 99, 122-143, 148, 151, 155, 163, 179, 225, 249, 272

C

Caregiving 1, 5, 16, 20
CARES Act (2020) 120
Cisgender 256
College Enrollment 102, 105, 115, 117
Color Blindness 216, 222, 256
Color Muteness 256
Community Engagement 145, 154, 186, 202
Community Leadership 186, 189, 202
Community of Inquiry (CoI) 13, 20
Computational Thinking 225, 385-386, 390, 398
Content Marketing 400-404, 406-409, 411-414

COVID-19 1-3, 6-7, 10-11, 13, 16-20, 22-26, 28-29, 31-34, 44-46, 48-49, 51, 53, 57, 59-62, 68, 70-71, 73-83, 85-86, 89-90, 97, 100, 102-103, 105-106, 110, 113-114, 120, 122-123, 126-127, 129-130, 133-134, 136-139, 141, 144-160, 171-172, 181-182, 186-187, 189-193, 198-202, 205-206, 227, 229, 242, 245, 250, 261-267, 270-281, 283-286, 288-289, 292-293, 300-303, 305, 310, 317, 320, 325, 352, 361, 363, 366, 369, 371-372, 381-382, 412
COVID-19 Pandemic 1, 3, 10, 13, 16-18, 20, 22, 34, 44-45, 48, 51, 59-60, 70, 73-74, 77-83, 86, 100, 102, 104, 110, 113-114, 120, 122, 126-127, 129-130, 133, 136, 141, 144-145, 149-150, 156-159, 171-172, 181-182, 186-187, 189-193, 198-201, 205-206, 227, 229, 245, 250, 261, 264-265, 267, 272-276, 284-286, 288, 292-293, 300-303, 305, 310, 320, 325, 361, 363, 369, 371-372, 382
Crisis-Driven Digitalization 34, 44, 58, 80
Critical Race Theory 103, 211, 250, 255-256

D

Digital "Homework Gap" 104-105, 114, 120
Digital Disparity 288, 292, 295, 299
Digital Divide 45, 102, 104, 114, 116, 120, 291-292, 294-295, 299-301
Digital Homework Gap 102
Discrimination 29, 119, 205-206, 212-214, 219-221, 223, 235-236, 238-240, 249, 256-257, 297, 300, 302
Dissertation 17, 140, 178-179, 183, 288, 292-293, 296, 299-300, 302, 332, 362, 412
Distance Education 17-18, 87, 126, 138-139, 143, 152-153, 155-157, 173, 181-182, 261, 263, 265-266, 272-275, 284, 286-287, 294, 317, 382
Distance Learning 49, 54-55, 74, 86, 106, 138, 147-148, 156-158, 169, 180, 182-183, 265, 277, 280-281, 286, 293, 302, 306, 316

Index

E

Education Transition 143

E-Learning 17, 45-47, 50, 75, 83, 124, 126, 138, 140, 142, 148-150, 157-159, 163, 178, 182, 225, 261, 263-265, 274-275, 281, 284-285, 307-308, 313, 316-317, 364, 381

Emergency Learning 276, 278-279

Emergency Online Learning 34, 44, 46, 49, 55, 73, 76, 274, 279, 314

Emergency Online Teaching 34, 44, 48, 50, 75, 78, 276

Enrolment 37, 45, 140, 144, 203

ENRRFM 288-290, 299

Ethnicity 10, 206, 211-212, 216, 218, 225, 239, 256-257

Ethnoracial Differences 239-240, 249, 257

F

Future Pull 34-35, 69, 72-73, 84

G

Gap Model 261, 267-268, 271-272

H

Higher Education 2-4, 7, 11, 15-20, 22-28, 30-35, 41, 51, 66, 68, 71-75, 77-83, 85-90, 98-99, 102-120, 122, 124-127, 130, 133-148, 151-152, 155-159, 162, 165-169, 171, 178, 180, 182, 188, 205, 211, 217-218, 222, 225, 229, 232, 239-242, 250, 253-254, 261-263, 266-268, 273-277, 280-289, 298-302, 306, 310, 317, 320, 329, 364, 368-371, 373-377, 379-381

Higher Education Act of 1965 108, 118, 120

Higher Education Institutions 11, 31, 66, 86, 98, 107-108, 124-127, 139-140, 143-145, 158, 166-168, 261-262, 276, 281, 283

Historical Guilt 257

Human Capital Theory 102, 104, 120

Humanizing 1-3, 8, 10-16, 21

Hybrid 2, 11, 19, 30, 35, 37, 42, 44, 46, 61, 65, 85-90, 92-94, 96-100, 102, 114, 124, 138-139, 141-142, 180, 263, 271-272, 278, 281-282, 284, 306, 308, 317, 322, 345

I

ICT Tools 161, 164, 166-168

Immersive Infographics 320, 322, 324, 351-352, 370, 384

Inclusive

Inclusive Education 63, 141, 222, 224-226, 248-257, 300

Inflation 6, 102-103, 105-106, 111, 113-114, 117, 146, 160, 227, 242, 247, 310

Infographics 321-369, 371-390, 396-398, 400-405, 407-414

Institutional Equity 205, 230

Instructional Design 6, 19, 28-31, 34-35, 59, 68-70, 169, 207, 224, 230, 240, 246-247, 258, 305-309, 311-318, 330, 346, 365

Interactive Infographics 320, 323-324, 327-328, 330, 338-340, 342-343, 349, 351-352, 360-361, 363, 367-368, 370, 384

Interactive Motion Infographics 320

Intersectionality 211-212, 238, 247, 250, 257

L

Learning Transition 18

Limited Resource 122, 124, 128, 135

M

Marginalization 206, 212-213, 218, 224, 248, 257

Mayo 28, 290, 304

Mental Health 3, 6-7, 10-12, 15-18, 21, 35, 44, 190, 201, 220, 239, 249, 259, 266, 371, 382

Microaffirmation 216, 257

Microaggression 205, 208, 212-217, 220, 226-227, 230, 239-240, 250-251, 253, 256-257

Microassault 205, 208, 230-231, 257

Midwestern University 34-35, 68, 306, 314

Mixteco 290, 304

Motion Infographics 320, 323, 341-342, 348-349, 352, 369-370, 375, 380-381, 384-386, 388-390, 396-398, 400-405, 407-411

Motivation 4, 14, 30, 32, 35, 37-57, 59-60, 62-68, 72-84, 98, 125, 128-129, 163, 184, 193, 219, 251, 264-265, 292, 335, 348, 362, 365, 372

N

Náhuatl 304

Narrative Inquiry Approach 85

Neutrality 245, 257

New Students 171, 177

Normal Rural School 288-289, 304

O

Online Education 2-4, 15-16, 45, 59, 62, 76, 79-80,

83, 87, 122, 125-127, 130-131, 142-143, 157, 169, 178, 261-266, 268-275, 285, 288, 291-294, 298-299, 313, 316

Online Learning 1-4, 11, 13-14, 16-20, 34-46, 48-62, 64-68, 71, 73-83, 97, 122-125, 127, 130, 133-134, 136-137, 139, 141, 145, 147-150, 152-153, 155, 157-158, 162-164, 170, 172-173, 180, 262-267, 274-287, 291, 295, 301-302, 305-306, 308, 314, 316-317, 334, 352, 361, 369

Online Learning Frameworks 1, 13

Online Library Services 171-179

Online Pedagogy 1-2, 9, 178

Overvalidation 214, 239, 257

P

Pandemic 1-7, 9-18, 20, 22, 24, 31, 34-35, 44-46, 48-49, 51-62, 64-65, 68, 70-74, 76-83, 86, 89-90, 100, 102-107, 109-110, 113-114, 118, 120, 122, 126-127, 129-130, 133, 136-138, 141, 144-159, 171-172, 179, 181-182, 186-187, 189-193, 198-202, 205-207, 227, 229, 231, 235-236, 240, 245, 247, 250, 259, 261-262, 264-267, 269-270, 272-282, 284-286, 288-293, 295-303, 305-306, 309-310, 314, 320, 325, 335, 361, 363, 371-372, 382

Pedagogy 2, 9-10, 18-19, 60-61, 86, 130, 133, 139, 149-151, 154, 157-164, 167-169, 178, 249, 256, 283, 285, 307-308, 331, 346, 361-362

PGF/TikZ 385, 387-388, 396

Pima 290, 304

Post-Acute Sequelae of SARS-CoV-2 (PASC) 22, 24

Post-COVID-19 Syndrome 22

Post-Pandemic 2-3, 9, 18, 96, 142, 190, 244, 305-306, 308-309

Programming Concepts 385

R

Racism 19, 205-208, 211, 213, 215, 219-222, 229-230, 232-234, 240, 243-245, 249, 251-252, 254, 256-257, 297

Racist Microaggression 205

Racist Trope 257

Relationship-Rich Education 2, 18, 21

Reparations 215, 257

Routine Learning 276, 279

S

SARS-CoV-2 22, 24, 33-34, 44-45, 68, 73, 157, 205-206, 227, 245, 288, 297, 299, 305, 310, 320, 325, 369

SARS-CoV-2 COVID-19 22

Self-Decentered Autoethnography 205, 208, 241

Servicemen's Readjustment Act (1944) 107, 120

Sexism 211, 213, 226, 229, 244-245, 253, 257

Singapore Institute of Technology 186, 189, 191, 202-203

Social Identity 214, 256-257

Social Impact 186-187, 189, 191, 196-203

Social Innovation 186-187, 189-192, 196-200, 203

Social Media 34, 39, 49, 54-55, 66, 76, 158, 161, 215, 248, 308, 315, 327, 342, 362-364, 373, 377, 407-408

Social Presence 13, 20-21, 35, 43, 50-52, 57, 61, 81, 265

Socioeconomic Gap 298-299

Stakeholder Engagement 400-404, 407-408, 411-414

Static Infographics 339, 342-343, 362, 367, 370, 373, 375, 384, 401-402, 413-414

Stereotype Threat 214, 248, 254, 257

Stigma 29, 219, 221, 249, 252, 257

Student Debt 102, 105, 107, 109, 113

Student Mental Health 10, 15

Student Motivation 34-35, 43, 56, 65, 74, 77, 79

Student Satisfaction 14, 57, 83, 140, 261-262, 266, 273-274, 302

Students' Perception 79, 81, 85, 141, 174, 265, 274

SWOT Analysis 76, 305, 310, 315, 317-318

Synchronous Learning 65, 80, 137, 277-278, 280, 287

T

Tarahumara 304

Teachers' Perception 122

Technology Acceptance Model 171, 173, 179-184, 267, 272, 287

Tepehuan 304

Thesis 99, 141, 288-290, 292-293, 295-297, 300, 302-303

Transitivity 85, 88-89, 94, 96

Tuition 36, 102-111, 147, 149, 265, 289, 298

U

Universal Design for Learning (UDL) 13-14, 17, 21, 224

University 1-3, 7, 10-12, 17-20, 22, 27-29, 32, 34-35, 45, 47-48, 50-51, 55-56, 58-59, 62, 65, 67-69, 71-75, 79-81, 99, 102, 105, 115-116, 118, 122, 126-136, 139, 141-142, 144, 146, 148-155, 157-159, 161, 169, 171-172, 175, 178, 180-184, 188-189, 192, 194, 199, 201-203, 205-208, 219, 222, 227, 229-231, 235, 237, 242-248, 254, 258-259, 261-262,

Index

264, 266, 268-271, 274, 283-285, 287-288, 295, 298, 301, 303, 305-306, 308, 310, 313-314, 320, 361-362, 368-369, 382, 400, 412-413

V

Values-Based Education 186-188, 203
Virtual Change 161
Vocational English Task-Based Language Teaching 85-86, 88, 97-98

W

White Fragility 214-215, 257

White Sensitivity 257
White Supremacy 207, 222, 257

Y

Youths 186-187, 189-191, 196-199, 203

Z

Zapoteco 290, 304

Recommended Reference Books

IGI Global's reference books are available in three unique pricing formats:
Print Only, E-Book Only, or Print + E-Book.

Shipping fees may apply.

www.igi-global.com

ISBN: 9781522589648
EISBN: 9781522589655
© 2021; 156 pp.
List Price: US$ 155

ISBN: 9781799840756
EISBN: 9781799840763
© 2021; 282 pp.
List Price: US$ 185

ISBN: 9781799855989
EISBN: 9781799856009
© 2021; 382 pp.
List Price: US$ 195

ISBN: 9781799864745
EISBN: 9781799864752
© 2021; 271 pp.
List Price: US$ 195

ISBN: 9781799875710
EISBN: 9781799875734
© 2021; 252 pp.
List Price: US$ 195

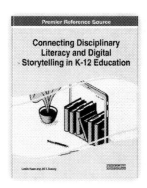

ISBN: 9781799857709
EISBN: 9781799857716
© 2021; 378 pp.
List Price: US$ 195

Do you want to stay current on the latest research trends, product announcements, news, and special offers?
Join IGI Global's mailing list to receive customized recommendations, exclusive discounts, and more.
Sign up at: **www.igi-global.com/newsletters.**

Publisher of Timely, Peer-Reviewed Inclusive Research Since 1988

www.igi-global.com   Sign up at www.igi-global.com/newsletters   facebook.com/igiglobal   twitter.com/igiglobal   linkedin.com/igiglobal

Ensure Quality Research is Introduced to the Academic Community

Become an Evaluator for IGI Global Authored Book Projects

 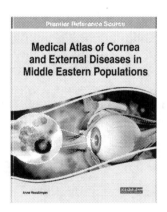 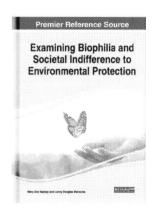 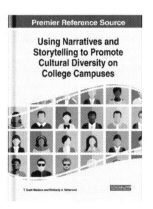

The overall success of an authored book project is dependent on quality and timely manuscript evaluations.

Applications and Inquiries may be sent to:
development@igi-global.com

Applicants must have a doctorate (or equivalent degree) as well as publishing, research, and reviewing experience. Authored Book Evaluators are appointed for one-year terms and are expected to complete at least three evaluations per term. Upon successful completion of this term, evaluators can be considered for an additional term.

If you have a colleague that may be interested in this opportunity, we encourage you to share this information with them.

Easily Identify, Acquire, and Utilize Published
Peer-Reviewed Findings in Support of Your Current Research

IGI Global OnDemand

Purchase Individual IGI Global OnDemand Book Chapters and Journal Articles

For More Information:
www.igi-global.com/e-resources/ondemand/

Browse through 150,000+ Articles and Chapters!

Find specific research related to your current studies and projects that have been contributed by international researchers from prestigious institutions, including:

- Accurate and Advanced Search
- Affordably Acquire Research
- Instantly Access Your Content
- Benefit from the InfoSci Platform Features

"*It really provides* an excellent entry into the research literature of the field. *It presents a manageable number of* highly relevant sources *on topics of interest to a wide range of researchers. The sources are* scholarly, but also accessible *to 'practitioners'.*"

- Ms. Lisa Stimatz, MLS, University of North Carolina at Chapel Hill, USA

Interested in Additional Savings?

Subscribe to
IGI Global OnDemand *Plus*

Learn More

Acquire content from over 128,000+ research-focused book chapters and 33,000+ scholarly journal articles for as low as US$ 5 per article/chapter (original retail price for an article/chapter: US$ 37.50).

6,600+ E-BOOKS.
ADVANCED RESEARCH.
INCLUSIVE & ACCESSIBLE.

IGI Global e-Book Collection

- **Flexible Purchasing Options** (Perpetual, Subscription, EBA, etc.)
- Multi-Year Agreements with **No Price Increases** Guaranteed
- **No Additional Charge** for Multi-User Licensing
- No Maintenance, Hosting, or Archiving Fees
- Transformative **Open Access Options** Available

Request More Information, or Recommend the IGI Global e-Book Collection to Your Institution's Librarian

Among Titles Included in the IGI Global e-Book Collection

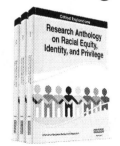

Research Anthology on Racial Equity, Identity, and Privilege (3 Vols.)
EISBN: 9781668445082
Price: US$ 895

Handbook of Research on Remote Work and Worker Well-Being in the Post-COVID-19 Era
EISBN: 9781799867562
Price: US$ 265

Research Anthology on Big Data Analytics, Architectures, and Applications (4 Vols.)
EISBN: 9781668436639
Price: US$ 1,950

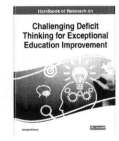

Handbook of Research on Challenging Deficit Thinking for Exceptional Education Improvement
EISBN: 9781799888628
Price: US$ 265

Acquire & Open

When your library acquires an IGI Global e-Book and/or e-Journal Collection, your faculty's published work will be considered for immediate conversion to Open Access *(CC BY License)*, at no additional cost to the library or its faculty *(cost only applies to the e-Collection content being acquired)*, through our popular **Transformative Open Access (Read & Publish) Initiative**.

For More Information or to Request a Free Trial, Contact IGI Global's e-Collections Team: eresources@igi-global.com | 1-866-342-6657 ext. 100 | 717-533-8845 ext. 100

Have Your Work Published and Freely Accessible
Open Access Publishing

With the industry shifting from the more traditional publication models to an open access (OA) publication model, publishers are finding that OA publishing has many benefits that are awarded to authors and editors of published work.

 Freely Share Your Research

 Higher Discoverability & Citation Impact

 Rigorous & Expedited Publishing Process

 Increased Advancement & Collaboration

Acquire & Open

 When your library acquires an IGI Global e-Book and/or e-Journal Collection, your faculty's published work will be considered for immediate conversion to Open Access *(CC BY License)*, at no additional cost to the library or its faculty *(cost only applies to the e-Collection content being acquired)*, through our popular **Transformative Open Access (Read & Publish) Initiative**.

- Provide Up To **100%** OA APC or CPC Funding
- Funding to Convert or Start a Journal to **Platinum OA**
- Support for Funding an **OA Reference Book**

IGI Global publications are found in a number of prestigious indices, including Web of Science™, Scopus®, Compendex, and PsycINFO®. The selection criteria is very strict and to ensure that journals and books are accepted into the major indexes, IGI Global closely monitors publications against the criteria that the indexes provide to publishers.

Learn More Here: For Questions, Contact IGI Global's Open Access Team at openaccessadmin@igi-global.com

Are You Ready to Publish Your Research?

IGI Global offers book authorship and editorship opportunities across 11 subject areas, including business, computer science, education, science and engineering, social sciences, and more!

Benefits of Publishing with IGI Global:

- Free one-on-one editorial and promotional support.
- Expedited publishing timelines that can take your book from start to finish in less than one (1) year.
- Choose from a variety of formats, including Edited and Authored References, Handbooks of Research, Encyclopedias, and Research Insights.
- Utilize IGI Global's eEditorial Discovery® submission system in support of conducting the submission and double-blind peer review process.
- IGI Global maintains a strict adherence to ethical practices due in part to our full membership with the Committee on Publication Ethics (COPE).
- Indexing potential in prestigious indices such as Scopus®, Web of Science™, PsycINFO®, and ERIC – Education Resources Information Center.
- Ability to connect your ORCID iD to your IGI Global publications.
- Earn honorariums and royalties on your full book publications as well as complimentary copies and exclusive discounts.

Join Your Colleagues from Prestigious Institutions, Including:

 Australian National University

 Massachusetts Institute of Technology

 JOHNS HOPKINS UNIVERSITY

 HARVARD UNIVERSITY

 COLUMBIA UNIVERSITY IN THE CITY OF NEW YORK

Learn More at: www.igi-global.com/publish

or Contact IGI Global's Aquisitions Team at: acquisition@igi-global.com

Printed in the United States
by Baker & Taylor Publisher Services